The Theology of God: Commentary

edited by

EDMUND J. FORTMAN, S.J.

PROFESSOR OF THEOLOGY
BELLARMINE SCHOOL OF THEOLOGY, NORTH AURORA, ILLINOIS

THE BRUCE PUBLISHING COMPANY / MILWAUKEE

230
FOt

Library of Congress Catalog Card Number: 67–29588

THE THEOLOGY OF GOD:

COMMENTARY

CONTEMPORARY COLLEGE THEOLOGY SERIES

GENERAL EDITORS: **J. FRANK DEVINE, S.J.**
BOSTON COLLEGE

RICHARD W. ROUSSEAU, S.J.
FAIRFIELD UNIVERSITY

THE THEOLOGY OF GOD: COMMENTARY is one of the volumes in the Historical Theology section of the Series

EDITORS' INTRODUCTION

Contemporary College Theology Series

THIS series begins with the presupposition that theology is necessary. It is necessary if Christian intelligence is to search for meaning in its dialogue with God, man, and the world. Since Christian intelligence is not the exclusive possession of the theological specialist or the cleric, the search must be carried on in all those areas of life, secular as well as religious, including the college situation, where meaning is to be found.

This search is a peaceful one for in some mysterious way it has already achieved its goal: the vision of faith and the fullness of love. Still it remains a relentless and universal search. Its inner certainty must radiate out not only to the edges of the mind but also into the farthest recesses of the world. We could call it "lay" theology but this word seems too pale a description for such an exciting enterprise of the Christian life.

In view of this the editors of this series are convinced that new questions had to be asked, new structures created, and new books written. These books would be neither catechetical nor apologetic. They would be purely and simply theological. The primary audience would be believers, but all thinking men would find them useful. In scope they would be broad enough to insure perspective. They would be scholarly enough to be intellectually relevant. They would avoid pedantry. In short, they would try to present a rich and deep understanding of Christian revelation in such a way that today's college students would be able to respond with a Christian faith and life that are both culturally mature and scientifically precise. Finally the authors of these books would be for the most part, teachers in colleges and universities where much of the contemporary theological dialogue is now going on.

The series falls into four parts: biblical, historical, ecclesial, and ethical. The divisions were not predetermined by the editors. They follow the shape of the most vigorous theological work now being done.

The books in the biblical section are intended to go beyond the traditional treatment of Bible history and the now familiar perspectives of salvation history. They concentrate on various books of the Bible. Their method has been especially designed for college work. Tentatively it might be called "exegetical theology." Every verse is not considered after the fashion of a commentary, nor are narratives developed as a biography, nor is there any attempt to create large theological syntheses. Rather the individual books are studied in chronological sequence; key passages are treated in detail and the rest are summarized. At the same time some attention is paid to the growing theological synthesis.

Since scholastic theology is already represented by individual works and sets of textbooks, the books in our historical section study dogmatic questions from a developmental point of view. In this way the editors hope to make the college students more aware of the great wealth of theological thinking that recent historicotheological studies have uncovered. This method, which is more inductive than deductive, should happily coincide with the thought processes of the college students. The three basic poles for synthesis are: God, Christ, and Man. In each area the historical development will be studied and a significant number of basic source texts presented. The problems raised in these studies will range all the way from Augustinian pessimism to Teilhardian optimism.

The textbooks for the third part of the series will deal with issues of great contemporary importance. They will examine questions discussed by the Second Vatican Council. As the name implies, ecclesial theology must first concern itself with the Church, what the Church knows herself to be as expressed in the insights of the new *Constitution on the Church* and with the more significant of the Church's allied concerns: other world religions, American Protestantism, its history, its motivating forces and spirit, and finally the new sacramental theology so enriched by the many magnificent liturgical advances. All of this growth has brought a wider and deeper appreciation of the nature of the Roman Catholic Church and her relationship, rooted in understanding and love, with the whole world.

The fourth and final section of the series is devoted explicitly to Christian moral response. The editors subscribe to the position that the proper place for the Catholic college or university to examine ethical questions is in a revelational rather than in a purely philosophical context. In addition to the "virtue" divisions of the *Summa* or the classic moral theology text, designed primarily for confessors, there is a need and a place for a "Christian ethics" that reflects the new insights which both biblical and dogmatic theology can provide. These books will strive to be openly Christian in spirit, ecclectic in approach, up to date in scholarship, and they will address themselves to those ethical problems which are most real to the modern American mind.

Finally, the editors would like to express their thanks to all those whose interest, advice, and cooperation have made this series possible. They are especially grateful to Mr. William May of The Bruce Publishing Company, who not only initiated the project and sustained it through the inevitable disappointments and complications, but contributed so much of his editorial skill to its final shape. To the individual authors who so graciously added to their heavy burden of academic responsibility by undertaking these books, we can only express the hope that their share in the shaping and influencing of the American Catholic community of today and of tomorrow will be far more meaningful to them than any meager thanks of ours.

The Editors,

J. FRANK DEVINE, S.J.
Boston College
RICHARD W. ROUSSEAU, S.J.
Fairfield University

ACKNOWLEDGMENTS

WE ARE grateful to the following for granting us permission to reprint copyrighted materials:

Barnes & Noble, Inc., New York, for excerpts from A. Wensinck's *The Muslim Creed;*

Basil Blackwell, Ltd., London, for excerpts from D. E. H. Whiteley's *The Theology of St. Paul;*

Benziger Brothers, New York, for excerpts from Jules Lebreton's *A History of the Dogma of the Trinity;*

Bobbs-Merrill, Inc., Indianapolis, for excerpts from *William of Ockham: Philosophical Writings,* translated by Philotheus Boehner, © 1964 by the Bobbs-Merrill Company, Inc., reprinted by permission of The Liberal Arts Press Division of the Bobbs-Merrill Company, Inc.

Cambridge University Press, England, for excerpts from James Gill's *The Council of Florence;*

The Clarendon Press, Oxford, for excerpts from D. N. Abercrombie's *The Origins of Jansenism;*

T. & T. Clark, Ltd., Edinburgh, for excerpts from Karl Barth's *Church Dogmatics,* II, 1, *The Doctrine of God;*

Columbia University Press, New York, for excerpts from Edward Dowey, Jr.'s *The Knowledge of God in Calvin's Theology;*

Concordia Publishing Company, St. Louis, and C. H. Beck'sche Verlagsbuchhandlung, Munich, for excerpts from Werner Elert's *Structure of Lutheranism;*

The Commonweal and Louis Dupre, for excerpts from Louis Dupre's article, "The God of History";

Desclée et Cie, New York, for excerpts from A. Cayre's *Manual of Patrology;*

The *Eastern Churches Quarterly* (now *One in Christ*), 58 Bocking Lane, Sheffield 8, England for excerpts from Paul Henry's "On Some Implications of the 'Ex Patre Filioque Tamquam ab Uno Principio' ";

Editions Xavier Mappus, Le Puy, for G. Salet's article "The Trinity: Mystery of Love," taken from his book, *Richesses du Dogme Chrétien;*

Fides Books, Notre Dame, Indiana, for excerpts from Barnabas Ahern's *New Horizons;*

Fordham University Press and Rev. Eric L. Mascall, for excerpts from Dr. Mascall's article on the secularization of Christianity from the Summer, 1966, issue of *Thought;*

The *Gregorianum,* for excerpts from Gustave Weigel's "The Theological Significance of Paul Tillich," Vol. XXXVII;

Harper & Row, Inc., New York, for excerpts from J. N. D. Kelly's *Early Christian Doctrines,* copyright © 1958 J. N. D. Kelly and © 1960 by John Norman Davidson Kelly (second edition), reprinted with the permission of Harper & Row, Publishers, Inc., New York; Christopher Mooney's *Teilhard de Chardin and the Mystery of Christ,* copyright © 1964, 1965 and 1966 by Christopher Mooney, S.J., reprinted with permission of Harper & Row, Publishers, Inc., New York.

Harvard University Press, Cambridge, for excerpts from Heiko Augustinus Oberman's *Harvest of Medieval Theology,* Copyright © 1963 by the President and Fellows of Harvard College;

Hawthorn Books, New York, for excerpts from B. Piault's *What Is the Trinity?* Copyright © 1959 by Hawthorn Books, Inc. and from L. Gardet's *Mohammedanism,* Copyright © 1961 by Hawthorn Books, Inc.;

B. Herder Book Company, St. Louis, for excerpts from R. Garrigou-Lagrange's *Reality;*

Helicon Press, Baltimore, for excerpts from K. Rahner's *Theological Investigations,* Vol. I; James Kritzeck's *Sons of Abraham;* P. Gelin's *Son and Saviour;* and David Knowles' *Evolution of Medieval Thought;*

Herder and Herder, Inc., New York, for excerpts from K. Rahner's *Spiritual Exercises;* Gabriel Moran's *The Theology of*

Revelation; and Leslie Dewart's *Future of Belief;*

Hodder and Stoughton, Ltd., for excerpts from George S. Hendry's *God the Creator;*

Humanities Press, Inc., for excerpts from C. R. S. Harris' *Duns Scotus;*

La Scuola Cattolica, Milan, for excerpts from Salderini's and Biffi's article "Le Tre Persone Divine nel Nuovo Testamento";

Lutterworth Press, London, for excerpts from Emil Brunner's *Dogmatics,* Vol. I;

Luzac & Co. and the Royal Asiatic Society for excerpts from A. S. Tritton's *Muslim Theology;*

Macmillan and Co., New York, for excerpts from J. Klausner's *From Jesus to Paul,* Copyright 1943 by The Macmillan Co.;

Manchester University Press and Watkin Williams for excerpts from Williams' *St. Bernard of Clairvaux;*

Paulist-Newman Press, New York, for excerpts from Ceslaus Spicq's *The Trinity and Our Moral Life;* M. Farrelly's *Predestination, Grace, and Free Will;* and William Grossouw's *Revelation and Redemption;*

Penguin Books, Ltd., Harmondsworth, for excerpts from G. R. Cragg's *The Church and the Age of Reason 1648–1798,* © Copyright 1966 by Penguin Books, Ltd.

Prentice-Hall, Inc., Englewood Cliffs, N. J., for excerpts from Wilfred Dewan's *The One God,* © 1963; and Matthew Spinka's *Christian Thought from Erasmus to Berdyaev,* © 1962;

Princeton University Press, Princeton, N. J., for excerpts from Ernst Cassirer's *The Philosophy of the Enlightenment;*

G. P. Putnam's Sons, for excerpts from Nicolas Zernov's *Eastern Christendom,* © 1961 by Nicolas Zernov;

Random House, Inc., New York, for excerpts from E. Gilson's *The Christian Philoosphy of St. Thomas Aquinas.* ©

Copyright 1956 by Etienne Gilson. Reprinted by permission of Random House, Inc.

Henry Regnery Co., Chicago, for excerpts from James Collins' *God in Modern Philosophy;* and Eugene Portalie's *Guide to the Thought of St. Augustine;*

S.C.M. Press, London, for excerpts from John Macquarrie's *An Existentialist Theology;* Claude Welch's *Trinity in Contemporary Theology;* and Bishop John A. Robinson's *Honest to God;*

Society for Promoting Christian Knowledge (SPCK), London, for excerpts from Oesterley's and Robinson's *Hebrew Religion;* E. K. Lee's *Religious Thought of St. John;* C. K. Barrett's *The Holy Spirit and the Gospel Tradition;* and Barrett's *The Gospel According to St. John;*

Charles Scribner's Sons, New York, for excerpts from Volumes I and II of Arthur McGiffert's *A History of Christian Thought,* pages 168–221 and 359–375. Copyright 1932, 1933, Charles Scribner's Sons; renewed copyright © 1960, 1961, Gertrude H. Boyce McGiffert; and from C. Welch's *In This Name* (U. S. title of *The Trinity in Contemporary Theology*), pp. 3–17. Copyright 1952, Charles Scribner's Sons;

Theological Studies, Woodstock, Md., for excerpts from J. J. Smith's "Primal Revelation and the Natural Knowledge of God"; P. De Letter's "The Theology of God's Self Gift"; and Gustave Weigel's "The Relevance of Paul Tillich";

Westminster Press, Philadelphia, for excerpts from Bishop John A. T. Robinson's *Honest to God,* © SCM Press Limited, 1963; and Thomas J. J. Altizer's *The Gospel of Christian Atheism,* © 1966, W. L. Jenkins.

Yale University Press, New Haven, for excerpts from John C. Murray's *The Problem of God.*

The World Publishing Company, New York (Meridian books), for excerpts from Jacques Maritain's *St. Thomas Aquinas.*

CONTENTS

THE THEOLOGY OF GOD:
COMMENTARY

I

GOD IN THE OLD TESTAMENT

1. **W. F. Dewan**[1] **studies the distinctive character of the God of the Old Testament. Even before monotheism is firmly established, life is what distinguishes Yahweh from other gods. At least in the latter part of the Old Testament, God is clearly seen as Creator and absolute Lord of the whole universe. Transcendence, glory, majesty, unapproachableness serve to underline the uniqueness of the Old Testament God.**

God is a Living Person. The beauty of the scriptural presentation of God is that he appears from the very beginning as a living person. It will later become the language of Christian theology to speak of three distinct persons in the divine essence, but for the moment the stress is on his personal nature. To Israel, Yahweh seemed "a person." To call him "living" is basic to the Hebrew concept of God: it is an immediate reaction in the face of all he did for them and to them. They are convinced of his life through the power he exercises so strikingly in their behalf. In fact,

[1] Wilfrid F. Dewan, C.S.P., is on the faculty of St. Paul's College, Washington, D. C. This excerpt is from his book, *The* *One God* (Englewood Cliffs, N. J.: Prentice-Hall, Inc., 1963), pp. 60–68.

1

when Yahweh[2] wishes to confirm threats or promises, he starts by first affirming that he is indeed alive; for example, "As I *live*," I will visit upon his head the oath he has despised and the agreement he has broken."[3]

Even before monotheism is firmly established, life is what distinguishes Yahweh from other gods. Israel is sure of the feebleness of foreign gods in contrast to their living God.[4] Some scholars think the title was devised against the nature gods of the gentiles who die and rise with the seasons, whereas Yahweh simply *lives*. The conviction that he is alive rests essentially on the fact that God is not a thing, a force, a power, but a *personal being*.[5] He is alive because of all the things he does for them, even to being the giver of life itself.[6] Their fondest hope is to be able to approach this living God.[7] It is their belief in this living God that leads them ultimately to affirm victory over death.

Their realization of God as a living person, acting powerfully in their lives, gives rise to anthropomorphic language. Even the highly spiritual theology of Second Isaiah and the New Testament often speaks of him as it would of a living human being. God speaks,[8] hears,[9] laughs,[10] uses organs suited to these acts: eyes,[11] hands,[12] arms,[13] ears,[14] feet,[15] which he places on a footstool. . . . He is shown as having all the human emotions: e.g., disgust,[16] regret,[17] jealousy.[18] . . .

God Is All-Powerful. Power impresses. Israel's realization of God's personality, uniqueness, and greatness comes in large measure through the overwhelming experience of his power. By his power the Hebrews come to know him first as vastly superior to any other god, then as the only possible God. True, he tells Abraham even from the start, "I am the almighty God,"[19] but it is actions more than words that convince his people. The theme of power is therefore a constant one running through all the other ideas of God.

God picks out a weak nation with little to recommend it, yet with his help it is able to do the impossible. He frees them from the bondage of powerful Egypt, establishes them in the Promised Land, and repeatedly helps them overcome their enemies. At first, his people seem to think of him as supreme within Israel itself; but slowly there dawns the realization that his power extends to the end of the earth.

At least in the latter part of the Old Testament God is clearly seen as Creator and absolute Lord of the whole universe. With a sign he calls

---

[2] Ex 3:14: the personal name he revealed to Moses.
[3] Ezek 17:19.
[4] Jer 10:9 f.
[5] 1 Sam 17:26, 36.
[6] Jer 38:16.
[7] Ps 41(42):3; 83(84):3.
[8] Gen 1:3.
[9] Ex 16:12.
[10] Ps 2:4.
[11] Am 9:4.
[12] Ps 138(139):5.
[13] Is 51:9.
[14] Is 22:14.
[15] Nah 1:3.
[16] Lev 20:23.
[17] Gen 6:6.
[18] Ex 20:5.
[19] Gen 17:1.

into being the heavens, earth, and seas; he cares for all things, and unless he sustains them, they fall back into nothingness.[20] He holds in his hands the destiny of all mankind. He has power over all nations,[21] he can drive the king of Assyria to chastise his people, then halt him powerless, before the walls of Jerusalem.[22] That God permits his people to be led into exile is recognized as punishment for infidelity; it is not due to any lack of power.

God Is One. Abraham's ancestors were pagans and polytheists. So, even after God revealed himself to him,[23] it probably took Abraham and his descendants a long time to understand just how unique this God was.

The first clear affirmation of God's oneness is made through Moses: "I, the Lord, am your God . . . you shall not have other gods besides me."[24] Yet even after this, there is some evidence that the Hebrews have not understood completely. They know that this is an absolute prohibition against worshiping any other gods, but belief in the existence of other gods for other nations lingered on.[25] Even in David's time, it was presumed that Yahweh's power ended at the frontiers of Israel.[26] For Israel, in her earliest period, however, two things are already clear: Yahweh is *the* God of Israel, and he is the *supreme* god.

Little by little, it becomes evident to the people through Yahweh's manifestations of power that he is not only superior to any other god, but totally unique. Moses confounds the gods of Egypt; foreign gods are seen as powerless to help their nations.[27]

It is thanks to the work of the prophets particularly, that the Hebrews outgrow any tendency to think of Yahweh as God of Israel only. They preach the Lord as creator of all, God of the whole world and of all history, as well as of the chosen people. Thus Deuteronomy has the classic formula, "Yahweh is God and there is no other God but him."[28] Jeremiah speaks of foreign gods as gods "who are not gods at all."[29] And Second Isaiah puts the final touches on the notion of monotheism. In proclaiming the almighty power of Yahweh,[30] he asserts that other gods not only have no power but are really nonexistent; he calls them "nonentities," empty breath, human creations which have no reality other than the material of which their idols are fashioned.[31]

God Is Eternal. Whereas other religions always presented a theogony [genealogy of the gods] as a first step in the organization of chaos, there is no trace of speculation among the Hebrews about the origin of God. Yahweh has no history, no consort (there is no Hebrew word for "goddess"), no family; he is just there from the start. His preexistence and endless continuance are taken for granted. The world has a beginning, God has

[20] Wis 11:26.
[21] Num 21:3; 1 Sam 14:22 ff.
[22] 2 Kg 19:35.
[23] Gen 17.
[24] Ex 20:2 f.
[25] 1 Sam 26:19; 2 Kg 3:27.
[26] I Sam 26:19; Mic 4:5.

[27] 2 Kg 18:33 ff.
[28] 4:35; 6:4; 32:39.
[29] 2:11; 5:7.
[30] 41:1-4.
[31] 43:10 ff.; 44:6 ff.; 45:20 ff.

none. "Before the mountains were brought forth and the earth and the world were born, from eternity to eternity, thou art, O God! for a thousand years in your sight are as yesterday which has passed."[32] Creative power is seen to imply eternal (or better, everlasting) existence.[33] . . . The Hebrews, of course, were not thinking philosophically about this term; Yahweh's eternity meant that his end and beginning were forever clouded by the unknown. The mysterious name "Yahweh" (related to "I am," "He who is," or "He who causes to be") implied life in unending actuality. The Hebrews do not have to be philosophers to grasp the significance of "He who is" as compared with the ephemeral nature of the seasons and years . . . and men whose bodies soon return to dust.

God Is Everywhere Present and Near. Once God entered into the dialogue of familiarity with his people, Israel's desire was to come to know this personal God as closely as possible; and knowledge, in its deepest sense, meant proximity, love, and communion. The sacred authors and prophets continually impress upon the people that God is not far off and remote — as they thought when building the golden calf[34] — but a God who is ever near.[35]

Even in the earliest books, God is seen as truly with his people, mingling in their lives, speaking to them, visiting Abraham. Israel is even seen as his "son," his "first-born."[36] Hosea

portrays God as a tender father.[37] In the later writings of the Old Testament the personal closeness with God is depicted by individual conversations with him.[38] One theory would even translate "Yahweh" precisely as "He who is present" to his people.

Once the notion of God as creator became clear, the Israelites began to realize that God is not only present to them, but present everywhere . . . "Where can I go from your spirit? From your presence where can I flee? If I go up to the heavens, you are there; if I sink down to the nether world, you are present there. . . . "[39]

God Is "Completely Other," Unchangeable, a Spirit. One-sided insistence upon God's immanence can lead to pantheism, the view that God is not personally distinct from man and the world. But if the men of the Bible are aware of God's presence, they are even more conscious of the fundamental distinction between God and man; that the distance is in fact infinite. God is, then, "completely other" or transcendent.

Though many anthropomorphic expressions are used to show God's closeness, and especially that he is a living person inviting us to personal relationship, nonetheless he remains wholly other. He is not a man but God.[40] This "otherness" of God is recognized in his unchangeableness.[41] . . . Everything else is fickle and changing, but not God.[42]

---

[32] Ps 89(90):2.
[33] Job 38:4 ff.; Pr 8:22 ff.
[34] Ex 32 ff.
[35] Dt 4:7.   [36] Ex 4:22.
[37] 11:1 ff.
[38] Ps 35(36):8 ff.; 71(72):1 ff.
[39] Ps 138(139): 8 ff.
[40] Hos 11:9.
[41] Mal 3:6.
[42] Num 23:19; Ps 101(102):27 f.

So aware are the men of the Old Testament that human expressions simply cannot capture the divine personality that they forbid any visual representations of Yahweh. To make an image of God to them meant to want to imprison him within certain limits — something that their awareness of God's transcendence clearly forbids. In fact, the sense of divine "otherness" grows steadily deeper in Israel's religion, till it comes to eliminate the very name "Yahweh," the proper, sacred, and dread name of their God, the name revealed to Moses. According to the Semitic mind, the name is part of the mystery of the being who is named. In the third century B.C. "Adonai" (my Lord) began to be substituted in public readings. The real basis for this "otherness" and unchangeableness of God, this big difference between God and men, is given us by Isaiah: namely, the one is Spirit, the other flesh.[43]

God Is Holy. The transcendence or "complete otherness" of God is most clearly expressed in the Bible by the notion of holiness. God is holy. He is "the holy one."[44] This is the most characteristic note of God for the men of the Bible. Holiness in God does not imply, however, effort or struggle against evil. It is more than a moral perfection: it signifies a mystery of absolute perfection and inaccessibility.

Certainly, God is pure, sacred, and untouchable, completely exempt from all faults, sins, or vices. From this results God's hatred of sin, and and his punishment of evil.[45] But the holiness of God is primarily a positive thing, absolute perfection. So much does it separate him from all creatures that even the seraphim must cover their faces as they sing "Holy, holy, holy."[46] He is "other" to the point of unapproachableness.

Thus, no matter how closely men are in touch with God, they are aware that the secret of God's own being can never be encroached upon. From this, there flows the natural attitude of "fear of the Lord," so often seen in the Old Testament. Indeed this awe which is reverent fear, not craven fear, is the "beginning of the knowledge of God."[47]

The positive side of holiness is expressed by majesty and glory. Glory is the radiant power of his being, a sort of external manifestation of his mysterious holiness; this glory radiates over all heaven and earth.[48] The New Testament account of the transfiguration of Christ is a striking example of this radiance of God's holiness. The Apostles fall to the ground overwhelmed by the evidence of his holiness and glory.[49]

Transcendence, glory, majesty, unapproachableness serve to underline the uniqueness of God. . . .

---

[43] 31:3.   [44] Is 5:24.

[45] Is 42:25; Ezek 28:22.
[46] Is 6:3.
[47] Ps 110(111):10; Pr 1:7; Job 28:28.
[48] Is 6:3.
[49] Mt 17:1 ff.

2. K. Kohler[1] **sees the God of Judaism as the One and Only God, the Holy God beyond all comparison. He is the world's great** *I Am,* **the living God and everlasting King, the Author of all existence and the self-conscious Ruler of both nature and history. Christianity adopted the pagan myths of the birth and death of the gods, and created a Christian plurality of gods in the place of the Graeco-Roman pantheon and sanctioned image worship.**

God in Judaism. Judaism centers upon its sublime and simple conception of God. . . . The God of Judaism is not one god among many, nor one of many powers of life, but is the *One* and *holy* God beyond all comparison. In him is concentrated all power and the essence of all things; he is the author of all existence, the Ruler of life, who lays down the laws by which man shall live.[2]

The pagan gods, and to some extent the triune God of the Christian Church, semi-pagan in origin also, are the outcome of the human spirit's going astray in its search for God. . . . Christianity succeeded by again dragging the Deity into the world of the senses, adopting the pagan myths of the birth and death of the gods, and sanctioning image worship. In this way it actually created a Christian plurality of gods in the place of the Graeco-Roman pantheon; indeed, it presented a divine family after the model of the Egyptian and Babylonian religions, and thus pushed the ever-living God and Father of man-

kind into the background. . . . Such is the lesson of history, that in polytheism, dualism, or trinitarianism one of the powers must necessarily limit or obscure another. In this manner the Christian Trinity led mankind in many ways to the lowering of the supreme standard of truth, to the infringement on justice, and to inhumanity to other creeds, and therefore Judaism could regard it only as a compromise with heathenism. . . .

The Names of God. . . . The Semites . . . perceived the Godhead as a power working from within, and accordingly gave it such names as *El* ("the Mighty One"), *Eloha* or *Pahad* ("the Awful One"), or *Baal* ("the Master").[3] *Elohim,* the plural form of *Eloha,* denoted originally the godhead as divided into a number of gods or godly beings, that is, polytheism. When it was applied to God, however, it was generally understood as a *unity,* referring to one undivided Godhead, for Scripture regarded monotheism as original with mankind. . . .

For the patriarchal age, the preliminary stage in the development of the Jewish God-idea, Scripture gives a special name for God, *El Shaddai* — "the Almighty God." . . . The name

[1] Dr. K. Kohler was president of Hebrew Union College of Cincinnati in 1923. In 1910 he had written a compendium of Systematic Jewish Theology. This excerpt is from his book, *Jewish Theology* (New York: The Macmillan Company, 1923), pp. 52–63, 72–84.

[2] Jer 10:10, 11, 16.

[3] Cf. Robinson Smith, *Religion of the Semites;* Max Mueller, *Chips from a German Workshop,* I, pp. 336–374.

by which God revealed himself to Moses and the prophets as the God of the covenant with Israel is JHVH (Jahveh). This name is inseparably connected with the religious development of Judaism in all its loftiness and depth. During the period of the Second Temple this name was declared too sacred for utterance, except by the priests in certain parts of the service, and for mysterious use by specially initiated saints. Instead, *Adonai* — "the Lord" — was substituted for it in the biblical reading, a usage which has continued for over two thousand years. The meaning of the name in pre-Mosaic times may be inferred from the fiery storms which accompanied each theophany in the various scriptural passages, as well as from the root *havah*, which means "throw down" and "overthrow."[4]

To the prophets, however, the God of Sinai, enthroned amid clouds of storm and fire, moving before his people in war and peace, appeared rather as the God of the Covenant, without image or form, unapproachable in his holiness. As the original meaning of JHVH had become unintelligible, they interpreted the name as "the ever-present One" in the sense of *Ehyeh asher Ehyeh*.[5] . . . In a number of the Psalms and in some later writings the very name JHVH was avoided probably on account of its particularistic tinge. . . . Instead, God as the "Lord" is impressed on the consciousness and adoration of men, in all

his sublimity and in absolute unity. . . . The name *Jehovah*, however, has no place whatsoever in Judaism. It is due simply to a misreading of the vowel signs that refer to the word *Adonai*, and has been erroneously adopted in the Christian literature since the beginning of the sixteenth century. . . .

Reverence for the Deity caused the Jew to avoid not only the utterance of the holy name itself, but even the common use of its substitute *Adonai*. Therefore, still other synonyms were introduced, such as "Master of the universe," "the Holy One," "the Merciful One," "King of the king of kings";[6] and in Hasidean circles it became customary to invoke God as "our Father," and "our Father in heaven."[7] . . .

The Essence of God. All efforts of philosophy to define the essence of God are futile. "Canst thou by searching find out God"? Zophar asks of his friend Job.[8] . . . Still, a divinity void of all essential qualities fails to satisfy the religious soul. Man demands to know what God is — at least, what God is to him. In the first word of the Decalogue God speaks through his people Israel to the religious consciousness of all men at all times, beginning "I am the Lord, *thy* God." This word *I* lifts God at once above all beings and powers of the cosmos, in fact, above all other existence, for it expresses his unique self-consciousness. . . . Thus the God of Judaism,

---

[4] Ex 3:14. Cf. Article "Jahweh" in *Protestantische Realencyclopaedie* and Cheyne's *Dictionary of the Bible*, art. "Names," pp. 109 ff.

[5] Ex 3:14.

[6] Under Persian influence — as the Persian ruler called himself the King of Kings.

[7] Cf. *Jewish Encyclopedia*, art. "Abba" and "Names of God."

[8] Job 11:7.

the world's great *I Am,* forms a complete contrast . . . to the lifeless powers of nature and destiny which were worshipped by the ancient pagans. . . .

The Jewish God-idea, of course, had to go through many stages of development before it reached the concept of a transcendental and spiritual god. It was necessary first that the Decalogue and the Book of the Covenant prohibit most stringently polytheism and every form of idolatry, and second that a strictly imageless worship impress the people with the idea that Israel's God was both invisible and incorporeal.[9] Yet a wide step still intervened from that stage to the complete recognition of God as a purely spiritual Being, lacking all qualities perceptible to the senses, and not resembling man in either his inner or his outer nature. Centuries of gradual ripening of thought were still necessary for the growth of this conception. This was rendered still more difficult by the scriptural references to God in his actions and his revelations, and even in his motives, after a human pattern. Israel's sages required centuries of effort to remove all anthropomorphic and anthropopathic notions of God, and thus to elevate him to the highest realm of spirituality.[10] . . .

Yet . . . while Judaism insists on the Deity's transcending all finite and sensory limitations, it never lost the

sense of the close relationship between man and his Maker. Notwithstanding Christian theologians to the contrary, the Jewish God was never a mere abstraction.[11] God is all in all; he is over all; he is both immanent and transcendent. His creation was not merely setting into motion the wheels of the cosmic fabric, after which he withdrew from the world. The Jew praises him for every scent and sight of nature or of human life, for the beauty of the sea and the rainbow....

The One and Only God. From the very beginning no Jewish doctrine was so firmly proclaimed and so heroically defended as the belief in the One and Only God. This constitutes the essence and foundation of Judaism. . . . The Judaism of the Torah starts with the proclamation of the Only One, and later Judaism marches through . . . the ages of history with a never-silent protest against polytheism of every kind, against every division of the Godhead into parts, powers, or persons.

It is perfectly clear that divine pedagogy could not well have demanded of a people immature and untrained in religion, like Israel in the wilderness period, the immediate belief in the only one God and in none else. Such a belief is the result of a long mental process; it is attained only after centuries of severe struggle and crisis. Instead of this, the Decalogue of Sinai demanded of the people that they worship only the God of the Covenant who had delivered them from Egypt to render them his

[9] Cf. D. F. Strauss, *Die Christliche Glaubenslehre,* I, pp. 525–553; Dillmann, *Handbuch der alttestamentliche Theologie,* pp. 226–235.

[10] Cf. *Jewish Encyclopedia,* art. "Anthropomorphism" and "Anthropopathism"; Schmiedl, *Studien über jüdische — arabische Religionsphilosophie,* pp. 1–30.

[11] Cf. Weber, *Jüedische Theologie,* pp. 149 f.; 157.

people.[12] . . . It is perfectly true that a wide difference of view exists between the prohibition of polytheism and idolatry in the Decalogue and the proclamation in Deuteronomy of the unity of God and, still more, between the law of the Pentateuch and the prophetic announcement of the day when Israel's God "shall be King of the whole earth, and his name shall be One."[13] Yet Judaism is based precisely upon this higher view. . . .

3. J. L. McKenzie[1] studies the divine names, creation, revelation, salvation, and monotheism. God is the creator but it is improbable that the author of Genesis affirms creation from nothing. Yahweh reveals himself in his deeds as lord of nature and of history, and saves by his own power. Salvation means a new Israel and by implication a new world; it approaches the idea of liberation from all evil, collective and personal, and the acquisition of complete security.

God. The existence of a divine being is never a problem in the Old Testament, and no discussion or demonstration is required. This conviction Israel shared with other peoples of the ancient Near East; the difference between Israel and these peoples turned on the identity of the divine being, not upon his reality and existence. . . .

The Hebrew words for divine being are *'el*, *'elohim,* and *'eloah*. The third of these is relatively rare and appears most frequently in poetry; there is no difference in meaning between *Eloah* and the first two words. *El* represents the common word for deity in the Semitic languages[2] . . . but appears as a personal name of the head of the pantheon of Ugarit. . . . Elohim . . . is plural in form and is often plural in sense; but it is also used of a single divine being, both of the God of Israel and of other gods. . . . Etymology furnishes no clue to the radical meaning of *El* and *Elohim;* most commentators and lexicographers believe that the words designate power, but this conclusion is drawn from the concept of deity rather than from etymology. . . .

Israel was aware that its ancestors had worshiped other gods,[3] presumably the gods of some part of the ancient Semitic world. The distinctive worship of the God of Israel begins with Abraham and is continued to Moses. It is the view of the E(lohist) and P(riestly) sources of the Pentateuch that the God of the fathers was known by another name than Yahweh before Moses. This name is Shaddai.[4] . . . Shaddai was rendered in the Septuagint by *panto-*

---

[12] Lev 19:4; 26:1; Is 2:8, 11; Ps 96:5.

[13] Zech 14:9.

[1] John L. McKenzie, S.J., is an eminent scripture scholar. At present he is teaching at the University of Notre Dame. He is the author of many books, among them *The Two-Edged Sword, The Power and the Wisdom, Myths and Realities, Authority in the Church*. This excerpt is from his *Dictionary of the Bible* (Milwaukee: The Bruce Publishing Company, 1965), pp. 315 ff.; 584 f.; 157 ff.; 735 ff.; 760.

[2] Akkadian *ilu*, Arabic *'ilah*, etc.

[3] Jos 24:2.

[4] In Pentateuch, Gen 17:1; 28:3; 35:11; 43:14; 48:3; Ex 6:3.

krator, "almighty," and as such has passed into English versions. W. F. Albright, followed by many, has interpreted it as "The One of the Mountain"; the cosmic mountain in ancient Semitic mythology was the home of the gods.[5] . . .

When the name *El* is applied to the God of Israel, it usually has a defining genitive: *El Bethel, El* of your fathers.[6] . . . *Elohim* likewise most commonly has a defining genitive when applied to the God of Israel. These genitives seem to express a desire to distinguish the God of Israel sharply from other beings to whom these names were applied.

The God of Israel is called by his personal name more frequently than by all other titles combined; the name not only identified the person, it revealed his character. This name is now pronounced Yahweh by scholars; the true pronunciation of the name was lost during Judaism when a superstitious fear of the name prevented its enunciation. In its place was read *Adonai,* "Lord"; the combination in writing of the consonants YHWH and the vowels of *Adonai,* a-o-a, created the hybrid Jehovah of the English Bibles. The meaning of the name etymologically is much disputed. The Septuagint rendered it by "He who is," and the Vulgate "I am who am." . . . W. F. Albright has interpreted the name as derived from the causative form (of the verb to be, *hawah*) and proposes that it is only the first word of the entire name

Yahweh-aser-yihweh, "He brings into being whatever comes into being." The name, therefore, designates him as creator, and this etymology is regarded as most probable by many scholars.

In the E(lohist) and P(riestly) (narratives) this name was first revealed to Moses on Mt. Horeb;[7] the J (Yahwist) source seems unaware of this tradition and uses the divine name Yahweh from the beginning of history. This name needs no defining genitive: Yahweh is the God of Israel without further definition. The name implies that a divine personal being has revealed himself as the God of Israel through the covenant and the exodus; it designates the divine personal reality as proclaimed and experienced. It affirms the unique Yahweh-Israel relationship and it affirms the unique character of Yahweh. . . .

Monotheism. Monotheism means the belief in the existence of one God only and exclusive worship of this one God. Monotheism in the Bible and in Israelite-Jewish-Christian religion is questioned by no one for the period after the 6th century B.C. The monotheism of Israel before this date has been questioned by many historians.

To answer the question, one must distinguish between the popular religion of early Israel and the religion of the Old Testament itself. The Old Testament is our chief source for the polytheism of the popular religion of Israel; the religious leaders of Israel whose utterances are preserved in the Old Testament engage in almost uninterrupted polemic against the adop-

---

[5] Cf. North.

[6] Gen 35:7; 49:25. Cf. Ps 68:36; 146:5; Gen 21:33; 33:20.

[7] Ex 3.

tion of polytheistic cults. The polytheism of early and monarchic Israel has been confirmed by archaeological exploration, which has disclosed numerous divine images in Israelite levels of occupation. The question is raised about the religion of the Old Testament and of the religious leaders of Israel; admitting that their conception of the deity differed from that of popular and Canaanite religion, does it deserve the name of monotheism as defined above? Here again a distinction must be made. A speculative philosophical affirmation appears nowhere in the Bible. Nor can we find in the Old Testament the monotheism which is evident in the New Testament. . . .

The religion of the patriarchs appears to have been the exclusive worship of a God who was conceived as the god of family or clan. This worship is represented in Genesis as given to him exclusively; but we here meet the problem of the gap in time between the patriarchs and the form in which these traditions appear in Genesis. Preserved and retold for many generations, including peoples who in all probability were not members of the original group of Israel, the patriarchal stories exhibit some retrojection of later religious ideas. This means that they are often represented as devout Israelites of a later period. This element should not be exaggerated, because in many respects the patriarchs are not represented as devout Israelites of a later period; but it does mean that caution is necessary in affirming that they were monotheists. In Genesis 14 Abraham is represented as present as the worship of a Canaan-

ite deity; his active participation is not explicitly mentioned, but it is highly improbable that he would be present and inactive. It would be impossible for a devout Israelite of a later period even to be present at such a sacrifice. The Israelites obviously identified the deity of Melchizedek with the deity of Abraham. Rachel stole the household gods of her father Laban, which gives a clue to his religion; yet Jacob was a member of his family for some years. Joseph was completely Egyptianized; the story of Joseph says nothing of his attitude toward Egyptian religion, but it hardly needs to be said. These elements in the patriarchal tradition suggest, although they do not demonstrate, that monotheism is scarcely the word to describe the religion of the ancestors of Israel.

Recent discussion of the question has centered about the monotheism of Moses. W. F. Albright has maintained from a study of biblical and comparative material that Moses must be called a monotheist, but not a speculative monotheist. A basic question is the first commandment of the decalogue. Some scholars maintain that this prohibition of worship is merely practical, with no affirmation implied; but this is difficult to maintain. The attitude of Israel toward other gods, as expressed in this commandment, is so singular that some affirmation must be implied. . . . Yahweh could be represented by no image, because he is like nothing else. . . . He was like nothing in the heavens or the earth, but he was also like no other god. Relevant here also is his solitary character. Alone of ancient Semitic deities he has no feminine consort and no divine family. . . . Therefore, scholars who do not believe that Israel reached this conception of God before the monarchy attribute the first commandment not to the period of Moses but to a later period. The attribution seems to be based on a theory of the development of Israelite religion rather than on critical analysis of the text. There is nothing in the history of early Israel to indicate that the first commandment goes beyond the belief and practice of early Israel. It must be granted that this monotheism is practical rather than speculative; but the first commandment can scarcely be interpreted as a selection of one god out of many. Other gods are totally rejected as simply irrelevant for Israel; they are not recognized as possessing any power or as active in any way, and Yahweh is not engaged in a combat with them.

Monotheism becomes more explicit in the ninth century. The combat of Elijah on behalf of Yahweh[8] is a more explicit rejection of the divinity of the Ba'al. In the eighth century Amos, Hosea, and Isaiah leave no doubt of their monotheism. But the most explicit and formal profession first appears in Isaiah 40–55. Here the gods of the nations are said to be nothing, nonexistent. This is not a departure from earlier belief, which never affirmed the reality of the gods beyond the images, but never formally denied it. The monotheism of Second Isaiah appears also in his presentation of Yahweh as lord of nature and lord of history — ideas which appear in

[8] 1 Kg 18.

earlier prophets also, but not explicitly connected with the unity of Yahweh.

Judaism distinguished itself from the Hellenistic world by its profession of belief in one God. Philosophical monotheism was taught by many Greek philosophers, but the religions of the Hellenistic world were still polytheistic. . . .

Creation. The Old Testament incorporated some motifs from the Mesopotamian and Canaanite myths of creation. The classic Mesopotamian account is found in the epic *Enuma Elish.* . . . The myth clearly exhibits the belief in the production of the universe from a pre-existing chaos. This chaos is the ultimate principle of the origin of all things, and itself arises from nothing. It is divine in character, for it is the parent not only of men but also of gods. Creation is the victory of the creative deity over this monster.

The Bible contains two accounts of creation at the beginning of Genesis, although the word is less properly applied to the second. The first in the book, although it is now generally regarded as more recent in origin, is found in Genesis 1:1–2:4a. . . . A comparison of this account with the *Enuma Elish* reveals that it is an explicit polemic against the Mesopotamian and Canaanite myths of creation. Chaos appears in Genesis, and the Hebrew word *tehom* is etymologically connected with the Akkadian *tiamat*; but it is no longer personified as a deity, nor does it exhibit the primeval principle of sex. Nor is it the source and origin of all things; the sole creator in Genesis is God. . . .

Man is the last of the creatures in both accounts, but his position is more significant in Genesis than it is in *Enuma Elish.* Here man is made in the divine image, and in virtue of this image receives dominion over the rest of creation. . . .

This creation account is marked by a serenity and undisturbed dominion of God over the things which he makes. Creation is accomplished by the spoken word, and not by work of any kind. God is the king who needs only speak to have his will accomplished; the creator, however, has no assistant in the execution of his creative work. . . . Hence there is no question of his entire supremacy; the author has represented it as best he knew how.

Whether the author represented God as creating from nothing is not easily answered. Creation from nothing is not denied by the author of Genesis; but it is extremely improbable that he affirms it. Creation from nothing as it is taught in modern theology presupposes a philosophy of nature which the Hebrews did not have. They did not answer the question because they were unable to raise it; but the metaphysical affirmation of creation from nothing rests upon an idea of the divine supremacy which is identical with the biblical idea. The word which is used for creation in Genesis 1 is *bara*. This word is used in the Old Testament only with the deity as the subject; hence it indicates a work which is distinctively divine, which no agent less than God can accomplish. . . . It does not of itself, however, indicate creation from noth-

ing, but the divine productive action. The Hebrew author was not able to go beyond the formless chaos which he has in common with Mesopotamian mythology. His imagination was unable to grasp a pure production from nothing. He did, however, reduce this chaos to mere shapeless matter with which God works, and in this way denied its divinity and that it was the primeval principle of creation. The account concludes with an affirmation of the goodness of all which God has made.[9] The author thus denies any dualism, which is implicit in Mesopotamian and Canaanite mythology. . . .

Revelation. By the term "revelation" . . . is understood the self-manifestation of the divine. . . . This self-manifestation is ultimately some kind of communication, but in the Bible it is not always the communication precisely of a proposition. . . . A fundamental presupposition of Old Testament revelation is that Yahweh is a living God.[10] The vitality of Yahweh is perceived in his words and his actions, which are his self-manifestation, his revelation. . . . This self-manifestation may be distinguished in several steps without attempting to determine which step is logically prior.

Yahweh manifests himself as the lord of history; this does not mean that man is not a free agent, but that history moves toward a term which Yahweh intends. He directs its movements, even when man is opposed to his purpose, in such a way that his end is attained. The fundamental event of history in which Yahweh

9 Gen 1:31.
10 Dt 5:23.

manifests himself as lord is the exodus of Israel from Egypt. In this event appears his power and his will to save Israel. . . .

Yahweh also manifests himself as creator and lord of nature. The typical poetic form in which Yahweh's manifestation in nature is conceived is the theophany. The presence and activity of Yahweh in nature is universal; all phenomena of nature are produced by Him.

Yahweh reveals himself in judgment; this is a particular aspect of his self-manifestation in history. He appears in the fall of nations.[11] He is revealed in his judgment upon Israel even more clearly than in his judgments upon the nations. . . .

The revelation of Yahweh is ultimately destined for all peoples through Israel.[12] Indeed all peoples experience the self-manifestation of Yahweh in history and nature, but they have not the peculiar manifestation of himself to Israel in election and covenant. In particular, they have not the "word" of Yahweh; and it is the word which makes it impossible to reduce the self-manifestation of Yahweh to his deeds in history and in nature, as some interpreters seem to do. The deeds of Yahweh need an interpreter; and in Israel one may distinguish a triple stream of revelation which interprets his deeds.

Moses stands at the head of this triple stream in an unparalleled position of face to face communication with Yahweh.[13] The first of the

streams is law, the revelation of the covenant will of Yahweh establishing standards of conduct for Israel. History and nature alone do not manifest the moral imperative which Yahweh lays upon Israel; this is explicitly stated by the founder of Israel as the community of Yahweh. Of the three this source is the best example of revelation preserved in tradition and codified in writing. Moses had no successor but the priests as the interpreters of the law were spokesmen of the revealed will of Yahweh.

The second stream is prophecy. Revelation in prophecy is normally conceived as the reception of the word. The prophet experiences the present activity of Yahweh in history and nature and interprets the deeds of Yahweh according to the word which is given him, the mystic intuition of the present divine reality. He discloses according to the word the will of Yahweh in the present and the plans of Yahweh for the destiny of Israel in the future, and gives directions how Israel must submit itself to these plans.

The third stream, and perhaps the weakest as revelation, is wisdom. Wisdom, however, is also a charisma and it is the gift of Yahweh. It does not deal with cosmic and historical events, but with the will of Yahweh as it governs the ordinary events of the life of the individual person. . . . Thus in all three of these sources of revelation, the self-manifestation of Yahweh as lord of history, creator and lord of nature, and source of law and wise conduct, is seen to be the governing factor of Israelite life and belief to the

---

[11] Is 13.
[12] Is 2:2–4; Mic 4:1–3.
[13] Ex 33:11; Num 12:6 ff.; Dt 34:10.

point where there is no other factor. Human intelligence and prudence best fufill themselves by learning what Yahweh is. Thus, the result of revelation in the Old Testament is knowledge which is not the philosophical knowledge of understanding but the knowledge of the living and active personal reality of Yahweh, experience of Yahweh as he is and as he acts. . . .

Salvation. The word and the idea of salvation are basic in the faith and theology of both Old Testament and New Testament. . . . That Yahweh saves is stated hundreds of times in the Old Testament. . . . Titles which employ the words "save" and "salvation" . . . can be called his most characteristic appellatives in the Old Testament. . . . Yahweh saves by his own power. . . . Yahweh does save through human means, but it is clearly understood that he raises men to be saviors and empowers them to save. . . . The saving power of Yahweh is exercised through his dominion over nature which is the instrument of his salvation and his judgment. . . . The most marvelous saving act of Yahweh is his deliverance of Israel in the exodus. . . . The power which is revealed in this work cannot be conceived as limited by any superior power. . . .

The idea of salvation is deepened and expanded after the exile; for the power and will of Yahweh to save must be exhibited in a manner which exceeds even the greatness of his saving deeds in the exodus if Israel is to survive this crisis. The simplest form in which this salvation is expected is the restoration of Israel to its own land.[14] . . . But the future salvation soon becomes messianic in character and is seen as a new creation of Israel, an event in which all the themes of victory and deliverance implied in the word are brought to their fullness. The messianic king is a savior in a way in which the historic kings never were.[15] The messianic salvation is eternal.[16] . . . Salvation means a New Zion and a new Israel, a new revelation of the character of Yahweh, and by implication a new world. Salvation approaches the idea of liberation from all evil, collective and personal, and the acquisition of complete security. . . .

[14] Ps 14:7; 69:36.
[15] Jer 23:6; 33:16; Zech 9:9.
[16] Is 45:7; 51:6, 8.

4. W. O. E. Oesterley and T. H. Robinson[1] think the worship of Yahweh was borrowed from the Kenites but profoundly developed by Moses and the prophets. The prophets saw Yahweh as Law, as Lord of Nature and History, as Lord of the End of Things and of Universal Morality and thus reached an absolute monotheism and a religion of the individual as well as of the community.

Yahweh, the God of the Hebrews. The beginning of the religion of Yahweh among the Hebrews centered in Moses; and it was the Sinai revelation to which was primarily due the acceptation of Yahweh as their God by the Hebrew people. . . . We have now to inquire by what means it was that Moses came to the knowledge of Yahweh. . . . There is a good deal in the later history of the Israelites which bears out the contention that Moses adopted the worship of Yahweh from the religion of the Kenites . . . that Yahweh was the God of Jethro, Moses' father-in-law, and his tribe, the Kenites.[2] Moses accepted Yahweh because he had learned about him from his priest Jethro; the Hebrews accepted Yahweh because, as they believed, he had shown forth his power and delivered them. . . .

The Kenites had worshiped Yahweh as their tribal God from time immemorial; and in course of time the Hebrews came to worship him too. But what a profound difference there was between the two in the use of the germ of revelation! In the case of the Kenites no religious development took place because the human response was wanting. In the case of the Hebrews how different! First through Moses, and later through the prophets, they gradually came to realize more and more fully the personality and character of Yahweh, and thus to apprehend, in some measure, the being of God. All through their history there was, in spite of setbacks, the slow yet continuous increase of this apprehension because of the human response to the divine prompting. True, it was never the nation as a whole that responded; that is always so. Elect instruments of God first come into touch with him; and they are the means of disseminating the knowledge of him. Moses, with all his limitations — and the Old Testament makes no secret of them — was one of those elect instruments, perhaps the greatest in pre-Christian times. . . . An insignificant man, belonging to an insignificant people, in an insignificant corner of the world, received through human means the divine spark of revelation; but he not only received it, he ac-

[1] W. O. E. Oesterley, Litt.D., D.D. (Camb.) and Theodore H. Robinson, Litt.D.(Camb.), D.D.(Lond.) are the authors of various books on Sacred Scripture, among these *The Jews and Judaism During the Greek Period, The Wisdom of Egypt and the Old Testament* by W. O. E. Oesterley; *An Introduction to the Books of the Old Testament* by W. O. E. Oesterley with T. H. Robinson; *The Book of Amos* by T. H. Robinson. This excerpt is from their book, *Hebrew Religion, Its Origin and Development* (London: Society For Promoting Christian Knowledge, 1930, 1949), pp. 146 ff.; 224 ff.; 337 ff.

[2] Ex 18:8 ff.

cepted and responded to it. . . .

The *Canonical Prophets.* There are certain features in the teaching of the prophets common to them all, of which the most important must be enumerated. (*a*) In the first place, the prophets saw *Yahweh as Law.* . . . His will might be absolute, but it was reliable; he did not change, and what was good in his sight today would not appear evil tomorrow. . . . Knowing Yahweh, they knew what he would do in any given set of circumstances, for they saw him as Law. (*b*) Further, the prophets saw Yahweh as the *Lord of Nature.* . . . By the middle of the eighth century, probably much earlier, the belief in Yahweh as the master of the physical universe had greatly developed and found expression in the myths of creation. . . . The prophets . . . as against all other nations, claimed Yahweh as the Creator-hero. Along with creation went also control, and the prophets, like all other Israelites, held Yahweh to be the master of all natural phenomena. . . . If Israel is faithful, and obeys the commands of Yahweh crops will be abundant. . . . Nothing happens in nature, great or small, except by his will. . . .

c) *Yahweh as Lord of History.* It is not only the world of physical nature but also the world of human relations, which is under his complete control. . . . The peculiar claim of the Hebrew prophet is that Yahweh is concerned to control not merely the fortunes of his own people but the destinies of all nations. . . . Even the great racial migrations are the work of Yahweh.[3]

[3] Am 9:7.

Within the nation itself, of course, Yahweh's power is absolute. . . . History is neither the result of the conflict between divine whims nor the outcome of human ambition; it is the development of a single great purpose.

d) *Yahweh as Lord of the End of Things.* . . . Eschatology is much older than the canonical prophets, and they found it necessary to correct men's ideas on the subject,[4] but they insisted with equal stress that Yahweh could and would make an end of things. . . . To some extent their views were apocalyptic in the strictest sense of the term, and there are passages which suggest that they looked forward to the great day when the heaven should fall and the earth be shattered, that a new world might be born from the ruins of the old. But there was a fundamental difference between the two points of view. The popular eschatology was political and national, while the prophetic was primarily ethical and religious. The people in general held to the doctrine that when matters reached their worst, when Israel was overwhelmed and oppressed by her enemies and was at the very last gasp, the great Day of Yahweh would suddenly dawn, Israel's God would appear in all his splendor and his might, to destroy the old universe of men and things and create a new one in which Israel and Yahweh should have sole pre-eminence. It was a part of the prophetic message to insist on the fundamental mistake of this view. Amos and his successors did not deny the coming of the Day of Yahweh, but for Israel it would be

[4] Am 5:18–20.

a day of darkness, rayless gloom, not a day of light and glory.[5] For when Yahweh came, it would not be to avenge his people on their foes, it would be to vindicate his own moral character by taking a final vengeance on his own people for their apostasy and immorality; it would mean the ruin of Israel, not her salvation. . . .

e) *Yahweh as Lord of Universal Morality.* The prophetic doctrine was sufficiently novel and significant in that it proclaimed the supreme place given to the moral element in Yahweh's demands on his own people. But it did not cease there. He was concerned to note the behavior of other nations as well as that of Israel. Wherever wrong, moral wrong, was done, whether it be to Israel or by Israel or by another people to a third, it was a violation of the Law of Yahweh, a contradiction of his glorious will, and must meet with his punishment. It is true that the geographical and political horizon of Israel in the eighth and seventh centuries was limited, and embraced few peoples outside the immediate environs of Palestine, but the principle was of universal application. . . . Yahweh is a moral being, and he is supreme over all races and lands, hence it follows as a matter of course that he must take their general behavior into consideration and call them to account. It is true that he will not be so strict with those whom he has not "known,"[6] but they are morally responsible to their own conscience. . . .

God and the Individual. The religion of the ancient world was primarily concerned with communities rather than with individuals; and this is true of the religion of Israel. But with Jeremiah . . . the individual human being begins to take on a new importance. The community as a whole is still, of course, the more prominent; but one man may reach God apart from his fellows. . . . In Jeremiah's struggles there is no thought of Israel as a whole . . . the man stands alone with his God. But on the other side we have the doctrine of individual responsibility. It is this latter which is especially emphasized by Ezekiel. . . . On the old "communal" view of religion, insisting as it did on the absolute solidarity of the race, the sins of the generation which preceded the Exile could be met only by the complete destruction of the whole nation; but Ezekiel, following Isaiah here, could not believe that Yahweh would destroy the people who represented him to the world, and thus believed profoundly in their ultimate restoration. A new start was possible, and was possible only because with the destruction of the actual sinners the sin was wiped out. Each generation, each individual, could begin life afresh, and could lay the foundations of a new order, in which Israel could achieve the great purpose for which she had been chosen and maintained in the world: the proclamation of Yahweh as the Lord of all mankind. . . .

[5] Am 5:18–20.   [6] Am 3:1–2.

5. J. Lebreton[1] **looks at the growth of the religious ideas by which God prepared his people for the revelation of the Trinity. What especially impresses him is the growth in monotheistic faith and messianic hope and in the conceptions of Spirit, Wisdom, and Word.**

If Christian theology was developed in a Hellenic environment, Christianity itself was born in Judaism; to discover the origin of its doctrines, we must study the beliefs of Judaism. Various relations may be discovered between them: certain Christian dogmas — for instance, the dogmas of creation and of the resurrection of the body, are established in the earlier dispensation; others, on the other hand, were unknown to the Jews, although, in spite of their ignorance of the fact, they were being prepared by God for the revelation which Christ was to bring them. Among these must be placed the dogma of the Trinity. . . . We do not ask of history to discover in the Old Testament what the most illustrious Fathers of the Church did not see; and, without looking in the books of the Jews for a revelation which God reserved to Christians, we will sketch the growth of the religious ideas by which he prepared his people for the revelation of the Trinity. . . . Here we propose to describe only the immediate preparation by which God

led his people to the revelation of the Trinity; it is therefore only in the last phase of its development, i.e., after their return from exile, that we shall study the progress of the idea of God.

God. All idolatrous worship had been abolished by that time. . . . For some time, Hellenic domination had stained the purity of this monotheism: in the ranks of the army of Judas Machabeus soldiers were found carrying votive objects consecrated to idols.[2] But the ensuing national reaction gave more vigor and vehemence to faith in the one only God. . . . This faith is expressed in the verse of Deuteronomy[3] which the Jews recite every day at the beginning of their prayers: "Hear, O Israel, the Lord our God is one Lord. . . ." This monotheistic faith was very inspiring and an efficacious preparation for Christianity.

It is true that even before the exile, Jahve was already recognized and preached as the all-powerful God.[4] After the exile it became customary to call Jahve God of heaven,[5] God of heaven and earth,[6] Lord of heaven,[7] King of the ages,[8] Master of the

[1] Jules Lebreton, S.J., was professor of Christian Origins at the Catholic Institute of Paris in 1939. He was born in 1873 and died in 1956. He was the author of many works, among them *A History of Early Church* and *The Spiritual Teaching of the New Testament*. This excerpt is from his book, *History of the Dogma of the Trinity*, trans. by Algar Thorold from the eighth edition (New York: Benziger Brothers, 1939), pp. 73–103.

[2] 2 Macc 12:40.
[3] 6:4.
[4] Is 7:18; 5:26; Jer 27:5. Cf. Kautsch, *Religion of Israel*, in *Dictionnaire Biblique*, Vol. 680.
[5] Ezra 5:12; Neh 1:4, 5; Jon 1:9; Dan 2:18.
[6] Ezra 5:11.
[7] Dan 5:23; 2 Macc 15:23.
[8] Tob 13:10.

world,[9] God and Master of all,[10] King of the whole creation.[11]

These are not empty epithets, and Persian influence is not enough to explain their use; they express one of the beliefs most dear to Israel, the universal domain of the creative God. Jewish piety, already fully formed and penetrated with the spirit of the Psalms, loves to find its nourishment in this thought that the whole world created by God belongs to him, and is filled by him.[12] "For what have I in heaven? And besides thee what do I desire upon earth? For thee my flesh and my heart hath fainted away. Thou art the God of my heart, and the God that is my portion for ever. For behold they that go far from thee shall perish: thou hast destroyed them that are disloyal to thee. But it is good for me to adhere to my God, to put my hope in the Lord God."[13] Father Lagrange writes: "We will not weaken by any commentary these words, the most beautiful of the Old Testament. . . . We are at the heart of the faith of Israel."[14]

Are we not also on the threshold of the Christian faith? Do we not recognize its accents in these appeals to the fatherly mercy of God for man whom he has created: "As a father hath compassion on his children, so hath the Lord compassion on them that fear him."[15] . . . In the book of Isaiah[16] Israel said with more assurance: "And now, O Lord, thou art our Father. . . . Be not very angry, O Lord. . . ." In Exodus[17] we read: "Thus saith the Lord: Israel is my son, my firstborn."[18] Deuteronomy[19] and the prophetic books often repeat this word,[20] God is the father of the entire people, he is also the father of the Israelites taken singly: and this is his title to filial veneration;[21] he recalls them to himself when they have sinned.[22] They, for their part, address him as sons, and appeal to his fatherly mercy.[23] . . .

These passages already strike a Gospel note. . . . But it is only in the Gospel that the dogma of the divine paternity will be fully displayed, and that the spirit of Christ will make the proper filial prayer of the Christian rise to God from the heart of the just.

The Spirit. The conceptions of the Spirit, Wisdom, Word are attached to the idea of God in the Old Testament; and if these various obscure and elementary conceptions are not sufficient of themselves to constitute a doctrine of the Trinity, they at least prepare the soul for the Christian revelation.[24]

The sacred writers represent the Spirit as a divine force or, rather, as

---

[9] 2 Macc 13:15.
[10] Ec 36:1.
[11] Judith 9:12.
[12] Ps 73:16; 103:13 ff.; 63:10 ff.; 144:15 ff.; 146:8 ff.; 138:7.
[13] Ps 72:25–28.
[14] *Revue Biblique* (1905), 195.
[15] Ps 102:13, 14.
[16] 64:8 ff.
[17] 4:22.
[18] See Dalman, *Die Wörte Jesu,* I, 150.
[19] 14:1; 32:5, 6.
[20] Is 1:4; 30:9; Hos 2:1; 11:1; Jer 3:4; Mal 2:10.
[21] Mal 2:10.
[22] Jer 3:14, 22.
[23] Is 64:7 ff.
[24] See Heinisch, *Personifikationen und Hypostases im Alten Testament und im alten Orient* (Münster, 1921); *Griechische Philosophie und Altes Testament,* Münster, 1913.

God himself in his action on man and the universe; and, inasmuch as the divine energy is more particularly manifested in the production and conservation of life, the Spirit is often regarded as a vivifying principle.[25] . . . The Spirit is the life-giving force which comes from God.[26] . . .

This conception of the life-giving Spirit will reappear in the New Testament, transformed, as the conception of life itself: the characteristic action of the Spirit will no longer have for its limit the natural life which we lead here below, but eternal life initiated at present in sanctity, consummated in heaven in glory. . . .

In the case of the most ancient heroes of the Bible, their more clearly divine actions are attributed to the Spirit of God.[27] This characteristic is more apparent in the inspiration of the prophets, which assumes an increasingly large place in the manifestations of the Spirit of God, and which later in Judaism and Christianity is looked upon as the special action of the Holy Spirit, the Spirit of the prophets.[28]

During the period of the prophets the characteristic of God's action in sanctification and illumination appears more manifestly. . . . Nevertheless, here, also, we find mentioned only the extraordinary charismata granted to certain privileged souls, to the "men

of the Spirit";[29] we do not find that the spirit of God extends his sanctifying action over all the Israelites;[30] and, in the case even of those whom he favors, he appears rather as a source of extraordinary gifts than as a principle of sanctity. It is another matter in the Psalms: the worshipper, addressing God . . . prays to God to "renew his Spirit within him."[31] . . .

The Spirit is sometimes represented as a force acting on men from without, bearing them, raising them up, leading them on;[32] more often he penetrates them either by his transitory influence[33] or by his permanent indwelling. Thus Joseph is full of the Spirit of God.[34] . . .

This belief in the immanence of the Spirit of God in the soul does not yet bear all its fruits, because . . . this presence of the Spirit is described more often as a privilege, accorded to heroes or prophets, than as a gift of God dispensed to all the faithful. From now on, however, this doctrine constitutes one of the most important and precious elements in the religion of Israel. . . .

Moreover, this belief in the Spirit of God, still very imperfect, is directed like all the religion of the Old Testament, toward the Messiah, and expects to find its perfection in him. It is principally in Isaiah that the relation of the Spirit to the Messiah is very explicit and accentuated.[35] The

---

[25] Gen 1–2; 6:3; Ps 103:29, 30; Is 32:15; Job 12:10; Zech 12:1.

[26] Is 31:3; Num 16:22.

[27] Joseph, Gen 41:38; Moses, Num 11:17; Samson, Jg 14:6, 7; Gideon, Jg 6:34; Saul, 1 Sam 11:6.

[28] See Weber, *Jüdische Theologie*, 192; Justin, *Apol.* I, 6; 1 Sam 10:6, 11.

[29] Hos 9:7.

[30] See Num 11:29.

[31] Ps 50(51):12, 13; 112:10.

[32] Cf. Ezek 3:12, 14; 8:3; 11:1, 24.

[33] As in most cases of prophetic inspiration.

[34] Gen 41:38.

[35] 11:1, 2.

Messiah is not the only one to receive these gifts of the Spirit; the time of his coming is foretold as a period in which divine graces will be poured forth.[36] . . . All these prophecies state clearly enough that the Spirit is, together with the Messiah, the supreme Messianic gift. . . .

It also becomes intelligible why, in all the doctrine we have surveyed, the personality proper of the Spirit is so faint. More often nothing is perceptible but the action of the Spirit, who is represented as a force communicated by Jahve;[37] on other occasions, instead of describing his action upon men, he is represented as united to Jahve, without a very clear distinction between the two terms.[38] . . .

Wisdom. . . . In the *Book of Proverbs* the theology of Wisdom is more developed. . . . We find in it two poems[39] . . . which indicate the divine character of Wisdom . . . and at first sight definitely emphasize the personal character of Wisdom.[40] It is evident here that the sacred writer does not intend to hypostatise folly, but only to personify it. We may ask ourselves if he wished to go further than this when speaking of Wisdom. . . . It is difficult to see in this passage[41] only poetical personification, and in fact, the majority of commentators agree in the view that Wisdom is presented here as already distinguished from

God, constituting a hypostasis or, at least, tending in that direction.[42] . . . No text of the Old Testament is more frequently quoted by the theologians of old in the course of their enquiries into the dogma of the Trinity. Already Jewish speculation had been occupied with it and gladly saw in it the affirmation of the pre-existence of the Law which was easily identified with the Wisdom of God.[43] St. Paul in his turn will apply it to the Son of God.[44] The apologists will make use of it as a chosen weapon to prove to the Gentiles or Jews the pre-existence of the Word and his role in the work of creation.[45] Later on the Arians will find there a decisive argument in favor of their heresy: "The Lord hath created me," they read in the Septuagint. It seemed to them the authentic consecration of their doctrine on the origin of the divine Word. . . .

This is not to say that the whole Trinity is to be found here. Wisdom alone is distinguished from God, and even so, has not all the clearness of a living personality. The Spirit, as we

---

[36] Is 32:15; 44:1 ff.; Ezek 11:19; 36:26; 37:12.

[37] See Hackspill, *Revue Biblique* (1902), p. 68.

[38] 2 Sam 23:2.

[39] Chaps. 8 and 9.

[40] 8:2–6; 9:1 ff.

[41] Pr 8:22–31.

[42] Examining this text in the light of traditional commentaries, it would seem that we could go beyond this prudent conclusion and assert a distinction of person. Historically considered, the text would not seem to admit of such an interpretation. It is true that it is suggested, but, considered in itself, neither its context nor its poetic form admit such a close interpretation of the expressions used. See Lagrange, *Revue Biblique* (1908), pp. 496, 494.

[43] *Berechith Rabba*, 17; *Exod. Rabba*, 30 (89d); Strack-Billerbeck, *Kommentar*, II, 353 ff.; Philo, *De ebrietate*, 31.

[44] Col 1:15. Cf. C. F. Burney in *Journal of Theological Studies*, XXVII (1926), 165 ff.

[45] Justin, *Dial.* 61:3; Athenag., *Legat.* 10.

have seen, is no more distinguished from God than the Logos. . . . However, it is in this book that we find the clearest foreshadowing of the Christian dogma. . . .

The Word. The sacred books often represent the creative act as a word of God.[46] The Psalms speak of the word sent by God, which heals.[47] . . . In all this, we may see nothing but bold figures of speech; the word of creation, or salvation, or reprobation is personified, it is not conceived as a hypostasis distinct from God. . . . It is chiefly in the Book of Wisdom that the personification of the word is dwelt upon: "For while all things were in quiet silence, and the night was in the midst of her course, thy almighty word leapt down from heaven from they royal throne, as a fierce conqueror. . . ." This last text, if taken by itself, would hardly have more significance than those of the Psalms or Prophets; but when it is found in a book which indicates so clearly the distinct personification of Wisdom, it is difficult not to give it more importance. . . .

The Messianic Hope. Side by side with the doctrines of the Spirit, Wisdom, the Word, a belief of a totally different character, the Messianic faith was developing. . . . We must, however, recognize that it is by means of the doctrine of Wisdom much more than by Messianism that the Jewish people was prepared for the revelation of the Trinity.[48]

Many liberal commentators, when they meet in the Gospel the name of the Son of God applied to Jesus, are disposed to consider it as simple equivalent of the word "Messiah";[49] it would seem from what they say that this title was frequently and traditionally used in this sense. This is a mistake:[50] very few texts are to be found in which Jahve calls the Messiah his Son; but neither in the Old Testament proper nor in the apocryphal books do we find the title "Son of God" applied by the writer to the Messiah.

We have seen above how God in the Old Testament loved to call the chosen people his *son:* the same title is given by him to David and to the heir who is promised to him.[51] The Messiah, in his turn, is called by God his *son* and all nations are given to him as his heritage.[52] It would be difficult to see in this text the eternal generation of the Word; the context suggests, on the contrary, the glorification of the Messiah and the inauguration of his reign. . . .

It seems, however, that texts are not wanting in the ancient prophets which might have revealed to the Jews the more than human dignity of the Messiah. In Isaiah he is called not only Emmanuel[53] — but "Wonderful, Counsellor, God the Mighty, Fa-

---

B. J. Warfield, "The Divine Messiah in the Old Testament," *Princeton Theological Review,* XIV (1916).

[49] Loisy, *L'Evangile et l'Eglise,* 42, 56, 57.

[50] See Dalman, *Die Wörte Jesu,* 223; Lagrange, *Revue Biblique* (1908), 491.

[51] 2 Sam 7:14.

[52] Ps 2:7 ff.

[53] 7:14, 8:8, 10

---

[46] Gen 1:3; Ps 32:9; Is 55:10, 11.

[47] Ps 106:20.

[48] See Touzard, *L'argument prophetique, Revue pratique d'apologetique,* VII (1908),

ther of the world to come, Prince of Peace.[54] . . . In his origin . . . as in his personal dignity, the predicted Messiah surpassed humanity.[55] . . . At last the visions of Daniel opened out new perspectives and the Messiah appeared in them on the clouds of heaven close to God.[56] . . .

We have discovered in the Old Testament many features which we shall find again in the doctrine of the Trinity; belief in the paternity of God, in the sanctifying action of his Spirit, the conception of his Wisdom . . . and of his Word . . . clearly enough personified, the affirmation of the transcendence of the Messiah. . . .

54 9:6.   56 Dan 7:13–14.
55 Mic 5:2.

II

GOD IN THE NEW TESTAMENT

A. A General Overview

K. Rahner[1] tries to find out how the men of the New Testament thought about God. Their unquestioning assurance of God's reality is based on the massive fact that God had revealed himself in his new activity in their own history. God is he who acts freely in an historical dialogue with men and tells about his "attributes" — which would otherwise remain hidden — only through this activity.

Unquestioning assurance of God's reality. The first thing that strikes us when we try to find out how the men

of the New Testament thought about God is the unquestioning assurance which characterized their conscious-

---

[1] K. Rahner, S.J., perhaps the most influential Catholic theologian today, editor of Denzinger's *Enchiridion Symbolorum* and co-editor of the new *Lexikon für Theologie und Kirche,* is the author of many articles and books, such as *Geist in Welt, Hörer des*

Wortes, Schriften zur Theologie, Nature and Grace, Mary, Mother of the Lord. This excerpt is from his book, *Theological Investigations,* Vol. I (Baltimore: Helicon Press, 1961) and is selected from pp. 94–99, 100–117.

ness of him. It never occurred to these men to raise the question of his existence as such. The New Testament knew nothing of all those characteristic features of our consciousness of God today . . . a fear that after all God may be nothing but a monstrous projection of man's subjective needs and yearnings. . . .

For the New Testament God is in the first place simply there. He is there: in spite of all his incomprehensibility and sublimity. . . . All they are concerned with is how this God, who has always been given and self-evident, actually behaves, so that man might for the first time learn how things really stand with himself and the world. . . . This unquestioning assurance of God's existence does not arise from any properly metaphysical considerations, nor is it troubled or put off balance by the awareness that this kind of genuine knowledge of God is absent in the rest of the New Testament world. . . . Proofs for the existence of God are never produced. . . .

In the second place, the unquestioning assurance of God's self-evident reality is not disturbed by the awareness of an ignorance of God in the pagan world round about.[2] For the New Testament this failure to apprehend God is always a moral fault and also its punishment. It knows of no ignorance or doubt about God which is morally neutral, any religious problematic which remains purely theoretical. . . . For Paul the failure is

thus a *refusal* to know God,[3] and the refusal is intrinsically and necessarily co-existent with actually knowing something about God all the time.[4] This is not the place to discuss this remarkable co-existence in man of a continual knowledge of God and a deliberate ignorance of him, and how we are to interpret it in logical and psychological detail; how it may be necessary to distinguish various layers in man's existential consciousness; how reference might be made to the phenomena of bad conscience, repression, self-deception, masked conscience. . . .

The men of the New Testament . . . were convinced that their Word did not encounter men to whom something till then simply unknown had to be brought home for the first time by careful instruction, but rather that it encountered men who had already had some kind of knowledge of God, even if they would not admit its truth, even if this truth was heavily overlaid in their minds by a settled ignorance — settled only in appearance. They brought tidings of the living God who had freely acted in history and so had disclosed himself to man as something infinitely beyond the capacities of the visible world; and at the same time their tidings laid bare a knowledge of God buried under original and personal sin — a kind of theological psychoanalysis, as it were.

Thus the revealed Word and natural knowledge of God mutually condition each other. The revealed Word presupposes men who really know something of God in spite of being

[2] Acts 17:30; Eph 4:18; Gal 4:8; 1 Th 4:5; 2 Th 1:8; 1 Cor 1:21.

[3] Rom 1:18 ff.
[4] Rom 1:19, 21, 28, 32; 2:14.

lying and lost through sinfully idolizing the world; and on the other hand, this concealed knowledge of God only becomes really conscious of itself when it breaks through men's hardness of heart and is released by the Word of the God who reveals himself as utterly beyond the world.

The inner reason. . . . For this unquestioning assurance which characterizes men's consciousness of God in the New Testament is the simple and massive fact that God had *revealed himself,* that by his action he had intervened in these men's history and so had given testimony to his own actuality. Above all else the men of the New Testament are convinced that God had revealed himself in the Old Testament history of the People of the Covenant.[5] But their knowledge of God is not derived just from his self-disclosure in the past history of their People; they experience the living reality of God in his new activity in their own history. God reveals himself anew to them too. God has spoken to them in his own Son *now.*[6] . . . The Son has declared God to them, whom no one has seen;[7] they have seen the Son of God with their own eyes, have heard him, and touched him with their hands.[8] . . .

God as Person. A further consequence . . . is that for the men of the New Testament God's personal being is a living reality. . . . The countless examples of living prayer in the New

Testament are so many testimonies to the personal God in whom primitive Christianity believed; and they indicate at the same time in what sense the concept of God's personality must be understood here: the God of the New Testament is a God whom men may address as *Thou,* in a way in which only a personal being can be addressed as *Thou.* We shall see in more detail what was involved in thinking of God as a Person by attempting to set out the individual elements in this conception of a personal God. God is he who acts; he who is free; he who acts in an historical dialogue with men; and he who in the true sense tells us about his "attributes" — which would otherwise remain hidden — only through this activity.

God as He who Acts. In metaphysical knowledge of God from the world, where God is apprehended in the sense of Vatican I's definition as *"principium et finis"* of all reality, God is also in a certain sense one who acts, he who sets up all reality. . . . But God's activity is in a certain sense concealed in "natural" theology by the mere fact that for the metaphysician absolutely *everything* is an objectivization of God's activity. In this way God's activity remains transcendent. . . . Because *everything* is God's action, this action fades as it were into the anonymity of the Always and Everywhere, as far as human knowledge is concerned, for human knowledge remains essentially dependent on recognizing something by bringing it into relief against other things of a different kind.

---

[5] Heb 1:1; Acts 3:13; 5:30; Mt 22:32; Lk 1:72; Mt 2:6; Rom 9:4; Gal 3:17.
[6] Heb 1:2; Tit 2:11; 3:4; 2 Tim 1:10; 1 Pet 1:21.
[7] Jn 1:18.
[8] 1 Jn 1:1.

Now what characterizes the experience of God in the New Testament (as of course it did in the Old Testament too) is that it knows of a definite and distinct activity of God *within* the world: it knows of God's saving activity in history, an activity which, as God's new, free initiative, neither instituted jointly with the world nor already contained in it, possesses a quite definite Here and Now in the world and in human history, distinct from all other being and becoming. . . . It is from this experience of God's free personal activity within history that the confession of God as *Creator of the world,* simply speaking, also acquires its specific vitality and clarity.[9] . . . The New Testament (like the Old) accepts its knowledge of the world's createdness in the strict sense from the God who speaks and reveals himself. . . . Thus knowledge of God's historical activity within the world and knowledge of his creative omnipotence through his mere Word over against everything which is not he, complete and support each other reciprocally. . . .

God as He who Acts freely. This God who acts in Nature and in human history is one who acts *freely.* God manifests himself as Person in his activity precisely by the fact that this activity is voluntary and free. . . . It is on the basis of a concrete experience of free irruptions into the historical course of the world, novel and unexpected and extrinsic to the world's immanent dynamism, that the men of the New Testament recognize God as

a free, transcendent Person. . . . And this is to say that God's freedom has determined from the very beginning a goal for the world and for men which is in fact infallibly pursued and attained in the history of the world. . . .

God is He who acts in an historical dialogue with Men. In the third place God shows himself as Person in that he deals with man in an historical *dialogue,* that he allows man, his creature, really to be himself a person. . . . It is almost impossible for metaphysics to avoid the danger of forgetting the two-sided personal relationship between God and the created spirit. . . . Further, this relationship between God and man, which is so obscure for metaphysics, is seen at its clearest precisely in the *saving* history of God's dealings with man. Man takes part in a real *dialogue* with God. He gives God's Word to him the answer which he, man, wants to give. And this may turn out contrary to God's will. Man can harden his heart,[10] he can resist the Spirit of God,[11] he can obey or not obey God's will,[12] he can contradict God,[13] he can shut the doors of his heart to God when he knocks,[14] he can set his will in opposition to God's plan of salvation.[15]

The attributes of God. We have to know God as Person before we can understand . . . that everything depends for man on how God in fact

9 Mt 11:25; Mk 13:19; Jn 1:3; Acts 4:24; Rom 11:36; 1 Cor 8:5 f.; Col 1:16.

10 Rom 2:5; Heb 3:13.
11 Acts 7:51.
12 Rom 15:18; 16:19.
13 Rom 10:21.
14 Apoc 3:20.
15 Mt 23:37 f.

behaves with regard to man, not just on how he necessarily is in himself. . . . The kernel of what the New Testament declares about God's "attributes," then, is not a doctrine about God as an abstract metaphysical entity, but an announcement about the concrete personal countenance which God shows to the world. . . .

The existentially personal and active character of God's behavior, in contrast to some fixed metaphysical attribute of his essence, is just as clear when he is called *good, merciful, loving,* and so on. He is forgiving,[16] merciful,[17] kind, [18] loving.[19] He is the

God of all grace,[20] the God of hope,[21] the God of peace,[22] the God of all comfort,[23] the God of love,[24] the Savior,[25] who in his compassion desires the salvation of all men.[26] . . . Properly and precisely, we know *who* God is . . . only from the activity in history of the free and living God, through which he showed us who he wished to be to us. Consequently the teaching of the New Testament in the ultimate analysis is not an ontology of God's attributes . . . but an historical account of the experiences in which man has come to know God.

B. God in the Synoptics

1. **B. M. Ahern**[1] **studies the vital continuity between the Old Testament and the New Testament. This living bond is best exemplified in the vital typology of Israel's exodus from Egypt. From the beginning the prophets saw that there had to be a new exodus and a new covenant. Christ fulfilled all the rich hopes of the prophets. In pondering the many Gospel applications of Exodus typology we come to a new, rich appreciation of the perfect deliverance that God wrought in and through Jesus.**

Upheaval stirred the world of Abraham. . . . All flesh had corrupted its way; God's clean sun shone on a pool full of death. But life still throbbed at Haran in northern Mesopotamia,

for Abraham lived there. . . . All future history would flow from him.[2] For one day at Haran, in the middle of the nineteenth century before Christ, God spoke to the heart of this

---

16 Mt 6:14; Mk 11:25.
17 Lk 1:72, 78; 6:36; 2 Cor 1:3; Eph 2:4; 1 Tim 1:2; Tit 3:5; 1 Pet 1:3.
18 Mt 19:17; Lk 11:13; 18:19; Jas 1:5.
19 Jn 3:16; 16:27; Rom 5:5; 8:37, 39; Eph 2:4; 2 Th 2:16; Tit 3:4.
20 Acts 20:24; Rom 5:15; 1 Cor 1:4; 3:10; 15:10; 2 Cor 1:12; Eph 3:2, 7.
21 Rom 15:13.
22 Rom 15:33; 16:20; 1 Cor 1:3; 2 Cor 1:2; Gal 1:3; Eph 1:2; Phil 4:9.
23 Rom 15:5; 2 Cor 1:3-4; 2 Th 2:16.
24 2 Cor 13:11.
25 Lk 1:47; 1 Tim 1:1; 2:3; 4:10; Tit 2:11; 2 Pet 3:9.
26 Mt 18:14; 1 Tim 2:3, 4; 4:10; Tit 2:11; 2 Pet 3:9.
1 B. M. Ahern, C.P., was born in 1915. Among his published works are *Mary, Queen of the Poor,* and *The Epistle to the Galatians and to the Romans.* This excerpt is from his book, *New Horizons* (Notre Dame, Indiana: Fides Publishers, Inc., 1963), pp. 29–46.
2 Rom 4:17.

tribal chief[3] and broke it wide open with a freshet of mercy, which gushed forth to cleanse all hearts by faith.

The divine word promised a blessed future, without telling its precise elements or the time of its coming. Long centuries were to pass before this pledge was fulfilled. But . . . hardly had he spoken when his promise began to send forth clean water that spread out in ever-widening circles of mercy and loving fidelity until it covered the earth.[4] The mercy of God touching each generation performs a univocal work of redeeming from death and of invigorating with life, so that all successive moments of history follow the same pattern: the wide outer circle of Christian fulfillment is of the same form as the small inner circle of God's promise to Abraham; and all the circles between bear similar shape. Thus a vital continuity binds fast the story of salvation; far from opposing the Old Testament, the New Testament, to use the apt phrase of Père de Vaux, "prolongs it."

It must be so, for God has shaped all to the full measure of his Christ. Through him the waters of divine mercy were to touch all shores; and so, the vast outer circle of mercy's worldwide expansion gives form to every inner circle, even to the first circle of the water's origin in the heart of Abraham. Christ's redeeming death is at once the cause and the pattern of every previous deed of divine mercy. Typology, then — mighty deeds foreshadowing mightier to come —inheres in the Old Testament as a necessary consequence of the Christian quality of all God's work. In his great deeds for Israel, God so kept his Son in mind that Søren Kierkegaard could speak of "the eternal contemporaneousness of Christ"; and the Master himself could say, "Abraham your father rejoiced that he was to see my day. He saw it and was glad."[5]

This living bond between the Old and New Testaments is best exemplified in the vital typology of Israel's exodus from Egypt. The event was of supreme importance, for it played a unique creative role in forming the nation, in fashioning its faith and way. . . . The basic historicity of the narrative cannot be questioned; it is an authentic witness to real events that marked the birth of Israel as a nation and of the worship of Yahweh. . . . It required centuries for Israel to taste the full flavor of the Sinai revelation and to understand how the name Yahweh was at once the source of all fear and of all hope. . . . It was the memory of the exodus that did most to convince Israel of God's power and pity. . . . Ever after, Israel looked back to the exodus and to the Sinai pact as the birth hour of the nation. Its history was often marred by infidelities, but no weakness of man could obliterate three dominant factors which Sinai burned into the Israelite soul: there is but one God; one chosen people; one country in which to work out the people's destiny. . . .

But there was a twofold orientation in Israel's faith. It centered in the historical exodus which has passed, but it looked forward also to an exodus

---

[3] Gen 12:1–3.
[4] Ezek 47:1–12.

[5] Jn 8:56.

yet to come. The reason is obvious. God had promised a full flowering, and the merciful pledge of Yahweh, the faithful One, is without repentance. Yet daily events brought bitter experience that the deliverance from Egypt and the covenant of Sinai were not definitive. . . . From the very beginning, then, the prophets saw that there had to be a new exodus and a new covenant.[6]

It was Christ who fulfilled all the rich hopes of the prophets. His very name held promise; for, as the angel explained to Joseph, this name was at once a symbol and a guarantee that, at long last, Yahweh had come to save his people.[7] It was but natural, then, that the writers of the New Testament should find in Israel's exodus from Egypt a leitmotiv for their own description of the work of Christ. Steeped as they were in the Scriptures, these men tended to locate the Savior in the biblical context of the great deliverance. The word "exodus," as used by them, always resounds with the full meaning of that historic event.

Often enough there is striking agreement among all the evangelists in handling the elements of this typology; such identifications were probably fixed and made permanent in the oral catechesis which preceded the writing of the Gospels. Yet, at the same time, there is also marked fluidity; Jesus is variously identified with the God of the exodus, with Israel itself, with Moses the leader, or with the chief factor in some incident of the exodus. Such divergence should

occasion no surprise; for all these different aspects merely stress that the basic typology of exodus must be sought in the mercy and fidelity of a saving God who, in solicitude for Israel, penetrated every person, event, and thing with his own divine power. Each element in the story of the exodus foreshadowed the much greater work of Christian redemption in which divine power penetrated the human nature and human deeds of Jesus, to work a definitive liberation from sin and an eternal covenant with God. Therefore, in pondering the many gospel applications of exodus typology, we come to a new, rich appreciation of the perfect deliverance that God wrought in and through Jesus.

Among the Synoptics, the Gospel of St. Matthew is especially rich with this typology. The avowed purpose of the author of the first Gospel was to stress the continuity between the Old and the New Law. It is obvious, then, that he would utilize the widespread Jewish expectation that "in the last days" God must work a new exodus. In developing this theme, Matthew, like Mark, stresses a similarity between the experiences of Christ and those of the chosen people of God. Thus, the return of the Holy Family from Egypt, after the death of Herod, is seen by Matthew as a new exodus; and so he captions it with the very words Hosea had used to describe the earlier event: "Out of Egypt I called my son."[8] The beginnings of the Savior's public life are also linked to similar incidents in the history of Israel.

---

[6] Hos 2:16–25.
[7] Mt 1:31.

[8] Mt 2:15; Hos 11:1.

As Israel was baptized into its new life with God by passing through the waters of the Red Sea, so Christ inaugurates his ministry for God by accepting baptism in the waters of the Jordan.[9] Thereafter both Israel and Christ live through a period of desert life and temptation. The forty days of Christ in the desert has its parallel in the forty years of Israel; his temptation accords with Israel's testing; his food is the word of God that comes down from heaven, just as Israel's food in the desert is not the bread of man's making but the manna of God's giving.[10] It is especially noteworthy that Christ defeats his tempter with texts from the book of Deuteronomy, all of them summing up the wisdom of God that guided and strengthened Israel.

After this early identification of Christ with Israel, Matthew prefers to emphasize the resemblance between Christ and Moses. Generalizations are, of course, always a risk. But there is some justification for saying that Matthew's chief concern is to represent Christ as a second Moses, greater by far than the first lawgiver of Israel. The keynote of this identification is sounded in Matthew's representation of Christ's first discourse, the Sermon on the Mount.[11] As Moses drafted the law of the Old Covenant, so Christ presents here the law of the New. This law is perfect in every way; and Christ himself is a lawgiver of divine holiness and authority. As a master he handles the earlier law with deft touch, changing at will and fashioning

to perfection. God had spoken through Moses; but this new Moses is more than an instrument, infinitely more than the mouthpiece of God. And so "the crowds were astonished at his teaching; for he was teaching them as one having authority."[12]

This resemblance between the two lawgivers dominates all the later discourses of Jesus in the first Gospel; indeed, the Master draws largely from Deuteronomy for the expression of his own thoughts. Moreover, there is likeness even in Christ's method of teaching. His soul, like that of Moses, was a limpid pool reflecting divine truth without distortion; in both men passion was controlled; nothing disturbed their tranquil grasp of truth or marred the clarity of its expression. For God said of Moses, "Moses was by far the meekest man on the face of the earth,"[13] just as Christ said of himself, "Learn from me, for I am meek and humble of heart."[14]

The wonders and miracles of Christ also point a likeness between himself and Moses. Through both lawgivers God wrought mighty works to authenticate their mission and to win for their law a hearing. It is not the meaning of the miracle that interests Matthew, nor its resemblance in kind to the miracles of Moses. Thus, he is content to tell the story of the multiplication of the loaves without referring, as John does, to the profound symbolism of bread coming miraculously from heaven. Matthew's concern is with the fact itself. Miracles

---

[9] Mt 3:13–17; Mk 1:9–11.
[10] Mt 4:1–11; Mk 1:12–13.
[11] Mt 5–7.

[12] Mt 7:28–29.
[13] Num 12:3.
[14] Mt 11:29.

are God's own work as he had wrought wonders through Moses, so now he was working in Jesus. Both were lawgivers mighty not only in word but also in deed.

It is especially in describing the Transfiguration that both Matthew and Mark bring into focus the typology of Moses.[15] Here the two great lawgivers of Old Covenant and New meet face to face; and the bright cloud that once overshadowed Moses[16] now descends upon Jesus. Heaven's authentication of the new Moses follows the pattern of its approval of the old.

The author of the fourth gospel is even more pointed in showing how Christ fulfilled the typology of Israel's exodus from Egypt. . . . Like Matthew, John too marks a resemblance between Christ and the lawgiver of Israel. . . . But in his treatment of the life and work of Christ many new aspects of similarity appear . . . The chief of these is the Paschal Lamb motif. . . . In John's eyes, Christ is the true Lamb of God who shed his blood on Calvary to save men from the death of sin and to liberate them for the promised land of heaven. . . . He finds also many other resemblances. For him, Christ is the light of the world[17]. . . . The manna from heaven was yet another element of Israel's exodus which St. John utilized as a type of Christ's beneficent action. . . . The brazen serpent, too, figures in the fourth Gospel as a type of the heal-ing power of Christ's redemption[18]. . . .

All in all, the story of Christ as told in the Gospels is understood when it is read in the biblical context of Israel's exodus. For Matthew, Mark, and John were all true Israelites, steeped in the Scriptures and sharing Israel's hope for an ineffable renewal of the divine mercy that led the chosen people out of Egypt. . . . It is the merit of the evangelists that they found in Christ the perfect fulfillment of all the Old Testament hopes — the "substance" that had cast out the shadows.[19]

The life and work of Christ are not over. Before he died, the Savior promised to abide with his Church always — ever the same Christ "yesterday, today, yes, and forever."[20] Strong is the bond between Moses and Israel, but stronger still, intimate as no other, is the union which binds Christ to his people in the Church. For the new Moses and the new Israel are joined together as head and members of one mystical body, as bridegroom and bride of a true marriage. In the mystery of his Church, Christ is personally present to every age and renders accessible to every follower the very substance of his life and work upon earth. . . . She is the tremendous Sacrament that brings the Christ of the first century into every age and into every heart. . . . What was wrought in Jesus during his earthly life is renewed in the soul of every Christian. . . .

---

[15] Mt 17:1–8; Mk 9:1–7.
[16] Ex 33:9–10.
[17] Jn 8:12.

[18] Jn 3:14; Num 21:9.
[19] Col 2:17.   [20] Heb 13:8.

2. G. Saldarini and G. Biffi[1] start their study of the three divine Persons in the New Testament from the "experience" and "formulas" of the apostolic community. In the Synoptic catechesis they see Jesus presented as the Messiah and with prerogatives proper to Yahweh, while the Holy Spirit appears at times as a personal being distinct from Christ. In the Infancy Gospels they find affirmation of the Messianicity of Jesus, adumbrations of his divinity and probably of the personality of the Holy Spirit.

The "experience" of the apostolic Community. The New Testament gives us secure data that the Christian community took its beginning from a characteristic *religious experience* that accompanied the annunciation of (kergyma) and the faith in the evangelic message. That experience is constantly marked by the presence of the Spirit who is offered[2] and "received."[3] A new Christianity was founded when this effusion of the Spirit took place.[4] The gospel is not the preaching alone but the experience of power and the Holy Spirit, as St. Paul said to the Thessalonians.[5]

These effusions allude to the "matrix" experience of the Holy Spirit on Pentecost[6] and recall Old Testament accounts of prophetic visions and theophanies[7] — and Christ's promises[8] and his Last Supper discourse. . . .

All these religious experiences are not described as generic divine possessions but are constantly referred to one mysterious agent, the Holy Spirit.

The "formulas" of the Apostolic community. If the experience provoked by the Spirit accompanied the announcement of the "word," what was this word? The content of this word was beyond doubt eminently *Christological* and concerned in the first place with Jesus of Nazareth.[9] The simplest profession of faith touched Jesus as the Messiah whom Israel had awaited and God had sent: Jesus is the Christ.[10] Another somewhat richer formula presented Jesus Risen and Lord as the object of faith.[11]

There is what we can call a trinitarian schema: God sent his Son. . . . and sent the Spirit of his Son.[12] In both of these, it is the Son that is directly considered in his work of salvation. The Father sends him and the Spirit comes as gift consequent on the Son's redemptive action. Father and

---

[1] G. Saldarini and G. Biffi are the authors of various theological articles in *La Scuola Cattolica* at Milan. One of G. Biffi's articles is "Colpa e libertá nell odierna condizione umana." This excerpt is from their article, "Le Tre Persone Divine Nel Nuovo Testamento," in *La Scuola Cattolica* 87–88 (1959–1960), pp. 241–277.

[2] Gal 3:5.
[3] Gal 3:2.
[4] Gal 3:2–4.
[5] 1 Th 1:2–6; cf. Acts 10:44–48.
[6] Acts 2:1–36.
[7] Ezek 1:4–28; 8:2–3.
[8] Lk 24:49; Acts 1:7–8.

[9] Cf. Y. Tremel, "Remarques sur l'expression de la foi trinitaire dans l'Eglise apostolique," *Lumière et vie*, n. 28, pp. 41–66; O. Cullmann, *Les premieres Confessions de foi chrétienne* (Paris, 1948).

[10] Mk 8:29; Acts 2:36; 3:20.
[11] Rom 10:9.
[12] Gal 4:4–6; cf. Acts 2:33–34.

Spirit are implied without being the direct object of the apostolic message: they are necessary for understanding what Christ has done. . . . The Holy Spirit as principle of the "experience" is very rarely included in the "content" of the Christological profession of faith. His function is rather to provoke this profession. He is rather in the line of subject than of object.[13]

Faith, i.e., the acceptance of the announcement, finds from the first instant of Christianity its ritual expression in baptism.[14] The salvific work of Christ and its ritual application seem to suggest three distinct sacred names: God (or Father), Lord (or Christ), and Spirit.[15] And anticipating we can add that the connection between Baptism and Trinity is confirmed by the ecclesial catechesis as fixed by the Synoptics at the baptism of Christ in a trinitarian epiphany.

These bonds between baptism and the Trinity were sanctioned (probably) by the ritual formula of baptism in the name of the Father and of the Son and of the Holy Spirit.[16] . . . This formula expresses both the faith of the baptized in the three divine Persons and the consecration of the baptized to them. The Son and the Spirit are placed exactly on the same level as the Father with a simplicity, a lucidity, and a force that could not be greater. . . .

The Synoptic Catechesis. This offers an ample development of the kerygmatic formula already considered. It begins with the baptism of

Jesus[17] and ends with the order of Christ to announce the remission of sins through baptism.[18] The content of this catechesis is clearly Christological: a presentation of Jesus of Nazareth as the Messiah, sent by God, who has died and risen for the salvation of sinners.

But there is also in it a clear intention to gather and express the exact relation between Christ and Yahweh — through a series of concepts that associate Jesus of Nazareth with the God of Israel in an indirect but progressively more marked manner. Jesus is not only a prophet and master but one with *power* over storms, maladies, demons, sinners[19] . . . and this power is what distinguishes him from all the rabbis.[20] A second indirect means is the confrontation of Jesus and the great ones of Hebrew history to show his superiority.[21] In the third place the Synoptists are intent on attributing to Christ the prerogatives proper to Yahweh. Just as Yahweh, so Christ is the only one who can work on the Sabbath — who disposes of angels — pardons sins — has the law under his dominion . . . and must be loved as Yahweh with a man's whole heart and power. But filiation is the category most emphasized by the Synoptists to express the relation between God and Jesus of Nazareth: *Jesus is the Son.*[22]

Not surprisingly the Holy Spirit is

[13] 1 Cor 12:3.
[14] Acts 2:38.
[15] 1 Cor 6:11; Eph 4:4–6; Tit 3:4–6.
[16] Mt 28:19.
[17] Mt 3; Mk 1; Lk 3.
[18] Mk 16:15–16; Mt 28:19; Lk 24:47.
[19] Mk 4:41; 9:25; Mt 9:1–8.
[20] Mt 7:29; Mk 1:27.
[21] Mt 12:41–42.
[22] Cf. A. George, "Le Père et le Fils dans les évangiles synoptiques," *Lumière et vie,* n. 29, pp. 27–40.

found even in the catechetical development of the kerygma somewhat in the shadow and only sporadically recorded. A first group of texts from the preaching of John the Baptist presents Christ as the one who baptizes in "the Holy Spirit."[23] Whatever these words may have signified in the mouth of the Baptist, it is certain that in the catechesis they allude to Pentecost and to the baptismal experience of the first Christian community.

In a second group of texts in the episode of Jesus' baptism and return to the desert,[24] the Spirit beyond doubt appears as a personal being distinct from Christ (and the Father).[25] In a third group of citations in the discourses of Christ[26] the personality of the Spirit is not proved apodictically from the parallel "blasphemy against the Son." This seems to be the trinitarian scheme of the Synoptics, but it must be taken cautiously. . . .

The Infancy Gospels. These narratives are complete in themselves and clearly independent of each other. They reveal a sufficiently clear intention of giving a Christian interpretation of some ideas of the Old Testament in a set of facts about the Infancy of Jesus.

The fundamental concept of Mt's text seems to be the affirmation of the Messianicity of Jesus of Nazareth through his kinship with David and Abraham[27] and through the narrative of the virginal birth.[28] Another idea that Mt's infancy narrative stresses is messianic universalism — in the episode of the Magi.[29] The divinity of Christ is adumbrated in the Messianic name of Emmanuel.[30] The two mentions of the Holy Spirit[31] signify the prodigy of the virgin birth. But it is difficult to say whether in the original redaction the term *pneuma* was used in the personal sense.

In Lk's text the connaturality of Christ, "Son of the most High," with the God of Israel is signified in the fundamental theme of the book: to show in the Infancy of Jesus the eschatological ingress of Yahweh in time that was prophesied by Malachy.[32] This is confirmed by the attribution to Jesus of terms traditionally reserved to God: "holy,"[33] "king,"[34] "great" without specification,[35] "salvation,"[36] "horn of salvation,"[37] "savior,"[38] and "glory."[39] We come to the same conclusion if we consider that Mary is here called "daughter of Zion" (where Yahweh is present).[40] The Holy Spirit is recorded with particular insistence in these pages to indicate — as is usual

23 Mk 1:8; Mt 3:11; Lk 3:16.
24 Lk 3:22; Mk 1:12; Mt 4:1.
25 Cf. I. M. Voste, *De baptismo, tentatione, et transfiguratione Jesus* (Romae, 1934); P. Van Imschoot, "Baptême d'eau et baptême d'Esprit," *Ephemerides Theologicae Lovanienses,* 13 (1936), pp. 653–666.
26 Mt 12:28–32; Mk 3:28–30; Lk 12:10.

27 1:1–7.
28 1:18–25; cf. Is 7:14.
29 2:1–12; Is 2:2; Mic 4:1–5; Zeck 8:20–23; Is 56:6–8; 60:1–22.
30 1:23.
31 1:18, 20.
32 Mal 3:1.
33 1:35.
34 1:33.
35 1:32.
36 2:30.
37 1:69.
38 2:11.
39 2:32.
40 1:28–33; Jl 2:21–27.

in the Old Testament — the divine origin of the prophetic state.[41] And in the account of the annunciation he is placed in relation with the conception of Jesus (the Holy Spirit will come upon thee) to signify primarily the revelation to Mary that she is to become the new Saint of Saints who is to host in herself Emmanuel (an affirmation of the divinity of Christ) and also to signify virginal birth.

The first readers of these pages, i.e., the Christians of the apostolic epoch, must have found natural enough the intervention at the beginning of the human life of Christ of the same personage who presided at the birth of Christianity (the Holy Spirit). Note too that a reading of the term *pneuma* in a personal sense —controvertible if one considers the infancy gospel as a document standing by itself — seems most probable at the moment of the incorporation of the document in the third Gospel.

3. B. Piault[1] thinks it was the intent of Jesus and the Synoptists to force men to recognize his presence, reflect on his words and examine his deeds closely, so that they might discover in them the mystery of his relationship to the Father and the mystery of his own person. And who can doubt that Matthew wishes to teach us the divine origin and nature of God's envoy?

The baptism of Jesus.[2] Jesus is baptized by John the Baptist. The Holy Spirit comes down upon him in bodily form, like a dove, and a voice is heard from heaven saying: "Thou art *my* beloved Son; in thee I am well pleased."

In order to understand this, it is necessary to go back once more to the Old Testament. The voice from heaven is that of the Father. . . . The voice quotes Is 42:1, changing two of the terms. Where Isaiah put "ser-

vant," the evangelists write "Son" and for "man of my choice," "beloved"; "Here is my servant to whom I grant protection, the man of my choice, greatly beloved."

Now in the Greek Septuagint version of the Old Testament the word "beloved" also means "only." For example, where the Hebrew of Gn 22:2 and 16 says that Isaac was Abraham's "only" son, the Greek version gives "beloved." The process becomes clear: Greek biblical language uses a word with two meanings: *beloved* and *only*. When the evangelists quote this passage of Is 42:1, they are proclaiming two things: First, that Jesus is the "servant of God" in the biblical sense, the Messiah who is spoken of in Is 42:1 and 53, the elect of God who is to bear the weight of the people's sins. But it also declares that this

---

[41] Of John 1:15; of Elizabeth 1:41; of Zachary 1:67; of Simeon 2:25–27.

[1] B. Piault was born in 1913 and teaches dogmatic theology at the Seminary of the Mission de France. Among his published works are "Le mystére du Dieu vivant, un et triune" and "La création et le péché originel." This excerpt is from his book, *What Is The Trinity?* trans. from the French by Rosemary Haughton (New York: Hawthorn, 1959), pp. 29–42.

[2] Lk 3:21–22; Mt 3:13–17; Mk 1:9–11.

servant is to be "the son." Second, they wish it to be understood that this "servant-son" is "beloved," that is, chosen above all,[3] hence "only." In other words Jesus is "God's only Son."

The teaching in this passage is now clear. When the bystanders who surrounded Jesus at his baptism heard the heavenly voice, they were being invited to recognize Jesus as the Messiah, a Son so privileged that he is even called the "only Son." There was enough in this to make the Israelites think deeply about the meaning of the sonship of Jesus. It is also possible that the bodily form like a dove had already given a hint of the presence of the Spirit of the Lord at work, because this form might well bring to mind the image of Genesis 1:2. . . . It is unlikely, however, that the Jews saw in this even a glimpse of a manifestation of the Trinity.

But when the evangelists assure us that the bodily form like a dove is the Holy Spirit, they are instructing us on the use and the nature of this manifestation as well as on the meaning of this whole theophany. In common with the whole Church we can be sure that in this passage the Gospel is teaching us that Jesus is the Son of the Heavenly Father in the exact sense of the word "Son" and that the third person of the Blessed Trinity rested upon him at his baptism. The pen of the sacred author was inspired in order to give us certainty on this point. . . .

The Son. It is around the person of Jesus in particular that the new teaching takes shape; and it is through

Jesus that the Three-in-One is to be imprinted on the mind and heart of man. Jesus announces his mysterious sonship unobtrusively, and his message is given more fully only as the end of his mission approaches. But it required nothing less than the whole of his earthly life to draw the attention of the Jews to the very special relationship which he claims with God, whom he calls his Father, and with the Holy Spirit. In this way, gradually the mystery is revealed.

All through his life Jesus strove to bring his disciples to the discovery of his special relationship with God the Father, a relationship utterly transcending their own.[4] Jesus claims to be "the son of God" on other grounds than those on which men may claim this title.[5] He is called "Son of God" by Satan,[6] by the devils,[7] and by the centurion when he is dying on the cross.[8] But it will be noticed that nothing in these passages makes it possible to say what kind of sonship unites Jesus with his Father. . . . Whenever the Messiah performs miracles, people are surprised that he should be able to do so. To make them ask questions, to encourage reflection about himself . . . is what Jesus wants. There was some mystery about him.

There was a beautiful text of great significance spoken by Jesus in Mt 11:25–27. In it he states that none knows the Father truly except the Son, and that he himself has a su-

[3] Cf. Transfiguration in Lk 9:35.
[4] Lk 2:49–50.
[5] Mt 6:32; 7:21; 10:32; 12:50; Lk 11:13; 12:32.
[6] Mt 4:1–11.
[7] Mt 8:20.
[8] Mt 27:54.

perior knowledge of the Father, a knowledge which is his to communicate to whom he pleases. This declaration has enormous force. It can only be interpreted as referring to knowledge in the most complete sense, which alone makes possible an unequalled intimacy between Father and Son. The Old Testament was certainly well aware that God alone knows his own plans.[9] If, then, Jesus knows them too, it is because he is God. We cannot help asking what echo his words can have found in the hearts of his disciples. What happened afterward shows clearly enough that they did not understand immediately. In fact, not long afterward Jesus and the twelve are at Caesarea Philippi and Jesus is trying to find out what they believe about him.[10] We must read this passage carefully. Peter's profession of faith still implies only a recognition of Jesus as Messiah. It is true that Matthew reports Peter as saying "Thou art the Christ, the Son of the living God," but Mark gives only "Thou art the Christ"[11] and Luke "The Christ whom God has anointed."[12] And that, at the time, was what Jesus wanted people to say about him. . . . Peter proclaims his faith in the Christ of God. For the time being that was enough because it was necessary for the community of Israel to recognize its Messiah . . . to recognize that the Messianic age had come. . . .

In the parable of the unfaithful vine-dressers[13] Jesus relates how they put to death first the servants, then the Son. This contrast between the Son, the heir to the vineyard, and the servants . . . emphasizes the pre-eminence of Jesus: he surpasses the prophets who preceded him. This is a transcendence which none of the Jews could fail to understand: from that moment they began to desire his death. . . .

To Caiaphas who is questioning him, Jesus declares that he is "the son of God." This statement is regarded as blasphemy. Why? Jesus asserts first of all that he is the Messiah spoken of in Dan 7:13: He "is seated at the right hand of God's power and comes on the clouds of heaven." But the characteristics of the Messiah in this passage are heavenly ones because of his mysterious origin: he will come "on the clouds of heaven." On the other hand Jesus' origins are known to all to be earthly: he is the son of Joseph and Mary. Hence in the eyes of Caiaphas the incredible nature of Jesus' words: how can he be the Messiah-Son of God of whom Daniel speaks? His pretension passes all bounds and issues in blasphemy. Here again the exact nature of the sonship of Jesus is almost certainly not even glimpsed, but who can doubt that Matthew, the inspired writer, wishes to teach us the divine origin and nature of God's envoy? . . .

We can only conclude that the early preaching of the apostles, or at least as much of it as was recorded in the Acts and in the Synoptic Gospels in the middle of the first century stated that Jesus was the *Christ of God*, the *Son of his choice*, the *only*

---

9 Is 40:13.
10 Mt 16:13–21.
11 8:20.
12 9:20.
13 Mt 21:33–46.

Son, beloved above all. We must certainly not see in this a lack, even after Pentecost, in the apostles' own knowledge of Jesus; it is rather a desire to present their Master in such a way that their hearers could accept him without scandal. They themselves knew quite well that the Master had acted in this way with them and with all the others, otherwise he would have been stoned on the spot. . . . But Jesus and the apostles after him . . . forced men to recognize his presence, to reflect on his words and examine his deeds closely, so that they might discover in them the mystery of his relationship to the Father and the mystery of his own person. . . .

4. J. L. McKenzie[1] studies the Father, Son, and Spirit of God. Jesus broadened and deepened the concept of the fatherhood of God, and speaks of the Father with an intimacy which appears nowhere in the Old Testament. Jesus has a unique relation to the Father, shared with no one, in virtue of which the Church proclaimed him Messiah, Lord, Son of God. The spirit of God is usually conceived as the mysterious divine impulse or power which it is in the Old Testament. But it is difficult to explain the Spirit in the theophany of Jesus' baptism in this way. And in the baptismal formula the listing of the three under "the name" is perhaps the most explicit declaration of the personal character of the Spirit in the entire New Testament.

The Father. It is evident that Jesus did not introduce the concept of the fatherhood of God as something entirely new. It is, however, broadened and deepened. The concept of God as father includes the notion of paternal love and care.[2] The love of the Father in heaven is a model of the love with which the disciples should love even their enemies.[3] The Father is the model of the perfection which the disciples should seek to attain.[4] . . . and an example of forgiveness.[5] Perhaps the supreme statement of God's paternal forgiveness appears in the parable of the prodigal son.[6]

Jesus often speaks of the Father with relation to himself in a different tone from that which he uses in speaking of the Father in relation to the disciples. . . . The difference is clearest in Mt 11:25–27, Lk 10:21 f. Here Jesus thanks the Father for what he has revealed to the little ones and concealed from the wise and knowing. He then affirms that the Father has revealed himself to the Son, i.e., Jesus, and that the Father and the Son know each other in a way which is not revealed and by implication cannot be revealed to anyone else.

Jesus and the Father. When we approach this question, we take the final step toward determining the identity of Jesus. It is a step at once easy and difficult: easy, because no theological problem has been the object

---

[1] J. L. McKenzie, S.J., Cf. Ch. I, 3, n. 1. This excerpt is from *op. cit.*, pp. 275, 830 ff., 842–843; 128 ff.; 132 ff.; 138 ff.

[2] Mt 6:5–8, 26 ff.

[3] Mt 5:43–45.   [5] Mt 6:14 f.

[4] Mt 5:48.   [6] Lk 15:1–32.

of so many declarations of the Church as the relations of Jesus to the Father; difficult, because these relations escape comprehension more than any other biblical truth. Jesus did certainly reveal God in a way which was revolutionary, more revolutionary than was perceived in the primitive Church. Yet one realizes at once that this relationship is incapable of comprehension from the outside. . . .

In the Gospels Jesus habitually refers to God as "the Father" or "my Father." This title is not entirely new; it occurs in the Old Testament perhaps about two dozen times; but it never receives a thematic treatment. The idea of God the Father is the dominant idea of God in the New Testament; it cannot be called dominant in the Old Testament. "Lord Yahweh," the most common invocation of God in the Old Testament, is the dominant Old Testament idea. . . .

It was not enough that Jesus should speak of the Father; it is the kind of fatherhood of which he speaks that is decisive. . . . The change . . . is a change in depth and not in quality. Jesus speaks of the Father with an intimacy which appears nowhere in the Old Testament. This flows from his own unique relationship with the Father. . . . His own intimacy is communicated to those who are identified with him.

The Son. The title "Son of God" is applied frequently to Jesus in the New Testament.[7] Modern writers point out

that the term is more congenial to a Hellenistic than to a Jewish background . . . but the New Testament use of the title does not reflect this Hellenistic background; Son of God is not a messianic title in Judaism. The title becomes a means by which the early Church expressed its faith in the absolutely unique character of Jesus. The use of the term reflects the developed faith of Easter and Pentecost. It is not obvious, however, that the title always meant precisely the same thing in all the New Testament writings, and it seems possible to trace a development.

The title appears in the annunciation narrative,[8] . . . in the confessions of the disciples[9] and Peter,[10] both occurring in exceptionally dramatic situations. The most solemn use of the title is in the scenes of the baptism[11] and in the transfiguration.[12] Here the title comes from the Father and authenticates the Son as his emissary. The sentence echoes the Servant Passage of Is 42:1; the servant of God turns out to be his Son. In the baptism the Spirit comes upon the Son.[13] Such a declaration from the Father obviously raises the sonship of Jesus above the common Old Testament use of the phrase. . . .

Jesus applies the title to himself. In the attestation demanded by the high priest Jesus accepts the title, and adds a prediction of his second coming in order to remove all doubt of its mean-

---

[7] Thirty-one times in the Synoptic Gospels, 42 times in the epistles, 23 times in John, where the title is most frequent, 3 times in Acts, once in Apoc.

[8] Lk 1:32, 35.
[9] Mt 14:33.
[10] Mt 16:16.
[11] Mt 3:17; Mk 1:11; Lk 3:22.
[12] Mt 17:5; Mk 9:7; Lk 9:35.
[13] Is 11:2; 61:1.

ing.[14] This obviously signifies a unique and supernatural sonship. In Mt 21:37f. and Mk 12:6 Jesus describes himself as the son of the owner of the vineyard slain by the vintners. Mt 11:27 ff. and Lk 10:22 ff. connect the title with a mutual knowledge of Father and Son which is shared by no one; only the Son in virtue of this intimate knowledge can reveal the Father. . . .

One may with P. Bonnard summarize the title in the Synoptics as indicating that Jesus is sent by the Father, possesses the Spirit, is the Son who realizes in his own person the sonship of Israel, the unique Son and heir who represents the Father to men, and who enjoys an exclusive and intimate union with the Father.

A unique relation to the Father. Jesus has a unique relation to the Father. . . . This relationship he shares with no one. When men are identified with Jesus Christ in the New Testament, they are adopted as sons of God; but adoption does not put them on the same plane with Jesus with reference to the Father. Jesus is the only-begotten Son. . . .

This relationship is designated by more than one term. The New Testament faithfully reflects the growth of faith and understanding in the primitive community. The Epistles . . . and the Gospel of John show a development of Christology which is not seen in the Synoptic Gospels. We have seen that the Church proclaimed Jesus Messiah and Lord in terms which he did not use himself; the Church also proclaimed Jesus Son in

[14] Mt 26:63 f.; Mk 14:61 f.

terms which he did not use himself. Here many critics . . . have said that the Church not only used language which was not the language of Jesus, but that it also made statements which did not reflect the teaching of Jesus. If this be true, one can only say that it is strange that the Church wrote and preserved in the Synoptic Gospels the only evidence which the critics have for asserting that the Church in other New Testament books was unfaithful to the teaching of Jesus. . . . It is far simpler to take the obvious course: that the New Testament is a document of growth, not of static assertions.

Son of God. We must remark that there were certain linguistic barriers to the New Testament use of the terminology of Nicaea and Chalcedon. The New Testament could not say simply that Christ was God until a development had been reached which is reflected in Jn 1:1 and not certainly in any other passage. "God" in Greek, *ho theos,* always means that Father whom Jesus revealed, identical with *ho theos* of the Old Testament, Yahweh. To call Jesus *theos* would be to identify him personally with the Father, a step which the primitive Church knew it must not take. When Jn 1:1 was written, the relations of Jesus and the Father were grasped with enough security to permit John to call Jesus *theos,* a divine being. Earlier, the phrase in a Jewish or Hellenistic context would have implied that the Word was another god. Hence Jesus can only be related to the Father obliquely; and the most common designation, which rests upon the words of Jesus in the Synoptic Gospels, is the Son of God. This title affirms personal distinction. It does not affirm identity of nature, for this philosophical term was not in the minds of the writers of the New Testament. It was sufficient for them that the title affirmed a unique sonship which is not the sonship of adoption communicated by Jesus to believers.

The title is exposed to that misconception which is called subordinationism, and this misconception appears early in the post-apostolic Church. In its most explicit form this heresy reduces Jesus to a level of being above the human but below that of the Father. . . . The New Testament did not encounter the danger of subordinationism and therefore did not couch its language deliberately in such a way as to neutralize the danger. Jesus speaks of his relationship to the Father in words which imply an intelligible conception of sonship: he is sent by the Father, he has a commission from the Father, he receives power from the Father, he does the will of the Father, he is the mediator between men and the Father. . . . In the Synoptic Gospels we find not that Jesus spoke of his unique sonship in the words of John and Paul, but that he assumed a position in the world which is unintelligible except as an exercise of unique sonship. . . . His teaching was invested with power and authority; this authority he takes no trouble to prove, but simply asserts. He is the one authoritative interpreter of the mind and will of the Father; he is the herald and the executor of the Father's plan of salvation. He treats the Law

of Judaism, the traditional revealed will of God, with a casual independence and assures those whom he addressed that the Law is insufficient to lead them to the Father. . . .

We have seen that Jesus exercises some reserve in the use of the titles of King and Messiah to designate his mission. It should not be surprising that he exercised even more reserve about his personal identity; but he did not exercise so much reserve that the Church could not discern that it gave its faith to a person like no other. Since the faith he demanded was the kind of faith given to no other, one can only say that there was a proportion between the two. In the sturdy Galilean peasant of wit and eloquence the disciples could discern a person of depths which they could not explore. To this person they committed themselves totally, and they did their best to convey to others the impact of the personality to which they had surrendered. The New Testament is the witness and the product of their faith. Jesus bore himself as the Son of his Father in a manner which was its own vindication. They who saw him saw the Father, and they knew that they had.

The Spirit. The spirit is given, first of all to Jesus himself in the baptism.[15] The repose of the spirit upon Jesus together with the word of the Father authenticates him as the Messiah.[16] In the infancy narrative of Matthew[17] the conception of Jesus is attributed to the holy spirit; this is

---

[15] Mt 3:13–17; Mk 1:9–11.
[16] Cf. Is 11:1 ff.
[17] 1:18, 20.

not only a denial of human paternity but also an affirmation that his coming is a work of the mysterious saving power of God so often mentioned in the Old Testament. . . .

The baptismal formula of Mt 28:19 is obviously a striking departure from these uses mentioned; and it is possible that this verse, like others in Matthew, represents a much more developed form of belief. The listing of the three under "the name" is perhaps the most explicit declaration of the personal character of the spirit in the entire New Testament; but it must be noticed that the very designation of spirit shows that the personality of the spirit is not to be conceived in the most obvious fashion.

The spirit is rare in Matthew and Mark compared to the writings of Luke, Paul, and John. E. Schweizer thinks this reflects their fidelity; they do not read back into the words of Jesus himself beliefs which became articulate only after Pentecost and the experiences of the primitive Church. The spirit in Matthew and Mark is generally the Old Testament spirit applied to the person and mission of Jesus. Outside of Mt 28:19 it cannot be called a personal being nor a being distinct from the Father. . . .

In the Old Testament spirit meant originally the movement of air, the breath, or the wind. It is a principle of life and of vital activity. . . . Like the word, spirit is a creative power. But the peculiar effects of the divine spirit are seen in men. Spirit is a power which moves men to do that which is normally impossible and enables them to rise above their capaci-

ties. . . . Spirit, then, is a mysterious divine force or impulse which explains the sudden and the unpredictable in human behavior; it is God at work in ways which are peculiarly his own. We must note that in the Old Testament this force is impersonal.

The Spirit in the New Testament. We observe a development of the idea of the spirit in the New Testament similar to the development of the idea of the person of Jesus. The word "Spirit" is used much less frequently in the Synoptic Gospels than it is in the Acts of the Apostles, the epistles, and the Gospels of John . . . and the reason the Spirit is more prominent outside the Gospels than within them is that Jesus himself spoke less of the Spirit than did the primitive community. But there is a passage of the Synoptic Gospels which could be called another meteor fallen from the Johannine or Pauline heaven. The theophany of the baptism[18] is represented as a revelation of the Father in a voice, of the Son in the flesh, and of the Spirit in a dove. This incident stands out in the Synoptic Gospels; for it is extremely difficult to point out passages in these Gospels where the Spirit is conceived as anything else than the mysterious divine impulse or power which it is in the Old Testament. . . . Even without the appearance of the Spirit in the epistles and the Gospel of John we would have difficulty in explaining the theophany of the baptism in the usual sense; for the theophany of the Spirit has no parallel in the Old Testament. What is more important, it has no

---

[18] Mt 3:13–17; Mk 1:9–11; Lk 3:21–22.

parallel in John and the epistles either. . . .

The novelty of the New Testament is as clear in its conception of the Spirit as it is anywhere. The prominence of the Spirit, the functions of

the Spirit, the relations of the Spirit to the Father and to Jesus are not derived from Judaism. And even less from any possible Hellenistic source. . . .

5. C. K. Barrett[1] studies the Holy Spirit and the Gospel Tradition, and asks why the Synoptic Gospels are almost silent about the Holy Spirit. He believes that direct emphasis upon the Spirit had to be avoided so that the Messiahship, the divine mission and status of Jesus of Nazareth might stand out.

No more certain statement can be made about the Christians of the first generation than this: they believed themselves to be living under the immediate government of the Spirit of God. After various necessary preliminaries, the most ancient book of Church History opens with a formal account of the inspiration of the disciples for their task, when, on the day of Pentecost, the Holy Spirit descended upon them in tongues of flame.[2] The note so impressively struck at the outset is not subsequently changed. There is hardly a chapter of the book in which the Spirit is not represented as at work. Every critical point in the Church's history, as here described, is made the scene of the Spirit's intervention. Thus, when the seven "deacons" were appointed, it was laid down that they should be men full of the Spirit.[3]

When Paul, in process of conversion and preparation for his mission, waited obediently at Damascus, Ananias was sent to him in order that he might receive the Holy Spirit.[4] When Peter first preached to the Gentiles, it was at the Spirit's command; and that he had rightly understood his instructions was indicated by a repetition of the event of Pentecost for the benefit of Cornelius and his circle.[5] The most critical point of the whole story — the separation of Paul and Barnabas for the purpose of undertaking missionary work of far wider scope than any that the original disciples had attempted — is recorded in these words: "The Holy Ghost said, 'Separate me Barnabas and Saul' . . . so they, being sent forth by the Holy Ghost, went down to Seleucia";[6] and the route of Paul's journey in Asia Minor, and his determination to make the decisive journey to Jerusalem, are attributed to the influence of the Spirit.[7] It is clear that the author of Acts thought of the history of the Church, at least in its

[1] C. K. Barrett has contributed articles to the *Journal of Theological Studies*, both the old and new series and is the author of *The Gospel According to St. John*. This excerpt is taken from his book, *The Holy Spirit and the Gospel Tradition* (London: S.P.C.K., 1960), pp. 1–4, 142, 157–159.
[2] Acts 2:1–4.
[3] Acts 6:3, 5.

[4] Acts 9:17.
[5] Acts 10:19 f.; 44–47; 11:12, 15 f.
[6] Acts 13:2, 4.
[7] Acts 16:6 f.; 19:21; 20:22 f.

early days, as governed from first to last by the Spirit of God.[8]

This picture of events cannot have been created by a late writer, of romantic inclination, who unblushingly idealized an entirely different state of affairs, since it is substantially the same as that suggested by much earlier documents. Paul's well-known account of spiritual persons and their gifts in 1 Cor bears it out. . . . The Pastoral Epistles preserve the same emphasis; and, much more important, so do the Johannine writings. . . . As markedly as does Acts, the Fourth Gospel points to a corporate reception of the Spirit as the beginning of the apostolic ministry of the Church.[9]

There is then no disputing our original statement that the Church of the first century believed that the Holy Spirit had been poured out upon it in a quite exceptional manner. It would therefore be surprising, were it not a fact to which we are well accustomed, to find that the Synoptic Gospels, on which alone we can rely for knowledge of the life and teaching of Jesus, are almost silent about the Holy Spirit, and that the teaching attributed to Jesus in them contains, on that subject, very few sayings, and those of doubtful authenticity. We have to ask whether this means that there is here a gulf between Jesus and the community which later professed allegiance to him. . . .

Dr. Leisegang[10] finds "The origin in Greek mysticism of the concept of

the Spirit in the Synoptic Gospels" . . . Dr. Windisch[11] first proves that the sayings of the Gospels which refer to the Spirit can be shown to be unauthentic (i.e., the saying of the Baptist; the baptism narrative; the temptation narrative; the expulsion of demons through the Spirit; blasphemy against the Spirit; the promise of the Spirit to the disciples); all are insertions due to editorial activity. . . . Dr. Flew[12] has another explanation: "There are few sayings about the Spirit, because Jesus saw that a richer and profounder understanding of the Spirit was needed than any which his disciples with their lack of insight could glean from the Old Testament; and this reinterpretation of the Spirit's work could only be lived out in his own ministry. . . . The whole conception of the Spirit in the Old Testament must needs be baptized into the death of Christ. Calvary was the only gateway to Pentecost. . . ."

Why do the Gospels say so little about the Spirit? . . . The faith — of the Evangelists — rested upon the Messiahship, the divine mission and status of Jesus of Nazareth. Hence, in comparison with the actual presence of the Lord's Anointed, and the operation of the powers of the kingdom of God, the commonplace phenomena of prophetic and other inspiration were insignificant and irrelevant. . . .

Accordingly, it is no more than should be expected that Jesus, who believed himself to be the divine deed to which the prophets had borne wit-

---

[8] Cf. Dr. Vincent Taylor in the Headingley Lectures on *The Doctrine of the Holy Spirit*, 41.

[9] Jn 20:22 f.

[10] In *Pneuma Hagion*.

[11] In *Studies in Early Christianity*, ed. by S. J. Case.

[12] In *Jesus and His Church*, 70 f.

ness, should refuse to detract from the significance of that divine event by laying stress upon his own inspiration, whether for prophetic speech or miraculous acts. It is markedly indicative of this attitude that he refused to give an account of his "authority" when it was demanded.

Direct emphasis upon the Spirit had to be avoided also because Jesus was keeping his Messiahship secret; to have claimed a pre-eminent measure of the Spirit would have been to make an open confession of Messiahship, if, as seems to have been the case, there was a general belief that the Messiah would be a bearer of God's spirit. But it was not merely that a secret had to be kept. Jesus acted under the necessity of a divine constraint.[13] Lack of glory and a cup of suffering were his Messianic vocation, and part of his poverty was the absence of all the signs of the Spirit of God. They would have been inconsistent with the office of a humiliated Messiah. . . .

If this be true, it is easy to understand why Jesus did not foretell the gift of the Spirit to the Church. There was no occasion for him to do so. The period of the humiliation and obscurity of the Messiah and his people was to continue until its climax and the day of final glorification. In the former period, the general gift of the Spirit was inappropriate; it would have divulged the secret of Jesus' Messiahship and it was not yet within the range of the kingdom, which was not yet *en dunamei*. In the latter period it was not a sufficiently significant feature of the eschatological hope to be mentioned. If the Messiah was coming on the clouds of heaven, what point was there in saying that he had the gift of the Spirit? He did not bestow the Spirit upon his followers, because that gift was a mark of the fully realized kingdom of God (not the germinal kingdom which corresponded to his veiled Messiahship). He did not prophesy the existence of a Spirit-filled community, because he did not foresee an interval between the period of humiliation and that of complete and final glorification. He did not distinguish between his resurrection and parousia, and accordingly there was no room for the intermediate event, Pentecost. . . .

C. God in St. Paul

1. J. Klausner[1] studies monotheism and the Messianicity and divinity of Jesus. He finds in Paul a monotheism that is blurred by the special function of the Pauline Messiah, a function which in Judaism is carried out by the one and only God himself. Through Jesus "are all things" and thus Jesus is second to God, though not actual deity.

---

[13] Mk 8:31; Lk 24:26.

[1] Joseph Klausner, Ph.D., was professor of Modern Hebrew Language and Literature in the Hebrew University, Jerusalem. Among his works are *Jesus of Nazareth*, translated from Hebrew into English by Dr. Herbert Danby, and a three-volume *History of Modern Hebrew Literature*. This excerpt is from his book, *From Jesus to Paul*, translated from the Hebrew by W. F. Stinespring of Duke University (New York: The Macmillan Co., 1944), pp. 467–485.

With regard to belief in a one and only God, Paul was still a Jew and not a Christian; belief in the Trinity still did not exist for him. There is only one God in the world, the God of Israel, whose children call him "Abba, Father"[2] there is "one God and Father of all, who is over all, and through all, and in all."[3] Paul says definitely, "God is one."[4] And still more definitely, ". . . the same God . . . worketh all things in all."[5]

We have in all this a thorough monotheism; yet it is not pure monotheism. The addition with regard to Jesus, that through him "are all things, and we through him"[6] . . . does not completely nullify the fundamental assumption that there is only one God . . . but it does weaken it. . . . Christ is subject to God the Father of all, who controls everything . . . yet God himself has subjected everything to Christ,[7] who is not subject to anything except to God alone — to the Father, whose son Christ is.

Jesus is, therefore, second to God — not actual deity, yet everything which God did in the world he did through (or by means of) Christ. . . . Even here we still have the Jewish belief in the unity of the Godhead, but it is blurred and made uncertain by the special function of the Pauline Messiah ("Christ") — a function which in Judaism is carried out by the one and only God himself. Belief in the Trinity is not yet present; but the first step toward such a belief has been taken.

The Jewish Messiah is a *political savior* of his enslaved nation, which is depressed and afflicted in an exile among peoples who hate and persecute it; the Jewish Messiah is also a *spiritual redeemer* of all mankind, which by the spirit of God which "shall rest upon him" and by the righteousness which "shall be the girdle of his loins"[8] . . . shall conquer heathenism. Then shall all peoples call upon the name of the one God[9] . . . and the "Kingdom of Heaven" shall be established upon earth forever.[10]

But it was never said in the old, original Judaism, that of the prophets and of the Tannaim, that the world was created by (or through) the Messiah, and that the one and only God has given up one of his most important functions and turned over to his Messiah his own essential prerogatives, such as the creation of the world and the supreme headship over all mankind. To be sure, even Judaism sees the Messiah as greater and higher than all the rest of mortal men; and as a symbol of righteousness, faithfulness, and goodness, he is the head of mankind according to the view of Judaism also. But this headship is entirely apart from that of the Deity. The Jewish Messiah is the head of humanity by reason of his ethical standards, but not because God has turned over to him his (God's) own headship, as Paul would have it. In-

2 Rom 8:15; Gal 4:6.
3 Eph 4:6.
4 Gal 3:20.
5 1 Cor 12:6.
6 1 Cor 8:4–6.
7 1 Cor 15:24–8.

8 Is 11:2–5.
9 Is 2:2.
10 The prayer *Shemoneh 'Esreh* for "Solemn Days" and the prayer *'Alenu*.

deed, Paul goes so far in this opinion that he dares to place God and Jesus on the same footing.[11] Here we have the essential and basic difference in Messianic belief as between Jews and Christians — even Pauline Christians.

How did Paul acquire this new Messianic belief? It would seem that it came to him *because of his fear of spirits*. Cosmic existence is, according to Paul, dualistic: there are in it *flesh* and *spirit*. The supreme spirit is the Spirit of God. Yet the spirit of Christ (the Messiah) is by nature closely related to it. There are in addition *good* spirits: ministering angels and angels of the presence — but there are also many *evil spirits* — devils and demons and angels of destruction, at the head of whom stands Satan, the leader of all evil spirits. Satan is the god of this world.[12] . . . This fear of Satan and his household — the evil spirits — was at least one of the fundamental causes of the function of the Jewish Messiah.[13] . . . And the Spirit of Christ, which is in a certain sense the Spirit of God, will conquer the spirit of uncleanness — Satan and the evil Spirits. This is the great importance of Christ in particular and of the Spirit in general. . . .

[11] 1 Cor 1:3; 2 Cor 1:2.

[12] 2 Cor 4:4. Paul knows only the term "Satan." The passages in the Epistles attributed to Paul in which we find the term "the devil" (*diabolos*) are suspected of being later. The Talmud calls Satan "Sammael," and the Midrash says of him that he is "the chief of all the accusing angels" (literally "Satans," Deut. Rabbah, XI, 10).

[13] On "God and Satan" see now W. O. E. Oesterley, "The Belief in Angels and Demons," *Judaism and Christianity*, I (London, 1937), 191–209.

Also, Jesus as Messiah is spirit and not flesh. To be sure, Paul speaks of him as "his (God's) Son, who was born of the seed of David according to the flesh."[14] And he makes it clear that Jesus is not only flesh, but also flesh and blood.[15] . . . Yet *this* Jesus had no real existence for Paul . . . for three reasons.

First, the Jesus of flesh and blood, Jesus, the Jewish Messiah (and the Jews never pictured the Messiah except in the form of flesh and blood) . . . strove to re-establish the kingdom of the house of David, although not by actual deeds of rebellion, not by the power of an army of revolutionaries, but by an army of penitents led by their Messiah. God was to take his stand by this Messiah and this army, and destroy from before them the rule of Rome (to be identified with the rule of Satan), then to restore to penitent Israel its land and its kingdom, and teach the Gentiles the ways of God — the ways of peace and love. Nothing of this entered into the calculations of Paul. . . .

Second, if the first disciples of Jesus, and Paul with them, had held to a Jewish Messiah like this, a Messiah who retained some measure of political function, everyone would have said to them that they were following a false Messiah, since he had failed to "restore the kingdom of Israel," just as the other false Messiahs had failed.

Third, and finally, Paul relied above all upon the vision on the road to Damascus, wherein he had seen not the earthly Jesus, but the Jesus who

[14] Rom 1:3.

[15] Rom 3:25; 1 Cor 10:16; Col 1:20.

had already ascended to heaven and then descended again and appeared to him in a "heavenly vision." So how could he hold to a Messiah like that pictured in the minds of the Jews of his time, or even like that pictured in the minds of the first Nazarenes, headed by near relatives of Jesus, who knew so much about Jesus' earthiness and humanness?

From these three considerations, Paul was *forced* to ignore Jesus the Jewish Messiah, the Jesus of flesh and blood . . . was forced to preach not the Jesus of the flesh, but the Jesus of the spirit, the heavenly Jesus. Therefore, the essential things for Paul became not the life of Jesus, nor even his ethical teaching, but *his death and resurrection,* and *his appearance on the road to Damascus.* . . .

Thus Jesus became for Paul more and more spiritual, and more and more heavenly. . . . To Paul, Jesus became "Christ Jesus" . . . the Son of God in a metaphysical sense, "the image of the invisible God,"[16] "the mystery of God,"[17] "the power of God and the wisdom of God."[18] . . . And of course, like the Philonic "Logos," Jesus is also "the first born of all creation,"[19] "the beginning, the firstborn from the dead."[20] Not once does Paul call Jesus "son of man," as Jesus called himself according to the Gospels; the reason being that for Paul "Jesus Christ" is not a man even in the most exalted sense, but is a heavenly figure,

the antithesis of the "son of man" in Ezekiel, or even in Daniel. Thus it is but a step from this spiritual and heavenly Messiah to complete equality with deity, as in the later doctrine of the Trinity.[21] . . .

The conception of Jesus as "Logos" or the "Word" was taught, apparently, by the Alexandrian Jew, Apollos, who was influenced by his fellow Alexandrian, Philo. . . . This conception that the Messiah is identical with the Logos, brought it about after a time that Jesus became one of the three members of the Trinity. Paul, who saw Greek philosophy . . . as something opposed to "the mystery of God"[22] did not accept this idea in its philosophic form. Nevertheless, the excessive and exaggerated adoration, going beyond all natural bounds, which Paul bestowed upon the crucified and risen Jesus, the heavenly and spiritual Jesus, who as a spirit would overcome Satan and the evil spirits, made Jesus equal to God in importance and superior to God in significant activities. . . .

Of the treatment of Jesus by Paul it might well be said, "Thou hast made him but little lower than God";[23] and this "little" that was lacking was quickly supplied . . . by Matthew and Luke . . . and John, a writer seeing in Jesus the "Logos" who existed at the beginning of all creation, and was with God, and was himself God. . . .

---

[16] Col 1:15; 2 Cor 4:4.
[17] Col 2:2.
[18] 1 Cor 1:24.
[19] Col 1:15.
[20] Col 1:18.

[21] Contrary to the view of Ernst Barnikol, *Mensch und Messias* (Kiel, 1932). See E. Lohmeyer, "Vom Problem paulinischer Christologie," *Theologische Blätter,* XIII (1932), 43–53.
[22] Col 2:2, 8 and elsewhere.
[23] Ps 8:6.

2. J. Lebreton[1] studies Paul and the infant Church. The source of Paul's doctrine is not religious syncretism but a revelation from Christ. The problem of salvation is the true center point of his theology and hence there are certain obscurities in Trinitarian theology and particularly in the doctrine of the Holy Spirit. The divine personality of the Holy Spirit, though certainly taught by Paul, remains in the background.

St. Paul and the infant Church. It is impossible to isolate Paul from the infant Church; he is no solitary theologian who creates a new doctrine and imposes it on the churches he founds; he is above all an apostle of Christ, who hands on the message which he had received, the deposit of faith which has been entrusted to him. Beyond doubt, his conceptions have a distinctive note . . . but in his conception of the nature and role of Christ and of his relations with God the Father and the Holy Spirit, he felt himself in full communion of ideas with all the Christians of his time. . . .

The problem of salvation has more than all the others captivated the attention of Paul; it is the true center point of his theology, and he has thrown a powerful but only a partial light on other dogmas; hence, certain obscurities in Trinitarian theology, and particularly in the doctrine of the Holy Spirit. . . . But we love to see the intense light which flashes on God and on Christ from the dogma of the redemption. . . .

The source of Paul's doctrine has been looked for in many quarters — in religious syncretism — Alexandrine theosophy — Hermetic philosophy — religious philosophy of Stoicism —

secret initiations of the mysteries. . . . Paul affirms to us that he had received this truth, which was the very essence of his teaching, by a revelation from Christ.[2] . . .

God the Father and Jesus Christ. . . . St. Paul begins almost all his letters with this salutation: "Grace to you and peace, from God our Father and from the Lord Jesus Christ."[3] . . . Even in the body of his letters he loves to associate God the Father and Jesus Christ, praying to them both at the same time or appealing to their witness.[4] . . .

God is the supreme Father, he is, as the Apostle loves to repeat, "The God and the Father of Our Lord Jesus Christ"[5] and it is from him as source and supreme ideal that every filial and paternal relation proceeds,[6] yet Jesus Christ alone is "his own Son,"[7] and others can only be his sons through incorporation with his firstborn Son. . . . We read in 1 Cor: "Yet to us there is but one God, the Father, of whom are all things, and we unto him: and one Lord Jesus Christ, by whom are all things and we

[1] Chap. I, 5, n. 1. This excerpt is from *op. cit.*, pp. 285–329.

[2] Gal 1:11–12.

[3] Rom 1:7; 1 Cor 1:3; 2 Cor 1:2; Gal 1:3; Eph 1:2; Phil 1:2.

[4] 1 Th 3:11; 2 Th 2:16; I Tim 6:13; 2 Tim 4:1.

[5] Rom 15:6; 2 Cor 1:3; Eph 1:3; Col 1:3.

[6] Eph 3:14–15.

[7] Rom 8:32.

by him."[8] It would be impossible to limit the significance of this text to the redemption of men: the parallelism of the phrases indicates clearly enough that everything that comes from God owes its existence to Christ. "God hath delivered us from the power of darkness, and hath translated us into the kingdom of the Son of his love: in whom we have redemption through his blood, the remission of sins: who is the image of the invisible God, the first-born of every creature: for in him were all things created in heaven, and on earth . . . all things were created by him and in him."[9] There is no need to insist on the supreme importance of this text; it is obvious enough at a first glance. We may, moreover, note that the Christological dogma is here expounded for its own sake, and not, as most frequently, merely glanced at by a rapid allusion. . . .

Paul does not separate the role of Christ in the Church from his role in the world: everywhere Christ is the first, everywhere he is the center, everywhere he is the principle of life. . . . This intimate union of man and the world helps us to understand the facility with which Paul passes from the conception of Christ as Head of the Church to that of Christ as Creator and support of the world: no doubt these two relations are by no means equivalent; Christians are "created in Christ Jesus"[10] in a very different way from that in which the world has been "created in him."[11] . . .

It does not follow from all this that one may not most legitimately, according to Paul's thought, distinguish between the relations belonging to Christ, as Creator, in his pre-existence, and, as Savior, in his human life, earthly or glorified. But it should be noted that all these relations are co-ordinated and directed toward one and the same end; the work of the incarnate Christ is at once the restoration (of man) and the consummation of the work of the pre-existing Christ; and the formula which expresses this work as a whole is: "All things were created by him and in him." And that is summed up for Paul in the fundamental dogma of the Christian faith, in that confession so efficacious that it suffices for salvation, so divine that the Spirit alone could have inspired it: *Kurios Iesous,* Jesus is the Lord.[12] . . .

This profession of faith . . . in the case of Paul, as in that of the other apostles, is inspired by memories of the Old Testament, and recognizes in the "Lord Jesus" the majesty of Jahve the Lord. But Paul affirms with peculiar energy certain divine features, of which this name of Lord reminded his Jewish or Pagan hearers; the Lord is the Judge.[13] . . . The Lord is the master to whom all belongs.[14] Thus the confession of the Lordship of Jesus is primarily a recognition of the absolute dominion which he has over his own, over his "slaves," as Paul loves to say.[15] . . . All Christians have the same Master,[16] and to him alone do

---

[8] 8:6.
[9] Col 1:12 ff.
[10] Eph 2:10.
[11] Col 1:16.

[12] Rom 10:9; Acts 16:29; 1 Cor 12:3.
[13] 1 Cor 4:5; 5:5.
[14] Rom 14:7–9.
[15] Rom 1:1; 1 Cor 7:22; Gal 1:10.
[16] Rom 10:12; 1 Cor 4:3, 4.

they owe obedience.[17] And just as this new servitude has redeemed them from every other, this responsibility to their Lord places them beyond every other jurisdiction. . . .

The Spirit. If the study of the theology of the Spirit in Paul is difficult, it is certainly not on account of the lack of texts, for they abound;[18] nor is it because this doctrine of the Spirit is not in the foreground of his thought; but it is because the Apostle uses the word "Spirit" to express very diverse conceptions . . . and chiefly because he reaches in one synthetic glance various, very distinct realities which have for long been disassociated by theological analysis. . . .

Paul's teaching transforms the whole doctrine of the Spirit. Moses said of old: "O that all the people might prophesy, and that the Lord would give them his spirit."[19] What to Moses was but a hyperbole has become a reality to Paul: the "man of the spirit" is no longer a solitary among the people of God: "in one Spirit we have all been made to drink."[20] This gift (of the Spirit) is so essential to the Christian that, without it, there is no union with Christ." If any man have not the Spirit of Christ, he is none of his."[21] . . .

The intimate alliance of the two concepts of spirit and power has been rightly pointed out[22] as one of the characteristic features of Pauline theology.[23] . . . The same observation is inevitable with regard to the concept of life.[24] Already in the Old Testament, the Spirit was considered as the principle of life; in Paul we find the same relation between the terms, but they have both been profoundly modified. The glorified life of the risen Christ is to Paul the type of all life, and the whole of his doctrine is transformed by this fundamental fact of Christianity.[25] . . .

This rapid description of the life of the Spirit, according to Paul, shows us clearly enough the origin of his doctrine; it is certainly in continuity with the theology of the Old Testament, and the greater part of the Pauline conceptions can be found in the prophetical books and the Psalms; there also, the Spirit is represented as light, strength, and life, and the source of extraordinary gifts and occasionally, though more rarely, as a principle of holiness.

But in Paul all these doctrines are transformed . . . and manifest a unity, up till then unsuspected. . . . All these transformations of the theology of the Spirit have their principle in the conception of Christ; in him God has revealed . . . wisdom, strength, life, and holiness. And since Christ is the firstborn of many brethren, since these divine gifts which he possesses in their plenitude are communicated by the Spirit to other men, we must recognize

---

[17] Eph 5:22; 6:7–8.

[18] According to Winstanley, *The Spirit in the New Testament*, p. 122, the word "Spirit" occurs 379 times in the New Testament, of which 146 are in St. Paul's writings, apart from Hebrews.

[19] Num 11:29.

[20] 1 Cor 12:13.

[21] Rom 8:9.

[22] Wendt, *Fleisch und Geist*, 146; Gunkel, 72.

[23] Rom 1:4; 15:13, 19.

[24] Strack-Billerbeck, III, 240.

[25] Rom 6:4.

that in all Christians the Spirit is the principle of a truly divine life.

As for the *Spirit himself and his nature*, it is evident, if we judge by his effects and action, that he is purely a divine principle. From one point of view . . . it might seem that he is no more than an impersonal force.[26] . . . On the other hand, we must consider the definitely personal role attributed to the Spirit by Paul.[27] Apostolic theology has reached a distinct conception of the personality of the Holy Spirit . . . not under the influence of Jewish or Hellenic ideas of intermediary beings, but in the light of Christ. . . . Jesus Christ, by revealing . . . himself as a divine Person distinct from the Father has given us a clearer conception . . . of the distinct divine Person of the Holy Spirit. In the case of John, whose doctrine on this point is more explicit, the influence of Christology will be still more manifest. The Holy Spirit will be "another Paraclete." But in Paul the influence of Christology is already certain. . . .

We must remember that the Father and the Son are united . . . by an infinitely close relation of dependence. . . . The Spirit also depends on God the Father. . . . He is sent, given, diffused by him. The frequent expression "the Spirit of God" makes known this relation of origin.[28] It is replaced once by an even more precise qualification: "the Spirit who comes from God."[29] . . .

It must be recognized . . . that the action of the Spirit appears much more definitely than his Person; the distinct personality of the Son is manifested very clearly in both his mortal and glorious life, and even in his preexistence. . . . The personality of the Holy Spirit, on the contrary, though certainly taught by the Apostle, remains in the background. That personality did not appear to us in an incarnation. . . .

3. **D. E. H. Whiteley**[1] **studies Paul's Christology and his doctrine of the Spirit. For Paul Christ attained to the exercise of Lordship at his resurrection, but the term Lord is applied to him during his life on earth. Paul did not consciously reject a "nature" Christology in favor of a purely functional Christology and came as near to asserting a metaphysical equality as his non-metaphysical framework of thought permitted. The Spirit plays a dominant part in his teaching, although no doctrine of the Spirit is worked out.**

Jesus is Lord. The full humanity of Christ is an essential element in the thought of Paul. . . . It is impossible to deny the centrality of Christ's death

---

[26] Rom 5:5; 1 Cor 6:19; Gal 3:5; Eph 1:7.

[27] Rom 8:9–12; 1 Cor 3:16; 6:19; Rom 8:26, 27.

[28] Rom 8:9, 14; 1 Cor 2:14; 3:16.

[29] 1 Cor 2:12.

[1] D. E. H. Whiteley, Fellow of Jesus College, Oxford, was the author of an article entitled "St. Paul's Thought on the Atonement" that was published in the *Journal of Theological Studies*. This excerpt is from his book, *The Theology of St. Paul* (Oxford: Basil Blackwell, 1964), pp. 99–129.

to Paul's soteriology, and Christ could not have died if he had not been human. . . . Paul displays no interest of a "biographical" nature in the earthly life of Jesus considered as past history; he is concerned with the acts and teaching of Our Lord only so far as they are relevant to the present and the future. . . .

We must now investigate those elements in his Christology which writers of a later period subsumed under the heading of the divine nature of Christ. Contemporary scholars very properly approach this subject by examining the titles and other terms which Paul applies to him, words, that is to say, such as "Lord," "Christ," "Son of God," "Image of God," "Glory," and many others. . . .

Of all the Pauline designations of Jesus Christ, Lord, *kyrios,* is most frequently employed. . . . Three questions must be asked. First, how did *kyrios* enter the vocabulary of the early Church and of the Apostle? Second, what meaning or meanings does it bear in the Pauline Epistles? Third, at what "point in time," if any, did Paul believe that Christ achieved lordship?

To the first question a clear answer is provided by Bultmann: "It is highly improbable that the title *Kyrios* as applied to Jesus is derived from the LXX. . . . Rather, the term *Kyrios* used of Christ is derived from the religious terminology of Hellenism, more specifically from that of oriental Hellenism."[2] . . . Bultmann's view can not be formally refuted, but it fails

to carry conviction, especially since *kyrios* is applied to Christ with such frequency in the two Thessalonian epistles, which were written barely twenty years after the resurrection.[3]

It is important to note that the early Christians were most reluctant to call Jesus God, whereas Lord is applied to him in many passages which in their present literary form date from the very middle of the first century. He is called God only in the Johannine writings and in the Pastorals, with the possible exception of Rom 9:5. The reason presumably is that for a Jew the word God could mean One Person only, while *kyrios* might be used of human beings; in using it, they confessed their personal relation to Christ.[4] The use of the word God would have seemed to be an infringement of monotheism, whereas by calling Jesus Lord they confessed that he was associated with his Father in the exercise of authority.

Cerfaux remarks that "Christ is Lord because he is God's vicegerent, exercising a power that belongs to God."[5] [This] quotation from Cerfaux . . . provides in summary form the answer to our second question, that of the meaning which *kyrios* bears in the Pauline Epistles when applied to Jesus Christ. . . . It is perfectly clear what has happened (in Rom 10:13, 9): Paul has transferred to Jesus as Lord words which in the Septuagint are

[2] *Theology of the New Testament* (New York: Scribners), Vol. I, pp. 124–125.

[3] See Vincent Taylor, *The Names of Jesus* (London, 1953), p. 47.

[4] See Vincent Taylor, *op. cit.,* p. 45.

[5] *Christ in the Theology of St. Paul,* trans. by Webb and Walker (New York: Herder & Herder, 1959), p. 466.

applied to God as Lord.[6] In both cases the subject matter is eschatological. The Apostle has not identified Christ with his Father: he has ascribed to him one of the functions of God. This is no isolated phenomenon, as we can see from 2 Th 1:8–10.

Since *kyrios* speaks of Christ as sharing in the exercise of God's authority, it is not surprising that it should be closely connected with the resurrection, the exaltation, and the parousia.[7] In answer to our third question, it would not be very wide of the mark to say that for Paul Christ attained to the exercise of Lordship at his resurrection, although the term Lord is applied to him during his life on earth.[8] . . .

In the Old Testament the term son of God is applied to angelic beings. . . .[9] To the king[10] . . . to Israel.[11] . . . We may accept without qualification Vincent Taylor's summary: "The significance of the phrase in Jewish thought is reasonably clear; it does not describe a divine being, but characterizes groups or individuals who stand in a peculiarly close relationship with God."[12] . . . Paul . . . though he calls Christ "Son of God" absolutely, never uses the phrase of Christians without qualification:[13] "The language postulates a relationship which is independent of any historical experience, one which is pre-

eminently ethical in character, and seems to involve 'a community of nature between the Father and the Son.' "[14]

In two passages only does Paul speak of Christ as the image of God, and in each of them the word refers not to any divine status, but to his function of revealing God to men.[15] . . . But although Paul explicitly speaks only of the revelatory function of Christ, it may fairly be argued that this function could not have been performed if he had not possessed that metaphysical relation to God which is expounded in the Patristic writings. . . .

There are undoubtedly traces of subordinationist language in Paul's Epistles. This language does not, of course, carry anything even remotely approaching the force that it would have done in the fourth century. Paul is not giving a considered answer in a subordinationist sense to questions which had been explicitly raised: rather, what he says about the problems of his own day suggests subordinationist answers to problems of whose very existence the Apostle was completely unaware. . . .

Again and again we have had occasion to remark that Paul is concerned, not to say that Christ is the equal of the Father in nature, but to assert that the Son is associated with the Father in his functions of creation, revelation and redemption. He says not that Christ is another Lord alongside God, but that he shares fully in God's Lordship. Cullmann brings

---

[6] Jl 3:5.
[7] See Cerfaux, *op. cit.*, p. 20.
[8] See *ibid.*, p. 469; cf. 1 Cor 7, 10, 15; 9:1; 11:23; 9:9; Gal 1:19.
[9] Gen 6:2.
[10] Ps 2:7.
[11] Ex 4:22.
[12] Vincent Taylor, *op. cit.*, p. 54.
[13] See Rom 8:14–17.

[14] Anderson Scott, *Christianity according to St. Paul* (Cambridge, 1961), p. 256.
[15] 2 Cor 4:4; Col 1:15.

this line of thought to its logical conclusion, and maintains that the Christology of all the New Testament writers, including Paul, is conceived wholly in functional terms: "Functional Christology is the only kind which exists."[16] His thesis has led to understandable misgivings, but Benoit[17] points out that dogmatic theology and biblical theology are not asking the same questions.

But further qualifications are essential. In our day we distinguish explicitly between a Christology of natures and a functional Christology, and we may consciously reject one in favor of the other. Paul did not consciously reject a "nature" Christology in favor of a purely functional Christology; and it is improbable that he would have comprehended the distinction. . . . It might be said that he came as near to asserting a metaphysical equality of community of natures as his non-metaphysical framework of thought permitted him to do. This, Barrett[18] adds, was the reason why the Church in the end was obliged to move on from a purely functional to an essential Christology.

The Holy Spirit. Although Paul cannot be said to have worked out a *doctrine* of the Spirit, yet the Spirit plays a dominant part in his teaching. . . . The teaching that the Spirit has been given to all Christians as such can be regarded as the fundamental teaching upon which all Paul's other utterances concerning the Spirit are based. . . . The Messianic Spirit . . . is the central concept from which all the others radiate outward. . . . Is the Spirit Divine and Personal? . . . To Paul the Spirit is at least the Spirit of a Personal God. Is the Spirit distinct from the Father? . . . In some passages, though they are a minority, Paul employs language which serves to distinguish the Spirit from God. Is the Spirit distinct from the Son? . . . It is generally agreed that Paul often applies the same language both to the Son and to the Spirit. Between Father and Spirit there is clear interaction. It is hard to find clear evidence for interaction between Son and Spirit. . . . Traces of a Trinitarian ground plan are common enough.[19] . . . Wainright is . . . justified in maintaining that, although God, Christ and the Spirit were in the forefront of Paul's mind he was not aware, unlike John, of a *problem* of the Trinity.[20]

---

[16] Oscar Cullmann, *The Christology of the New Testament* (London, 1959), pp. 181, 235, 293, 306, 326; cf. L. Malevez, S.J., "Functional Christology" in *Theology Digest*, Spring, 1962, pp. 77 ff.; Oscar Cullmann, "Functional Christology: A reply," *Theology Digest*, Autumn, 1962; R. H. Fuller, *The Foundations of New Testament Christology* (New York: Scribner's, 1965).

[17] *Revue biblique*, 1958, p. 274.

[18] *Journal of Theological Studies*, N. S., X (1959), p. 397.

[19] J. N. D. Kelly, *Early Christian Creeds* (London, 1960), pp. 21 f.

[20] A. W. Wainwright, *The Trinity in the New Testament* (London, 1962), p. 249.

4. J. L. McKenzie[1] studies the Father, Son, and Spirit. The pre-existence of the Son becomes evident especially in Phil 2:5–11. The title of Son affirms the divinity of Jesus and differentiates him from the Father. The identity between Jesus and the Father is everything but personal. The theology of the Spirit is more elaborate but still unreflecting and consequently not always entirely consistent.

God the Father is invoked in the exordium of each of the thirteen epistles attributed to Paul and he is invoked as God our Father in the body of each of them except Gal, 1–2 Tm, Tt. . . . The Father is the Father of our Lord Jesus Christ.[2] The characteristics of the divine paternity noted in the Gospels are usually implicit in Paul. . . .

The Son. To a remarkable degree the divine sonship of Jesus is associated with his redeeming death; to perceive fully the meaning and efficacy of the redemption, it is necessary to understand who he is that dies.[3] . . . As the Son, Jesus is the revealer of the Father surpassing the prophets;[4] here are added the attributes of the supremacy of the Son and his function in creation. For Paul Jesus is declared, i.e., revealed as the Son of God in his resurrection; before this event men might question the title, but not after it. He is the term to which creation tends and is the one through whom all creation becomes subject to the Father.[5] The sonship of Jesus is the operative principle of the adoption of Christians. . . . Faith in the Son of God[6] and knowledge of the Son of God[7] are things by which the Christian lives. Salvation is the transfer into his realm.[8]

In the epistles the pre-existence of the Son becomes evident, an idea not explicit in the Synoptics. The divine nature, the divine origin, and divine power of the Son are such that we cannot suppose that these are the fruits of adoption. The only Son cannot be distinguished from other men unless his personal relation to the Father antecedes his appearance in the flesh. In the epistles the title affirms the divinity of Jesus and differentiates him from the Father, who is signified by the title "God" (Greek *ho theos*).

It is not surprising that the apostolic Church began to profess its faith in the person of Jesus as well as in his mission in more explicit terms. The teaching was the instruction given to the baptized about him in whom they had believed. The earliest statement of the New Testament in which the *pre-existence* of Christ is affirmed appears in Paul, and this is early enough; the major epistles of Paul are earlier than the Synoptic Gospels. The pre-existence of Christ

[1] Chap. I, 3, n. 1; *op. cit.*, pp. 276, 831–832, 943–844; *The Power and the Wisdom*, 135.

[2] 2 Cor 1:3; Eph 1:3; Col 1:3.

[3] Rom 5:10; 8:32; Gal 4:4; Col 1:13; Heb 6:6.

[4] Heb 1:2.

[5] 1 Cor 15:28.

[6] Gal 2:20.

[7] Eph 4:13.

[8] Col 1:13.

is not affirmed even in the infancy narratives of Matthew and Luke. It is not found everywhere in the writings of Paul; but Phil 2:5–11 is so clear and so much in harmony with the language of Paul elsewhere that there can be no doubt that it belonged to his teaching. Paul was not proposing any idea excogitated by himself; while he is the principal literary witness, there is no reason to think that the entire Church was not saying the same thing. The Church perceived that the Father had to have an eternal Son. If the Son were not eternal, then it would be impossible to see how he could have a unique sonship not shared with other men. . . .

The sonship revealed the meaning of the saving act of Jesus and explained the solidarity which made the saving act possible. Sonship was a revelation of the love of the Father; for God was mysteriously involved in suffering. The power manifested in Jesus was not conferred upon him; he possessed it by eternal nativity. He was in virtue of his person the creator of the new man. The dignity of lordship which came to him in his resurrection was an actualization of a dignity of which he had, again in the words of Philippians, emptied himself in his incarnation as a slave. But in all this he is the Son; the Father works in him, and Jesus does nothing which the Father does not accomplish through him. . . .

When Jesus is called the power of God and the wisdom of God[9] or the reflection of his glory and the stamp of his nature,[10] the language but not the thought of the personified attributes is used. . . . By the use of these titles the identity between Jesus and the Father is more firmly stated, an identity which is everything but personal.

The Spirit. The theology of the spirit becomes still more elaborate in Paul; but it is still unreflecting and consequently is not always entirely consistent. The spirit is basically the divine and heavenly dynamic force; it is conceived as peculiarly existing in Jesus (and specifically in the risen Jesus), as pervading the body of Jesus which is the Church, and as apportioned to the members of the Church. Jesus is the son of David in the flesh but the son of God in power according to the spirit;[11] the unique possession of the spirit by Jesus and the unique power which flows from this possession reveal his true reality, which is the reality of the spiritual sphere, i.e., the divine and heavenly sphere. . . .

The spirit is not obviously and explicitly conceived as a distinct divine personal being in Paul. The occasional personifications which he employs do not go beyond the personifications found in the Old Testament and in Judaism. *The prevailing* conception is that of the pervading new divine life communicated to the Church by Jesus. Here[12] we meet an enumeration of Jesus, God (i.e., the Father) and the spirit[13] which goes beyond the general idea of the spirit in Paul and opens the possibility of

[9] 1 Cor 1:24.　[10] Heb 1:3.
[11] Rom 1:3.
[12] As in Mt 28:19.
[13] 2 Cor 13:13.

seeing that the new life is ultimately the work of a personal reality, like the creative and saving deeds of the Father and of Jesus Christ. As is noted above, the name of spirit and the character of the reality and the works of the spirit demand that we enlarge our idea of the divine personality.

5. C. Spicq[1] studies the Trinity and our moral life according to Paul. Grace can be given to each one only by a free and unforeseeable initiative of God the Father. In terms of His Son God the Father conceived and accomplished all things. "To live in Christ Jesus" is made possible because the Holy Spirit "comes to help our weakness." The Holy Spirit is the life-giving principle of the moral life, a life that responds to the movement of the Holy Spirit.

From the Father. The entire Epistle to the Romans reveals or manifests[2] God's plan of salvation and underlines its singular appropriateness: God decided to grant pardon and salvation to all men who believe in the proclamation of the Gospel. This is nothing other than the manifestation of the grace of the Father in Jesus Christ. . . .

The secret of the divine plan is, in a word, grace. When we say that God gives his grace, we understand that he takes the initiative in granting favors. . . . For Paul, grace is not a thing; it is God himself, living and giving himself; or, if one prefers, it is his relationship of charity and generosity with men. . . . At the origin of our being as Christians, men saved and redeemed, there is pure gratuitousness. . . .

Because God wishes to save all men and because our Lord did indeed die for the salvation of the human race,[3] sometimes grace is treated as a sort of gift made once and for all to all men, so that it would be in the power of each one to draw on it by means of good will. It is true that the efficacy of the redemption is universal; but grace, a love, can be given to each one only by a free and unforeseeable initiative of God the Father. To those who have not received it, God owes nothing; for their sins are as so many obstacles to grace; and who is without sin among the sons and daughters of Adam? . . .

Here we reach the heart of the inviolable divine liberty. God loves whom he wishes, and he has his preferences. The thought of God's love for the elect, for those he has preferred, is overwhelming. Grace is freely and lovingly given to each one of those who receive it; it is an effusion of God's goodness.[4] . . . "Those whom he has predestined, he has called; and those whom he has called, he has sanctified, and those whom he

[1] Ceslaus Spicq, O.P., was born in 1901. Among his published works are *Agapé dans le Nouveau Testament, The mystery of godliness* and *L'épitre aux Hébreux.* This excerpt is from his book, *The Trinity and Our Moral Life,* trans. by Sister Marie Aquinas, O.P. (Westminster, Md.: The Newman Press, 1963), pp. 27–35, 39–46, 50–53, 63–68.

[2] 2:17; 3:21.

[3] 1 Tim 2:5–6.

[4] Rom 3:24; cf. Rom 11:6.

has sanctified, he has glorified."[5] . . .

Far from thinking that everything was lost, the converts to Christianity, who knew the gift of God and possessed it, were assured of triumph. Not only was salvation possible, but sinners were loved! They were able to enjoy divine intimacy even on earth and to approach the throne of grace in all confidence:[6] God loves men; he wills their happiness. In Christ he opens the way for them and sets everything to work for the realization of his plan of salvation.[7] . . . Consequently, the Christian life, even in the worst trials, is lived in an atmosphere of confidence and magnanimity. Since "God makes everything work together for the good of those who love him" and since "grace is superabundant" and "we are filled with the fulness of God," we are conquerors, able to do all in him who strengthens us.[8]

But our essential reaction in the face of the divine goodness, the one which will be the inspiring force of our moral life, is clearly that of gratitude[9] . . . the permanent attitude of a sinful creature who has been mercifully saved, who knows that he is the object of an infinite love, and who receives this love, lives by it, and sings its praises.[10] . . . The Father who first loved them has given all; his sons should give back all in a fervent cult of praise. . . . Paul considers what return the Christian should make for this divine love. He presents the virtues to be practiced, obedience, humility, charity, etc., as so many forms of gratitude toward God, as a consecration and an offering of thanksgiving.[11] . . . This consecration of ourselves as a thank-offering is the only response possible to the divine kindnesses . . . this living out of our gratitude becomes an obligation. . . .

In Christ Jesus. Gratitude is clearly the dominant inspiration of the moral life. This being true, we must determine how Christians are to express their gratitude to God and to live their lives in charity before him. The all-inclusive response of Paul is: *in Christ Jesus.* It is in terms of his Son that God the Father conceived and accomplished all things.[12]

Since it is in Christ that God, out of love for us, conceived and executed his plan of salvation, it is clear that no supernatural reality can exist or can even be thought of apart from Christ. It is in Christ that God chooses and predestines his elect,[13] that he manifests his grace,[14] that he communicates his charity[15] and peace,[16] liberty[17] and light,[18] knowledge and strength.[19]

Not only does God give everything through Christ; he receives only what is united to Christ, what passes through Christ, and what comes from Christ. There is, then, only one moral problem for the Christian: participation or union with Christ, in whom

---

[5] Rom 8:30–39.
[6] Cf. 2 Cor 3:12; Eph 3:12; Phil 1:20; Heb 3:6; 4:16; 10:19, 25.
[7] 2 Cor 2:14; cf. Col 2:15; Eph 3:20; Phil 4:19.
[8] Phil 4:13.
[9] Col 1:12–14.
[10] 1 Cor 14:18; Phil 4:16; Col 4:2; 1 Tim 2:1.

[11] Rom 12:1.
[12] Eph 2:4–7.
[13] Eph 1:4, 5, 11.
[14] Tit 2:11; 3:4.
[15] Rom 8:35–39.
[16] Phil 4:7.
[17] Gal 2:4.
[18] Eph 5:8–14.
[19] Eph 4:21; 6:10.

he possesses all the treasures of salvation and by whom alone he rejoins God.[20] . . .

Paul coined the expression "in Christ" which he uses more than one hundred sixty times. What precisely does it mean? First of all, it must be emphasized that he is speaking not of the Christ *according to the flesh*,[21] but of the risen Christ, living now in heaven. . . . Sharing the same nature and the same attributes of power and glory as the Father, Christ is able to endow His disciples with life and make them divine.[22] . . . Therefore, from the moment he believes, the Christian is defined as one united to the glorious Christ.[23]

But how are we to understand this vital relationship? To call it mystical explains nothing, for mystical means merely secret. . . . In designating the Christian as a "being in Christ," thus directly excluding the notion of fusion or absorption, Paul presents much more than a psychological relationship of knowledge and love. He describes a union that is personal, a communion that is reciprocal; or better, an organic and living relationship, a union of life that is the result of our incorporation into Christ. He declares explicitly that we have been grafted onto Christ and implanted in him,[24] so that we constitute but one being with him. . . . Just as every creature is completely dependent upon his Creator and has being only in this "relationship," so the Christian exists super-

naturally only in his relationship to Christ. . . . A Christian has his being of grace through dependence on Christ. . . . Without Christ he would not exist, that is, supernaturally.[25] . . .

Baptism unites the Christian so completely to his Savior that not only does he live "in Christ" and in union with him, but his life is henceforth that of Christ himself living in him. Christ died and rose again, and the baptized person shares in this death and resurrection. He relives them for himself, and renews them so truly that it can be said that he dies and is buried with Christ, and then rises, lives again, and reigns with Christ.[26] The consequence is evident. The Christian life — a symbiosis with the Lord[27] — will be nothing other than the living and the putting into effect of this baptismal grace, a continuous, progressive death to sin and a life of renewal and victory.[28]

This double rhythm of the crucifixion and resurrection of the Savior[29] . . . marks his whole existence. What he has acquired once and for all ontologically, he must develop and perfect psychologically and morally.[30] Such is the end to strive for. . . .

Here we reach the heart of Pauline ethics: the moral life is a prolongation, an extension, an unfolding of the life of Christ in his disciples. The "rule of life" of the Christian is to *conform* his thought and his conduct to Christ, who is the perfect model, and thus

20 1 Cor 1:30; 6:11.
21 Rom 1:3–4; 1 Tim 3:16.
22 1 Cor 15:45–49.
23 Rom 10:5–10; Eph 3:17.
24 Rom 6:5.

25 2 Cor 5:17.
26 Rom 6:3–4.
27 Rom 6:8; Col 2:13.
28 2 Cor 4:10–11; Col 2:12.
29 Gal 6:17.
30 Rom 6:5–14.

to become ever more perfectly incorporated into him. This is the express will of God, the reason for the creation of the world and the predestination of the faithful. . . . This law of the imitation of Christ is so truly the unique moral rule of Christianity that it applies to all ages, all conditions, and all stages of life.[31] . . . They must adopt his manner of thinking and judging,[32] be inspired with his sentiments, copy his virtues, imitate his charity, and have the same filial piety toward the Father.[33]

By the Holy Spirit. How can Christians live "in Christ Jesus" and imitate his virtues, especially his charity? How can they serve God alone, joyfully expressing their gratitude to him all day long and seeking only his glory? . . . "To live in Christ Jesus" is made possible because the Holy Spirit "comes to help our weakness."[34] . . . Initially, it is the person of the "Holy Spirit" who creates in us all the faculties and works of the Christian life. . . . The Holy Spirit is the specific gift[35] that God grants to each baptized person at the intercession of his Son.[36] He is the Spirit of the risen Christ by whose life his members live.[37] . . .

According to Paul, the Holy Spirit is much more than the "gift of God" that sums up all the other gifts of salvation, more even than the agent of our sanctification, who communicates grace to us and incites us to vir-

tue. He is the very source of our spiritual life, so much so that the new morality, contrasting markedly with Israelite morality which was based on the Commandments, is a life that responds to the movement of the Holy Spirit.[38] The new morality is defined as "the law of the Spirit."[39] This means that we are dependent on the Holy Spirit alone, on his inspiration and on his impulse.[40] . . . In a word, it is because "we render service to God which is new and according to the Spirit"[41] that the economy of the new alliance is specifically different from the old. . . .

Because a baptized person belongs to his Lord, he is consigned to his service; the relationship is sealed by the gift of the Holy Spirit. Thus this new creature, who lives by the Holy Spirit, has within him the sign of his incorporation into the new alliance, and consequently the assurance of obtaining all its promises. . . . The Holy Spirit both establishes between the baptized person and God the relationship of child to Father and guides his moral life so that it is led not in a slave's spirit of indifference or fear but in the spirit of an adopted son: in fidelity, love, and confidence. . . . For a life dependent upon the movement of the Holy Spirit cannot but assure entrance into heaven.[42] . . .

---

[31] Col 3:9–11; Gal 3:28.
[32] 1 Cor 2:16.
[33] Rom 15:5; Phil 2:5.
[34] Rom 8:26.
[35] Rom 5:5.
[36] Cf. Jn 14:16, 26.
[37] Rom 8:9–11; Gal 4:6; 1 Cor 12:13.

[38] St. Thomas Aquinas writes: "The principal element in the Law of the New Testament, that in which all its value lies, is the grace of the Holy Spirit," *Summa Theologiae,* I–II, q. 106, a. 1.
[39] Rom 8:2.
[40] Rom 8:10.
[41] Rom 7:6.
[42] 2 Cor 5:1–5.

D. God in St. John

1. W. Grossouw[1] studies the terms light, life, and love in the Gospel of St. John, and Christ as the focal point of this Gospel. The Incarnate Logos is really the true Light, the unfathomable fountain of life for mankind, and the supreme revelation and realization of God's love. As Logos, he exists from all eternity and as Son, as the Only-begotten who was sent into the world, He is the Redeemer of the world.

Light. Nothing is more characteristic of John's way of thinking and, indeed, of his entire Gospel than his use of the term *light.* This is perhaps one of the points wherein we understand him least. He does not use the word with unreasonable frequency;[2] but he *always* uses it in very significant passages and *never* in the common, physical sense of the word.[3] If we classify the texts in which he uses this term, we may divide them into three categories:[4] those pertaining to God;[5] those pertaining to Christ;[6] and those in which the term light is applied to man.[7] Yet this differentiation must not be made too strictly, for Christ is the Light of men.

Such a combination is typical of John. Whereas, our theology is constructed systematically in horizontal fashion with successive tracts on the existence of God, the Trinity, Creation, Christ the Redeemer, the Church, Grace, and so forth, John draws his line of thought vertically through the three spheres of God, Christ, and Christians. God is the Light, and the Logos is the Light of men, and the Christian is in the Light. Just as the Father has Life in himself, so the Son is Life, and the Christian possesses this Life in faith. This ordering of ideas gives a strong cohesion to John's theological thought and draws the believer directly into the sphere of the divine life. On the other hand, it also brings with it that interchangeableness of concepts which we have mentioned above.

The incarnate Logos is really the true Light. In John's way of looking at things, it is self-evident that the Father is the fullness of Light.[8] . . . Christ is our divine light precisely because he is the revelation of the Father. The Apostle insists upon this constantly.[9] This is the great event in history which John contemplates with respectful astonishment and loving gratitude: the plenitude of divine Life and Light has come forth from the

[1] Dr. William Grossouw of the University of Nijmegen, The Netherlands, was born in 1906. Among his published works are *Spirituality of the New Testament, In Christ* and *Biblische froemmigkeit.* This excerpt is from his book, *Revelation and Redemption* (Westminster, Md.: The Newman Press, 1955), pp. 27–92.

[2] Twenty-two times in the Gospel and 6 times in the First Epistle.

[3] 11:9–10 is only an apparent exception.

[4] Here we must make exception for 11:9–10 and for 5:35 where light is an ordinary metaphor for John the Baptist.

[5] 1 Jn 1:5–7.

[6] 1:4–5, 7–9; 3:19–21; 8:12; 9:5; 12:46.

[7] 1:4; 8:12; 12:35; Jn 1:7; 2:8–11.

[8] 5:26.

[9] 1:1–4.

bosom of the divinity[10] and has appeared among us in the person of Jesus Christ. Almost as great is the tremendous and incomprehensible tragedy of the world: "the world knew him not," for from the very beginning the darkness has been opposed to the Light.[11] The darkness consists in the denial and overthrow of divine revelation. Just as the Light is the manifestation of the divine truth, so the darkness is a futile but terrible attempt to blot out the operation of the Light. The stage of this struggle is the spirit of man. . . .

With Christ the Light came into the world;[12] and when he returned to the Father whom he had never left, the Light remained shining in the darkness through Christians who have within themselves his Spirit and the principle of divine life.[13] . . . The Light has its origin in God, it appears in Christ, it gleams in the Christian revelation, it is the beneficent glow of Christian life and love. Christ is the unifying element in this diversity. In giving a definition of the Johannine concept of Light, we might best offer this: The Light is Christ as the revelation of the divinity.[14]

Life. The notion of life occupies the central position in John's theology. "And this is the testimony, that God has given us eternal life, and this life is in his Son."[15] This is the essence of the message of salvation as presented by John: "Christ, the Son of God, is the source of life for mankind. The imperishable gift of Christian salvation is *life.* . . .

The incarnate Word is for mankind the unique and unfathomable fountain of life, a veritable spring from which life pours forth.[16] . . . The Logos is the Life Eternal. Without distinction, John says both that Christ is the life,[17] and that life is in Him.[18] Christ's life is "with the Father." He possesses life as independently as does the Father; his life is also a source of life for others, yet he receives it from the Father.[19] . . .

---

[10] 1 Jn 1:2 ff.

[11] 1:5 ff.

[12] 12:46 and elsewhere.

[13] 1 Jn 3:9–24; 4:13.

[14] It is precisely this specifically Christian character, its relationship to the historical person of Christ, which distinguishes John's representation of light from all forms of Gnosticism. In the Gnostic doctrine Light is looked upon as something almost physical, as the sphere, the habitation, or the materialization of the principle of good (e.g., among the Mandeans); or in a more philosophical sense as being identical with the faculty of thinking and with the divine spirit (*Corpus Hermeticum*), but always in opposition to "darkness" which is ultimately limited by or identified with matter. It is clear that the Gnostic antithesis of spirit and matter is not to be found in John. "The Word was made flesh." Christianity, even the Christianity of John, with its Incarnation (1:14), Eucharist (6:48 f. and also 6:64), resurrection of bodies (5:28–29) is not a gradual liberation from matter, but from sin; and sin, which is apostasy from God par excellence, constitutes in John's way of thinking a rejection of the Light, an obstinate refusal to believe in Christ. On the other hand, it cannot be maintained that the Johannine use of the term light differs in no essential point from the diction of the rest of the New Testament. The absolute aspect of such expressions as "God is Light" and "I have come a light into the world" (12:46) have no parallel in the Bible and may have been formally influenced by Gnosticism.

[15] 1 Jn 5:11.

[16] 1 Jn 1:2.

[17] 11:25; 14:6; 15:20 (?).

[18] 1:4; 15:11.   [19] 5:26; 6:27.

The Christian life, which the believer possesses because of his union with the Son, is of the same kind as that which the Father has "in himself" . . . for it is a participation in the plenitude of the divine being and activity. . . . Through Christ man shares in this divine gift, which is nothing less than a communion with the Father and the Son. This communion is already begun here on earth through faith in the Christian revelation. . . .

Love. To the ancient world, Christendom revealed itself as love — and Christians of all ages must remain lovers or cease to be Christians. In Greek, the international language at the time of the Apostles, this Christian love was called *agapē*. . . . The Greeks . . . used the word *eros* to express their type of love. . . . *Eros* signifies passionate love, that elementary ardor, that joy in the good things of life, that appetite of the flesh, that impetuous desire, that invincible god which triumphs over everything. No one has ever praised *eros* as did Plato in the *Symposium*. In his view, love is basically the desire for corporal beauty, but this is not its final objective. It rises from the body to the Spirit, and from the Spirit to "divine beauty" itself, to the eternal ideas. By this admirable dialectic Plato attempts to avoid the excessively corporal and passionate elements which are inherent in the *eros*. . . .

The Christian *agapē*, on the other hand, is not the fruit of a gradual development or the result of a spiritual progress. It is not a purified passion. It comes from God and is his gift.[20]

It does not ascend from some human principle, but descends from the bosom of God only to return again. . . .

By centering his *agapē* in God — and this is worth repeating — by fixing it in the Father who has revealed himself through Christ, John has exceeded both the narrowness of the Jew who loved only his fellow countryman, and the *eros* of the Greek which had lost in stability and purity what it had gained in universality.

It is in John that we have that admirable phrase, which has had no precedent and will never be surpassed: "God is love" (though it must be honestly admitted that the Johannine formula did find an anticipation in the Old Testament. One need only think of the loving Father and the tenderly loving Bridegroom of the Prophets.[21] . . .

If the essence of God is love, and if Christ is the supreme revelation of God, *the Incarnate God,* then he must also be the supreme revelation, the highest realization of God's love. This is precisely what St. John teaches.[22] Jesus is the incarnate love of God, especially in his death whereby he *has saved the world,* that is, man, who so needed salvation.[23] . . .

Thus Jesus is the mediator of divine love. This love is entirely focused upon the Son and through him it reaches men.[24] The *agapē* does not lose its peculiar nature in man. It remains in the believer a divine energy ever tending toward a sharing of itself, toward action, toward unity,

[20] 1 Jn 4:7.

[21] 1 Jn 4:7–8, 16.
[22] 1 Jn 4:9–10, 16.
[23] 1 Jn 1:7.   [24] 17:23 ff.; 14:21 ff.

toward the completion of the divine circle: Father — Son — believer. . . . Jesus' entire work of salvation is directed to this one end: that the believers may share in that love which is the essence of God.[25] . . .

Christ, the Focal Point of the Fourth Gospel. Jesus is the central point of John's view on the world. His adorable and always vivid personality has broken the rigidity of expression and formula which might otherwise have easily led to some system of Gnosticism. . . . It goes without saying that in all the Gospels Jesus is the central personality; but the fourth Gospel far exceeds the others in stressing this focalization. . . . We must be mindful, however, that to express this fruitful contemplation of Christ John uses expressions and formulas which differ from ours. For centuries we have been accustomed to the clear-cut formulas of the great dogma of Jesus as a divine person existing in a twofold nature — divine and human. This precise formula only came into being in the course of ages after much theological thought and dispute. It presupposes certain philosophical concepts, such as nature and person, and is manifestly the fruit of theological reflection. Hence we must not think it strange if we do not find these formulas in the New Testament, not even in John. Nor may we conclude that, because these formulas are not expressed as such in the sacred books of the New Testament, the *substance* of the dogma is not contained there. On the contrary, it was these very writings, and especially the Gospel of John, which

supplied the scriptural foundation for this Christological dogma. . . .

For the writers of the New Testament, Jesus was undoubtedly both true man and true God — for he is the only Son of the Father — but they were not wont to make an explicit distinction between the divine and the human nature or between these natures and the divine person. For that matter, Jesus himself did not make these distinctions either.[26] . . . Perhaps we may formulate it as follows. We are accustomed to distinguishing clearly between the human and divine in Jesus. But John sees Christ as a unity, as a totality. He sees the human as permeated and transfigured by the divine, as a revelation of God. The divine radiance, the *glory* of God shines through him, and whoever has seen this glory and has believed may give testimony of it. . . . It is not a human story that opens the Gospel of John, but the mysterious and exalted song of a divine generation; and as it ends, there arises before our astonished eyes the figures of the risen Savior bearing the marks of his suffering, the Lamb which has been slain for the sins of the world. And we? We are left with only that one word, which St. Thomas spoke in behalf of us all: "My Lord and my God."[27] . . .

The Logos. The Prologue of John[28] . . . is in every respect the most exalted, and the most Johannine passage

---

[25] 17:26.

[26] Though at times he did suggest such a distinction; for example, see Mt 22:41–45.

[27] 20:28. This is the real end of the Gospel, the final chord. What follows on this is a double epilogue (20:30–31) and all of chapter 21.   [28] 1:1–18.

of the fourth Gospel. . . . It precedes the Gospel because it is principally concerned with the pre-existence, the pre-human existence of Christ. . . . The statements of John concerning the Logos may be summarized as follows: the Logos exists from all eternity; he is with God from all eternity; he is God. An absolutely universal causality in the creation of things is attributable to him.[29] Lastly, this Logos became man. . . . "The Word was made flesh." And with that the term Logos as a proper name disappears from the Gospel. One may thus conclude that John intends "Logos" to indicate the pre-human existence of Christ, the eternal background of his appearance in time on this earth. . . .

The Son. Jesus is the Son and he is also the Redeemer. . . . It is precisely as Son, as the Only-begotten who was sent into this world, that he is the Redeemer of the world. . . . Christ is the *only-begotten* Son. . . . The divine Sonship of Jesus possesses an entirely unique character. It is not to be identified with the adoptive sonship of the Christian. The Apostle expresses this unique character by the adjective *only-begotten.*[30] By this term he means the identity of nature and the intimate love which exist between the Father and the Son, which is the efficient source of all divine filiation. . . . From this sonship in the strict sense there follows the unity of nature with the Father. . . . "I and the Father are one,"[31] or as John lets Jesus himself express it in one of his favorite

sayings: "The Father is in me and I in the Father."[32] This communion is thus comparable to a mutual penetration, to a perfect reciprocity to each other in knowledge and in love, in their whole life and being. . . .

The Savior. In Jesus there is no disjunction between Sonship and redemption; he is the redeemer of mankind precisely as Son. . . . For this he came into the world. This is the work which the Father gave him to do. . . .

Jesus, the Savior of the world, is the topic of the Gospel. "That believing in him, you may have life." Life here means Christian salvation in its fullness. Thus John sees Jesus as the Savior, who, in his adorable personality, through the revelation of the Father which he is and which he brings to us, grants life through the love with which he surrenders his earthly life. . . . Christian salvation is not only a freeing from evil; it is at the same time and especially a good gift, a renewal, a power, a new and better life. . . . In Paul's view Christian life consists in experiencing both mystically and morally, the two great mysteries of Jesus' life: his death and resurrection. In Paul's mind, the crucified and risen Lord is the Redeemer. John views salvation as inseparably united to the person of the Logos become man without stressing particular phases of his earthly life. Christ is in his own person the life, which was revealed by the Incarnation and in which faith — taken in the Johannine sense — makes us partakers. "He who has the Son has the life."[33]

---

[29] 1:3.   [31] 10:30; 17:21–23.

[30] See 1:14, 18; 3:16–18; 1 Jn 4:9. This term is not used by Jesus himself, since 3:16–18 is part of a reflection by the writer.

[32] 10:38; 14:10–20.   [33] 1 Jn 5:12.

2. D. Mollat[1] studies the divinity of Christ in terms of Jesus' glory, work, and titles of Son of Man, Son of God, Word. He sees Jesus' pre-existence given clearer formulation in John than in any other New Testament writing. And nowhere else in the New Testament, not even in the hymn to Christ in Colossians, is there to be found such a magnificent expression of faith in the divinity of Jesus as in John's Prologue.

The word which in John's writing most closely approximates to our abstract noun "divinity" is that of "glory." It is admittedly a much less precise word, but it possesses an infinitely greater range of highly concrete overtones. It derives from the Old Testament, where the "glory of God" described the terrifying brightness and overpowering intensity of the divine Presence. It was God himself, revealing himself in all the majesty and all the power that is his.

The New Testament applied this to Christ. The Synoptic Gospels, however, nearly always reserve it to the Son of Man coming on the clouds of heaven at the parousia, in the splendor of his power. . . . John, on the other hand, ascribes glory to the Jesus "dwelling among us" as a habitual characteristic; John had "seen" his glory and gives testimony of it;[2] glory was evident in Jesus' miracles, which were like signs "manifesting" it and revealing the supreme power bestowed on him by the Father and indicating that God was present and acting in him.[3] But, for John, glory shone out most clearly at the passion, his "hour" properly so called, the hour of the "exaltation" and "glorification" of the Son of Man.[4] This exaltation was itself the sign of the invisible glorification wrought in Christ by his resurrection, by which he was finally re-endowed with the glory he possessed with the Father before the creation of the world.[5] . . .

Any study of Christ's divinity in John turns upon an understanding of what the evangelist meant by this concept of Jesus' glory. Such an understanding will clearly not be derived in sufficient detail merely from a study of the word "glory" alone. So we must try to examine the mystery of Jesus' personality as John portrays it, and the formulas like Messenger, Son of Man, Son of God, and Word, by which he expressed it. The word "glory" is really in the nature of a synthesis of all these other expressions. We may merely note that when John uses this word of Christ on earth — the word which the synoptists reserve for the eschatological glorification of the Son of Man — this is already an indication that for John "the glory" belongs to the very being of Jesus, belongs to that in him which is hidden from sight and is revealed

---

[1] Donatien Mollat, S.J., is the author of *L'Evangile et les epitres de saint Jean.* This excerpt is from his portion of the book, *Son and Saviour,* edited by A. Gelin, P.S.S. (Baltimore and Dublin: Helicon Press, 1962), pp. 125–127; 134–135; 138; 155.

[2] 1:14.

[3] 2:11.

[4] 12:33–34.

[5] 17:5.

only to faith. We may also note the astonishing new departure in applying to a man a word which formerly described God himself revealing himself in power. No name like this had ever before been bestowed upon prophet, king, priest or any other man in the Bible. . . . By applying it to Jesus, only one thing could be meant: that God had appeared on earth and had been revealed in all his power in Jesus. John actually underlines the essential sameness of the glory of God and the glory of Jesus.[6]

It remains for us to specify the nature of the bond which binds these two "glories" into one. John tells us what it was in his prologue: it is the bond between Father and Son; Jesus' glory was "glory as of the only Son from the Father, full of grace and truth."[7] From the very beginning, then, this word glory tells us that for John the Gospel is the account of a theophany, where fire, thunder, and lightning have given place to the appearance of a son of man, Jesus, who called God his Father. . . .

The Fulfillment of Scripture. . . . The Gospel of John takes as its framework the solemn liturgical feasts in order to point implicitly to Jesus as the fulfillment of all ancient religion. Not only the history of the chosen people, but also the worship of Israel was brought to its close in the person of Christ. The Sabbath disappeared before him, the feasts reached perfection at his coming, and the Temple itself, the focus of the whole religion, gave way to the temple of his risen

body, from which poured the fountain of living water to renew the world. Jesus revealed the religion "of spirit and of truth" in its fullness. The whole of sacred history was the slow, step-by-step introduction to it. He adopted as his own, and disposed of as its lord, the entire religious inheritance of Israel, and he alone had the power to make it fruitful as God intended it should be. . . .

Such are the characteristics of John's view of Christ. He is the consummation of his people's destiny; its history converged on him and its religion reached perfection in him. More than that, however, in him the fullness of divine truth was offered to every man, divine life was given without restriction, and the pitiless light which shone from him revealed the whole universe in its true colors.

What then is Jesus? John's Gospel asks this question with more insistence than the other Gospels. . . . The Jewish leaders . . . admitted that the mystery was beyond them: "We do not know where he comes from."[8] The Greeks who came "to see Jesus" seemed dumbfounded by the same enigma, and it intrigued Pilate too: "Where are you from?" he asked, meaning not "from what country?" but "who are you, what is the mystery of your origin?" Even the pagan caught the suggestion of a more than human greatness.

Foremost among the formulas which express John's answer to the problem raised in the previous section is that Jesus of Nazareth was "the one sent," the one whom the Father consecrated

---

[6] 13:31; 11:40.
[7] 1:14.

[8] 9:29.

and "sent into the world."[9] To recognize him as such is the prerequisite for the possession of eternal life.

The expression is not in itself a statement of his divinity. It had already been used, for example, of the prophets.[10] . . . Yet there is a radical difference between Jesus and the prophets who had been sent by God. The latter were told of their mission on some particular day; until then they lived like other men; then suddenly the Word of God was made known to them by a sign, or in a vision, or by the dispatch of someone to inform them of their vocation. Moreover, the Bible tells us of the shocked amazement with which they often greeted the revelation of God's call. . . . Nothing like that happened with Jesus. . . . A modern scholar has put this point brilliantly in the words: "Jesus did not only live for his mission, but he lived *on* it."[11] The overriding difference between Jesus and the prophets was therefore this, that whereas the latter were sent to convey a definite message or to carry out a well-defined assignment, his mission — the very fact that he was sent — constitutes his message and the work he had to do.[12] He proclaimed his coming

into the world as the object in which men must believe in order to achieve salvation. . . . The work of God which he had to do was simply his coming into the world. . . . Jesus' mission as recorded in the Gospel of John is actually closer to the mission of the Word or of Wisdom in the Old Testament than to that of the prophets, for like the Word of Wisdom his mission is not subordinate to — is not "for" — anything else. The very presence of Jesus is the light which illumines and saves the world. . . .

Son of Man. Both John and the synoptists use the term Son of Man to describe Christ. . . . The expression retained its transcendent importance for John; it designates Jesus as the supreme judge whose summons would bring all men back from the grave on the day of the last judgment. But in John, more clearly even than in the synoptists, it expresses the heavenly origin of Jesus. The Son of Man was more than the figure of mystery "who comes upon the clouds of heaven"; he was the one "who descended from heaven"[13] to reveal "the things of heaven" to men and to give them "the true bread of heaven."[14] His heavenly origin serves as a guarantee for the divine and spiritual mysteries he reveals.

---

[9] 10:36.

[10] Jer 1:5–6.

[11] R. Bultmann, *Das Evangelium des Johannes* (Göttingen, 1941), p. 143 ff.

[12] Jean Guillet has recently put forward similar ideas with regard to Jesus and the Holy Spirit: "In Jesus the fullness of the Spirit indwells. . . . No prophet had ever possessed the Spirit to this extent. . . . The Spirit had come upon the Judges and Prophets as a strange power from on high. . . . They knew they were being held spellbound by someone stronger than themselves and being led by him wherever he wished

---

them to go. Not so with Jesus in whom there was never any suggestion of compulsion. He did not regard the Spirit as an invader from outside, but freely held conversation with him. Moreover, the Spirit was present at Jesus' bidding for he had power over this all-mighty Power. He left his followers so that he could bestow this Spirit upon them." In *Lumen Vitae*, VIII, 1953, pp. 28–30.

[13] 3:13.   [14] 6:32.

The title "son of Man" in John, then, even more clearly than in the synoptists, endows Jesus' messianic actions with a heavenly, transcendent, mysterious, and divine quality. It presents Jesus as the being come from on high, who was in the world without being of it, who descended from heaven and ascended there again, who belonged to heaven and not to earth. . . . Heaven and earth were united in him. . . .

Son of God. The title Son of God, as found in the Bible or in the extrabiblical thought of the first century, did not inevitably suggest sonship in the strict sense of the word, that is, a sonship as the term of generative activity by which a father's nature is transmitted to another. The title often expressed no more than a special relationship between a man and God in virtue of the mission with which the man had been entrusted, or in virtue of the special love God manifested in his regard. . . . It would, therefore, be reasonable to agree with Dupont that in John "the title Son of God is related on one side to the title Messiah,[15] and on the other to that of Son of Man,[16] and that furthermore, it has a close connection with Jesus' divine mission."

This statement does not, however, exhaust all the significance of the title. The argument which begins to develop in chapter ten about the Son of God reveals that the Jews as well as Jesus regarded it in this instance not only as a messianic title, but also as an affirmation of divine sonship in the strict sense of the word.[17] . . . This is confirmed by the nature of the relations between Jesus and the one of whom he claimed to be the Son, by the way he speaks of his Father. Jesus was "the only Son" given to the world by God as a living proof of his love. . . . He puts himself on a different footing from other men. The Temple is his Father's house. Jesus proclaimed his mission in his Father's name; he related what he had seen with the Father, who had given him to the world as the true heavenly bread. His Father glorifies him. . . . A bond of unequalled intimacy linked Jesus and the Father, a bond of mutual love, of knowledge, of joint activity, and of mutual sharing in the possession of all good. . . ." The Father knows me and I know the Father."[18] "The Father is in me and I am in the Father."[19] "The Father and I are one."[20] . . .

As a recent writer has expressed it: "Christ was able to give us the power to become children of God precisely because he was the Begotten of God. . . . The function which Christ fills originates from his nature, from his essence."[21] The nature of the Son of God is the keystone upon which the whole building depends. As for Paul, the building depended on the glory of the risen Lord, so for John it rests upon the glory of the Only Son of God.

A modern critic can, nevertheless,

[15] 3:14–17.
[16] J. Dupont, *Essais sur la Christologie de saint Jean* (Bruges, 1951), pp. 283–293.
[17] 10:22–40.
[18] 10:15.
[19] 10:38.
[20] 10:30.
[21] M. E. Boismard, *St. John's Prologue* (London, 1957), p. 94.

claim that the description of Jesus as Son of God does not connote any metaphysical statement. The paradox of the Christian faith, he claims, is that divine revelation is present in a man, in this man Jesus; there is no real difference between him and other men except that he is the "Chosen One of God," "the one who is sent," the revealer in whom God speaks to man, and only to this extent, the Son.[22] . . . But this extrinsic and nominalist explanation of Christ's nature and work does not correspond to the evidence of the Gospel. The Gospel did not, of course, define Christ's nature in the metaphysical language of later theology, any more than did the other writings of the New Testament. . . . But there existed a unity between Jesus and the Father which was more than the moral union of an obedient servant or a perfect envoy. . . . When Christ announced his oneness with the Father, the Jews wanted to stone him: "For no good work, but for blasphemy; because you being a man, make yourself God."[23]

Before the Incarnation. The assertion that Jesus is God is supported by the declaration that he pre-existed, a concept which is given clearer for-mulation in John's Gospel than in any other of the New Testament writings. Like Wisdom, Jesus is regarded as pre-existing before his earthly, temporal life. . . . The language used in Chapter six . . . leaves no room at all for doubt: "What if you see the Son of man ascending to where he was before?"[24] And this is reinforced by the solemn proclamation in Chapter eight: . . . "Truly, truly, I say to you, before Abraham was, I am."[25] . . . The Jews made no mistake about it. They understood him so well that they picked up stones to kill him as a blasphemer. . . .

The Word of God. In the prologue to his Gospel, John has made a synthesis embracing all his christological reflection. . . . We can find there . . . a vision of tremendous scope which begins with eternity and embraces the whole history of revelation. . . . Jesus: the eternal Word, God, creator of the universe, the Son, only begotten of the Father, who came on earth as a human being to make God known to us and to make us his children. Nowhere else in the New Testament, not even in the hymn to Christ in Colossians, is there to be found such a magnificent expression of faith in the divinity of Jesus. . . .

[22] R. Bultmann, *Theologie des Neuen Testaments* (Tübingen, 1951), p. 413.
[23] 10:33.
[24] 6:62.
[25] 8:57–58.

3. E. K. Lee[1] finds that John's favorite name for God is "the Father," but that this Fatherhood is limited to those whom Christ has chosen out of the world. Jesus is the unique Son of God and demands belief in his absolute pre-existence. The Paraclete sayings carry us farther than any other writings in the development of the New Testament doctrine of the Godhead.

The Father. That John thought of God as "personal" is a sure deduction from the Hebrew cast of his thought; but it is also determined by the fact that God revealed himself in a person, Jesus Christ. Therefore, in spite of all the use he made of such abstract terms as light and truth, terms which may have been determined by contemporary religion, and which may equally describe an impersonal deity, his favorite name for God is "the Father." . . .

A distinction is to be observed between God as Father in a real sense and as Father in an ethical sense. The doctrine that God is the Father of all men in virtue of their material creation is not a Biblical idea at all.[2] There is only one passage in the whole of the New Testament which can be claimed to support the idea . . . Acts 17:28. And even this probably means no more than "made in the image of God."[3] . . .

While, therefore, John does not follow contemporary thought in thinking that God's children are his offspring in the carnal sense, he has points of contact with Greek and Jewish thought in his teaching on the "new birth:" "Except a man be born of water and the Spirit, he cannot enter the kingdom of God."[4] The expression . . . means that the spiritual man or members of the kingdom of God owe their existence as such to the procreative power of God symbolized by the sacrament of Baptism.[5] It follows that such a new birth involves more than just a moral change in man: just as one must be born as a physical organism in order to enter into the physical world, so one must be born as a spiritual organism in order to enter into the divine world. This involves also a new standard of values, for the new realm entered is the realm of truth in contrast to falsehood, of light in contrast to darkness.[6] . . .

John describes the relation of the children to the Father in the same terms as he uses to describe his relation to the Son. The favorite expres-

[1] Edwin Kenneth Lee, M.A., M.Litt., Vicar of Lofthouse, Leeds, wrote his book, *The Religious Thought of St. John* in the midst of the busy life of a colliery parish. The book was published in London by S.P.C.K., in 1950. This excerpt is from pp. 42–45; 49–53; 64–65; 68–73; 74; 76–83; 91–92; 210–216; 219.

[2] *Pater* is occasionally used in the more general sense of Creator — Jas 1:17; Heb 12:9.

[3] See Rackham, *The Acts of the Apostles*, p. 317; cf. Lk 11:13, where the earthly father of children is parallel with the heavenly Father.

[4] 3:5 ff.

[5] A symbol is that which partakes of the nature of the thing symbolized.

[6] Cf. Odeberg, *The Fourth Gospel*, pp. 48 ff.; see Schlatter, *Der Evangelist Johannes*, p. 87, and Büchsel, *Theologisches Wörterbuch zum Neuen Testament*, ed., G. Kittel, Vol. I, pp. 378.

sion which John uses to describe Christ's nature and privilege is that of Son[7] and Jesus himself claims no higher title.[8] "The only begotten Son" is an expression which John uses[9] to denote his unique relation of love and privilege. Both terms indicate likeness; and Christ's fitness to reveal God rests upon this unique acquaintance of the only begotten Son with the Father and upon his union with him.[10] Yet notwithstanding this uniqueness in position and nature, notwithstanding also the fact that the children are never called sons, there is a very close analogy between the position of the Son and the children. . . .[11]

This conception is founded upon God as the source of all life, and is intimately connected with John's idea of eternal life as the preeminent gift of God in Christ. That God is life, is with John an idea coordinate with "God is love," "God is light," and the "true God." The idea of the divine Fatherhood is compounded of the two ideas, life and love: the true God is also eternal life.[12] . . .

It is very clear that the more richly the idea of God's Fatherhood is developed, so much the more impossible is it to think of it in relation to the world in general. As defined by the whole range of ideas with which Fatherhood is associated in the Johannine writings, the relation is limited to those whom Christ has chosen out of the world.[13] It is evident that the

ideas of begetting, of the new birth and of eternal life, were not realized in the case of all men. . . . God's love as an attribute of the Father is, in this deeper sense, limited to the children.[14] . . .

Son of God. John regards Jesus as the Son of God in a unique way that differentiates him in kind from all other "sons of God." . . . The begetting of Jesus as the Son of God was something quite different from both Hebrew and Hellenistic usage. For him the term has a value absolutely *sui generis;* Jesus is the "only begotten Son of God."[15] Only John in the New Testament applies the word *monogenes* to Jesus, and he does this four times in the Gospel and once in the Epistle.[16] . . . When he applies the term to Christ, he means that Jesus is the "Son of God" in a unique sense; the other sons of God are different not only in degree but in kind. The use of the term prevents us from thinking of the Logos as a diffused, impersonal force working in nature and history. The Logos does not dwell in Christ as in men; the Logos is "only begotten," is Jesus Christ. The Logos and the only begotten Son refer to the same person. . . . It would seem, therefore, reasonable to say that the ethical relation which is everywhere prominent in the expression we are studying rather suggests than excludes a substantial relation. We must, however, be careful when using nonscriptural terms to express Biblical ideas. . . .

---

[7] 1:34; 20:31; 1 Jn 2:22, 23; 5:23.
[8] 3:35, 36; 5:23; 19:7.
[9] 1:14; 3:16, 18.
[10] 1:18.
[11] 1:12; 1 Jn 3:2; 5:1.
[12] 1 Jn 5:20.   [13] 15:19.

[14] 1 Jn 3:1.
[15] 1:14.
[16] 1:14; 1:18; 3:16; 3:18; 1 Jn 4:19.

The Pre-existence of Jesus. Another question arises: Did Jesus express the fact of his pre-existence in so many words, or did he leave it to be inferred from his claim to be perfectly at one with the Father? The fact is that Jesus' consciousness of pre-existence is so clearly expressed that one wonders how it could be called into question. . . . It is not proved by the frequent expressions which represent him as "sent" or even "sent into the world," for such expressions are used of John the Baptist and others. Nor is it indubitably expressed in the claim of learning from the Father, of doing and saying what he has seen and heard from him; for this might conceivably be the result of inspiration and inspired vision. There are other expressions that denote derivation from God, but not pre-existence.[17] . . .

We may, however, with more confidence point to those expressions which represent Jesus as coming down from heaven.[18] . . . There are also other statements which would seem to admit of no misunderstanding.[19] In the High Priestly prayer he says: "for thou lovedst me before the foundation of the world";[20] and he speaks of the "glory which I had with thee before the world was."[21] Glory was the term which designated the radiant being of the Deity. . . . Christ, therefore, claims

to have shared from all eternity the divine nature of God. . . .

But Jesus' testimony does not end with a claim for relative pre-existence. He demands belief in his absolute pre-existence.[22] . . . The phrase "before Abraham was, I am," signifies even more than pre-existence.[23] By it Jesus claims to be the ever-existent and ever-central Son, to whom everything and every being of the spiritual world are constitutively and essentially related. . . .

The Logos. John was . . . faced with two problems for which he was seeking not so much an explanation as a name. The name he found in the term *Logos,* and the problems were as follows: (*a*) There was the problem which had worried all religious philosophers from time immemorial: How can God reveal himself to man? Israel's problem was religious as the Greeks' was metaphysical. . . . (*b*) The second problem was a peculiarly Christian one. John, with the other Christians, was convinced that Jesus was God. . . . This belief seemed to be set in irreconcilable contradiction to the fundamental monotheism of the Jewish religion from which Christianity had sprung. . . . The name Son was unsuited to meet this precise diffi-

---

[17] 8:42; 1 Jn 4:4. The question whether the title Son of Man includes in itself the idea of pre-existence is discussed later in this book. As a negative answer is there given, nothing further need be said at this point.
[18] 3:31; 6:33, 38, 41, 42, 51.
[19] 6:62; 16:28.
[20] 17:24.
[21] 17:5.

[22] 7:24; 8:58.
[23] Cf. Stauffer, *Theologisches Wörterbuch zum Neuen Testament,* Vol. II, p. 352; "In the 1st-person speeches of the Gospel of St. John, Jesus contends with the pseudo-saviours and pseudo-gods of the polytheistic world for the claim to soteriological 1st-person predication. He excels them all, and reveals himself as the only valid representative of God in the absolute divine formula *ego eimi,* the purest expression of his unique and still utterly inconceivable significance."

culty, because its chief stress lay upon the idea of personality, and so upon distinction in the Godhead. What was wanted was a name which would designate Jesus according to his nature, and in eternal communion, not only with God in the abstract but with the God of the Old Testament.

It so happens that the term Logos had been used in such a way that it could be adapted to provide a solution to both these problems. Dr. E. Krebs suggests that the term may have been selected deliberately in opposition to the various Logos doctrines of heathenism.[24] It would certainly appear that John was offering to the pagan world a reasoned answer to a problem that had exercised the best minds in Greek philosophy and Jewish religion. John crowns and completes the Pauline doctrine [of the Logos] by his definite and absolute identification of Jesus with the Logos. He thus shows that in Jesus Christ, God and man, time and eternity, were brought together; he also showed that the belief in Jesus as the Logos was a reasonable deduction from the Jews' own teaching about God's relation with the world. . . .

In Greek thought . . . the Logos comes to occupy the position of an intermediary between the Supreme God and the created world. . . . The Johannine proclamation is in complete contrast to such a conception. . . . The Word is not an inferior and subordinate agent. His Father is associated with all he does: "My Father worketh hitherto and I work"; "I and the

Father are one." Thus God is not isolated from the world with which he makes contact in and through the Son. The Father and the Son do not stand over against each other as a principal and a secondary god, the former remaining apart from the world while the latter creates, organizes, and sustains. But they are related to one another in terms of absolute harmony and identity of purpose. . . .

In the Old Testament the Word of God is regarded as being effective not only at the initial moment of creation, but in accomplishing his will in the world at all times. . . . But the Word of the Lord is specially regarded as the means of revelation. He is a messenger who reveals the will of God.[25] . . . When, therefore, John proclaimed that Jesus was the Logos and that he was one with the Father, it is difficult to avoid the conclusion that he had in mind the kind of relationship that existed between God and the Word in the Old Testament. . . .

The Paraclete. We must not make the mistake of Dr. E. F. Scott, who thinks that the Johannine teaching about the Holy Spirit is superfluous.[26] . . . It would be more accurate to say that the Holy Spirit is the abiding *representative* of Christ, in whom he himself returns to his flock. For John makes it quite clear that in his own mind it is "another Paraclete" who shall be with his disciples when Jesus withdraws his visible presence.[27] The judgment of Dr. H. B. Swete seems

---

[24] *Der Logos als Heiland im ersten Jahrhundert,* pp. 98 ff.

[25] Ps 147:15.

[26] *The Fourth Gospel,* pp. 347, 388; cf. Gardner, *The Ephesian Gospel,* p. 159.

[27] 14:16; 16:7. The Sinai Syriac renders: "He will give you another, the Paraclete."

conclusive: "It cannot be maintained that Christ is speaking in John 14–16 merely of a new operation of divine power in man[28] or of his own spirit as perpetuating itself in the lives of his disciples. For he proceeds to distinguish him both from the Father and from himself. . . . The differentiation is perfect; the Spirit is not the Father, nor is he the Son; as a person he is distinct from both."[29] . . .

John lays greater stress than any other Evangelist upon the work of the Holy Spirit and more clearly than any other Evangelist he shows what constituted the distinctive operation of the Holy Spirit. . . . An examination of all the relevant passages in the New Testament shows that the article is invariably used when the Holy Spirit is regarded as an agent operating upon man from the outside, as it were, or as a divine Being. When the article is omitted, the Holy Spirit is regarded as an inward inspiration working as an impersonal divine power within men. The fourth Gospel is no exception to this rule, and it is important to notice that in Chapters 14–16, where the distinct personality of the Holy Spirit is most clearly described, the article is used in every case. . . .

It is as Paraclete that the Spirit is most characteristically represented by John. The term is used only five times in the New Testament, and that only in the Johannine writings,[30] and it is translated in two ways: by Advocate, in the sense of pleader or defender, and by Comforter, in the sense of consoler.[31] . . . The Paraclete shall guide the disciples unto all truth[32] and reveal to them what they were unable to bear from Jesus' lips.[33] . . .

This conception of the Paraclete, as the teacher of truth, constitutes a most important element in John's doctrine of the Spirit, and brings it into line with his philosophy of salvation. . . . The Paraclete as the Spirit of Truth is no abstract moral quality, but signifies the revelation in history of the ultimate truth of God.[34] . . . In the relative independence which John ascribes to the Paraclete we see reflected the high significance of the Spirit as the medium of revelation which Jewish theology had already dimly recognized, and which the Christian theology expressed in the Trinitarian formula. To quote Dr. W. F. Howard, "Though with St. John we are still in the pre-dogmatic stage of the Trinitarian teaching, the sayings about the Paraclete carry us a degree farther than any other writing in the development of the New Testament doctrine of the Godhead.[35]

---

[28] Cf. Ps 139.

[29] Hasting's *Dictionary of the Bible*, article "The Holy Spirit," Vol. II, p. 408. The manner in which the neuter *Pneuma* is connected with the masculines *os, ekeinos,* and *autos* is very striking.

[30] 14:16, 26; 15:26; 16:7; 1 Jn 2:1.

[31] See Westcott, *St. John*, pp. 211 ff.; Hasting's, *Dictionary of the Bible*, Vol. III, pp. 665 ff.; A. Jülicher, *Enc. Bib.*, 3567 ff.; Field, *Notes on the Translation of the New Testament*, pp. 102, 103.

[32] 16:13.

[33] 16:12.

[34] Cf. Hoskyns, *The Fourth Gospel*, p. 552.

[35] *Christianity according to St. John*, p. 80.

4. J. L. McKenzie[1] studies the Father, Son, Word, Spirit. Jesus and the Father are one, but the Father is greater than Jesus. "Son of God" is a soteriological rather than a metaphysical title, but with metaphysical implications. Word as used by John has become almost the technical designation of the Second Person in theology. The personal reality of the Spirit is not subject to debate.

The Father. In John the Father appears almost entirely as the Father of Jesus in contrast to the Father of the disciples. Jesus has a unique relationship with the Father, who communicates himself to men through Jesus his Son and confers upon him power and authority to execute his mission. Jesus is the only-begotten of the Father;[2] he is the object of the peculiar love of the Father.[3] Jesus alone knows the Father,[4] and Jesus and the Father are one.[5] To know and to see Jesus is to know and to see the Father,[6] because Jesus is in the Father and the Father in Jesus.[7] Jesus teaches what he has learned from the Father[8] and does the works of the Father.[9] No one can come to the Father except through Jesus.[10] The Father is greater than Jesus,[11] as the father is always superior to his son, and the sender to the one sent; but Jesus has received all power and authority from the Father,[12] so that he can grant any request which the disciples may make.[13] Jesus is sent by the Father and lives through

the Father[14] and thus is able to communicate life to those who believe in him; and he can send his disciples with the fullness of power as he himself was sent by the Father.[15] . . .

The Son. The use of the title in John presupposes the reflection evident in the epistles. In the confessions of Nathanael[16] and of Martha[17] it is possible that the title has acquired a messianic significance. More commonly, it expresses the intimate union of the Son with the Father; this is a perfect union of their operations, in virtue of which the Son receives from the Father the power to judge and to confer life.[18] Because of the close union of the Father and the Son, John emphasizes that the Son is entitled to the glorification proper to his sonship and that the Father will glorify him.[19] The Son is the redeemer whom the Father has given; the love which the Father has for the Son makes him the medium through which the world is saved and men receive eternal life.[20] To this purpose the Father has committed all things to him.[21] Hence it is faith in the Son which

---

[1] Chap. I, 3, n. 1. This excerpt is from his book, *Dictionary of the Bible*, pp. 276, 831, and his book, *The Power and the Wisdom*, pp. 137, 142.

[2] 1:14, 18.
[3] 3:55; 5:20; 10:17.
[4] 1:18; 6:46; 10:15.
[5] 10:30.
[6] 14:7–9.
[7] 10:38; 14:10.

[8] 8:28–38.
[9] 10:32; 14:10.
[10] 14:6.
[11] 14:28.
[12] 16:15.
[13] 16:23.

[14] 6:57.
[15] 20:21.
[16] 1:49.
[17] 11:27.
[18] 5:19–26.
[19] 11:4; 17:1.
[20] 3:16–18; 1 Jn 4:9, 13.
[21] 3:35 f.

brings eternal life.[22] The sonship of Jesus is the principle of the adoption of Christians;[23] fellowship with the Son is fellowship with the Father.[24] Confession of the Son brings men to union with the Father, and without union with the Son no one reaches the Father.[25] Throughout the Johannine writings the pre-existence of the Son as a divine condition is evidently supposed.

In the New Testament "Son of God" is a soteriological rather than a metaphysical title. The unique relation of Jesus the Son of God with the Father enables him to mediate between the Father and mankind and gives his saving acts and his intercession a unique efficacy. Were he not the Son, it is inconceivable that men should receive the adoption which he confers, which is a far more intimate union with God than the Old Testament adoption of Israel. Were he not the Son, the Father could not have for him the love which makes his offering of himself so acceptable. There are, of course, metaphysical implications in the title, and these implications are the source of the great theological discussions of the 3rd–5th centuries A.D.; but the New Testament itself is not explicitly conscious of these metaphysical implications and therefore does not answer explicitly the metaphysical questions which can be asked. . . .

The Word of God. Word as designation of Jesus is used only by John, and rarely by this author; the peculiar force of the term is seen in the fact that although the term is rare, it has become almost the technical designation of the Second Person in theology. The term has a long history not only in the Old Testament but in the religions of the ancient Near East. The word is conceived as a projection of the person. Once emitted it acquires an enduring reality of its own. . . . It reveals the identity of the thing to him who knows the name. The divine word is a creative force. . . .

John's use of the term is clearly the "fulfillment" of the Old Testament in the finest sense of the word; and it owes nothing to Platonic or Stoic conceptions of the *logos*. In the world of thought [common to John's hearers] Jesus as the Word of the Father takes his place easily. He is the revelation of the Father and the embodiment of his power. He is the projection of his personality as an enduring reality. He makes the Father intelligible; in him men experience a personal encounter with the Father. He is the creative word, bringing into being a new man and a new world. It is no wonder that the term has acquired such significance in theology, even though the rich Old Testament background of the term has not always been considered. And as well as any other term it expressed the divine pre-existence of Jesus. . . .

The Spirit. The Spirit in John differs sufficiently from the Spirit in Paul to demand our attention. The identity between Jesus and the Spirit in John is closer than in the other New Testament books. This is not an identity of person, nor is the Spirit a metaphor for Jesus himself; the two

22 6:40; 20:31; 1 Jn 5:13.
23 1:12.
24 1 Jn 1:3.
25 1 Jn 2:22–24.

remain quite distinct. But it is no doubt because of this close identity that where Paul conceives the Spirit as dwelling in the individual believer, John describes the Spirit more as an external reality which operates upon the believer. John is extremely explicit that the Spirit is the successor of Jesus who continues the work of Jesus; the Spirit cannot come until Jesus is glorified, which is exactly parallel to the conception of Luke.

Peculiar to John is the Spirit as "Paraclete," the advocate, the intercessor, or helper. It is as the Paraclete that the Spirit is sent by Jesus; that he is sent by both the Father and by Jesus is the historic point of doctrinal difference between the Latin and Greek churches. It is also as the Paraclete that personal actions are more frequently attributed to the Spirit; the Spirit is the revealer, the teacher, the witness. . . .

It is an article of Catholic faith that the Trinity of persons exists in unity of nature; the personal reality of the Spirit is not subject to debate. Nor is the distinct personal reality of the Spirit from the Father and the Son subject to debate. . . .

5. J. Lebreton[1] studies the Son and the Spirit. He sees a strict cohesion of the Johannine texts that stress the Son's complete dependence on the Father and those that stress his complete unity with the Father in action and being. From the supper discourse texts the Holy Spirit emerges as much a living Person as Jesus himself.

The Father and the Son. No one doubts the divinity of Christ on the pages of John, but many recognize merely a divinity subordinated to that of the Father: for them, as for the Arians, all the theology of the fourth Gospel is dominated by the phrase: "The Father is greater than I"; if they recognize that other texts yield a different impression, the most that they will admit is that the Gospel contains two currents of doctrine, one tending toward the subordination of the Son to the Father, an the other toward their equality.[2] Such a dualism would be surprising in a work of such profound unity. . . .

In order to determine the relations of the Father and the Son, we ought to be able to establish the precise relations of origin connecting them. This is a vain hope. The Gospel does not furnish any additional data to those contained in the prologue. Several of the Fathers . . . think they see the eternal generation of the Word referred to when Christ declares: "from God I proceeded and came":[3] it seems more probable that the reference is to the mystery of the Incarnation: the Son who was in the "bosom of the Father" came forth thence, so to speak, to fulfill his mission here

---

[1] Chap. I, 5, n. 1. This excerpt is from *op. cit.,* pp. 390–404.

[2] Reus, *Theologie chrétienne,* Vol. II, 440–444; Holtzmann, *Neutestamentliche Theologie,* Vol. II, Part 2, 490 ff.

[3] 8:42.

below.[4] What is in any case perfectly clear in these passages is the mission of the Son by the Father, and the Son's dependence on the Father.

This dependence is shown as stricter and more complete in the writings of John than in any other book of the New Testament. Occasionally, it seems to refer immediately to the humanity of Christ, manifested in the loving subjection of Jesus to God his Father.[5] . . . a dependence full of love, confidence, intimacy, but at the same time, strict and total. Jesus presents this dependence to his disciples as a model,[6] and rightly, not only because it is perfect, but because it is truly a human model. . . .

Certain details of these texts, however, do . . . transcend the narrow limits of human life. Thus the mission mentioned in John 12:49, refers to the Son as pre-existing, and the words which immediately follow those quoted above do so even more clearly.[7] The fact is, to John perhaps in a higher degree than to Paul, the chief object of contemplation is the *unity of the person* of Christ; John is well aware of the distinction of natures in that unity — he knows that the "Word has become flesh; he remembers the diversity of relations which they set up — he would never say of the pre-existing Son that "the Father was greater than he"; but above all he is anxious not to "divide Christ." Nothing then is more natural than for him to recognize in the same sentence

the human subjection of Jesus and the eternal dependence of the Son.

"Amen, amen, I say unto you, the Son cannot do anything of himself, but what he seeth the Father doing: for what things soever he doth, these the Son also doth in like manner."[8] . . . Evidently, there is no question here of the human actions of Christ, but of his eternal and divine activity. It is the same throughout this discourse; the divinity of the Son is its principal topic, although here and there his humanity is mentioned.[9] . . . If Christ is the life, he is so only by communication from and by dependence on the Father.

On the other hand, the knowledge of the Son is perfect, universal, and in the strict sense of the word, divine.[10] . . . It is evident that for John[11] the power of the Son is identical with that of the Father; he never represents the Son as a mere instrument of the Father; he even refrains — and the fact is remarkable — from the phrases occurring so frequently in the other books of the New Testament, which indicate in the divine action the hierarchy of the divine Persons.[12] . . . We do not read in John's pages that God has created the world through his Word, nor that the Father works miracles through his Son. To convey this idea, he makes use of two mutually complementary series of expressions which help us to understand his Trinitarian theology.

---

[4] Cf. 13:3; 16:28.

[5] 4:34; 8:29, 55; 12:49–50; 14:31; 15:10; 17:1–2.

[6] 15:10.

[7] 17:5; cf. 8:28.

[8] 5:19–23.

[9] Cf. 5:26; 6:58.

[10] 16:30.

[11] 5:17, 21; 10:28–30.

[12] Acts 2:22; 10:36; Rom 2:16; 1 Cor 15:57; Heb 1:2.

All that the Son has and does has been given him by the Father,[13] This gift made by the Father to the Son is universal, as well as eternal and irrevocable; by which John gives us to understand, as far as human language can, this double truth, that all comes from the Father, and the Son himself also possesses the plentitude of everything. . . . The works of the Son are the works of the Father, not only because the Father has bestowed on the Son the power of doing them, but because he dwells in the Son, producing them continuously.[14] . . .

St. John thus shows in a clear light the unity of the Father and Son in action as in being. This unity also manifests itself in glory, the natural fruit of the divine works: the Father is glorified *in* the Son rather than *by* the Son.[15] In the same way Christian worship will reach the Father *in* the Son rather than *by* the Son. . . .

It is difficult, I think, not to recognize the strict cohesion of all these theses; it is no doubt possible to make two parallel series of Johannine texts, establishing on the one hand the dependence of the Son, and on the other his unity with the Father, and conclude that they are incoherent; one may go further and distinguish two influences, one of religious experience, and another, of metaphysical speculation. All such hypothetical interpretations merely glance to and fro on the surface of the Johannine doctrine without touching, so to speak, its soul. . . .

In later days, particularly from the fourth century onward, theologians will show that these relations of origin and dependence alone enable us to distinguish between persons whose nature is possessed in common, and that consequently this dependence of the Son on the Father, which seems at first sight to threaten the unity and even the equality of the two persons, is, on the contrary, the consecration of that unity and the condition that enables us to conceive it. . . .

The Supper Discourse. There are no other [texts] in the whole of the New Testament which contain such explicit teaching on the Holy Spirit and his personality: John 14:15–19; 25–26; 15:26; 16:7–15. From these texts taken together, a definite and irresistible impression results: the Holy Spirit promised by Jesus is not merely a gift, a force, but as much a living Person as he is himself, and one whose action is so divine that his presence will for the disciples advantageously replace the visible presence of Jesus himself: "It is expedient to you that I go."

This impression is strengthened by an attentive examination of the texts in detail. . . . John, in spite of the proximity of the neuter word *to pneuma* (the spirit), always uses the masculine pronoun *ekeinos* (he) to designate the Holy Spirit.[16] . . . John loses sight of the grammatical term he has selected, and only sees the Person whom he is describing. For it is evidently a Person whose acts he is describing: it is a Paraclete, an ad-

---

[13] 5:36; 26, 22, 27; 17:2; 3:35; 13:3; 16:15; 17:10.

[14] 14:10; 17:21; 14:11.

[15] 13:31, 32; 14:13.

[16] 14:26; 15:26; 16:13, 14. Cf. Swete, *Holy Spirit*, 292, n. 1.

vocate; he will teach everything to the Apostles, he will remind them of all that Christ has said to them; he will give testimony of Christ; he will convince the world. . . . One cannot imagine a more personal role; but what is even more decisive is the analogy between the Spirit and himself presented by Jesus: "I will ask the Father, and he shall give you another Paraclete that he may abide with you forever"; the whole of the rest of the discourse does but accentuate this parallelism. All the attempts to reduce the significance of this discourse to a "metaphorical personification"[17] fail on this point: the personality of Jesus is the measure of the personality of the Holy Spirit; they must both be denied or both accepted. . . .

The analogy, however, is not so close as not to admit essential differences. Sonship characterizes the relations of the Son and the Father; it does not appear in the theology of the Spirit. The Father is the sole origin of the Son; this is not the case in the relation between the Son and the Spirit: the Son sends the Spirit, but "from the Father."[18] . . . Thus, even in his relations with the Spirit, the Son is dependent on the Father. . . . The Father is the sovereignly independent first principle. . . .

6. **C. K. Barrett[1] sees John as more conscious than the synoptic writers of the centrality of Christology. Jesus' sonship involves a metaphysical relationship with the Father. Jesus is an ontological mediator between God and man and no less a mediator of true knowledge and salvation. The Paraclete passages are best treated as genuine parts of the last discourses, not as insertions. Though even in these no doctrine of the Trinity is formulated, yet the materials are present out of which such a doctrine might be formulated.**

Christology. The Christology of the fourth Gospel is not "higher" than that of the Synoptic Gospels; but it is true that John was a profound and responsible theologian, more conscious than the synoptic writers of the importance and centrality of Christology. . . . What John perceived with far greater clarity than any of his predecessors was that Jesus *is* the Gospel and that the Gospel *is* Jesus. . . . It was intolerable therefore that the person of Christ should remain undefined. Paul, who had recognized the same truth, evidently felt the same obligation.

None of the Synoptic Gospels presents a developed and systematic Christology, but they are full of the raw material of Christology. In particular, they all affirm, in predominantly eschatological terms that it was in Jesus that God caused the life and activity of the "other" world to break

---

[17] This is the expression of W. Beyschlag; cf. Reville; Goguel; Holtzmann; Stevens; Swete.

[18] 15:26.

[1] Chap. II, B, 5 n. 1. This excerpt is from his book, *The Gospel according to St. John* (London, S.P.C.K., 1960), pp. 58–62, 74–78.

through into this world. . . .

The question of Messiahship in general holds a prominent place in the Gospel.[2] But what does John mean by representing Jesus as Messiah? In the Synoptic Gospels the Messiahship of Jesus is concealed. He nowhere claims the dignity for himself, and discourages the proclamation of demons. . . . The Synoptic and especially the Marcan presentation of Messiahship is governed by the theme of the messianic secret; Jesus is truly Messiah, but a Messiah as bound to humility and obscurity as he is obliged in the end to suffer. . . . So far John runs parallel to Mark; but the parallelism is far from complete. . . . There is an element of concealment in Jesus' Messiahship, but it is also openly confessed from the beginning of the Gospel.[3] It is hidden from the unbelieving and revealed to the believers whom God has called. . . . Christ is not manifested to the world, but he is manifested to his own (as indeed he is in Mark). . . .

It is clear that John, though he retains messianic language, restates its content. This is true also of his treatment of the other principal synoptic descriptions of Jesus — Son of God and Son of man. Superficially it might seem that the two are almost reversed in meaning, for while in the Synoptic Gospels "Son of God" draws attention to Christ's obedience to God, and "Son of man" means a heavenly being, in John "Son of God" means at times one who shares the nature

of God, "Son of man" one who shares the nature of man. To draw the contrast so sharply would however be misleading.

For John, Jesus' sonship does indeed involve a metaphysical relationship with the Father. The charge that Jesus, by claiming to be the Son of God and to work continuously with him, makes himself equal to God, is never rebutted. John does not mean to rebut it. . . . Undoubtedly, he believes that the Son of God who was incarnate in Jesus of Nazareth inhabited eternity with the Father. But these notions are always qualified by the thought of a fundamentally moral relationship, in which the Son is obedient to the Father. . . . By thus showing its two aspects, John brings out more clearly than the synoptists the meaning of sonship: both moral likeness and essential identity are included.

The use of the term Son of man in the Synoptic Gospels is one of the greatest puzzles of New Testament theology and criticism.[4] Jesus as Son of man lives a humble human life, will suffer and die, will appear in glory. These are the most characteristic synoptic uses of the title. . . .

Death is a central feature of John's Son of man doctrine, but . . . for him the death of Jesus is at the same time his glory.[5] . . . The Son of man was (pre-existent) in heaven, descended from heaven, and ascended into heaven. Of no other can this be said.[6] . . . All this means that the

---

[2] 1:20; 3:28; 7:25; 12:34; 4:29 f.; 1:41; cf. 4:29; 6:69.
[3] 1:41, 45, 49.

[4] For a good summary see M. Black, *The Expository Times*, LX (1948), 11–15, 32–6.
[5] 3:14.   [6] 3:13; cf. 6:62.

Son of man is the one true mediator between heaven and earth; he passes from the one to the other, and through his earthly sojourn he bestows upon men the revealed knowledge and the eternal life in virtue of which they in turn come to the life of heaven. . . . The Son of man in John is . . . not only a mediator in that he is the redeemer of men, but is also a mediator in an ontological sense, since he is related both to God and to men.

The idea of mediation involves a further relation of Jesus Christ to men: he is a revealer. It is at this point that John's characteristic description of Jesus as the Logos may be introduced. . . . The term Logos is seen to describe God in the process of self-communication — not the communication of knowledge only, but in a self-communication which inevitably includes the imparting of true knowledge. The Logos is a Word of God which at the same time declares his nature and calls into being a created life in which a divine power circulates. Unlike Philo, who equates the Logos with an archetypal man in whose image the whole human race was made, John conceives the relation between the Logos and the human race soteriologically. Men are not in their own nature born of God, but those are so born who receive the Logos in his incarnate mission; these become a new humanity of which the Logos, or Son of God, is the source and pattern. . . .

The synoptic Christology lacks clarity of definition, both regarding the relation between Christ and God and regarding the relation between Christ and men. "Son of God" does not necessarily align Jesus with God, nor does "Son of man" declare him to be true and complete man. This is not to say that the synoptists are either Ebionite or docetic in intention; they simply view Jesus in the light of the eschatological crisis which he precipitated, and they describe the whole situation in appropriate terms. John releases himself from a purely apocalyptic interpretation of Jesus, while he continues to use eschatological language (though not exclusively). Jesus is the beginning and the end, the first creator and the final judge; also he is the ultimate truth both of God and of humanity. Being truly God and truly man, and being also the image of God and the archetype of humanity, he is an ontological mediator between God and man; he is no less a mediator of true knowledge and of salvation.

The Holy Spirit. The superficial contrast and underlying unity which exist between John and the Synoptic Gospels appear perhaps most markedly in their treatment of the Holy Spirit. It is well known that in the Synoptic Gospels (especially in Mark) references to the Spirit are very few; in John they are numerous and striking. In this, John no doubt stands nearer to the belief and interests of early Christian piety, but it is not for this reason alone that doubt is cast upon the genuineness of the sayings about the Spirit which he ascribes to Jesus. The question is not so much whether the Jesus who is presented in the Synoptic Gospels did speak them as whether he could have spoken them.

They presuppose a considerable perspective of continuing Christian history, and it must be asked whether room for this can be found in the eschatological thought and teaching of Jesus himself.

John's doctrine of the Holy Spirit may not be reconcilable with the oldest Christian eschatology, but it is certainly integrated into his own. The sequel to the earthly life of Jesus was his return to the glory he had enjoyed before the creation of the world, and the earthly counterpart of this heavenly event was the gift of the Spirit. Previously the Spirit had not been at work (except in Jesus himself 7:39); now he became the means by which the eternal life which is God's gift to his own is realized, and herein is John's equivalent for the "realized" eschatology which (along with futurist eschatology) is found in the Synoptic Gospels. . . .

A number of important references to the Spirit may be collected from the last discourses, characterized by the use of the terms *parakletos* and *Spirit* of truth.[7] It has been held that they are all to be regarded as insertions [and] that they interrupt the contexts in which they are placed. . . .

This view can hardly be considered well founded. In the first place, it must be acknowledged that a simple

consecutiveness of thought is not to be looked for in John's writing. . . . In the second place, if the Paraclete passages were removed there would remain not one reference to the Holy Spirit in the last discourse. It is, of course, conceivable that John should have written a set of discourses without speaking of the Spirit, but it does not seem probable. In the third place the Paraclete passages stand where they do without the smallest evidence of textual dislocation, and no convincing hypothesis of their origin, and of the reason and method of their insertion, is forthcoming. It seems then on the whole best to treat these passages as genuine parts of the last discourses. . . .

None of the earlier references in the Gospel to the Spirit show the same measure of personalization as do the last discourses. It is true that even in these no doctrine of the Trinity is formulated; but the materials are present out of which such a doctrine might be formulated. The three divine Persons are mentioned side by side, distinct from one another, yet akin to one another as they are not akin to man. . . .

It may be that some of John's language is unguarded; the Arians found 14:28 very useful; but more than any other New Testament writer he lays the foundations for a doctrine of a co-equal Trinity.

---

[7] 14:16 ff; 15:26; 16:7–15.

III

GOD IN PRE-NICENE AND NICENE THEOLOGY

1. J. N. D. Kelly[1] studies the Apostolic Fathers, the Apologists, Irenaeus and Tertullian and Origen, as well as the Nicene crisis, theology and aftermath. In the Apostolic Fathers he finds no sign of a Trinitarian doctrine. The Apologists were the first to try to frame an intellectually satisfying explanation of Christ's relation to God the Father. Irenaeus had the most complete vision of the Godhead before Tertullian. Tertullian went further than Irenaeus in describing the Three as Persons. Origen's Trinitarianism was a brilliant reinterpretation of the traditional triadic rule of faith in terms of middle Platonism, but involving a thoroughgoing subordinationism. While Nicea decisively banned Arianism, its positive teaching is more difficult to determine, especially as to numerical identity of substance.

The Church's Faith. The doctrine of one God, the Father and creator, formed the background and indisput- able premise of the Church's faith. Inherited from Judaism, it was her bulwark against pagan polytheism,

---

[1] J. N. D. Kelly was Principal of St. Edmund Hall, Oxford University, Lecturer in Patristic Studies, and Canon of Chichester Cathedral. Among his published works are *Early Christian Creeds* and *Rufinus, A* *Commentary on the Apostles' Creed.* This excerpt is from his book, *Early Christian Doctrines* (New York: Harper & Brothers, 1958), pp. 87–132, 223–269.

Gnostic emanationism, and Marcionite dualism. The problem for theology was to integrate with it, intellectually, the fresh data of the specifically Christian revelation. Reduced to their simplest, these were the convictions that God had made himself known in the Person of Jesus, the Messiah, raising him from the dead and offering salvation to men through him, and that he had poured out his Holy Spirit upon the Church.

Even at the New Testament stage ideas about Christ's pre-existence and creative role were beginning to take shape, and a profound, if often obscure, awareness of the activity of the Spirit in the Church was emerging. No steps had been taken so far, however, to work all these complex elements into a coherent whole. The Church had to wait for more than three hundred years for a final synthesis, for not until the Council of Constantinople (381) was the formula of one God existing in three co-equal Persons formally ratified. Tentative theories, however, some more and some less satisfactory, were propounded in the preceding centuries. . . .

Before considering formal writers, the reader should notice how deeply the conception of a plurality of divine Persons was imprinted on the apostolic tradition and the popular faith. Though as yet uncanonized, the New Testament was already exerting a powerful influence; it is a commonplace that the outlines of a dyadic and a triadic pattern are clearly visible in its pages.[2] It is even more marked

in such glimpses as are obtainable of the Church's liturgy and day-to-day catechetical practice. . . . The ideas implicit in these early catechetical and liturgical formulae, as in the New Testament writers' use of the same dyadic and triadic patterns, represent a pre-reflective, pre-theological phase of Christian belief. This in no way diminishes their interest and importance. It was out of the raw material thus provided by the preaching, worshiping Church that theologians had to construct their more sophisticated account of the Christian doctrine of the Godhead.

The Apostolic Fathers. The earliest writers we have to consider, the Apostolic Fathers, appear as witnesses to the traditional faith rather than interpreters striving to understand it. Nevertheless, their deliverances, usually fragmentary and often naïve, furnish useful insight into the lines along which the Church's unconscious theology was developing; and this insight is all the more valuable because, so far from being a homogeneous group, they were the spokesmen of widely differing trends.

Little can be gleaned from the first of them, Clement of Rome. He coordinates the Three in an oath.[3] . . . As for Christ, he takes[4] his pre-existence prior to the incarnation for granted. . . . The Holy Spirit Clement regarded[5] as inspiring God's prophets in all ages. . . . The chief interest of "Barnabas" theology is the prominence it gives to Christ's pre-existence.

---

[2] See J. N. D. Kelly, *Early Christian Creeds* (London, 1950), Chap. 1.

[3] 58,2.
[4] 22,1; 16,2.
[5] 8,1; 13,1; 16,2; 63,2.

Ignatius and Hermas are rather more revealing. . . . The center of Ignatius's thinking was Christ. It is true that he assigned a proper place to the Holy Spirit. He was the principle of the Lord's virginal conception,[6] it was by him that Christ established and confirmed the Church's officers;[7] he was the gift sent by the Savior, and spoke through Ignatius himself.[8] Further, the triadic formula occurs thrice[9] at least in his letters, the most notable example being a picturesque simile comparing the faithful to stones forming the temple built by God the Father; the cross of Jesus Christ is the crane by which they are hoisted up, and the Holy Spirit the hawser. . . . Christ is the Father's "thought" (*gnome*). . . . He is "our God," "God incarnate" and "God made manifest as man."[10] . . . In his pre-existent being "ingenerate,"[11] he was the timeless, invisible, impalpable, impassible one who for our sake entered time and became visible, palpable, and passible. His divine Sonship dates from the incarnation.[12] . . .

Hermas clearly envisages three distinct personages — the master, i.e., God the Father, his "well-beloved son," i.e., the Holy Spirit, and the servant, i.e., the Son of God, Jesus Christ. The distinction between the three, however, seems to date from the incarnation . . . so that before the incarnation there would seem to have been but two divine Persons. . . .

The evidence to be collected from the Apostolic Fathers is meager, and tantalizingly inconclusive. Christ's pre-existence . . . was generally taken for granted, as was his role in creation as well as redemption. Of a doctrine of the Trinity in the strict sense there is of course no sign, although the Church's triadic formula left its mark everywhere.

The Apologists and the Word. The apologists were the first to try to frame an intellectually satisfying explanation of the relation of Christ to God the Father. They were all ardent monotheists, determined at all costs not to compromise this fundamental truth. The solution they proposed, reduced to essentials, was that, as pre-existent, Christ was the Father's thought or mind, and that, as manifested in creation and revelation, he was its extrapolation or expression. In expounding this doctrine, they had recourse to the imagery of the divine Logos, or Word, which had been familiar to later Judaism as well as to Stoicism, and which had become a fashionable cliché through the influence of Philo. . . . The Apologists' originality lay in drawing out the further implications of the Logos idea in order to make plausible the twofold fact of Christ's pre-temporal oneness with the Father and his manifestation in the world of space and time. In so doing, while taking up the suggestion of such Old Testament texts as Ps 33:6, they did not hesistate to blend with them the Stoic technical distinction between

---

[6] *Eph.*, 18,2.
[7] *Philad. inscr.*
[8] *Eph.*, 17,2; *Philad.*, 7,1.
[9] *Eph.*, 9,1; *Magn.*, 13,1; 13,2.
[10] *Eph.*, 3,2; *Rom.*, 8,2; *Eph. inscr.*, 18,2; *Trall.*, 7,1; *Rom. inscr. Eph.*, 7,2; 19,3.
[11] *Agennetos*: the technical term reserved to distinguish the increate God from creatures.
[12] *Eph.*, 7,2; *Poly.*, 3,2; *Smyr.*, 1,1.

the immanent word (*logos endiath-
etos*) and the word uttered or expressed (*logos prophorikos*).

Their teaching appears most clearly
in Justin, although his theology is far
from being systematic. . . . The Logos
. . . had become incarnate in his entirety in Christ.[13] The Logos is here
conceived of as the Father's intelligence or rational thought . . . but he
was not only in name distinct from
the Father . . . but "numerically distinct too."[14] . . . The incarnation apart,
the special functions of the Logos . . .
are to be the Father's agent in creating and ordering the universe[15] and
to reveal truth to men.[16] As regards
his nature, while other beings are
"things made"[17] or "creatures"[18], the
Logos is God's offspring, his "child"
and "unique Son":[19] "before all creatures God begat, in the beginning, a
rational power out of himself."[20] By
this generation Justin means, not the
ultimate origin of the Father's Logos
or reason (this he does not discuss),
but his putting forth or emission for
the purposes of creation and revelation; and it is conditioned by and is
the result of, an act of the Father's
will.[21] But this generation or emission
does not entail any separation between the Father and his Son . . . does
not involve any partition of the latter's
essence. . . .

There are two points in the apolo-

13 *1 Apol.*, 46,3; 5,4; *2 Apol.*, 10,1.
14 *Dial.*, 128,4.
15 *1 Apol.*, 59; 64,5; *2 Apol.*, 6,3.
16 *1 Apol.*, 54,4; 46; 63,10.
17 *2 Apol.*, 6,3.
18 *Dial.*, 61,1; 100,2.
19 *1 Apol.*, 21,1; *Dial.*, 125,3; 105,1.
20 *Ibid.*, 61,1.
21 *Ibid.*, 61,1; 100,4; 127,4; 128,4.

gists' teaching which, because of their
far-reaching importance, must be
heavily underlined, viz. (a) that for
all of them (i.e., Justin, Tatian, Theo-
philus, Athenagoras) the description
"God the Father" connoted, not the
first Person of the Holy Trinity, but
the one Godhead considered as author
of whatever exists; and (b) that they
all, Athenagoras included, dated the
generation of the Logos, and so his
eligibility for the title "Son" not from
his origination within the being of
the Godhead, but from his emission
or putting forth for the purposes of
creation, revelation and redemption.
Unless these points are firmly grasped,
and their significance appreciated, a
completely distorted view of the apologists' theology is liable to result. Two
stock criticisms of it, for example, are
that they failed to distinguish the
Logos from the Father until he was
required for the work of creation,
and that, as a corollary, they were
guilty of subordinating the Son to
the Father. These objections have a
superficial validity in the light of
post-Nicene orthodoxy, with its doctrine of the Son's eternal generation
and its fully worked out conception
of hypostases or Persons; but they
make no sense in the thought-atmos-
phere in which the apologists moved.
It is true that they lacked a technical
vocabulary adequate for describing
eternal distinctions within the Deity;
but that they apprehended such distinctions admits of no doubt. Long
before creation, from all eternity, God
had his Word or Logos, for God is
essentially rational; and if what later
theology recognized as the personality

of the Word seems ill-defined in their eyes, it is plain that they regarded him as one with whom the Father could commune and take counsel. Later orthodoxy was to describe his eternal relation to the Father as generation; the fact that the apologists stressed that his generation or emission resulted from an act of the Father's will . . . was not so much to subordinate him as to safeguard the monotheism which they considered indispensable. . . . That the Logos was one in essence with the Father, inseparable in his fundamental being from him as much after his generation as prior to it, the apologists were never weary of reiterating.

The Apologists and the Trinity. What the apologists had to say about the Holy Spirit was much more meager, scarcely deserving the name of scientific theology. . . . Nevertheless, being loyal churchmen, they made it their business to proclaim the Church's faith, the pattern of which was, of course, triadic.

On several occasions Justin coordinates the three Persons[22] . . . References to "the holy Spirit" or "the prophetic Spirit" a bound in his writings; and although he was often hazy about the relation of his functions to those of the Logos . . . he regarded the two as really distinct. . . .

Yet, as compared with their thought about the Logos, the apologists appear to have been extremely vague as to the exact status and role of the Spirit. . . . In spite of incoherencies, however, the lineaments of a Trinitarian doctrine are clearly discernible. . . . The

Spirit was for them the Spirit of God; like the Word, he shared the divine nature, being (in Athenagoras's words) an "effluence" from the Deity. . . . The image with which the apologists worked, viz., that of a man putting forth his thought and his spirit in external activity, enabled them to recognize, however dimly, the plurality of the Godhead, and also to show how the Word and the Spirit, while really manifested in the world of space and time, could also abide within the being of the Father, their essential unity with him unbroken.

Irenaeus. The theologian who summed up the thought of the second century, and dominated Christian orthodoxy before Origen, was Irenaeus. He for his part was deeply indebted to the Apologists. . . . He approached God from two directions, envisaging him both as he exists in his intrinsic being, and also as he manifests himself in the "economy," i.e., the ordered process of his self-disclosure. . . . The Son and the Spirit are his "hands," the vehicles or forms of his self-revelation. . . .

Where he was in advance of the apologists, from whom he also diverged in his deliberate avoidance of philosophical jargon, was (a) in his firmer grasp and more explicit statement of this notion of "the economy," and (b) in the much fuller recognition which he gave to the place of the Spirit in the triadic scheme. . . . He also throws[23] into much more striking relief than they the Word's coexistence with the Father from all eternity . . . and he certainly conceived

---

[22] Cf. *1 Apol.,* 61,3–12; 65,3.

[23] *Haer.,* 2,30,9; 3,18,1.

of the Word's relationship to the Father as eternal, but he had not reached the position of picturing it as generation.

With the Son Irenaeus closely associated the Spirit, arguing[24] that, if God was rational and therefore had his Logos, he was also spiritual and so had his Spirit.[25] Naturally, the Son is fully divine.[26] The Spirit, too, although Irenaeus nowhere expressly designates him God, clearly ranked as divine in his eyes, for he was God's Spirit, ever welling up from his being.[27] Thus, we have Irenaeus's version of the Godhead, the most complete, and also most explicitly Trinitarian to be met with before Tertullian. Its second-century traits stand out clearly, particularly its representation of the Triad by the imagery, not of three coequal persons (this was the analogy to be employed by the post-Nicene fathers), but rather of a single personage, the Father who is the Godhead itself, with his mind or rationality, and his wisdom. . . . The whole point of the great illustrative image . . . of man with his intellectual and spiritual functions, was to bring out, however inadequately, the fact that there are real distinctions in the immanent being of the unique, indivisible Father, and that while these were only fully manifested in the "economy," they were actually there from all eternity.

Third-Century Trinitarianism. The third century saw the emergence of conflicting tendencies in Trinitarian thought which were to provide the material for later controversies. Hitherto the overriding preoccupation of Christian theism had been with the unity of God; the struggle with paganism and Gnosticism thrust this article well into the foreground. As a result, while theologians were obscurely aware of distinctions within the one indivisible Godhead . . . they showed little disposition to explore the eternal relations of the Three, much less to construct a conceptual and linguistic apparatus capable of expressing them. Their most fruitful efforts . . . were expended in considering the Triad as manifested in creation and redemption, and in attempting to show how the Son and the Spirit, revealed in the "economy" as other than the Father, were at the same time inseparably one with him in his eternal being. . . .

The very success — of this Economic Trinitarianism — brought to the surface a powerful reaction in circles which fought shy of the Logos doctrine and suspected that the growing emphasis on the triplicity disclosed by revelation imperiled the divine unity. This current of thought was chiefly evident in the West; it was called monarchianism because its adherents, as Tertullian phrased it,[28] "took fright at the economy" and sought refuge in "the monarchy," i.e., the axiom that there was one divine source and principle of all things. At the same time a diametrically opposite movement was under way in the East . . . which tried, without sacrificing the basic tenet of monotheism, to do justice to the reality and distinction of the

---

[24] *Dem.,* 5.
[25] Cf. Ps 33, 6; Wis 1, 6; 9, 1 f.
[26] *Dem.,* 47.
[27] Cf. *Haer.,* 5,12,2.

[28] *Adv. Prax.,* 3.

Three within God's eternal being — in other words, to their subsistence as "Persons." . . .

Tertullian. Tertullian exerted himself to show . . . that the threeness revealed in the economy was in no way incompatible with God's essential unity . . . in no way involved any division or separation; it was a *distinctio* or *dispositio* (i.e., a distribution), not a *separatio*, and he quoted the unity between the root and its shoot, the source and the river, and the sun and its light as illustrations. His characteristic way of expressing this was to state that Father, Son, and Spirit are one in "substance." Thus, Father and Son are one identical substance which has been, not divided, but "extended."[29] . . . The Son is *unius substantiae* with the Father,[30] and the Son and Spirit are *consortes substantiae patris*.[31]

Using crudely materialistic language (his background of ideas was Stoic, and he regarded the divine spirit as a highly rarefied species of matter), Tertullian can say[32] that "The Father is the whole substance, while the Son is a derivation from and portion of the whole" — where the context makes it plain that "portion" is not to be taken literally as implying any division or severance.

Thus, when he sums the matter up, he dismisses[33] the idea that the Persons can be three in "status" (i.e., fundamental quality), substance or power; as regards these the Godhead is indivisibly one, and the threeness applies only to the "grade" (*gradus*) or "aspect" (*forma*) or "manifestation" (*species*) in which the Persons are represented.

Hippolytus and Tertullian were . . . in advance of Irenaeus (*a*) in their attempts to make explicit the oneness of the divine power or substance of which the Three were expressions or forms, and (*b*) in their description of them . . . as Persons (*prosopa; personae*). This latter term, it should be noted, was still reserved for them as manifested in the order of revelation; only later did it come to be applied to the Word and the Spirit as immanent in God's eternal being.

There has been much discussion about the precise meaning of their terminology, some arguing that for Tertullian, at any rate, with his legal upbringing, *substantia* signified a piece of property which several people could jointly own. In fact, however, the metaphysical sense was foremost in his mind, and the word connoted the divine essence, that of which God is, with the emphasis on its concrete reality. As he remarks,[34] "God is the name for the substance, that is, the divinity." . . . Hence when he speaks of the Son as being "of one substance" with the Father, he means that they share the same divine nature or essence, and in fact, since the Godhead is indivisible, are one identical being.

On the other hand, the terms *prosopon* and *persona* were admirably suited to express the otherness, or independent subsistence, of the Three. After originally meaning "face," and so "ex-

---

[29] *Apol.*, 21,12.
[30] *Adv. Prax.*, 25.
[31] *Ibid.*, 3.
[32] *Adv. Prax.*, 9.
[33] *Adv. Prax.*, 2,19.

[34] *Adv. Hermog.*, 3.

pression" and then "role," the former came to signify "individual," the stress being usually on the external aspect or objective presentation. The primary sense of *persona* was "mask," from which the transition was easy to the actor who wore it and the character he played. In legal usage it could stand for the holder of the title to a property, but as employed by Tertullian, it connoted the concrete presentation of an individual as such. In neither case, it should be noted, was the idea of self-consciousness nowadays associated with "person" and "personal" at all prominent. . . .

Origen. Meanwhile an immensely significant development was taking place in the East. This drew its initial inspiration from the catechetical school at Alexandria, the two thinkers responsible for it being Clement (fl. 200) and Origen (c. 185–254). . . . Origen's Trinitarianism was a brilliant reinterpretation of the traditional triadic rule of faith, to which as a churchman he was devoted, in terms of the same middle Platonism.

At the apex of his system, as the source and goal of all existence, transcending mind and being itself, he placed God the Father.[35] He alone is God in the strict sense (*autotheos*), being alone "ingenerate" (*agennetos*); . . . Being perfect goodness and power, he must always have had objects on which to exercise them; hence has brought into existence a world of spiritual beings, or souls, coeternal with himself.[36]

To mediate, however, between his

absolute unity and their multiplicity, he has his Son, his express image. . . . Being outside the category of time, the Father begets the Son by an eternal act so that it cannot be said that "there was when he was not";[37] further, the Son is God, though his deity is derivative and he is thus a "secondary God."[38]

Third (and here he realizes that Christianity parts company with philosophy, relying on revelation alone), there is the Holy Spirit, "the most honourable of all beings brought into existence through the Word, the chief in rank of the beings originated by the Father through Christ."[39]

The Father, the Son, and the Holy Spirit are, Origen states[40] "three Persons" (*hupostaseis*). This affirmation that each of the Three is a distinct hypostasis from all eternity, not just (as for Tertullian and Hippolytus) as manifested in the "economy," is one of the chief characteristics of his doctrine, and stems directly from the idea of eternal generation. . . . The Son is "other in subsistence than the Father" . . . but "one in unanimity, harmony, and identity of will." . . . As the passage just quoted[41] shows, Origen sometimes represents the unity of the Three as a moral union; their wills are virtually identical.[42] Elsewhere[43] he argues that Father and Son are one God in much the same way as man and wife form one flesh,

---

[35] *De princ.*, 1,1,6; *C. Cels.*, 7,38.
[36] *De princ.*, 1,2,10; 1,4,3.

[37] *De princ.*, 1,2,4.
[38] *C. Cels.*, 5,39.
[39] *In Joh.*, 2,10,75.
[40] *In Joh.*, 2,10,75.
[41] *Dial. Heracl.*, 2.
[42] *In Joh.*, 13,36,228 f.
[43] *Dial. Heracl.*, 3.

and the righteous man and Christ one spirit. . . .

The pivot of his teaching was that the Son had been begotten, not created by the Father.[44] . . . As the Father's offspring, he is eternally poured forth out of the Father's being and so participates[45] in his Godhead. He issues from him as the will from the mind, which suffers no division in the process.[46] According to Wis 7:25, he is "a breath of the power of God, a pure effluence of the glory of the Almighty"; and Origen points out[47] that "both these illustrations suggest a community of substance between Father and Son. For an effluence would appear to be 'homoousios,' i.e., one substance with, that body of which it is an effluence or vapour." Whether or not the term "homoousios" is original in this passage (there seems to be no cogent reason why it should not be), the idea expressed is authentically Origenist. . . .

He attempts to meet the most stringent demands of monotheism by insisting that the fullness of unoriginate Godhead is concentrated in the Father, who alone is "the fountainhead of deity." The Son and Spirit are divine . . . but the Godhead which they possess and which constitutes their essence, wells up and is derived from the Father's being.

In a more limited field the impact of Platonism reveals itself in the thoroughgoing subordinationism which is integral to Origen's Trinitarian scheme. The Father . . . is alone *autotheos.* . . . The Son is simply . . . *theos,* not *ho theos.* . . . He merits a secondary degree of honor. . . . The same goes for his activity; the Son is the Father's agent, carrying out his commands, as in the case of creation.[48] . . . Whereas the Father's action extends to all reality, the Son's is limited to rational beings, and the Spirit's to those who are being sanctified.[49]

The Nicene Crisis. The end of the third century marked the close of the first great phase of doctrinal development. With the opening of the second phase we resume consideration of the central dogma of the Godhead, and can plunge without more ado into a controversy which, in retrospect, we can see to have been uniquely decisive for Christian faith. This was the embittered debate which, touched off by the flaring up of Arianism, was to culminate . . . in the formulation of Christian orthodoxy. . . .

The villain of the piece (to use the language of orthodoxy) was the archheretic Arius. . . . Arius was presiding as presbyter over the church district of Baucalis in Alexandria when he began to publish his daring conclusions about the nature of the Word in 318.[50]

The fundamental premise of his system is the affirmation of the absolute uniqueness and transcendence of

---

[44] Where he seems to speak of him as a creature, his language is a conscious concession to the usage of Prov 8:22 (The Lord created me . . .)

[45] *In Joh.,* 2,2,16.

[46] *De princ.,* 1,2,6; 4,4,1.

[47] *Frag. in Hebr.,* PG 14, 1308.

[48] *C. Cels.,* 7,57; *De princ.,* 1,2,13.

[49] *De princ.,* 1,3,8.

[50] Our chief sources of information about Arius's ideas are some letters of his own and such fragments of his *Thalia,* or "Banquet," a popular medley of prose and verse, as Athanasius has preserved in his own polemical writings. Cf. R.J. 648–651.

God, the unoriginate source of all reality. . . . By God he means, of course, God the Father. What then of the Son or Word, whom the Arians agreed that the Father, because the world of contingency could not bear his direct impact, used as his organ of creation and cosmic activities? The attitude of Arius and his colleagues can be summarized in four propositions which follow logically from the premises stated above.

First, the Word must be a creature, a *ktisma* or *poiema,* whom the Father has formed out of nothing by his mere fiat. . . . Second, as a creature the Word must have had a beginning. . . . Third, the Son can have no communion with, and indeed no direct knowledge of his Father . . . because in himself he is, like all other creatures, "alien from and utterly dissimilar to the Father's essence and individual being." . . . In what sense could the Word be called God or Son of God? . . . He is called God in name only and Son by grace (these are only courtesy titles). The holy Triad consists of three Persons (*hupostaseis*), but these Three are entirely different beings not sharing in any way the same nature or essence. . . . The net result of this teaching was to reduce the Word to a demigod. . . .

The Theology of Nicaea. From the negative point of view there can be no doubt what the attitude of the Council was as expressed principally in the creed it drafted. Arianism, it is clear, at any rate in its original form, was placed under a decisive ban. The Son, the creed states emphatically, is begotten, not made. Anyone who affirms that the Father pre-existed the Son, or that the Son is a creature produced out of nothingness, or is subject to moral change or development, is formally declared a heretic. . . .

Much more difficult to determine is its positive teaching. The creed supplies some hints, stating that as begotten the Son is "out of the Father's substance" and that he is "of the same substance as the Father" (*ek tes ousias tou patros — omoousion to patri*). . . . As regards "out of the Father's substance" we can be fairly confident . . . that the original purport of these words was that the sonship was a real or (if we may use the term) metaphysical one, entailing that the Word shares the same divine nature as the Father from whose being he is derived. . . .

But . . . are we to understand "of the same nature" in the generic sense in which Origen, for example, had employed *homoousios,* or are we to take it as having the meaning accepted by later Catholic theology, viz., numerical identity of substance? The root word "ousia" could signify the kind of stuff or substance common to several individuals of a class, or it could connote an individual thing as such.

There can be no doubt that, as applied to the Godhead, *homoousios* is susceptible of, and in the last resort requires, the latter meaning. As later theologians perceived, since the divine nature is immaterial and indivisible, it follows that the Persons of the Godhead who share it must have, or rather be, one identical substance.

But the question is whether this

idea was prominent in the minds of the Nicene fathers, or rather of that group among them whose influence may be presumed to lie behind the creed. The great majority of scholars have answered unhesitatingly in the affirmative. Indeed, the doctrine of numerical identity of substance has been widely assumed to have been the specific teaching of the Nicene council.

Nevertheless, there are the strongest possible reasons for doubting this. The chief of these is the history of the term *homoousios* itself, for in both its secular and its theological usage prior to Nicaea it always conveyed,[51] primarily at any rate, the "generic" sense. . . .

In view of all this, it is paradoxical to suppose that the Nicene fathers suddenly began employing what was after all a familiar enough word in an entirely novel and unexpected sense. The only reasonable inference is that, in selecting it for insertion in their creed, they intended it to underline, formally and explicitly at any rate, their conviction that the Son was fully God, in the sense of sharing the same divine nature as his Father. . . . We know that afterward, when the identity of substance of the Three Persons was fully acknowledged, the most orthodox theologians continued to use *homoousios*, in the appropriate contexts, with the sense of generic unity.

The theology of the council, therefore, if this argument is sound, had a more limited objective than is sometimes supposed. If negatively, it un-

equivocally outlawed Arianism, positively, it was content to affirm the Son's full divinity and equality with the Father, out of whose being he was derived and whose nature he consequently shared. It did not attempt to tackle the closely related problem of the divine unity, although the discussion of it was inevitably brought nearer. The deeper implications of *homoousios*, as applied to the unique and indivisible Godhead, may already have been apparent to some. . . . It is highly probable that the handful of Western bishops at any rate, led by Ossius of Cordoba, took it for granted the unity of substance was entailed. . . . They must have welcomed *homoousios* as a convenient translation of the formula *unius substantiae* which they had inherited from Tertullian. . . .

The Aftermath of Nicaea. On one side stood the group headed by Athanasius, small in numbers but strong in the consciousness that the Western church was solidly behind them. They were devoted advocates of the *homoousion*, and had come to perceive that identity of substance must follow from the doctrine that Father and Son share the same Godhead. . . . Ranged against them was a much larger group . . . comprising by far the greater portion of Greek-speaking churchmen. Held together by dissatisfaction with Nicaea, it included representatives of markedly different standpoints. A small, determined minority were definitely Arian, although they deemed it politic at first to veil their intentions. The great majority, however, were as far removed from Arianism as their opponents from Sabellianism; the

---

[51] See G. L. Prestige, *God in Patristic Thought*, Chap. 10 for the evidence.

typical Arian theses were, in fact, anathema to them. Origenist in outlook, they thought naturally in terms of three hypostases, and were easily induced to believe that the *homoousion* imperiled them. . . . They were conservatives who preferred the traditional lack of definition and objected to the Nicene key-word as a departure from pure Biblical standards. . . .

Conversion of the Homoiousians. The figures largely instrumental in this were Athanasius and Hilary of Poitiers. . . . Both of them realized that, as regards the fundamental issues, the gap between the Homoiousians[52] and the Nicene party was extremely narrow, and that the final success of the latter could be ensured by establishing a rapproachment between them.

So[53] Athanasius made a conciliatory gesture, saluting the Homoiousians as brothers who in essentials were at one with himself. . . . Hilary[54] went even further. . . . He even allowed the propriety of *homoiousios*, especially in view of its anti-Sabellian emphasis on the three Persons, since it had to be understood in the sense of perfect equality and that strictly entailed unity of nature. His conclusion was that, since they acknowledged the distinction of persons, the Catholics, i.e., the Nicenes, could not deny the Homoiousian, while the Homoiousians for their part were bound to allow

unity of substance if they believed seriously in the perfect likeness of substance.

A further practical step of great importance was taken in 362 at the council of Alexandria, which met under Athanasius's chairmanship. . . . The formula "three hypostases," hitherto suspect to the Nicenes . . . was pronounced legitimate, provided . . . it merely expressed the separate subsistence of the three persons in the consubstantial Triad. . . . By this statesmanlike decision . . . the union between the two parties was virtually sealed, and we can see foreshadowed in it the formula which became the badge of orthodoxy, "one *ousia*, three *hypostaseis*." . . .

The Homoousion of the Spirit. Since Origen's day theological reflection about the Spirit had lagged noticeably behind devotional practice. . . . Arius considered him a hypostasis, but regarded his essence as utterly unlike that of the Son. . . . The later Arians, Aetius, and Eunomius . . . regarded him merely as the noblest of the creatures produced by the Son at the Father's bidding. . . .

It was in 359 or 360 that Athanasius was instigated to expound his own theology of the Spirit. . . . A group of Egyptian Christians . . . argued that the Spirit was a creature brought into existence out of nothing. . . . Athanasius's teaching in rejoinder . . . is that the Spirit is fully divine, consubstantial with the Father and the Son. . . . He comes from God, bestows sanctification and life and is immutable, omnipresent, and unique. . . . He belongs to the Word and the

---

[52] *Homoiousian,* which is derived from *homoios* ("similar" or "like") and *ousia* ("substance" or "nature") thus differs from *homoousian,* derived from *homos* ("same") and *ousia.*

[53] In his *De Synodis* (359).

[54] *De syn.,* 67–71.

Father and shares one and the same substance with them (*homoousios*). . . .

The task was completed, cautiously and circumspectly, by the Cappadocian Fathers — against — the Macedonians. . . . Basil[55] urged that the Spirit must be accorded the same glory, honor, and worship as Father and Son. . . . Gregory of Nyssa emphasizes the "oneness of nature" shared by the three persons. . . . Gregory of Nazianzus throws off all inhibitions. "Is the Spirit God"? he inquires, "Yes, indeed. Then is he consubstantial? Of course, since he is God." . . .

A problem of the Cappadocians was to differentiate between the mode of origin of the Son and that of the Spirit. All that Basil can say is that the Spirit issues from God, not by way of generation but "as the breath of his mouth." . . . Gregory of Nazianzus is satisfied with the Johannine statement[56] that he "proceeds" from the Father. . . . It was Gregory of Nyssa who provided what was to prove the definitive statement: the Spirit is out of God and is of Christ; he proceeds out of the Father and receives from the Son; the three persons are distinguished by their origin, the Father being cause (*to aition*) and the other two caused (*to aitiaton*) . . . one directly produced by the Father, the other proceeding from the Father through an intermediary. . . . There is no trace of subordinationism. . . .

The Cappadocians and the Trinity. The essence of their doctrine is that the one Godhead exists simultaneously in three modes of being or hypostases. . . . Each of the divine hypostases is the *ousia* or essence of the Godhead determined by its appropriate particularizing characteristic . . . : for Basil . . . respectively "paternity" . . . "sonship" and "sanctifying power" or "sanctification." . . . For the others — "ingenerateness" . . . "generateness" . . . and "mission" or "procession." . . . Thus the distinction of the Persons is grounded in their origin and mutual relation.

They are, we should observe, so many ways in which the one indivisible divine substance distributes and presents itself, and hence they come to be termed "modes of coming to be" (*propoi huparxeos*). Amphilochius of Iconium, after stating his belief in "one God made known in three forms of presentation" (*prosopois*), suggests that the names Father, Son, and Holy Spirit do not stand for essence or being (God does) but for "a mode of existence or relation." . . .

A modern theologian[57] has aptly summarized their thought in the sentence: "The whole unvaried substance, being incomposite, is identical with the whole unvaried being of each Person. . . . The individuality is only the manner in which the identical substance is objectively presented in each several Person." . . .

The Cappadocians have often been charged with accepting the *homoousion* while interpreting it in a merely specific or generic sense. . . . The fundamental point which should be remembered is that for these writers the

[55] In his *De Spiritu sancto* (375).
[56] Jn 15:26.

[57] G. L. Prestige, *God in Patristic Thought* (2nd ed., 1952), p. 244.

ousia of Godhead was not an abstract essence but a concrete reality . . . simple and indivisible. . . . The corol-lary of this simplicity is that tritheism is unthinkable. . . .

2. J. C. Murray,[1] studies the Nicene problem of the Son of God in his relation to the Father. Tertullian had resolved the problem in the plastic terms of imagination, Origen in terms of the Platonist dyadic conception. Then came the Arian form of the question: new, inevit-able, legitimate, and exigent of an answer of faith. Nicea gave the definitive answer not in the empirical categories of experience, the rela-tional category of presence or even the dynamic categories of power and function but in the ontological category of substance, which is a category of being. It defined what the Son is.

The issues. The patristic era . . . was a brilliant epoch in the history of thought, which rivaled and perhaps surpassed the fifth century B.C., when the Greek mind reached the height of its powers. The roster of the Fa-thers of the Church is a roll call of memorable names. And these great minds were not engaged in trivial logomachy. They carried on what was perhaps the last great religious argu-ment of the Western world. Certainly in no subsequent argument have the issues been wrought out so clearly and argued with such amplitude for stakes that were incalculably high. In the third, fourth, and fifth centuries, the Christian mind, tutored both in faith and philosophy, clashed in stern en-counter with its two deadliest enemies, Gnostic syncretism and Hellenistic ra-tionalism. For some of us, these still are the enemies; in new forms, they are recognizable among us today.

What were the issues? Three stand out. First, there was the issue of Chris-tian faith in its relation both to He-brew religion and to Greek culture. Was it possible to combine, in some harmonious synthesis, these three di-vergent modes of thought and styles of life, so as to create a new style of life and thought, the Christian style? Second, there was the issue of the nature of reality and of the power of intelligence to reach it. What are the ultimate categories of the real in terms of which the mind conceives and af-firms that which is? Are they the categories of space, time, and matter as in Stoic materialism or the cate-gories of ideas as in the Platonic tra-dition? Are they the intersubjective categories of Hebrew thought, "I and Thou," or are they the categories of being and substance as in the tradi-tion of metaphysical realism that origi-nated in Aristotle and was renewed and transformed by its contact with the tradition of biblical realism? Third, there was the issue of scriptural exe-

[1] John Courtney Murray, S.J., was born in 1904. An eminent theologian, he made an outstanding contribution to the Religious Liberty Decree of the Second Vatican Coun-cil. Among his published works are *Moral-ity and Modern War* and *We Hold These Truths.* This excerpt is from his book, *The Problem of God* (New Haven: Yale University Press, 1964), pp. 32–52.

gesis. What is the sense (or the senses) of Scripture? How does one construct a valid hermeneutic by which they may be reached? Included prominently here was the issue of symbol and reality and their relation. Specifically, what is the reality that the symbols of Scripture symbolize? . . .

The Nicene Problem. In and through these three pervasive issues runs the fundamental problematic theme, which was the problem of God in its new form, the problem of the Logos, the Word, the Son of God, in his relation to the Father. In order to grasp the new problematic fully, one must have in mind the three component elements contained in the Christian conception of God at the time. First, there was the heritage from the Old Testament. There is one Lord, who is the living God, the Holy One hidden in the midst of the people, known through his active existence in their history. Second, there was the New Testament heritage. The same one God of the Old Testament is the Father of the Lord Jesus Christ. The Father is *the* God, God with the definite article (in Greek, *ho theos*), the one God, as Christ is the one Lord.[2] . . . Third, there was the heritage common to both Old and New Testaments which is also, in some form, the patrimony of human reason itself. The one God is the Lord of the cosmic universe as its Creator, and he is likewise the Lord of history as its Ruler. This one Lord is radically distinct from the whole realm of his creation, both cosmic and historical. His power is of an order totally differ-

ent from that of the forces that operate in the material universe or in the temporal process. In the customary images, he is above the world as he is outside of time. . . .

This common heritage was contained in the notion of God as *Pantokrator*. We translate this Greek word[3] as "the Almighty." We hear in the word the notion of omnipotence, a power that is without limit: "God can do everything." This, however, is a post-Augustinian notion. The Israelite and the early Christian heard in the word a more concrete meaning: "God the *Pantokrator* does everything." The reference is to an actuality of power, to the fact that the divine action, both creative and provident, is universal in its scope, extending over the whole world of nature and of man and including under its dominion all processes whatever, whether cosmic or historical.

Today, when we want to express the heritage common to the Old and New Testaments and also to the tradition of reason, we use the term *monotheism*. Its connotations are static, or, if you will, ontological. The early Christian, however, used the term *monarchy*. It is a technical theological term whose connotations are dynamic or historical. When, for instance, Dionysius of Rome[4] speaks of the "most venerable preaching of the Church of God, which is the Monarchy," he means the traditional Hebraic and Christian doctrine of the *Pantokrator* — that the one Lord God

²1 Cor 8:6.

³ Taken from the Septuagint, the Alexandrian Greek translation of the Hebrew Scriptures.
⁴ Ca. A.D. 260.

is the supreme, universal, actively ruling Power over all things. It was this doctrine of the Monarchy that sustained the Christian polemic against Manichaean dualism, against the Stoic World-Soul, against the Platonic Idea of the Good, against the Gnostic Pleroma, and against all other false or faulty theologies. It was a doctrine full of mystery, inspiring awe. It was also a doctrine that presented complications, which in turn gave rise to questions. The complications were inherent in the data of Christian faith, which were chiefly three.

First, as Dionysius has just told us, the doctrine of the divine Monarchy — that there is one *Pantokrator* — is to be maintained as the true teaching of the Church. Second, also to be maintained as true, is the teaching that Jesus Christ is the Lord, that is, he is the *Pantokrator*. Third, no less to be maintained, is the truth that is evident on every page of the Gospel, that Christ, the *Pantokrator,* is the Son; he is from the Father and therefore is other than the Father, who is *the* God, the *Pantokrator*. These data of faith which affirm a mystery, also give rise to a problem. The issue is clear. How is the ancient doctrine of the Monarchy to be maintained so as to leave intact the new doctrine that Christ, the Father's Son and Word, is equally *Pantokrator,* as the Father also is? This was the Nicene problem of God. It was the problem of the Logos, the Son, within the divine Monarchy. It does not rise formally in the plane of the religious existence but on the plane of theological understanding.

It is impossible to give here even a sketch of the swirling dialectic of thought that was released when Christian thinkers confronted the problem of God in its first specifically Christian form. I shall mention, however, the two major attempts at solution — by Tertullian[5] in the West, and by Origen[6] in the East.

Tertullian resolved the problem in the plastic terms of imagination. He cast two analogies to explain how the Son is Lord and *Pantokrator* simultaneously as the Monarchy remains one and undivided. Tertullian's first analogy was biological; he took it from Stoic physics, which explained the constitution of the world by analogy to the living body. The Monarchy, he said, is preserved by apprehending it as an organism. The Father and the Son are indeed parts of it, but the organism itself is undivided and its Power is one. The trouble here is that to speak of God as an organism is to use a metaphor, an analogy from the material world, to which God bears no likeness at all. Therefore, the metaphorical solution leaves the problem just as it was. The metaphor of organism serves to restate the problem in an image, but metaphors, here as everywhere else, explain nothing.

Tertullian's second analogy was anthropological. The Monarchy, he said, is preserved by apprehending Father and Son as united in a complete harmony of mind and will. The trouble here is that this is anthropomorphism, an analogy taken from the world of men. The one God, Father and Son,

[5] Ca. A.D. 160–222–23.
[6] Ca. A.D. 185–254–55.

is utterly unlike two men who are one in spirit, united in some common enterprise. Again, the problem is left intact. Both of Tertullian's imaginative efforts fail precisely because they are imaginative. They transpose the problem to the plane of images, where no solution is available, since the problem exists in the order of thought.

In the East, Origen, the greatest genius of the third century and perhaps of any century, attacked the problem in higher terms. He made use of a concept borrowed from the most popular contemporary philosophy, Middle Platonism. It was the dyadic conception, derived from Plato himself. There is the One, the Goodness that is divine. There is also the Logos, which emanates from the One and participates in the One as the Image of the divine Goodness. The Christian doctrine of the Father and his Logos is then interpreted in terms of this platonist scheme. The Father is *the* God; only of him does Origen use the definite article. The Logos is not *the* God; he is simply God, and he is God by emanation and participation in a Platonist sense. Therefore, he is a God "of the second order," as Origen calls him. He is a diminished deity, since emanation, in Platonist thought, involves some measure of degradation in the order of being.

This, with drastic brevity, is Origen's answer to the pre-Nicene problem of God, the Logos in the Monarchy. The trouble is that it destroys the terms of the problem. In Origen's solution, the Logos is subordinated to the Father as an inferior god who does not merit and cannot properly be given the divine Name. This is contrary to the terms of the problem as set by Christian faith, which affirms the Logos-Son to be *Kyrios,* Lord, the bearer of the divine Name *Pantokrator* in an undiminished divine sense.

Origen himself, I should add, made this Christian affirmation with complete fidelity and great vigor. But he undertook a further task, which was to set forth a theological understanding of this affirmation. His failure, like Tertullian's, was of the order of understanding. The best philosophical instrument of understanding within Origen's reach — the Middle Platonist theory of the emanation of the Logos from the One — broke in his hands. It delivered only a subordinationist theory of the Logos. This is not an understanding of the Christian doctrine of the Logos. The Christian Logos is not subordinate or inferior to the Father; to attempt to understand him thus is not to understand him at all. Origen's genial speculations had an enormous influence on subsequent theological thought, but they left the pre-Nicene problem of God standing, still awaiting the construction of a theology that would be adequate to the problem.

As a matter of fact, the issue of the alternatives, which is essential to the notion of a problem, had not yet been stated with precision. This was finally done by Arius . . . an able dialectician, a disciple of Lucian of Antioch. . . . His greatest historical significance was that he ruthlessly clarified the problem of the Logos and set it in its proper terms.

. . . Arius impatiently discards all

metaphor and all anthropomorphism; he dismisses all Platonist speculation. Instead, he posits the question in categories completely alien to all the philosophical and religious systems of the ancient world. He asks his question in the Hebraic-Christian categories of Creator and creature. Arius' question was luminously clear. Given that the Son is from the Father, is the Son of the order of the Creator, who is God, or of the order of creature, who is not God? And to the question thus put, in altogether decisive form, he returns an unequivocal answer. The Son, he says, is from the Father as the "perfect creature." He came to be as all creatures come to be, through a making, through an act of the Father's will. When he thus became, he came to be out of nothing. And before he came to be, he was not. Therefore, "there was when he was not" (this last phrase is the celebrated Arian tessera that shocked the Christian world).

This was Arius' answer to the problem of the Logos within the Monarchy. He rescues the Monarchy by extruding the Logos from it. It was the answer of the rationalist who eliminates the seeming contradictions within the Christian statement of the mystery of God, by evacuating the mystery itself. In the end, for Arius, the Logos-Son has only the status of a creature; he is no more a mystery than you or I.

We need not be concerned here with the case Arius made for his view. It was essentially a dialectical, not a scriptural, case. It was based on the notion of God as the Unoriginate and on the conclusion that what originates from God, as the Son from the Father, must necessarily be created. It is more to our purpose here to note the mode of thought in which Arius raised the problem of the Son. His question asked whether the Son *is* God or not. The correlative questions were, what does it mean to say that the Son *is-from* the Father as Son, that is, what *is* his mode of origin from the Father and what therefore *is* his relation to the Father? I add emphasis to illustrate the fact that these were ontological questions. They raised the issue of the being and substance of the Son as he *is*, in himself and in relation to the Father. Moreover, the alternative answers which Arius presented and from which he chose were cast in ontological categories, God or creature. These are categories of being and substance. They transcend the Stoic materialist categories, the idealist categories of Platonist devising, and the intersubjective categories of Hebraic thought.

Four comments need to be made on Arius' position of the problem of the Son. It was new, inevitable, legitimate, and exigent of an answer that would have to be an answer of faith.

In the first place, the Arian question was new in the form and mode of thought in which Arius raised it. The New Testament problem had been that of the presence of the Son, and with him the Father, in the midst of the people as Savior and Judge. Explicitly, therefore, the problem had been stated in the intersubjective category of presence with its attendant dynamic categories of power, function, and action. The Christology of the New Testament was, in our contemporary word for it, functional. For instance, all the titles given to Christ, the Son — Lord, Savior, Word, Son of God, Son of man, Messiah, Prophet, Priest — all these titles, in the sense that they bear in the New Testament, are relational. They describe what Christ is to us; they detail his functions in regard to our salvation. They do not explicitly define what he *is*, nor do they explicitly define what his relation to the Father is. Therefore, in asking whether the Son *is* God or not, Arius altered the scriptural state of the question. He moved the problem into a different universe of discourse. In effect, he asked a new question.

In the second place, it was inevitable that the new question should have been asked. If Arius had not asked it, someone else would have. There are two reasons for its inevitability.

The first lies in the essential dynamism of human intelligence. When it functions without any bias induced by faulty or prejudicial training, the mind moves inevitably from the question of what things are to us (the phenomenological question) to the deeper question of what things are in themselves (the ontological question). The human mind moves from description to definition. In this case, it moves from inquiry into the reality of God's presence to inquiry into the reality of the God who is present. . . .

The second reason for the inevitability of Arius' question lies in the realist conception of the word of God contained in Scripture and unani-

mously held in the Church of the Fathers. At that time, there was no doubt in anyone's mind that the Scriptures were not simply the record of the religious experience of Isaiah or Ezekiel, of Paul or John. In the patristic era, the Christian did not consider that his faith was based on religious experience, his own or that of anyone else. It was based on the events of the sacred history — the event of Christ supervening on the ancient events of the history of Israel. He knew that in these events, which were irruptions of the divine into history, God was the "speaking God" of the Letter to the Hebrews.[7] He knew that the word spoken by God came from intelligence and was addressed to an intelligence. It was suffused with mystery, but it was nonetheless compact of conceptions that were somehow intelligible and of affirmations that were unconditionally true. He knew, finally, that, since they were true (as warranted by the "speaking God"), the affirmations in the word of God put him in touch with reality. They had for him an ontological reference. They were not mere symbols whose value would be as vehicles of man's religious experience, which would itself then be the ultimately real. The value of the word of God was in its truth, in the fact that it affirmed what is, what exists in an order related to man's religious experience but only because it is itself antecedently real. So, when the Christian cried, "Lord Jesus!" he was not simply uttering his religious experience of the risen Jesus. He was affirm-

---

[7] 1:1.

ing that Jesus did rise from the dead and that he is the Lord.

It was this conviction of the realism of the word of God — that it is a real word with a real meaning — that sustained Athanasius in working out the celebrated formula which explained the sense inherent in the dogma stated by the Council of Nicaea. His study of the Scriptures disclosed to him, as to Basil later, a general proposition. All the affirmations made by the Scriptures about the Father are also made about the Son, with one exception. The Scriptures never say that the Son is the Father. In particular, the Scriptures affirm about the Son what they affirm about the Father, that he has as his own the two powers that are uniquely divine and proper only to God — the power to give life and the power to judge the heart of man. If, then, everything that is true about the Father is likewise true about the Son, except that the Son is not the Father, it follows that the Son is all that the Father is, except for the name of Father.

This was the Athanasian rule of faith, based on the Scriptures, which the Council of Nicaea had stated in a dogmatic formula, as we shall see. The point at the moment is that behind the Athanasian rule lay the universal patristic conviction that, to put the matter in our technical terms, a realist epistemology and ontology are implicit in the conception of the word of God which the Scriptures exhibit. The word of God is true; therefore it expresses what is.

In the third place, it follows that the Arian form of the pre-Nicene

question, whether the Son is God or a creature, was entirely legitimate. The reason is that it was stated in ontological categories that were undeniably scriptural. If the Old and New Testament affirm anything at all, they affirm that the Creator is God that the creature is a creature. These affirmations are not a matter of religious experience but of ontology. These two categories, Creator and creature, are classifications of being. They define things that are and that are radically distinct in the order of substance. It was, therefore, legitimate to state the problem of the Logos in these ontological terms.

In the fourth and final place, because the Arian ontological question was new and had not been explicitly answered, because it was inevitable and had to arise, because it was legitimate and could not be declined, it demanded an answer. More than that, the answer had to be the answer of faith. The Arian question had not been raised in the spirit of detached Hellenistic speculation, as an interesting problem for leisurely and inconclusive discussion in the school. On the contrary, upon the answer to the question hung the whole issue of human salvation.

All through the Arian controversy runs the soteriological argument for the full divinity of the Son. Its premise was the doctrine, as old as the Old Testament itself, that only God can save us. Only he is the Power that can rescue us from death in all the forms that death takes and bring us to life in the land of integrity and peace that he has promised to the

faithful. Hence, from Athanasius onward, the Fathers argue that, if the
Son is not God, fully the *Pantokrator,*
wholly situated within the order of
the divine power and being, then he
is not our Savior and we are not saved.
It was clear to the Fathers that there
was no salvation in the Arian Son,
a time-bound creature such as we are,
out of the Father by a making as we
are, Son only by a grace that holds
no grace for us.

The imperious Arian question received its definitive answer at the
Council of Nicaea in 325, at the
hands of the Fathers assembled in the
legendary number of three hundred
and eighteen. . . . "We believe," they
wrote, "in one God the Father, the
Pantokrator, Maker of all things visible and invisible; and in one Lord
Jesus Christ, the Son of God, begotten
out of the Father, the Only-begotten."
So far one hears only the echo of
earlier creeds, themselves the echo of
the scriptural formulas. Then comes
the cutting edge of the Nicene dogma
that thrust through all the Arian eva-
sions to the essential issue: "Begotten
out of the Father, that is, out of the
substance of the Father, God out of
God, Light out of Light, true God out
of true God." The Son is not out of
the Father's will, as the creature is,
but out of his substance, by a unique
mode of origination radically different
from the creative act. The Christian
alternative in the Arian dichotomy,
God or creature, is selected and posited: "Begotten, not made." The Son
is not the perfect creature, placed, by
a making, outside of the divine order.
He is begotten within the divine order

and he remains within it. His being
is untouched by createdness. Finally,
there comes the famous word to which
a century of argument had inevitably
moved: "Consubstantial (*homoousion*)
with the Father."

In the adjective *homoousion* the
Nicene problem of God finds its definitive answer. The answer is given,
as it had to be given, not in the empirical categories of experience, the
relational category of presence, or
even the dynamic categories of power
and function but in the ontological
category of substance, which is a category of being. Nicaea did not describe; it defined. It defined what the
Son is, in himself and in his relation
to the one God the Father. The Son
is from the Father in a singular, un-
shared way, begotten as Son, not made
as a creature. The Son is all that the
Father is, except for the Name of Father. This is what *homoousion* means.
This is what the Son is.

Two aspects of the Nicene dogma
call for comment. It was not new,
and it was new.

It was not a new truth, not a new
revelation. The intention of the Nicene Fathers was simply to state the
sense of the Scriptures against the
Arian dialectical distortion. Athanasius
is explicitly clear on this point. The
difficulty was that the sense of the
Scriptures with regard to what the
Son is was scattered in a multiplicity
of affirmations about him. It was contained in all the titles given him, in
all the symbols and images used of
him, in all the predicates that describe
his role and function concerning our
salvation. All that Nicaea did was to

reduce the multiplicity of the scriptural affirmations to the unity of a single affirmation. The Son, begotten from the Father, not made by him, is consubstantial with the Father — this was the sense of everything that the Scriptures had to say about the Son. Therefore, it was nothing new. It had already been said.

The Nicene dogma was new, however, in that it stated the sense of the Scriptures in a new mode of understanding that was not formally scriptural. The Scriptures had affirmed that Jesus Christ, the Son, is here with us as Lord of us. Nicaea affirmed that the Lord Jesus Christ is the consubstantial Son. The sense of both affirmations is the same, but the mode of conception and statement is different. A passage has been made from a conception of what Christ the Son is-to-us to a conception of what the Son, Christ, is-in-himself. The transition is from a mode of understanding that is descriptive, relational, interpersonal, historical-existential, to a mode of understanding that is definitive, explanatory, absolute, ontological. The alteration in the mode of understanding does not change the sense of the affirmation, but it does make the Nicene affirmation new in its form.

At the Council itself the reason for the passage to the new ontological mode of conception and statement was altogether practical. Athanasius is again explicit on this point. The old efforts to state the doctrine of the Son and Logos used scriptural formulas; this had been the traditional practice, visible in the earlier creeds. The trouble was that the Arian party was quite willing to recite the scriptural affirmations at the same time that it read into them an Arian understanding, the conception of the Son as a creature. The Fathers had, therefore, to go beyond the letter of the scriptural formulas to their sense. They stated the sense in new formulas: "out of the substance of the Father," "consubstantial with the Father." These formulas would not bear the Arian understanding. The latter was excluded from the formulas by the new mode of understanding the Scriptures that the formulas embodied.

The new formulas were not adopted without opposition, either at the council or in the course of the long controversy that ensued. They were opposed, of course, by the men of the radical Arian Left and by their leftist successors, the so-called Half-Arians. But they were also opposed by the men of the conservative Right, the "men around Eusebius of Caesarea." . . . The conservative position is stated thus: "We say that the Son is like (*homoios*) in all things to the Father, just as the Scriptures say and teach." The same essential conservative position is visible in the formula of the Synod of Constantinople in 361. The *homoousion*, it said, is not a scriptural word; therefore the Nicene formula cannot be a formula of faith.

The prime objection of the Right was to the word, but the issue went much deeper, below the level of language, to an issue of most weighty substance. The real issue concerned development in the understanding of the Christian revelation and faith. It concerned progress within the tradition. This was the issue that the Eusebians, after the immemorial custom of conservatives, failed to see, or, perhaps, refused to see. They pretended to be protagonists of the tradition. In fact, they were only defenders of the status quo, which is quite a different thing. They were fundamentalists, or biblical positivists. They were in their own way the first proponents of the maxim, *Sola Scriptura,* in their insistence that only in the formulas of Scripture may the Christian faith be proposed. The Right . . . was reactionary, or, to put it more elegantly, they were the victims of the fallacy of archaism.

At the root of the fallacy is the rejection of the notion that Christian understanding of the affirmations of faith can and indeed must grow, at the same time that the sense of the affirmations remains unaltered. Arius had cast the old question in a new mode of conception, the ontological mode. It was no longer to be answered simply by repeating the formulas of Scripture, which did not directly meet the new issue because their affirmations were made in a different mode of understanding. . . .

What the Eusebians further failed to see was that the fallacy of archaism inevitably breeds its contrary, which is the fallacy of futurism. The futurist fallacy rests on the notion that the affirmations of Christian faith never have a final sense. . . .

The Nicene homoousion avoids both fallacies, archaism and futurism. It transposes the scriptural affirmations concerning the Son into a new mode of understanding — what we now call the Nicene or dogmatic mode for the reason that the Nicene dogma was its first historical illustration. But there is no discontinuity or incoherence between the dogmatic mode and the scriptural mode. The transition from one to the other was not made violently — from the descriptive, relational, interpersonal, historical-existential, scriptural mode, to the definitive, absolute, explanatory, ontological, dogmatic mode. The passage was made with ease and naturalness on the internal authority that it is in accord with the native dynamism of intelligence. Between the two modes there is harmony, even homogeneity. The sense of the affirmation, as made in both modes is identical. The sense of Scripture, that Jesus, the Son, is present as our Lord, is identically the sense of Nicaea, that Jesus, our Lord, is consubstantially the Son. The tradition is maintained. But there has been progress within it, growth in the understanding of it. The *homoousion* formulates the traditional faith; it is a formula of faith. But the faith is so formulated as now to be more fully understood. The Christian who affirmed that Christ is with us as the Lord still makes this affirmation, only now he has come to understand more fully what Christ, the Lord with us, *is.* He has transcended archaism, and, in so doing, he has also avoided futurism. The homoousion represents a limit in the understanding of the faith. As there is no stopping short of it on peril of archaist imprecision in the faith, so there is no going beyond it on peril of futurist adulteration of the faith. . . .

Five aspects of the Nicene definition . . . should be noted. First, . . . the Nicene definition was a rejection of Eusebian archaism and its effort to restrict the Christian faith to the formulas of Scripture. Second, the definition formally established the statute of the ontological mentality within the Church. It was the precedent for the Councils of Ephesus and Chalcedon, which resolved the issue of the internal constitution of Christ, the Son Incarnate, in the ontological categories of nature and person . . . and forbade the freezing of the Christian faith in patristic formulas. . . . Third, by its passage from the historical-existential categories of Scripture to the ontological or explanatory categories exhibited in the *homoousion* Nicaea sanctioned the principle of the development of doctrine — the phrase is Newman's. . . . One might better speak of growth in understanding of the primitive affirmations contained in the New Testament revelation. . . . Fourth, . . . thus Nicaea established a bridge between Scripture and conciliar dogma . . . , Scripture states the faith of the Church; so does dogma, but in another mode of conception and statement so organically related to the scriptural didache as to merit the name of growth. Fifth, . . . by sanctioning the status of the ontological mentality in the field of faith, Nicaea also established the statute of the philosophical reason in the field of theology. Thus, it laid down the charter of Scholasticism. Without Nicaea there would have been no Chalcedon . . . no Aquinas . . . no Augustine.

IV

GOD IN ST. AUGUSTINE

1. J. N. D. Kelly[1] looks at the Trinity in the West and at Augustine's contribution. Augustine gave the Western tradition its mature and final expression. Probably his most original contribution to Trinitarian theology was his use of analogies drawn from the structure of the human soul, to deepen our understanding of the mystery.

The Trinity in the West. . . . Western theological reflection about the Trinity, virtually quiescent since Novatian . . . [began] to bestir itself [during the fourth century]. . . .Hilary, as a result of his sojourn in the East, was able to collaborate with Athanasius in winning over the Homoiousians, himself teaching a doctrine which, while absolutely clear as

against Sabellianism on the distinction of the persons, insisted on their consubstantiality. . . . A little later we find Ambrose conceiving[2] of three Persons who are one (*unum sunt*) through their having one substance, one divinity, one will, one operation; the idea of a universal with its particulars does not suffice to explain their unity. . . . Far the most original

[1] Cf. Ch. III, 1, n. 1. This excerpt is from *op. cit.*, pp. 269–279.

[2] Cf. *De fid.*, 1,2,17–19; 4,34; 5,42; *De incarn. dom. sacr.*, 8,81–88.

and interesting figure, however, in the middle decades of the fourth century was Victorinus, the Neo-Platonic philosopher who after his conversion ca. 355 set himself to defend the *homoousion* against Arian criticisms. Important for their own sake, his ideas are also noteworthy for the impact they had on Augustine.

Victorinus draws his inspiration from Plotinus, although his devotion to Scripture and the Christian revelation obliges him to make drastic modifications in the Neo-Platonic scheme. In harmony with the biblical idea of a living God, he thinks of the Deity as essentially concrete and active; God is eternally in motion, and in fact his *esse* is equivalent to *moveri*.[3] In relation to the contingent order, this movement takes the form of creation, while in relation to the Word it is generation.[4] He is thus able to develop a doctrine of eternal generation which evades the Arian objection that generation implies change. At the same time he holds[5] that the immanent dialectical process within the Godhead is intrinsically triadic; God is *tridunamos,* "possessing three powers — being, living, understanding" (*esse, vivere, intelligere*). From this point of view, the Father is the divine essence considered as absolute and unconditioned . . . invisible and unknowable. . . . The Son is the "form" by which the Godhead determines or limits itself, thereby coming into relation with the finite and making itself knowable.[6] . . . He is

related to the Father as act to potency,[7] or as Word to eternal silence.[8] The Spirit, about whom Victorinus has less to say, is distinguishable from the Son as intelligence is from life, as the voice from the mouth which utters it. So Victorinus can write that[9] "the Father is silence eloquent, Christ is his voice, and the Paraclete is the voice of the voice." . . . In one of his hymns[10] he sums up the characters of the Persons as "Existence, Life, Knowledge — O Blessed Trinity"; and affirms, "God is substance, the Son form, the Spirit concept."

Yet these three dynamic characters are shared alike by all three persons; each with the others is only one substance, one will and life, one knowledge.[11] Again and again he insists on the circuminsession, or mutual indwelling of the persons.[12] They are one with the unity which transcends number;[13] yet there is a distinction between them which Victorinus would prefer to express by *tres subsistentiae* than by *tres personae,* or else by saying that the absolute Godhead subsists *tripliciter.*[14] . . .

Victorinus finds[15] the best analogy to, or expression of, the Triune Godhead in the soul, which on his view exists in man as a part, as it were, of God. In it can be seen the triad *esse, vivere,* and *intelligere,* determinations or distinctions which are related to

---

[3] *Adv. Ar.,* 1,43.
[4] *De gen. verb.,* 29 f.
[5] *Adv. Ar.,* 4,21.
[6] E.g., *Adv. Ar.,* 3,7; 4,20.

[7] *Ibid.,* 1,41.
[8] *Ibid.,* 1,13; 1,4.
[9] *Ibid.,* 3,16.
[10] *Hymn* 3.
[11] *Adv. Ar.,* 3,4; 3,17.
[12] *Ibid.,* 1,15 f.
[13] *Ibid.,* 3,1.
[14] *Ibid.,* 2,4; 3,4.
[15] *Ibid.,* 1,32; 1,62–4.

each other as the Persons of the Trinity of which it is the image, and which, like them, are consubstantial.

The Contribution of Augustine. It was Augustine, however, who gave the Western tradition its mature and final expression. All his life as a Christian he was meditating the problem of the Trinity, explaining the Church's doctrine to inquirers and defending it against attack, and perhaps his greatest work is the long and elaborate discussion known as the *De trinitate,* which he put together at different dates between 399 and 419. He accepts[16] without question the truth that there is one God who is Trinity, and that Father, Son, and Holy Spirit are at once distinct and co-essential, numerically one in substance; and his writings abound in detailed statements of it. Characteristically, he nowhere attempts to prove it; it is a datum of revelation which, on his view, Scripture proclaims on almost every page[17] and which "the Catholic faith"[18] hands on to believers. His immense theological effort is an attempt at comprehension, the supreme example of his principle[19] that faith must precede understanding (e.g., *praecedit fides, sequitur intellectus*). Here there is space to single out only the salient features of his exposition.

1) While Augustine's exposition of Trinitarian orthodoxy is scriptural throughout, his conception of God as absolute being, simple and indivisible,

transcending the categories, forms its ever-present background. So in contrast to the tradition which made the Father its starting point, he begins with the divine nature itself. It is this simple, immutable nature or essence (he prefers "essence" to "substance," for the latter suggests a subject with attributes, whereas God for Augustine is identical with his attributes)[20] which is Trinity.[21] The unity of the Trinity is thus set squarely in the foreground, subordinationism of every kind being rigorously excluded. Whatever is affirmed of God is affirmed equally of each of the three persons.[22] Since it is one and the same substance which constitutes each of them, "not only is the Father not greater than the Son in respect of divinity, but Father and Son together are not greater than the Holy Spirit, and no single person of the Three is less than the Trinity itself."[23]

Several corollaries follow from this emphasis on the oneness of the divine nature. First, Father, Son, and Spirit are not three separate individuals in the same way as three human beings who belong to one genus[24] . . . rather each is identical with . . . the divine substance itself.[25] . . . Second, whatever belongs to the divine nature as such should, in strictness of language, be expressed in the singular, since that nature is unique.[26] . . . Third, the Trinity possesses a single, indi-

---

[16] E.g., *De fid. et symb.,* 16; *De doct. christ.,* 1,5; *De trin.,* 1,7.

[17] Cf., *De trin.,* Bks. 1–4.

[18] E.g., *Serm.,* 7,4; *Ep.,* 120,17; *Joh. tract.,* 74,1.

[19] E.g., *Serm.,* 118,1; *De trin.,* 15,2.

[20] *De trin.,* 5,3; 7,10.

[21] *De civ. dei,* 11,10; *Ep.,* 120,17.

[22] *De trin.,* 5,9.

[23] *Ibid.,* 8,1; cf. 6,9.

[24] *Joh. tract.,* 39,2–4.

[25] *De trin.,* 6,9; 7,11; 8,1.

[26] *Ibid.,* 5,10 f.; 8,1.

visible action and a single will; its operation is inseparable.[27] In relation to the contingent order the three persons act as "one principle,"[28] and, "as they are inseparable, so they operate inseparably."[29] In his own words,[30] "where there is no difference of natures, there is none of wills either." In illustration of this, Augustine argues[31] that the theophanies recorded in the Old Testament should not be regarded, as the earlier patristic tradition had tended to regard them, as appearances exclusively of the Son. Sometimes, they can be attributed to the Son or to the Spirit, sometimes to the Father, and sometimes to all three; on occasion, it is impossible to decide to which of the three to ascribe them.

Lastly, Augustine faces the obvious difficulty which his theory suggests, viz., that it seems to obliterate the several roles of the three persons. His answer[32] is that, while it is true that the Son, as distinct from the Father, was born, suffered, and rose again, it remains equally true that the Father cooperated with the Son in bringing about the incarnation, passion, and resurrection; it was fitting for the Son, however, in virtue of his relation to the Father, to be manifested and made visible. In other words, since each of the persons possesses the divine nature in a particular manner, it is proper to attribute to each of them, in the external operation of the Godhead, the role which is appropriate to him in virtue of his origin. It is a case of what later Western theologians were to describe as appropriation.

2) This leads us to the distinction of the persons, which Augustine sees is grounded in their mutual relations within the Godhead. While they are identical considered as the divine substance, the Father is distinguished as Father because he begets the Son . . . and the Spirit is distinguished from Father and Son inasmuch as he is "bestowed" by them; he is their "common gift," being a kind of communion of Father and Son, or else the love which they together pour into our hearts.[33]

The question then arises what in fact the three are. Augustine recognizes that they are traditionally designated persons, but is clearly unhappy about the term; probably it conveyed the suggestion of separate individuals to him. If in the end he consents to adopt the current usage, it is because of the necessity of affirming the distinction of the three against Modalism ("the formula 'three persons' was employed, not so that that might be said, but so as to avoid having to say nothing at all"), and with a deep sense of the inadequacy of human language.[34]

His own positive theory was the original and, for the history of Western Trinitarianism, highly important one that the Three are real or subsistent relations. His motive[35] in formulating it was to escape a cunning di-

[27] Ibid., 2,9; C. serm. Ar., 4; Enchir., 38.
[28] De trin., 5,15.
[29] Ibid., 1,7; cf. 2,3.
[30] C. Maxim., 2,10,2.
[31] De trin., 2,12–34; cf. 3,4–27.
[32] Serm., 52 passim: cf. De trin., 2,9; 2,18; Ep. 11,2–4.
[33] Ep., 170; De trin., 5,6,8,12,15–17; 8,1; Joh. tract., 74,1–4.
[34] De trin., 5.10; 7,7–9; De civ. dei., 11,10; C. serm. Ar., 32.
[35] De trin., 5,4.

lemma posed by Arian critics. Basing themselves on the Aristotelian scheme of categories,[36] they contended that the distinctions within the Godhead, if they existed, must be classified under the category either of substance or accident. The latter was out of the question, God having no accidents; the former led to the conclusion that the three are independent substances. Augustine rejects both alternatives, pointing out that the concept of relation still remains. The three, he goes on to claim, are relations, as real and eternal as the factors of begetting, being begotten and proceeding . . . within the Godhead which give rise to them. Father, Son, and Spirit are thus relations in the sense that whatever each of them is, he is in relation to one or both of the others.[37] . . . The advantage of the theory from his point of view was that, by enabling him to talk meaningfully about God at a new language level, it made it possible simultaneously to affirm unity and plurality of the Deity without lapsing into paradox.

3) Augustine was always puzzled[38] to explain what the procession of the Spirit is, or wherein it differs from the Son's generation. He was cer-

tain,[39] that the Spirit is the mutual love of Father and Son, the consubstantial bond which unites them. His consistent teaching, therefore, was that he is the Spirit of both alike. . . . Thus, in relation to the Holy Spirit the Father and the Son form a single principle: inevitably so, since the relation of both to him is identical, and where there is no difference of relation their operation is inseparable.[40]

Hence Augustine, more unequivocally than any of the Western fathers before him, taught[41] the doctrine of the double procession of the Spirit from the Father and the Son (filioque): "The Son is from the Father, the Spirit . . . is the Spirit of both since he proceeds from both. . . . The Father is the author of the Spirit's procession because he begot such a Son, and in begetting him made him also the source from which the Spirit proceeds." The point is that, since the Father has given all he has to the Son, he has given him the power to bestow the Spirit.[42] It should not be inferred, he warns us,[43] that the Spirit has therefore two sources or principles; on the contrary, the action of the Father and Son in bestowing the Spirit is common, as is the action of all three persons in creation. Further, despite the double procession, the Father remains the primordial source, inasmuch

---

[36] A feature of Aristotle's (B.C. 384–322) logic was his analysis of the ways in which the mind thinks about things. These he called Categories, and he enumerated ten in all: substance (ousia — in the sense of individual thing), quantity, quality, relation, place, date, position, state, action, passivity.

[37] For the theory of relations see Joh. tract., 39; Enarr. in ps., 68,1,5; Ep., 170; 238–41; De civ. dei, 11,10; De trin., Bks. 5–7.

[38] E.g., De trin., 9,17; 15,45.

[39] Ibid., 15,27; cf. 5,12 (ineffabilis quaedam patris filiique communio).

[40] Ibid., 5,15.

[41] E.g., Ep., 170,4; De trin., 5,12; 15,29; 15,45.

[42] C. Maxim., 2,14,7–9; Joh. tract., 99,9; De trin., 15,47.

[43] De trin., 5,15.

as it is he from whom the Son derives his capacity to bestow the Spirit.[44]

4) We come lastly to what is probably Augustine's most original contribution to Trinitarian theology, his use of analogies drawn from the structure of the human soul. The function of these, it should be noted, is not so much to demonstrate that God is Trinity (on his view revelation provides ample assurance of that), as to deepen our understanding of the mystery of the absolute oneness and yet real distinction of the three. Strictly speaking, according to Augustine,[45] there are "vestiges" of the Trinity everywhere, for insofar as creatures exist at all they exist by participating in the ideas of God; hence everything must reflect, however faintly, the Trinity which created it. For its veritable image, however, a man should look primarily into himself, for Scripture represents God as saying, "Let *us* (i.e., the three) make man in *our* image and *our* likeness."[46]

Even the outer man, i.e., man considered in his sensible nature, offers "a kind of resemblance to the Trinity."[47] The process of perception, for example, yields[48] three distinct elements which are at the same time closely united, and of which the first in a sense begets the second while the third binds the other two together, viz., the external object, the mind's sensible representation of it (*visio*) and the intention or act of focusing

the mind. Again,[49] when the external object is removed, we have a second trinity, much superior because located entirely within the mind and therefore "of one and the same substance," viz., the memory impression (*memoria*), the internal memory image (*visio interna*), and the intention or setting of the will.

For the actual image, however, of the Triune Godhead we should look to the inner man, or soul, and in the inner man to his rational nature, or *mens,* which is the loftiest and most Godlike part of him.[50] It has often been assumed that Augustine's principal Trinitarian analogy in the *De trinitate* is that disclosed by his analysis[51] of the idea of love (his starting-point is the Johannine dictum that God is love) into the lover (*amans*), the object loved (*quod amatur*), and the love (*amor*) which unites, or strives to unite them. Yet, while expounding this analogy, he himself reckons[52] that it affords only an initial step toward our understanding of the Trinity, at best a momentary glimpse of it. . . .

What he considers his all-important analogy is based on the inner man, viz., the mind's activity as directed upon itself or, better still, upon God. This analogy fascinated him all his life, so that in such an early work as the *Confessions*[53] (397–398) we find him pondering the triad of being,

[44] *Ibid.*, 15,47.
[45] E.g., *De ver. relig.*, 13.
[46] E.g., *Serm.*, 52,17–19.
[47] *De trin.*, 11,1.
[48] *Ibid.*, 11,2–5.

[49] *Ibid.*, 11,6 f.
[50] E.g., *Enarr. in ps.*, 42,6; *Serm. de symb.*, 1,2.
[51] *De trin.*, 8,2–9,2.
[52] *Ibid.*, 15,5; 15,10.
[53] 13.11.

knowing, and willing (*esse, nosse, velle*). In the *De trinitate* he elaborates it at length in three successive stages, the resulting trinities being (*a*) the mind, its knowledge of itself, and its love of itself;[54] (*b*) memory or, more properly, the mind's latent knowledge of itself, understanding, i.e., its apprehension of itself in the light of the eternal reasons, and the will, or love of itself, by which this process of self-knowledge is set in motion;[55] and (*c*) the mind as remembering, knowing, and loving God himself.[56] Each of these, in different degrees, reveals three real elements which, according to Augustine's metaphysics of personality, are coordinate and therefore equal, and at the same time essentially one. . . . It is the last of the three analogies, however, which Augustine deems most satisfactory . . . for — it is only when the mind has focused itself with all its powers of remembering, understanding, and loving on its Creator, that the image it bears of him, corrupted as it is by sin, can be fully restored.

While dwelling at length on these analogies and drawing out their illustrative significance, Augustine has no illusions about their immense limitations. In the first place, the image of God in man's mind is in any case a remote and imperfect one: "a likeness indeed, but a far distant image. . . . The image is one thing in the Son, another in the mirror."[57] Second,

while man's rational nature exhibits the trinities mentioned above, they are by no means identical with his being in the way in which the divine Trinity constitutes the essence of the Godhead;[58] they represent faculties or attributes which the human being possesses, whereas the divine nature is perfectly simple. Third, as a corollary from this, while memory, understanding, and will operate separately, the three persons mutually coinhere and their action is one and indivisible.[59] Lastly, whereas in the Godhead the three members of the Trinity are persons, they are not so in the mind of man. "The image of the Trinity is one person, but the supreme Trinity itself is three persons": which is a paradox when one reflects that, nevertheless, the three are more inseparably one than is the trinity in the mind.[60] This discrepancy between the image and the Trinity itself merely reminds us of the fact, of which the Apostle has told us, that here on earth we see "in a mirror, darkly"; afterward, we shall see "face to face."[61]

[54] *De trin.*, 9,2–8.
[55] *Ibid.*, 10,17–19.
[56] *Ibid.*, 14,11–end.
[57] *Serm.*, 52,17; cf. *De trin.*, 9,17; 10,19.

[58] *Ibid.*, 15,7 f.; 15,11–13.
[59] *Ibid.*, 15,43.
[60] *Ibid.*
[61] It will be noted that different authors give Patristic and Thomistic citations in different forms. Thus J. N. D. Kelly cites Augustine's work *On the Trinity* as *De trin.*, 5,9, Portalie-Bastian as *De trin.*, 5,1(42,947) McGiffert as *De trinitate*, X.12(19) and other authors in still other ways. We have left these Patristic citations as the authors give them so that the reader may get a glimpse of a less and more detailed form of citation. We have also done this with regard to citations of the works of St. Thomas.

2. E. Portalié[1] studies Augustine's doctrine about God: His existence, nature, Trinity. No one can be completely ignorant of God . . . the source of all being, truth and good. God is by his essence pure actuality of being and therefore all perfection. God is the God-Trinity, that is, the basic divinity unfolding itself into three persons, Father, Son, and Holy Spirit, without succession of time or nature, but not without an order of origin.

The Existence of God. In Augustine's mind, the existence of God is one of those truths on which Providence has thrown such light that it is inescapable. No one can be completely ignorant of God: "God is hidden everywhere; he is manifest everywhere. No one can know him as he is, but no one is permitted not to know him."[2] Even atheists refuse to believe only because of passion, "in their hearts."[3] Moreover, there are very few of them, "a rare type of man,"[4] for it is really a kind of insanity: "That madness belongs to only a few."[5]

God is not, however, for us the object of our direct and immediate intuition. . . . According to St. Augustine's theory of knowledge, we receive knowledge neither from an immediate contemplation of God nor from innate ideas. He describes in his commentary on Genesis how our soul, starting with the knowledge of sensible things, rises all the way to the "invisible things of God" through the illumination of the Word.[6]

Although he mentioned all the classic proofs for the existence of God, rarely is a systematic demonstration to be found in his writings. He places particular emphasis upon the consensus of the human race: "Except for a few whose human nature is too depraved, the whole human race acknowledges that God is the author of this world."[7] The ancient proof through finality and the order of the world was developed by him with an inimitable delicacy, grace, and feeling: everywhere in the beauty of nature he sees the name of the divine architect. . . . His eloquence is especially admirable when he develops the metaphysical proof of the finite and changeable world crying out for an infinite and changeless Creator.[8] . . .

Augustine's outstanding proof, however, is the one developed explicitly in *On Eighty-three Different Questions*,[9] more fully in *On Freedom of*

---

[1] Eugene Portalié, S.J., was born in 1852 and died in 1909. In 1899 he held the chair of positive theology at the Institut Catholique of Toulouse. Most of his writing was done for the Jesuit periodical, *Etudes*. This excerpt was taken from R. J. Bastian's translation of his article on Augustine in the *Dictionnaire de Théologie Catholique* and entitled *A Guide to the Thought of St. Augustine* (Chicago: Henry Regnery Co., 1960), pp. 125–141, 213–219.

[2] *Enarr. in ps.*, 74,9 (36,952).

[3] *Enarr. in ps.*, 13,2 (36,141).

[4] *Enarr. in ps.*, 52,2 (36,613).

[5] *Serm.*, 69,2,3, (38,441).

[6] *De gen. ad. lit.*, IV, 32,49 (34,316–317).

[7] *In Joh. ev. tract.*, 106,4 (35, 1910).

[8] *Serm.*, 141,2,2 (38,776); *Conf.*, X, 6,9 (32,783), XI, 4,6 (32,811).

[9] *De div. quaest.*, 83, 54 (40,38).

Choice,[10] and finally in the *Confessions.*[11] It rests upon the comprehension of an eternal and unchangeable truth, superior to man, and can be formulated in this manner: if the mind of man (and the angelic mind),[12] occupying the highest level in the hierarchy of beings in the universe, discovers a being more perfect, that being must be God. Now my mind ascertains that there is an eternal and unchangeable truth above itself which it does not create, but which it contemplates. This truth is not mine nor in me because others contemplate it as well as I do and without my assistance. This truth is, therefore, God himself or, if one supposes that there is a yet more elevated being, it at least leads us to this being, the source of all truth.[13] Jules Martin sees in this proof the foreshadowing of St. Anselm's argument. But he is mistaken in that, for Augustine does not conclude to the existence of God from a concept about him. Rather, analyzing the characteristics of truth, he finds that they are inexplicable unless there is an unchangeable being behind them, the source of unchangeable truth. . . . Basically, this proof, like the others, is reducible to the famous trilogy in which God is conceived by the great doctor as the source of all being, truth, and good: "The cause of existence, the ultimate

reason for the understanding, and the order of life."[14]

The Divine Nature. The limitations of our knowledge about God — the inability to comprehend his nature and to talk about it in human language — is one of the favorite themes of the great doctor. . . . he is far from being an agnostic, but he does feel more than others the torments of the divine mystery which surrounds us. He never wearies of saying that neither our concepts nor our words can exhaust the infinite; "If you understand, it is not God,"[15] "God is ineffable." "We can more easily say what he is not than what he is."[16] The truest concepts will be those which are most general, provided that we know how to clarify their vague outlines. For Augustine, God is being, the absolute being, being in its fullness and perfection, being above which, beyond which, and without which nothing at all exists.[17]

Among the attributes of God simplicity is the trait he focuses on. Since God is by his essence pure actuality of being and so cannot ever be conceived as being in potency and gradually transformed into act, he is therefore all perfection. Augustine goes so far as to regret the use of the word *substance* when speaking of the divine essence, as if it introduced a distinction between the essence of the being and its accidental qualities.[18]. . . To exclude all appearances of metaphysical composition from the divine being,

---

[10] *De lib. arb.,* II, 3–15, 7–40 (32,1243–1263).

[11] *Conf.,* VII, 10,16 (32,742).

[12] *Retract.,* I, 26 (32,627) .

[13] Cf., *De lib. arb.,* II, 3–14, nn. 7–12, 13–14, 15–38 (32,1243–1261). Jules Martin, *Augustin,* pp. 101–188.

[14] *De civ. dei,* VIII, 4 (41,228–229).

[15] *Serm.,* 117,3,5 (38,663).

[16] *Enarr. in ps.,* 85,12 (37,1090).

[17] *Sol.,* I, 1,3–4 (32,870–871).

[18] *De trin.,* 7,5,10 (42,942).

he takes delight in describing the absolute identity which does not make each one of his attributes (such as goodness, wisdom, or justice) just accidents joined to his being, but his very being itself: "Whatever he has he is. . . . Thus he possesses wisdom in such a way that he is Widom."[19] He also insists on the identity of these attributes among themselves.[20] . . .

The relationship of God to time and space is explained more easily in the light of the ineffable simplicity. Eternity is such a perfect actuation of all the divine life that, no change being possible, neither yesterday nor today nor tomorrow can be distinguished. For time is not born of the revolutions of the stars as Plato thought, but of the change which is inherent in every creature: "Time is the movement of a creature from one state to another."[21] His simplicity likewise shows that God is elevated above all space, present everywhere but unextended and incommensurable.[22]

The theory of the divine knowledge is summed up by Augustine in this grand conception: In one single, unchangeable glance God contemplates every being, every truth, every possible or real object. This knowledge is an eternal intuition before which the past and the future are as real as the present, but each for that portion of time in which it really exists. God encompasses all time and therefore can know the future (whether produced freely or necessarily) as infallibly as he knows the present.[23] Today no one any longer denies that Augustine admitted the knowledge of conditioned future (pure futuribles) in God, events which will never take place, but which would have taken place if certain conditions had been fulfilled. It would seem at first glance that these purely hypothetical objects can never be present to the divine mind, since they represent nothing in reality. But, along with the other Fathers, St. Augustine admitted this knowledge in God. Moreover, as we shall see, he made this knowledge serve as the well-spring of divine providence. When the Semipelagians misinterpreted this knowledge and thought that they found traits in it which annulled the gratuity of grace and the gift of predestination, the great doctor of grace denied such applications of this knowledge, but he always admitted the knowledge itself.[24]

The Trinity. According to Schwane, Augustine would have merited the first place among the doctors of the patristic age no less by his teaching on the Trinity than by his teaching on grace.[25] His work of fifteen books *On the Trinity* certainly synthesizes and adds the finishing touches to the most profound and exact statements which had been made about this great mystery, especially in harmonizing the divinity of the Son and the Holy

---

[19] *In Joan. Evang. tract.*, 48,10,6 (35, 1743).

[20] *De trin.*, 15,5,7–8 (42,1061–1062); cf. 5,10,11 (42,918); 6,7,8–9 (42,929).

[21] *De gen. ad lit.*, 5,5,12 (34,325).

[22] *Ep.*, 137,2,8 (33,519).

[23] *De lib. arb.*, 3,2–4, 4–10 (32,1272–1276).

[24] *De praed. sanct.*, 9,17 (44,973); *De dono persev.*, 9,23 (44,1005–1006).

[25] Schwane, *Histoire des dogmes*, II, 265.

Spirit — never afterward to be questioned — with the unity of the divine being. The outstanding characteristic of his Trinitarian teaching is that it clearly manifests the progress of the Latin mind in its thought about the Trinity, a progress opposed to that of the Greek or Eastern Fathers. Father de Regnon has traced this divergence in conception between the East and West, but the reader should remember that de Regnon's admiration for the Greeks did not permit him to appreciate the full value of the progress accomplished or at least initiated by the genius of Augustine.[26]

This development of the dogma is all the more remarkable because the Trinitarian teaching of Augustine as molded by Scholasticism was to direct the thought of all the Western theologians. The principles held in common by the Greek and Latin Fathers at the time when Augustine wrote were the dogma of the three persons participating fully and equally in the same divine nature and the explanation of the dogma by this axiom, implicitly formulated by the Greeks themselves: "In God everything is one where there is no distinction by relative opposition," a formula in which unity is referred to the nature and distinction to the persons.[27] . . .

Three traits characterize the Latin way of conceiving the Trinity and the progress brought about under the influence of the great doctor: (1) the concept of the nature before the persons; (2) the insistence on attributing all the operations *ad extra* to the entire Trinity; (3) the psychological explanation of the processions.

1) *Nature Before Persons.* In his explanation of the Trinity, Augustine conceives the divine nature before the persons. His formulation of the Trinity was to read: one single divine nature subsisting in three persons. The Greeks, on the contrary, put it this way: three persons have the same nature. Up to that point the attention of the Greeks was centered directly on the persons. . . . It was only through reflection that the Greek mind considered directly the one identical divine nature in these three persons. St. Augustine, on the other hand, foreshadowing the Latin concept which the Scholastics borrowed from him, considered the divine nature before all else and investigated this nature until he attained its complete reality in the persons. God, for him, did not directly mean the Father, but the more general notion of the Godhead, conceived concretely and personally no doubt, but not as any one person in particular. It is the God-Trinity, that is, the basic Divinity unfolding itself into three persons, Father, Son, and Holy Spirit, without succession of time or nature, but not without an order of origin.

This special character of Augustine's Trinitarian theory alone explains the novel form of the pseudo-Athanasian Creed which it inspired. All the ancient creeds,[28] even those in vogue at the time of Augustine and used by

---

[26] De Regnon, *Etudes de théologie positive*, pp. 300–429.

[27] Cf. *De trin.*, 5,5–6,6–7 (42,913–915); 5,1 (42,947).

[28] Denzinger, *Enchiridion Symbolorum*, nn. 39:75.

him at Milan and in Africa,[29] are drawn up according to the old idea beginning with faith in one God who is the Father and concluding with the Holy Spirit, speaking of the Trinity in no other way.[30] . . . But the *Quicumque* Creed, based on Augustinian inspiration, opens by professing faith in the Godhead common to the three persons: "This is the Catholic faith, that we worship one God in the Trinity and the Trinity in unity."[31]

The doctrine is certainly the same, but it is plain that the Augustinian conception anticipates and averts objections in advance because it emphasizes the unity of nature. Never, up to this time, had the divine unity been set in relief so strongly in its relation to the three divine persons. The Greeks, accentuating the role of the persons, were constantly harassed by accusations of tritheism and consequently felt obliged to recapitulate the whole Trinity in its primal source, the Father.[32] With St. Augustine, however, the oneness of the divinity appears immediately; later, this way of considering the question was to result in the distinction between the two treatises *De Deo Uno* and *De Deo Trino*, a distinction which the Greek view would never have inspired.[33]

The equality of the divine persons likewise shines forth with greater clarity. The ancient concept brought into prominence the role of the Father as the sole source of the divinity, and, according to the expression of St. Denis, the source of every being, the source and origin of the other persons, so that the divinity seemed to belong properly to him alone. He is God to a supereminent degree. . . . Such insistence, however, carried with it the danger, for minds not too keen, of a subordination of the Son and the Holy Spirit. Therefore, Augustine concentrated his attention first on the divine nature with all its absolute perfections, existing identically the same in each of the three persons. Augustine can say of this great identity that "the equality is so absolute that not only is the Father not greater than the Son . . . but neither is any one person of the Trinity less than the Trinity itself."[34]

There is, it is true, another danger. Once one has become accustomed to conceiving the divinity independently of the three persons, will one not gradually come to conceive it as a personal God before becoming the Father, Son, and Holy Spirit, thus entailing either a fourth person in God or absorbing the three persons in a new kind of Sabellianism? The theory of Cajetan[35] and Durandus[36] which affirms a subsistence common to the three persons could never have arisen

---

[29] Hahn, *Bibliothek der Symbole*, nn. 33–47.

[30] Denzinger, *Enchiridion Symbolorum*, nn. 1–13, 1–44.

[31] Denzinger, *Enchiridion Symbolorum*, nn. 39:75.

[32] Cf. the words of Pope St. Dionysius to St. Dionysius of Alexandria quoted by St. Athanasius, *De decretis Nicaenae synodi*, 26, PG, 25,464.

[33] Cf. *De trin.*, 7, especially chaps. 4–6 (42,939–946).

[34] *De trin.*, 8,1 (42,947).

[35] Cajetan, *In Summam S. Thomae*, III, q.3, a.2; I, q.39, a.4.

[36] Durandus, *In III Sent.*, d.1, q.2, n.7,

from the ancient concept, although it was a natural enough product of the Latin spirit. Augustine sensed this danger and acted to prevent it when he denied that the divinity had any reality distinct from the reality of the divine persons.[37]

Operations ad extra. Another step forward initiated by Augustine in his Trinitarian theory is his insistence on making all the divine action *ad extra* the work of all three persons indistinctly. Only according to the special way in which each person possesses the divine nature can one attribute to each of them the role in external operations which is proper to the character of its origin: simple "appropriation" is the phrase the Latins after Augustine will use. The Greek Fathers, it is true, also affirmed this unity of operation (*energeia*) in God, for it was their great proof of the unity of nature. But this was the fruit of reflection, for in their direct description of the Trinity, they emphasized, on the contrary, the part of each person in the operations performed in community of action until it became almost a distinct role. Hence arose those expressions which sounded quite strange to Latin ears: "From the Father through the Son in the Holy Spirit." . . . Hence in particular arose that popular explanation of the visible manifestations of God in the Old Testament according to which the Son alone had appeared to the ancient patriarchs. St. Augustine proclaims first that in reality the manifestations are necessarily the work of the whole Trinity, although one of the persons could occasionally be manifested in a special way.[38] . . .

Psychological Theory of the Processions. Finally, Augustine laid the foundations for the psychological theory of the processions. In this conception, brought into systematic form later by Anselm and completed by St. Thomas, the mind tries to penetrate into the inner life of God and, contemplating the divine nature endowed with intellect and will, explains through these two operations the number and nature of the processions concerning the origin of the Son and the Holy Spirit. The Son is born of the Father as the *Verbum* of the divine intellect, "after the manner of the act of understanding," St. Thomas was to say.[39] The Holy Spirit proceeds from the Father and the Son as the substantial term of their love, "a procession of love."[40] With these two processions the cycle of what can be called the divine evolution is completed because only these two operations demand a substantial term. This is the profound metaphysical study which St. Augustine inaugurated by his subtle analysis of the human soul, which he liked to see as the most beautiful image of the Trinity. . . .

Creation and Creatures. The main features of creation *ex nihilo* [are] that it is distinct from God and the work of the divine free will. . . . There

---

[37] *Letter 120 to Consentius,* written about 410 in answer to Letter 119, insists on the infinite simplicity which does not permit singling out some one thing as the "divinity of the Trinity" which would be other than the Trinity itself.

[38] *De trin.,* 2,17,32 (42,866).
[39] *Summa Theologiae,* I, q.27, a.2.
[40] *Ibid.,* a.3.

remains to be considered here his theory of the Hexaemeron, a theory which testifies to the amplitude of his views in exegesis and his originality in the very difficult problem of the creation of the world.

Simultaneous Creation? Did St. Augustine hold that the entire universe was created simultaneously? . . . All his pondering has resulted in the following conclusions.

All systems affirming the eternity of the world, even though a created world, are in his mind contrary to reason. He does not admit the theory of St. Thomas that only faith informs us that the world had a beginning.[41] . . . The account of the six days of creation in Genesis cannot be taken literally and in its natural meaning. After 389 Augustine excludes the sense of ordinary days.[42] . . . In reality the creative action was instantaneous and the six days of Genesis correspond to the indivisible instant when everything was created.[43] Relying on the saying of Ecclesiasticus.[44] "He created all things at the same time," Augustine rejects the idea of any new creation by God, although admitting new intervention on his part.[45]

Contrary to most of his contemporaries, however, he does not presume that the instantaneous act of the Creator produced an organized universe such as we see today. He distinguishes

between creation properly so called and the formation or development of the world. This second action is due, at least in great part, to forces placed by the Creator in the depths of nature which have gradually and progressively passed through the various phases to which the Mosaic account gives an approximation.[46]

Primitive Elements and Seedlike Principles. How does Augustine conceive the primitive elements of the world and the seedlike principles (*rationes seminales*)? At the beginning, in his theory, God created the elements of the universe in the state of a confused and nebulous mass — the word is his: "A nebulous form appears."[47] These elements, according to Aristotelian terminology, he calls matter and form, or better, formless matter.[48] . . . Among the elements created on the first day Augustine distinguishes two types. Some were definitely constituted in their specific natures while others existed only in germ in their pre-existing causes. Thus, everything was created in the beginning but the majority of beings were only in potency and enveloped in their causes.[49] . . .

Elsewhere he compares the evolution of the world as it blossomed forth from the primitive elements to the development of a seed which becomes a great tree.[50] . . . These seedlike principles (*rationes seminales*), a term

[41] *De civ. dei*, 11,6 (41,322); 12,15,2 (41,364); 12,12 (41,359); 11,5 (41,321).

[42] *De gen. contra manich.*, 1,23,41 (34, 193).

[43] *De civ. dei*, 11,9 (41,324).

[44] 18:1.

[45] *De gen. ad. lit. lib. XII*, 5,4,10 (34,325).

[46] *Conf.*, 12,8,8 (32,829).

[47] *De gen. ad lit. lib. XII*, 1,12,27 (34,256).

[48] *Conf.*, 12,8,8 (32,829); *De gen. ad lit. lib. imperf.*, 1,15,29 (34,257).

[49] *De gen. ad lit. Lib. XII*, 7,28,41 (34,371).

[50] *Ibid.*, 5,23,45 (34,338).

undoubtedly borrowed from the Neo-platonists[51] and to become quite famous later in the Scholastic era, are nothing else than the energy latent in the germs which are destined to develop not just during the six days of creation but during all the centuries of the history of the world.[52] . . .

At the risk of surprising some readers, we must add that St. Augustine extended his system to man also. How, he asks, did Adam and Eve exist from the beginning of the world? "I answer: invisibly, potentially, causally, in the way that future things which are not yet made exist."[53] . . . From this potential existence, once the time had come, "Adam had to be made from the slime of the earth, and woman from the side of man."[54] To avoid mistake in this matter the reader must take heed of two important reservations. Augustine will say that the soul could not have been enclosed in any "causal principle";[55] furthermore, God will intervene in the formation of the body of man.

Augustine an Evolutionist? The question whether Augustine is an evolutionist would be ridiculous if one meant atheistic evolution or material evolution without a soul, for Augustine makes God and the soul the very center of his entire cosmogony and anthropology. But there is a theistic evolution which could appeal to the authority of the Doctor of

Hippo, and with some show of truth. For when he so absolutely denies successive creations, does he not admit that the Creator has endowed matter with the power of gradual differentiation and transformation which constitutes a type of evolution? Many have thought as much. Zahm congratulates the great doctor for having anticipated modern science in granting nature this power of transformation.[56] . . . This interpretation, nevertheless, is completely inaccurate in both parts.

1) Augustine did not think that transformation was possible; on the contrary, affirming the immutability of species, he makes no allowance for the possibility that "different realities could come from the same primitive principle or the same seed."[57] . . . Thus, the seedlike principles do not constitute potencies in the elements to evolve "from homogeneity to heterogeneity," as Zahm thinks,[58] but presuppose as many seeds as there are to be different species. . . .

2) Augustine demands the immediate intervention of God for the formation of the universe, something different from the ordinary divine concurrence. God certainly creates no longer, but his direct action is sometimes necessary to make up for the powerlessness of cosmic energies and to bring about the full development of such and such a seed at the desired moment. Now, whether this divine influence introduces new matter into the universe (a hypothesis rejected by

[51] Grandgeorge, *Augustin*, p. 114.
[52] *De gen. ad lit. lib. XII*, 9,17,32 (34,406).
[53] *Ibid.*, 6,6,10 (34,343).
[54] *Ibid.*, 5,8 (34,342).
[55] Cf. Book VII of the *Literal Commentary on Genesis*.

[56] Zahm, *Bible, science et foi* (Paris, 1894), pp. 58–66.
[57] Jules Martin, *Augustin*, p. 314.
[58] Zahm, *L'evolution et le dogme* (Paris, 1897), p. 124.

Augustine) or whether at various intervals it gives a new stimulus (as he insists), it is always a deficiency in natural law and recourse to a miracle.

It is true that the great doctor does not specify the instances when God must intervene in this miraculous manner. But he accepts the principle. . . . He categorically affirms this miraculous intervention for the formation of the body of Eve and gives his general theory in that connection.[59] . . . The same is true of the intervention of God to introduce the soul of Adam into his body and also, it seems, for the formation of his body.[60]

Augustinian Predestination. To understand Augustine's attitude it will be better to compare the various answers which have been made since his time to the question he raised: Does God, in His creative decree and before any act of human liberty, determine by an immutable choice the elect and the reprobate? Must the elect during eternity thank God for having rewarded their merits or must they also thank Him for having, before any meritorious act on their part, chosen them to merit this reward? Three answers have been given to the above question.

1) *Semipelagian Answer.* The Semipelagian system decides the problem in favor of man. God predestines everyone equally to salvation and gives to all an equal measure of graces. Only the free will of man, by resisting or consenting to grace, decides whether one will be saved or lost. All special predestination, if it is not founded on the real or conditional merit of the elect, would be opposed to the justice of God and to human liberty. They go so far as to insinuate (and later theologians were to repeat this) that the number of the elect is neither determined nor certain.

2) *Predestinarian Answer.* The predestinarian system (which the Semipelagians attributed to St. Augustine and which others think is really to be found in his writings) asserts not only a preferential choice of the elect by God from all eternity (rightly understood, this is the Catholic dogma), but at the same time the predestination of the reprobate to hell and the absolute powerlessness of both classes to escape from the irresistible impulse which leads them on to either good or evil. These two assertions constitute the essential character of the predestinarianism attributed to St. Augustine by the Semipelagians and really taught by Calvin.

3) *Catholic Answer.* Midway between these two extreme opinions, the Catholic dogma, which was not fabricated but only formulated by Augustine, simultaneously asserts these two truths: The eternal choice of the elect by God is very real, very gratuitous, and constitutes the grace of graces; this decree, however, does not destroy the divine will to save all men and moreover is realized only through human freedom of choice, leaving full power to the elect to fall and to the non-elect to rise again.

Solution of St. Augustine. Does this last system truly represent the thought of Augustine? Our answer will con-

[59] *De gen. ad lit. lib. XII,* 9,17,31–32 (34,405–406).
[60] *Ibid.,* 7,24,35 (34,368).

sist in an analysis of the divine decree as Augustine understood it.

1) *Knowledge of God Before the Decree of Predestination.* Before any divine decree to create the world, the infinite knowledge of God presents to him all the graces and different series of graces which he can prepare for each soul, along with the consent or the refusal which would follow in each circumstance — and that in millions and millions of possible combinations. Thus he sees that St. Peter, if he had received a different grace, would not have been converted, and Judas, if a different divine call had sounded in his heart, would have done penance and been saved.

Our actual world, with all its history from Adam to the Last Judgment, is only one of millions and millions of worlds which God could have brought into being. Among these worlds there are some in which all would be saved, others in which all would be lost, and others in which the damned and elect are mixed. . . . This is the knowledge which, according to Augustine, precedes and enlightens the choice of God. . . . This knowledge showing him the different ways of saving Judas was not the knowledge of vision which beholds only future events (the conversion of Judas was never a future event), but another type of knowledge — whatever name it is given — whose object embraces the conditional responses of each free will to each call from God. Without this knowledge neither Augustine nor predestination can be understood.[61]

Tenor of the Divine Decree. Faced

with all these possible worlds, God, by an absolutely free act, decides to bring this actual world into existence just as it appeared in the midst of the possible worlds with all the circumstances of its historical evolution, with all the graces which in fact have been or will be distributed until the end of the world, and finally with all the elect and reprobate who God foresaw must exist in it once he really created it. Now, according to Augustine and the Catholic faith as formulated by him, in this decree of complex unity an analysis will disclose two elements between which an essential distinction must be drawn.

The first element of this decree is the certain determination of the elect in virtue of an entirely gratuitous benevolence (before any merits) in their regard. God, in fact, in decreeing to create this world and to give this series of graces . . . decides at the same time the name, the place, and the number of all the citizens of the future Jerusalem. The following factors comprise Augustinian predestination: (1) The election according to his purpose of which Augustine spoke so frequently.[62] (2) God's immutable choice which obliges one to state: "The number of the elect is certain and will neither be increased nor decreased."[63] It is evident, in fact, that only those will be saved who God knows will wish to cooperate with the grace decreed for them. The list of the elect and the reprobate is closed, and known only to the eyes of God.

---

[61] Wolfsgruber, *Augustin*, p. 828.

[62] *De cor. et grat.*, 9,23 (44,929–930); *de praed. sanct.*, 16–18, 32–37 (44,983–987).

[63] *De cor. et grat.*, 13,39 (44,940).

Although all the elect *could* fall and the non-predestined *could* be converted, as a matter of fact none of the elect will wish to be lost and none of the reprobate will wish to yield to grace. . . . (3) This election is the gratuitous gift above all others which, far from being merited, is the source of all merit, the gift of gifts, in virtue of which "even man's merit is a gratuitous gift."[64] . . . (4) It is a predestination which forces one to say that neither God nor Jesus Christ had the absolute will to save all men. God could, if he had willed, have chosen a world where all souls would be saved. . . . Why did he not will to? That is his own mystery.[65] (5) Predestination is the mystery of mysteries not because it interferes with freedom of choice but because there is only one response Augustine could give to this question: "Why did God, when he saw that Judas could have been saved with another grace, not give it to him"? Augustine's answer is: "O the depths."[66] . . .

One should notice at this point that this theory of predestination proposed by Augustine is exactly the same as the Catholic dogma which all the schools teach under this undisputed formula: Predestination taken as a whole is absolutely gratuitous (before any merits). This point is worth mentioning because many have seen in these truths only an expression of Augustine's severity. All the schools also agree in their proclamation of the sec-

ond element in the divine decree.

The second element is the sincere will of God to give all men the power of saving themselves and the freedom of damning themselves. In the elect there is no irresistible impulse of grace toward paradise; in the wicked, no obduracy toward damnation. According to Augustine, God in his creative decree has explicitly excluded every set of events in which grace would take away man's liberty and every situation in which man would not have the means to resist sin. That is the essential point of the system: by it he refutes the predestinarian heresy which has been ascribed to him. Indisputably there is absolute certainty that only the elect will wish to be saved. But to say that there is no possibility of salvation for the others is contrary to the uninterrupted teaching of Augustine in his last works as well as his early ones.[67] . . .

Such are the two essential elements of Augustinian and Catholic teaching on predestination. This is the dogma common to all Catholic schools (save for the mode of reconciliation concerning which the Church allows complete freedom). Once these two points are settled, the long debates of the theologians on predestination before or after merits are far less important than many people think. . . .

Damnation. A more serious exaggeration made by Augustine concerns the very degree in which the sin of Adam is transmitted to his descendants, that is, the inmost nature of the

---

[64] *Ep.*, 186,10 (33,820).

[65] *De gen. ad lit. lib. XII*, 11,10,13 (34,434).

[66] *Rom* 11:33; *de spir. et lit.*, 34,60 (44,421).

[67] *De gen. contra manich.*, 1,3,6 (34, 176); *Retract.*, 1,10,2 (32,599); *De div. quaest. VII ad Simpl.*, 1,2,13 (40,118).

damnation of the children of Adam. . . . He calls the line of Adam a mass of slime; a mass of sin, of sins, of iniquity; a mass of wrath, of death, of damnation, of offense; a mass totally vitiated, damnable, damned.[68] But all this constitutes the dogma of the Fall, not its explanation. If there is sin, there is damnation, and that to the same degree in which there is sin; no Catholic can doubt this. But are this sin and damnation of the same nature as personal sin and the damnation which it merits? . . . Augustine's thought must be sought for in his theory about the fate of infants who have died without baptism. There, despite the efforts of certain theologians and even of the great Scholastic doctors to soften his statements, his theory is really too severe, although less cruel than some have thought.

His theory is too severe, for he consigns these souls to hell and condemns them to eternal punishment there. In the beginning he hesitated or even granted the possibility of an intermedi-

ate place between heaven and hell,[69] but later his doubts are resolved and he always speaks of the punishment which they have to suffer.[70]

His theory is less cruel than has been thought, for he always proclaimed the mildness of this punishment; he calls it the "gentlest punishment,"[71] the "lightest condemnation."[72] And this is not to be understood merely in comparison to the punishment of the other souls in hell, for Augustine immediately adds that he does not dare to decide whether their lot is not preferable to simple annihilation.[73] It remains certain that in his thought the damnation due to original sin alone is essentially different from that which personal sins merit.

Theology has progressed since then and expressed in clearer terms the thesis that original sin deprives one solely of supernatural benefits, leaving nature intact.

---

[68] Cf. the exact citations in Rottmanner, *Der Augustinismus*, p. 8.

[69] *De lib. arb.*, 3,23 (32,1303).

[70] *Ep.*, 166,6,16 (33,727); cf. *De dono persev.*, 12,30 (45,1010); *Serm.*, 294,4,3 (38,1337), a very severe statement.

[71] *Enchir.*, 93 (40,275).

[72] *Contra jul.*, 5,11,44 (44,809).

[73] *Ibid.*

V

GOD IN MUSLIM THEOLOGY

1. L. Gardet[1] looks at Mohammed, the rise of Islam, and the Koran. The Koran is not a theological exposition of God's nature and attributes. Its three prevalent themes are: (1) God is the creator, judge, and re-munerator; (2) he is unique and one in himself; (3) he is at one and the same time omnipotent and merciful, Lord of the worlds, Lord of the East and the West.

Mohammed and the Rise of Islam. Mohammed, of the Quraish tribe and the Banu Hashim clan, was born at Mecca in the year A.D. 570.[2] The Banu Hashim clan was highly respected and allied to influential circles, but it would seem to have been greatly impoverished. It was not one of the ruling families. Mohammed never knew his father, for he died before he was born. He lost his mother when he was five or six years old. . . .

[1] Louis Gardet (pseud.) has written a good deal about Mohammedanism. Among his published works are *La cité musulmane* and *Connaitre l'Islam*. This excerpt is from his book, *Mohammedanism*, trans. from the French by William Burridge, W. F. (New York: Hawthorn Books, 1961), pp. 19–25, 29–41.

[2] Other dates have been put forward, 567, 569, 572, 573. For the social economic and political background to the origins and expansion of Islam, see W. Montgomery Watt, *Muhammad at Mecca* (Oxford, 1953), and *Muhammad at Medina* (Oxford, 1956).

Mohammed the orphan grew up in poverty. . . . He had a Beduin nurse, of whom Muslim tradition speaks with affection. With her he led the life of a nomad. In his youth and early manhood he lived at Mecca and was employed in connection with the trading caravans. . . . He was engaged by Khadija, the young widow of a rich merchant. It appears that he looked after her business for her. Then, although she was considerably older than he was, he married her. As long as she lived, he took no other wife. . . .

He frequently retired for long spells to caves in Mount Hira, close to Mecca. It was there that one day his first "revelation" descended on him, at first frightening and disquieting him. According to the most frequently accepted Muslim tradition, this "revelation" was to become the ninety-sixth *Sura* of the Koran. . . .

Frightened and fearing he might be a prey to illusions, Mohammed confided in Khadija. She believed he was genuine and had faith in the words of the "revelation." Other "revelations" followed, and a small group of followers was formed. . . . Mohammed, the "announcer," preached amidst the irony and growing hostility of the Meccans. . . . For well-nigh ten years, his few adherents and his numerous opponents in Mecca heard the recital of the first *Suras* (chapters) of the Koran, telling how God is merciful, almighty, creator, remunerator, supreme and just judge, inaccessible, benevolent, ready to grant pardon; stressing relentlessly that the hour of judgment was at hand, proclaiming, in the face of the Meccan polytheism,

that there is only one single God; promising paradise to the believers and the torments of hell to the unbelievers; claiming as predecessors a long line of prophets, especially those of the Bible, from Adam to Christ; affirming a living and vital continuity of this new faith with the faith of Abraham, the friend of God.

It is toward the end of Mohammed's preaching at Mecca that, so tradition alleges, two great events took place which were to be a constant stimulus to Muslim piety. The first is what has come to be known as the nocturnal journey of Mohammed from Mecca to Jerusalem. The other was his "ascension" from Jerusalem to the throne of God. Some people admit that this journey and "ascension" were "in spirit," but it is more widely held that they were miraculous, bodily phenomena.[3] . . .

The believers left Mecca in successive groups. Mohammed, Abu Bakr, and, undoubtedly, Ali, were the last to leave. Thus came about the famous flight, the *Hegira,* of the Prophet and Abu Bakr, pursued by the Meccans and escaping thanks to the shelter of a cave. They reached Quba, a suburb of Yathrib, on September 24, 622. This date marks the year one of the Mohammedan era (abbreviated as A.H.).

And indeed, this Hegira of Mo-

---

[3] The "nocturnal journey" is generally commemorated on the 27th of the month of *rajab,* the "ascension" on the 17th or, preferably, on the 17th of the month of *ramadan* or at the end of *ramadan* during the night of destiny (*laylat al-qadr*), when the heavens are supposed to open and angels come and go between heaven and earth.

hammed and his companions, leaving their tribe and family and their native town to go and live in Yathrib, is the beginning of the Muslim community. . . . 10 A.H., the small enclaves of Christians and Jews in the north of the Arab peninsula accepted Muslim protection. . . . It may be said that by this date the Muslim Community extended over the whole of Arabia. . . . Mohammed died in the arms of his favorite wife, Aysha, on the 13th day of the month of Rabi in the year 10 A.H. (Monday, June 8, A.D. 632). . . .

The Koran. From its very inception Islam was to be directly centered on the Koran. For the Christian Christ came to perfect all things, and revelation is brought to a close with the death of the last of the apostles. For the Muslim, it is the Koran that completes and closes the earthly cycle of the envoys of God. The Koran was spoken by the prophet, it was stored safely in the memory of the companions, written down by such as were able to write and eventually it was all drawn up in an official recension by Uthman, the third of the caliphs.

The one hundred fourteen chapters (*Suras*) of the Koran were arranged according to their length, the shortest first, and the whole text was prefaced by the *Sura* called *al-Fatiha,* the "opening," which became the model of Islamic prayer: "Praise be to God, Lord of the worlds! The compassionate, the merciful! King on the day of reckoning! Thee only do we worship, and to thee do we cry for help. Guide thou us on the straight path. The path of those to whom thou hast been gracious; With whom thou are not

angry, and who go not astray." . . .

Each of the chapters of the Koran, every one of its 6,226 verses, are looked on as "signs from God" (*ayat Allah*) and the sincere Muslim regards it as a supernatural dictation communicated to Mohammed, the inspired Prophet. It is for the Muslim the subsistent word of God, the distinction between good and evil. . . . The prophet, the whole community after him, is consecrated to the services of this world. Mohammed himself is first and foremost the messenger, the "warner," to whom the transmission of this deposit is entrusted. As Louis Massignon puts it, the Muslims have always considered that the excellence of the literary form of the Koran is the ultimate proof of the personal prophetic inspiration of Mohammed: for them the style is a miracle surpassing all physical miracles. And so the unsurpassable beauty of the Koran, in the eyes of Islam, is its own witness to its authenticity.

The Koran recognizes that the Torah and the Gospel are "revealed." It accuses the Jews and Christians of falsifying their books, but despite this they remain "keepers of the Scriptures." The later teaching of Islam declared that the word of God is Torah and Gospel and Koran. But Mohammed is the "seal of the Prophets,"[4] so much so that the Koran sums up all anterior prophecies and gives them a definitive form.

But in the course of all this, the Koran does not, as one might expect, retrace God's plan for mankind. The story of mankind is not presented as

---

[4] *Koran,* 33,40.

a progressive unfolding of events but as a succession of disjointed interventions on the part of God. These, through the voice of the prophets, reiterate the truths and the conditions set down in the primordial covenant, leading on to the fulfillment of that covenant at the supreme hour.

The primordial covenant is the pact which God, from eternity, before the creation of bodies, granted to Adam's race. . . . This self-same covenant rendered to God, was recalled by each of the prophets against the incredulity and wickedness of men. It reaches its culminating point in the faith of Abraham and is of the very essence of the Muslim community.

Thus the entire Koran looks toward man's ultimate end and is dominated by eschatology. Its teaching can be grouped under two heads, each of which can be subdivided into two parts. Under the first head comes what may be termed a non-temporal or supra-temporal teaching. This deals, on the one hand, with the inaccessible mystery of God-One and, on the other, with the imminence of the hour of annihilation, the resurrection, the great "gathering," the final judgment, the torments promised to the reproved and the reward promised to the elect. Under the second head come the disjointed temporal events identified with the successive prophetic missions; and lastly there is the delineation of the pattern of life within the framework of Muslim prophecy.

God. The Koran is not a theological exposition of the existence of God, his nature and attributes. God is there the unfathomed mystery, the inaccessible,

ascertained in his transcendent perfections and in his interventions in the world. Three themes are prevalent throughout; they have to be taken as parts of one whole. (1) God is the creator, judge, and remunerator; (2) he is unique (*wahid*) and one in himself (*ahad*); (3) he is at one and the same time omnipotent and merciful. He is Lord of the worlds, the Lord of the East and the West, in his omnipotence which is accepted unquestioningly. This, in its turn, draws the believer to see in him a protector and to laud this divine power of mercy and forgiveness: a thought most vividly emphasized in the Koran.

The absolute precept of love, Thou shalt love the Lord thy God with thy whole soul, is not formulated in the Koran. What is brought out, first of all, is the inscrutable sovereignty of God and then, total and blind surrender. . . . Guided by God, man's reason will discover in the perishable world the irrefutable evidence of the necessary and transcendent existence of the Creator.

It is the perfections showing forth his unicity and omnipotence in regard to this order in the world that God reveals. He possesses the most beauteous names. He is One and Unique, the Living One, the Subsistent, the True-Reality, the Sublime, the Most High, the Redoubtable, the Light and Light upon light, the absolute Creator who ceases not to create, the one unlike all created things, he that Heareth, the All-seeing, the Omniscient, the Witness, the Benefactor, the Protector, the Generous, the Merciful, the Pardoner who ceases not to absolve, the Compassionate, the Well-Wisher, the best of Judges. . . .

The hour of reckoning is ever imminent, and when it strikes, man, in response to the primordial pact, will find himself face to face with his Lord. . . . In this treatment of the last day, the Koran keeps two things constantly in perspective: the implacable omnipotence of God "who has no account to give of himself" and the just retribution of the works of man. . . . The Koran does not set itself the theological problem of predestination nor the philosophical problem of the nature of the freedom of human acts. Indeed, it does not set itself problems at all. What it is doing is emphasizing the mystery of the relationship between the creature and the Creator. Even the problem of the nature of evil is not taken up. . . . The reprobate are those who refuse divine help. On the day of judgment every soul shall be judged according to its deserts.[5] . . . God grants his favors to whom he will. . . . The responsibility of man and the absolute decree of God, these are two capital assertions running through the teaching, each reaching, still with no attempt at conciliation, their culminating point in the announcement of the judgment, where before the eyes of all shall shine forth the omnipotence and the mystery of the Most High God, who knows each and every creature and the thoughts of man. . . .

The Prophets. . . . All revelation is given word for word to the prophet upon whom it "descends." Hence if there is identity between the Koran

[5] Koran, 40,17; cf. 92,16; 4,79; 52,96.

and the texts of the "possessors" of the Scriptures, it is because, according to Muslims, God has repeated to the Prophet of Islam, through the agency of the angel of revelation[6] what he had already communicated to previous prophets. If there are divergences, it is either because the manner of teaching is different or because the ancient Laws have since been distorted by man. In any case it is the text of the Koran, seal of all prophecy, that must be taken as authentic.

Of all the prophets brought into the Koran, predominance is given to those called the "apostles endowed with constancy." These are, in chronological order, Noah, whose ark symbolized the maintenance and renewal of the primordial pact; Abraham, the friend of God; Moses, the interlocutor of God; Jesus, Son of Mary and "Word of God." Each of them became the prototype of a religious disposition. Abraham is the witness to faith in the Unique and is the breaker of idols. With Ishmael he rebuilt and purified the temple of the Kaaba, which had been destroyed by the deluge. He was ready to sacrifice that very son whom God had given him in answer to his prayer. The "solemn sacrifice" which was offered instead is perpetuated in

[6] "The faithful spirit" (26,192); "the spirit of sanctity" (16,102). In 2,97 it is the Angel Gabriel who is mentioned. The ministry of the angel, sometimes seen by Mohammed, sometimes only heard by him, was to become for Islam the specific modality of prophetic revelation. It is this that distinguishes it from personal divine inspiration, which may also be experienced by a prophet but also by some just or holy man who is not a prophet. "Inspiration" pure and simple does not imply a mission to transmit a religious law to men.

the community by divine command. It is thus that the central Muslim religious act, the sacrificial pilgrimage at Mecca, was to be linked with the memory of Abraham. Moses retired to the desert for forty days. God spoke to him in the burning bush on the mountain and gave him the Torah for the children of Israel. . . . Among the passages referring to Jesus in the Koran, two stand out from the rest: his birth beneath a palm tree and the laden table that came down from heaven at his prayer when the apostles asked him for a sign.

It is to this faith of Abraham that the faith-and-witness in the Unique, demanded of the believer, looks back as to its type and exemplar. Islam has unremittingly claimed Abraham as its father, according to the flesh through Hagar and Ishmael, spiritually through the recovery of faith. In the face of all the revolts and apostasies of the peoples visited by the prophets, the Koran proclaims a fundamental identity between the announcement that sums up all announcements and the faith of Abraham. Some traditions name Isaac, but the common teaching speaks only of the sacrifice of Ishmael. . . .

The Koran and Christian Dogmas. . . . At various times, passages from the Koran have been looked on by Muslim apologists as the refutation of the Christian dogma of the Trinity and Incarnation. But when we come to examine these passages more closely, we discover that their statement of the Christian dogmas they propose to refute is far from accurate. What they are refuting is not orthodox Christian

belief at all but heretical views which the Church herself repudiates.

Thus, in regard to the Trinity: "Say not Three: God is one only divinity."[7] And in another *Sura*[8] we read: "They surely are infidels who say God is the third of three." The way the Incarnation is represented varies. Sometimes Christ is spoken of as a human person clad in divinity — a statement suggestive of the Nestorian heresy. Sometimes, and this is more frequent, he is spoken of as a humano-divine person engendered according to the flesh by the divinity itself.[9] . . . Muslims who later sought to refute Christian dogma wrongly took the definition of the Trinity to mean that there was plurality of substances in God. On the other hand, Muslim writers who set out to take a sympathetic approach to Christianity by showing that Christians were indeed monotheists — thus Ghazali, Ibn Rushd, Ibn Qayyim — did little else than present the Trinity as erroneously taught by the Modalists and spoke of the Incarnation as merely the language of theopathy. . . .

Muslim piety toward Christ and his mother, based on the Koran, is remarkable. There is a store of narratives, reminiscent of the apocryphal Gospels: the story of Mary in the Temple, her marriage to Joseph, the birth of Christ under a desert palm tree, the miracles supposed to have

---

[7] *Koran,* 4,169.
[8] 5,177.
[9] Thus, 4,177: "Far be it from him that he should have a son"; 5,16: "O Jesus, son of Mary, hast thou said unto mankind, Take me and my mother as two Gods beside God?"

been performed by our Lord as a child and a youth. . . . But in the Medinan *Suras* there is a solemn affirmation of the virgin birth of Christ and the assertion that Christ *is* the "Word of God" (*Kalimat Allah*) conveyed by God to Mary, and a "spirit proceeding from God."[10] . . . Yet all this without any allusion to the Incarnation. . . . But the function of the "son of Mary" is that of every prophet: to transmit the warning of God. . . .

He is "different from other men," for he is born of the Word of God conveyed to Mary; but he is prophet among the prophets, one of the greatest of them, and his task is not yet ended, since he is to return at the end of time. . . . While Islam records the Fall of Adam in the Garden,[11] the dogma of original sin is wanting. Hence, there could be no place in Islamic teaching for the dogma of redemption.

2. J. Kritzeck[1] studies Islam's Judaeo-Christian background. A. Geiger argued for a dominant Jewish influence on the Koran, J. Wellhausen for one that was chiefly Gnostic. There also seem to be a few specifically Nestorian influences. Contrary to orthodox Moslem belief, Mohammed did have knowledge of the biblical narratives before his call to prophethood, and that knowledge was, no doubt, secondhand.

One might suppose that Islam, simply because it is so much younger than Judaism or the Christian Church, would pose fewer or at least less difficult historical problems. Such is not the case. "Islam, it used to be said, grew up in the full light of history. Within a single lifetime that light has grown steadily dimmer. Under critical examination the foundations of the old tradition have dissolved into enigmas and hypotheses."[2] Scholars have found it necessary to reconsider many

time-honored generalizations, particularly those concerning Mohammed's integrity and his followers' methods. This task has barely been begun in most fields of Islamic research.

One thing, however, is certain: Islam can never be disengaged from the life of the man who was called Mohammed.[3] He was born at Mecca in Arabia about the year 570. When he was about forty years of age, he began to make a series of very remarkable claims. He maintained that he was the "reciter" of a "recitation" (Arabic *qur'an*, hence Koran), transmitted to him by the angel Gabriel. This "recitation," he claimed, was the final redaction of what Allah, "the

---

[10] *Koran*, 4,177.

[11] *Second Sura.*

[1] James Kritzeck, is the editor of an Anthology of Islamic Literature and with R. B. Winder the author of *The World of Islam.* This excerpt is from his book, *Sons of Abraham — Jews, Christians and Moslems* (Baltimore-Dublin: Helicon Press, Inc., 1965), pp. 31–47.

[2] Hamilton A. R. Gibb, *Mohammedanism* (London: Oxford University Press, 1949), p. 23.

[3] Arabic *Muhammad,* "the praised one." The standard Moslem biography, the *Sirat Rasul Allah* of Ibn-Ishaq (d. 767), has recently been translated by Alfred Guillaume, *The Life of Muhammad* (London: Oxford University Press, 1955).

God of Abraham, Ishmael, Isaac, and Jacob and the Tribes . . . and Jesus"[4] wished to communicate to mankind. It carried in itself, as he was ultimately compelled to insist, the power to invalidate the former Scriptures wherever they disagreed with his "recitation." He further regarded himself as the last of a series of prophets and "messengers" whom God had sent to restore the purity of his religion, for not only had it been deformed by Jews and Christians, but it had also remained unknown to others. In 622 he and his followers fled to Medina (then called Yathrib), a city some distance north of Mecca, a flight[5] from which Moslems date their era. And not without reason. At Medina Mohammed both added to the number of his followers and welded them together into a community, indeed into a military power, which, at the time of his death in 632, was nearly ready to extend itself by rapid conquest to mastery over much of Asia and Africa.

Various questions concerning Islam's origins and, more particularly, concerning the sources of the notions and stories contained in the Koran, impose themselves on us. The Orthodox Moslem position is a flat denial that such sources could exist. Moslems do not deny that Mohammed knew Jews and Christians; what they do deny is that Mohammed is, in any sense at all, the author of the Koran. No matter how interesting Mohammed's opinions on the number of the angels or the proper way of combing one's

hair may be, they enjoy less authority than God's revelation through him.[6] Many Moslems do not even deny that there were slight variants in the first versions of the Koran, or that the arrangement of the chapters is an arbitrary one, but they hold that the present form, which was established early, is the true one, corresponding to a heavenly archetype.[7] The Islamic concept of revelation is thus considerably more rigid than is the Catholic Christian or even the orthodox Jewish, for it excludes the idea of human, though divinely inspired authors.

Needless to say, non-Moslem scholarship takes a different view, denying the Koran exemption from that rigorous scrutiny to which nothing that comes to human ken is immune. The

---

[4] 2,136, p. 336.
[5] Arabic *hijrah*, hence Hegira, and more accurately "emigration."

[6] Mohammed's "opinions" are preserved in the immense tradition (Arabic *hadith*) literature, on which Ignaz Goldziher, *Muhammedanische Studien* (Halle: M. Niemeyer, 1890), II, 1–275, and Alfred Guillaume, *The Traditions of Islam* (Oxford: Clarendon, 1924) may be consulted. An idea of the subject matter can be gleaned from Arent J. Wensinck, *A Handbook of Early Muhammadan Tradition* (Leiden: E. J. Brill, 1927).
[7] Theodor Nöldeke, Friedrich Schwally, Gotthelf Bergsträsser, and Otto Pretzl, *Geschichte des Qor'ans*, 3 vols. (Leipzig: Dietrich, 1909–1938) is still, and will doubtless long remain, the best history of the *Koran*. The chapters of the *Koran* are arranged, with the exception of the first, roughly according to length, a particularly unsuitable arrangement in view of the fact that the longest are usually the latest. Many learned attempts have been made to rearrange them. Some scholars think that the heavenly archetype to which the Koran is said to correspond is referred to as "preserved tablet" (85,22, p. 48), "hidden book" (56,77, p. 109), and "eternal book" (43,3, p. 145; 13,39, p. 143), though others have given other meanings to these allusions.

origin of Islam has engaged good scholars for many centuries; within the past century it has engaged great scholars.

It has nearly always been held that the major influences on Mohammed must have been principally, but not exclusively, Jewish and Christian, and that they were colored by Mohammed's own character and remade to conform to aspects and needs of the pre-Islamic Arabian mind. Within this broad framework, however, opinions have clashed. It was the prize dissertation of Abraham Geiger, the leader of Jewish reform, which stimulated much of the modern discussion; in it he argued for a dominant Jewish influence on the Koran.[8] An opposing view, which held the influence to be chiefly Gnostic, was given the powerful support of Julius Wellhausen.[9] This view was followed to a greater or lesser extent by Theodor Nöldeke, Henry P. Smith, and Wilhelm Rudolph, to name only a few, and strengthened by Carl H. Becker, Richard Bell, Tor Andrae, and Karl Ahrens. It is that of the standard history by Carl Brockelmann.[10] Once the

incompleteness of Geiger's source materials had been overcome, a reaction toward his earlier view was led by Hartwig Hirschfeld, Israel Schapiro, and Eugene Mittwoch, and sympathetically regarded by Davis S. Margoliouth, Alfred Guillaume, and Erwin Rosenthal.[11] Charles C. Torrey went considerably beyond them in emphasizing the Jewish influence, while the recent work of Abraham Katsh shows how well and in what detail such a view can be substantiated.[12] Probably the safest and soundest view is the moderate opinion outlined by Johann

---

[8] See Abraham Geiger, Was hat Mohammed aus dem Judenthum aufgenommen? (Bonn: F. Baaden, 1833); translated by F. M. Young as Judaism and Islam (Madras: M.D.C.S.P.C.K., 1898).

[9] Chiefly in his Reste arabischen Heidenthums, 2nd ed. (Berlin: G. Reimer, 1897), pp. 204–212.

[10] See Nöldeke, op. cit., I, 7 and passim; Henry P. Smith, The Bible and Islam (New York: Scribner, 1897), p. 315; Wilhelm Rudolph, Die Abhängigkeit des Qorans von Judentum und Christentum (Stuttgart: Kohlhammer, 1922), pp. 63–71; Carl H. Becker, Islamstudien (Leipzig: Quelle und Meyer, 1924), I, 386–431, 450–471; Richard Bell, The Origin of Islam

in its Christian Environment (London: Macmillan, 1926); Tor Andrae, Der Ussprung des Islams und das Christentum (Uppsala: Kyrkohistorisk Arrskrift, 1926); Karl Ahrens, "Christliches im Qoran," Zeitschrift der deutschen morgenlandischen Gesellschaft, Neue Folge IX (1930), 15–68, 148–190; Carl Brockelmann, Geschichte der islamischen Völker und Staaten (Munich: R. Oldenbourg, 1939), p. 15.

[11] See Hartwig Hirschfeld, Jüdische Elemente im Koran (Berlin: Im Selbstverlag, 1878) and Beiträge zur Erklärung des Koran (Leipzig: Otto Schulze, 1886); Israel Schapiro, Die Haggadischen Elemente im erzählenden Teil des Korans (Leipzig: G. Fock, 1907); Eugen Mittwoch, Zur Entstehungsgeschichte des islamischen Gebets und Kultus (Berlin: G. Reimer, 1913); David S. Margoliouth, The Relations between Arabs and Israelites Prior to the Rise of Islam (London: Oxford University Press, 1924); Alfred Guillaume, "The Influence of Judaism on Islam," The Legacy of Israel, edited by Edwyn R. Bevan and Charles Singer (Oxford: Clarendon, 1928), pp. 129–171; Erwin Rosenthal, "Islam," Judaism and Christianity, edited by H. Loewe (London: Sheldon, 1937), II, 147–185.

[12] See Charles C. Torrey, The Jewish Foundation of Islam (New York: Jewish Institute of Religion Press, 1933); Abraham Katsh, Judaism in Islam (New York: New York University Press, 1954).

Fück and Julian Obermann,[13] but in all likelihood the last word on the problem will never be said.

The Arabians of Mohammed's time were still overwhelmingly pagan, which is to say in modern usage, polytheistic and idolatrous. In company with many peoples before and since, they lived in a world which they believed to be "populated" with many worshipful gods and demi-gods occupying places in a rather informal and fluid hierarchy of spirits.

> Every tribe worshiped its own god, but also recognized the power of other tribal gods in their own sphere. Among the Arabs, in any case, the bond between a tribe and its god was not so intimate as that in Israel, for instance, between Yahweh and his people. Individual clans sometimes named themselves after other gods than those of the tribe, and the same divinity was worshiped by various tribes. The gods had fixed abodes, in which, after the tribe departed, they enjoyed the worship of its successors; the tribe returned to them once or twice a year on holidays. . . .

> In addition to all these gods and goddesses the Arabs . . . believed in a God who was creator of the world, Allah, whom the Arabs did not, as has often been thought, owe

to the Jews and Christians. At first, to be sure, the ritual bond applied only to those gods who were closer to the Arabs than Allah, the great god of the worlds, but on the eve of Islamic times this cult no longer filled, as it did among primitive men, the entire religious consciousness of the Arabs. The more the significance of the cult declined, the greater became the value of a general religious temper associated with Allah.[14]

Yet pre-Islamic Arabia contained many Jews and Christians, and their influence was felt upon Arabian religion. There is no special difficulty in accounting for the presence of Christians by the sixth century. It is even easily explained why these Christians, far removed by their ancestors' choice from the reprovingly orthodox influences of the two Romes, tended to be Nestorians and Monophysites mainly — in a word, heretics. It is more difficult to explain why the number of Christian communities was not larger than it was. The foremost among them was Najran, under the Nestorian influence of the king of Hira.[15]

There were also Jewish trading settlements at Teima, Khaybar, Medina, and again farther to the south. They are occasionally mentioned in rabbinical literature, and may have dated back to the seventh century B.C.[16] . . . There is evidence, too, of a considerable number of Jewish proselytes among the Arabs. They do not seem

---

[13] See Johann Fück, "Die Originalität des arabischen Propheten," *Zeitschrift der deutschen morgenländischen Gesellschaft*, Neue Folge XV (1936), 509–525; Julian Obermann, "Islamic Origins: A Study in Background and Foundation," *The Arab Heritage*, edited by Nabih A. Faris (Princeton: Princeton University Press, 1946), pp. 58–120.

[14] Brockelmann, *op. cit.*, pp. 8–9.
[15] See Guillaume, *The Life of Muhammad*, pp. 14–16.
[16] See Torrey, *op. cit.*, pp. 10–15, 26–27.

to have had, however, any higher Jewish learning; it has been suggested that even the "city Jews" were affected by some forms of heterodox Jewish thought in which both Christian and heathen notions had been incorporated.[17]

What did the presence of Jews and Christians mean to the young "messenger to the Arabs," who, by his own admission, had been an idol worshiper? It is difficult to sift the Koran or the tradition literature for exact information; we are faced, moreover, with various stages in the development of Mohammed's attitudes. It is highly probable that as a boy and young man he knew, and was on friendly terms with, both Jews and Christians. He is said to have heard the bishop of Najran preach, and to have met on a caravan a monk "well versed in the knowledge of the Christians."[18] Material soon to be published in full by Guillaume points to an early impression left on Mohammed by some Coptic Christian wall paintings in the Kaaba itself. The first encouragement Mohammed received after his prophetic call, if we except that of his wife, came from her cousin Waraqa, "who had become a Christian and read the scriptures and learned from those that follow the Torah and the Gospel."[19] He was also familiar with various classes of Jewish Scholars, whom

he could name accurately, and there is reason to believe that many Jews, expecting the imminent advent of a messiah in Arabia, showed a special interest in him.[20] Apparently, he was also somehow connected with a mysterious group, called *Hunafa,* "the pure ones," who, repelled by the evil of idol worship, favored a monotheism tending neither to Judaism nor to Christianity.[21] . . .

In the early Meccan period Mohammed liked to appeal, though somewhat vaguely, to Jewish and Christian authority for his teachings on the unity of God and on judgment: "All this is written in earlier scriptures; the scriptures of Abraham and Moses."[22] The only way in which he then admitted differing from the ancient Scriptures was that his teachings were in Arabic. "Before it (the Koran) the Book of Moses was revealed, a guide and a blessing to all men. This book confirms it. It is revealed in the Arabic tongue."[23] It is my conviction that the late Meccan and early Medinan periods saw the greatest readiness to ab-

---

[17] See Margoliouth, *op. cit.,* pp. 57–83. An opposing view is held by Torrey, *op. cit.,* pp. 23–25. Goitein, *op. cit.,* pp. 46–61, suggests that there was a Karaite group among those Jews.

[18] Guillaume, *The Life of Muhammad,* pp. 79–81.

[19] *Ibid.,* p. 107.

[20] See *ibid.,* pp. 93–94.

[21] See the *Koran,* 2,135, p. 335; 3,67, p. 400; 3,95, p. 402; 4,125, p. 367; 6,79, p. 418; 6,161, p. 427; 10,105, p. 71; 16,120,123, p. 303; 22,31, p. 391; 30,30, p. 190; 98,5, p. 29. See also Richard Bell, "Who were the Hanifs?" *The Moslem World,* XX (1930), 120–124; Nabih A. Faris and Harold W. Glidden, "The Development of the Meaning of the Koranic *Hanif," Journal of the Palestinian Oriental Society,* XIX (1939), 1–13. W. Montgomery Watt, *Muhammad at Mecca* (Oxford: Clarendon, 1953), pp. 162–164, points out that three of the four most famous *Hunafa* mentioned in the traditions eventually became Christians.

[22] 87,18, p. 32.

[23] 46,12, p. 125.

sorb Jewish elements into Islam, for at that time Mohammed's special aim was to win Jewish converts, especially among the influential Jews of Medina.

For a time, then, he went out of his way to model Islam on the Scriptures, but later he took a sharply different attitude; it stemmed, one suspects, from the unwillingness of Jews and Christians to accept his teaching, at least in large numbers. The koranic chapters of that time clearly show Mohammed's wish to disassociate Islam from both Jewish and Christian orthodoxy and to establish the supremacy of his religion by vigorous disputation and the use of force. Incidents such as are recorded in the *Sirah,* a semi-official biography, speak volumes:

> When the Christians of Najran came to the apostle [Mohammed] the Jewish rabbis came also and they disputed one with the other before the apostle. Rafi said, "You have no standing," and he denied Jesus and the Gospel; and a Christian said to the Jews, "You have no standing," and he denied that Moses was a prophet and denied the Torah (*sic!*). So God sent down [the following verse from the Koran] concerning them: "The Jews say the Christians have no standing; and the Christians say that Jews have no standing, yet they read the scriptures. They do not know what they are talking about."[24] . . .

Unsuccessful in his attempt to convince these "Scripture folk," Moham-med began to attack them intellectually and physically. Only the Jews offered organized opposition; moreover, in the beginning they seem to have provided a goodly number of false disciples.[25] But they were incapable of long and effective resistance to the growing Moslem power and within a few years Khaybar and the other Jewish colonies in North Arabia had been brutally vanquished.

My sketch of Jewish and Christian elements in Isalm must perforce be brief and the identifications tentative, for Julian Obermann has rightly said: "What with the vast overlapping of Jewish and Christian lore, especially in the period and area involved (the general impression of greater Jewish influence) may be illusory or at least inexact, unless it is borne out by detailed evidence for each element under discussion. Obviously, Old Testament and even rabbinical materials might have been transmitted to Arabia by Christian channels, since Christianity had been steadily and successfully proselytizing among the Jews. Seemingly, New Testament material might easily have been derived from rabbinical homilies, which had been including such material, largely but not exclusively for polemical purposes, for many centuries. Indeed, the situation is of a kind that in a considerable number of instances we can go only as far as to demonstrate a given element in Islam as of Judaeo-Christian origin, but not further."[26]

Mohammed's monotheism began, no doubt, as a rejection of paganism; still,

---

[24] Guillaume, *The Life of Muhammad,* p. 258. (Cf. *Koran,* 2,113, p. 333.)

[25] See *ibid.,* pp. 246–270.

[26] Oberman, *op. cit.,* pp. 59–60.

it was not vague. It was, as he never ceased to repeat, the monotheism of Israel. He probably never heard an authentic exposition of the mystery of the triune God, for in his mind the Trinity seems to have included the Virgin Mary and to have made Christ both Son and Spirit. He denied the incarnation: "Allah is One, the Eternal God. He begot none, nor was he begotten."[27] There was for him no redeemer, no need for redemption, no original sin.[28] Although there is only one indisputable quotation from the Bible in the Koran,[29] scores of Old Testament stories are repeated, in the main accurately, with many reminiscences of their Hebrew wording.

There are, however, a few discrepancies.[30] Despite the honor in which Abraham is held, the predominant figure in the Koran is Moses. If one follows Theodor Nöldeke's chronology of the chapters, which all told is probably still the best, he is mentioned more than one hundred times in the Meccan period alone. . . . About twenty Hebrew prophets are mentioned, but not Isaiah, Jeremiah, Ezekiel, or any of the minor prophets except Jonah.[31] . . .

Christ, by contrast, is mentioned in only two chapters of the Meccan period, and references to him in the whole Koran are sparse. His most important utterances are never men-

---

[27] 112,3, p. 257.

[28] It is therefore surprising to find often repeated, even by so eminent an authority as Gibb, op. cit., p. 45, that Moslems believe in the Immaculate Conception of the Virgin Mary. There is only one passage in the Koran (3,37, p. 398) and a hadith rated as "most reliable" by both Al-Bukhari and Muslim which refer to the Virgin Mary, as well as to Christ, as being (uniquely, in the case of the hadith) exempted at their births from any association with Satan. Although it seems very likely that these passages represent a direct borrowing from Christian doctrine, they nevertheless did not serve as the basis for any dogma of original sin or of the Immaculate Conception in Islamic theology, since the koranic treatment of Adam would have contradicted such dogmas. As J. Windrow Sweetman says in Islam and Christian Theology (London: Lutterworth, 1947), Vol. II, Part I, p. 186: "The usual explanation of the story of the temptation of Adam (in the Koran 2,33–37, p. 326, and 7,18–24, pp. 240–241) is that Adam really did not wilfully sin, but was deceived by Satan and was immediately pardoned. Thus there can be no thought that Adam's fault involved his descendants. . . . Man was created weak (cf. Koran 4,32, p. 358) rather than sinful in the Muslim conception."

[29] That of Ps 37:29 in 21,105, p. 294.

[30] Thus Joseph's well apparently had water in it (12,19, p. 39; cf. Gen 37:24); Joseph's father and mother went down to Egypt to be reunited to him (12,100, p. 46; cf. Gen 46:1–27; Rachel's death is mentioned in 35:19); Haman was Pharaoh's vizier (28,5, p. 74; 40,38, p. 161; cf. Est 3–9); Pharaoh's wife brought up Moses (28,8, p. 74; cf. Ex 2:10); and Moses married one of Jethro's two daughters (28,23,27, pp. 75–76; cf. Ex 2:21; 2:16 mentions seven daughters). There is apparently some confusion about Jacob; Saul and Gideon are confused (2,248–252, pp. 348–349), and the Virgin Mary is sometimes thought to have been confused with Mary, the sister of Moses and Aaron, on the basis of the vocative "Sister of Aaron" in 19,28, p. 33, although Moslem commentators have taken this merely as establishing Mary's blood relationship to the high-priestly family.

[31] I say "about" twenty because there are some problems concerning the precise identification of one or two; in addition, four "Arab" prophets are mentioned. There is no cogent intentional reason I have ever seen advanced why the omitted prophets were in fact omitted; my guess is that Mohammed simply had no acquaintance with them, which may itself tell us more about the Arabian Jewish community and its canon; see Torrey, op. cit.

tioned, and those that are mentioned frequently deviate from the text of the New Testament. To the end, Mohammed regarded the Gospel — in the singular — as a book revealed *to* Christ.[32] Some of the stories, such as Christ's speaking in the cradle[33] and making a live bird out of clay,[34] echo apocryphal writings such as the Protoevangel of James the Less, the Gospels of Thomas the Israelite and of Nicodemus, and especially the so-called "Infancy Gospels," all of which are known to have existed in Coptic, Syriac, and even Arabic. There also seem to be a few specifically Nestorian influences.[35] That Christ was not crucified was a belief common among some Gnostics; the same notion is found in the Koran: "[The Jews] declared: 'We have put to death the Messiah Jesus the son of Mary, the apostle of Allah.' They did not kill him, nor did they crucify him, but they thought they did."[36] From what is missing in the Koran, Charles Torrey argues that much of Mohammed's information about Christ must have come from Jewish informants.[37]

Contrary to orthodox Moslem belief, Mohammed did have knowledge of the biblical narratives before his call to prophethood, and that knowledge was, no doubt, secondhand. Probably he had heard improvised translations of the Jewish scriptures by learned men, and of the Christian by unlearned ones. It is quite possible that information concerning one group may have come from the other, and more than possible that wherever scripture is misrepresented or distorted, Mohammed followed homiletical embellishments by Jews or Christians.[38]

In the realm of religious legislation, the Jewish influence seems clearly to predominate. Like Judaism, Islam is a religion not only of a book, but also of a law minutely regulating day-to-day living of its believers.

> Law is thought of, not as a product of human intelligence and adaptation to changing social needs and ideals, but of divine inspiration and hence immutable, . . . the practical aspect of the religious and social doctrine preached by Mohammed.[39]

Both the Islamic profession of faith, the *shahadah*: "There is no god but Allah, and Mohammed is Allah's messenger," and Chapter 112 of the Koran: "Say: Allah is One"[40] bear a resemblance to the Jewish *shema*, and may have been modeled after it.[41]

---

[32] See Giuseppe Gabrieli, "Gesù Cristo nel Qorano," *Bessarione*, IX (1901), 32–60; James Robson, *Christ in Islam* (London: John Murray, 1929), and Charles J. Ledit, *Mahomet, Israel, et le Christ* (Paris: La Colombe, 1956).

[33] 19,30–34, p. 34; 5,109, p. 386.

[34] 3,43, p. 399; 5,110, p. 386.

[35] Several are discussed by Thomas O'Shaughnessy, *The Koranic Concept of the Word of God* (Rome: Pontificium Institutum Orientalium Studiorum, 1956).

[36] 4,156, p. 370.

[37] See Torrey, *op. cit.*, pp. 80–81.

[38] See Obermann, *op. cit.*, p. 94; and D. Masson, *Le Coran et la révélation Judéo-Chrétienne*, 2 vols. (Paris: Adrien-Maisonneuve, 1958).

[39] Gibb, *op. cit.*, p. 73.

[40] P. 257.

[41] See Torrey, *op. cit.*, pp. 133–134.

3. A. S. Tritton[1] **looks at three problems of Muslim theology, the problem of predestination and free will, the created or uncreated nature of the Koran, and the divine attributes. Then he studies the Mu'tazila, the men of unity and justice, whose task was to defend the unity and providence of God against all encroachment.**

Beginnings of Theology. Three questions came to the front, as it seems, about the same time. The relation between God's omnipotence and men's life or the problem of predestination and free will; the nature of the Koran, whether it was created or not; and the question of the divine attributes.

Those who took the side of free will were called *kadariya*.[2] . . . Was it Christian influence which started the discussion of the problem? Probably it arose inside Islam for very little study of the Koran would bring into prominence the conflicting statements contained in it on this point. Contact with Christians probably hastened developments. There are indications that the discussion began in Syria. . . . Of Syria . . . it is said, "We attacked this land and met those who say that there is no providence."[3] All agree that Ma'bad al-Juhani was a *kadari* and,

though he lived in Basra, it may have been in Damascus that he was executed in 80/699.[4] . . . A letter of Marwan II is preserved in which he says, "I will gird up my loins against the *kadaris* and smite them with my sword."[5] It was quite natural that the government should support the doctrine of predestination; all that is, including the state, has the favor of God. . . .

The doctrine of an uncreated Koran is strange and seems an intrusion on the unity of God, yet it arose at an early date. John of Damascus noted that it was heresy to say that the Koran was created.[6] A tombstone from Mosul, perhaps of 200 A.H., declares that the Koran is the word of God, revealed not created.[7] It may be that the explanation is to be sought in the tendency which puts the law beside or above the lawgiver. The Greeks had the Fates and the Babylonians the tablets of fate. Among those who came in contact with the Muslims, the Jews believed that the Law had been created before the world. On another side the Christians taught that the Logos existed eternally in God. . . . In the meaning of word, the Logos may well have provoked the doctrine of the uncreated Koran. . . .

---

[1] A. S. Tritton, M.A., D.Litt., was born in 1881 and Professor Emeritus of Arabic since 1947. Among his published works are *Islam, Beliefs and Practices,* and *Rise of the Imams of Sanaa.* This excerpt is from his book, *Muslim Theology,* published for the Royal Asiatic Society (London: Luzac & Co., Ltd., 1947), pp. 54–57, 79–82.

[2] The name is taken from *kadar* "arrangement" and then "providence." The movement was so called because it raised the question of the extent of God's government, just as the early *Khawarij* were called *Muhakkima,* those who questioned the rightness of the arbitration.

[3] Subki, 1,50; also *Mudawwana,* 1,407.

[4] Abu'l-Mahasin, 1,222.

[5] Tabari II, 1851.

[6] Migne, 96, 1341.

[7] *Repertoire Chron. d'Epigraphie,* 1, 95.

One source of the doctrine of the divine attributes may be the usage of the Koran, which joins to the mention of God such epithets as wise, powerful. This in its turn may go back to the custom of poetry. The Christians had elaborated a system of attributes. As the idea of God is much the same in both religions, it is not surprising that the lists of attributes largely agree; still, it is natural to suppose that the earlier influenced the latter. John of Damascus teaches that they belong to God by nature and are not taken from elsewhere, anticipating the Muslim doctrine that they are not other than God.[8]

John of Damascus gives a list of the divine attributes and, with one or two exceptions, they have Muslim equivalents. The following list might have been taken from John or from Muslim divines: — Uncreated, immortal, eternal, without beginning, boundless, immaterial, creator, not liable to feeling, not confined by space, without bounds, without limits, unseen, incomprehensible, self-sufficient, lord, supreme, infinite in power, generous, endless, changeless, preceeding phenomena, simple, uncompounded, without body, giver of life, all powerful.[9]

Mu'tazila. . . . The true Mu'tazila . . . called themselves the men of unity and justice. In their eyes their task was to defend the unity of God against all encroachment and to show that no shadow of evil fell on his providence. Assent to five propositions made the Mu'tazila: that God is one, is righteous, rewards good and

punishes evil, that sinful Muslims are corrupt, and that men must uphold right and resist evil.[10] They could not tolerate the semi-independent attributes of popular theology so they are called the strippers (*mu'attila*), those who deprived God of his attributes. They affirmed that God was alive, wise, powerful, etc.; they denied that these qualities had a separate existence of their own.[11] They inclined to describe God by negatives. . . . We must not imagine any secret thought, any motion of satisfaction or anger, or rest in God.[12] . . . In God, who is perfect, knowledge passes at once into act without the help of any other quality. . . . Later they divided the attributes into two classes, those of essence and those of action, or those belonging to himself and those involved in his activities. They could not decide in which class to put generosity. The attributes of action were originated, phenomenal.

They were rationalists insofar as they held that God was amenable to reason; so the essential facts about him are known by reason without revelation. There is a natural religion, the worship of the one just Creator whom all intelligent men must know. Further, God's acts must have a cause; he created men that they might worship him. . . . Revelation supported reason and went beyond it. A man who, by the fact of his being a man, was bound to worship God, was not responsible for knowing the laws of

---

[8] Migne, 94, 860.
[9] Migne, 94, 792.

[10] *Intisar*, 126; *Muruj al-Dhahab*, 6,20 f.
[11] God has no quiddity.
[12] Guidi, *La Lotta tra l'Islam e il Manicheismo*, 38.

Islam if he had never heard of the prophet. Some said that the punishment of sinners in hell was known by reason while the eternity of punishment was known by revelation. . . .

As God is righteous, he cannot be the author of evil, so it must be the work of men or devils who are both responsible for their acts. God has given them power to use as they like and they are answerable for it. . . . Some held that this is the best of all possible worlds and saved the divine omnipotence by asserting that God could repeat this best forever. Some

taught that any infidel would be converted if God turned on him the full force of His grace. . . . A man might know about God by hearsay, by the report of parents or teachers, and some held that such knowledge was no better than unbelief. Faith was usually defined as a knowledge of the divine commands and the amount of disobedience, which would make up wickedness, was carefully calculated. Some held that a detailed knowledge of all God's commands was essential while others were content with an outline acquaintance with the chief.

4. A. J. Wensinck[1] studies the Muslim theology of God and the world. The movement of the Kadarites was followed immediately by that of the Mu'tazilites, for the discussions of predestination and free will could not fail to call forth the question of the justice of God, and the latter must necessarily lead to that of his essence and qualities. Though Mu'tazilism was rejected, it tinged Islam with rationalism.

The movement of the Kadarites was followed immediately by that of the Mu'tazilites, for the discussion of predestination and free will could not fail to call forth the question of the justice of God, and the latter must necessarily lead to that of his essence and qualities.

The period in which these questions were debated covers the second and third centuries A.H. This period is that of the dogmatic crisis of Islam. There were moments, especially in the first part of the third century, when it might have seemed that Islam, from the stern, uncompromising

religion which manifests itself in Koran and Tradition, would take a turn toward the mild, ethical attitude of post-Augustine Christianity, as well as toward the rationalistic tendencies that lingered in the air as a legacy from antiquity. It was without doubt a momentous period in the life of Islam. Nor did it pass without leaving enduring traces. Though Mu'tazilism was rejected, it tinged Islam with rationalism. . . . Had not mysticism in course of time acquired a place in official Islam, chiefly through the influence of al-Ghazali, the Muslim religion would have become a lifeless form.

The answer given in Tradition to the question of predestination did not go beyond the emphatic statement that

[1] A. J. Wensinck, is the author of *La pensee de Ghazzali*. This excerpt is from his book, *The Muslim Creed* (New York: Barnes & Noble, Inc., 1965), pp. 58–70, 83–101.

everything that happens, human acts inclusive, is the product of the divine decree that had settled all things before the creation of the world. This answer gave rise to an objection which could not easily be parried. If all human acts are the product of the divine decree, how is it that man is punished for them? . . .

The Mu'tazilites took over the view of the Kadarites, that man is the author of his acts, a view which originated in the tendency to safeguard the ethical nature not of man, but of God . . . The importance attached to grave sins, the denial of Allah's authorship of human acts, and the emphasis laid on man's will as the cause of sin, resulted in man being punished severely for his evil deeds. The Mu'tazilite view regarding the retribution of sin is consequently very severe as compared with that of orthodox Islam, which made an extensive use of the idea of intercession on behalf of sinners, to such an extent that it was held that everyone in whose heart an atom of faith had subsisted would be brought back from Hell.[2] With an eye to the Mu'tazilites, who denied this doctrine, it is declared that Muhammed's intercession will be valid even on behalf of those who had committed grave sins.[3] . . . The Mu'tazilites taught that anyone who had entered hell could not be delivered from it.[4] . . .

We now turn to the second principle of the Mu'tazilites, the unity of Allah. The discussions of this principle include the whole doctrine of God. It may be that they started from the question whether Allah will be seen by the faithful in Paradise. . . . al-Nawawi opens his comment upon these traditions with the following passage: "The position of all the people of the *sunna* is that seeing Allah is possible and not absurd,[5] further that this will happen in the next world and that only the faithful, not the infidels, will see him. Some of the schismatics, namely, the Mu'tazilites, the Kharidjites and some of the Murdjites, maintain that Allah will not be seen by any of his creatures and that this would be absurd. . . . As to the question of seeing Allah in this world, we have already said that this is possible; yet the large majority of the ancient and later *mutakallimun* and others maintain that the vision of Allah will not happen in this world". . . .

The Koran is full of descriptions of heaven and hell, which are not used in a metaphorical sense. To heaven belongs the throne of Allah, he is the Lord of the throne,[6] the noble, large, exalted throne,[7] which is borne by the angels.[8] "But those who shall have feared their Lord shall be driven on in crowds to Paradise until they reach it, and its gates shall be opened, and its keepers shall say to them, Peace be on you! . . . And thou shalt see the angels circling around the throne,

---

[2] Muslim, *Iman*, trad. 148.
[3] F. Tirmidhi, *Kiyama*, p.11. The tradition is not in the *Sahih's*.
[4] al-Baghadi, *Fark*, p. 99; *Encyclopaedia of Islam*, art. "Shafa," at the end; Ibn Hazm, *Kitab al-Fisal*, iv, 63 ff.

[5] On the opposition "possible," "absurd," cf. *Fikh Akbar* II, art. 16 and commentary.
[6] *Sura* 17,44; 40,15; 43,82; 81,20.
[7] *Sura* 23,117; 9,130; 85,15.
[8] *Sura* 40,7; 49,17.

uttering the praises of their Lord: And judgment shall be pronounced between them with equity: and it shall be said, Glory be to God the Lord of the worlds."[9] . . .

According to al-Ashari,[10] Hisham ibn al-Hakam[11] was of the opinion "that Allah has a body, defined, broad, high and long, of equal dimensions, radiating with light, of a fixed measure in its three dimensions in a place beyond place, like a bar of pure metal, shining as a round pearl on all sides, provided with colour, taste, smell and touch, so that its colour is its taste and its smell its touch, absolute colour which does not admit any other colour, and that it moves or is at rest, rises and sits down."

The Mu'tazilites held the opposite view and so were anxious to avoid anthropomorphic expressions. . . .

If, as a matter of fact, the discussions on God's essence started from the question of anthropomorphism, as we have supposed, it is only natural that they should follow this course throughout. The next point may well have been the idea of God's being infinite and exempt from the idea of place . . . [Here is] al-Ashari's description of the views of the Mu'tazilites on this point: "Some of them say that God is every place. Others say, the Creator is no place, but he is where he is dwelling from eternity. Others say the Creator is in every place, that is, he comprises all places

and his being is found in all places."[12] It will be seen later that orthodox Islam confessed God's being to be infinite and exempt from the limitations of time and place[13] . . .

The Crisis of Islam and its Outcome. The Mu'tazilite movement was a powerful one, which succeeded for a time in gaining a hold upon the higher circles in matters temporal and spiritual. . . . The second and third centuries witnessed a heroic war with rationalism, which proclaimed itself the highest principle in theology. The victory was won by orthodox Islam, which finally took possession of the dogmatic fortresses of the enemy. Yet it could not refrain from making use of the weapons which it found there. So there developed a likeness between the orthodox and their opponents, which to many seemed to be of more than a superficial kind. . . .

In the long run, however, logic could not but influence philosophy and theology. It was just the discrepancy between this new element and the genuine conception of Islam that was to bring about a new crisis in Muslim theology in the teachings of al-Ghazali. In ethical mysticism, that is, in exchanging its former Aristotelianism for a Platonic tendency, he found his personal salvation. But al-Ghazali did not radically reject *kalam*,[14] and so Aristotelianism kept its place side by side with Platonism. . . .

---

[9] *Sura* 39,73,75.

[10] *Makalat,* i, 197; cf. p. 146.

[11] Cf. Arnold, *al-Mu'tazilah,* pp. 26, 31, 32.

[12] *Makalat,* i. 202.

[13] Ali-al-Kari, p. 35.

[14] The scholastic method in Arabic is called *kalam.* It was the spirit of Aristotle to which Christianity and Islam paid homage by accepting his logical method and distinctions and by raising them to the rank

To him is ascribed the final triumph of the Ash'arite system in the East. We are fortunate in possessing much authentic material regarding his position. One of the most brilliant scholars of the Islamic world in the second half of the eleventh century A.D., he had written books that were to become standard works in two fields, those of *fikh* and *kalam*, with their collateral theological and philosophical branches. Among his works of *kalam* may be mentioned the *Iktisad fi'l-I'tikad*, which has been trans-

---

of their official philosophy and the foundation of their dogmatics.

Regarding the origin and literal meaning of this term several opinions have been expressed (cf. Macdonald, art. "Kalam" in the *Encyclopaedia of Islam*). It will be sufficient to remind the reader of two facts.

The first is the temporal coincidence of the rise of scholasticism with the debates on the *kalam Allah*, the speech or word of God, an expression which is used or implied in the passages of the Kuran (*Sura*, vii, 139 etc.), in which God is represented to have spoken with Moses. This coincidence has inevitably caused some confusion in the discussions on the origin of *kalam* in the sense of scholasticism. It must therefore be borne in mind that the coincidence is merely fortuitous and of no value whatever for the question with which we are concerned at the moment.

The second is this, that *kalam* in the sense of scholasticism has nothing to do with the Greek *logos* or any of its derivations, but was prepared by the development of Arabic terminology. *Kalam* is, in the first place, speech, and *takallama* speaking. These terms have the cognate meaning of discussion and disputation (cf. Muslim, *Aiman*, trad. 38) . . . The *mutakallimun* were thus characterized, not as theologians, but as rationalists and philosophers, and the fact that *kalam* in the course of time received the meaning of dogmatic theology is an indication of the rationalistic direction which Muslim theology has gradually taken . . . The Mu'tazilites . . . introduced rationalism and the system of *kalam* into Islam.

lated into Spanish by Asin Palacios. . . . The *Iktisad* is a regular treatise on dogmatics, preceded by four prefaces on the use and methods of *kalam*.

The first chapter deals with the essense of Allah, his existence, his eternity, his being neither substance nor *accidens*, his being infinite, not subject to any modality; with the possibility of his being attained to by sight, as he is attained to by knowledge; with his being one.

The second chapter deals with the qualities of Allah, his living, knowing, being powerful, willing, hearing, seeing, speaking; his possessing life, knowledge, power, will, hearing, sight, and speech; with the nature of these qualities and their mutual relation; with their being additional to his essence, yet eternal, essentially connected with his essence; with the false opinion of those who say that they have been originated.

The third chapter deals with the acts of Allah. In seven propositions it is shown that there does not rest on him any obligation to give laws, to create, to give reward, to take into account what is salutary for his servants; that it is not absurd that he should command them to do what is above their power; that he is not obliged to punish sin; that it is not absurd that he should send Prophets. This chapter is preceded by a preface on the ideas of necessary good and evil. The fourth chapter deals with the Apostles and with the traditions on the last things, on the headship of the community, on heresies and their criterion.

The *Iktisad* is a work of al-Ghazali, the intellectualist, who treated dogmatics with a skill which may have corresponded to the depth of his conviction. . . . At any rate, in the thirty-seventh year of his life he passed through an intellectual and religious crisis, in which the edifice of his spiritual existence crumbled down to its very foundations. They were never built up again, but replaced by a "religion of the heart" of a mystic character. When the crisis was passed, he gradually recovered the faculty of estimating the relative importance of *fikh* and *kalam*.[15] . . .

al-Ghazali next expounds his views on the exoteric and the esoteric side of religion. . . . "One of the parties, trying to follow a middle way, opens the door of allegorical interpretation regarding all that is related to the qualities of Allah; whereas they take in the literal sense the descriptions of the last things . . . these are the Ash'-

arites. The Mu'tazilites go farther. They explain away Allah's being seen, and his being possessed of hearing and sight; Muhammad's ascension, which they deny to have taken place in a bodily way; the punishment in the tomb, the balance, the bridge and other eschatological representations.[16] Yet they confess the resurrection of the body, Paradise and its sensual pleasures, hell and its bodily torments. The philosophers go farther than the Mu'tazilites. They interpret all eschatological representations as allegories denoting mental and spiritual pain, and mental and spiritual delight. They deny the resurrection of the body, but say that the soul is immortal and that it will be punished or made happy by punishments and delight of a non-sensual nature. They are extremists. The true middle path between a complete allegorism and rigid Hanbalism is narrow and obscure. It is found only by those who enjoy divine help and who reach the heart of things by divine light, not by hearsay. Then when the mysteries of things are revealed to them, so that they see them as they are, they return to Scripture and Tradition and their wording; whatever accords with what they have witnessed by the light of certainty they affirm and whatever does not accord with it they interpret allegorically." . . .

[15] The use of *fikh* (cf. Sachau, *Zur ältesten Geschichte*) in the original sense of "insight" became antiquated when the word acquired the technical sense of "jurisprudence." *Fikh* in the sense of "insight" does not occur in the Kuran, but frequently in Tradition. . . . In a well-known tradition the term is applied to religious matters. . . . In another tradition *fikh* is mentioned side by side with faith.

It is a remarkable fact that *fikh* in the technical sense of jurisprudence hardly occurs in canonical Tradition. . . . Apparently the application of the term *fikh* to jurisprudence had not yet acquired general currency in the first century A.H.

[16] Cf. Wasiyat Abi Hanifa, art. 18 ff.

VI

GOD FROM AUGUSTINE TO AQUINAS

1. A. C. McGiffert[1] studies God in Eriugena, Anselm of Canterbury and Abelard. Eriugena's system surpassed in orginality and profundity anything produced in the western church for many a century. Anselm was important particularly for his theological method and his confidence in the rationality and demonstrability of Christian truth. For generations to come Christian thinkers were affected both by Abelard's achievements and by his failures.

John Scotus Eriugena. During the century and a half succeeding the death of Gregory the Great there was

comparatively little theological activity in the Western Church. Theology shared, however, in the intellectual renaissance and in the awakened interest in the antique, which marked the Carolingian period, and in the centuries following there was considerable theological discussion and a

---

[1] Arthur Cushman McGiffert, is the author of *Protestant Thought Before Kant* and *Rise of Modern Religious Ideas.* This excerpt is from his book, *A History of Christian Thought* (New York: Charles Scribner's Sons, 1954), pp. 168–221.

good deal of heated controversy. Even now, to be sure, there was not much original or creative thinking; theologians were almost exclusively engaged in appropriating the heritage of the past and adapting it to the needs of the new age.

But one man stood out from his contemporaries as a speculative genius of the first rank. In the entire history of Christian thought there are few more striking figures than John Scotus Eriugena. . . . Born in Ireland early in the ninth century, he made his way to France where he enjoyed the friendship of Charles the Bald and became the most famous scholar and teacher of the day. . . . His knowledge of Greek and his acquaintance with Greek philosophy and with certain eastern Fathers not well-known in the West gave him a great advantage over the scholars of the continent. It is not surprising that his restless and brilliant intellect, working with materials largely unfamiliar to his contemporaries, should lead him to opinions out of line with theirs and should create the impression that he was an exceedingly dangerous teacher. The fact is, he was a bold and venturesome thinker, and while he recognized the authority of the Scriptures and the Fathers, he put reason first and insisted that it must be followed at all costs. Though authority is earlier in time than reason, the latter is by nature older than the former and superior to it. . . . Authority must have the support of reason.[2] The Fathers found truth by the use of reason and we must find it in the same way. To

follow reason, however, does not mean to break with authority, since both come from God and cannot contradict each other.[3] . . .

Eriugena was primarily a philosopher and as such he is dealt with in most histories of philosophy. But in his hands philosophy and theology were one, and the historian of Christian thought can ill afford to neglect him. At the beginning of his work on predestination he declares that philosophy and religion are identical.[4] . . .

Though Eriugena was largely influenced by earlier thinkers, his system of philosophy or theology — for it may be called either — was truly his own and surpassed in originality and profundity anything produced in the Western Church for many a century. . . . In his principal work *On the Division of Nature* (*De divisione naturae*) . . . the term Nature . . . includes both God and the universe, everything that can be thought about whether existent or non-existent.[5] . . .

Under the influence of Neoplatonism and particularly of Pseudo-Dionysius, Eriugena emphasized the transcendence and incomprehensibility of God.[6] God is above all being. He is wholly unknowable and can neither be perceived nor conceived. We can know that he is but not what he is. The affirmative theology which ascribes to God all perfections is symbolical only. When we declare that God is omnipotent, omniscient, and the like, we are only trying to say in figurative language that he is greater

---

[2] *De divisione naturae*, Bk. I, ch. 69.

[3] *Ibid.*, I. 66.

[4] *De praedestinatione*, ch. 1, no. 1.

[5] *De divisione naturae*, I (beginning).

[6] Cf. e.g., I.3 ff.; 66 ff.

than can be said or thought. The only true theology is the negative theology which denies that God is, not because he is below being but above; and which denies that he is powerful and wise and beneficent, not because he is less but more than all these, so much more that none of them can be truly said of him.[7] . . .

Though influenced largely by Dionysius, he was not a mystic and was not concerned with the practical question of how men may be brought into oneness with God. While he gave his conditional approval to the negative theology, he apparently cared nothing about the *via negativa,* by which alone, according to Dionysius, men may reach mystical union with the divine. . . . Eriugena's interest . . . lay elsewhere. Not the transcendence but the immanence of God was his fundamental postulate, immanence amounting to genuine pantheism.[8] The divine nature embraces everything; apart from God or outside of him there is nothing. He is Being unlimited and undifferentiated; the world is Being circumscribed and divided.[9] When we say that God created everything, we mean that he is in everything as its essence, the common substance of all that is.[10] He cannot be seen in himself but only in the things that he inhabits.[11] Spirits and bodies, all things that exist are but manifestations of

him; each is a genuine theophany.[12] And not only is God in everything, he is identical with all that is, for God and the creature are not two but one and the same.[13]

Language could not well go further than this. But though Eriugena asserted unequivocally that God is in all and is the essence of all and that he and the creature are one and the same, he yet declared that God is at the same time above all, as man is above as well as in the world of things.[14] Eriugena's pantheism was therefore not thoroughgoing. In spite of his strong statements, he did not identify God and the world completely and without qualification. But it was on the identity rather than the distinction that he laid stress and the pantheistic character of his system as a whole is abundantly evident. . . .

I have said that Eriugena's fundamental tenet was the immanence of God, or rather the oneness of God and the universe. But this is only half the story, for his philosophy was not simply pantheistic; it was also dynamic. With the idea of divine immanence he combined the idea of evolution. The universe is not static or at rest, it is continually developing. Out of God, the great All, all things come and back to him they all find their way. Everything, Eriugena says, tends naturally to return to its source and the universe which comes from God tends naturally to return to him. The process of evolution and involution in reality goes on within the divine

---

[7] I.14 ff.; 39.

[8] The very use of the term Nature in the title of his principal work to include God as well as the world is significant of his general attitude.

[9] I.12; III.17.

[10] I.72.

[11] I.10.

[12] III.4.

[13] III.17.

[14] E.g., III.20; IV.5.

nature itself, for God is all and the universe is but an expression or manifestation of him. In the unfolding of the divine essence the world comes into existence — a phenomenal universe in space and time — to return ultimately to the source whence it came.

In the evolutionary process there are no new or extraneous factors. In the cause all its effects are already present. God is the one and only source and all comes from him. When it is said that he created all things out of nothing, it is meant that he created all things out of himself,[15] the phrase *ex nihilo* being used to indicate not that which is below but that which is above being. The process of evolution is not a matter of choice with God. . . . Creation is a necessity and God could not have refrained from it if he would. His nature is such that it must unfold itself, must express itself in the world of ideas and in the world of space and time. It has within itself the potentiality which means the actuality of an endlessly developing universe.[16] We are dealing here, evidently, not with a static but with a dynamic pantheism, the pantheism of a Hegel rather than a Spinoza. . . .

In his work *On the Division of Nature*, Eriugena, with a sweep of imagination seldom equaled, set himself to expound the eternal process of evolution and involution, in which all being is embraced. At the beginning

of the work he divided nature, or the all, into four parts: first, that which creates and is not created, namely, God; second, that which is created and creates, namely, the world of ideas or primordial causes; third, that which is created and does not create, the phenomenal world in space and time; and fourth, that which is neither created nor creates, the return, that is, of all to God from whence all came. . . . Not that the all is made up of four parts, but that it passes through four stages, from the primeval oneness through the world of ideas and the world of things back again to the primeval oneness, or God, from unity through multiplicity back to unity. . . .

In the first book of *On the Division of Nature* Eriugena deals with God, the one who creates and is not created. . . . Goodness . . . is God's principal attribute from which all others flow. It was goodness that led him to create; in fact the whole process of evolution roots itself in the divine beneficence. "God is properly called love because he is the cause of all love . . . and brings to an end in himself the loves of every creature."[17] . . . That creation is due to the goodness of God does not make it any the less necessary; goodness is not a matter of will with God but of nature. . . .

The second stage of being, that which is created and creates, Eriugena, in agreement with Augustine and the Neoplatonists, identified with the world of ideas, or primordial causes. This contains the prototypes of all existing things, the forms according to which the actual world was

---

[15] Cf., III.19–23. This is in striking contrast with the position of Origen and many others who distinguished "made from the nature of God" (as Christ is) and "made out of nothing" (as the universe is).

[16] III.6.

[17] I.74.

made.[18] . . . The world of ideas, according to Eriugena, exists in the divine Son or Logos.[19] It is eternal as he is eternal and represents, as from another point of view he represents, the first stage in the unfolding of the Absolute. The connection of the world of ideas with the Logos shows the influence of Christian tradition. . . . He did not begin with the Logos, as many earlier thinkers had done, and find in philosophy a justification and application of the Logos doctrine; he began with philosophy and used the Logos only to give his philosophy Christian standing. . . .

The next stage in the process of the divine unfolding, or manifestation of God, was the creation of the sensible world including angels as well as men and things. It had its cause in the world of ideas and took its pattern therefrom, but it exists in space and time as the world of ideas does not. . . . Man is a microcosm of the whole creation both visible and invisible.[20] Not only was the world made for his sake that he might rule and control it, in a sense the whole world truly exists in him, for it is his idea of it that gives it reality as it is God's idea of him that gives man reality.[21]

Eriugena's system provided . . . not simply for the coming of all things from God but also for the return of all things to God. To this, the most difficult part of his task, he devoted the fifth and longest book of his great work. . . . The return will include the whole creation, not men and angels alone but brutes as well, and all things animate and inanimate. The process of evolution . . . was from higher to lower: first the eternal world of ideas, then the phenomenal world of space and time, and in the latter, first angels, then men, then animals, and so on down the scale. In the return to God, the process will be reversed. The lower creation will be absorbed in man and with him will ascend to the world of ideas . . . and this in turn with all that has come from it — space and time, matter and spirit, the visible and invisible — will make its way back to God, gathering up everything in him until he becomes finally all in all again as he was at the beginning.

In this grandiose vision Eriugena's religion came to expression as well as his philosophy. And his religion took the form of Christianity, for he found in Christ the one in and through whom the return is accomplished. Having by his incarnation become a part of the created universe, he prefigures and foreshadows by his resurrection the return to God not of some men alone but of the whole human race and of the entire universe as well.[22] From Eriugena's point of view the incarnation and the resurrection were the important matters; other events in Christ's career he had little interest in.[23] To have connected Christ, the incarnate and risen Word with the return of all things to God, as he had connected the eternal Word with the creation of the universe, seemed to him enough to guar-

---

[18] II.34.

[19] Cf., II.21; III.6 ff.; IV.7.

[20] II.3 ff.

[21] IV.7; cf. II.9.

[22] V.22,38.

[23] What he says about Christ's death in V.38 and elsewhere is wholly perfunctory.

antee the Christian character of his system. . . .

Eriugena's was the first great philosophical system of the Middle Ages and for some centuries there was no other to compare with it. Indeed for sweep of imagination and breadth of vision it has seldom been approached in ancient or modern times. . . . *On the Division of Nature* was . . . condemned . . . by Pope Honorius III.

Anselm. A thinker of an entirely different type was Anselm, Archbishop of Canterbury . . . who died at his post in 1109. . . .

As a theologian Anselm took his motto from Augustine of whose writings he was an eager student. Not "I know that I may believe," but "I believe that I may know."[24] He insisted that all Catholic doctrines are true because divinely revealed, and that the Christian must accept them on the authority of the Church, but he maintained that they are also rational, meaning thereby that they may be understood and may be proved true, without recourse to revelation, by the use of the reason alone. The theologian, therefore, has a double task, to explain and elucidate the truths of revelation for the sake of believers and to prove them true for the sake of unbelievers. In this connection it is interesting to note that Anselm made little use of the customary authorities in his theological works. As a matter of fact, most of his writings are singularly free from references to the Bible and the Fathers.

Anselm was an accomplished dialectician and insisted that a thorough training in logic was indispensable to the theologian. He was also something of a philosopher, but philosophy interested him not for its own sake but only for the sake of theology. . . . He was a genuine realist of the Platonic type and was convinced that unless a theologian recognized the reality of universals he could not be an orthodox believer. . . . His realism . . . appears clearly in his little dialogue *On Truth* in which he maintains that there are not many truths but only one, that truth is unchanging and eternal, that it has real existence, and that things are true only because they partake of it.[25]

His realism appears also in his work on the Trinity which was written against Roscellin, Abbot of Compiegne. "Those dialecticians, or rather dialectical heretics, of our time," he says, "who think that universal substances are nothing but words (*flatum vocis*), and are unable to distinguish color from bodies or the wisdom of man from his soul, should be wholly excluded from the discussion of spiritual questions. For in their souls reason which ought to be the ruler and judge of all that is in man is so involved in corporeal images that it is not able to escape from them or to discriminate between them and the things that should be contemplated by reason simply and alone. For how can he who does not yet understand that many men are in species one man

---

[24] "Neque enim quaero intelligere ut credam, sed credo ut intelligam." (*Proslogion*, ch. 1.) Augustine's words are "credimus ut cognoscamus."

[25] Cf. *De veritate*, 13, where Anselm summarizes his position.

comprehend how in that most lofty and mysterious nature a plurality of persons, each of whom singly is perfect God, are one God."[26] Anselm was entirely right in believing that the orthodox doctrine of the Trinity presupposed philosophical realism, and it was historically of great importance that he pointed this out so clearly. Otherwise, his brief treatise was of no special significance.

Roscellin's work on the Trinity is lost, but he was evidently a nominalist — one of those "heretical dialecticians" who maintained that individuals alone are real and universals nothing but words. Applying his nominalism to the doctrine of the Trinity, he claimed that the three persons (Father, Son, and Spirit) were real but that the common divine nature which they were supposed to share had no actual existence. Anselm consequently accused him of tritheism. "Either he wishes to confess three gods or he does not understand what he says. If he confesses three gods, he is not a Christian; if he says what he does not understand he is not to be trusted."[27] To be sure, according to Anselm, Roscellin taught that the three persons of the Trinity are one in will and purpose and equal in power, but they are not one in essence or substance. Indeed they could not be, for there is no such thing as divine essence or substance. In his emphasis on the threeness, in which he went so far as to liken the persons of the Trinity to three angels or three men, Roscellin resembled the Cappodocian

Fathers, but he differed with them radically in denying to the three persons a common divine nature.

Anselm was not a systematic theologian and did not attempt to cover the whole range of Christian doctrine. His theological writings, all of them short and concise, deal only with subjects that happened to interest him or were forced upon him by controversy. They are, however, by no means casual in character and content. Their author had evidently thought the Christian system through in the most thoroughgoing fashion and in all of them his fundamental principles clearly appear.

His earliest theological treatise, the *Monologium* or *Soliloquy*,[28] reveals the twofold purpose referred to above, the apologetic and the religious. In it, he undertook in the first place to demonstrate the existence of God on the basis of reason alone without appealing to authority. Since there are many goods of various kinds, it is necessary to believe that there is one supreme good through which they are all good. In the same way we are compelled to recognize that there is one being greater and higher than all others through whom they all exist. An infinite regress, Anselm claims, is unthinkable and we must therefore assume an original self-existent being to which all else is due. This is the familiar cosmological argument from contingent to necessary being, though phrased, it must be admitted, in somewhat awkward fashion. . . .

Having proved to his satisfaction the existence of God, Anslem devoted

---

[26] *De fide trinitatis*, 2.
[27] *Ibid.*, 3.

[28] *De divinitatis essentia monologium.*

the remainder of the work to a consideration of his nature, thus carrying out the second purpose of his treatise. The original, self-existent Being, through which all others exist and to which they owe such excellence and such greatness as they possess must be the greatest and best of all beings. "It is necessary that it be living, wise, powerful and all-powerful, true, just, blessed, eternal, and similarly whatever is better than all that is not it."29 . . . "It is supreme being, supreme life, supreme reason, supreme safety, supreme justice, supreme wisdom, supreme truth, supreme goodness, supreme greatness, supreme beauty, supreme immortality, supreme incorruptibility, supreme immutability, supreme blessedness, supreme eternity, supreme unity, which is nothing else than to be supremely, to live supremely and the like."30 . . .

The moderation of Anselm's statements in contrast with those of many other theologians is noticeable. Though his doctrine of God, in the *Monologium* at any rate, was more philosophical than religious, he did not indulge in the speculative flights, for instance, of an Eriugena. The truth is he had no such grandiose conception of the universe as Eriugena had. So far as he philosophized he did so within the limits of the traditional thinking of his day.

Having dealt with the nature of God, Anselm turns next to God's expression of himself, the divine Word through whom all things were created. An amusing example of his habit of

rationalizing accepted doctrines is his explanation of why it is fitting to speak of God and his Word as father and son rather than mother and daughter. The first and principal cause of offspring, he says, is in the father, and the son is always more like his father than the daughter is, "Hence, it is most true that the supreme spirit is father of his offspring" and "that his offspring is not a daughter but a son."31

The supreme Being loves himself, and this love Anselm identifies, in traditional fashion, with the Holy Spirit. Though he discusses the doctrine of the Trinity at some length and tries to rationalize the distinction of the three persons (or substances as he prefers to call them) by comparing them with human memory, intelligence, and love,32 he admits finally that the mystery is incomprehensible and that the most one can do is to accept the truth of the doctrine, which is beyond all question. . . .

After writing his *Monologium*, which Anselm says was made up of many arguments, he began to ask himself whether there might not be found a single proof of the existence of God which would require no other for its support.33 The result was his famous ontological argument, a contribution of his own, which he set forth in a treatise entitled *Proslogion* or *Ad-*

29 Ch. 15.
30 Ch. 16.

31 Ch. 42.
32 As Augustine had done before him. Cf. *De trinitate*, X.12 (19); XIV.8 (11); also IX.2 (2) and XV.6 (10).
33 As a matter of fact the *Monologium* contains only one general argument for God's existence though phrased in different forms.

dress.[34] The *Proslogion* is even briefer than the *Monologium* and the greater part of it is devotional rather than argumentative in character and takes the form of an address to God after the style of Augustine's *Confessions*. The argument is contained in the second chapter and runs as follows — to give Anselm's summary of it in his own words. "Even the fool is convinced that there is something, at any rate in the understanding, than which nothing greater can be conceived, for when he hears this, he understands it, and whatever is understood is in the understanding. And certainly that than which a greater cannot be conceived cannot exist in the understanding alone. For if it be in the understanding alone, it is possible to conceive it as existing in reality, which is greater. If, therefore, that than which a greater cannot be conceived is in the understanding alone, that very thing than which a greater cannot be conceived is one than which a greater can be conceived. But this assuredly cannot be. Without any doubt, therefore, there exists something both in the understanding and in reality than which a greater cannot be conceived."

Anselm's argument called forth a brief reply from a contemporary, the monk Gaunilo of Marmoutier, who took up the cudgels in behalf of "the fool who says in his heart there is no God." . . . Though Gaunilo's reply was acute and of a sort to throw suspicion on all argumentation from idea to reality, it did not touch the heart of Anselm's argument that to exist both in the understanding and in reality is greater than to exist in the understanding alone. It was not until Kant indeed that the unsoundness of this cardinal assumption was fully exposed.[35] But though no adequate answer was forthcoming for seven hundred years, the argument did not generally commend itself and was used by none of the great schoolmen of the Middle Ages. . . . The only other work of Anselm's that needs mention is his *Cur deus homo*, the most famous of all. In it, again with unbelievers in mind, he undertook to show the necessity of the incarnation by the use of reason alone without appealing to authority as he had undertaken in the *Monologium* and *Proslogion* to demonstrate the existence of God. The work, which is about the same length as the *Monologium*, . . . is repetitious and ill-arranged. . . . Anselm's general theory, however, is clear enough and may be summarized as follows.

Every rational creature is bound to obey God. If he always paid God what he owed him he would never sin. To sin is nothing else than to withhold from God his due. But this is to rob and dishonor him.[36] Justice (justice both to God himself and to the general order of things) demands either that God be repaid for the loss he has incurred or that the offender be punished. In either event his authority over the creature is maintained and thus his honor vindicated. But to

[34] *Proslogion seu alloquium de Dei existentia.*

[35] See my *Rise of Modern Religious Ideas*, pp. 55 ff.

[36] Bk. I, ch. 11. The argument begins with this chapter.

punish all men everlastingly — and justice demands that the punishment of the wicked be everlasting as the reward of the good is — would defeat the divine purpose in creation, for man was made to be eternally happy in the enjoyment of God. Consequently, for his own sake, quite apart from any consideration for the human race, God must save at least some men, enough at any rate to make up for the number of fallen angels. This he can do only if adequate satisfaction be given. Man cannot give it, since all men are sinners and one sinner cannot justify another. Indeed a man cannot even atone for his own sins, for all the self-denial and asceticism he may practice in the effort to do so he owes in any event to God who rightfully demands of him all that he has and is and can become.[37] Moreover, even the least of sins is greater than can be compensated for by the whole world or by an infinity of worlds. Only a being superior to all that is not God, only God himself in fact, is great enough to render satisfaction even for the smallest sin. But it is man that owes it, for he is the offender. Therefore only one who was both God and man, that is, Christ alone, could render the needed satisfaction and he could do it in no other way than by offering God something that he did not owe him and that God could not demand as his right. But God justly demands of every rational being complete obedience to his will. Christ, therefore, owed him obedience

on his own account and could not atone for others' sins even by a life of perfect holiness. One thing, however, he was under no obligation to do and that was to lay down his life, for as he was not a sinner, death had no claim upon him.[38] Consequently, by dying, he could make satisfaction for human sin and he could do it in no other way. As his life, the life of the God-man, was of infinite value, his death was sufficient to atone not for some sins merely but for the sins of all the world and even infinitely more. In order that his sacrifice of himself might be efficacious, it was necessary that he be not only sinless, and hence under no obligation to die, but also omnipotent and hence able not to die. In other words, he must die not under compulsion but of his own free will. As a reward for freely offering up his life, all are saved that accept him and are his. His death does not avail for the reconciliation of Satan and the fallen angels; they could be reconciled only by the death of a God-angel, not of a God-man.

Thus Anselm undertook to prove that the incarnation and death of the Son of God were necessary and grounded in the very nature of things. In this he went beyond all his predecessors. Some of his ideas were anticipated by others, but the notion that God must have saved man in this particular way and in no other was wholly new and was typical of Anselm's general attitude. His theory was

[37] I.20. This really undermines the assumption on which the whole theory of penance is based, but there is no sign that Anselm drew the application.

[38] Though Christ took on human nature he was not a sinner, for Mary was purified from sin before his birth (II.16). Cf. Anselm's *Liber de conceptu virginali et originali peccato*, ch. 8 ff.

important also among other things because it excluded the old notion shared
even by Augustine that Christ by his
death paid a price to the devil and
thus made it possible for God to re-
lease men from his control. Anselm
attacked the notion directly[39] and the
whole weight of his theory was against
it. . . .

Anselm was the first Western theologian to bring clearness out of obscurity and to frame a consistent and
coherent theory. The contrast with
the theory of Irenaeus which underlay
all Eastern thought upon the subject
is very striking. While with Irenaeus
the emphasis was on the incarnation,
with Anselm in spite of the title of
his work the emphasis was on the
death; and while Irenaeus thought
chiefly in physical and mystical terms,
the thinking of Anselm was control-
lingly ethical and legal.[40] The two
theories are genuinely typical, the one
of the Eastern, the other of the Western way of looking at things.

Abelard. "He that believes quickly
is light minded." These words from
Ecclesiasticus . . . were quoted by
Abelard in his so-called *Introduction
to Theology* and they admirably represent his general attitude. Born in
1079 at Le Pallet in Brittany, the
eldest son of a noble house, he early
turned his back on the career of a
feudal lord and gave himself to the
pursuit of learning. With a high regard for his own powers and a contempt for the abilities of others, he
combined a contentious temper which
kept him constantly at war. . . .

He was a pupil for a time of the
nominalist Roscellin . . . and later of
the famous realist William of Champeaux. . . . He broke with both of
them, however, and they were for
many years among his bitterest foes.
His own doctrine of universals — in
effect, a moderate Aristotelian realism
— is set out with sufficient clearness
in his *Glosses* on Porphyry,[41] the best
example of his dialectical method. He
repudiated William's realism, denying
that universals exist before particulars
and independently of them, but he
also rejected the extreme nominalism
of Roscellin who maintained that universals are mere words and devoid of
all reality. . . .

Abelard early set up for himself as
a teacher of philosophy, that is, particularly of dialectics or logic. In that
age logic . . . had the same standing
as the scientific method has now. . . .
Abelard's success as a teacher was immediate and extraordinary. . . . He
soon became the most celebrated
teacher and the most formidable dialectician of his generation and as his
fame grew William's steadily declined.
Ambitious to try his powers in what
was generally recognized as the high-

---

[39] Cf. I.7.

[40] In this connection attention may be
called to Anselm's statement (*De fide trinitatis,* 4) that in the incarnation man was
brought into union not with the divine
nature but with a divine person, the Son
of God. "For he who rightly understands his
incarnation, believes that he took man up
into a unity not of nature but of person."
The difference of emphasis between this and
the eastern idea of salvation through deification is very marked.

[41] Aristotle's *Categories* and Porphyry's
Isagoge, both translated into Latin by
Boethius, were the principal text books on
logic in Abelard's day.

est intellectual pursuit he turned finally to theology, studying for a brief period with a certain Anselm of Laon, not to be confounded with his greater namesake of Canterbury. Though Anselm of Laon was the most famous theological teacher of the day, Abelard speedily decided that he was unworthy of his high reputation and treated him with his usual disdain. . . . By his contemptuous attitude he won Anselm's hostility and made lifelong enemies of some of his pupils, a circumstance, as the event proved, of tragic consequence for Abelard. . . .

As a teacher of theology he repeated his earlier success, this time in Paris. . . . Abelard's tragic love affair with Heloise, which drove him humiliated and disgraced into a monastery, while it destroyed all hope of high preferment, did not put an end to his career as a scholar or his influence and popularity as a teacher. His most important theological work was done after he became a monk and his reputation as a theologian grew apace. . . .

From the time he became a monk, his career was a troubled one. . . . In the famous abbey of St. Denis near Paris . . . he made permanent enemies of his superiors and his fellow monks. . . . In 1121 at the Council of Soissons, as the result of a campaign instituted by two pupils of Anselm of Laon, his work on the Trinity, possibly his first theological production, was condemned and he was compelled with his own hand to consign it to the flames. . . . In later years he was unfortunate enough to incur the animosity of Bernard of Clairvaux, ecclesiastically the most influential man

of the day and religiously of an altogether different type from Abelard. It was due chiefly to Bernard that Abelard himself was condemned as a heretic at the Council of Sens in 1141 and that Pope Innocent II approved the decision of the Council. To be sure, the sentence was not carried out. Abelard still had his friends and supporters and found refuge at the famous monastery of Cluny where he was highly honored and was given charge of the studies of his fellows. The following year, however, he died a disillusioned and broken man.

. . . While personal animosity had something to do with the harsh treatment accorded him by the ecclesiastical authorities, his general theological attitude was chiefly responsible for it, that is, not so much heretical views on particular doctrines as the rationalistic tendency and temper which marked much of his work and seemed to many to threaten the very foundations of the faith. . . .

Abelard opposed all compulsion in matters of faith. Belief, he maintained, should be free and no one should be forced to accept what seemed to him untrue or condemned for not accepting it. . . . Even heretics he insisted should be reasoned with, not subjected to force. To be sure, his denunciation of Roscellin as a heretic to the Bishop of Paris was hardly in accord with this principle, but he was moved in that case by personal animosity and by the report that Roscellin was about to treat him in the same way.

Though he insisted on the application of reason to the doctrines of the Christian system he was not, . . . a thoroughgoing rationalist, for he believed in a divine revelation and recognized the authority of the Scriptures. What was plainly written in the Bible, he maintained, was to be accepted without question. He deprecated, however, the practice of reading into the sacred text all sorts of things that were not there, and his own exegesis was as a rule uncommonly sober and restrained. Moreover, he had a broad view of inspiration. It was not confined, so he held, to the biblical authors, but was shared by philosophers and sages of many lands. And it did not consist in external control or in the imparting of truth from without, but in such enlightenment of the mind as enables a man to discover truth for himself. This inspiration the biblical writers had in large measure — some to be sure in larger measure than others — and, as a consequence, they could speak with peculiar authority.

Abelard's view of inspiration was very modern, but it did not lead him to doubt the full authority of the Bible.[42] At this point he was one with the common sentiment of the Church. On the other hand, he disagreed with the Church at large in his estimate of the Fathers whose writings were generally recognized as authoritative, and whose opinions were supposed to be binding on the conscience of all Christians. Though he made large use of them and was as glad as anyone else to claim their support when he found himself in harmony with them, he did

not regard them as infallible. He was well aware that they differed with each other in many and important matters and he made it his business to point out their disagreements in order to undermine the belief in their infallibility, which he was convinced tended to destroy all independence and make the free use of reason in religion impossible.

His famous work entitled *Sic et non* (*Yes and No*) was compiled with this end in view. In the prologue he declares that many seeming discrepancies among the Fathers are apparent only. Sometimes they are due to a corruption of the text, sometimes the fault is ours. . . . But if after all allowances are made contradictions still remain, we ought not to accuse the Fathers of sin but only of ignorance. In so vast a mass of writings it is not strange that there are mistakes and we should not be troubled by them, for we are under no obligation to follow the Fathers as we are to follow Scripture. On the contrary, we are at liberty to pass judgment upon their opinions and to reject those that seem erroneous.

The work *Sic et non* itself is made up wholly of patristic quotations so arranged as to show the disagreements of the Fathers, real or apparent, on a large variety of topics, theological, ethical, ecclesiastical, historical, and the like. The topics are phrased in the form of propositions, of which there are no fewer than a hundred and fifty-eight. Among them are such as the following: That we should believe in one God; that he is triune; that he is the cause of evil; that Christ

---

[42] He recognized, it is true, that some of the biblical writers might conceivably have erred but he nowhere treats this possibility as an actuality.

became flesh; that he was ignorant; that the creature is to be worshiped; that all the Apostles had wives except John. . . .

In spite of his attitude toward them, it was not Abelard's wish, as many of his contemporaries supposed, to undermine Christianity or to get rid of the supernatural element in it. He was an apologist for Christianity not an opponent of it. Like many a modern liberal he simply desired to make it more acceptable to intelligent men and, with this end in view, he undertook to show its rationality and where necessary to interpret it in such ways as to bring it more fully into accord with the best thinking of the age. His brief treatise on the Trinity,[43] which was condemned at the Council of Soissons in 1121, admirably illustrates his general interest. It was not intended as an attack on the Trinitarian dogma. On the contrary, it was written at the request of his students to make the doctrine more comprehensible and thus strengthen rather than weaken faith. In support of it, he quotes from the Bible, both Old Testament and New, from the Fathers, and even from pagan philosophers.[44] With the evident intention of justifying himself for appealing to the philosophers, he declares that they taught faith and

immortality and virtue and he emphasizes the nobility of their lives and their contempt of the world which contrasts favorably with the conduct of many Christians.[45] . . .

After . . . clearing the way for the use of dialectics, Abelard employs it freely in the remainder of the work, undertaking to show that the oneness and the threeness of the Godhead if properly understood do no violence to sound reason. His own interpretation of the doctrine was similar to Augustine's though not identical. The three persons he represented not as individual beings or substances, and not as persons in the ordinary sense, but as attributes or properties of the one individual and simple substance God. The Father is power, the Son wisdom, the Holy Spirit beneficence or goodness.[46] God is triune in that he is all-powerful, wise, and good. If omnipotence or wisdom or goodness be lacking, he is not truly God; only as his power is directed by wisdom and used for beneficent ends, is it divine power. Thus God is necessarily triune. . . .

Abelard's interpretation of the Father as power, of the Son as wisdom and of the Spirit as goodness did not mean that he thought of the Father alone as powerful, of the Son alone as wise and of the Spirit alone as beneficent. On the contrary, though power is the characteristic mark of the

---

[43] De unitate et trinitate divina; discovered and published by R. Stölzle: Abaelards 1121 zu Soissons verurtheilter Tractatus de unitate et trinitate divina (1891).

[44] He refers particularly to Plato's doctrine of the anima mundi and to ideas of the Logos current among the Greeks. His quotations from pagan writers came to him chiefly by way of Augustine and Lactantius. His knowledge of Greek, as he elsewhere confesses, was meager and his acquaintance with Greek authors limited.

[45] De unitate et trinitate divina, Bk. I, ch. 5 (pp. 15 ff.).

[46] In speaking of the Holy Spirit he uses the words benignitas, caritas, and bonitas. It is interesting that goodness or love is made the characteristic mark not of the Father but of the Spirit, fatherhood being taken to connote power rather than affection.

Father, wisdom of the Son, and goodness of the Spirit, it is the one God who is powerful and wise and beneficent all at once.[47]

In his *Historia calamitatum* (Chapter 9) Abelard tells us that he was accused at Soissons of teaching tritheism. Certainly, there is no sign of anything of the kind in his treatise on the Trinity. On the contrary, it looks rather in the direction of Sabellianism and we are not surprised to learn that some criticized it on that account. The accusation of tritheism was probably due to the fact that Abelard was known to have rejected the traditional realism and to the consequent assumption that he must agree with his teacher Roscellin, the famous nominalist, who had been attacked by Anselm of Canterbury and whose "tritheism" had been condemned at an earlier council of Soissons. The truth of the matter is that Abelard agreed neither with Anselm nor with Roscellin. He did not conceive of God as a universal divine substance which is individualized in three persons, Father, Son, and Spirit, but as a unique, single, and individual substance which is possessed of three properties: power, wisdom, and goodness. Thus he avoided the tritheism of Roscellin without adopting the realism of Anselm.

Abelard was really as sound on the doctrine of the Trinity as Augustine and there was no reason why he should have been accused of heresy, at any rate for anything said in his extant treatise, unless because he tried to penetrate, as Augustine and many

[47] *Ibid.*, Bk. II, ch. 5.

Fathers before him had done, the mysteries of the faith, and to make more comprehensible and thus profane a doctrine which multitudes of devout Christians believed should be accepted without investigation or elucidation. It is significant that, when his opponents at Soissons tried to show his work heretical, they were unable to do so and that it was finally condemned only because it had been issued without ecclesiastical license.[48]

Already in this little work there appears Abelard's interest, which he

[48] Cf. *Historia calamitatum*, 9.

Editor's additional note: R. S. Storrs: *Bernard of Clairvaux*, p. 451: "at a Council held at Soissons A.D. 1121, with an unjust violence at which many at the time were offended . . . he was, without any fair examination or any opportunity to reply to his assailants, condemned as a Sabellian . . ."; Concerning the Council of Sens, A.D. 1140: Storrs, 493; "Bernard had collated passages from the writings of Abelard, seventeen in number, which he judged heretical and contrary to the faith of the Church. . . . On the following days . . . the various passages . . . were discussed, and fourteen of them were condemned, especially those concerning the Trinity, the Divine Nature of Christ, his redemptive work, etc."; F. Cayre, A.A. *Manual of Patrology*, II, 419: "The *Capitula haeresum P. Abaelardi* . . . were nearly all (12 out of 18) condemned as heretical. These errors mainly concerned the Trinity (modalism), creation (exaggerated optimism), Christ (Nestorian leanings), redemption (transformed in practice into a simple lesson in charity. . . . Particularly grave was his error on the Redemption which did away with all objective value in the Passion of Christ"; *Denzinger*, 368:721 ff.: "The Errors of Peter Abelard: (1) That the Father is complete power, the Son a certain power, the Holy Spirit no power; (2) That the Holy Spirit is not of the substance of the Father or of the Son; (3) That the Holy Spirit is the soul of the world; (4) That Christ did not assume flesh to free us from the yoke of the devil etc."

never lost, in the moral character of God. It was his desire to ethicize the idea of God through and through. Anything like pantheism — the identification of God with nature — was abhorrent to him. It was in part because of its pantheistic tendency that he opposed the realism of William of Champeaux. Always he insisted on the personality of God, his uniqueness and individuality, his freedom, his independence of the world, and the control of all his activities by moral ends.

A similar ethical interest appears very clearly in his doctrine of Christ's work which he set forth in his notable commentary on Paul's Epistle to the Romans.[49] In agreement with Anselm, whom however he did not mention, he repudiated the traditional notion that Christ by his death paid a price to Satan, but he also rejected Anselm's own doctrine. Instead of following him in teaching that the purpose of Christ's incarnation and death was to make it possible for God to forgive human sin without impairing the divine honor, Abelard maintained that there was nothing in the nature of God to hinder the free exercise of forgiveness and that the only impediment to it was in men not in God. Christ took on flesh and lived among men and

died on the cross in order to reveal the love of God and thus arouse in them an answering love which is their reconciliation and redemption. . . .

Some time after Abelard's tractate *On the Divine Unity and Trinity* had been condemned at Soissons he issued a revised edition of it under the title *Theologia christiana.*[50] . . . The work on the Trinity exists in still a third edition, a considerable part of the *Theologia christiana* being reproduced in a somewhat abbreviated form in a general treatise on theology to which Abelard himself refers simply as *Theologia,* but which is commonly though incorrectly called *Introductio ad theologiam.*[51] . . .

In spite of his many enemies and his condemnation by both council and pope, Abelard was enormously influential. His career indeed marked an epoch in the development of Christian thought. . . . Consciously or unconsciously, willingly or unwillingly, Christian thinkers for generations to come were affected both by his achievements and by his failures. His general way of looking at things, the problems he raised and the methods he employed in dealing with them, all helped to transform the intellectual climate of the age and to determine its interests.

2. W. Williams[1] studies the trinitarian doctrine of Gilbert de la Porrée, the bishop of Poitiers. He was charged with teaching that there is in God a form or essence that is not God. At the Council of Rheims in 1148 he abjured the four propositions ascribed to him.

---

[49] *Ep. ad Romanos*, Bk. II, ch. III and V (Migne, Vol. 178, cols. 831 ff. and 859 ff.).
[50] In Migne, Vol. 178, cols. 1123–1330.
[51] Under the latter title in Migne, Vol. 178, cols. 979–1114.

[1] Watkin Williams, was the author of *Studies in St. Bernard of Clairvaux.* This excerpt is from his book, *Saint Bernard of Clairvaux* (Manchester: Manchester University Press, 1952), pp. 313–319.

Gilbert de la Porrée was born at Poitiers in the year 1076. Otto of Freising, under the date of 1142, describes him as having "recently attained to the height of episcopal rank at Poitiers"[2] and as a man "whose habit it was, owing to the subtilty of his mind and to the keenness of his reasoning faculty, to state many propositions in a quite unusual way."[3] . . .

In 1147 Gilbert was opposed, not only by St. Bernard but also by . . . Adam of Petit-Pont, Canon of Paris, . . . Hugh of Champfleuri, Chancellor of the King, and Hugh of Amiens, Archbishop of Rouen, who all three deposed to having heard damaging statements fall from his mouth.[4] The principal charge against him, derived rightly or wrongly from his commentary on the *De Trinitate* of Boethius, would seem to have been that he taught "that the divinity is not God; that there is in God a form or essence which is not God."[5] This, writes Geoffrey,[6] "was the origin of his wrong doctrine. He propounded that there is in God a form by which God exists, but which is not God; just as humanity is the form of man, not what he is but that by which he is man."[7]

[2] *Gall. Christ.*, II.1178.

[3] Otton. Frising, *Gesta Frid. I Imp.*, I.xlviii; Waitz, *op. cit.*, 67 seq.; cf. Joann. Sares. *Hist. Pontifical.*, VIII.17 seq., ed. Poole.

[4] Otton. Frising, *op. cit.*, I.liii.

[5] Gaufr, *Ab. Clar. Ep. ad Alb. Card.*, 2, PL, CLXXXV, 587 seq.; cf. Mans, *Concil.*, XXI, 711.

[6] Geoffrey, fourth Abbot of Clairvaux, in a letter written to the Cardinal Bishop of Albano, Albino by name. Cf. n. 55.

[7] Gaufr, *Libell. contra Cap. Gilb.*, PL, 185, 595 seq.; De Cap. Primo; *Ep. ad Alb. Card.*, 4.

After a discussion which lasted for several days, the Pope decided to postpone the matter for further consideration at a council to be held at Rheims on mid-Lent Sunday, March 21, in the following year, 1148. . . .

Gilbert presented himself — at the Council of Rheims — attended by the clergy of his household bearing a large collection of patristic and other works. . . . We should remember that Gilbert was a man of immense learning, possessed of one of the finest libraries of his day.[8] . . . After much discussion, in which many joined but apparently few shone, for Gilbert was an accomplished fencer — and the Pope was beginning to weary of the prolonged and fruitless logomachy, St. Bernard put the trenchant question. "The origin of this scandal is," he remarks to Gilbert, "that many think that you believe and teach that the divine essence or nature, the divinity of God, his wisdom, goodness, greatness, is not God, but the form by which he is God. If you believe this, say so plainly or else deny it." The reply was prompt. "The form of God, the divinity by which he is God, is not itself God." "Now" says St. Bernard, "we have got what we have been looking for; let his confession of faith be written down." Gilbert raised no objection and formally attested his belief in writing. "Now do you write," he says, turning to the Abbot of Clairvaux, "that the divinity is God." Calmly St. Bernard replies: "Let it be written with an iron stile of adamantine point, or if you will engraved on flint, that the divine essence, form, nature, deity,

[8] *Planctus Laurent.*, R.H.G.F., XIV, 380.

goodness, wisdom, virtue, power, greatness, is truly God."[9] St. Bernard pressed the point that, if the form of God is not God, it is something higher than God, seeing that from it God derives his being, founding himself upon such passages in the *De Trinitate* of St. Augustine as "God is great, not by partaking of greatness but by being himself greatness."[10]

Gilbert continued to produce his authorities, Greek as well as Latin. . . . We may recapitulate in the words of Geoffrey the statements charged against him. "I. That the divine essence, substance and nature which is called the divinity, goodness, wisdom, greatness of God, and the like, is not God but the form by which he is God. II. That the three persons, Father, Son, and Holy Spirit, are neither one God nor one substance nor one anything. III. That the three persons are three by their three unities, and are distinguished by three properties which are not the same as the persons themselves; but that there are three eternal units, differing both from one another and from the divine substance. IV. That the divine nature was not incarnate nor did it assume human nature." Whether this be a fair statement or not, there is little doubt but that the four articles are theologically associated. Gilbert contended that his view offered the only escape from the dilemma presented by the Arian doctrine of plurality of essences and the Sabellian doctrine of one essence which is one person; and

his view he based upon the distinction between the *subsistens,* God, and the *subsistentia* or *substantia qua est subsistens,* the divinity. Theodoret, he declared, had held that "whosoever understands the nature and the person to be the same, falls either into Arian division or into Sabellian confusion." . . . Finally, the council was dissolved. . . .

Shortly afterward an assembly was held in a hall of the archiepiscopal palace. . . . The Pope himself unmistakably adopted a tone of supreme authority, and Gilbert was decidedly more submissive than he had been hitherto. When called upon to abjure freely the four articles charged against him, his reply was: "If you believe otherwise, so do I; if you state otherwise, so do I; if you write otherwise, so do I." Thereupon the Pope on his apostolic authority and with the consent of all present condemned the articles and gave strict injunctions that none should dare either to read or to transcribe Gilbert's commentary on the *De Trinitate* of Boethius until the Roman Church had corrected it.[11] . . . Thus, Gilbert was reconciled to the Church. . . .

Gilbert died in 1154 but he lived on in his works, in particular in his *Liber Sex Principiorum* which was in effect a completion of the *Categories* of Aristotle. . . . His theology, or rather his conception of theological data was perhaps influenced by the peculiar character of his realism. It was, moreover, impossible for him to regard theological data when treated metaphysically as exempt from the

---

[9] *Gaufr Ep.,* 3; cf. Joann. Sares., *Hist. Pontifical.,* IX, 21, ed. Poole; *Gaufr, Ep.,* 4.
[10] *Op. cit.,* 5; S. Aug. *De trin.,* V, x (11).

[11] Joann. Sares, *Hist. Pontifical.,* XI, 25 seq., ed. Poole.

treatment applied to any other data. He was probably incapable of doing so. If in his view the *subsistentia* humanity was not man, the *subsistens*, then by no process of reasoning intelligible to him could the *subsistentia* divinity be proved to be God the *subsistens*. Perhaps we shall say that his opponents were equally incapable, and that in fact they cut rather than untied the knot. . . . It was not that he held the formal teaching of the Church to be theologically untrue, but rather that he felt the matters with which he dealt to be no concern of theology proper. Let the theologians mind their business and he would mind his. In truth it was as yet too soon for the *synthesis;* it awaited a St. Thomas of Aquino.

3. R. S. Storrs[1] studies Bernard of Clairvaux as a theologian. He lacked Anselm's power of metaphysical analysis and original theological speculation. But he was called "the last of the Fathers" and "the man of Love." Of his theology, as of his heart, it might truly be said that its home was in the heavens.

Bernard of Clairvaux. His genius was sensitive and practical, rather than dialectical, sympathetic with truth, and with truth in mysterious forms and relations, rather than patient and profound in analysis. . . . If we fail to find in him the extraordinary power of metaphysical analysis, with philosophical coordination of ascertained conclusions, which Anselm showed for example, or Aquinas afterward, we need not be surprised. His life, on the whole, seems to me among the noblest phenomena of his age; but I by no means affirm that in the department of original and enlightening theological speculation he had no superiors.

He is, in fact, chiefly important . . . as representing in its best form, and with a halo projected upon it from his radiant spiritual life, the doctrine which he had learned in his youth, which seemed to him confirmed by experience and illumined by the Scripture, and in which his soul found nourishment, rest, and exaltation. He left no *"Summa Theologiae."* . . .

The doctrine which he had early accepted . . . he held and loved . . . with the entire force of his nature. He was intensely, though not timidly, conservative of it; and he looked with a certain sensitive jealousy, born of a deep and controlling affection on anything which might tend to lower its dignity or obscure its splendor before the eyes of the world. This is really the significance of the title which I have mentioned as affectionately given to him, "The last of the Fathers"; while Anselm, on the other hand, though the most profound theologian of his time, is also fairly to be regarded as the first, and among the greatest, of the schoolmen.

. . . He accepted, without reserve, the system of Christianity as it had

[1] R. S. Storrs, is the author of the book entitled *Bernard of Clairvaux,* which was published in New York by Charles Scribner's Sons in 1907. This excerpt is from pp. 294–298, 322–324, 341–346.

come to him from the past. . . . He believed it because he felt it. . . . That he was a firm and fervent supernaturalist, in his conception of religious truth, need not be said. It would have seemed just as credible to him that man had built the sun and stars as that he had framed the Gospel of Christ out of fancies and myths. . . . Not dryly logical, nor on the other hand philosophically discursive, the warmth of his heart and the imaginative glow of his mind, gave light and color to all his system. . . . He was, if we may express it in a sentence, a contemplative yet a most practical Mystic; apprehending secret sublimities in truth . . . an occult life in the Christian truth, which analysis cannot grasp, any more than the hand can clutch the sunbeam; yet preserved from extravagance by his study of the Scriptures, by that constant activity which kept his mind alert and watchful, and by that earnest Christian love, and that eager desire to bless mankind, which kept his heart faithful and sound. . . .

He was called by his contemporaries "the man of Love," because he so conspicuously sought it in himself, insisted on it in others; . . . he thought no love of God perfect until one had come to love himself only on account of the Divine One by whom he had been created, and by whom redeemed . . . the soul then pours itself forth upon God, thinking only of him, and cleaving to him in the perfect unity of the Spirit. "Blessed and holy would I call him," he says, "to whom it is granted to experience something like this in this mortal life, though it be

but once, or only occasionally, and for hardly more than a moment. To lose thyself utterly, as if thou wert not . . . this is the part of heavenly converse, not of mere human affection." . . .

It was for this most supreme experience that Bernard labored and prayed; . . . when such a final transfiguring love should be vitally present God would be revealed not to the soul only, but within it. It would have the immediate intuition of him, as declared in its ecstatic consciousness; and in that would be perfect felicity. . . .

It is very plain, therefore, that the purpose of Christianity was not satisfied in his view by any dexterity in ritual practice, by any philosophical apprehension of truth, by any careful adjustment of the conduct to ethical precepts, by any occasional gladness of hope, or transient experience of penitence or of praise. It was not satisfied, indeed, by a free development of those noble and beautiful elements of character which constitute for us Christian manhood. He looked beyond these. He desired and sought a superhuman exaltation of the soul, above sense and flesh, above logical thought or ardent sentiment, toward or into the vision angelic. The subjugation of the body, almost to the point of its nullification, was in his view intimately connected with this. The absorption of the mind on spiritual themes was essentially involved in it. With him, as with others sympathetic with his temper, the only perfect attainment of the soul was in its union with the Divine, while personal consciousness was to be maintained even in that ecstatic tranquility. For this, he prayed; toward this, he aspired and incessantly labored; not waiting, as some one has scornfully said, "to swoon into Divine repose," but seeking to arise, by contemplation, prayer, assiduous self-discipline, noble service, to a point where, by God's grace, through the indwelling of his Spirit, he might discern him in the soul, become a partaker of the divine nature, be changed into his image from glory to glory, be filled even unto his fulness. . . . It was the radiance of this immense aspiration which glorified his life; which shed at the time, and has shed ever since, its heavenly luster upon his career. . . .

It has been said, not unfrequently, that Bernard was a Reformer before the Reformation; standing, substantially, in spirit at least, with Tauler, Eckhart,. Ruysbroeck, and the German "Friends of God"; almost with Huss, and Jerome of Prague. I do not so conceive his position; though in regard to papal infallibility, to justification by faith, to supererogatory works, to the Immaculate Conception of Mary, he stands in line with such Reformers. In many particulars, of teaching, experience, evangelical practice, he plainly agreed with them; and his sharpest words of censure and of threat were reserved for those who, having forsaken conspicuous sins, trusted in external works and in ritual practice, moving in a mechanical performance of duty, with no conspiring impulse of the heart; omitting no iota of outward service, while the spirit within continued the servant of self-will, greedy of fame, loving ambition. The iniquity of such may deceive

themselves, he says, but God is not mocked; only true piety and spiritual endeavor can bring men to him.[2] In some elements, both of doctrine and of spirit, Melanchthon seems to have almost reproduced him, though with certainly far less of the superlative intensity which belonged to Bernard.

But it is not so much through his relation to any who came after him that we are now to regard him, as in the expression which is evident in him of the most vital and quickening theology which prevailed in his time; mystical, spiritual, supremely devout, transcending reason in the uplift of faith, contemplating as its practical end the Beatific Vision, and offering itself as the divine means to enable men to attain that. . . . Of his theology, as of his heart, it might truly be said that its home was in the heavens. . . . It gave him a strange supremacy among men. . . . Every force of his soul was exalted and energized by the touch of this theology upon him; and its ethereal sovereign power lived for long in other minds. Indeed, it never was lost, or will be, from the consciousness of the Church. . . .

The essential life of that theology never will cease to be exhibited among men, or to do its transcendent work

[2] "Vis videre mundatam, ornatam, et vacantem domum? Hominem intuere qui confessus est, et deseruit manifesta peccata praecedentia ad judicium, et nunc solas movet manus ad opera mandatorum, corde penitus arido, ductus consuetudine quadam . . . In corde enim servus est propriae voluntatis, cultor avaritiae, gloriae cupidus, ambitionis amator; et mentitur iniquitas sibi, sed Deus non irridetur . . . Sed inveniatur utilis ad omnia pietas, et exercitium spirituale. — *Opera*, vol. prim. Ser. in Assump. B. V. Mariae, iii. col. 2142.

upon them, while the Gospel continues. The more we have of its temper at least in our own hearts, the more clearly will the person and work of Christ be apprehended by us, the more devoutly will the divine benignity as manifested in him be adored, the more shall we also in thought and hope transcend the world, and be eager to enter, with illumined and purified spirits, the spheres of the celestial life. . . .

As nearly, perhaps, as any one of the great Church-teachers, he approached that beloved disciple who wrote of Christ more sublimely than others, as having a clearer intuition of his glory; who saw him in the Apocalypse, and who was, by eminence, the Apostle of Love.

VII

GOD IN AQUINAS, SCOTUS, ECKHART

1. D. Knowles[1] looks at Aquinas, the prince of scholastics, who created a wholly new and original Christian philosophy. For him God is a dynamic existential reality, the creator and source of all being, goodness and truth, the one subsistent being in whom alone essence and existence are one — in a trinity of persons.

St. *Thomas Aquinas* has been hailed by common consent in the modern world as the prince of scholastics . . . the *doctor angelicus* . . . the *doctor communis*. To Thomists of pure blood, as to many others besides, he appears as the authentic voice of reason, interpreting and defending tradition, as the greatest medieval representative of the *philosophia perennis*, the way of thinking that is ever ancient and ever new. . . .

Greatness is there. The judgment of his contemporaries and posterity has not been false. As we read, with sympathy and a receptive mind, on and on in the two great *Summae*,

[1] David Knowles, O.S.B., was born in 1896. He is the author of *The English Mystical Tradition, Saints and Scholars, The Benedictine*. This excerpt is from his book, *The Evolution of Medieval Thought* (Baltimore: Helicon Press, 1962), pp. 255–268.

the pattern unfolds and the cardinal principles of thought recur and are used, like keen knives, to separate truth from all else. . . . The peculiar greatness of Aquinas, as a master of technical method, lies in his combination of fearless strength of reasoning with an entire absence of personal bias, and in his ability to recognize and produce harmony and order — to recognize them in the universe and to produce them in his own thought — to a degree without parallel among the great philosophers of the world. . . .

His significance appears in two principal achievements. He integrated Aristotelian philosophical principles with traditional speculative theology, and he created by remoulding and rethinking existing materials and old problems, a wholly new and original Christian philosophy. . . .

Aquinas did not merely adopt and "baptize" or "Christianize" Aristotle. He had, indeed, no hesitation in extending his thought, in filling gaps within it and interpreting it in accord with Christian teaching. . . . But he did more than this. . . . He stood the system of Aristotle on its head or, to speak more carefully, supplied the lack of higher metaphysics in Aristotle by framing a conception of the deity which was in part drawn from Judeo-Christian revelation and which, when proposed in Thomist terms, embodied all that was most valuable in the metaphysic of Platonism. . . . Aristotle's God is a shadow, an unseen, unknown, uncaring force and reason necessary to give supreme unity to the universe. In the Aristotelian system reality, existential real-ity, is strongest in the world of everyday experience; the loftier the gaze, the weaker the reality. With Thomism, on the other hand, the infinitely rich, dynamic existential reality is God, the creator and source of all being, goodness and truth, present in all being by power and essence, holding and guiding and regarding every part of creation, while as the one subsistent Being, the uncaused cause, the *ens a se* in whom alone essence and existence are one, He takes the place of the Platonic forms and exemplars. . . .

Yet though Aquinas followed Aristotle, he also went beyond him with new intuitions and principles, such as the unicity of form in all beings, man included, and the distinction between essence and existence. . . . The leading idea running through his whole system is that every finite being is made up of act and potency, essence, and existence. Existence brings the potency of an essence into act, but is itself limited by that potency. This distinction between essence and existence is vital; it is the shibboleth of Thomism. It is because God alone is subsistent being, without distinction between his essence and existence, that he is all-perfect, and it is ultimately from contingent being that we deduce the existence of God. . . . Subsistent being is above all created natures, it is, therefore, supernatural being, unattainable by any created or creatable intelligence. God is, therefore, in essence transcendent, though he is also by essence, power and presence immanent. But if God is a supernatural being, how can we have any knowledge of him by natural powers?

Aquinas answers this question by his profound doctrine of analogy, which again depends upon the distinction between essence and existence. . . . Goodness, for example, is not predicated of God and ourselves univocally — men are not good as God is good — nor is it predicated merely equivocally — the same word with a different meaning — but analogically. It is thus that Aquinas avoids both agnosticism and anthropomorphism. . . .

Aquinas' acceptance of Aristotle, though thorough and epoch-making, is neither uncritical nor absolute. He accepts his metaphysics almost in entirety, but his world-system only with reservations, and for all the higher levels of Christian life he repeatedly asserts Aristotle's incompetence. Similarly, while taking over bodily from the Jewish Maimonides much of his natural theology, he takes only part (and that with cautious reservation) of his and others' Jewish and Neoplatonist teaching on the information of the heavenly spheres by intelligences or angels, and he firmly rejects the series of creative causes posited by Avicenna, and the emanations of the Neoplatonists. At the same time, Aquinas admits far more from non-Aristotelian sources than appears at first sight. Thus the Platonic ideas, resolutely banished in their familiar form from epistemology and metaphysics, remain "in the heavens" (to use a Platonic phrase) where Augustine had seen them, as the eternal, exemplary, creative ideas in what we call "the mind of God." Moreover,

as we have seen, the "exemplary" and participatory function of the ideas is assumed by the Thomist doctrine of essence and existence. . . .

Indeed, Aquinas makes so much use of ways of thought that are ultimately Platonic that it may almost be said of him that he achieves that fusion of the Academy and the Lyceum that so many of his predecessors and contemporaries were attempting. He accomplishes this, however, not by a synthesis, but by using elements from Platonism mainly in the higher levels of metaphysics. Thus by his use of the principle that all creatures participate in being, though in varying measure, by his use of exemplarism in which the creature reflects the creator, by his doctrine of metaphysical composition, and by his assertion of the self-sufficing being of God, he makes of God the center and cause of a universe of manifold being, and in ethics the creator, lawgiver and providential Father of each human soul, thus placing the center of gravity, so to say, at the summit of being, and revealing a radiating center, a living principle and a final goal where Aristotle points merely to an abstract postulate. In this way he adds all that is true in Plato's idealism, other-worldliness and spirit of love to the common-sense, rationalistic empiricism of Aristotle.

To this copious fund of material taken from older thinkers, and to the many, and as yet not fully catalogued, debts which Thomas owed to his immediate predecessors and masters, another rich source must be added, the self-revelation of God in the Old and

New Testaments. This revelation is not indeed philosophy, but, as Gilson has finely shown, it gives clear and simple answers to several of the problems that all philosophers must face; it directs attention to the sovereign importance of others which they might neglect; and it brands as false many conclusions to which some thinkers in every age are prone. In all these ways, the Christian religion, in a mind profoundly receptive of its influence, must present the philosopher with a view of the universe different in many respects from that of Plato and Aristotle. . . .

From all these constituents of Aquinas' thought there emerged the first original philosophical system that Christianity had seen — neither Platonism, nor Aristotelianism, nor Augustinism, but Thomism. Henceforward this presentation of the universe of reality could be regarded, not only as a phase in the ever-changing outlook of thinking man, and as a phenomenon of thirteenth-century intellectual life, but as a system to which men could return to study, to adopt and to amend. . . .

The preceding observations, as indeed the whole tenor of the modern presentation of Thomas, have stressed his significance as a philosopher to the detriment, or at least to the overshadowing, of his wider reputation. We must not forget that Thomas was also, indeed was primarily, a great theologian. Though, true to his own principles, he uses philosophical arguments to defend and explain some of the most obscure mysteries of the faith, such as the Trinity, the personal union of the divine and human natures in the Incarnate Word, and the real presence in the Blessed Sacrament . . . the careful reader of the *Summa* becomes aware of other qualities in the philosopher, of a wide and living knowledge and an unusually felicitous use of Scripture wholly different from that of St. Bernard, but no less impressive; of an unexpected tolerance of Dionysian elements of thought, and of a clarity of exposition which makes many of the Trinitarian articles unrivalled as precise statements of the Christian faith. . . .

2. J. Maritain[1] looks at the wisdom of Aquinas that has become the common property of the Church and of men. His novelty *par excellence* was the integration of Aristotle into Catholic thought. Better than any other thinker he established the rights and value of the science of being and the transcendence of him who is being, intelligence, goodness, life, beatitude.

[1] Jacques Maritain was born in Paris in 1882 and with his wife, Raissa entered the Catholic Church in 1906. In 1914 he was called to the chair of philosophy at the Institut Catholique in Paris. He is widely regarded as the greatest living Catholic philosopher. Among his many published works are *The Degree of Knowledge, True Humanism, Christianity and Democracy, Existence and the Existent, Approaches to God* and *The Person and the Common Good*. This excerpt is from his book, *St. Thomas Aquinas* (New York: Meridian Books, Inc., 1958), pp. 25–29, 32–37, 42–46, 64–65, 99–100, 103.

He came into the world at the beginning of a century in which Christian civilization — already threatened and on the verge of collapse — was in the process of recovering itself in order to bring forth its best fruits. . . . He had asked: What is God? He had to find the answer, to gather together the principles of wisdom in the unity of a doctrine destined ever to grow. A privileged moment of history rendered possible such a synthesis. Yesterday Christian thought was not yet ripe, tomorrow it will begin to decay. . . . He is sent for the salvation of the intellect. . . .

The novelty *par excellence,* prepared by some of his elders, above all by Albert the Great, but whose accomplishment was reserved for him, was the integration of Aristotle into Catholic thought. . . . What the fifteenth and sixteenth centuries failed to achieve in the order of art and the allurements of the senses, the thirteenth, thanks to Thomas Aquinas, achieved in the order of metaphysics and theology. It did not excommunicate Aristotle and the whole effort of reason; it did not yield nor apostatize before them; it converted them. Thomas transfigured Aristotle without deforming him, not contenting himself with restoring his true meaning against the alterations of commentators, with completing and correcting him wherever he makes a mistake or hesitates, but working the miracle of disengaging from the historic Aristotle . . . a pure Aristotelian form much more purely Aristotelian than Aristotle himself had known. Aristotle, moreover, is above all for Thomas the treasurer of natural reason; with Aristotle it is the whole of antiquity that he assumes, not without also retaining all the good that the Jews and Arabs were able to discern. He likewise gathered all the testimonies of Scripture and the Fathers, the whole of Christian thought, in such a way that "for having profoundly venerated" the Fathers and holy Doctors who preceded him, "he in a way inherited the intellect of all."[2] . . . He is not only the disciple of uncreated Wisdom, of the wisdom of saints and . . . philosophers. . . . He is also the disciple of the human race.

The universal heritage grasped completely and completely redone, born anew in the intellect; this is quite the contrary of eclecticism or a mosaic of opinions. An immaterial world, endlessly complex in its structure and perfectly one in its being, is vitally engendered in the womb of the spirit. Nothing loftier than such a synthesis, nothing that demands a greater independence and a purer personal strength of thought! But neither is there any work more impersonal in itself. The doctrine of Thomas . . . is the common property of the Church and of men. . . .

Theology makes use of philosophy, illuminates it as it judges it in its own light. It is by this means that Thomas transplanted Aristotelian concepts to a new climate — the supernatural — where faith impels them to yield in our mind some understanding of the mysteries of God. . . . He is not only, nor principally, a philosopher; essen-

---

[2] A saying of Cajetan taken up by Leo XIII and Pius XI.

tially, he is a theologian. It is as a theologian, from the peak of architectonic knowlege *par excellence*, that he definitively secures the order of the Christian economy. . . .

Thomas, in his probing the intimate nature of knowledge and the peculiar life of the intellect, establishes better than any other thinker — against positivism, but respecting the full role played by the immanent and constructive activity of the mind — the objectivity of knowledge, the rights, and the value of the science of being. But he establishes also — against the false systems of metaphysics which threaten to assail us, against the pantheistic immanentism which some would impose on us in the name of the Orient, against the pragmatism of the West, against the Hegelian divinization of becoming and against the diverse forms of radical atheism which have sprung up in the world since Feuerbach, Auguste Comte, and Karl Marx — he establishes, I say, the transcendence of him whom we know through his creatures but who is without common measure with them; who is being, intelligence, goodness, life, beatitude, but who overflows and surpasses infinitely our ideas of being, goodness, and all the other perfections. . . . Thus metaphysics rises in his hands above agnosticism and rationalism; it starts with experience and mounts right up to Uncreated Being, and thus re-establishes in the human spirit the proper hierarchy of speculative values, and initiates in us the order of wisdom. . . .

Thomas leaves truth all its grandeur, a grandeur the measure of which is the Son of God. Philosopher and theologian, he . . . casts his net over the universe and captures all things, to bear them, vivified in the intellect, toward the Beatific Vision. This theology of the peaceful is, under the light of faith, an immense movement of thought between two intuitions: the intuition of being and the first principles of reason, whence it starts and which is given to it here on earth; and the intuition of God clearly seen, toward which it advances and which will be given to it in the hereafter. Ordering the whole discourse to an ineffable supreme end . . . it asks us to pay tribute both to the rights of being over our spirit and to the divine sublimity. This is why it is so serene and so universal, so open and so free, the most boldly affirmative and the most humbly prudent, the most systematic and the least biased, the most intractable and the most receptive to all the nuances of the real, the richest in certitudes and the most careful to respect the part of the probable and of opinion. . . .

Thomas loves God more than the intellect, but he loves the intellect more than all the philosophers have loved it.

3. É. Gilson ponders Aquinas' existential interpretation of Exodus. There is no doubt that St. Thomas thought that God had revealed to men

---

[1] Étienne Gilson was born in Paris on June 13, 1884. In 1932 he inaugurated the first Chair of the History of Medieval Philosophy at the Collége de France. In

that his essence was to exist. Hence Thomistic existentialism concerned not merely natural theology, but theology in the strict sense.

Haec sublimis veritas. It is hardly credible that the existential nature of the problem of the existence of God ever had to be discovered. It is even less credible that Christian theologians had to discover the existential nature of the Christian God. Was it not enough to open the Scriptures in order to discover it there? When Moses wished to know the name of God in order to reveal it to the Jewish people, . . . God said to Moses: "I am Who Am" . . . "Thus will you reply to the children of Israel: He Who Is sends me to you."[2] . . . How could Christians ever have been ignorant that their God was the supremely existing being? . . .

Certainly the identification of God and Being is the common possession of Christian philosophers as Christian.[3] But the agreement of Christians upon this point did not prevent philosophers from being divided on the interpretation of the notion of being. Holy Scripture provides no treatise on metaphysics. . . . It is easy to understand how Christian thinkers had to struggle a long time to clarify the meaning of this basic text of Exodus. It was only gradually that a metaphysical interpretation was found. . . . History permits us to make a living analysis by comparing the essentialist interpretation of the text of Exodus at which Augustine finally stopped, with the existential interpretation of the same text developed by Thomas Aquinas.

Augustine was so sure that the God of Exodus was Plato's being that he wondered how to explain the coincidence without admitting that Plato had somehow or other known Exodus.[4] . . . Clearly, the Being of Exodus is here conceived as the immovable entity of Plato.[5] . . . To identify thus the true being which God is with "immovable being" is to assimilate the "I am" of Exodus to the *ousia* of Platonism. . . . The Latin equivalent of *ousia* is *essentia* and it seems, certainly, that Augustine identified in his mind the God of Abraham, of Isaac, and of Jacob with that alone which, being immovable, can be called *essentia* in all the fullness of the

---

1947 he was received into the Académie Francaise to become one of the French immortals. In 1951 he resigned from his chair at the Collége de France to devote all his time to the direction of research at the Toronto Institute of Mediaeval Studies. He has a world-wide reputation as historian and philosopher. Among his many published works are *The Spirit of Saint Bonaventure, John Duns Scotus, God and Philosophy, The Spirit of Mediaeval Philosophy* and *Christianity and Philosophy.* This excerpt is from his book, *The Christian Philosophy of St. Thomas Aquinas* (New York: Random House, 1956), pp. 84 ff.

[2] Ex 3:13–14. On the meaning of the expressions from *Exodus* see E. Gilson, *The Spirit of Mediaeval Philosophy,* 1936, p. 433, n. 9.

[3] On the agreement of Christian thinkers on this point see *The Spirit of Mediaeval*

Philosophy, pp. 51–52, ch. 3; "Being and Necessity," pp. 42–63.

[4] St. Augustine, *De civitate Dei,* 8, 11; PL, 41, 236.

[5] St. Augustine, *De doctrina christiana,* I, 32, 5; PL, 34, 32.

term. How would it be otherwise since to be is "to be immovable"?[6] . . . Hence the divine name of names, "I am" is best translated into philosophical language by the abstract term *essence* which itself denotes the immutability of *"that which is."* . . .

To pass from this philosophical interpretation of the text of Exodus to the one Thomas was going to propose, it was necessary to bridge the gap between being of essence and being of existence. . . . Thomas' proofs for the existence of God . . . prepared that bridge. It only remains to recognize the proper nature of the God whose existence they have demonstrated, to recognize him as the supreme act of being. . . . What can we hope to find at the end of the analysis . . . if not *being,* free from all that is not being? . . . We do not say that he has no essence but that his essence is his act of being.[7] To grasp in one glance the extent of Thomas' reform on the plane of natural theology, we have only to measure the distance separating the God *essentia* of Augustine from the God of Thomas whose *essentia* is, as it were, absorbed by its *esse.*

However, this pure act-of-being which Thomas the philosopher met

at the end of metaphysics, Thomas the theologian had met too in holy Scripture. It was no longer the conclusion of rational dialectic but a revelation from God himself to all men that they might accept it by faith. There is no doubt that Thomas thought that God had revealed to men that his essence was to exist. Thomas is not lavish with epithets. Never did a philosopher yield less frequently to the temptation to wax eloquent. Here, however, seeing these two beams of light so converging that they fused into each other, he was unable to withhold a word of admiration for the overwhelming truth blazing forth from their point of fusion. He saluted this truth with a title exalting it above all others: "God's essence is therefore his act-of-being. Now this sublime truth,[8] God taught to Moses when . . . the Lord replied: I am Who Am. You may say this to the children of Israel: *He Who Is* has sent me to you. Thus he showed that his proper name is *Who Is.* It remains then that the divine act-of-being itself[9] is the essence or nature of God."[10]

Let us note well that for Thomas this revelation of the identity of essence and existence in God was the equivalent of a revelation of the distinction between essence and existence in creatures. . . . "It is impossible that the substance of any being other than the First Agent be its very act-of-being."[11]

These positions have two principal

[6] St. Augustine, *De Trinitate,* VII, 5, 10, PL, 42, 942. Other texts may be found in M. Schmaus, *Die psychologische Trinitätslehre des hl. Augustinus* (Münster i.W., 1927), 84, 1. In St. Thomas the immutable presence of the divine essence is no longer the first and direct sense of the *Qui est* of *Exodus.* As it concerns time, and as time is "cosignified" by the verb, this meaning is only a "cosignification" of the *Qui est.* Its "signification" is given as *ipsum esse. Summa Theologiae,* I, 13, 11.

[7] *De Potentia,* 7, 2, ad 1.

[8] *Summa Contra Gentes,* I, 22.
[9] *Ibid.*
[10] *Ibid., ipsum igitur esse Dei est sua essentia.*
[11] *Summa Contra Gentes,* II, 52.

consequences. First, Thomistic existentialism concerned not merely natural theology but theology in the strict sense. It is here indeed a question of a literal interpretation of the word of God. . . . When Augustine read the name of God, he understood "I am he who never changes." Thomas reading the same words understood them to mean "I am the pure act of being."

Whence this second consequence, that no historian can consider Thomas' thinking to be a combination of distinct schools of thought. Neither identity of essence and existence in God nor the distinction between essence and existence in creatures belongs to the *revelatum*, properly so-called, since neither of these truths is beyond the range of natural reason considered as a judging faculty. . . . Time was necessary for reason to do its work. Augustine was on the right path; Thomas but followed the same road to its end. . . . But . . . is it Thomas the theologian who, reading in Exodus the identity of essence and existence in God, taught Thomas the philosopher the distinction between essence and existence in creatures? Or is it Thomas the philosopher who, pushing his analysis of the metaphysical structure of the concrete even as far as the distinction between essence and existence, taught Thomas the theologian that *He Who Is* in Exodus means the *Act-of-being*?

4. F. Cayre[1] gives a brief sketch of Aquinas' doctrine about God's existence and his nature. In his demonstrations Aquinas stresses metaphysical principles and bases his doctrine on the highest principles drawn particularly from the nature of God, his independence and his universal action.

Existence and nature. Thomas does not admit St. Anselm's a priori argument. The latter supposes that the existence of God is a self-evident truth, or at least capable of becoming so, without reference to contingent reality.[2] But the first thesis of the Angelic Doctor in his *Summa* states that the proposition "God exists," while evident in itself, is not evident for us.[3] It is nevertheless capable of being demonstrated a posteriori by proceeding from the effects to the cause, by means of the principle of causality.[4] Such demonstration is strictly metaphysical "provided it proceeds from the right effect to the right cause, i.e., the cause on which the effect necessarily and immediately depends."[5]

Thomas distinguishes *five ways* by which the existence of God may be established. They differ mainly in the created concrete object which is used

---

[1] F. Cayré, A.A. is an honorary professor at the Institut Catholique of Paris and editor of *L'Anné Theologique*. Among his publications we mention *Spiritual Writers of the Early Church*. This excerpt is from his two-volume *Manual of Patrology* (Paris, Tournai: Desclée & Co., 1936), Vol. II, pp. 585–590.

[2] Anselm, *Proslogion*, c. 2–3, PL, 158, 223–242.

[3] *S.T.*, I, q. 2, a. 1.

[4] *Ibid.*, a. 3.

[5] *Ibid.*, I, q. 104, a. 1. See Garrigou-Lagrange, *Dieu*, pp. 72–76, 763–773.

as the starting point of each demonstration: (1) the movement of beings that surround us; either movement in its strict meaning or any kind of change: (2) their efficient activity manifested in the constant production of fresh beings; (3) their contingency which touches their deep reality, and is ephemeral as regards existence; (4) the relative imperfection of their essences, which is shown by the manifold degrees of being that can be distinguished; (5) lastly, the order of the universe; order in the whole and in the least detail, in the smallest creatures and in the greatest. All this supposes a *raison d'être*, a cause; yet on the other hand in a series of causes it is not possible to proceed to infinity. Such are the two essential principles that form the kernel of the argument and lead to the conclusion: there is a First Cause; God exists.[6]

What is most striking here is the concrete and objective character of the starting point. The metaphysical principle alone makes the demonstration possible, but Thomas seems to have exercised especial care in order to find for it a trustworthy and easily verifiable foundation. In this, he differs sharply from the Augustinians who preferred to stress psychological realities, notably the most profound metaphysical truths considered at one and the same time as psychological facts and as principles of objective demonstration.[7] Thomas appears to have used

a similar method with slight modifications in his fourth way. But his demonstration of God's existence, being less dependent on subjective data, is clearer and more sober. It may be that the greater complexity of the Augustinian method rendered it in a sense more rich.

Nature and attributes. Thomas' teaching as to what formally constitutes the divine nature,[8] is a matter of dispute even among Thomists.[9] Some make it consist in his subsisting intellectual thought,[10] others his aseity, the *esse a se*.[11] But it would seem that Thomas really takes it to be subsistent being[12] and there is no doubt that he deduces all the other divine attributes from the being of God. These attributes concern the nature and the operations of God, in himself and *ad extra*.

The attributes relating to the very being of God are first the properties of being in general, raised to their supreme perfection: simplicity or oneness, truth, goodness or perfection. Then come infinity that excludes all

---

III–XIV, 7–38; *De div. quaest.*, LXXXIII, q. 54; *Confess.*, Bk. VII, c. X, 16.

III–XIV, 7–38; *De div. quaest.*, LXXXIII, q. 54; *Confess.*, Bk. VII, c. X, 16.

[8] R. Garrigou-Lagrange, *Dieu*, pp. 343–370. "The divine perfections, such as they are *in themselves*, not distinct, are equal, in the sense that none is more perfect than another and each implies the others. But inasmuch as they are distinct as regards our manner of knowing them, and analogically similar to created perfections, it is not impossible to discover an order among them, relative to the first." *Ibid.*, p. 349.

[9] Scotus differs from St. Thomas by taking God's Infinity as the fundamental attribute.

[10] John of St. Thomas, Billuart. St. Augustine should probably be classed with this group: he gives special importance to Truth and to Wisdom.

[11] Capreolus, Bañez, Contenson.

[12] See R. Garrigou-Lagrange, *op. cit.*, pp. 356–370.

[6] *S.T.*, I, q. 2, a. 3. See Garrigou-Lagrange, *Dieu*, pp. 241–338.

[7] See St. Anselm, *Monologion*, c. 1–4; St. Augustine, *De libero arbitrio*, Bk. II, c.

limitations of essence, immensity and ubiquity excluding all limitations of space, and eternity, excluding temporal limitations. Lastly, with regard to our natural knowledge, the Being of God is invisible and incomprehensible, yet nevertheless knowable by analogy.

The attributes relating to the divine operations may be divided accordingly as they concern the immanent divine operations or those that cause an effect exterior to God. The former are Wisdom, and Providence, for the intelligence and love for the will, and his two great virtues, Mercy and Justice. The immediate principle of the exterior divine works is Omnipotence, creating and preserving, on which depends the divine co-operation necessary to all created beings so that they may act and attain their end.[13]

The distinction of positive and negative divine attributes is less important than the foregoing since it is made "from a secondary point of view, more relative to our mode of knowledge."[14]

It should be well understood how these perfections that we know through created things, have their being in God. They are not in him only inasmuch as he is able to produce them,[15] but according to their nature.[16] Nevertheless, they are in him eminently, "that is to say, according to a modality, infinitely superior to created modality, which is known to us only negatively and relatively and which enables us to identify them with the formal essence of God without destroying them."[17]

This modality is to be explained by the analogical character of our knowledge which goes beyond equiv-

ocal prediction but does not reach univocacy.[18] Though identical with the divine essence, they are nevertheless distinct from one another "virtually," that is to say, according to a distinction of reason founded in reality, but subsequent to the consideration of the mind. The basis of this distinction is twofold: (1) the eminence of the Deity by which he can identify in himself perfections that are really distinct in creatures; and (2) the imperfection of our minds that cannot attain to God's absolute simplicity.[19] This virtual distinction, however, could not be allowed, were it to be based on a potentiality in God: such would be the distinction between essence and existence, intelligence, and the act of knowing, will and the act of willing.[20]

The operations of God relating to creatures form one of the most characteristic points of theological Thomism. God's knowledge is universal: it has for its primary object the divine essence inasmuch as this explicitly contains all his attributes and the relations of the Trinity. But it also extends to every other object, both the "possibles"[21] and all beings actually called into existence in the past, present, and future.[22] God perceives

[18] Duns Scotus though admitting the univocal nature of transcendental ideas applied to God, has to admit that the perfections expressed are in him *really* and are distinguished *formally*.

[19] R. Garrigou-Lagrange, *ibid.*, p. 521. Cf. *In I Sent.*, D. 11, q. 1, a. 3.

[20] *Ibid.*, pp. 552–558. Cf. *S.T.*, I, q. 3, a. 4; q. 14, a. 4; q. 54, a. 1–2.

[21] Knowledge of simple intelligence.

[22] Knowledge of vision. *S.T.*, I, q 14, a. 2, 9; *De Verit.*, q. 3, a. 3, ad 8; *C.G.*, c. 60, 69.

[13] Garrigou-Lagrange, *op. cit.*, p. 371.

[14] *Ibid.*, p. 372.

[15] *Causaliter, virtualiter.* Against Maimonides, *De potentia*, a. 7; *S.T.*, I, q. 13, a. 2. Garrigou-Lagrange, *ibid.*, p. 516 ff.

[16] *Formaliter.*

[17] Garrigou-Lagrange, *op. cit.*, p. 521.

these latter, not in themselves[23] but in himself in the decree that makes them present to him for all eternity.[24] To say that God's knowledge of things derives from things themselves would be to ascribe imperfection to God: infinite intelligence would depend on the finite.[25] Man's free will, moreover, is not prejudiced by this universal intuition[26] even though it be based on a decree, for the divine will is essentially transcendent: its efficacy is sovereign, both as regards the effects that it produces and their mode of being; God uses proportionate causes for the production of necessary or contingent effects.[27]

Divine causality extends to every action of his creatures; God creates the power of acting, preserves it, applies it to its action and finally as first agent, moves it so as to produce in each thing according to its nature the most universal effect, the very being of the thing in question.[28] This divine movement is more exactly explained in the *Summa* where

mention is made of a threefold causality: final, efficient, and formal.[29] This movement in no wise excludes the action of a secondary cause, which, considered as an action of the First Cause, is thus subordinated to it.[30] The divine motion is total cause of the effect, as is also the secondary cause in its own order.[31]

These important principles are used as a basis for the solution of other associated questions, closely linked up with the divine knowledge and will. Such is Providence, which by an act of knowledge and will, regulates the order of the universe, as a whole and in its slightest detail.[32] Providence is an extension of Divine Wisdom. With both of these is associated predestination, a special Providence touching the elect, whom God knows and for whom he prepares glory and the means of attaining it. And this without injustice to those who do not attain glory.[33] Later theology bitterly disputed the question of predestination to glory alone.[34]

---

[23] S.T., I, q. 14, a. 8. Garrigou-Lagrange, *op. cit.*, p. 402.

[24] *Ibid.*, p. 408. The author remarks that the *medium* is the divine decree, presence being merely the *condition* of intuitive knowledge. Cf. S.T., I, q. 14, a. 13 (complement of a. 8).

[25] According to Vasquez, on the contrary, it is more perfect for God to know created things in themselves. According to Suarez, God knows them at one and the same time in Himself as in their cause and immediately in themselves. See L. Mahieu, *Suarez*, pp. 229–230.

[26] C.G., I, c. 68.

[27] *Cum igitur voluntas divina sit efficacissima, non solum sequitur quod fiant ea quae Deus vult fieri, sed et quod eo modo fiant quo Deus ea fieri vult.* S.T., I, q. 19, a. 8.

[28] *De potentia*, q. 3, a. 7. Cf. C.G., III, c. 67.

[29] S.T., I, q. 105, a. 5.

[30] *Ibid.*, ad 2. This motion of the First Cause implies a *priority*, not of time, but of *nature*, over the action of the second cause; the word motion itself indicates this, and St. Thomas is content with that. His school has judged it opportune to stress this point by adopting the words *premotion* and *predetermination*. These terms have aroused lively opposition.

[31] Molina and his school generally look upon divine causality and human causality as two parallel and co-ordinated causalities.

[32] S.T., I, q. 22, 4 articles.

[33] *Ibid.*, q. 23, 8 articles.

[34] Since the first graces are quite gratuitous, and as final perseverance cannot be the object of strict merit, predestination taken as a whole is all gratuitous; this is

This magnificent Thomist system- atization is the supplement of the Augustinian theology, especially from a philosophical point of view and the Augustinian trend is faithfully followed. The doctrine is based on the highest principles drawn par- ticularly from the nature of God, his independence and universal action. Here the theologian comes face to face with mystery, but is not dis- mayed, for he is aware of the weak- ness of the human mind and its powerlessness before the transcend- ency of the First Cause.[35] The Molin- ist school, starting from other prin- ciples arrived at somewhat divergent conclusions. It did not, however, suc- ceed in avoiding the difficulties of the mystery, and perhaps aggravated them, despite appreciable advantages that were otherwise gained.

5. R. Garrigou-Lagrange[1] studies Aquinas' contribution to trinitarian doc- trine. Augustine had taken a great step forward in the theology of the Trinity by the road that leads from unity of nature to trinity of per- sons. Aquinas followed this road but added precisions and distinctions to the doctrine of divine processions, relations and persons, and answered many difficult questions.

Augustine and Thomas. In his commentaries on the New Testament, Thomas carefully examined the prin- cipal texts regarding the Blessed Trin- ity, in the Synoptic Gospels, in the Gospel of St. John and in the Epistles of St. Paul. He analyzes with special emphasis the formula of baptism, our Lord's discourse before his passion, and especially John's prologue. His guides throughout are the Fathers, Greek and Latin, who refuted Arian- ism and Sabellianism.

These scriptural studies led him to see clearly the part played by Augus- tine in penetrating into the meaning of our Lord's words on this supreme mystery. This debt of Thomas to Augustine must be our first study. We find here a very interesting and im- portant chain of ideas. Unless we recall both the advantages and the difficulties presented by the Augus- tinian conception, we shall not be able to understand fully the teaching of Thomas.

Sabellius had denied real distinc-

---

admitted by all theologians. Their differ- ences concern only *predestination to glory in se* (prescinding from its preparation by faith and grace). Bossuet regarded these "abstractions" as being "useless enough after all." Even should one be less critical than Bossuet as regards these Scholastic discus- sions, it must be admitted that they place the problem on a very different plane from that which was usual with the Fathers, even the Augustinians, in the 5th century.

[1] Reginald Garrigou-Lagrange, O.P., was a famous Dominican Master of Theology. For many years he was Professor of Dog- matic Theology in the Collegio Angelico in Rome. Among his many works may be noted *God: His Existence and His Nature, The One God, The Three Ages of The Interior Life.* This excerpt is from his book, *Reality* (St. Louis: B. Herder Book Co., 1950), pp. 135–138, 140–147, 152.

---

[35] A powerlessness that gradually di- minishes as man forms a purer idea of God, free from unconscious anthropomorph- ism, to which our intellectual difficulties are due in a large measure.

tion of persons in the Trinity. Arius, on the other hand, had denied the divinity of the Son; Macedonius, that of the Holy Spirit. In refuting these opposite heresies, the Greek Fathers, resting on scriptural affirmation of three divine persons, had sought to show how this trinity of persons is to be harmonized with God's unity of nature. This harmony they found in the term "consubstantial," a term which by controversy grew more precise, and was definitively adopted by the Council of Nicea. The Son, said the Greek Fathers, led particularly by St. Athanasius,[2] is consubstantial with the Father, because the Father who begets the Son communicates to that Son his own divine nature, not a mere participation in that nature. And since this Son is the Son of God, his redemptive merits have infinite value. And the Holy Spirit, proceeding from the Father and the Son, is likewise God, consubstantial with the Father and the Son, without which consubstantiality he could not be the sanctifier of souls.[3]

Now these Greek Fathers thought of the divine processions rather as donations than as operations of the divine intelligence and the divine will. The Father, in begetting the Son, gives to that Son his own nature. And the Father and the Son give that divine nature to the Holy Spirit. The mode, they add, of this eternal generation and spiration is inscrutable. Further, following the order of the Apostles' Creed, they spoke of the Father as Creator, of the Son as Savior, of the Holy Spirit as Sanctifier. But their explanations left the road open to many questions.

Why are there two processions, and only two? How does the first procession differ from the second? Why is that first procession alone called generation? Why must there be one Son only? And why, in the Creed, is the Father alone called Creator, since creative power, being a characteristic of the divine nature, belongs also to the Son[4] and to the Holy Spirit? The Latin doctrine of appropriation is not found explicitly in the Greek Fathers.

Thomas, reading Augustine's work,[5] realized that this greatest of the Latin Fathers had taken a great step forward in the theology of the Trinity. Augustine's point of departure is the unity of God's nature, already demonstrated philosophically. Guided by revelation, he seeks the road leading from that unity of nature to the trinity of persons. This road, followed also by Thomas, is the inverse of that followed by the Greek Fathers.

In John's prologue, our Lord is called "the Word" and the "Only-begotten." These terms struck Augustine. Did they not offer an explanation of that generation which the Greek Fathers called inscrutable? The Son, proceeding from the Father, is called the Word. That divine Word is, not an exterior, but an interior word, a mental, intellectual word, spoken by the Father from all eternity. The Father begets the Son by an intel-

---

[2] *Cont. Arianos*, I, 14, 16, 25, 27; II, 24; III, 6.

[3] St. Athanasius, *Epist. ad Serapionem*, I, 23 ff.; III, 1–5.

[4] *Omnia per ipsum (Verbum) facta sunt.* St. John's prologue. Thus similarly in St. Paul's epistles.

[5] *De trinitate.*

lectual act, as our spirit conceives its own mental word.[6] But while our mental word is an accidental mode of our intellectual faculty, the divine word, like the divine thought, is substantial.[7] And while our spirit slowly and laboriously conceives its ideas, which are imperfect and limited and necessarily manifold, to express the diverse aspects of reality, created and uncreated, the Father, on the contrary, conceives eternally one substantial Word, unique and adequate, true God of true God, perfect expression of all that God is and of all that God does and could do. Much light is thus thrown on the intimate mode of the Word's eternal generation.[8]

The saint also explains, in similar fashion, the eternal act of spiration.[9] The human soul, created to the image of God, is endowed with intelligence and with love. It not only understands the good, but also loves the good. These are its two highest faculties. If then the only-begotten proceeds from the Father as the intellectual Word, we are led to think that the Holy Spirit proceeds from both by a procession of love, and that he is the terminus of this latter procession. Here, then, enter the divine relations.[10] The saint speaks thus: "It is demonstrated that not all predicates of God are substantial, but that some

are relative, that is, as belonging to him, not absolutely, but relatively to something other than himself." The Father is Father by relation to the Son, the Son by relation to the Father, the Holy Spirit by relation to the Father and the Son.[11] This doctrine is the basis of Thomistic doctrine on the divine relations.

So far, then, we have the reason why there are two processions in God, and only two, and why the Holy Spirit proceeds, not only from the Father, but also from the Son, just as in us love proceeds from knowledge. Augustine, however, does not see why only the first procession is called generation, and why we are not to say that the Holy Spirit is begotten. On this point, and on many others, Augustine's doctrine awaits precision by Thomas.

A similar remark must be made on Augustine's doctrine concerning the question of appropriation. Starting from the philosophically demonstrated unity of God's nature and not from the trinity of persons, he easily shows that not the Father alone is Creator, but also the Son and the Holy Spirit, since creative power is a characteristic of the divine nature, which is common to all three persons. This doctrine, through the course of centuries, becomes more precise by successive pronouncements of the Church.[12] Thomas is ever recurring to it. The three persons are one and the same

---

[6] *Ibid.*, Bks. IX and X.
[7] *Ibid.*, V, 5, 16, 17.
[8] See especially *ibid.*, XV, 10–16.
[9] *Ibid.*, Bks. IX and X; XV, 17–28.
[10] *Ibid.*, Bk. V (in toto) and XV, ch. 4, 5, where he speaks thus: *Demonstratur non omne quod de Deo dicitur secundum substantiam dici, sed dici etiam relative, id est, non ad se, sed ad aliquid, quod ipse non est.*

[11] *Ad Filium, ad Patrem. Ad Patrem et Filium. Ibid.*, V, 16, 17. Cf. J. Tixeront, *Hist. des dogmes*, II, 364–366.
[12] See Denz., nos. 19, 77, 254, 281, 284, 421, 428 (new: 188, 171, 501, 531, 535, 790, 800).

principle of external operation. If then, in the Apostles' Creed, the Father is in particular called the Creator, he is so called by appropriation, by reason, that is, of the affinity between paternity and power. Similarly, the works of wisdom are appropriated to the Word, and those of sanctification to the Spirit of love. This theory of appropriation, initiated by Augustine,[13] finds final precision in Thomas,[14] and definitive formulation in the Council of Florence.[15] . . .

The Divine Processions, Relations, Persons. Following revelation, particularly as recorded in John's prologue, Thomas shows that there is in God an intellectual procession, "an intelligible emanation of the intelligible Word from the speaker of that Word."[16] This procession is not that of effect from cause,[17] nor that of one subjective mode from another[18] . . . but is a real procession . . . by which the Word has the same nature as has the Father. . . . And the Word is not like our word, accidental but substantial, because God's act of knowledge is not an accident, but self-subsisting substance. . . .

Further, this procession of the only-begotten Son[19] is rightly called generation. The living thing, born of a living thing, receives a nature like that of its begetter, its generator. In

the Deity, the Son receives that same divine nature, not caused, but communicated. Common speech says that our intellect conceives a word. This act of conception is the initial formation of a living thing. But this conception of ours does not become generation, because our word is, not a substance, but an accident, so that, even when a man mentally conceives his own substantial self, that conception is still but an accidental similitude of himself, whereas the divine conception, the divine Word, is substantial, is not merely a similitude of God, but is God. Divine conception, then, is rightly called generation. Intellectual conception, purified from all imperfection, is an "intellectual generation," just as corporeal conception terminates in corporeal generation. . . .

There is in God a second procession, by the road of love, as love in us proceeds from the knowledge of the good.[20] But this second procession is not a generation,[21] because love, in contrast with knowledge, does not make itself like its object, but rather goes out to its object.[22] . . .

If there are real processions in God, then there must also be real relations. As in the order of nature, temporal generation founds two relations, of son to father and father to son, so likewise does the eternal generation of the Word found the two relations of paternity and filiation. And the procession of love also founds two relations, active spiration and "passive"

---

[13] *De trin.,* VI, 2.
[14] I, q. 39, a. 7, 8; q. 46, a. 3; q. 45, a. 6, ad 2.
[15] *In Deo omnia sunt unum et idem ubi non obviat relationis oppositio.* Denz., no. 703 (new: 1330).
[16] *Secundum emanationem intelligibilem Verbi intelligibilis a dicente.* I, q. 27, a. 1.
[17] Arianism.
[18] Modalism.
[19] I, q. 27, a. 2. Cf. Jn 1:18.

[20] I, q. 27, a. 3.
[21] *Ibid.,* a. 4.
[22] *Amor meus, pondus meum* (Augustine).

spiration.[23] . . . Real relations in God are four: paternity, filiation, active spiration, "passive spiration." But the third of these four, active spiration, while it is opposed to passive spiration, is not opposed to, and hence not really distinct from, either paternity or filiation.[24] This doctrine, perfectly self-coherent, shows the value of Augustine's conception, which is its foundation and guaranty. . . .

Since person signifies substance in its most perfect form, it can be found in God, if it be stripped of the imperfect mode which it has in created persons. Thus made perfect, it can be used analogically of God, analogically, but still in its proper sense, in a mode that is transcendent and preeminent. Further, since revelation gives us two personal names, that is, the Father and the Son, the name of the third person, of the Holy Spirit, must also be a personal name. Besides, the New Testament, in many texts, represents the Holy Spirit as a person.[25]

Now, since there are three persons in God, they can be distinct one from the other only by the three relations which are mutually opposed (paternity, filiation, and passive spiration), because . . . all else in God is identical. These real relations, since they are subsistent,[26] and are, on the other hand, incommunicable,[27] can consti-

tute the divine persons. In these subsistent relations we find the two characteristics of person: substantiality and incommunicability. . . . These three opposed relations, then, paternity, filiation, and passive spiration, belong to related and incommunicable personalities.

A divine person, then, according to Thomas and his school, is a divine relation as subsistent.[28] Elsewhere the saint gives the following definition: A divine person is nothing else than a relationally distinct reality, subsistent in the divine essence.[29] . . .

The three persons, purely spiritual, are open to possession one by the other, being distinguished only by their mutual relations. The Father's entire personality consists in his subsistent and incommunicable relation to the Son, the ego of the Son is his relation to the Father, the ego of the Holy Spirit is his relation to the first two persons.

Thus each of the three persons, since he is what he is by his relationship to the others, is united to the others precisely by what distinguishes him from them. . . . The three divine persons are the exemplar of the life of charity. Each of them speaks to the others: All that is mine is thine, all that is thine is mine.[30]

---

[23] I, q. 28, a. 1.
[24] I, q. 28, a. 4.
[25] I, q. 29, a. 3.
[26] Not accidental.
[27] Being opposed.

[28] I, q. 29, a. 4.
[29] *De potentia*, q. 9, a. 4: *Persona nihil aliud est quam distinctum relatione subsistens in essentia divina.* Cf. I, q. 40, a. 1, 2.
[30] Jn 17:10.

6. C. R. S. Harris[1] studies Scotus' view of the ideal theology and his mediating position between the older and the newer scholasticism. He looks at his formal distinction and the charge of extreme voluntarism brought against him, especially in connection with his account of the Trinitarian process.

The frontier line between metaphysics and theology can . . . never be defined with complete accuracy without destroying the fundamental unity of knowledge and ultimately of consciousness itself. We shall be forced, therefore, to stray somewhat into the no man's land which throughout the history of medieval thought is occupied on a precarious tenure, now by one, now by the other of these departments of learning. And in the case of Scotus himself our task is doubly difficult. For the critical character of his thought often renders it impossible to decide with any degree of certainty the exact ground on which any particular thesis which he is defending is ultimately based, and to distinguish arguments founded purely on natural reason from those which rest in the last resort on some revealed truth. For the syllogistic method of argumentation is applied to theology and philosophy alike, and the insoluble question then arises whether the premises of a particular series of inferences can or cannot be reduced to propositions which are knowable by the sole light of the active intellect. . . .

Perhaps the most lucid account of the scientific character of theology and of the limits of human knowledge is given in the *Quodlibeta* in a discussion on the demonstrability of the divine omnipotence. Scotus distinguishes first of all between intuitive and abstractive knowledge. In intuition the object is directly given; it is known immediately as actually present in the same way as the object of sense-perception in the act of perceiving. But abstractive knowledge is a knowledge mediated by concepts, and the concept as such is indifferent to the existence or non-existence *in re* of the content which it symbolizes.[2] Now of God, during the period of our earthly existence, we can have no intuitive knowledge, for it is this very knowledge of vision, the *lumen gloriae*, which goes to constitute the beatific state. Our knowledge of God, then, can only be abstractive, mediated through the instrumentality of a conception. The question, therefore, arises as to how far a conceptual knowledge of God is possible. The answer which Duns gives illustrates very clearly his notion of the ideal theology which shall be perfectly scientific. It is possible for man *in statu viae* to have a

[1] C. R. S. Harris, M.A., D.Phil. (Oxon.), Ph.D. (Princeton) was Fellow of All Souls College (Oxford), and Jane Eliza Procter Visiting Fellow Princeton University, U.S.A., 1922–1923. This excerpt is from his book, *Duns Scotus*, Vol. II, The Philosophical Doctrines of Duns Scotus (Oxford At The Clarendon Press, 1927), pp. 147–151, 171–172, 176–177, 186–187, 207–208, 214–216, 219–220, 222–224.

[2] *Quodl.*, q. 7, n. 8: "*Et breviter hic repetitur, quia etsi cognitio abstractiva possit esse non existentis aeque sicut et existentis, tamen intuitiva non est nisi existentis, ut existens est; cognitio autem hominis abstractiva et definitiva potest esse non-existentis et existentis.*" Cf. *De Cognitione Dei*, q. 1, n. 2.

conception of God which shall include "virtually" all the necessary truths concerning the divine being, and this knowledge is consistent with the earthly state, for it is not an intuitive knowledge. But of the contingent truths of God's nature there can be no scientific knowledge, for knowledge is only of the necessary, and these contingent verities depend on no necessary principles, but solely on the divine will, whose freedom is unlimited save by its own nature, and whose actions are not predictable. But even concerning these contingent truths there is a kind of necessary knowledge which is possible; for a man possessed of the type of knowledge of which we have been speaking would know the necessary truth that God is able to create, to raise from the dead, to beatify, and so forth.[3] His theology would be scientific, for the ideal of scientific knowledge is the knowledge of the properties of a subject as belonging to its essence and

known as "necessary," and would stand midway between the knowledge of vision, the "light of glory," and the "light of faith." He would have attained, in fact, to the theological ideal of Anselm, Abelard, and Hugo of St. Victor, and perceived the *rationes necessariae* which are the ground of the Triune Unity.

But such a theology, though not absolutely inconsistent with the earthly condition of humankind, is not vouchsafed to men. We cannot reach a conception of the divine nature from which the necessary truths pertaining to it can be deduced and demonstrated *propter quid* by the use of natural reason.[4] Nor can such a conception be given us by faith, for faith can only move us to assent to certain propositions concerning the being of God which cannot be shown to be self-evident: it can yield us no simple notion or concept of God which transcends the concept of the metaphysician.[5] And the metaphysical concept of God which we can form is wholly inadequate to express the divine nature in its fullness, *sub ratione deitatis*. Such a knowledge of the divinity belongs only to God himself.[6]

---

[3] *Ibid.*, n. 10: *"Juxta istam conclusionem potest haberi corollarium quomodo Theologia potest esse scientia in intellectu viatoris, stante simpliciter statu viae, quia intellectus potens habere conceptum virtualiter includentem omnes veritates de ipso necessario ordinatas . . . potest de ullo objecto habere scientiam completam, sicut autem potest intellectus viatoris habere de Deo. Minor patet, quia distinctissimus conceptus subjecti Theologiae, quod est Deus, potest haberi citra cognitionem intuitivam, et ille conceptus et virtualiter et evidenter continet omnes veritates necessarias de subjecto; contingentes autem non potest includere quia illae non natae sunt includi in ratione alicujus subjecti . . . Tamen de contingentibus sunt quaedam veritates necessariae, non quidem de actu eorum sed de possibilitate, et illae etiam modo praedicto sciri possunt, utpote, Deus est potens creare, potens resuscitare, potens beatificare, et sic de aliis articulis fidei respicientibus contingentiam."*

[4] *Quodl.*, q. 7, n. 11, 10.

[5] *Ibid.*

[6] *Op. Ox.*, lib. I, dist. 3, q. 2, n. 16: *"Dico quod non cognoscitur Deus naturaliter a viatore in particulari et proprie, hoc est sub ratione hujus essentiae ut haec et in se. . . , quia sub ratione talis cognoscibilis est objectum voluntarium et non naturale, nisi respectu sui intellectus tantum."* The phrase *"objectum voluntarium"* is highly suggestive, but it is difficult to see what exactly it is that Scotus is trying to convey. Does he mean that such a knowledge of God can only be vouchsafed to man by a special act of the divine will, or that it is only by a mystical effect of grace upon our will that we can attain such a knowledge?

Scotus' treatment of the arguments for the existence of God shows once more his mediating position between the older and the newer scholasticism. His attempted rehabilitation of the ontological argument and his insistence on the self-evidence of the divine existence for a mind endowed with a clear conception of the divine essence, which, as Werner remarks,[7] endows the notion of God with a potential apriority, point clearly to the traditions of the Franciscan school. But in the main he follows the newer empiricism of the Thomists in his emphasis on the inability of the human mind to attain to any but a posteriori demonstrations of the divine existence, and his denial of any innate idea of God. He thus differentiates himself sharply from the first great Franciscan doctor, Alexander of Hales, and from the Augustinian tradition with its half-mystical ontologistic theory of knowledge. . . .

The conception of God as infinite being is the fundamental notion of the Scotist natural theology. The idea of infinity receives a much more positive content at the hands of Duns than at those of Thomas. For infinity signifies not merely the removal of all limits of an external nature, and the subtle Doctor tries hard to give it a positive significance. For though, he tells us, when speaking of the divine perfections we call them infinite, thus using a negative term, we do so only because their positive nature is less known to us than the finite qualities which they negate.[8]

Yet in the last resort Scotus' notion remains purely abstract, and he is unable to use it as a starting point for a dialectical advance in which the idea of the divine essence and its attributes can be developed. For from the idea of infinite being, as from the infinite substance of Spinoza, no transition can be mediated to the finite world, and no content of intrinsic attributes can be developed. He is thus arrested by the very same problem which Hegel attempted to solve at the beginning of his dialectic, and the progress of his argument is brought to a stop. Consequently, the deduction of the divine attributes is merely descriptive and wholly unsystematic, being pieced together out of fragments of traditional scholastic theology, somewhat awkwardly grafted on to a truncated and distorted Aristotelianism. . . .

Thomas had repudiated the notion that the divine names were synonymous, and he had conceded that the distinctions were contained "virtually" in the divine essence.[9] But this will not satisfy the critical Duns. He agrees with Aquinas that God's intellect and will are each identical with his essence,[10] but they are not therefore identical with each other. So, too, with the divine goodness and the divine wisdom. Here, as elsewhere, he attempts to mediate between the ultrarealistic *distinctio realis* and the nominalistic *distinctio rationis* by means of his notion of the *distinctio formalis a parte rei*. The distinction between the divine attributes is not

[7] *Geschichte der späteren Scholastick,* vol. I, "Duns Scotus," p. 334.

[8] Cf. *Quaest. Miscell.,* q. 5, n. 20.

[9] *De Potentia Dei,* q. 7; *S.T.,* I, q. 13, a. 4.

[10] *Op. Ox.,* I, dist. 2, q. 2, nn. 20 ff.; *Rep. Par.* I, dist. 45, q. 2, n. 7.

purely conceptual in origin; it is one which exists prior to the operation of human thought. For, notwithstanding the identity of the divine goodness and wisdom with the divine essence, wisdom and goodness are different, and their difference is not obliterated by the fact that both are infinite. There is a formal non-identity which cannot be transcended.[11] Yet we cannot regard them as separate qualities, accidental, as it were, to the divine essence, for in God there is no accident, and such a categorization would be inconsistent with the divine simplicity. They are, therefore, identical *realiter* insofar as they are one with the divine essence, but distinct *formaliter* in so much as their notions are non-identical.

And furthermore this formal distinction is of the profoundest importance to the Scotist theology, for on it is founded his whole conception of the Trinitarian process. The distinction between the divine attributes is the basis of the personal emanations. Were the divine intellect identical with the divine will there could be no distinction between the Son and the Holy Ghost. For the Son is the Word of the Father, and proceeds from him *nascendo* even as the idea springs from the intellect. But the Holy Ghost proceeds from the Father and the Son *spirando,* as love flows forth from the will.[12] Now the distinction between the divine Persons is real and not merely conceptual — hence the distinction between the divine attributes is also in some sense real.[13] . . .

In all this long and tedious controversy there is not one word to justify the commonly accepted notion that, according to Duns' teaching, the essences of things are dependent for their being on the divine will — as a matter of fact the divine will is not even mentioned in this connection at all. The charges of extreme voluntarism brought against him by Baur,[14] Ritschl,[15] Vacant,[16] Pluzanski,[17] De-Wulf,[18] Seeberg,[19] and most recently by Landry,[20] thus turn out to be utterly unfounded. In fact, Scotus goes out of his way to repudiate the notion that the divine ideas depend in any way on the divine omnipotence. They are solely the product of the divine intelligence,[21] which conceives them prior to the divine will, and that necessarily,[22] and it would do so even if, *per impossibile,* God were not endowed with a will at all.[23] . . .

As in the case of the human will, so also in that of the divine, Duns is anxious to maintain what we might call a moderate indeterminism in con-

---

[11] *Op. Ox.,* I, dist. 8, q. 4, n. 17.
[12] *Ibid.,* n. 7.

[13] *Ibid.,* n. 10.
[14] Cf. Baur, *Die christliche Lehre von der Dreieinigkeit und Menschenwerdung Gottes,* p. 642.
[15] A. Ritschl, *Jahrbücher für deutsche Theologie,* 1865, Bd. 10, p. 307.
[16] Vacant, *Compte rendu,* etc. (Freibourg, 1898), p. 643.
[17] Pluzanski, *Essai sur la Philosophie de Duns Scot,* p. 182.
[18] De Wulf, *History of Mediaeval Philosophy,* Eng. trans., p. 374.
[19] Seeberg, *Die Theologie des Duns Scotus,* p. 178.
[20] Landry, *Duns Scot,* p. 344.
[21] *Op. Ox.,* I, dist. 36, n. 4.
[22] *Op. Ox.,* I, dist. 3, q. 4, n. 20.
[23] *Op. Ox.,* Prol., q. 4. Cf. *Rep. Par.,* I, dist. 48, q. 1, n. 12.

trast to the extreme and arbitrary libertarianism which has so often been ascribed to him. . . . The volition of God is not purely arbitrary, a sort of willing *in vacuo*. For the will cannot of itself be a first agent.[24] God can only will objects presented to him by his intellect.[25] The divine omnipotence is thus limited to the possibilities provided by the divine intelligence . . . bound by the law of contradiction . . . and restricted to the logically possible.[26]

In view of these considerations, it is therefore inaccurate to maintain with Ritter, Kahl, and others,[27] that according to Scotus the divine will is unmotived, cut loose, as it were, from the divine intelligence, even from the divine essence itself. . . . For the divine willing though not determined by the divine intellect, is yet influenced by it. It is the intellect which presents to the will the objects to be willed,[28] and without it no act of will at all would be possible. The divine freedom must not, therefore, be interpreted as a kind of transcendent irrationality. The whole meaning of the identity of will and intellect with the divine essence lies in the fact that the divine will is necessarily rational, for it is in the last resort the power to create things after the pattern of the divine ideas.[29] . . . Thus

Duns' theory of the divine will follows throughout very closely the teaching of Thomas. . . .

Trinitarian process. . . . In his account of the Trinitarian process we shall find a final answer to those critics who would see in the conception of "absolute will" the central notion of Scotus' theology. It is true that according to Duns' teaching the Triune Unity can be proved neither a priori nor a posteriori: we can demonstrate it neither through our notion of the divine essence nor by arguments drawn from the nature of the created world. Yet the dogma is not altogether removed from the realm of human reason; it can be shown on rational grounds to be credible, and the philosophical objections which are brought against it can be shown to be fallacious.[30]

In his speculative construction of the Trinitarian process Duns abandons for a moment the dualism of intellect and will in the divine being, and returns to the older tripartite division of Augustine: *memoria, intellectus,* and *voluntas.* The concept of *memoria* is somewhat difficult to define, so nearly does it coincide with that of the intellect; it is, according to Scotus, the divine intellect considered not in the act of positing its intellectual object, but rather as having that object present to it, *in actu secundo,* as opposed to the *actus primus* or *intellectio.*[31] The memoria, and not the intellect as such, is, according to its formal notion, the principle of the immanent production or generation[32]

[24] *Quodl.*, q. 16, n. 15.

[25] *Op. Ox.*, I, dist. 2, q. 2, n. 22.

[26] *Rep. Par.*, I, dist. 43, q. 1, n. 13; *Op. Ox.*, I, dist. 2, q. 2, n. 20.

[27] Ritter, *Geschichte der Philosophie,* 8er Teil, p. 393; W. Kahl, *Die Lehre vom Primat des Willens bei Augustinus, Duns Scotus und Descartes,* p. 105; Schwane, *Dogmengeschichte der mittleren Zeit,* p. 78.

[28] *Op. Ox.*, IV, dist. 46, q. 1, n. 10.

[29] *De Rerum Principio,* q. 6, n. 8.

[30] *Op. Ox.*, I, dist. 2, q. 7, n. 3 ff.

[31] *Quodl.*, q. 1, n. 21.

[32] *Ibid.,* cf. Henry of Ghent, *S.T.,* art.

and is, therefore, called the *memoria fecunda,* inasmuch as it produces the *notitia genita* or *verbum.* Now this product of the *memoria perfecta* is a "perfect production" only if the *notitia genita* is adequate to the principle which produces it. But the *memoria* of the divine essence is infinite, and must, therefore, have an infinite *notitia* corresponding to it.[33] This *notitia infinita,* the *Verbum* or *Filius,* the Second Person of the Trinity, is thus generated within the divine essence itself, for outside of it there is no infinite. Hence the immanent production is called the *productio ad intra,* which, being wholly within the ground of the divine essence and possible, is also necessary.[34] The Third Person is produced by the Father and the eternal Word, *per modum spirandi,* the principle of spiration being the divine will, which is identical in both Persons and operates on the divine essence by loving it. This act of the divine volition has as its object an infinite love, which is the *amor spiratus* or Holy Ghost.[35] There is not a word here of the primacy of the divine will over the divine intellect; both participate equally in the Trinitarian process, and there is no foundation whatsoever for the view that Scotus regarded one as a more fundamental aspect of the divine nature than the other.

7. **A. C. McGiffert[1] studies Eckhart and the mystics. Eckhart's significance was due not only to the extreme character of his mysticism but also to his grounding of it in a speculative theology of a very daring type. Tauler and Suso were less extreme and paradoxical than Eckhart in their writings.**

Mysticism of one or another type has existed in every period of Christian history and in every part of Christendom. . . . No one country has a monopoly of them, though in Germany and the Netherlands they seem to have been more numerous than elsewhere; at any rate we know more about them there, particularly in the thirteenth and fourteenth centuries when their numbers were increasing rapidly. Of all of them there is none more interesting or better worth studying than Meister Eckhart, as he was called. He was born in central Germany . . . about 1260 and early joined the Dominican Order in which he later held important administrative posts and wielded considerable influence. . . . He was a follower of Thomas Aquinas and belonged ostensibly to his school, but he felt other influences as well and departed widely in some respects from the teaching of the great Dominican doctor.

The chief difference between them lay in the fact that Eckhart was a mystic of the most thoroughgoing kind, while Thomas, though he read

---

27, qq. 6 and 7; Thomas, *S.T.,* I, q. 27, a. 1 and 2.

[33] *Op. Ox.,* II, dist. 1, q. 1, n. 13.

[1] Ch. VI, 1, n. 1. This excerpt is from *op. cit.,* pp. 359–375.

[34] *Op. Ox.,* I, dist. 2, q. 7, n. 3.

[35] *Op. Ox.,* II, dist. 1, q. 1, n. 13.

the future life of the saved in mystical terms, was far from being a mystic in his interpretation of the present life. Compared with this fundamental contrast all theological divergences were of relatively minor importance. Nevertheless, to understand Eckhart, we must acquaint ourselves with certain aspects of his theology, for his significance was due not only to the extreme and uncompromising character of his mysticism but also to his grounding of it in a speculative theology of a very daring type. . . .

Eckhart's great aim as a preacher and religious teacher was to promote the Christian's union with God. This he counted the end of all religion and the essence of salvation as brought to the world by Jesus Christ. In his own person Christ united God and man and thus made it possible for man in his turn to become one with God. Union with God Eckhart interpreted in the most intimate possible sense. It is not simply communion with God, or oneness of will and affection with him, but a complete fusion of man's nature with the nature of God. "God must become I," Eckhart declares, "and I must become God."[2] . . . This union with God, this transformation into God, Eckhart speaks of frequently as deification: the man united to God "is deified"; "he is a deified person. . . ."[3] This does not mean that man loses his individual consciousness. However closely united with God and however completely transformed into God, he still retains

something of himself; his personal identity is not destroyed but rather conserved and enriched.[4]

Union with God was possible, so Eckhart believed, because man and God are at bottom really one. Man came from God and is himself in some sense truly divine. It is not simply that he was made in the image of God and still retains vestiges of the divine likeness, but that he shares the being of God. Upon this essential oneness of God and man Eckhart laid great emphasis. . . . God, Eckhart insisted, is within man and is to be found not by traveling to some distant sphere but by turning one's gaze upon one's inner self, where the soul of man and the Spirit of God are inseparably joined.

The union with God which Eckhart preached he was fond of calling the birth of Christ in the soul. There is a twofold begetting of the Son: his eternal generation as the second person of the Trinity, and his generation in the soul of man. . . . "The Father begets his Son in the soul in the same way as he begets him in eternity and not otherwise. He must do it whether he likes it or not. The Father begets his Son without ceasing; and I say furthermore he begets me as his Son and the same Son. I say more: he begets me not alone as his Son, he begets me as himself and himself as me — me his essence and his nature."[5]

There is a faculty in the soul by which a man may know God directly.[6] . . . The faculty by which one knows

---

[2] In a sermon on "Renewal in the Spirit" in Pfeiffer's *Meister Eckhart*, Sermon 99, p. 320.

[3] Pfeiffer, Sermon 76, p. 240, 643.

[4] Cf. Lasson: *Meister Eckhart der Mystiker*, pp. 212 f.

[5] Pfeiffer, Sermon 65, p. 205.

[6] *Ibid.*, Sermon 69, p. 221.

God is not merely human like the senses, or the reasoning power, but divine. . . . "My eye and God's eye are one eye — one seeing, one knowing, one loving."[7] Eckhart had many names for this faculty: divine spark, power, eye of the soul, ground of the soul, uncreated light, and so on. . . .

There are three kinds of knowledge: sensible, rational, and super-rational. . . . Man . . . must renounce and rise above both the sensible and the rational, that is all ordinary human knowledge, in order to know God. This he can do because of the divine faculty just referred to, the faculty that makes him truly one with God and opens to him the vision of the divine. The vision of God which Thomas put into the future life, when man shall have laid off the flesh with its limitations, Eckhart put into the present (not the perfection of it to be sure, but its real beginning), for even here we are one with God, if we but know it. Few, to be sure, are aware of it, and hence few now enjoy the vision, but all might if they only would, for God is not apart from us but in us. . . .

Eckhart, as I have said, was a philosopher as well as a mystic and he did not content himself with asserting the essential oneness of God and man. He made it part of a general system of philosophy and read it in the light of a larger whole. God he represented as the fountain from which all things flow and to which all things return. God is being and the source of all being. The universe is not simply

his creation; it is God unfolded and revealed. It is not of another nature but of the nature of God himself, for God alone truly is. All things are in God and outside of him there is nothing. God and the world together are no more than God alone. Everything is in God and is identical with him. . . .

The whole universe, spiritual as well as material, is part of an eternal process, the process of the divine unfolding and refolding.[8] In begetting the eternal Word, God begets the eternal ideas in which every thing, from angels down to the lowest creatures, has its eternal existence. The visible world is but the temporal manifestation of this eternal world of ideas. Out of the fullness of God all things came and to him all things return. The process is circular not rectilinear — God is not simply the source, but the goal of all things, not simply the beginning but the end of the process. . . . All creatures long for unity and desire to return to the source whence they came. There there is complete rest. Movement belongs to the imperfect. Through the imperfect and the finite the process goes on until it reaches the perfect quiescence of Deity in which all things are eternally at peace. All this reminds us of Eriugena. Whether Eckhart drew directly upon that great thinker, or only felt the influence, as Eriugena did, of Plotinus and the Neoplatonists, at any rate his thought moved along similar lines. Not altogether inappropriately

---

[7] *Ibid.*, Sermon 96, p. 312.

[8] For this and what follows see the quotations in Karrer: *Meister Eckhart*, pp. 84 ff.

he might be called a mystical Eriugena or Eriugena become mystic.[9]

To God in himself — the undifferentiated unity lying back of the process of evolution — Eckhart gave the name *deitas* or *Gottheit* (Deity or Godhead), distinguishing him from the personal God, the creator of the world.[10] Of God in himself, or Deity, we can speak truly only in negative terms. He is not this or that or anything that we can say or think. He is pure being without qualities or attributes of any kind. To define him is to limit him. If he were comprehensible, Eckhart says, he were no God. . . . That God is incomprehensible and beyond all human understanding was no new idea. From the beginning it had been recognized by Christian theologians, but some made more of it and others less. Like Dionysius the Areopagite, who influenced him largely, Eckhart went further than most in his emphasis upon this aspect of the divine. . . . "If I say God is a being, it is not true: he is a transcendental essence, a super-essential nothing."[11]

This Being who is above all being and utterly beyond human comprehension Eckhart distinguished, as I have said, from the personal God, the creator and ruler of the world. The latter, the triune God of the Christians, has been revealed; the former remains hidden. The latter is Deity manifest, Deity in relations; the former is Deity apart and alone, the Absolute, out of touch with anything else that is.[12] . . .

The practical significance of all this lies in the fact that Eckhart taught that union with the personal God revealed by Christ was not enough and that Christians should not be content with it. They should press on until united with the ultimate fountain of being, the oneness that lies back of all differences, the unknown and unknowable Deity. . . . Knowledge in the ordinary sense is impossible at this level. The relationship between the soul and the absolute is superrational and indefinable but it means the closest possible union and the highest conceivable beatitude. . . .

Not Christ himself and not the Christian God, the God revealed by Christ and in him, was the supreme object of Eckhart's desire, but a mysterious Being unknown and unknowable lying back of God, a Being who though called Deity is really nothing but a metaphysical abstraction, the conception of unity in which the phi-

---

[9] Denifle (*Meister Eckeharts lateinische Schriften und die Grundanschauung seiner Lehre*) attempts to show that practically all Eckhart's teaching is to be found in Thomas and was the common property of the schoolmen. But though Eckhart quoted largely from Thomas and though parallels to many of his utterances can be found in him the emphasis lies elsewhere and the general impression is very different. We are moving indeed in another realm of thought, the Neoplatonic not the Aristotelian, and that despite the fact that there is no little Aristotelianism in details.

[10] See the quotations in Büttner: *Meister Eckeharts Schriften und Predigten aus dem Mittelhochdeutschen übersetzt*, 1903, I, 198 f.

[11] From Evans' translation of Pfeiffer's *Eckhart*, p. 246.

[12] The difference between the two is similar to that marked by Clement's use of the terms God and Logos: his God is Eckhart's Deity, his Logos Eckhart's God.

losopher finds satisfaction in the midst of all the disunities and diversities and inconsistencies of the phenomenal universe. It has been said that Eckhart's mysticism was more philosophical than religious. The statement is not without truth, but it implies a distinction between philosophy and religion which is hardly justified.[13] . . .

Eckhart had much to say about . . . the conditions prerequisite to union with God. And first of all, surprisingly enough, he put the imitation of Christ in his life of active Christian service rather than solitude and separation from the world. . . . Notwithstanding his recognition of the importance of love for others expressing itself in deeds of charity and helpfulness, he commonly spoke of the contemplation of God as the noblest of all exercises. . . . Motionless detachment makes a man superlatively Godlike. Eckhart's mysticism led him to value somewhat lightly the sacraments and other external means, of grace, as also the priesthood, the appointed ministers of salvation.[14] . . . Much the same is true of his attitude toward good works. Man is not saved by them but by love for God alone.[15] . . .

Toward the close of his life, he

fell under the suspicion of heresy and after his death several propositions drawn from his writings were condemned by Pope John XXII who denounced him for "wishing to know more than he should."[16] . . . Eckhart himself, to be sure, had no thought of heresy. He was a loyal son of the Church . . . and when the storm began to gather, he declared himself ready to make full submission if that should be desired. His death, however, spared him the humiliation of a recantation.

In spite of his condemnation, his name continued to be revered and his memory cherished by multitudes. Among those who felt his influence were the German Dominicans, Henry Suso, and John Tauler . . . and the Flemist mystic John Ruysbroeck. . . . While they reproduced many of his ideas, they were not so profound and philosophical as he; and Tauler and Suso, at any rate, were much more careful not to offend the weaker brethren. Their writings which are thoroughly devotional in spirit are less extreme and paradoxical than Eckhart's and better calculated to promote a type of mystical piety in harmony with Catholic tradition, though the independent and venturesome spirit of the great master shines through now and then.

---

[13] Eriugena, it should be remembered, identified philosophy and religion.

[14] Cf. Pfeiffer, Sermon 76, p. 239.

[15] Pfeiffer, p. 560.

[16] Cf. Denz. 501–529 (new: 950–980).

VIII

GOD IN THE FOURTEENTH AND
FIFTEENTH CENTURIES

1. P. Boehner[1] gives us a glimpse of William of Ockham, the central figure of the nominalist movement. Ockham is first and foremost a theologian who views the world from the standpoint of the absolute. By his theory of univocity he puts a link between creatures and God, and between ontology, natural theology and revealed theology. His philosophy had enormous influence.

The great Scottish philosopher John Duns Scotus is in many respects the connecting link between the thirteenth and the fourteenth centuries. . . . He is the builder of one of the most impressive systems of the Middle Ages; but at the same time his work reveals many characteristics of the period which follows him. . . . A prodigiously varied school, composed mostly, though not exclusively, of members of the Franciscan Order,

[1] Philotheus Boehner, O.F.M. was Late Professor of Philosophy, The Franciscan Institute, St. Bonaventure, N. Y. He died May 22, 1955 while engaged in laying the foundation for the first comprehensive critical edition of Ockham's philosophical and theological works. This excerpt is from his work, *Ockham: Philosophical Writings* (New York: The Bobbs-Merrill Co., Inc., 1964), pp. x–xxii, xxxix–xlvi, li.

achieved the firm entrenchment of Scotus' doctrine in scholasticism for centuries to come. It was natural that the followers of the older scholastics, in particular Thomas, should strongly oppose the innovations of Duns Scotus and his criticism of their own position. But these were not his only critics; some of those who readily acknowledged their great indebtedness to him nevertheless felt free to go their own way. Two of these independent-minded followers are known as the originators of conceptualism, viz., the saintly French Franciscan, Archbishop Peter Aureoli (d. 1321 or 1322), and the English Franciscan, William Ockham.

Aureoli and Ockham have many doctrines in common. . . . Both reject the realistic interpretation of universal concepts and the connected doctrine of "formal" distinctions so characteristic of Scotus's teachings, and both went far beyond the work of the great Master.

Though we must not underrate the importance of Aureoli for medieval thought . . . it nevertheless seems justifiable to consider Ockham as the central figure of a new movement, known as the school of the nominalists. . . . This school grew to such importance that every historian of fourteenth-century scholasticism is forced either to go back to, or to start with, the Doctor plusquam subtilis, the Venerabilis Inceptor, William Ockham.[2]

He lectured at Oxford and was accused of teaching dangerous doctrines. . . . Pope John XXII called him to Avignon where his trial dragged on for three years. . . . In the debate over Franciscan poverty . . . he took sides with his superior against the Pope, and fled with him to the German Emperor, Louis of Bavaria. . . . The fugitive Franciscans were excommunicated by the Pope and by their own Order. . . . After the death of Louis . . . there is good evidence that Ockham sought a reconciliation with the Pope and his Order . . . but whether he signed the formula of submission or not we do not know. . . . Thus ended the career of one who was a brilliant philosopher, a great theologian, and too modern a politician. . . .

Ockham is first and foremost a theologian. . . . For him there can be only one absolute in this world. . . one reality which is completely self-sufficient, namely God, the supreme author alike of creation and of revelation. . . . And by God Ockham means a God of absolute unity and simplicity, and at the same time a God threefold in his personality. . . . God's revelation, whether as deposited in holy

---

[2] William of Ockham was probably born at Ockham, near London, perhaps closer to 1280 than 1290. It is most probable that he pursued his higher studies in theology at Oxford from about 1309 to 1315, lectured on the Bible from about 1315–1317, lectured on the Sentences from about 1317 to 1319. It seems that he died c. 1349 (or 1347?), probably a victim of the Black Death. Cf. Guillelmi de Ockham Opera politica, accuravit J. G. Sikes (Manchester, 1940); Fritz Hoffmann, Die erste Kritik des Ockhamismus durch den Oxforder Kanzler Johannes Lutterell (nach der Hs. CCV der Bibliothek des Prager Metropolitankapitels), in Breslauer Studien zur historischen Theologie, Neue Folge Band ix (Breslau, 1941); Rudolf Höhn, O.F.M., "Wilhelm Ockham in München," in Franziskanische Studien, xxxii (1950).

Scripture or as embodied in the living tradition of the Church, is accepted by Ockham as the rule of faith. . . . However, Ockham is also a logician, perhaps the greatest logician of the Middle Ages. Reason is something sacred, a gift from God; hence the laws of reason are to be respected. . . .

Ockham's philosophy is empirical, but he is no empiricist. He is an empirical thinker, because he is a Christian firmly believing in the contingency of this created world of ours. . . . Ockham never loses sight of this basic Christian idea — so radically opposed to the necessitarian view — that there is no *inherent* necessity for anything in this world to be what it is. Even in his investigation of the problems of physics or psychology, Ockham never forgets that this world is absolutely dependent on the will of God; always he takes the stand of a Christian, who firmly believes in the omnipotence of God and the contingency of creatures.

Thus the following maxims are the guiding principles of all Ockham's work: (1) All things are possible for God, save such as involve a contradiction. . . . (2) Whatever God produces by means of secondary, (i.e., created) causes, God can produce and conserve immediately and without their aid.[3] . . . (3) God can cause, produce and conserve any reality, be it a substance or an accident, apart from any other reality.[4] . . . We are not allowed to affirm a statement to be true or to maintain that a certain

thing exists, unless we are forced to do so either by its self-evidence or by revelation or by experience or by a logical deduction from either a revealed truth or a proposition verified by observation. That this is the real meaning of "Ockham's razor" can be gathered from various texts in Ockham's writings.[5] It is quite often stated by Ockham in the form: "Plurality is not to be posited without necessity." . . . The form usually given, "Entities must not be multiplied without necessity,"[6] does not seem to have been used by Ockham. (5) Everything that is real, and different from God, is contingent to the core of its being.

If we bear in mind these guiding principles of Ockham, then his philosophical work becomes intelligible as the effort of a theologian who is looking for absolute truth in this contingent world, viz., for truth independent of any of those thoroughly contingent worlds which are equally possible. He is a theologian who views the world from the standpoint of the absolute. . . . The actual order of creatures remains contingent; the possible order of creatures is above contingency. Hence, the tendency of Ockham to go beyond the investigation of the actual order, by asking what is

---

[3] Cf. *Quodlibeta*, vi, q. 6, of the Strasbourg edition.

[4] Cf. Reportatio, ii, q. 19 f.

[5] Cf. *De sacramento altaris*, cap. 28; ed. Birch, p. 318; *Ordinatio*, d. 30, q. IE; *Reportatio*, II, q. 150. It should be noted that various formulations of "Ockham's razor" are already found before Ockham, for instance in Duns Scotus. The oldest scholastic thinker, so far as we know, who formulated it, gives this version: "Frustra fit per plura quod potest fieri per unum"; Odo Rigaldus, *Commentarium super Sententias*, MS. Bruges 208, fol. 150a.

[6] *Entia non sunt multiplicanda sine necessitate.*

possible regardless of the state of the present universe. . . . Thus the work of Ockham also becomes intelligible. . . . . as the effort of a philosopher who is constantly reminded by the theologian in himself that he must not call any truth necessary unless it can be shown that its denial implies a contradiction.

Such a theologian, and such a philosopher, stands in need of a refined and powerful logic, since he is always looking beyond facts and the actualities toward absolute being and absolute possibility. Ockham was, therefore, bound to be more interested in logic than any of his predecessors. . . .

Metaphysics. It has been said that Ockham's basic ideas in logic and epistemology are opposed to the development of an ontological philosophy . . . i.e., he cannot have a metaphysics. Ockham himself would have been surprised at this insinuation. The best answer to it is Ockham's own metaphysics. . . .

Metaphysics is a real science, or a science concerned with real things. . . . Its main subject is the term "being," which stands for beings. There is no "being as such" in the universe outside the mind; there are only *beings.* . . . Thus there is one concept which can be predicated about everything that exists or can exist. The spoken or written term "being" is univocal. In fact, to deny this univocity of the term "being," i.e., to maintain that to the term "being" there does not correspond one and the same concept, predicable about any real things, would, according to Ockham, entail agnosticism in regard to God. . . .

However, and this is of equal importance, this univocity of the term "being" and of others used in metaphysics, does not imply that any reality is common to God and creatures. In fact, there is no common feature whatever in reality. There is something common only in the conceptual order. There is not even a real similarity between God and creature, neither in their substantial being, nor in accidental being (since God has no accidents). There is, we would say, only a structural similarity that transcends any concrete content of the things conceived as "beings," somewhat as a melody can be the same, though every note is different when played in a different key. Thus we can grasp in one concept things which are entirely dissimilar in their actual being: for the modes of infinity and finitude establish an infinite dissimilarity. Nevertheless God is a "nonfinite" (i.e., infinite) "being," and a creature is a "finite being," and every corresponding term in these expressions is univocal. . . .

Once Ockham's theory of univocity is established, the link is secured between creatures and God, and in consequence between ontology and natural theology, and also between natural theology and revealed theology. It is strange that Ockham should have been accused of having separated theology from philosophy. Really, he made their common basis explicit. It is obvious that the Christian theologian would speak a language totally different from that of a pagan philosopher, were there not a common concept, at least of "being" which they could both use. For, in fact, if there were no common concept, they could not even contradict each other. But it is also clear that we have no concept of God that is both simple and at the same time proper to God. Not even the theologian has such a concept, for such a simple and proper concept is reserved to one who has an intuitive cognition of God or a special revelation from God.

On the proofs of God's existence. Ockham, therefore, has paved the way for a natural theology. He demonstrates that we *can* know something about God — little though it may be if we demand the utmost certainty. The question thus arises, *what* can we know about God with our unaided natural reason?

We can know something about God either by way of a demonstration . . . or by way of a persuasive (probable or dialectical) argument. The latter argument does not proceed from evident premises; but its premises are accepted by all, or at least by all acute and trained minds. The conclusion may be *certain*, but it is not *evident*. Evidentness and certitude are by no means equivalent. We can be certain who our parents were, but the fact itself cannot be evident to us.

About God, there are only a few conclusions which can strictly be demonstrated. One is the truth that God exists. Ockham gives a proof for this truth in the *Ordinatio* and in his *Questions on Physics,* but he nowhere goes into a detailed presentation of it. In both places he starts with a criticism of the proof advanced by Duns Scotus, which in our opinion is the most powerful and most developed proof of this kind elaborated by any scholastic in the Middle Ages. Ockham, the logician, directs his criticism mainly against the idea of efficient causality used by Duns. Ockham does not deny that God is the first efficient cause, but he believes it is difficult to prove that, in the order of efficient causes, an infinite series of causes is impossible, so that a first efficient cause must be asserted. Ockham argues, however, that this difficulty does not arise if we consider conservation instead of origination. In a series of *efficient* or *producing* causes we are not logically bound to postulate co-existence in time of all the causes belonging to the same series; but in a series of *conserving* causes, where one thing maintains another in being, and the former is being maintained, and so on, it follows *ex hypothesi* that the whole series must be simultaneously existing. Hence an infinite series would, in this case, entail the actual co-existence of an infinity of separate beings, and that is considered impossible.

Ockham's criticism of Duns Scotus is directed, therefore, against the actual form, but not against the main principle of this proof. This idea of conservation used in Ockham's proof is distinctively Christian; it is entirely foreign to Aristotelian thought, since Aristotle has no idea of creation, nor of any relation of efficient causality between God and the world. We only regret that Ockham did not elaborate this proof in detail and did not connect the idea of conservation with that of the essential temporality in every creature. . . .

According to Ockham, there are certain divine attributes that can be demonstrated, for instance, that God is an intellectual nature. For it follows formally that if God is the highest being, God must have both intellect and will. . . . [But] according to Ockham, we cannot *demonstrate* that there is only one God. . . . Duns Scotus tried hard to demonstrate it, but seems to have been left unsatisfied by all his demonstrations. For his part, Ockham denies the possibility . . . and falls back on a persuasive argument. . . . Similar arguments, probable or persuasive . . . can be made for the truth that God knows things outside himself, and that God is free as regards producing creatures. . . . The same holds for God's infinity, for God's omnipotence (in the Christian sense), and for other attributes of God. . . . In a strictly scientific metaphysics Ockham wants only demonstrative conclusions. . . . What the neo-scholastics would call physical or moral

certitude, he leaves to apologetics. . . . A Christian thinker . . . must not present his well-founded arguments as strict demonstrations; for in so doing he would expose his faith to the danger of being ridiculed. . . .

Ockham's philosophy had an enormous influence. But it seems that he had few disciples. It is difficult to find an "Ockhamist" school in the same sense as we encounter a Thomist or Scotist school. Ockham's teachings had, rather, a stimulating effect. They awakened many somewhat independent thinkers who were united at least against the realism of the older scholastics. These *"Nominales"* (in the medieval sense) constituted the *via moderna,* which was not so much a school as a trend of thought. It is still too early to pass judgment on this great intellectual movement. One historical fact, however, seems to be quite securely established: it was the physics of the *via moderna* which gave birth to modern physics.[7]

2. H. A. Oberman[1] studies Gabriel Biel's doctrine of predestination. Biel marks the spirit of late medieval nominalism. He taught an essentially Pelagian doctrine of justification, rejected Scotus' supralapsarianism and followed his master, Ockham, in understanding predestination as foreknowledge, as "post praevisa merita."

[7] Ockham's Works on Theology: *Ordinatio Ockham; Reportatio Ockham; Quodlibeta septem; Tractatus de corpore Christi; Tractatus de sacramento altaris; Tractatus de praedestinatione et de praescientia Dei et de futuris contingentibus; Quaestiones variae.* Select bibliography of works on Ockham: a useful bibliography of publications before 1950 is found in L. Baudry, *Guillaume d'Occam. Sa vie, ses oeuvres, ses idées sociales et politiques;* Ph. Boehner, *Medieval Logic* and *Collected Articles on Ockham;* G. Buescher, *The Eucharistic Teaching of William Ockham;* R. Guelluy, Philosophie et Theologie chez Guillaume d'Ockham;* M. C. Menges, *The Concept of Univocity regarding the Predication of God and Creatures according to William Ockham;* P. Vignaux, "Occam," in *Dictionnaire de Théologie catholique,* t. xi, col. 876–889; 718–783.

[1] Rev. Dr. Heiko A. Oberman, is the author of *Archbishop Thomas Bradwardine: A Fourteenth-century Augustinian: A Study of his Theology in its Historical Context*

Introduction. It is a curious — and dangerous — coincidence that the late medieval period is one of the least known in the history of Christian thought *and,* at the same time, a period in the interpretation of which there are a great many vested interests. . . . One can substantiate this observation by pointing to at least three significant schools of interpretation. Reformation scholars have been inclined to view the later Middle Ages merely as the "background of the Reformation" and have too often been guided in their evaluation by statements of the Reformers — especially Martin Luther — which by their very nature tend to be informed by a conscious departure from particular developments in the medieval tradition. There is a tendency in this school to stress contrasts between Luther and late medieval theologians and in general to assign Luther more to the tradition of Paul and Augustine than to that of William of Occam and Gabriel Biel.

There is, secondly, what one may loosely call the Thomistic school of interpretation which holds that in the thought of Thomas Aquinas, the Middle Ages reached its apex. It states that the thought of the succeeding period, beginning with Duns Scotus and culminating in nominalism — the work of Occam, Biel, and their disciples — is characterized by the disintegration and rapid collapse of the Thomistic synthesis. The idea that

nominalism is an essentially anti- or at least a non-catholic movement leading up to the Reformation, and that, for example, Luther, however catholic in intention, became a heretic unwittingly because of his distorted, nominalistic training, is very often connected with this hypothesis. In this school late medieval thought is merely seen as the "aftermath of high scholasticism."

Finally, there is a third school which can be called the Franciscan school of interpretation. This school is apt to stress the orthodoxy and theological contribution of "new" Franciscans such as Scotus and Occam. And since this is a relatively young, and, until recent years, a decidedly less vocal school of interpretation, it is not as yet clearly committed to one particular approach. There are, however, signs which indicate that this group is willing to defend the orthodoxy of nominalism; it explains the theology of Luther as an erroneous interpretation of the theology of such a nominalist as Gabriel Biel, due to other elements in Luther's thought unrelated to the nominalistic tradition. While the Thomistic school locates the break in the medieval Catholic tradition somewhere between Aquinas and Scotus, this third school searches for the decisive rupture somewhere between Biel and Luther. . . .

In view of the limited use made of the sources to date, it is fair to say that the case of Gabriel Biel has been prejudged. This may also be true of of the thought of Gabriel Biel neces-William of Occam. . . . The analysis

and *Forerunners of the Reformation.* This excerpt is from his book, *The Harvest of Medieval Theology.* (Cambridge, Mass.: Harvard University Press, 1963), pp. 1–6, 185–196, 206, 211, 215–216.

sarily leads us to investigate medieval thought as a whole. The indebtedness of Biel to Duns Scotus and Jean Gerson at the one hand, and the obedient discipleship of Bartholomaeus von Usingen, professor at Erfurt — and in this function teacher of Luther — at the other, mark the time span of our more detailed investigation. . . .

At certain points we believe we have brought new perspectives to the study of late medieval thought, not so much because we proclaim Biel to be a great innovator, but because in Biel we are provided with a strategic vantage point. From here we see spread out before us, not the barren wastelands of sterile debates which we had been led to expect by traditional late medieval scholarship, but a richness of deep pastoral and searching theological concern. . . . Biel marks the spirit of late medieval nominalism in conscientiously probing all the great theological traditions, harvesting those fruits which seemed ripe enough to nourish the Christian faith in search of understanding. . . .

Biel's vast knowledge of medieval theology in all its variety appears from the fact that apart from his great debt to Occam, he listens throughout his works most intently to the voices of other medieval theologians — among whom should be mentioned especially Bernard of Clairvaux, Peter Lombard, the old Franciscan school (Alexander of Hales and Bonaventura), Albert the Great, Thomas Aquinas, and Duns Scotus. . . .

Most surprising has been the discovery that Biel's own understanding of the Christian faith incorporates both the essence of nominalistic theology and traits which one cannot avoid classifying as mystical. The usual assumption that nominalism and mysticism are mutually exclusive would therefore seem no longer tenable.[2] . . .

Predestination and Justification. It is a reliable rule of interpretation for the historian of Christian thought that the position taken with respect to the doctrine of predestination is a most revealing indicator of the understanding of the doctrine of justification. It is not surprising therefore to discover in the theology of Gabriel Biel how closely his treatments of these two major doctrines correspond. . . .

We have seen that Biel could teach simultaneously a justification by grace alone and a justification by works alone due to the eternal procession from compassion and mercy to justice, temporally reflected in the procession from Incarnation to judgment. God's compassion finds its eternal expression in the proclamation of two eternal decrees by which an order of justice was established.

The order *de potentia absoluta* signifies . . . God's mercy according to which he chose, absolutely free from

[2] While generally the opposition of scholasticism and mysticism is rejected by scholars today as untenable, nominalism and mysticism are still supposed to be mutually exclusive. As great an historian of Christian thought as Reinhold Seeberg felt that though these two movements share a psychological interest, they form the sharpest possible contrast: empiricism versus idealism. Cf. Seeberg, DG III, p. 675; Albrecht Ritschl, *Geschichte des Pietismus*, I (Bonn, 1880), 467 ff.; Adolf von Harnack, DG III, **443.**

exterior interference, undetermined by any cause whatever apart from himself, to accept man's moral virtue as meritorious for his salvation. The order *de potentia ordinata,* on the other hand, proves to be the "dome" within which the actual life of the *viator* unfolds, where justice reigns and judgment day looms large as the day on which it will be disclosed whether the *viator* has indeed done his very best.

One cannot but admire the unity and consistency of this structure of thought.[3] As the history of theology can well be written in terms of a constant effort to reconcile or relate God's love and God's wrath, it is impressive to see how Biel tries to give both their due by joining them organically. Nevertheless, God's gratuitous self-giving love, expressed in his willingness to commit himself, the uncreated, to deficient creatures is not operative existentially *within* the order chosen, but *in the fact that* he chose this particular order in eternity. . . . An understanding of the organically joined but dual form of justification — at once by grace alone and by works alone — paves the way for a proper evaluation of Biel's doctrine of predestination.

Two doctrines of predestination in Biel? Viewed in isolation there *seem to be* two mutually exclusive doctrines of predestination in Biel's theology.

On the one hand there is what appears to be a doctrine of absolute predestination *ante praevisa merita,* in the form thus in which Augustine, Thomas Bardwardine, and Gregory of Rimini understood predestination — God's unprecedented and uncaused eternal decision with respect to the salvation of his creation. On the other hand, predestination seems oftentimes to be understood as foreknowledge.

We must note immediately that the problem of reprobation does not trouble Biel. The solution is so clear for him that he usually calls the reprobate the foreknown, *praesciti,* according to the maxim *Deus non prius sit ultor quam aliquis sit peccator* which constituted for Scotus and Occam sufficient grounds to reject a doctrine of double predestination.[4] Biel does not labor the point that the foreordination of the reprobate cannot be admitted without making God a tyrant. Reprobation is foreknowledge of guilt and preparation of the corresponding punishment.[5]

Apart from the issue of reprobation, therefore, Biel can speak in terms of an absolute predestination: all the elect are predestined from eternity and entered in the books of life and death from which they cannot once entered, be stricken. No change in the elect or reprobate could ever affect or in-

---

[3] We are unable to discover any evidence which would support Joseph Lortz's judgment that late medieval theology in general and Occamism in particular, are marred with "Unklarheit." Cf. Lortz, *Die Reformation in Deutschland,* 2 ed., 2 vols. (Freiburg i.Br., 1941), I, 139 f., 205ff.

[4] *Ox. I Sent.,* d. 41, q. 1, n. 11; *I Sent.,* d. 41, q. 1 D. For Scotus' position see the excellent study of Wolfhart Pannenberg, *Die Prädestinationslehre des Duns Skotus* (Göttingen, 1954); for Occam, Paul Vignaux, *Justification et prédestination,* pp. 127–140; for Bradwardine and Gregory of Rimini, Oberman, *Bradwardine,* pp. 95–122, 211–223.

[5] *I Sent.,* d. 40, q. 1, a. 1, n. 2 B.

fluence God since there is no cause for predestination outside God.[6] God's eternal decision to predestine a man is due to the contingent will of God who has the power to accept and reject.[7] . . .

When "cause" is understood in the strict sense of the word,[8] one has to say that a creature can never cause his own election or reprobation since this is a free decision of God which stands from eternity. Only in the second sense, when "cause" is understood to mean the order of priority, can one say that God's decisions are "caused" by merit or guilt. . . . The sacraments also are causes in the second sense of the word; they derive their effectiveness not *ex natura rei* but *ex voluntate dei*.[9] Since this revealed will of God is to be understood *de potentia ordinata* and constitutes therefore a commitment on God's part, there is no reason to subscribe to the traditional verdict of occasionalism as applied to the nominalistic concept of causality.

Predestination and foreknowledge. The application of the distinction between the two kinds of causes takes us already into what seems to be a second doctrine of predestination which stresses that predestination is really not more than God's foreknowledge of man's future behavior. The indicated maxim, *Deus non prius sit ultor quam aliquis sit peccator,* is not merely applied to reprobation but encompasses now also the predestination of the elect. Just as God foresees that the stubborn sinner will persevere in sin and will be, "therefore," condemned, thus God also foresees that the righteous man will persevere in love and "therefore" he predestines him.[10]

In some exceptional cases there is indeed no reason whatsoever . . . not even in the second sense of the word "cause" — for predestination: Paul and the Virgin Mary had no chance to do their very best and thus to earn *de congruo* the infusion of grace. In both cases special prevenient grace was given, to the Virgin at the time of the infusion of her soul into her body, to Paul even at the time that he was persecuting Christians.[11]

Usually — *regulariter!* — however, God does not grant salvation without merits. God created man with a free will which enables him to choose between good and evil. God, now, has decreed that no one will be damned unless for personal guilt, and that acceptation will require personal merits. To enable man to acquire merits, God has committed himself to assist all those who do their very best with the infusion of grace which is necessary for salvation.[12] . . .

---

[6] *Lect.,* 33 F.

[7] *I Sent.,* d. 40, q. 1, a. 2, concl. 2 C.

[8] A cause in the strict sense of the word implies that when it exists, something else follows as its effect. In the larger sense of the word one can say that "cause" refers to an order of priority between two situations which are nevertheless not related by an efficient, material, formal or final cause.

[9] *IV Sent.,* d. 1, q. 1, a. 1, concl. 1; cf. d'Ailly, *IV Sent.,* q. 7, a. 7. For a discussion of Occam's position, cf. Hochstetter, *Studien zur Metaphysik und Erkenntnislehre von Ockham,* p. 153.

[10] *I Sent.,* d. 41, q. 1, a. 2, concl. 1, 2.

[11] *I Sent.,* d. 41, q. 1, a. 2, concl. 3. Occam, *I Sent.,* d. 41, q. 1, a. 2 G.

[12] *I Sent.,* d. 41, q. 1, a. 3, dub. 3. Occam, *I Sent.,* d. 41, q. 1, a. 2 G. The identification of predestination and foreknowledge is most explicit in *Lect.* 31C:

Biel's single doctrine of predestination. When we now survey the two series of considerations which stressed respectively predestination *ante* and *post praevisa merita,* we can see that Biel, far from leaving us with two unrelated doctrines of predestination, presents us again with the same organic construction as we discovered in his doctrine of justification. . . . There is a direct parallel between "the two kinds" of justification and "the two kinds" of predestination. Justification by grace alone and its protective complement, predestination *ante praevisa merita,* are stressed insofar as God in all eternity ruled as a full sovereign with unlimited power. He freely decided to delegate some of his power to his creatures: *de facto,* therefore, the *viatores* live an existence conditioned by justification by works and by predestination *post praevisa merita.*

The organic unity of the doctrine of justification reappears in the doctrine of predestination: there is no trace of the often-claimed ambiguity and lack of clarity in this understanding of the movement from eternity to history as a movement from freedom to commitment.[13] This commit-

ment implies that man on his part has to rely on his resources; he has to do his very best in order to acquire the habit of grace. . . . In the case of the *normal viator . . . predestination is foreknowledge.*[14]

As we can gather from the absence of any discussion of predestination in his sermons, this doctrine does not really function in Biel's theology. This should not surprise us. It is the traditional task of the doctrine of predestination to form a protective wall around the doctrine of justification by grace alone — a doctrine which does not necessarily imply justification by faith alone. Since we have found that Biel teaches an essentially Pelagian doctrine of justification, absolute predestination is not only superfluous but would even be obstructive. And seen against the background of justification, we can well understand that

ebenso unwohl zu fühlen wie in der Erbsündenlehre. Darum wohl seine Kürze und Unklarheit." *Die Rechtfertigungslehre,* pp. 88, n. 268; 87, n. 259. Feckes could have referred for the same opinion to Ferdinand Kattenbusch, *Luthers Lehre vom unfreien Willen und von der Prädestination nach ihrem Entstehungsgründe untersucht* (Göttingen, 1875), p. 83, and to Albrech Ritschl, "Geschichtliche Studien zur christlichen Lehre von Gott," *Jahrbücher für deutsche Theologie* 10 (1865), 317 f.

[14] Therefore even the careful conclusion of Ernst Wolf is not precise enough: "Der Widerstreit zwischen der Kontingenz göttlichen und menschlichen (natürlichen wie übernatürlich geförderten) Handelns wird deutlich: man könnte fast sagen, alles liege an Gottes Entscheid aber ebenso auch an dem des Menschen. Praktisch genommen kann bald der eine, bald der andere Gesichtspunkt jeweils für den einzelnen massgebend werden . . ." *Staupitz und Luther: Ein Beitrag zur Theologie des Johannes von Staupitz und deren Bedeutung für Luthers theologischen Werdegang* (Leipzig, 1927), p. 175.

". . . . ab aeterno deus vidit petitionem hominis futuram . . . determinavit se ab eterno remissurum peccatum. . . ." See also Erich Seeberg, *Luthers Theologie in ihren Grundzügen,* 2 ed. (Stuttgart, 1950), p. 37.

[13] In this sense Feckes' conclusion has to be revised: "Gottes Allwerksamkeit und menschliche Verdienste sind nicht miteinander in Einklang gebracht, so dass man nicht weiss, ob man Biel für die zweite Art (Biel's *regulariter*) der Prädestination zu den Vertretern einer Prädestinationslehre *ante* oder *post praevisa merita* rechnen soll." "Biel scheint sich in der Prädestinationslehre

foreordination would in Biel's hands have to be transformed into foreknowledge.[15] . . .

Biel's marked theological interest along with his *regulariter* thesis constitute here the only two points on which he deviates from Occam. Essentially, therefore, we may say that Biel in his understanding of predestination — and as we also found with respect to justification — follows faithfully his master Occam in understanding predestination as foreknowledge. . . .

Therefore, it is clear that since the arguments brought forth by Seeberg[16] and Vignaux[17] in favor of an absolute doctrine of predestination are not convincing, we have to say that *Occam and Biel teach a predestination*

"post praevisa merita." . . .

The rejection of Scotus' psychology implied for Biel finally also a rejection of Scotus' supralapsarianism. Like many a theologian before him,[18] Scotus found it hard to see in the supreme moment of the history of salvation, the Incarnation, merely an *ad hoc* decision of God to neutralize the horrid consequences of Adam's fall. . . . (Hence) the election of Jesus Christ was decided irrespective of the fall. . . . In answer to the challenge of Scotus, Biel subordinates the passion of Christ to the redemption of the elect. God had foreseen that the glory of the elect would be acquired by means of the passion of Christ which was ordained for this particular purpose.[19]

3. N. Zernov[1] gives us a glimpse from the Orthodox point of view of the *Filioque* clause of the Council of Florence. There Mark of Ephesus attacked it but Bissarion of Nicaea and other Greeks under urging by the emperor accepted the theology of the double procession and agreed to restore their unity with Rome.

The Florentine Council. During the years of the Empire's agony the

Basileus had continued to make desperate efforts to secure military help

---

[15] Though Erich Seeberg did not see the forceful unity of Biel's thought and therefore his argumentation is not flawless, we have to agree with his main conclusion: "Das Gesagte wird es deutlich gemacht haben, dass die Prädestination letzten Endes auf die Präsziens reduziert und damit aufgehoben wird. . . " *Luthers Theologie*, I, 28. Cf. p. 30. See also Otto Scheel whose section on the theology of Biel is the most reliable interpretation to date: *Martin Luther: Vom Katholizismus zur Reformation*, II: *Im Kloster* 3rd and 4th printing (Tübingen, 1930), p. 181.

[16] Seeberg, DG III, 769 f. (Reinhold Seeberg).

[17] Paul Vignaux, *Justification et Predestination*, p. 138; cf. also "Occam," in DTC, vol. XI, col. 881 f.

[18] Bonaventura, III *Sent.*, d. k, q. 2; Thomas, *S.T.*, III, q. 1, a. 3; III *Sent.*, d. 1, q. 1, a. 3. The discussion of what we termed "conceivable sacred history" is by no means a nominalistic innovation! For an interesting comparison with patristic thought on this point, see Georges Florovsky, "Cur Deus Homo? The Motive of the Incarnation," in *Festival Volume Hamilcar Alivisatos DD* (Athens, 1957), pp. 3–12.

[19] III *Sent.*, d. 19, q. 1, a. 2, concl. 4.

[1] Nicolas Zernov was Spalding Lecturer in Eastern Orthodox Culture, at the University of Oxford in 1961. Among his published works are *Three Russian Prophets*, and *The Russians and Their Church*. This excerpt is from his book, *Eastern Christendom* (London: Weidenfeld and Nicolson, 1961), pp. 126–129.

from the West. This was to be purchased only by submission to the Pope, and negotiations for such a surrender went on all the time. Once they seemed to have succeeded at the Council of Lyons in 1274. . . . But the Byzantines recovered their ecclesiastical freedom by repudiating the union with Rome concluded at Lyons.

The last attempt at reconciliation with the papacy was made on the eve of the fall of the Empire. The Emperor, John VIII,[2] was determined to obtain reinforcements from the West, the last hope of saving his realm. . . . On 24th November 1437, the Basileus, accompanied by his brother Demetrius, the Patriarch Joseph II,[3] and twenty-two bishops, set sail for Italy. They reached Venice on 8th February 1438, and at once opened negotiations with the Pope, Eugenius IV,[4] who convoked a Council for the purpose of restoring unity with the Greeks. The first sessions of this synod took place at Ferrara, but on 10th January 1439, the assembly was transferred to Florence where the act of reunion was signed by both sides in July of the same year.

The Council of Florence was a representative gathering; the Patriarchs of Alexandria, Antioch, and Jerusalem sent envoys, and Isidore, Metropolitan of Moscow,[5] acted in the name of the Russian Church. The Orthodox Bishops were divided. One section led by Bissarion, Archbishop of Nicaea,[6] and Isidore of Moscow, who was a

Greek, desired reunion with the Latin West, not only for political but also for religious reasons. The other section, led by Mark, the Archbishop of Ephesus,[7] thought that surrender to Rome meant betraying the apostolic tradition preserved by the Christian East. The Latins were led by Cardinal Julian Caesarini.[8] The trivial points which had loomed so large in the polemic between Greeks and Latins in the preceding centuries were brushed aside. The whole problem of the schism was considered from a purely doctrinal point of view. It was believed that if theological understanding could be achieved the unity of Christendom would be immediately restored and the Islamic menace eliminated.

Five main items were selected for deliberation, the *Filioque* clause, purgatory, papal primacy, Eucharistic bread, and the words of consecration of the elements for Holy Communion. Consideration of the *Filioque* clause took the longest time. Mark of Ephesus attacked the Western addition, both on the ground of its theological implications and also as a violation of the agreement reached at the earlier Ecumenical Councils not to alter the creed sanctioned by the synods. This doctrinal debate was opened on 2nd March and lasted until June. It ended with a Western victory. The scholastic theologians had by that time elaborated an intellectual scheme defending the double procession of the Holy Spirit; they were well equipped for the dispute and

[2] 1425–48.
[3] 1416–39.
[4] 1431–47.
[5] D. 1463.
[6] 1395–1472.

[7] D. 1443.
[8] 1398–1444.

drove Mark of Ephesus and his supporters into a merely defensive position. The Orthodox tried by quotations
from the Fathers to prove that the
original formula alone represents
the apostolic tradition which excluded
the doctrine of double procession, but
the Latins showed that a number of
ancient and revered ecclesiastical
writers had described the Holy Spirit
as proceeding from the Father through
the Son. On the strength of these
expressions, Bissarion of Nicaea and
other Greeks, being urged by the
Emperor to make concessions to the
Latins, accepted the theology of the
double procession and agreed to restore their unity with Rome. The
minority, led by Mark, protested in
vain.

The other points of divergency, the
bread of the Eucharist, Purgatory, and
the words of Consecration, were ami-
cably solved, both sides accepting the
Eastern and Western practice and
teaching in these matters as traditional,
and therefore lawful.

The most interesting side of the
Florentine Council was the solution
of the papal problem. . . . The Greeks
were genuinely surprised when the
Latins raised it toward the end of
the discussions. . . . The Greeks were

unaware of the centrality of the papacy for the West. This fact was proved
by the quick agreement reached by
both sides. The Orthodox accepted a
formula proposed by the Latins with
the proviso that the privileges and
rights of the Eastern Patriarchs should
remain unaltered. . . .

The Florentine Council was concluded by a solemn proclamation of
the unity achieved. Mark of Ephesus
refused to sign the declaration of reunion, however, and his defiance indicated the strength of Byzantine resistance to the surrender to Rome made
by the hard-pressed Emperor and his
prelates.

The reconciliation proved to be an
illusion. The returning Greek dele-
gates were met with undisguised hostility. People openly said they would
rather be ruled by the Turks than by
the Pope. . . . Even more uncompromising was the reception of the news
in Moscow; the Metropolitan Isidore
had to flee from Russia. Both Prince
and people unanimously repudiated
the terms of capitulation; only Bissarion and his supporters stood firm
in defense of the Florentine union.
They eventually joined the Roman
Church, and Bissarion ended his life
as a prominent Cardinal.

4. J. Gill[1] maintains that the Council of Florence changed the course of
history and achieved its aim of reunion, even if its results were short-
lived. The conviction of the Greeks that the Saints, Latin and Greek,
could not err in the faith and so must agree, is both the explanation

---

[1] Joseph Gill, S.J., was Professor of the
Pontifical Oriental Institute in Rome in
1959. He is the author of many articles in
Orientalia Christiana Periodica. This excerpt
is from his book, The Council of Florence
(Cambridge: The University Press, 1959),
pp. vii–viii, 189–194, 207–209, 213–221,
225, 229–232, 291–294.

and the justification of their accepting union without being open to a true charge of insincerity and of inexcusable moral cowardice.

The Council of Florence made the Reformation inevitable. A dictum like that is a challenge to discussion. . . . It is, however, certain that the Council of Florence changed the course of history. . . . It was the last and the greatest endeavor [until John XXIII] to unite the separated Churches of East and West. . . . It envisaged union of the Latin Church with all the Christians of the East, Greeks, Russians, Armenians, Copts, Ethiopians, Chaldaeans, Maronites, Nestorians. And the attempt succeeded, even if its results were short-lived. The delegations of Armenians and the rest accepted that same decree augmented and applied to their separate cases. . . . It is one of the General Councils recognized by the Western Church. Its decree of union with the Greeks abides as the definition of certain theological truths and as a norm of doctrine to guide the minds of those who hope . . . to heal the schism yet. It has, indeed, already served as such in the union with Rome of Churches of oriental rite, such for example, as the Ruthenian (1596) and the Rumanian (1700), arranged on the basis of the principles enunciated at Florence. . . .

In a great hall of the Convent of S. Maria Novella . . . the Pope, the Emperor, and 40 representatives of each of the two Churches met. . . . The root of the trinitarian differences between the Churches was the Procession of the Holy Spirit. The Scripture clearly asserts that the Spirit proceeds from the Father. The Greek Doctors had for the most part been content to repeat the declaration of Scripture, for there was no need to go further to meet their adversaries, though a few had employed the phrase "proceed from the Father through the Son." Later Greek theologians had made the silence of the Fathers into a positive doctrine — the Holy Spirit proceeds from the Father alone — though meantime Latin theology with its more psychological approach had formulated western teaching into "proceeds from the Father and the Son." . . .

The sixth session took place on 17 March, when Mark Eugenicus . . . started by commenting on St. John's words: "But when the Paraclete cometh . . . who proceedeth from the Father, he shall give testimony of me,"[2] pointing out that that passage showed the Holy Spirit's origin from the Father alone. . . . St. Paul says no less: "Now we received . . . the Spirit that is of God."[3] . . . Athanasius says the same. . . . The Fathers, therefore, are in complete accord with the Holy Scriptures in rejecting that the Son is cause of the Spirit. . . . The Councils no less than the Fathers profess this same doctrine. . . . The second Council, developing the Credo of the first, ordained in its Creed: "We believe also in the Holy Spirit, the Lord and giver of life, who proceedeth from the Father, who together

[2] Jn 15:26.
[3] 1 Cor 2:12.

with the Father and the Son is adored and glorified." . . . That profession of faith was final. No other Council added "from the Son": indeed all addition was forbidden as if there was a foreboding of what one day the Latin Church would do. . . . The third Council both in word and deed was conformed to the second. . . .

In the seventh session . . . Montenero[4] regretted that Eugenicus would not hear the confutation of his arguments: however, he proposed to treat the subject under four heads — the Scriptures, Latin doctors held in respect by the early Councils, Greek doctors of the greatest repute, reply to Greek objections. The Scriptures call the Spirit the Spirit of the Son.[5] That usage implies a relation or respect of the Spirit to the Son. . . . It must be a relation of origin. Again John records Our Lord's words: "the Paraclete . . . whom the Father will send in my name."[6] . . . This temporal mission of the Holy Spirit necessarily presupposes his origin from that Person by whom he is sent. . . . Montenero's second line of proof was the testimony of the ancient Latin Fathers. . . . Leo the Great . . . Pope Damasus . . . Hilary . . . Jerome . . . Ambrose . . . Augustine . . . Pope Hormisdas. . . . Among Greek doctors Montenero quoted . . . Basil . . . Epiphanius . . . Didymus . . . Athanasius . . . Cyril of Alexandria. . . .

George Scholarius . . . shared Bessarion's views as to the solidity of the

Latin presentation of their doctrine and the complete inadequacy of the Greek reply: "But you all see that the Latins have contended brilliantly for their faith. . . . They brought forward from the common Fathers of the Church the six most renowned in dignity, wisdom. . . . They argued so precisely and clearly, expressing the question in exact words and as befits teachers, appending also the reasons and the texts of Holy Scripture from which they had drawn that doctrine as an inevitable conclusion. . . . Besides, they put forward others . . . of the East, adorned with equal wisdom and honour, who said just the same as those others, though not so plainly. . . . On our part nothing was said to them to which they did not manifestly reply with wisdom, magnanimity and truth, and we have no Saint at all who clearly contradicts them. . . . Who is so simple-minded as to believe that the Latins wish to destroy the faith and to adulterate the trinitarian theology of all the Doctors"? . . .

Montenero's display of metaphysical niceties . . . far from clarifying the thoughts of most of his Greek hearers . . . served only to mystify them the more and to make them cleave the most tenaciously to their sheet-anchor in trinitarian theology — "from the Father alone" — feeling that Latin thought on the Blessed Trinity was far removed from the simple tradition they had inherited. But the Lombard Provincial had done two things that had impressed them. He had roundly affirmed western belief in there being but one cause of the Holy Spirit and . . . he had produced an array of

---

[4] Saturday, 21 March. Giovanni Montenero was the Dominican Provincial of Lombardy.
[5] Gal 4:6; Rom 8:9; Acts 16:7.
[6] Jn 14:26.

Fathers both Latin and Greek to support his assertions. . . . A seed had been sown that could bear fruit. The saints of both Churches had written at length on the doctrine of the Trinity. . . . No saint could err in matters of faith, for they all . . . were inspired by the one Holy Spirit. . . . If, therefore, the Latin Saints really did say "From the Son" and the Greek Saints "Through the Son," then these two expressions must mean the same thing and no obstacle could remain to prevent union between East and West at least as regards the doctrine of the Blessed Trinity. . . .

It is important to appreciate this conviction of the Greeks, that the saints could not err in the faith and therefore must agree, for it is both the explanation and the justification of their accepting union (which they did accept) without being open to a true charge of insincerity and of inexcusable moral cowardice. It was for them an axiom and it was accepted by all without exception. . . . Mark Eugenicus accepted the principle as much as anyone else. . . .

But it was some time before this promising line of agreement was seriously taken up and pursued. . . . It was not till nearly the end of May, more than two months after the last public session, that the possibilities for union latent in the agreement of the Saints were thoroughly investigated. Bessarion and a few others then exploited them to the full. The rest, unable to controvert the facts exposed and unwilling to deny a principle they deemed true, were led to admit the equivalence of "Through the Son"

and "From the Son," and to subscribe to a profession of faith that embodied that acceptance. So the main obstacle that divided the Churches was overcome. . . .

The Greeks signed the decree . . . Sunday, 5 July.[7] . . . At last the day of union dawned, Monday, 6 July. . . . When the Mass was finished . . . a pulpit had been placed near the papal chair, into which Cesarini and Bessarion mounted to read out the decree. As Cesarini finished his recitation, he asked first the Pope if he agreed and Eugenicus replied *Placet,* then the Latin prelates who also exclaimed *Placet.* Similarly Bessarion, when he had finished reading, interrogated the Emperor and the Greeks who replied "Agreed." Whereupon His Holiness intoned the *Te Deum.* . . . As he went out, Latins and Greeks in turn praised God with the chant of psalms.

---

[7] The decree as it is given in Denz. 691:1300 f.: "In the name of the Holy Trinity, of the Father and Son and Holy Spirit, with the approbation of this holy general Council of Florence we define that this truth of faith be believed and accepted by all Christians, and that thus all profess that the Holy Spirit is eternally from the Father and the Son, and has His essence and His subsistent being from the Father and Son simultaneously, and proceeds from both eternally as from one principle and one spiration; we declare that what the holy Doctors and Fathers say, namely, that the Holy Spirit proceeds from the Father through the Son, tends to this meaning, that by this is signified that the Son is also according to the Greeks the cause, and according to the Latins the principle of the subsistence of the Holy Spirit, as is the Father also. . . . We define in addition that the explanation of those words *Filioque* has been lawfully and reasonably added to the Creed for the sake of declaring the truth and because of an urgent necessity at that time."

5. P. Henry[1] **ponders some implications of the "*Filioque tamquam ab uno principio.*" Both points are simply a corollary of the principle that in God everything is one except where "opposite" relations intervene. They imply that God acts according to the structure of his Being in every mission *ad extra*.**

Both Councils, Lyons and Florence, solemnly defined . . . not only that the Holy Spirit proceeds from the Father *and the Son* alike, but that in this procession Father and Son are *not two* distinct principles but only *one principle,* and that there is only one spiration of the Holy Spirit. . . . It is expressly stated that the processions are eternal and that the proceeding Persons are equal to their Principle. . . .

That there are relations, and those of origin, in the Godhead, belongs, I think, to the deposit of Faith and Revelation, at least insofar as they immediately arise from and are really identical with the Processions in God. On the other hand, it is not defined and does not evidently belong to the deposit of Faith that the Relations constitute and characterize the Persons, and even less, although it is most certain and true, that in God there is no distinction between the Persons except that which is involved in the complementary "opposition"[2] of

the relations. *"Omnia sunt unum ubi non obviat relationis oppositio"*[3] is not part of the definition of the Council of Florence, although it is essential to its systematic exposition of the doctrine of the Holy Trinity — essential rather as the keystone than as the corner stone. Therefore, it is of very great importance, not only for theological thought, but also for spiritual life.

The Council of Florence gives only one main argument for the *Filioque;* and for the *tamquam ab uno principio* only a comparison. But both complementary points are simply a corollary of the principle just recalled: in God everything is one except where "opposite" relations intervene. . . . The argument for the *Filioque* given by the Council is quite in keeping with this metaphysical principle, and moreover has the advantage of having an explicit scriptural background. It runs as follows. All that the Father has or is and does, he gives to the Son, except his fatherhood (it is easy to recognize the Johannine setting of this major premise). . . . Now the Father produces . . . the Spirit. . . . Therefore the Father also gives to the Son

[1] Paul Henry, S.J., was born in 1906. He is the author of *St. Augustine on Personality,* and editor of *Traités théologiques sur la Trinité.* This excerpt is from his article, "On Some Implications of the 'Ex Patre Filioque Tanquam Ab Uno Principio," in *The Eastern Churches Quarterly,* Supplementary Issue, Vol. VII, 1948 (London: Geo. E. J. Coldwell, Ltd.) pp. 17–29.

[2] The English "opposition" is not a felicitous translation of the Latin "oppositio." At the meeting "contrast, contrasted," was suggested but did not meet with general ap-

proval. We mean "mutual relations" "facing one another," but so very far from excluding one another that the one cannot exist or be thought of without the other.

[3] "And everything is one where relative opposition does not intervene": Denz. 703 (1330).

his active spiration of the Spirit. . . .

There are many devotional and doctrinal implications of the *ex Patre Filioque tanquam ab uno principio*. . . . First, the *Filioque* is another instance of the perfect equality of Father and Son, not only with regard to anything or anybody outside the Godhead, but with regard to everything connected with the inner life of God himself. . . . Second, rightly understood, the *tamquam ab uno principio* would tend to correct a popular but not strictly accurate description of the Holy Spirit. It is generally agreed that the Spirit is the mutual Love of Father and Son. But this statement is often (and falsely) taken to imply that the Spirit unites the first two Persons, previously considered as distinct: he is thought to be the bond between Father and Son, the means by which they love one another. That is not the case. He is the expression, the fruit, the result of their love and unity. . . . He is not the giver but the gift of unity. . . .

Third, systematically considered, the doctrine of the *Filioque* as well as that of the *tamquam ab uno principio* can be traced . . . to one fundamental principle, viz., that distinction and distinctions in the Godhead rest on complementary opposition of relations, or, more concretely that in God Persons are relations and relations are Persons. . . . The doctrine forces us to a thorough revision of our natural and instinctive egoistical and fragmentary conception of personality. We naturally think of persons as conscious beings turned inwards and following a centripetal impulse. . . . In God,

personality essentially has its center of reference in another. The Father is Father, that is himself, only because he is so to another: *ad alium*. The Son is Son inasmuch as he is the Son of the Father. And the Spirit is the Spirit only because he is the common Spirit of their perfect unity, dynamic and fruitful. . . .

Fourth, another conception implied in the same complete doctrine is that, in objective terms, any mission, visible or invisible, of a divine Person *ad extra* involves a corresponding procession *ad intra*: God acts according to the structure of his Being. The same notion may be stated thus in terms of reflex knowledge: any "economic" conception of the Trinity, viz., one defining and describing God in relation to his work in the Creation, redemption and glorification of Man and the Cosmos, must rest on a strictly "theological" conception of the Godhead. . . .

The *Filioque tanquam ab uno principio* is only a particular instance of the legitimacy of expressing more clearly the content of revelation, even to the point of including the new expression in the ancient and traditional Creeds. This is one of the points, apparently canonical but in truth dogmatical, which was discussed at the Council of Florence. The right to define so-called "new dogmas" is seen operative in the constant practice of the early Church and it is one of which the Catholic Church makes a very large use, seeing in it more a duty than a right. In its eyes, *homoousios* and *Filioque* are of the same type and one is quite as "scriptural" as the other: as far as Scripture goes, *Filioque* would be perhaps even more scriptural than *homoousios*. . . . Let it be borne in mind that the initiative of introducing the *Filioque* was not due to the Papacy; as long as they could, the Popes, faithful to a liturgical conservatism, checked the other Western churches and tried to stop them from adding the *Filioque* to the Creed. It was only when the *Filioque* was opposed on dogmatic grounds and contradicted by "From the Father alone" (*ek monou tou patros*)[4] that "for truth's sake" the Roman see promoted the Hispano-Gallican Creed. . . . In my opinion the Catholic Church could suppress the *Filioque* from the Creed or add to the Creed the *tanquam ab uno principio* which has been twice solemnly defined. A suppression such as this would not be without precedent, for the Council of Constantinople in 381 dropped from the Nicene Creed the important "from the substance of the Father" (*tout estin ek tes ousias tou patros*)....[5]

---

[4] If this *ek* is meant to express that the Father is the *first* principle of the Godhead, the *principium sine principio*, the Catholic Church cannot but agree that the Spirit proceeds *ek monou tou patros*.

[5] Cf. Denz. 86 (150).

If the facts are here recorded faithfully and interpreted without too pronounced a bias, one might feel justified in drawing from them conclusions — not unimportant conclusions — concerning the possibility or necessity of expressing one and the same dogma by means of more than one set of metaphysical categories. If this instance is justified, the much controverted dogma of the procession of the Spirit is not or should not be, as is generally thought, the main dividing line between Eastern and Western Christianity, but, paradoxically, their central, God-centered, uniting point. East and West would here not exclude each other but come together to express fully and perfectly in union what they can express only imperfectly in "division": the doctrine of the Spirit of the Father and the Son's Unity. On theoretical lines, it would appear that one dogma at least is officially expressed by the Catholic Church, united at Lyons and Florence, in two formulations which are not strictly equivalent or identical but complementary. If this plurality of systematic exposition is possible or even necessary for one revealed truth, it might not be impossible or unnecessary for other data of the one divine revelation.

IX

GOD IN THE REFORMERS

**1. G. S. Hendry[1] studies Luther's theology of the Godhead of God. It was
in radical opposition to all philosophical theology and natural theology.
For Luther was brought face to face with the living, personal God,
the Creator, who stands in such a relation to man that it cannot be
conceived in intellectual terms at all. God is to be encountered by
faith alone in his revelation of himself in his Word.**

Luther was the first to realize to the
full the profound incompatibility of
Greek intellectualism with Christian
dogma and to make the definitive
separation between them.

Luther was trained as a theologian

[1] George S. Hendry gave the *Hastie Lectures* in the University of Glasgow in 1935.
They are printed substantially as they were
given in his book, *God the Creator* (Nashville, Tenn.: Cokesbury Press, 1938). This
excerpt is from that book, pp. 76–83, 85–
87, 91–96, 110, 113–122.

in the nominalist tradition in the form
it had received from Ockham. . . . The
doctrine of God which he learned
there provided the form for the new
content he was to instill into it.[2] Of
course, the difference between Luther
and the Nominalists is great, as he
himself was well aware, and he in-

[2] Cf. F. W. Schmidt: "Der Gottesgedanke
in Luthers Römerbriefvorlesung" in *Theologische Studien und Kritiken,* 1920–1921,
p. 129.

cludes them in his general condemnation of the philosophical theologians.[3]

The truth is, however, that Luther broke decisively with all his immediate antecedents: for he broke out of the trammels of that Greek intellectualism which characterizes the scholastic theology. He realized that the problem of God is not an intellectual problem, but it is a, or rather the, existential problem. The intellectual approach to the problem of God leads entirely wide of the mark. Faith is not an intellectual faculty, it is not a supernatural enhancement of reason; it is a totalitarian personal decision and act which is absolutely unique. . . .

After long wrestling with the Epistle to the Romans, he made the discovery, or rather rediscovery, of the gospel of justification by faith. It was equivalent to a rediscovery of the Godhead of God, of the proper dimension of Godhead. The relation between God and man is not one of parity; it initiates with God and it is altogether of grace. . . .

This was Luther's theological starting point. It bears a superficial resemblance to the teaching of the Ockhamists, but the decisive difference is that to them it was a skeptical conclusion, while for Luther it is a positive foundation on which he took his stand and proceeded to work, casting down and building up. He does not content himself with saying that we cannot know God except he reveals himself; his whole emphasis is on the fact that God does reveal himself;

but he reveals himself as God, as personal Creator-Lord. In revealing himself, God does not present himself as an object of human thought, he does not put himself at the disposal of man in any sense at all. He does not enter into the sphere of the competence of the human mind so that it becomes able to comprehend him. In his revelation God reveals himself as God, he exhibits his own sole authority and pronounces judgment on man. The assumption of the scholastic theology of the Middle Ages — and of the present day, for scholasticism, which is identical with intellectualism, is the abiding menace of Christian theology — is that the revelation of God is a communication of knowledge which we can add as a supplement to our existing store of knowledge. It need not always be formulated in precisely that way, but it always rests upon the same fundamental idea. . . .

If God in revealing himself became an object of knowledge like other objects, he would cease to be God, he would become a part of what we call "the world." But that is precisely the scholastic-intellectualistic misunderstanding; intellectualizing revelation, it reduces God to the status of an object belonging to the world. This is what Luther clearly saw. He realized as no other that revelation means: God reveals himself as God, and it is just in that that our salvation lies. It does not mean our attaining knowledge of God, it means God's taking knowledge of us. To know God is rather to be known of God.[4] The apprehension of God's revelation of him-

[3] Luther's *Römerbriefvorlesung*, ed. Ficker (Rom. Fi.), ii, 110.

[4] Gal 4:9.

self is not a kind of knowledge or any enhancement of it by any means, supernatural or otherwise; it is not knowledge at all; it is acknowledgment.[5] It is not an activity but a passivity. "Be still, and know that I am God."[6] Faith is for Luther the great *passio*. The relation of man to God is not a *facere*, it is a *fieri*. He learned this in his personal discovery of justification by faith, and he found it was a key to open many doors. . . .

The theological significance of Luther derives from the fact that he discovered the fatal flaw in the medieval synthesis and shattered it beyond repair. He discovered the fact of sin, its gravity, and its consequences.[7] . . . By his unrelenting insistence on this "magnifying of sin" Luther opens a comprehensive attack on the theology and the Church of his time. . . . He desires to make room for the Gospel, for Christ and his righteousness. . . . By his apprehension of the revelation of God's grace in Christ he learned that the only way of access to God is through the Mediator — there is no immediate way.[8]

Luther's theology is Christocentric; that is its first and fundamental characteristic. "Faith in Christ is its be-

ginning, middle, and end."[9] It is Christocentric in the fullest sense of the term; for Christ is not merely the Mediator through whom we are restored to fellowship with a God of whom we have antecedent knowledge from some other source, but Christ is the only Mediator of knowledge of God and we can have no knowledge of God apart from Christ. . . . If we are to be admitted to the knowledge and presence of God at all, God must present himself to us as a God for sinners. This he does in Christ. He veils his holy majesty, he clothes himself in the lowly vesture of Christ's humanity and reveals himself to us as gracious, forgiving love.

This apprehension of God entailed a reversal of the method which prevailed in the scholastic and mystical theology. The scholastic method was to begin at the top and proceed downwards; Luther's method is to begin at the bottom and proceed upwards. . . .[10]

Luther's insistence on the sole sufficiency of the revelation of God in Christ was accompanied by a radical opposition to all philosophical theology and natural theology. Christ alone is the door to the knowledge of God, and every attempt to reach a knowledge of God by reason or the "light of nature" is excluded. . . . "I am not opposed to philosophy being taught and learned. . . . But to mingle it with theology as if it belonged there is not right and is not to be tol-

---

[5] *Anerkenntnis* rather than *Erkenntnis;* cf. K. Barth: *Kirchliche Dogmatik,* no. 6.
[6] Ps 46:10.
[7] "Reformation is identical with the knowledge that the medieval synthesis is impossible, because man is not only sinful, he is a sinner, because we walk by faith and not by sight. Every system is an anticipation of the heavenly vision, at the cost of the truth that contradiction is the permanent character of this earthly, sinful existence." Brunner, *Gott und Mensch,* p. 2.
[8] Glanke, Art. "Luther" in *Die Religion in Geschichte und Gegenwart,* iii, 1764.

[9] Theodosius Harnack: *Luther's Theologie* (1927 edition), i, 41.
[10] "But philosophy and the worldly-wise people desired to begin at the top — and thereby they have become fools. We must begin at the bottom and work upwards": Weimar edition of Luther's works, 21, 22.

erated."[11] . . . Our knowledge of God is entirely mediate, and we must hold fast to the *media* which he has given us. This is the *theologia crucis* which Luther opposes to the *theologia gloriae* of the scholastics and all who presume to seek an immediate knowledge of God. . . ." "He who wishes to think or reason about God soundly must lay everything aside except the humanity of Christ. . . . For in no other way does God desire to be approached. Persevere in that way, and in a short time you will be a profounder theologian than all the scholastics."[12] . . .

To his condemnation of philosophical theology Luther adds a similar condemnation of "natural theology" and "natural religion" which are closely connected with it. As the problem of natural revelation has recently come into the forefront of theological controversy, Luther's thought upon it may be reproduced somewhat more fully.[13] Luther admits a natural knowledge of God: "Nature shows that we should worship God, and the heathen indicate it also; for there has never been a heathen who did not worship his false gods. . . . The Jews had also false gods like the heathen. . . ."[14]

This natural knowledge of God, however, is so meagre and so vitiated and corrupted by sin that it is totally inadequate for our need.

Luther's strong evangelical interest saves him from the pitfall of the purely intellectualistic consideration of the universality of religion. He sees with an unerring eye the fatal defect in all natural religion, its impotence to avail the sinner for salvation — and this no less even where natural religion is strongly "ethical"; Luther thinks always in terms of sin and grace, and this cuts across the distinction of ethical superiority and inferiority. . . .

"There are two sorts of knowledge of God; the one is called knowledge of the law, the other knowledge of the gospel. . . . But that is not the true knowledge of God which is reached by the law, whether it be that of Moses or that implanted in our nature. For men do not follow it. . . . The other knowledge of God is reached through the gospel: that the whole world by nature is an abomination to God and eternally condemned under the wrath of God and the power of the devil from which it was not able to be saved; then that the son of God, who is in the bosom of the Father, became man, died and rose again from the dead, and has destroyed sin, death and the devil. This is the true and solid knowledge, fashion, and thought of God; it is called the knowledge of grace and truth, the evangelical knowledge of God. But it does not grow in our garden; reason knows not a jot about it."[15] . . .

---

[11] Weimar edition, *Tischreden* (TR), 5, 25 f.

[12] Luther's Letters, ed. Enders (En), i, 416.

[13] See Karl Barth: *Das erste Gebot als theologisches Axiom, Zwischen den Zeiten*, 1933, 297–314; Emil Brunner: *Natur und Gnade, zum Gesprach mit Karl Barth*, 1934; Karl Barth: *Nein! Antwort an Emil Brunner*, 1934; Ernst Wolf: *Martin Luther, das Evangelium und die Religion*, 1934; Peter Barth: *Das Problem der natürlichen Theologie bei Calvin*, 1935; Peter Brunner: "Allgemeine und besondere Offenbarung" in *Calvins Institutio* in *Evangelische Theologie*, 1934, 189–215.

[14] Weimar edition, 24, 9.

[15] Weimar edition, 46, 667 ff.

Luther realized that our knowledge of God is always a knowledge of God in his hiddenness. For in all his dealings with us God remains God, our Creator and Lord, and we cannot apprehend him as an object in the world. It is by faith we apprehend God. . . . There are two features in his apprehension of God on which he lays repeated emphasis and which illustrate how, as a modern writer has expressed it, "Luther treated the Godhead of God seriously."[16] (1) Luther insists on the majesty of God and his essential superiority to man. In his exposition of the Magnificat he traces the condescension of God to the fact that "because he is the all-highest and there is nothing above him he cannot look above him, and he cannot look beside him because there is no one equal to him; he must of necessity look within and beneath him."[17] . . . Luther's insistence on the majesty of God, however, rests upon another, more positive element — viz., his apprehension of the nature of God as living will. This is the deep root of the hiddenness of God. Luther's "voluntarism" or emphasis on the centrality of the will in God has been traced to his training in the Ockhamist theology. Only, he is not concerned primarily to assert the irrationality and incalculability of the divine will but simply its vitality, its ceaseless and all-pervading activity. . . . The activity of the divine will is the ground of all existence. . . .

[16] Helbig in Preface to: Luther, Theologie des Kreuzes.
[17] Weimar edition, 7, 547.

Luther does not hesitate to apply this doctrine to human activity, and the whole of his treatise, De servo arbitrio, against Erasmus, is devoted to the exposition of it: if the activity of God is all-efficacious, then the activity of man plays a secondary and subordinate role. . . . But . . . a full-fledged determinism would be inconsistent with his basic position. Man must be conceded liberum arbitrium in regard to what is beneath him; it is only in regard to what is above him that it must be denied him.[18] Even here, however, the servitude of the "will" is not to be understood as psychological determinism or compulsion; that would destroy the essential nature of the will. . . . In other words, the will must be accorded freedom of choice. Luther repeatedly acknowledges that. But this formal aspect of freedom is of little interest to him. What Luther is concerned with is the question of "material freedom," whether the will is free to realize its choice, whether it is a "vis efficax."[19] . . . For Luther, God and the devil . . . contend in deadly enmity for the possession of the will, which they goad and drive as their slave.[20] . . . In seeking the freedom of neutrality, man breaks away from God only to fall a victim to the devil. Thus man's supposed freedom proves to be only freedom to sin[21] and the loss of the true freedom to realize his destiny as the child of God.

[18] Weimar edition, 18, 638.
[19] Weimar edition, 18, 636.
[20] Weimar edition, 18, 750.
[21] Weimar edition, 18, 752.

2. W. Elert[1] sketches Luther's doctrine of God. Luther's whole theology appears as the answer of a man with whom God himself has spoken. All knowledge of God depends on revelation; consequently, it is possible only in faith. There is also a revelation of God in nature, in the creation and preservation of the world. But what or who God is the Holy Spirit alone teaches.

The Doctrine of God.[2] According to Luther, all "natural" knowledge of God comes to an end before the "hidden God" (*Deus absconditus*). Melanchthon thought he could give it a friendlier assignment. The dogmaticians of the seventeenth century followed him in this. The upshot was the Enlightenment. This difference seems to refer only to the assumptions of the knowledge of God, not to its content.

But in accordance with the impact of the gospel, all knowledge of God depends on revelation. Consequently, it is possible only in faith. But according to everything that has been said about revelation, the knowledge of God resulting from faith must take a different course from that which results from rational meditation.

"Faith is the creator of a divine quality," says Luther, "not in the Person but in us. Apart from faith God loses his justice, glory, power, etc., and there is no majesty or divine quality where there is no faith."[3] This really says everything. What at first seems to be a monstrous power — the power to be the creator of a divine quality in us — Luther may ascribe to faith without being misunderstood, because to him faith itself is nothing vis-a-vis God. After all, it lives only because God invokes it and calls it into being. God is in us only in such a way that we hear his call. According to Luther, knowledge of God is possible only in this reciprocal relation, this dialog between the God who calls and the faith which hears. . . . For him every confession, every dogma, takes on the character of a personal answer to God's revelation. He extols the so-called Ambrosian Hymn of Praise, which he counts among the "three creeds or confessions of the faith of Christ" because it teaches "not only to confess the true faith but also to praise and thank God in this faith."[4] . . .

Luther's whole theology appears as the answer of a man with whom God himself has spoken. To him the fact

---

[1] Werner Elert was born in 1885 in the village of Heldrungen. In 1923 his university, Erlangen, made him professor of church history and, after the death of Philip Bachman, also of systematic theology. He died in 1954. His literary output was great. Among his works are *Der Kampf um das Christentum* and *Abendmahl und Kirchengemeinschaft in der alten kirche, hauptsächlich des Ostens*. This excerpt is from his book, *The Structure of Lutheranism*, transl. from the original German *Morphologie des Luthertums* (St. Louis, Mo.: Concordia Publishing House, 1962), pp. 211–221.

[2] Cf. E. Hirsch, *Luthers Gottesanschaung*, 1918; Carl Stange, *Der christl. Gottesglaube im Sinne d. Reformation, Studien z.Theologie Luthers*, I, pp. 235 ff.

[3] Weimar edition of Luther's works; 40, I, 360, 5.

[4] Weimar edition, 50, 263, 10.

that God is a person is no problem and cannot be a problem, because his faith has a personal relationship to God. . . . It is true that Luther must speak about God's wrath with reference to his own evangelical relationship to God and as one who is under the earnestness of the divine law. . . . But faith knows, of course, that the Son has appeased the wrath of the Father and therefore that God, by imputing the righteousness of the Son, lets his mercy be victorious over his wrath. This is the case over against the believer. Therefore faith views "doing good and saving"[5] as the "proper office of God." . . .

Nowhere is what appears to be the completely anthropomorphic character of Luther's conception of God as evident as it is here. But this character has not only been taken from the usage of the Bible; it is also the only possible way to do justice to the fact that faith is addressed by a divine "You" (*Du*). Every attempt to construct God's "essence" (*Wesen*) hypothetically from his "attributes" must run aground on the diastasis of wrath and mercy. . . .

For Luther, of course, the efficaciousness of mercy is actually bound to the historical work of redemption. But, in the first place, this points back to an eternal decree which already presupposes the reality of God's love. In the second place, however, the efficaciousness of mercy has become a reality in what resulted from his wrath on the cross of Christ — an event which likewise has eternal significance. . . . It leads necessarily to the thought of

[5] Weimar edition, 25, 190, 2.

predestination and any desire to go to the bottom of this is equivalent to a battle against God.[6] . . .

His doctrine of God's effective work in man is emphasized in a distinctly soteriological manner. From the standpoint of predestinarian thinking the goal of this work is determined by the destruction or salvation of men. It is altogether from the standpoint of faith that God performs his works in the service of love for his creatures. Of course Christ's work gives us the certainty of divine love.[7] . . .

Luther knows that "reason," too, must trace everything that is good back to God. But he knows that reason lacks two things. In the first place, trust in God's good will. It permits misfortune to divert it from this trust.[8] In the second place, reason is not capable of "properly ascribing or attributing divinity to the only One to whom it is due." . . . It knows, of course, that there is a God. But "what or who God is . . . the Holy Spirit alone teaches."[9] There is also a revelation of God in nature, in the creation and preservation of the world. But in themselves man's relationships do not let God be known as the One he is. It is not until the Divine Spirit has

[6] Weimar edition, 18, 690, 26.

[7] Weimar edition, 20, 402, 31 ff.

[8] Weimar edition, 19, 206, 14: "In the first place, it (reason) believes that God can do this and knows how to do it, to help and to give. But that he desires or is willing to do this for it too — this it cannot believe. Therefore it does not remain firm in its opinion. For it believes and knows that God has the power; but it is in doubt about the desire, because it feels the opposite when there is adversity."

[9] Weimar edition, 16, 206 f.: "was odder wer Gott ist . . . leret alleine der heylige geyst."

done his work that the connection between revelation and faith is established here. This work assures you, the human being, that the Creator and Preserver of the world is *your* Creator and Preserver, that he is your Father.[10] . . .

These were the principles that guided Luther when he accepted the doctrine of the Trinity as taught by the early Church. "On the outside the works of the Trinity are undivided."[11] Luther traced this statement back to St. Augustine. What it says was self-evident to him. Over against his creatures God is absolutely One.[12] Luther is equally certain of the revelation of three Persons.[13] Here the personality is assured above all by the name

---

[10] Weimar edition, 17, I, 430, 26; 38 ff.

[11] *Opera trinitatis ad extra sunt indivisa:* Weimar edition, 54, 57, 35, and frequently.

[12] Weimar edition, 37, 291, 7. Weimar edition hereafter is: WA.

[13] Above all, in the expositions of the Apostles' Creed. For these and later for Luther's doctrine of the Trinity the following presentations, which go into greater detail, should receive special consideration: *A Brief Form of the Ten Commandments,* 1520, WA 7, 204 ff.; *A Simple Way to Pray, Written for a Good Friend,* 1535, WA 38, 358 ff.; the Smalcald house sermon on the articles of the Creed, 1537, WA 45, 11 ff.; the sermon for Trinity Sunday in the same year, WA 45, 89 ff.; *The Three Creeds or Confessions of Christian Faith,* 1538, WA 50, 262 ff.; *Concerning the Last Words of David,* 1543, WA 54, 28 ff.; and the Catechisms. For Luther's view concerning the development of the Trinitarian dogma also *On the Councils and the Churches,* 1539, WA 50, 509 ff. — About the writing *Concerning the Last Words of David.* Gregorius Joestel wrote from Wittenberg: "As long as the world has stood, no book has been written that extolled the article of the Trinity more than this one does." WA 54, 21. — In addition, cf. the *Disp. de divin. et humanit. Christi* of Feb. 28, 1540.

"Father"; that of the Son, by the historical person of Christ; that of the Spirit by the fact that he "speaks" to me and performs in men God's personal work of sanctification through the forgiveness of sins.[14] It is true that whenever Luther speaks of the doctrine of the Trinity as such, he puts the strongest emphasis on the "oneness" of God; but he does not let this tone down the "threeness" to a mere Trinity of revelation. On the contrary, he adopts the doctrine of immanent relationships.[15] It is true that he makes no attempt to penetrate it on the basis of the understanding he has because of faith. The connecting link is the concept of substance (*Wesen*); the traditional "works on the inside" (*opera ad intra*) constitute the immanently distinguishing factor. Of course, Luther adduces ample proof from Scripture, even from the Old Testament; and he makes use of the old analogies from nature and psychology, particularly those of Augustine. In general, however, the doctrine of the Trinity came to a standstill in his theology like an erratic boulder. But one cannot say that he was unaware of its significance prior to the emergence of opposition on the part of fanaticism with its unitarian tendencies. As early as 1520 he calls this doctrine the "highest article in faith — the article on which all the others depend."[16] When later, on the other hand, he says in his explanation of the Trinitarian creeds of the "main article, the one concerning Jesus

---

[14] WA 54, 41, 5; WA 38, 374, 35.

[15] Cf. the argument, WA 45, 91, 5 ff.

[16] WA 7, 214, 27: "höchst artickell ym glauben darynnen die andern alle hangen."

Christ" that "all the others attach themselves to it- and firmly support it,"[17] one can sooner conclude from this that he recognized more and more the Christological approach to the doctrine of the Trinity as the only one that was compatible with his theology.

Subsequently, Melanchthon provided the systematic program. In the Augsburg Confession the article "On God" was put ahead of all the other articles. It retained this position throughout early Lutheran dogmatics — if one leaves out of account the prolegomena, which, to be sure, were gradually inflated to an enormous degree.[18] . . . Melanchthon himself was the only one to make an exception. In the final edition of the Loci he finds in the doctrine of the Trinity a place for Christology in its entirety. His closest pupils followed him in this. Here at least a focal point of the doctrine of the Trinity had been found — a focal point which could have provided a sure foundation for the entire conception of God. But this possibility did not materialize either; for the arrangement still kept Christology separated from the real doctrine of salvation, which would have had to be its starting point if the impact of the gospel was to come into its own at all.

Apart from subtler turns of expression, like the sharply individualizing way in which Melanchthon worded the Trinitarian concept of Person,[19] the doctrine of the Trinity as taught by the early Church was reproduced to a greater extent at first than it was really thought through anew. Melanchthon himself made cautious attempts to understand it in a speculative manner, in accordance with Augustinian and medieval patterns. While thinking about himself — so he argued in the Loci of 1535 — the Father begets a thought which becomes his image, and into this image he pours his essence (Wesen). This is the "Word." With respect to the Spirit, of course, Melanchthon merely adds that he is an impulse or a driving, moving, and life-giving force.[20] In the final edition of the Loci this is explained by saying that just as the Son was begotten by means of the Father's thinking, so the Holy Spirit proceeds from the will of the Father and the Son; for to impel and to love are matters of the will.[21] . . . It is the purpose of the revelation of the Spirit, he wrote, to call forth in believers emotions identical with him: love and peace that rests in God.[22] . . .

Yet one surely should not interpret the reticence of the early dogmaticians over against a speculative development of the doctrine of the Trinity as mere incompetence. Early Lutheranism as a whole regarded this doctrine not only as an inheritance which one dared not leave to others to preserve. No, this teaching was recognized as the expression of a truth which the

---

[17] WA 50, 266, 37.

[18] Of course, it is completely missing in the Loci Theologici of Urban Rhegius as edited in 1545 by Johann Freder. In the main this book observes the procedure of Melanchthon's first Loci.

[19] Corpus Reformatorum 21, 1076, in connection with 21, 614.

[20] 21, 258.

[21] 21, 616.

[22] 23, 360.

reformational approach itself did not let them evade. . . . In the defensive action which all the churches of that time took against the anti-Trinitarian theology of the Socinians, the Lutheran dogmaticians stood in the very front rank. Wherever they scented approaches to this theology in Calvinism, they attacked. Rome's insinuation that neither they nor the Lutheran confessions took the doctrine of the Trinity seriously but had accepted it merely for reasons of prestige were indignantly rejected.[23] The reason for their certainty in this matter was by no means their formal agreement with the old creeds; it was their conviction that they were standing on unimpeachably biblical ground.[24] They devoted an enormous amount of work to the scriptural proof of the Trinity. *And this is the contribution which early Lutheranism actually made to a real appropriation of the doctrine of the Trinity in the Western World.* At that time this was

undertaken largely with insufficient exegetical resources. Nevertheless, the dogmaticians stated the basic question correctly in the evangelical sense. It was not a question of formal differences in rank between church doctrine and Scripture doctrine; it was a question of what gave rise to the doctrine of the Trinity. The struggle for scriptural proof caused them to realize that it was not the historical heresies which gave rise to this doctrine, as Luther still believed, but the economy of divine revelation itself. If they did not know how to make more of it dogmatically, the reason is to be found in the first place — as stated — in the arrangement of their dogmatics, which began with the doctrine of the Trinity instead of letting this doctrine arise in and with the doctrine of salvation, but, in the second place, in the doctrinaire abridgement of the concept of revelation. . . .

3. E. A. Dowey, Jr.[1] studies the knowledge of God the Creator and God the Redeemer in Calvin's theology. The special revelation of God the

[23] Against what the Socinians had to say in opposition: Joh. Gerhard, *Loci* III, 322 f. — Fr. Balduin, *Sol. Refutatio Catechismi Ariani, qui Rackoviae*, etc., 1620, pp. 49 ff. Against the supposed or actual weakening: Ag. Hunnius, *Calvinus, Judaizans*, Wittenberg, 1593. — Against the insinuations on the part of Rome: L. Hutter, *Aug. Conf. . . . Analysis methodica*, Wittenberg, 1602, pp. 51 ff. — Joh. Hülsemann, *Manuale Aug. Conf.*, Wittenberg, 1631, pp. 1 ff.

[24] Cf. especially Abr. Calov, *Exegema Aug. Confessionis*, Wittenberg, 1665. Sebastian Schmidt, *Collegium biblicum prius, in quo Dicta Veteris Testamenti . . .*

Argentor, 1676. L. III, *de s. Trinitate.* Cf. also Schmidt's *Exercitationes theologicae de Deo et eius attributis item de Theologia naturali cum clave Jobaea*, Guelpherbyti (Lüneburg), 1690.

[1] Edward A. Dowey, Jr., completed the research and writing for the first printing of this work on the knowledge of God according to Calvin in 1951. With some minor corrections that work reappears in its second printing under the title, *The Knowledge of God In Calvin's Theology* (New York and London: Columbia University Press, 1965). This excerpt is from this book, pp. 131–135, 142–145, 205–219.

Creator in Scripture clarifies and also complements, by the addition of new content, what can be known of God the Creator in creation. For Calvin, God the Redeemer is a God of gratuitous love, and his doctrine of double predestination does not change this.

Knowledge of God the Creator. Both revelations — general and special — are presented to the mind objectively in creation and Scripture, and subjectively in the *sensus divinitatis,*[2] conscience, and the internal testimony of the Holy Spirit. The content is identical up to a point: both teach the eternity and self-existence, power, wisdom, truth, goodness, righteousness, justice, mercy, and holiness of God, and both reveal identically God's or-

derly will for his creation, the former in conscience and the latter in the Mosaic moral law. The revelation in Scripture, however, goes beyond what can be learned from creation since the Fall (1) in teaching of the Trinity, (2) in giving the time and manner of creation, plus an angelology, a demonology, and a picture of man's original state, and (3) in revealing the full scope of God's particular providence. The purpose of both revelations is the eternal felicity of men in glorifying the Creator, while the actual function of the revelation in creation is solely to leave man inexcusable before God. In short, Scripture repeats by objective source and subjective witness everything that creation teaches about the Creator, and then adds to it. Further, it contributes to the true purpose of this revelation rather than the accidental function of condemning.

Then has Scripture, according to Calvin, entirely supplanted the revelation in creation for the believer? Has the revelation in creation no continuing constructive function or constitutive theological value for the man of faith?

These two questions, in spite of the possibility of an affirmative answer implied in the foregoing summary, embody an idea strange to Calvin: the idea that the Creator's revelation in creation ceases to be relevant to the

---

[2] The *sensus divinitatis* in man does not mean a special organ or faculty of the soul. It is not the product of ratiocination nor is it adequately described as a "religious a priori."

The noetic element does exist in it: this is knowledge of God. It is not a mere notion, or presentiment, and it does not originate from within us but has its source in God. "God *himself* has endued all men with some knowledge of his deity" (I.iii.1 [OS III.37.19]). This knowledge issues in a proposition: "God exists," or "some God exists." And "God" means the One God Himself, for this revelation is not so vague as to allow polytheistic interpretation. Hence, the intellectual element, formulable in the necessary proposition one God exists, is part of the primitive *sensus,* which thereby has a brief but extremely important knowledge content. But we cannot go further. Calvin's major occupation with the *sensus divinitatis* is not in analyzing the how and what of its knowledge content, but with its empirical effects.

The empirical effects of the *sensus divinitatis* are (1) the universality of religion, which because of sin means the universality of idolatry (I.iii.1), accompanied by (2) the servile fear of God (I.iv.4) and (3) the troubled conscience (I.iii.2.3). These three together are implicated in the inexcusability of all men (I.v.15).

believer who has scripture.[3] We must consider these two questions, not because they arise from a study of Calvin, but because they have arisen as a problem of Calvin interpretation under the influence of Karl Barth. The motive has been to clear Calvin of all suspicion of natural theology, that is of constructing an independent avenue to God that stands outside special revelation. This can be done legitimately. But the zeal with which it has been pursued — partly in an effort to set the theology of Calvin in clearer opposition to Thomism, to Neo-Protestantism, and to the "German Christian" movement of the last decade — resulted in a statement of the case which falsifies Calvin by not admitting, or by minimizing, the degree to which Calvin as a reader of Scripture finds himself referred by Scripture and under the guidance of Scripture to God's revelation in creation.[4] As we shall now see, Calvin

calmly and without polemic, considered the revelation in creation as part of the believer's knowledge of God.

Calvin calls seeing God in nature a "way of seeking God" that is "common to aliens and to those of his family."[5] And the fact that the Jews had the moral law in addition to the general revelation meant that they were bound by a "double tie to honor God."[6] Were the God of nature known to the Christian exclusively in Scripture, Calvin's[7] comparing the two revelations and maintaining the identity of their content would be frivolous.[8]

This is a recurrent theme of the Commentary on First Corinthians, where Calvin joins Paul in setting the "wisdom of this world" and the "foolishness of God" in sharp opposition. But Calvin never fails to make the further allowance that once faith has done its work, this formerly rejected wisdom is not to be scorned.[9]

---

[3] "But Calvin has not the least intention of setting up a kind of opposition between the Biblical and natural revelation. Rather, God's word elucidates his revelation in nature." Wernle, *Der evangelische Glaube*, p. 175.

[4] Wilhelm Niesel's *Die Theologie Calvins* is a good example. Niesel's chapters follow the order of discussion of ed. '59 throughout, with one exception: Chapter II, "The Knowledge of God," reverses the order that Calvin followed without exception from ed. '39 through '59, by placing the doctrine of Scripture (pp. 19–36) before "The Question of the Natural Knowledge of God" (pp. 36–49). His justification for doing this is the primacy of Scripture in Calvin's theology as stated in his preface to the *Institutes* and to the French Bible and even in the opening words of ed. '36 . . . Granting, of course, both that Calvin's theology is derived exclusively from Scripture and that the chief aim of it is to point through Scripture to the encounter with God in Christ — we

still cannot use these central ideas like swords to slash away problems. We must still explain why Calvin, in spite of this, persisted for twenty years in beginning his systematic work with the general revelation. Why did he in edition after edition develop his doctrine of the word and Spirit with little mention of Christ . . . Why, finally, was the knowledge of the Creator always kept separate from that of the Redeemer? . . .

[5] *Institutes* I.v.6 (OS III.51.13–21).

[6] Com. Ps. 19:7 (CO XXXI.199b).

[7] I.x.

[8] I.x.1 (OS III.85.7–12).

[9] From this commentary Karl Barth, *No!*, and also Niesel, *Die Theologie Calvins*, cite only places which demonstrate man's inabilities where the saving mysteries of God are concerned. But Calvin makes perfectly clear that man's abilities as such are not to be scorned. Cf. Com. 1 Cor 1:17 (CO XLIX.321b); 1:20 (pp. 324 f.); 1:21 (pp. 326 f.) is the strongest condemnation of human intellectual pretense; 3:19 (p. 359d–

A section of the "Argument" to the Commentary on Genesis is directed specifically to our problem. . . . Calvin points out that although Paul belittles the "wisdom of the world" and teaches that we must be carried on high above the world to behold those things which eye has never seen. . . . where natural nourishment and the light of the sun and stars are replaced by Christ, and the air by his Spirit — that nevertheless, we are not to conclude that God's revelation in nature no longer concerns us.[10] This is, of course, a denial of any "natural theology," for only in Christ do we see even the "hands and feet of God." Yet we see these "hands and feet" actually before our eyes in the works of creation. . . .

Granting, then, that the spectacle of creation is not superfluous to the Christian, but that in Calvin's understanding the Scriptures urge the believer to see the world as a revelation of God, and that Calvin goes so far as to use the older science of his day, derived largely from non-Christians, as an aid in the exegesis of Scripture, we still face the question of the exact relationship between the general and the biblical revelations of God as Cre-

ator. Several visual metaphors of Calvin give an indication of the answer. Calvin refers to creation as a mirror[11] or theater[12] in which is reflected or displayed or written the revelation of the Creator. Man, however, because of sin, has weak sight and must use the "spectacles" of Scripture to see what is before him.[13] This metaphor would imply neither the substitution of a new object of vision for an old one nor a complete cure of the eyes, but the use, because of a permanent defect in sight, of an aid in perceiving the original object, the revelation in creation. . . .

The relation, thus, is one of clarification, in which Scripture is a pair of eyeglasses or a guide and teacher. The special revelation of the Creator in Scripture is not a substitute revelation, a completely new picture placed before the eyes. It does not make irrelevant God's other works which Christians have objectively in common with all men, but it is an aid in understanding these works — an indispensable aid. . . .

But over and above this, Scripture also presents a new knowledge content about the Creator in the doctrines of the Trinity, creation, and particular providence. Here the metaphor of the spectacles is no longer useful, because since the Fall these teachings are no longer communicated by creation, but only by Scripture. Scripture here is the sole source, not a lens held up to nature. It goes without saying that Calvin's doctrine of the Trinity is exclusively biblical in origin. As for

---

360a), the world's wisdom is a "handmaid," subject to Christ; 8:1–2 (pp. 427d–430).

[10] CO XXIII.10d–11a, and *passim*. Since Wilhelm Niesel calls it "unpardonable" that Gloede should cite this passage after Peter Barth in *Das Problem*, p. 25, had proved it unusable, one feels called upon to remark that Peter Barth's comment consisted solely of italicizing the sentence in which Christ is mentioned and leaving in small type the preceding and following sentences that make the point. See Niesel's review of Gloede's work in *Theol. Literaturbeilage der Reform. Kirchenstz.*, pp. 15 f.

[11] I.v.1 (OS III.45.26).
[12] I.xiv.20 (OS III.170.23).
[13] I.vi.1 (OS III.60.25–30).

creation, man sinfully forgot, except for the patriarchal tradition which God kept alive, the details of the six-day creation which had been especially intended for his instruction. This creation process is not to be deduced from or observed in creation today by the "aid" of Scripture, as is, for example, the wisdom of God. Scripture teaches it *de novo*. The same is true of particular providence. While a Plato[14] can see that the world and the life of men is upheld by the will of God, only the man of faith, instructed by Scripture, can penetrate to the knowledge of God's particular providence, the "special care" of God by which alone his "paternal favor" is known.[15] . . .

Thus, the special revelation of God the Creator in Scripture not only clarifies but also complements, by the addition of new content, what can be known of God the Creator in creation. The doctrines of the Trinity, creation, and particular providence, are a special revelation of God with regard to both the means of communication and the content, and yet neither surpasses the bounds of the knowledge of God the Creator. We have not yet come to the specific knowledge of the Redeemer, although we are in an area of Calvin's thought where faith in Christ is presupposed. . . .

The Content of the Knowledge of God the Redeemer. In the case of the revelation of God the Creator, we found two sources of knowledge, creation and Scripture, which conveyed up to a point identical information about God, and we also noted a cer-

tain special content of the scriptural revelation. . . .

. . . The revelation of God the Redeemer is [centers] in a single main theme of Scripture. Its knowledge content is both easier to epitomize and more difficult to give in detail than the knowledge of the Creator. It is, simply, Christ. But this special theme is encased in the whole of Scripture, it is involved in successive forms of historical presentation, and it ramifies into the subjects of the person and the work of Christ, the whole of the so-called *ordo salutis*, and the "external means" of fellowship with Christ: the church and the sacraments. . . .

God's attributes are for the most part, as Warfield says, "in solution" in Calvin's theology, rather than "in precipitate."[16] This is even more true of Calvin's soteriology than of his doctrine of God the Creator. We shall here, however, "precipitate" the two most prominent attributes of God the Redeemer, that is to say, of what the work of redemption makes known to us of God. To say "two," however, is already to falsify the case, for it is the very unity, mysterious[17] unity of the "two" which we mean, following Calvin, to emphasize. The two are really one. . . .

We have observed Calvin binding together in a single conception of amazing scope the entirely personal, existential assurance of salvation through the Holy Spirit's application of the work of Christ in faith, with

[14] Com. Ps. 104:29 (CO XXXII.95c).
[15] I.xvi.1 (OS III.188.29).

[16] B. B. Warfield, *Calvin and Calvinism*, p. 143.
[17] In the sense of the New Testament *musterion*, suprarational reality.

the most utterly objective *jenseits* of all theological ideas: the eternal decrees. The faithful man, in which Christ now dwells, is the elect man, chosen of God in Christ before creation for a salvation that is still largely in the future. He knows God to be merciful, absolutely and forever merciful, in the present certainty of his own personal salvation. But he knows this mercy as utterly gratuitous, because it rests, not in any conditionedness of creation or any merit of sinful man, but in the eternal counsel of God. Gratuitous mercy, then, is the two-in-one attribute of God to which we are pointing. These two words represent the two poles of saving knowledge "of God" as Redeemer and "of ourselves" as redeemed. Both poles are on one axis: Christ. Apart from Christ neither God's forgiving mercy nor his gratuitous decree is known. Through Christ both are known and inseparable. The gratuitousness of mercy is revealed in election,[18] and the benevolence or mercy-quality of election is seen in the assurance that faith has of personal salvation.[19] . . .

Gratuitous-goodness, gratuitous-mercy, or gratuitous-love — any one of these is the appropriate epithet for God the Redeemer in Calvin's theology. We can, since Nygren, express this characteristic of God in a single term, *agape*. However, if we wish to

keep to the idiom of Calvin, the word-pair is more accurate. . . . In the single word "agape" we see graphically the unity behind Calvin's double word. Both signify the same thing. Calvin, like Luther,[20] and in part like Augustine, was a theologian of *agape*, gratuitous-love. God the Redeemer is above all the God of grace.[21] . . .

It has often been said that the leading characteristic of Calvin's theology is his doctrine of predestination, understood particularly in terms of the sovereignty, the absolute freedom of God, who can damn his creatures for his own glory. But for Calvin, God is never merely sovereign.[22] He is sovereignly good, sovereignly just, sov-

---

[18] "We shall never be clearly convinced, as we ought to be, that our salvation flows from the fountain of God's gratuitous mercy, till we are acquainted with his eternal election, which illustrates the grace of God by this comparison, that he adopts not all promiscuously to the hope of salvation, but gives to some what he refused to others." III.xxi.1 (OS IV.369.25 ff.).

[19] III.xxii.10 (OS IV.391.25 ff.).

[20] This is not to overlook the differences between Luther's and Calvin's conceptions of the love of God. Köstlin points out that there are no such words about love filling the heart of God in Calvin as in Luther and that while the fatherly love of God is the center of the Christian experience, it is not so clearly the dominant motif as in Luther, "Calvins Institutio nach Form und Inhalt," pp. 424–426. How true this is, does not concern us here; but the reference will serve to show that caution must be exercised.

[21] Cf. Seeberg, *Lehrbuch der Dogmengeschichte*, p. 517. This fine statement, however, is outweighed in Seeberg's treatment by his search for the "universal metaphysical elements" of Calvin's God idea, which he finds in the properties of God the Creator as we have outlined them in the last chapter. This God as a metaphysically conceived determiner of all events, thus is seen as the regulator of providence and special providence (predestination), whose every act is for the sake of his "holiness" or "glory" displayed in grace and justice within creation (pp. 575–578) and his "sovereignty" as seen in salvation and damnation (pp. 579–582).

[22] Beyerhaus, *Studien zur Staatsanschauung Calvins*, pp. 48–77, is particularly guilty of this, also Kampschulte, *Johann Calvin*, I, 251–278.

ereignly merciful and gracious.[23] The dimension of sovereignty or gratuitousness is never permitted to condition or to control the mercy of God, so that he might become suddenly and arbitrarily not merciful, not just, and not good. When misunderstood, this very characteristic leads to a concept of God as a divine and arbitrary dictator who can and may do anything — or worse, who has already decided everything and has decided it arbitrarily; in Calvin's theology it is the very apex of trust in God's trustworthiness,[24] nonarbitariness, the complete unconditionedness and therefore eternal unchanging truth of what he has revealed, namely, his mercy in Christ. . . . For Calvin, God the Redeemer is not the God whose mercy may be withdrawn. Nor is he the God who deals with men solely in terms of the double decrees. . . .

Now problems loom up. Is it not curious to call Calvin a theologian of love? Where is love in the best-known statement of his theology, namely: "Predestination we call the eternal decree of God by which he has determined in himself what he would have

to become of every individual of mankind. For they are not all created on equal terms, but eternal life is foreordained for some and eternal damnation for others. Every man, therefore, being created for one or the other of these ends, we say he is predestined either to life or to death."[25]

These words, like the definition of faith, were carried unchanged from the edition of 1539 into the final redaction. They must be taken seriously, but they must not be taken out of context. The context, without exception, both formally and theologically, is Calvin's soteriology, and in 1559 the doctrine comes at the end (but for the doctrine of the resurrection) of the *ordo salutis*.

For Calvin the doctrine of double predestination does not in any way change the picture of the God of gratuitous love. Rather it emphasizes it. We cannot here enter into a thorough study of the doctrine of the decrees and his basic formulation of it, but we can show the fact that and the way in which, within that formulation, the element of reprobation is subordinate to that of election, despite their apparent equality in the above statement. Our grounds are two, epistemological and logical. . . .

First, the epistemological ground. . . . It is simply this: the doctrine of reprobation is known only to the believer who knows himself as elect to salvation and looks upon his neighbor as potentially elect. That is to say, the doctrine of reprobation enters into neither the relation to God nor the relation to one's fellow man,

---

[23] "In a word, with all his emphasis on the sovereignty of God, Calvin throws an even stronger emphasis on his love: and his doctrine of God is preeminent among the doctrines of God given expression in the Reformation age in the commanding place it gives to Divine Fatherhood. 'Lord and Father,' — fatherly sovereign, or sovereign Father — that is how Calvin conceived God." Warfield, "Calvin's Doctrine of God," *op. cit.*, p. 176; cf. Doumergue, *Jean Calvin*, IV, 88 ff.

[24] The three functions of the doctrine of predestination are to promote humility, to give the believer a sense of his obligations to God, and to bestow a "firm confidence," III.xxi.1 (OS IV.369.33–35).

[25] III.xxi.5 (OS IV.374.11–17).

neither the worship nor the ethics, of the only one for whom it is a doctrine: the believer.

Calvin teaches the supralapsarian decree of reprobation, that before creation each of the reprobate was determined by God for his end.[26] That is all. No more can be said on the subject.[27] This is a flat, isolated, although necessary statement for him. Beyond this, he has no positive teaching. . . . This decree may not be scrutinized, and God may not be questioned on the basis of it. If the decree of election is to be explained only by God's mercy revealed in Christ, the decree of reprobation is not to be investigated at all. . . .

Second, there is a logical or systematic peculiarity within the doctrine of reprobation itself that robs it of the right to be set parallel to election as if, according to Calvin, these were two modes of God's dealing with men that are of equal directness and of equal strength in the believer's knowledge of God. . . . It is clear that Calvin is trying to show that God takes direct responsibility for all good in creation, including the essential created goodness of Satan, but that evil, while it never happens outside of his omnipotence, cannot be attributed to his intent, for his will is good.[28] The wrath of God is not such a basic characteristic of his relation to men as is his mercy.[29] . . . Finally, the damnation of the reprobate is not so directly a contribution to the glory of God as is the salvation of the elect, for he reprobates them in such a way that they fall by their own fault, and their punishment, not their sins, redounds to his glory.[30] . . .

Reprobation is an isolated doctrine for Calvin, literally in its place in the *Institutes,* in its comparative rarity in Calvin's commentaries and sermons,[31] as well as in its theological scope. It has no power within Calvin's theology . . . to do anything but emphasize the incomprehensibility and supernaturalness of the whole work of salvation, that is, the utter gratuitousness of God's love. . . . Here is a radical, one might say reckless consistency in the working out of the Biblical teaching of the gratuitousness of divine mercy.[32] . . .

4. E. Brunner[1] sketches the development of the doctrine of predestination from Augustine through Luther and Calvin to modern times. Luther

[26] III.xxiii.4.7.

[27] "I reply with Paul that no account can be given of it, for its greatness far surpasses our understanding." III.xxiii.5 (OS IV. 398.26–28).

[28] I.xviii.3–4.

[29] Com. Rom 1:18 (CO XLIX.23a).

[30] III.xxiii.8 (OS IV.402.31 ff.) and par. 9.

[31] Jacobs, *Prädestination,* p. 56.

[32] A criticism of this variety is that of Köstlin.

[1] Emil Brunner, one of the outstanding theological reformers, was born in 1890. For many years he lectured on dogmatics at Zurich. Among his numerous published works we mention *The Divine Imperative, A Study in Christian Ethics; Faith, Hope and Love; Man in Revolt, A Christian Anthropology; The Mediator, A Study of the Central Doctrine of the Christian Faith; The Theology of Crisis; The Philosophy of Religion From the Standpoint of Protestant Theology.* This excerpt is from his *Dogmatics,* vol. I, *The Christian Doctrine of God* (Lutterworth Press: London, 1949), pp. 340–346.

came to think that the doctrine of predestination was speculative, natural theology. But Calvin, as a dogmatic theologian, taught a supralapsarian doctrine of double predestination.

Before Augustine there was no doctrine of predestination. In a world like that of declining antiquity, dominated by the idea of fate, it was far more important to stress the freedom and responsibility of man than the fact that he is determined. This concern led the early Church Fathers to the other extreme from that of the doctrine of predestination: to the doctrine of free will, which they developed in connexion with the Stoic idea of *autexousion* as the presupposition of moral responsibility.

Augustine's great achievement was the rediscovery of the biblical *sola gratia;* this was why he meant so much to the Reformers. Augustine, was, however, also responsible for connecting the doctrine of election (against the teaching of Scripture) with the psychological-anthropological problem of freedom. From the time that Augustine came decidedly under the influence of Pauline thought, the idea of grace predominated in his theology. As a genuine disciple of the great apostle, he saw how man was hopelessly entangled in the net of sin, and he understood the gospel message more and more as the doctrine that God, by his grace, sets man free from this bondage to sin. In all this he remained true to the genuinely New Testament line of thought. . . . (But) Augustine is not so much concerned about the *gracious action of God* in Jesus Christ, as he is in the *transformation of man,* who was in bondage

to sin, into a free *man,* by the working of grace. . . .

From this transformation which takes place in man he proceeds to argue further, in terms of causality. If this transformation is really due to grace alone, then this divine factor, which alone counts, must be traced back to its eternal origin. This origin is the divine choice in grace. Then election is no more the state of "being-elect-in-Christ" than faith is the state of "being-justified-in-Christ." Rather, the psychological separation of grace from Christ (*gratia infusa*) corresponds to the separation of election from Christ. Election is that pre-temporal act of God to which the *causal* consideration of the divine work of grace leads. Election is wholly severed from the revelation in Christ; it is the metaphysical postulate which results from the causal consideration of the experience of grace.

The great gulf, in Augustine's thought, between faith in Christ and election, comes out very clearly in the fact that — for Augustine — "faith" does not necessarily imply the certainty of salvation and election.[2] . . . This severance of election from faith in Christ now means that election is more narrowly defined as the selection of a *numerus praedestinatorum* from the *massa perditionis.* This misunder-

---

[2] *Quis enim ex multitudine fidelium quadiu in hac mortalitate vivitur, in numero praedestinatorum se esse praesumat?* Opp. X, 999.

standing of the scripture passage,[3] which contrasts the great number of those who are "called" with the small number of those who are "chosen," seemed to provide a scriptural basis for this view. Actually, this passage does not refer to the subject of eternal *election* at all, but merely to the separation of one group from another at the judgment.

Otherwise Augustine does not yet develop the idea of predestination to its most ruthless conclusion of a *gemina praedestinatio*. Rather, in his thought, we can still detect a trace of the unequal emphasis of the Bible, in that he speaks of a "praedestinatio," to salvation, but not of a "predestination" to destruction; he only speaks of a "foreknowledge" of rejection and of the reprobate. This distinction makes it possible for him to understand predestination in an infralapsarian and not in a supralapsarian sense: out of those who were affected by the Fall of Adam God chooses some to be saved; the rest he leaves to their self-chosen fate.

The first man to pronounce the terrible phrase *praedestinatio gemina* was a monk named Gottschalk, in whose writings we already find the expression *pariter,* which Calvin's formula revived. The fight against Gottschalk and his champion Ratramanus, shows that the Catholic Church was still less inclined to accept this extreme idea of Predestination, since in practice it was moving far more in the direction of Semi-Pelagianism. On the other hand, Aquinas adopted again the doctrine of Augustine on

this point; he, too, speaks of a *certus numerus praedestinatorum;*[4] he, too, distinguishes between the *predestination* of the elect and the *foreknowledge* of the non-elect. . . .

If we are to estimate Luther's and Calvin's doctrine of predestination aright, we must start from the fact that for them the problem was regarded entirely from the standpoint of the question of Augustinianism *versus* Pelagianism. Thus from the very outset they adopted the position of the "Either-Or" set up by Augustine, and thus they accepted that fatal perversion in the idea of election, which we have seen to be present in the thought of Augustine. Once they had embarked on this path, they followed it to the bitter end, to the *horribile decretum* of a double predestination. Calvin expressed this view in terms which exactly convey his meaning: *"non pari conditione creantur omnes, sed aliis vita aeterna, aliis damnatio aeterna praeordinatur."*[5] This formula leaves us in no doubt whether Calvin really taught this doctrine in the Supralapsarian sense or not. Luther, too, in his work, *De servo arbitrio,* argued the strict determinism of Bradwardine through to the bitter end, with extreme, one might even say brutal, logic.

In Luther's teaching, however, this was not his last word. This predestinarian determinism was later contradicted by his new understanding of

---

[3] Mt 22:14.

[4] *S.T.,* I, q. 23, a. 7.

[5] *Institutio,* III, 21, 5: "they are not all created on equal terms, but eternal life is foreordained for some, and eternal damnation for others."

election, gained from a fresh insight into the New Testament. Luther, it is true, never revoked what he said in *De servo arbitrio;* but from 1525 onwards his teaching was different. He had freed himself from the Augustinian statement of the problem, and from the causal thinking of Augustine. He saw that this doctrine of predestination was speculative, natural theology, and he understood the Biblical idea of election in and through Jesus Christ. Since this change in Luther's thought is still too little known — in spite of Th. von Harnack's remarkable evidence[6] — and since we are here concerned with a most important, not to say fundamental truth, we must now deal with this subject in greater detail.

Whereas before 1525, and especially in *De servo arbitrio*, Luther explicitly denies the universalism of the divine will of salvation . . . he now makes an explicit distinction between the universalism of the promise and the particularism of the way in which the world will end. "For the Gospel offers to all men, it is true, forgiveness of sins, and eternal life through Christ; but not all men accept the promise of the Gospel . . . but the fact that all men do not accept Christ is their own fault. . . . *"Interim manet sententia Dei et promissio universalis. . . .* For it is the will of God that Christ should be a *communis thesaurus omnium.* . . . But the unbelieving withstand this gracious will."[7] . . .

Luther perceives that the question of predestination lies outside the

sphere of Christian revelation and faith, and that it is a question of speculative natural theology. It is the scholastic speculative theology which makes the distinction between a *"voluntas signi"* (the revealed will) and the *"voluntas beneplaciti,"* the unsearchable divine election or rejection. "No one ought to dispute about the *nuda Divinitas* (that is, about the will of God that has not been revealed). . . . In the *Verbum Dei* alone do we have the true knowledge of the will of God: *aliae cogitationes de voluntate beneplaciti — occidunt et damnant.* . . . "If thou dost believe in the revealed God and dost receive his Word, then soon also the hidden God will reveal himself unto thee. . . . If thou dost cling with firm faith to the revealed God, . . . then art thou certainly predestined and thou knowest the hidden God."[8]

In all this Luther had perceived two truths: first of all, that the traditional doctrine of predestination, as he himself had taken it over from Augustine, is *speculative* theology, and thus does not create a real knowledge of God, but on the contrary, drives men to despair — and second, that the true doctrine of predestination is simply the knowledge of election in Jesus Christ through faith. Thus at this point, as at so many others, Luther had freed the Gospel from the burden of tradition which had almost entirely obscured it, and he once more bases theological truth upon the revelation of God in Jesus Christ.

With Calvin the situation is different. In so far as he was a preacher

---

[6] *Luthers Theologie*, I, pp. 148–190.
[7] Erlangen edition, 26, 300.

[8] *Ibid.*, 43:460.

of the Gospel, for him, too, election in Jesus Christ through faith was the centre round which all his thinking circled.[9] As a dogmatic theologian, however, he was entirely of the same opinion as Augustine, whose doctrine of predestination he intensifies in the sense of the *gemina praedestinatio*, and the Supralapsarian equation of foreknowing and fore-willing. The biblical inequality of election and rejection is in his *theory* entirely removed, but in *practice* it appears in the fact that apart from a very few exceptions, Calvin never preached about the double decree, but only about election. Calvin fails to perceive the real origin of this doctrine of double predestination — that is, speculative natural theology — from the application of the causal concept to unbelief — owing to the fact that he believes that he has derived his doctrine entirely from the holy Scriptures, in that he combines certain Bible passages with one another — no one of which really contains this doctrine — in such a way that, together, they appear to provide the Scriptural proof for the *gemina praedestinatio*. . . .

The controversy between the Lutherans, who, following Luther's later utterances, reject the *gemina praedestinatio* and teach the universalism of the Gospel, and the Calvinists — as well as the controversy between the Supralapsarians and the Infralapsarians among themselves — is of no interest for us here. The doctrine of Calvin

to some extent culminates in the Articles of Dordrecht.[10] With this statement the doctrine of predestination returns to its origin, to the doctrine of Augustine, without, however, actually condemning the more extreme doctrine of Calvin.

In modern times the doctrine of Augustine had found a champion in Schleiermacher's deterministic speculative theology — certainly with pantheistic modifications — and has found its historian in one of the most outstanding of his pupils, Alexander Schweizer.[11] Otherwise in later theology the less-biased view of the doctrine of the New Testament is emphasized. Even the Reformed theologian Böhl no longer speaks of a *double* decree, but of "the" decree of God, even when he is contending against the Lutheran "universalism," which he evidently confuses with the general theory that "everyone will be saved."[12] Only within the strictly Calvinistic theology of Holland,[13] and in America, has the Calvinistic doctrine of the double decree, mostly, however, in the modified form of the Articles of Dordrecht, been maintained.

---

[9] Cf. the fine Zürich Dissertation of G. Jacobs, *Erwählung und Verantwortlichkeit bei Calvin*, 1927.

[10] Cf. Müller: *Die Bekenntnisschriften der reformierten Kirche*, pp. 845 ff.: "non omnes homines esse electos, sed quosdam non electos, sive in aeterna dei electione praeteritos quos scilicet deus ex liberrimo, justissimo . . . irreprehensibili et immutabili beneplacito decrevit in communi miseria, in quam se sua culpa praecipitarunt, relinquere."

[11] Alexander Schweizer: *Die protestantischen Zentraldogmen.*

[12] Böhl: *Dogmatik*, p. 289.

[13] Kuyper and his school.

X

GOD IN THE SIXTEENTH AND
SEVENTEENTH CENTURIES

1. N. Abercrombie[1] studies Molina's doctrine of divine concurrence, knowledge, and predestination. In the matter of concurrence Molina holds the necessity of a divine influx that flows into the effect, and not into the second cause itself. He is the first to investigate thoroughly the divine *scientia media* whereby God, before the issue of any creative decree, has a certain knowledge of hypothetical future contingents. Predestination includes a conditioned foreknowledge of the way in which man will use his free will in certain circumstances.

Molina.[2] The theologians of the sixteenth century fall roughly into three groups. The first, which includes Baius and the Reformers, deliberately,

---

[1] Nigel Abercrombie, M.A., D.Phil. (Oxon.), was lecturer in French, Magdalen College, Oxford in 1936. This excerpt is from his book, *The Origins of Jansenism*

(Oxford: The Clarendon Press, 1936), pp. 93, 100–103, 106–112.
[2] Luis de Molina (1563–1600), was born at Cuenca and joined the Society of Jesus

and more or less completely, broke with the traditional scholasticism of the Middle Ages. The second, which is represented by the Order of Preachers, deliberately and more or less faithfully, held to that tradition, and attacked the new theology solely from the standpoint of the old. The third group was the Society of Jesus, with the theologians who openly allied themselves therewith: this was the "left wing" of the intellectual counter-Reformation. These men, no less than their Protestant opponents, were sons of the Renascence, in that they were not content with the conclusions and methods of the medieval schools; they differed from the first group in the degree of their tenacity to that corpus of belief and opinion which, in their time, constituted Catholic thought. The most interesting representative of this third group is Luis de Molina.

Molina published at Lisbon, in 1588, as the result of a lifetime of thought and study, his *Concordia*.[3] . . . It would be difficult to name a single treatise of dogmatic theology which has more profoundly affected the history of dogma. . . . The *Concordia* falls easily into five divisions. In the first, Molina investigates the nature, value, extent, and limitations of human liberty, especially of the liberty of fallen man. In the second, he discusses in general the relation between the activity of the first cause and the activity of second causes; that is, the nature of the *concursus divinae potestatis*, in virtue of which all secondary causality is operative. In the third part of his work he treats of "actual grace." In the fourth, he propounds and defends the notion of *scientia media*. In the last, he gives an account of Predestination and Reprobation—which is, in some ways, the least valuable part of the *Concordia*. . . .

Concurrence. In the matter of the concurrence of the first cause with second causes, as in the matter of human freedom, there are two opposed capital errors to be avoided: namely, the opinion that second causes have no real efficacy, but only mask the immediate operation of God; and the other, that second causes are quite independent, in their proper activity, of the Creator, and have in themselves all that is required for causal action.

Molina is not satisfied with the account of this matter given by Aquinas[4] and discovers two things which seem unintelligible or misleading. The first, that Aquinas teaches a divine "motion and application to action" of the second cause. Molina confesses that he cannot understand this. . . . That created agents . . . which are operative of themselves, by reason of their nature and existence,

---

at Alcala. For nearly twenty years he taught theology at Evora. His writings are the *Concordia* (1588), the commentaries on the *Prima Pars of the Summa* (1592), and *De justitia et jure* (1593, 1596, and posthumously).

[3] *Concordia liberi arbitrii cum gratiae donis, divina praescientia, providentia, praedestination, et reprobatione, ad nonnullos primae partis D. Thomae articulos.*

[4] He alludes to *Pars Prima*, q. 105, art. 5.

such as a flame . . . stand in any need of "motion and application to action," Molina is unable to admit. His second complaint . . . is that Aquinas appears to omit altogether to notice any *concursus* which should "give being" to the effect of the second cause. . . .

Molina himself will not admit a divine "motion and application" as any part of the ordinary relation between first and second causes, but confines this relation to the divine *concursus*. This he defines as an influx of being from God into the effect of the secondary agent. This *influxus* forms one cause with the *influxus* of the second cause itself, and receives its specific determination from the latter. Each influx is as necessary as the other, for the effect proceeds only from the total cause. The necessity for the divine influx depends upon the metaphysical incapacity of a created agent in the domain of being. Its most important characteristic is that it flows into the effect, and not into the second cause itself, which remains wholly unaffected by its action. . . . "The influx of the first cause is neither prior nor posterior, in time or in the order of reason, to the influx of the second cause."

From this account it follows that the action of the divine *concursus* is not such as to affect, in any degree, the freedom of the second cause. An equally important consequence is that God cannot in any way be called "the author of sin." . . . The *influxus* of the first cause is in no way specified or particularized, except by the second cause, into whose own and proper effect it flows, in order to give

reality to the creature's causal action. . . . The general *concursus* is provided in order that good actions may be accomplished by creatures; and in this way God is the cause of all natural acts, and of all morally good acts, and doubly the cause of all supernatural acts. But man is free to act as he pleases, and thus has the power to abuse the general gift of the divine *concursus:* he could not sin, any more than he could exist, without an emanation of being from God, but the fact that he sins is his own doing, and not in any respect the work of God. . . .

Scientia Media. . . . If Molina was not actually the first theologian to teach that God possessed this "knowledge," he was the first to devote a thorough investigation to the subject, to give it its due importance, and finally to carry it, in a book, outside the lecture rooms of one or two isolated professors. . . .

The Lord's own words,[5] in which he gives evidence of certain knowledge concerning what particular free agents — the people of Tyre and Sidon — would have done, if their circumstances had been different, are in themselves a sufficient proof that God possesses this perfect knowledge of hypothetical future contingents, or conditioned free actions. Confirmatory evidence is provided by the fact that the ignorance, which is the only alternative to this knowledge must confirm our belief in this knowledge still farther: for God knows things in the

[5] Mt 11:21: "Woe to you, Chorazin! woe to you, Bethsaida! for if the mighty works done in you had been done in Tyre and Sidon, they would have repented long ago in sackcloth and ashes."

comprehensive intellectual vision of his own essence, and not, as we do, by contemplating them from without; therefore it is not the existence of things which enables him to know them, but his own. Nothing, therefore, should prevent him from knowing things "before" they exist in eternity; but rather we should be led to suppose that their existence in no way alters the certainty and perfection of the knowledge he has of them. . . .

Molina concludes this section of his work with a summary and application. There are three kinds of divine knowledge, according to our abstractive and analytical mode of understanding. The first, *scientia naturalis,* has for its subject matter everything possible, that is, all being, and all possible being, in whatsoever determinations it could possibly receive; the scope of this knowledge is the scope of the power of God. The second, *scientia libera,* is the knowledge of everything that was, is, or ever shall be; this is called the *scientia visionis,* and its scope is that of the free creative decree of God. The third, *scientia media,* is the kind of knowledge which we have just been discussing; it is the certain knowledge of the behaviour of every free second cause in all possible circumstances, and all the consequences of such behaviour; it depends upon, and is only limited by, God's "most high and inscrutable comprehension of every free will." The existence of this kind of knowledge in God is the reconciliation of eternal omniscience with human liberty; for the certitude of this knowledge is divinely perfect, while our freedom is

in no way prejudiced or affected by the fact that God knows what we shall do "through the infinite and illimitable perfection and sharpness of his understanding." For this fact indeed makes it necessary, in *sensu composito,* that we do what we do; but necessity *in sensu composito* is no more than the application to our actions, as modes of being, of the principle of contradiction, and is universally admitted to be compatible with the most perfect and indeterminate contingency. . . .

Predestination. . . . Predestination, as Aquinas said, is a part of providence. It is defined as the *"ratio transmissionis creaturae rationalis in beatitudinem."*[6] . . . The effects of the decree of predestination in the elect themselves comprise everything which in any way tends toward their beatitude, except sin itself. . . . The effects of reprobation are exclusion from the beatific vision, and the infliction of the pains of hell; sin is not the effect, but the cause of reprobation. The scholastic tradition is to be upheld, that the effect of predestination as a whole has no cause *ex parte praedestinati.* Predestination necessarily implies and involves *scientia media,* since it includes the will to assist free men with graces which will sort with their behavior in hypothetical circumstances. *Scientia . . . visionis* follows upon the decree of predestination, for God thus sees the effects

[6] *Sum. Theol.,* I, q. 23, a. 2: "quaedam ratio ordinis aliquorum in salutem aeternam, in mente divina existens": "a kind of plan of the ordering of some persons towards eternal salvation, existing in the divine mind."

of his decree in their own proper existence. . . .

As regards the natural events which contribute to the salvation of the elect, Christ, apart from his terrestrial existence, is not the cause of the effects of predestination in man. . . . But as regards our dispositions to grace, our consecution of grace, and our increase and growth in grace, he is the principal cause of these effects to our election and predestination . . . The sole cause of . . . reprobation, *ex parte hominis,* is final impenitence in the state of mortal sin.

2. M. J. Farrelly[1] sketches Bañez's view of God's plan and causality that lead man to his eternal beatitude. The complementary truths that form the foundation of this view are the complete primacy of God as first cause and the complete dependence of the creature upon God in its action. Bañez vigorously rejects Molina's doctrine of God's knowledge as false to the principles of St. Thomas as well as to the principles of sound philosophy.

Bañez. The complementary truths that form for Bañez[2] the foundation for any adequate explanation of the revealed mystery of God's plan and causality that lead man to his eternal beatitude are the complete primacy of God as first cause and the complete dependence of the creature upon God in its action. God is the source of all the perfection of the creature. He gives to the creature, not only the power of acting which it then puts into effect, but also the act itself of the creature. Its action is a passage from potency to act, and it is thus a gain of being, of goodness, and of perfection. Since its act is an act of potency and every created perfection is a participation of the perfection of God, the creature's act itself is a participation in the act of God through God's causality. What is true of the creature as such does not cease to be true when the creature considered is man, for this is a metaphysical truth that depends upon the nature of the creature as creature and God as God. . . .

This, of course, is not to say that God's action or will destroys the contingency of the acts of contingent created causes. God's perfection does not militate against the perfection of his creature, nor does his causality

---

[1] M. J. Farrelly, O.S.B., of St. Anselm's Abbey, Washington, D. C., submitted a work entitled, *Predestination and Grace: A Re-examination in the Light of Modern Biblical and Philosophical Developments,* to the Catholic University of America as his dissertation for a doctorate in theology. This excerpt is from that work, published as *Predestination, Grace, and Free Will* (Westminster, Md.: The Newman Press, 1964), pp. 5–19.

[2] Dominic Bañez (1528–1604) became a Dominican at Salamanca in 1546. He taught at Salamanca, at Avila, at Alcala, at Valladolid. He returned to Salamanca (1577) where he spent the remainder of his life, occupying the second chair of theology and then the first, from 1580 to his death in 1604. His work consists either of commentaries on the *Summa Theologiae* or writings occasioned by the Molinist controversy. Cf. *Scholastica commentaria in primam partem Summae theologicae s. Thomae Aquinatis 1* (Madrid, 1934).

diminish the causality of his creature. In fact, God has willed that some acts of creatures take place contingently, and hence he has fitted contingent created causes for these effects, as he has willed that other acts take place necessarily and hence has fitted necessary created causes for them. . . .

It follows from what we have said of the divine causality that, as Thomas expressed it, "the will of God is the cause of goodness in things. And hence from this fact are some things better, that God desires for them a greater good; so it follows that he loves more those things that are better."[3] . . . If one is more perfect than another, it is because God has freely willed a greater good for it. . . . Corresponding somewhat to the different effects of God's love for the predestined, Bañez states that one can imagine in the simple unity of God various acts. "The acts which we can imagine being in the divine mind both with reference to all and those proper to the predestined are these. God knew all possible men, among whom he loved certains ones with reference to natural existence, and these he willed to create. Among these, he loved some still further for the supernatural end. This divine love is called choice insofar as he separated these for himself from among others whom he willed to create. And finally he predestined these chosen ones; that is, he foresaw and ordained that through definite supernatural means, they would effectively arrive at the supernatural end."[4] . . .

Bañez vigorously rejects Molina's doctrine of God's knowledge as false to the principles of Thomas as well as to the principles of sound philosophy. Thomas rejected any explanation of God's knowledge of the creation and its acts that would put within God's intellect a passive determination brought about by the creature. And he taught that divine knowledge was, like that of the artist with reference to his work, a causative knowledge. . . . As the artist knows what color and shape his work will take because he decides it, so too God knows all creatures and their acts because by his own divine will he determines efficaciously what they will be. It is, then, the decree of the divine will that is the medium of God's knowledge of what the creature will do. . . .

Bañez's doctrine on predestination itself is wholly contained in the principles on the gratuity of the gift of eternal life, the divine will as the first and efficacious cause of this gift, and the divine knowledge as causative and as depending upon the intrinsically effective decree of the divine will. . . . Predestination, which is God's providence over the elect, presupposes God's will of the term of beatitude for the predestined subject; and of its nature it consists in a "plan pre-existing in the divine mind about the efficacious means to achieve the end."[5] The supernatural means by which the end is gained for the adult are the supernatural acts he performs; but since they are means to the end, "good works are not foreseen as preceding predestination but as infallibly fol-

[3] S.T., I, q. 20, a. 4.
[4] In S.T., I, q. 23, a. 2, p. 480.

[5] In S.T., I, q. 23, a. 2, p. 481.

lowing it,"[6] for it is characteristic of prudence to determine the means only after the end has been determined.

But so far this leaves untouched the problem of how there can be in God a truly universal salvific will asserted by Paul who taught that *God wishes all men to be saved and to come to the knowledge of the truth* (1 Tim 2:4). It also does not explain how the divine will and intellect are related to the evil of sin and of man's loss of eternal beatitude. In short, what is the lot of those for whom there does not exist an eternal divine decree of predestination or of determination to a supernaturally or naturally good act? Here Bañez admits there is a mystery, but it is a mystery made, not by man's theory, but by God's revelation.

Some light is cast upon this mystery through the distinction drawn by Thomas in dependence upon St. John Damascene between God's antecedent and consequent will. Antecedent to his consideration of all the particular circumstances, God wills that all men be saved; but consequent upon such consideration, he wills to reprobate some men. In other words, he does not choose them for eternal life. Scripture itself teaches this.[7] Since by his consequent will[8] God permits some to be reprobated, his universal salvific will is really God's antecedent will.

While Bañez holds that it can safely be held that this will exists formally in God, "it seems much more probable that the will that is signified by this name *velleity* does not formally exist in God; but it is enough that such an antecedent will be said to be eminently in God."[9] What God actually wills, he fulfills; but since he does not actually fulfill his antecedent will, it is better that this not be said to exist formally in God. On the other hand, the disposition to save all men was in Christ who died for all and in the prayers of the saints. Since what exists in the creature pre-exists eminently in God, its cause, this universal salvific will should be said to exist eminently in God, as in the one who caused the disposition in Christ and the saints. From this salvific will, God gives sufficient grace to all moral adults and commands them to do nothing impossible.[10] . . .

Bañez rejects Molina's doctrine of God as a partial cause of the effect with the will, and he shows that God is the total first cause who moves the will itself from potency to act by a physical created causality that both moves and determines the will and

---

[6] *In S.T.*, I, q. 23, a. 5, p. 523.

[7] As the statement Paul quotes from Malachi indicates in its context in the ninth chapter of *Romans: Jacob I have loved, but Esau I have hated*: Rom 9:13. He also quotes 1 Cor 9:27; 2 Cor 13:5; 2 Tim 2:20; Mt 7:23.

[8] I.e., consequent upon God's knowledge, not of the individual's sins, but of the purpose of the universe as a whole.

[9] *In S.T.*, I, q. 19, a. 6, p. 421. This both as a doctrine and as an interpretation of St. Thomas is rejected by all Thomists now. Basing themselves on the statement of St. Thomas in *De Veritate*, 23.3, *"voluntas de Deo proprie dicitur, et haec est voluntas beneplaciti, quae per antecedentem et consequentem distinguitur,"* they hold that a universal salvific will is formally in God. See R. Garrigou-Lagrange, *The One God*, pp. 535–538.

[10] *In S.T.*, I, q. 23, a. 3, p. 495. Bañez holds: *"Possibile est secundum legem ordinariam quemlibet hominem dum est in hac vita, salvari."*

does so by a natural antecedence to the act of the created will. This antecedent movement is not simply the moral movement of the object upon the will, as Suarez believed, but a physical movement, since the effect is itself a physical act of the will.[11] If asked more specifically what this passive premotion is, Bañez answers: "I indeed confess that I do not understand what that divine premotion is, if it is considered passively, other than the very power of the intellect placed in completed act by the author of nature, who works in all things according to the plan of his providence."[12]

With the rather small changes indicated above, the doctrine of Bañez has remained the doctrine of Thomists generally down to the present. In the present century particularly, however, there have been some attempts by those who claim to be Thomists to explain the problem of moral evil more adequately than it is felt Bañez has done. For example, Guillermin in a series of articles[13] developed once more the doctrine of J. Gonzalez de Albeda that sufficient grace does more than simply place the will in first act. It also gives "an impulse to second act, although it does not remove the impediments to this act, and, in fact, is resisted; thus it is a physical premotion, even a predetermination, but impedible, not infallible."[14] Marin-Sola goes further and holds that "sufficient grace gives in addition to an infallible beginning of the virtuous act an impulse to second act that can itself often result in second act if it is not resisted."[15] . . . Maritain, too, in an

---

[11] Bañez, "Tractatus de vera et legitima concordia liberi arbitrii creati cum auxiliis gratiae Dei efficaciter moventis humanam voluntatem," in *Comentarios inéditos a la prima secundae de santo Tomás*, 3 (ed. V. B. de Heredia, Madrid, 1948), c. 3, n. 3, p. 370. Cf. *In S.T.*, 1–2, q. 109, a. 1, n. 2, p. 22: "*Deus enim applicat nostram voluntatem ad actionem bonam et consensum liberum applicatione reali seu physica, ut ipse dicit, et non solum applicat ut causa moralis proponendo objectum sub ratione appetibilis.*" The expression *praedeterminatio physica* was used for the first time in the *Apologia fratrum praedicatorum* composed by Bañez, Peter Herera, and Alvarez and sent to Pope Clement VIII with the dossier of the Grand Inquisitor of Spain on the controversy about 1599. See E. Vansteenberghe, "Molinisme," DTC, 10.2 (1929), 2157.

[12] Bañez, "Tractatus," 2, c. 2, n. 2, p. 384. It seems that the physical causality that reduces the will from potency to act is not exercised through the object of the will in Bañez's opinion, as the quotations in the previous note show. Cajetan (*In S.T.*, 1. 80. 2, n. 6) holds that while the object presented to the will specifies the will, it is not the cause of the exercise of the will. This is the appetite itself. Garrigou-Lagrange ("Predestination," DTC, 12.2 [1935], 2983) rejects the Augustinian explanation of grace as a *delectatio victrix* because this "*n'etant qu'une motion morale, par maniére d'attrait objectif, et non pas une motion physique, ab intus quoad exercitium*' ne

saurait étre intrinséquément et infailliblement efficace." Grace moves the will to act "*par une 'motion qui applique notre volonté a poser vitalement et librement son acte* (I, q. 105, a. 4 and 5),' et qui, pour cette raison, par opposition á la motion morale, est dite prémotion physique. Les Thomistes ajoutent méme: cette motion est prédéterminante, en tant qu'elle assure infailliblement l'exécution du decret éternel prédéterminant.*" Ibid., 2984.

[13] H. Guillermin, "De la gráce sufficante," *Revue Thomiste*, 9 (1901), 505–519; 10 (1902), 47–76, 377–404, 653–674; 11 (1903), 20–31.

[14] The summary given of this doctrine by R. Garrigou-Lagrange in *Grace*, p. 230. See concerning Gonzales de Albeda in H. Lange, *De Gratia* (Freiburg i.Br., 1929), p. 482.

[15] See F. Marin-Sola, "El sistema tomista sobre la moción divina," *Ciencia Tomista*, 32 (1925), 5–54 (esp. 28–32). He gave

effort to show more clearly than Thomism does the initiative of the creature in evil, explains grace as susceptible to rejection on the part of man.[16] . . . One criticism that even admits difficulties with the traditional theory is given by M. -J. Nicolas, who admits: "The whole problem then lies in this point of the relation between the divine permission and the evil initiative, the failure of the creature. I see the two ways that are open to explain this, and each of them seems impossible to follow to the end."[17] If the ultimate priority belongs to the creature, then how does God know this evil initiative? This would make God passive before creatures. If, on the other hand, God knows our failure in his permission, there is a necessary connection between that permission and our failure. If this is so, how can God be absolved from responsibility for man's sin? He suggests that the difficulty lies in attempting to gain too profound an understanding of the mystery.

3. M. Spinka[1] studies Descartes' mechanistic view of the physical universe, and Spinoza's deterministic pantheism. He concludes that Descartes' philosophy set in motion the natural theology of Deism and ultimately led to the dispensing with God altogether, and that Spinoza contributed mightily to the present-day secularism.

Descartes.[2] The second basic truth of the Cartesian metaphysics is the existence of God: for Descartes found within himself a clear idea of God.

his answers to objections raised in "Respuesta a alguna objeciones acerca del sistema tomista sobre la moción divina," *Cien. Thom.*, 33 (1926), 5–74, and in "Nuevas observaciones acerca del sistema tomista sobre la mocion divina," *ibid.*, pp. 321–397. See for a favorable judgment on this, G. Bavaud, "La doctrine du P. Marin-Sola sur la gráce est-elle une concession au Molinisme?" *Revue Thomiste*, 58 (1958), 473–483. The author concludes by stating: "Le refus de la gráce de la persévérance finale, Dieu la décide seulement aprés la prevision de multiples resistances? À notre avis, rien n'empéche un thomiste de defendre cette position."

[16] J. Maritain, "L'existant libre et les libres desseins eternels," *Court traité de l'existence et de l'existant* (Paris, 1947), pp. 141–195.

[17] M. J. Nicolas, "Simple reflexions sur la doctrine thomiste de la gráce," *Revue thomiste*, 58 (1958), 649. Others criticize these new theories without showing uncertainty concerning the adequacy of the Thomist explanation. See Garrigou-Lagrange, *op. cit.*, p. 231; and J. H. Nicholas,

O.P., "La permission du péché," *Revue thomiste*, 60 (1960), 5–37, 185–206, 509–546. A recent Thomist critique of Suarez is found in T. Mullaney, O.P., *Suarez on Human Freedom* (Baltimore, 1950).

[1] Matthew Spinka served as a member of the faculties of the Chicago Theological Seminary and of the Divinity School of the University of Chicago. This excerpt is from his book, *Christian Thought from Erasmus to Berdyaev* (Englewood, Cliffs, N. J.: Prentice-Hall, Inc., 1962), pp. 23–40.

[2] René Descartes (1596–1650), heads the list of modern French philosophers. Like many French philosophers — Pascal, Condorcet, Comte — he was an accomplished mathematician. His *Rules for the Direction of the Mind* was written in 1628 but published posthumously in 1701. His metaphysical masterpiece, *Meditations on First Philosophy* was issued in 1641. Among his other works are *The World* or *Treatise on Light, Dioptrics, Meteors*, and *Geometry, Discourse on Method, Principles of Philosophy, The Passions of the Soul.*

But to have an *idea* of God does not yet prove that God *exists*. In order to prove the latter, Descartes adduces two arguments: the first of these consists in the affirmation that his idea of God "is also very clear and distinct." "By the name of God I understand a substance that is infinite (eternal, immutable), independent, all-knowing, all-powerful, and by which I myself and everything else, if anything else does exist, have been created."[3] And since the idea of an infinite being could not be produced by Descartes, who was only a finite being, he concluded that it was given him by intuition from God himself. *Ergo*, "we must conclude that God necessarily exists."[4]

But, u n f o r t u n a t e l y, Descartes' "proof" of the existence of God is not conclusive, if we admit no other factors than those allowed by his *Method*. He was undoubtedly sincerely convinced of the truth of his proposition and as such was a genuine believer in a philosophical religion. Nevertheless, a keen thinker like Blaise Pascal clearly understood the far-reaching implications of Descartes' postulates and realized that they were essentially destructive of the very bases of spiritual religion and of faith. . . .

Pascal's judgment was indeed right; for although superficially it may appear that Descartes was but repeating the argument of the great Christian thinker, Anselm, this appearance is deceptive. The very essence of Anselm's

view is that faith is primary and reason subsidiary, i.e., secondary. Anselm's faith was "seeking to know . . . I believe in order to understand."[5] . . . In other words, Anselm's argument presupposes faith, does not in itself result in faith. It is this aspect of the Anselmic, ontological proof which is subverted by Descartes as well as by all who followed him in seeking to base the proof of the existence of God on reason rather than on faith. "This criticism holds good," writes Erich Frank, "for all the attempts of modern metaphysicians to prove the existence of God through logical arguments alone and without the presupposition of faith; it is unavoidable that at some point reason will discover the illusory character of its purely speculative proofs of God."[6]

That Descartes' proof of God, although absolutely basic to his system, was actually soon discarded by the subsequent thinkers of the critical school is a matter of common knowledge. Of his first proof — namely, that his idea of God was most clear and distinct and since it was not derived from himself, it must have been implanted in him by God himself — the subsequent philosophers made short shrift. They simply denied that *they* had any such idea of God in their consciousness and thus exposed the basic weakness of the Cartesian proof, namely, that the existence of God depends upon our having a clear and dis-

[3] E. S. Haldane and G. R. T. Ross, transl., *The Philosophical Works of Descartes* (New York: Cambridge University Press, 1931), "Meditations," III, I, p. 165.
[4] *Ibid.*

[5] Cf. his *Proslogion* and its subtitle: *Fides quaerens intellectum*, PL, 158, 223–242.
[6] Erich Frank, *Philosophical Understanding and Religious Truth* (New York: Oxford University Press, Inc., 1945), p. 37.

tinct innate idea of it. Moreover, once Descartes' own view of the physical universe as wholly mechanical became generally accepted, and as men discarded the notion that only God could have given the machine its initial momentum, the need for God disappeared.

In the next place, the ontological argument put forth by Descartes was thoroughly discredited by Kant.[7] Kant held that one cannot argue on the basis of the phenomenal in order to prove the existence of the noumenal. He was followed in this matter by most of the later philosophers. The net result was the virtual abandonment of the attempt to prove God's existence by these means and the consequent conclusion: that since he cannot be proved by intellectual arguments, he does not exist.

Having established the existence of the Creator and the Prime Mover of the universe, Descartes felt no difficulty in asserting, as the third undoubted verity, the existence of the material world. He defined matter, in distinction from the mental substance, as spacially extended, while mind was not. The basic mode of the material world is mechanistic. The universe is one vast, immensely complicated machine, governed wholly by mechanical laws. Accordingly, it can be rationally understood, for there is nothing in it which transcends natural laws of geometry and physics. This, of course, has been essentially the view of the natural sciences down to Planck and Einstein. . . .

The Cartesian view of the physical

universe . . . has failed even more dismally than his other supposed verities. . . . The "new" physics, derived from the discoveries of Einstein and Planck and other investigators, has supplanted the "mechanistic" explanations of the universe by the theories of relativity and quantum, and has in addition swept away the confident materialism of the nineteenth century. . . . There is practically no proposition of the Cartesian physics which is still held. Sir James Jeans sums up his judgment of it in the terse remark: ". . . the system was mostly erroneous."[8]

Thus although most of Descartes' specific achievements in natural sciences have been transcended by the new physics, his basic assumption that all nature may be comprehended by scientific method and reason has remained the guiding principle of the natural sciences. In this respect Descartes has contributed to the revolution in science and is one of the pathfinders of modern philosophy. Not only is the idea of mechanism in nature due to him, but also the application of this idea to man as well. The atheistic materialists of the second half of the eighteenth century — La Mettrie, d'Holbach, and others — could derive their whole concept of man as machine from Descartes. Thus the basic humanistic character of the Renaissance was already undermined by the essential anti-humanism of mechanistic rationalism.

In such a universe there is no room not only for man, but for God as well. For as has already been indi-

---

[7] Frank, *op. cit.*, p. 51, n. 32.

[8] Sir James H. Jeans, *Physics and Philosophy* (New York: Cambridge University Press, 1943), p. 108.

cated, the idea of God was actually undermined by the Cartesian metaphysics, although Descartes himself did not foresee such a result. He remained outwardly a faithful Catholic, yet his actual position could not but repudiate the Church's faith. His aim was to attain knowledge — including that of God — by reason alone. His philosophy has set in motion the natural theology of Deism and ultimately has led to the dispensing with God altogether, when he was thought to be no longer needed. As Étienne Gilson sums up this aspect of the matter: "the mechanical world of Descartes rested upon the assumption of the conservation of the same quantity of motion in the universe; hence the God of Descartes had to be an immutable God and the laws established by his will could not be allowed to change, unless this world itself be first destroyed. In short, the essence of the Cartesian God was largely determined by his philosophical function, which was to create and preserve the mechanical world of science as Descartes himself conceived it."[9]

Spinoza. The greatest of the rationalistic philosophers after Descartes was Baruch Spinoza.[10] . . . He wrote his celebrated, posthumously published *Ethics* in conformity with the dictum

that philosophy can demonstrate its propositions with as great a logical cogency and irresistible clarity as the geometrical axioms of Euclid. But if he follows the Cartesian method[11] in this matter, he departs from Descartes in the basic concept of the source of our knowledge; instead of starting with the certainty of his own mind and deriving the concept of God therefrom, Spinoza begins with the certainty of God and derives all the rest from that axiom. To put it in another way, Spinoza denies the fundamental Cartesian dualism — the radical difference between thought and matter — in favor of radical monism.

He postulates as his starting point God as the sole existing substance, of which thought and matter, as well as an infinite number of other modes, are attributes. In this way he indeed escapes the irreconcilable contradictions of Cartesian dualism, in which the two realities, mind and matter exist side by side but cannot interact. Spinoza's God, then, represents the ultimate essence of all things, and in him all contradictions are reconciled. "By God," he writes, "I understand Being absolutely infinite, that is to say, substance consisting of infinite attributes, each one of which expresses eternal and infinite essence."[12] This basic presupposition is affirmed as a self-evident axiom of

---

[9] Étienne Gilson, *God and Philosophy* (New Haven: Yale University Press, 1941), pp. 87–88.

[10] Baruch or Benedict Spinoza was born in 1632 and died in 1677. He was excommunicated from his Jewish community in 1656. Among his works are *Parts I and II of René Descartes' Principles of Philosophy, Ethics, Treatise on the Healing of the Understanding, Short Treatise on God, Man, and His Well-Being.*

[11] See Harry A. Wolfson, *The Philosophy of Spinoza* (Cambridge, Mass.: Harvard University Press, 1934), 2 vols. Also Richard P. McKeon, *The Philosophy of Spinoza* (New York: Longmans, Green and Co., Inc., 1928), esp. Chapter I.

[12] W. Hale White, *Ethic of Benedict de Spinoza* (Oxford: The Clarendon Press, 1943, 4th ed.), I, def. vi.

rationality; Spinoza speaks of no necessity of doubting all things before one may attain to a certainty of knowledge. For him it is a rationally necessary assumption that substance exists. He defines substance as that "which is in itself and is conceived through itself," i.e., its existence is necessarily included in its essence.[13] To deny existence to substance would be to affirm that nothing exists — which is manifestly absurd. . . . Moreover, there is only one substance, outside of which nothing can be conceived. Spinoza calls this substance God, although one must not jump to the conclusion that this God is the God of Abraham and Isaac, or the Father of Jesus Christ.

Thus Spinoza has no difficulty in asserting the existence of God, and no need of resorting to any of the traditional proofs for his existence. Nevertheless, he did retain the proof that the idea of God is immediately, intuitively given. Hence no other proof is needed; so that " . . . while his essence is unknown, the fact of his existence, that he is a real being and not a mere figment of our imagination, is known to us — and it is known by a direct and immediate kind of knowledge which of all the kinds of knowledge is the most valid."[14] . . .

Having established the a priori starting point, Spinoza proceeds to dispose of the medieval concepts of God's non-materiality as well as of Cartesian dualism by designating mind and matter (or as he called the latter, extension) attributes of the divine substance. To be sure, God is not limited

to these two attributes: since he is infinite, his attributes are likewise infinite. But these two — thought and matter — are the only two apprehended by our knowledge. . . . Therefore God is both thought and matter, both mind and body.

The ascription of materiality (although not corporeality) to God is the daring new aspect of Spinoza's thought. The finite manifestation of God's attributes are called modes, of which man is one. God then is the immanent cause of all existent things; they depend on him not only for the beginning of their existence, but for its continuation as well. Moreover, all things are determined by God, so that nothing in nature is contingent. There is no such thing as free cause. In fact, God himself is determined by his own nature, and should not be thought of as possessing "free will."[15] All that exists, therefore, exists necessarily and cannot exist otherwise than it does.

This concept of God clearly reveals the pantheistic nature of Spinoza's thought. God is Nature — Deus sive Natura. God is identified with the universe, for he is its immanent cause and does not transcend it.[16] He is not the Creator producing the world ex nihilo, or in the sense that he willed to created the sort of universe as he pleased. Spinoza's chief argument against the notion of God as creator is that since he is material, he does not need to create matter. Furthermore, since God is eternal, the universe is likewise being produced eternally by his inner necessity.

---

[13] Ibid., def. iii.
[14] Harry A. Wolfson, op. cit., II, p. 353.

[15] White, op. cit., I, prop. xxxii, cor. 1.
[16] Ibid., I, prop. xviii.

Natural laws, therefore, necessarily are what they are and from all eternity cannot be otherwise.[17] This then is determinism with a vengeance: the universe governed by inexorable, unchangeable laws from which no deviation is possible.[18]

Moreover, there is no teleology in Spinoza's system, no "far-off divine event to which all creation tends"; "nature does nothing for the sake of an end, for that eternal and infinite Being whom we call God or Nature acts by the same necessity by which he exists; . . . since, therefore, he exists for no end, he acts for no end."[19] It is we, human beings, who delude ourselves into thinking that we aim at an end. We interpret — although mistakenly — all things from the point of view of our advantage, and regard natural objects, yea, even God as means toward an end.[20]

However, if all things are necessarily what they are, how is it possible for man to pursue a purpose in a purposeless universe? Does not this imply freedom which Spinoza so strenuously denies? And furthermore, if man acts toward an end, does he not regard this end as good? But how can there be a distinction between good and evil in a universe governed by necessity? Spinoza lamely affirms that these terms indicate no positive quality in things themselves, but are mere modes of thinking which men form from comparing one thing with another. Nevertheless, he retains the terms, although he redefines them:

by "good" he means things that are useful to us, and by "evil" the opposite.[21]

And yet, he is genuinely interested in providing an ethic whereby a reasonable man could conduct himself to the greatest advantage. The amazing thing about the whole undertaking is that Spinoza proceeds as if a man *could* choose one way or another, that is to say, as if he possessed ethical freedom, a postulate which he vigorously denies. . . . After all that has been said of the necessity under which God and man act . . . , it seems almost incredible that Spinoza should still undertake to construct an ethical system which must basically rest on the assumption of moral freedom. This appears to me as a fundamental and insurmountable contradiction which vitiates his whole system. . . .

In summing up Spinoza's views, let us first of all note that all the essentials of modern naturalism and philosophical determinism are already present in them. From that point of view, he is one of the most important modern thinkers who has contributed mightily to the present-day secularism. His system is essentially Stoic morality, but without its presuppositions, for it is predicated on rationalistic pantheism. Despite that, it is incomprehensible how Bertrand Russell could say of Spinoza that "ethically he is supreme."[22]

In further stages of secularization of Western culture, the term "God" has dropped out altogether and the alter-

---

[17] *Ibid.*, I, appendix, p. 38.
[18] *Ibid.*, I, prop. xxxiii, schol. 1.
[19] *Ibid.*, IV, preface, pp. 177–178.
[20] *Ibid.*, I, appendix, p. 40.

[21] *Ibid.*, IV, def. I and II.
[22] Bertrand Russell, *A History of Western Philosophy* (New York: Simon and Schuster, Inc., 1945), p. 369.

native term "Nature" has been adopted exclusively. In this sense, Goethe, the greatest of Spinoza's disciples, concluded that he is no longer a Christian.[23] Spinoza himself certainly was not an atheist, although his religious views were incompatible with any of the historic creeds, even with that of Judaism. Nevertheless, his ecstatic disciples, such as Novalis, conferred upon him the epithet of "the God-intoxicated man." Yet the sober judgment of Etienne Gilson, with the exception of the ascription of atheism, is justified: "A religious atheist, Spinoza was truly inebriated with his philosophical God."[24]

4. W. E. May[1] studies the God of Leibniz and finds that the idea of God plays a central, dominating role in his thought as in the thought of Descartes and Spinoza. The God attained by Leibnizian reason bears a remarkable resemblance to the God in whom the man of faith believes. But he is much closer to the Plotinian One than to the Christian God.

The God of Leibniz. As in the thought of Descartes and Spinoza, so too in that of Leibniz the idea of God plays a central, dominating role.[2] One of the reasons for Leibniz' concern with God undoubtedly is rooted in his ambition to reconcile the scientific advances of his day with the Judaeo-Christian heritage of western civilization. Thus, we find in his writings several arguments for the existence of God.[3] Moreover, we discover that he describes the God reached through rational demonstration as omnipotent, omniscient, good,[4] as the ultimate source of the perfections found in contingent existents as well as of the necessity and infallibility of the truths of reason,[5] as the supreme being who wills only the good and permits evil only in order to draw from it some greater good,[6] as infinite,[7] wise,[8] and as exerting fatherly

---

[23] Goethe in his letter to J. K. Lavater, quoted in Erich Frank, *op. cit.*, p. 20.

[1] William E. May is an editor for The Bruce Publishing Company. This excerpt is from his article, "The God of Leibniz," in *The New Scholasticism*, XXXVI (1962), pp. 506–528.

[2] Gottfried Wilhelm Leibniz was born at Leipzig in 1646. He died in 1716. He has been hailed as a forerunner of symbolic logic, as a metaphysical genius, and as a religious apologist. He is well known for his doctrine of monads, of pre-established harmony, and of the best possible world. Among his works are *On the Ultimate Origin of Things, The Principles of Nature and Grace, The Monadology, Discourse on Metaphysics,* and *Theodicy.*

[24] Gilson, *op. cit.*, p. 102.

[3] For the demonstrations which Leibniz offered to prove God's existence, see *On the Ultimate Origin of Things* (W. 345–350), *The Principles of Nature and Grace,* 7–8 (W. 527–528), *The Monadology,* 36–38, 43–45 (W. 540–542) etc. W. stands for *Leibniz: Selections,* ed. P. Wiener (New York, 1951). Cf. J. Jalabert, *Le Dieu de Leibniz* (Paris, 1960), pp. 54–127 for a detailed study of these arguments.

[4] See *The Principles of Nature and of Grace,* 9 (W. 528). See also *Discourse on Metaphysic,* I (W. 290–291).

[5] *The Monadology,* 41 (W. 541).

[6] *Theodicy,* 21 (Huggard transl., 136).

[7] *The Monadology,* 41 (W. 541).

[8] *Discourse on Metaphysics,* I (W. 290–291).

concern over those creatures to whom he has imparted a spiritual principle.[9]

Obviously, the God attained by Leibnizian reason bears a remarkable resemblance to the God in whom the man of faith believes. But are they, in fact, identical? The answer to this question demands a careful scrutiny of the Leibnizian theology. One of the finest contemporary Leibnizian scholars, Jacques Jalabert, has recently undertaken this task, concluding at the end of his detailed and painstaking study, that "the God of Leibniz is indeed the God of the Christians."[10] Yet Jalabert attaches some interesting reservations to his conclusion,[11] and the question itself is worthy of further reflection and study. . . .

His . . . favorite proof for God's existence is drawn from the possibility of his essence. For Leibnez, *if* God is possible, he must necessarily exist. And we can show that God is possible, because his possibility or essence is conceived as being that of a being which "possesses no limitations, no negations, and consequently, no contradictions."[12] . . . For Leibniz the concept of God "most full of meaning" is that which conceives of him as the absolutely perfect being.[13] . . . But the elements which enter into our concept of God, namely, those of being, of knowledge, and of power, are susceptible of perfection in the highest degree, for it is not absurd to speak of the greatest being, the greatest knowledge, and the omnipotent.[14] Thus there is nothing to hinder a being so conceived from existing, for there is no possible clamoring for existence which could contain greater perfection than this possible being which is, by definition, the greatest possible.[15]

Thus, Leibniz holds, nothing is more necessary than the actual existence of the greatest possible being. For only if this being exists can there be any reality in the possibility of beings other than himself. And there must be some reality in their possibility, otherwise how could we explain their actuality? That is a given datum of experience. But what is the nature of this God of Leibniz? . . . Are we to look upon him as a Creator God? . . . Or is he in some way different from a Creator God? . . .

Perhaps the best way to gain an insight into the nature of Leibniz' God and the way in which he is related to this contingent universe is to examine Leibniz' teaching on "creation." Here the first point to observe is that Leibniz quite regularly calls this universe a "created" universe, and the individual existents within it "created" monads or substances. But he is very reluctant to call his God a "creator" or to term the act whereby he brings the world into being "crea-

---

[9] *The Monadology*, 84 (W. 550).

[10] Jalabert, *op. cit.*, p. 221: "Transcendant et personnal, le Dieu de Leibniz est bien le Dieu des Chrétiens."

[11] Jalabert admits, for example, that Leibniz' doctrine that God's creation of a best of all possible worlds was morally necessary runs counter to "l'orthodoxie catholique," and that his position on the divine choice lies midway between the blind necessitarianism of Spinoza and the "traditional" indeterminism (*ibid.*).

[12] *The Monadology*, 45 (W. 541–542).

[13] *Discourse on Metaphysics*, I (W. 290–291).

[14] *Ibid.*

[15] Compare *Discourse on Metaphysics* I (W. 290–291) with *The Monadology*, 45 (W. 541–542).

tion." His favorite way of designating this act is to call it an "emanation,"[16] a "fulguration" of the "Divinity."[17] This manner of speaking is significant. . . .

Leibniz would agree that "creation" is a free act of God and that the beings "created" by him are not made out of his own substance. Yet Leibniz does regard the existence of this contingent universe as a morally necessary fact. Indeed, he even maintains that a kind of moral necessity obliging God to create "is a good thing, conformable to the divine perfection."[18] . . . It is absurd that absolute power, the omnipotence of God, be impotent. Consequently, it must be operative, and it can operate only upon the objects of God's understanding. These are the antecedent possibilities of things.[19] It is possible for there to be beings other than God, if only he wills to fulfill their exigency to exist. It is within his power so to will, and thus will he must — although this "must" is moral only, not metaphysical. . . . There is thus, in Leibniz, a kind of

necessity in God impelling him to create, and to create in a definite manner. Although Leibniz argues that creation is a free act, inasmuch as it is not grounded on any metaphysical or absolute necessity, the constraint under which his God must create in order to preserve his own perfection has important implications for locating his thought within the perspective of Christian faith.[20] . . .

If we now look to the actual contingent universe, we discover that the only true beings are complete substances which Leibniz calls monads. . . . Each of these monads, in addition, is in reality an objectification or realization of a certain viewpoint of the entire universe as seen by God.[21] They cannot, furthermore, be said to be made from nothing. Prior to their creation, these monads existed in the possibles or essences in the mind of God, that is, in the possible limitation or "finitization" of the divine attributes of power, knowledge, and will. There is, in other words, a subject of creation in Leibniz, namely, the antecedent possibility of things.

[16] On the Ultimate Origin of Things (W. 350): "We have thus the ultimate reason of the reality of essences as well as of existences . . . but it is evident that it is from this source that existing things continually emanate."

[17] The Monadology 47 (W. 542): "Thus God alone is the primitive unity or the original simple substance; of which all created or derived monads are the products, and are generated, so to speak, by the continual fulgurations of the Divinity."

[18] Letters to Samuel Clarke (W. 239).

[19] The Monadology, 43 (W. 541): "The understanding of God is the region of eternal truths, or of the ideas upon which they depend." On the Ultimate Origin of Things (W. 349): "They (the essences of things or the possibles) exist in a certain region of ideas, if I may speak thus, that is in God himself."

[20] See Jalabert, op. cit., p. 221.

[21] Discourse on Metaphysics, XIV (W. 309): "Created substances depend upon God who preserves them and can produce them continually by a kind of emanation just as we produce our thoughts, for when God turns, so to say, on all sides and in all fashions, the general system of phenomena which he finds it good to produce for the sake of manifesting his glory, and when he regards all the aspects of the world in all possible manners, since there is no relation which escapes his omniscience, the result of each view of the universe as seen from a different position is a substance which expresses the universe conformably to this view, provided God sees fit to render his thought effective and to produce the substance."

Moreover, since the actually existing monads limit their antecedent possibilities in a determinate manner, there is a sense in which we can say that there is more reality in their possibility than in their actuality.

The results of this analysis, we believe, show us a natural theology that is, in its most fundamental inspiration, Neo-Platonic in character. . . . An amazing feature of Leibniz' doctrine of God is his teaching that God is, properly speaking, his own cause.[22] The principle of sufficient reason pervades the entire Leibnizian universe. Even God has a sufficient reason or cause of his own being—namely, the divine essence. . . .

In conclusion, the God of Leibniz, like the One of Plotinus and the First Cause of the *Liber de causis*,[23] is best regarded under the aspect of perfection or goodness.[24] He is the

Infinite Unlimited Principle of all.[25] Things proceed from God, as they do from the One of Plotinus, necessarily, precisely because the God of Leibniz, like the One of Plotinus, is unlimited Power and the supreme God who cannot suffer any jealousy[26] and is, morally at least, constrained to bring into being[27] a universe whose individual components or monads each reflect and mirror, in a finite manner, the totally indeterminate perfection that superexists in God.[28]

To us, the God of Leibniz is much closer to the Plotinian One than to the Christian God. The universe of Leibniz, we should recall, is an existential blank, for existence adds nothing

---

[22] In his *Colloquy with Eckhard*, for example, Leibniz writes: "necesse est esse Ens a se, seu quod existentiam suam a se ipso, nempe a sua essentia, habeat" (cited by Jalabert, 127). Cf. also *Discourse on Metaphysics*, XXIII (W. 324), and *The Monadology*, 44 (W. 541–542).

[23] Apropos a comparison between *The Monadology* and the *Liber de causis*, Gilson's observation is of interest. He remarks: "Every time a philosophical or theological opuscule consists of concise aphoristic statements, often alliterative, and attended or not by a short commentary, the influence of the *Book of Causes* can be at least suspected" (*A History of Christian Philosophy in the Middle Ages* [New York, 1955], p. 236). *The Monadology* of Leibniz surely falls under the heading of the philosophical opuscule described by Gilson.

[24] Compare, for example, the *Discourse on Metaphysics*, I (W. 290–291), with *Ennead* VI, 9. Leibniz writes: "The conception of God which is the most common and the most full of meaning is expressed well enough in the words: God is an absolutely perfect being." Plotinus, through-

out the ninth tractate of the sixth *Ennead*, stresses the One, his supreme principle, as the beatifying object toward which we tend, our true Good, the source of all the perfections found in us. See, e.g., *Ennead*, V, 6, 4.

[25] *The Monadology*, 41 (W. 541: "God is absolutely perfect, *perfection* being only the magnitude of positive reality taken in its strictest meaning, setting aside the limits or bounds in things which have them. . . ." *Ennead* V, 1, 7: "The totality of things must come after the One, because the One itself has no determinate form. It simply is one, while Intelligence is what in the realm of Being constitutes the totality of things. Thus, the One is not any of the things that Intelligence contains. It is only the source from which all of them are derived."

[26] *The Principles of Nature and Grace*, 9–10 (W. 528): "This primitive simple substance must contain in itself eminently the perfections contained in the derivative substances which are its effects; thus it will have perfect power, knowledge, and will . . . It follows from the supreme perfection of God, that in creating the universe he has chosen the best possible plan, in which there is the greatest variety together with the greatest order. . . ."

[27] See *Letters to Samuel Clarke* (W. 239).

[28] Compare *The Monadology*, 56–60 with *Ennead* V, 3, 15, and 16.

new to the antecedent possibilities of things.[29] . . . God's essence as the *summum possibile* precontains all things in a supereminent, that is, *undetermined* way. Cannot the same be said for the One of Plotinus, the unlimited principle from whom all things emanate as radiations?[30]

5. R. A. Tsanoff[1] studies Pascal's Despair of Reason, and his immortal wager. Choose for God: you thus insure yourself against the hazard of damnation. Even if there were only one chance that God exists and ten thousand chances that there is no God, still the infinite disparity between the hazards involved would warrant your staking your life on God's existence.

Pascal's Despair of Reason.[2] How are we to prove God's existence? "If there is a God, he is infinitely incomprehensible, since having no parts nor limits, he is out of touch with us. We are thus incapable of knowing what he is or whether he exists. Accordingly, who would dare to undertake the solution of this question? Not we, we are out of touch with him altogether."[3] The Christian who believes without pretending to prove his faith is after all right, for how are proofs possible here? "God exists, or he does not exist. Now, to which side shall we incline? Reason can settle nothing here: an infinite chaos is in our way. A throw is being cast, at the end of this infinite distance, which will come out heads or tails. What will you wager? By reason you can make neither the one nor the other; by reason you can support neither side."[4]

We have now come to the famous wager of Pascal, which has occasioned endless controversy. Is this a dialogue with an unbeliever, or is Pascal disputing God's existence with himself? Certain it seems that if knowledge

---

[29] *De Veritatibus Primis* (E. 99). E. stands for the J. E. Erdmann edition of *Gottfried Wilhelm Leibniz Opera Philosophica quae extant latina gallica germanica omnia,* first published in 1840, reprinted with other texts and an introduction by R. Vollbrecht in 1959 by Scientia Aalen.

[1] Radoslav A. Tsanoff, Ph.D., was professor of Philosophy at the Rice Institute in 1931. He has written for the *Rice Institute Pamphlet* and the *Philosophical Review,* and is the author of *The Problem of Immortality: Studies in Personality and Value.* This excerpt is from his book, *The Nature of Evil* (New York: The Macmillan Company, 1931), pp. 76–81, 85.

[2] Blaise Pascal (1623–1662), mathematician, physicist, moralist, and philosopher, was perhaps the most fascinating genius in a century that counted many. It is said of him that at twelve he created mathematics, at sixteen he wrote his treatise on conic sections, at eighteen he invented a calculating machine, at twenty, demonstrated the phenomena of air-pressure. In 1646 he became interested in the Jansenists and thereafter lived a life of asceticism within the Jansenist walls of Port Royal where he wrote an attack on the Jesuits (*Provincial Letters*) and an apology for the Christian religion (*Pensées*). He also wrote *Of the Geometrical Spirit* and the *Preface to the Treatise on the Vacuum.*

[30] *Ennead* V, I, 6–7: "Why did the One not remain within itself, why did it emit that manifoldness that we find to characterize Being and which we seek to trace back to the One? . . . It [this act of emitting] must be conceived as a radiation [Leibniz' "fulgurations of divinity"?] which though it proceeds from it, leaves undisturbed its self-sameness. . . ."

[3] *Oeuvres,* Vol. XIII, p. 145.

[4] *Ibid.,* p. 146.

about God is beyond the reach of our reason, then the recognition of its helplessness is the only reasonable course open to reason, and agnosticism the true wisdom. Does God exist or not? I do not know; I cannot say; how then can I wager? "The right thing is not to wager at all."[5]

But this agnostic withdrawal from the wager of eternity, is it not in effect itself a wager? To act so as to ignore the issue whether God exists or not is virtually to deny God's existence. This is indeed the most reckless of choices: to move blandly in the face of possible eternal ruin. Theoretically Pascal's reason counselled skeptical in-action, but he found the agnostic practice intolerable. If we were to wait upon certainty before acting, could we act at all? We must act today in preparation for tomorrow, although we may never see the mor-row. Every step we take is a step in the dark. Whether we march or whether we stand still, we are in-variably gambling on the uncertain. It behooves us to use our poor reason in determining the nature of the hazard we run in this world of uncertainties.

God exists, or God does not exist — and by God's existence Pascal under-stands here the whole of the Christian religion — God exists or God does not exist. This is of all issues the most solemn and fatal; it imposes itself on you; you cannot shirk it; willy-nilly, Pascal says, you must wager, *il faut parier*. On which side will you stake your life, your soul? Since you must choose, let us see on which side your

5 *Ibid.*

interest lies? Whether you choose the one or the other is as far as reason goes, indifferent, for there is no reason either way. But what about your fortune, your beatitude or your irre-trievable ruin? Either there is a God, perfect goodness and wisdom and power, and this world-course is a solemn drama of Divine Providence governing all destiny; or else there is no God, and this world is a vast machine of matter-in-motion, or else immense and irremediable chaos. Either there is a God, and your life and death are but the prelude to an eternal career of bliss or damnation; or there is no God, and your lot is as the lot of all other clods of moist earth.

What have you to gain and what to lose if you choose one way or the other, heads or tails? Suppose you live your life as if God existed: you may, of course, miss the so-called pleasures of this brief life; but, again, you may gain an eternity of heaven. On the other hand, live your life as if there were no God: you may then have your sinful way here and now, and then death and nothing more; but, my soul, it is also possible that you may face eternal damnation. Staked against possible heaven and hell, what are the pleasures of this life worth? Nothing at all. The in-finite is staked against the finite, today and tomorrow against eternity. How can you then hesitate about your choice? Choose for God: you thus in-sure yourself against the hazard of damnation, you stake your brief life on the chance of eternal bliss. Even if there were only one chance that

God exists and ten thousand chances there is no God, still the infinite disparity between the hazards involved would warrant your staking your life on God's existence.

Behold Pascal's immortal wager. But the soul of man replies: Be it as you say; all the same, you are forcing me to yield my life against my will. The fact is, I am so made that I cannot believe in God. Will you damn me for my inability? What am I to do? Even if my reason accedes, my heart resists the call of faith?

True, Pascal answers: if reason cannot help you here, habit and custom shall. Your heart is resistant because it is wedded to passion, to the lusts of this world. Break down the resistance to faith, curb your passions. You cannot believe? Enter anyhow upon the path of the believer, do as he does, act as if you were a believer, go to mass, take holy water. "This will make you believe and will stultify you, *cela vous abétira.*"[6] The word is terrible; we shudder as it comes from Pascal's lips and we dare not look at him lest we see on his face the ironic grin of the mocking unbeliever. Port Royal could not bear, or did not dare, to print this word. But there is no grin of mockery on Pascal's lips: terrible exhorter though he be, he never loses sight of the other side. To the unbeliever such artificial acquiescence seems debasing stultification. Mechanically to go through the motions of a ritual, to drug and stupefy myself into alien piety: "This is just what I fear, the soul protests." "And why," Pascal replies: "What have you to lose."[7] Eternity is at stake for you, and you are worrying over your sorry dignity and self-respect. Your supreme interest counsels the wager; close your eyes and plunge forward, blindly if need be; habit will sweep aside the obstacles in your way while you wait for the grace of God to illumine you with the higher light, to humble and transfigure and exalt you all at once.

Pascal is one of the most defiant warriors for the Christian faith; but his wager has proved a precarious bulwark for orthodoxy. Orthodoxy demands a different sort of assurance. Different is the assurance of Paul: "I know him whom I have believed, and I am persuaded that he is able to guard that which I have committed unto him against that day."[8] Here is straightforward, unquestioning trust. . . . Believe without understanding if you must, Clement of Alexandria would say, but if you believe with understanding, all the better. To the simple assent of faith the gnosis of Christian intelligence is as the man full grown is to the infant. This is the great confidence in the intellect which distinguishes the best of scholastic thought, particularly the great succession of Dominican philosophers of the thirteenth century: philosophy is the handmaiden of theology, but it is a necessary introduction to it.

There has been an opposite sort of believer who has felt that his faith is somehow compromised, if it leans on intelligence. Defiantly he has scorned all proofs, as if to reassert the solidity of his faith by rejecting all

---

[6] *Ibid.*, p. 154; cf. p. 271.

[7] *Ibid.*, p. 154.

[8] 2 Tim 1:12.

rational basis for it. This is the view of Tertullian: Separate Jerusalem from Athens, the Church of Christ from the Academy of Plato. What are proofs and arguments to me? Do you say that what I believe is undemonstrable, that it is absurd? Well, I believe it just because it is absurd, *Credo quia absurdum est*. This type of mind is not exclusively Christian. You find it in Islam, in India. Here is al-Ghazzali of Bagdad . . . here are immemorial mystics of India. . . .

But there is danger in this defiant faith, danger of results wholly unintended by its champions. Do you disdain in your religion to rely on reason? Would you separate theology from philosophy and science? Well enough: you remain then wholly devoted to your faith by fiat; your religion cannot be proved and does not have to be proved. But after you come others who take you at your word, that religion does not admit of proof, but who, unlike you, are mainly interested in what has to be and can be proved. They leave you to your undemonstrable faith and they go their own secular way. So it is that Duns Scotus, arch-believer himself, became a factor in the disintegration of belief which marked the collapse of scholasticism and the beginnings of the scientific Renaissance. . . .

Deeper wisdom lies in Pascal's amazing treasury of thought. He is communing with the Savior: "Be comforted," the Savior says to him, "you would not seek me, had you not found me. I was thinking of you in my agony; I have shed such drops of blood for you. . . ."[9] . . . Here, we venture to think, is the most poignant as it is the most profound note in Pascal, poignant in the white heat of the phrase: "I have shed such drops of blood for you!", profound and luminous in the initial, immortal words: "You would not seek me had you not found me." The soul groping in the dark marshes of doubt pushes on and refuses to sink back. In thus pushing on and refusing to sink back, in holding its course ever solidly ahead, it is itself proof eternal that there is solid ground ahead. Is God's truth done and finished and stored away on divine pantry-shelves beyond our reach; is it done and dead and laid out under divine seals which we may never break? Or is it not rather ever in the making? Is God himself the unreadable Preface of the book of creation, or is he not rather the living, careering heart of the book, ever to be sought and found, yet never encased in a formula: the infinite, eternal, every-present Beyond?

[9] *Oeuvres*, Vol. XIII, p. 438.

XI

GOD IN THE EIGHTEENTH AND
NINETEENTH CENTURIES

1. G. R. Cragg[1] studies God in the Age of Reason for Voltaire and the *Philosophes*. The *philosophes* denied the fact of revelation, detested dogma, attacked the Church and Christianity, and held to a God that Deism could countenance. For Voltaire God was the God of nature, the great geometrician, the architect of the universe. The idea of providence he dismissed as absurd.

Voltaire[2] *and the Philosophes.* The eighteenth century was self-consciously an enlightened and emancipated age. Throughout much of its course,

---

[1] Gerald R. Cragg is professor of Historical Theology and Director of Studies at Andover Newton Theological School, Boston, Mass. This excerpt is from his book, *The Church And The Age of Reason* (Eerdmans Publishing Co., 1962), pp. 234–246.

[2] Francois Marie Arouet, self-titled De

it was not a period remarkable for creative thought. Its debt to the seventeenth century was immense; it drew upon medieval sources to a far greater extent than it realized. The ingredients of eighteenth-century thought were borrowed from others, the pattern which they assumed was original and new. The Age of Reason was remarkable less for the doctrines which it propounded than for the manner of thought which it encouraged. It was secular in spirit and destructive in effect. It diffused a skepticism which gradually dissolved the intellectual and religious patterns which had governed European thought since Augustine. It proclaimed the autonomy of man's mind and his infinite capacity for progress and perfectibility. In the principle of causality it believed that it had found the key which would open all the secrets of knowledge and lay bare the essential nature both of the universe and of man. The thought of the period was largely English in origin but predominantly French in character. Its basic concepts had been fashioned by Locke and Newton; they were publicized by Bayle and Montesquieu, Voltaire, and Diderot. . . .

The zest which marked eighteenth-

century thought was due to its confidence, and this confidence was inspired by the belief that man's mind had discovered a new and marvellous instrument. This much-prized tool was reason — not man's mind as such, but the way in which his rational faculties could be used to achieve certain specific ends. Descartes had relied on deduction; Newton had used inductive analysis in penetrating to the great secret of nature's marvelous laws, and the spirit and method of Newtonian physics ruled the eighteenth century. Nature was invested with unparalleled authority, and it was assumed that natural law ruled every area into which the mind of man could penetrate. . . . The emphasis fell increasingly on the practical consequences of knowledge: man is endowed with reason, said Voltaire, "not that he may penetrate the divine essence but that he may live well in this world". . . . The Age of Reason was chiefly interested in the elaboration, elucidation, and exposition of this analytical procedure derived from Newtonian physics. Its most brilliant achievement was the *Encyclopedia*.[3] Diderot, the direcing genius of the enterprise, explained its purpose. He and his colleagues were not primarily interested in communicating a specific body of knowledge; rather they aimed at effecting a fundamental revolution in the prevailing pattern of thought.

This was a deliberate challenge to accepted beliefs. The theology and ethics of the churches were subjected to a criticism more merciless than any which they had hitherto faced. The

Voltaire, was born in 1694. In a three years' exile to England, he matured from 1648–1789 (Grand Rapids, Mich.: Wm. B. a witty poet into a philosopher. His admiration for things English occasioned the *English Letters* (1733) and is evident in his *Elements of Newton's Philosophy* (1738). A visit to Paris in 1778 occasioned a triumphal celebration which hastened his death. Among his works are *Philosophical Dictionary, The Ignorant Philosopher, Remarks on M. Pascal's "Thoughts," Essay on the Manners and Spirit of Nations.*

[3] 1750–1770.

appeal to reason and to natural law was closely related to the desire for freedom from traditional patterns of authority. What men wanted, however, was a change, not a revolution. For all its destructive appearance, the thought of the Enlightenment was curiously conservative.

The *philosophes*[4] were members of the middle class, believing in order and security and wanting a stable society. The idea of a disordered universe was abhorrent to them. Hence, for convenience' sake, they retained the kind of God that Deism in its later phases could countenance. He was scaled down and domesticated; his majesty was no longer disconcerting, and he was useful as a guarantor of order. He was abstract and remote; he was no longer inconvenient because he no longer encountered man with an exacting personal demand.

"I believe in God," said Voltaire, "not the God of the mystics and the theologians, but the God of nature, the great geometrician, the architect of the universe, the prime mover, unalterable, transcendental, everlasting." Such a God stood entirely outside the drama of human history; he could not be connected with anything that happens on this insignificant planet. He built the machine and set it in motion,

but the machine now runs its predetermined course in complete independence of its maker. The *philosophes,* therefore, denied the fact of revelation. They dispensed with the holy Scriptures and the holy church. The God they retained inevitably faded into the abstraction of a first cause. This was the natural consequence of their glorification of the Newtonian revolution; having "deified nature," they "denatured God." . . .

The influence of Voltaire encouraged a complete denial of God. . . . For the better part of half a century he was the most powerful influence in European thought. . . .

In his earliest phase, he drew heavily (and not always exactly) on the English Deists, and gave their views the widest possible circulation. Long after they had been virtually forgotten at home, they were affecting the intellectual climate of the continent. From the Deists, Voltaire drew the arguments with which he attacked miracles, prophecy, and the authority of Scripture. He popularized the views of Locke and Newton. Here, too, he was profoundly influential in determining the pattern of eighteenth-century thought. He emphasized the simplicity and sublimity of Newton's laws — and gave a superficial and inaccurate account of them. The inferences which he drew from them were important: man's mind, he claimed, has now been emancipated from authority, from innate ideas, and from revelation. Into the place thus left vacant, reason stepped and brought with it a method which used a few simple principles to account for everything that could be

---

[4] The Philosophes were not formal philosophers but men of letters who were also men of the world. Some of them were scientists, some were historians, economists, psychologists, while some were merely able publicists. Among them were men of great talent, a few were men of genius. For these men philosophy was not one branch of knowledge among many, but the spirit which animated every branch. Their aim was the diffusion of knowledge and the creation of an emancipated spirit.

explained. As concerning other things — the inscrutable regions of mystery or paradox — Voltaire airily dismissed them as of no account.

In the early stages of his long career he accepted the abstracted kind of deity in whom Deists could plausibly believe. "I am not an atheist," he said, "nor a superstitious person; I stand for common sense and the golden mean." But as time progressed, Voltaire's golden mean was increasingly obscured by violent antipathies. The idea of providence — of God's watchful care of individual lives — he dismissed as absurd. His attacks on the organized church grew more and more vitriolic. In this respect Voltaire did not stand alone. All the *philosophes* participated in this bitter vendetta. . . .

The failings of the priesthood were magnified into a deliberate conspiracy against reason and the elementary rights of man. *Ecrasez l'infáme* was Voltaire's battle cry; he repeated it with the monotony of an unvarying refrain. "L'infáme" was not God, nor Christ, nor Christianity, not even Catholicism. Probably what Voltaire meant by it was privileged and persecuting orthodoxy. . . . Voltaire wasted no sympathy on democratic aspirations, and both his hatred of Christianity and the deliberate class-consciousness of the Age of Reason are admirably conveyed by his words to Frederick the Great: "Your majesty will do the human race an eternal service in extirpating this infamous superstition [Christianity], I do not say among the rabble, who are not worthy of being enlightened and who are apt for every yoke; I say among the well-

bred, among those who wish to think." . . .

The *philosophes* were anti-Christian but not necessarily irreligious. They attacked the church with every weapon at their disposal, and fashioned the kind of anti-clericalism which has had such a vogue in certain European countries. Clearly in attacking God they were attacking the pretensions of priestcraft; it is equally obvious that in their own way they cherished beliefs and aspirations which can only be described as religious. They detested dogma but hankered after an awareness of God which would be as all-embracing as the universe itself. In the very process of seeking to define these non-Christian truths, the Age of Reason laid bare the insufficiency of reason. The problem of evil in a world apparently so good could neither be evaded nor resolved. They repudiated the explanations advanced by the theologians, but had nothing to substitute for them. . . . "It is not enough," said Diderot, "to know more than [the theologians] do; it is necessary to show them that we are better, and that philosophy makes more and better men than sufficient or efficacious grace." . . .

The religious concern of the *philosophes* carried them beyond an emphasis on ethics and an interest in practical studies. They rejected traditional doctrines but did not necessarily repudiate religion itself. Holbach might parade his atheism but he spoke for a relatively limited coterie. The chief ingredients in the outlook which the *philosophes* encouraged are clearly religious in implication, however far removed they may be from Christian belief. To begin with, they taught that by nature man is good, not bad. There is no native bias which predisposes him to evil; he is not born with a propensity to sin. The right comes as naturally to him as the wrong; encourage him with a favorable environment, and his propensity to good will assert itself. It will then be seen that he is easily enlightened, susceptible to reason's guidance, and disposed to be generous and humane. . . .

In the second place, the *philosophes* insisted that our primary concern is with the life we now live, not with some hypothetical existence hereafter. They were contemptuous of preoccupation with heaven, though many of them retained a belief in the immortality of the soul. They wanted to alter the center of interest; instead of regarding this life as a mere probation

for another, men should strive to achieve the good life here and now. And this good life is within our reach; with the light of reason and the guidance of experience to show us the way, we can reasonably expect to achieve perfection. . . . .

If the *philosophes* regarded the Christian past with aversion, they looked to the philosophic future with confidence. Man's true fulfillment lay neither behind him (in the golden age of antiquity) or ahead (in the Christian expectation of paradise). It would be achieved when men substituted true values for false ones — self-fulfillment for vicarious atonement and the love of humanity for the love of God. . . . God had been dethroned as judge, and posterity was exalted in his stead. . . . "Posterity," wrote Diderot, "is for the philosopher what the other world is for the religious man." . . .

2. **E. Cassirer**[1] **studies English deism and Hume. The aim of this deism was to banish mysteries, miracles, and secrets from religion and to expose religion to the light of knowledge. It built its concept of natural religion on its "dogma" of human nature. Hume broke its hold on contemporary thought by assailing this dogma from the viewpoint of experience and pure factual knowledge.**

English Deism. English deism, despite all the variety and deviations within individual presentations, shows essentially the same basic tendency. Deism begins as a strictly intellectual-

ist system; its aim is to banish mysteries, miracles, and secrets from religion and to expose religion to the light of knowledge. Toland's book *Christianity*

---

[1] Ernst Cassirer was a historian of philosophy and especially interested in the philosophy of the Enlightenment. Among his other works are *Individual and Cosmos in the Philosophy of the Renaissance* (1927) and *The Platonic Renaissance in England*

(1932). This excerpt is from his book, *The Philosophy Of The Enlightenment*, a translation of his *Die Philosophie der Aufklärung* made by F. C. A. Koelln and J. P. Pettegrove (Princeton, N. J.: Princeton University Press, 1951), pp. 171–181.

Not Mysterious[2] describes in its title the theme which hereafter appears over and over again in the writings of the deistic movement. The philosophic meaning of deism consists primarily in that it maintains a new principle in the formulation of its problem. For deism assumes that the question of the content of faith cannot be isolated from that of the form of faith, that both questions are soluble only in common. It is then not only the truth content of individual dogmas, it is rather the religious type of certainty as such toward which the question is now directed. On this matter Toland believes he can refer to Locke and introduce the basic concepts and principles of Locke's theory of knowledge into the problems of religion. For what is true of religious knowledge in general, must also hold for religious knowledge in particular. Locke had defined the act of knowing in general as an awareness of agreement or disagreement between ideas. Hence it follows that knowledge by nature involves a relation; above all, the terms of the relation must be given in, and clearly understood by, our consciousness. For without such understanding of the basic elements of the relation it loses all meaning.

According to Toland, this methodological consideration represents an essential principle and a necessary limit for the objects of religious faith. Absolute transcendence of these objects is forestalled; for how could our consciousness, as a knowing, believing, and judging subject, concentrate on

an object if this object were not somehow present in some phenomenon of consciousness? . . . The objection that one can be very sure of the existence of a thing without knowing any of its predicates is unsound. For even if such a form of knowledge were possible, what religious significance could we attribute to it? If belief is not to become completely vain and meaningless, its object must somehow be meaningful — it must include certain elements which can be clearly understood. That which is in every respect mysterious and by definition beyond all understanding, must therefore remain as alien to faith as to knowledge. "Could that Person justly value himself upon being wiser than his Neighbors, who having infallible Assurance that something call'd *Blictri* had a Being in Nature, in the mean time knew not what this *Blictri* was?"[3]

Toland concludes that there can be mysteries only in a relative, not in an absolute sense. He refers to content which is beyond the reach of a certain mode of comprehension, not to content which is beyond all possibility of understanding. So far as the word "mystery" is concerned, Toland declares that it had originally meant a doctrine which was not contrary to reason but which involved a known truth that for some reason was to be kept secret from a part of mankind. The concept "revelation" accordingly, cannot be opposed to that of natural religion in the sense that the two terms are different in their specific content. It is not the content of that which is manifested which distinguishes these concepts but

[2] J. Toland, *Christianity Not Mysterious*, London, 1696.

[3] *Ibid.*, p. 133.

the nature and manner of the manifestation. Revelation is not a unique ground of certainty; it is only a particular form of communication of a truth whose ultimate proof and verification must be sought in reason itself.

Tindal, too, in his book *Christianity as Old as the Creation*,[4] starts from this principle. He points out that natural and revealed religion do not differ in substance but in the manner of their becoming known; the former is the inner, the latter, the outer manifestation of the will of an infinitely wise and good being. In order to conceive such a being, it is necessary to free it from all merely athropomorphic limitations. It would indicate an incomprehensible narrowmindedness in this being to withhold part of its nature and activity, or to employ them to the advantage of a particular time and of a particular people above all other peoples. Just as God is always the same and human nature is one and unalterable in itself, revelation too must dispense its light equally in all directions. God would not be God if, as for example the dogma of election by grace has it, he could, as it were, conceal his nature within himself — if he could enlighten one part of mankind and leave the other in darkness. The most important criterion of the genuineness of all revelation can, therefore, consist only in its universality, in its transcendence of all local and temporal limitations.

Christianity is, therefore, true to the extent that it satisfies this fundamental condition. It exists insofar as it is bound to no particular place or time, insofar as it is as old as the world. Between natural law and Christian law, so far as content is concerned, there is no difference; the latter claims to be nothing more than the reassertion of that which is set down in the first. Such a "republication of the Law of Nature" is given to man especially in his knowledge of morality. Here then lies the truly infallible revelation which exceeds all others in value and certainty.

Tindal thus arrives at a definition of religion which Kant later could adopt unchanged in his work on *Religion within the Bounds of Mere Reason*. For Tindal religion is the recognition of our duties as divine commands; it consists in starting with generally valid and generally accessible norms and then in relating these to a divine Author and looking upon them as expressions of his will. The center of gravity has now shifted, even in the development of English deism, from the sphere of the purely intellectual to that of "practical reason"; and "moral" deism has now replaced "constructive" deism.[5]

The extraordinary effect which English deism had on the whole intellectual life of the eighteenth century depends essentially on this transition. In the light of its purely theoretical content, the intensity of this effect is

[4] Tindal, *Christianity as Old as the Creation*, 1730.

[5] Concerning the details of this development see especially Leslie Stephen, *History of English Thought in the Eighteenth Century*, two volumes, second edition, London, 1881; see also Troeltsch, "Deismus," *Gesammelte Schriften*, vol. iv, pp. 429 ff., and Hermann Schwarz, "Deismus," *Paedagogisches Lexikon*, ed. Velhagen and Klasing.

scarcely credible. For among the leaders of this movement there is no thinker of real depth and of truly original stamp, and the purely theoretical deductions on which deism bases the defense of its viewpoint are often questionable and involved in half-truths. The attitude of deism, the honest desire for truth, and the moral seriousness with which it undertook its criticism of dogma, were more effective than all these deductions. Such are the real inner motivating forces. Bayle, who lived at the beginning of the deistic movement, recognized this clearly and prophesied victory for the ethos of deism.[6] . . .

Despite the exertion of all energies and despite the flood of polemical literature which grew from year to year, the final victory of deism seemed inevitable. But now fresh and unexpected aid came to the rescue of the threatened system of orthodoxy. One of the bitterest opponents of this system became an ally on this point. It was not theological dogmatics but radical philosophical skepticism which repelled the attacks of deism and stalled its advance. In England Samuel Clarke with all his logical acumen had once more undertaken to establish the truth of the whole body of Christianity by deducing it from universally valid premises.[7] Even Voltaire was compelled to admire Clarke's ability; in his *Letters on the English* he describes Clarke as a "real thinking ma-chine" capable of the most difficult tasks.[8] . . . But all this labor with strictly logical demonstrations seemed to make no impression on deism; it seemed rather to make the weakness of orthodox doctrine stand out more conspicuously than before. In his defense of free thinking, Anthony Collins remarks ironically that until Clarke undertook to demonstrate the existence of God nobody had ever entertained any doubts on this point.[9]

Hume.[10] Yet what the logician and metaphysician could not do, the radical opponent of all logical and metaphysical dogmatism succeeded in doing. It was Hume who confronted deism with a new problem, and in doing so he broke its hold on contemporary thought. In founding its concept of natural religion, deism proceeds from the presupposition that there is a human nature which is everywhere the same, and which is endowed with a certain fundamental knowledge of a theoretical as well as of a practical sort on which it can absolutely rely. But where do we find such a human nature? Is it an empirically given fact, or is it not rather

---

[6] Bayle, *Commentaire Philosophique, Oeuvres Diverses*, The Hague, 1737, vol. ii, p. 366.

[7] Cf. Clarke, *A Demonstration of the Being and Attributes of God*, London, 1705–1706.

[8] See *Lettres sur les Anglais*, Letter vii, *Oeuvres*, Vol. xxvi, pp. 33 f.

[9] Collins, *A Discourse of Freethinking Occasioned by the Rise and Growth of a Sect Called Freethinkers*, London, 1713. See Leslie Stephen, *op. cit.*, Vol. i, p. 80.

[10] David Hume was born in 1711 and died in 1776. Before 1737 he had already finished his major work, *A Treatise of Human Nature. An Enquiry concerning Human Understanding* high-lighted the problems of causality and skepticism (1748). His *Dialogues concerning Natural Religion* (not published till 1779) set forth his mind upon the problem of God's existence. He left for posthumous publication his *Two Essays on Suicide and Immortality* (1777).

simply a hypothesis? And does not the main weakness of deism lie in the fact that it trusts implicitly in this hypothesis, and that it raises a hypothesis to the status of a dogma?

Hume assails this dogma. His opposition to deism is concerned neither with its doctrine of reason or revelation; he aims merely to evaluate it from the viewpoint of the standards of experience, of pure factual knowledge. His evaluation proves that the whole proud structure of deism stands on feet of clay. For that apparent "human nature" on which deism proposed to base natural religion is itself no reality but a mere fiction. Experience reveals human nature to us in an entirely different light from all the constructive attempts of the deists. Here we find human nature not as a storehouse of fundamental truths, of a priori verities, but as a dull confusion of instincts; not as a cosmos, but as a chaos. The more penetrating our knowledge of the nature of man and the more accurate our description of this nature, the more it loses the appearance of rationality and order.

Hume had reached this conclusion even in the realm of theoretical ideas. . . . For the very concept of cause, which was supposed to stabilize our knowledge, is itself without foundation. It is supported by no immediate evidence, and by no a priori significance and necessity; it is itself merely a product of the play of ideas which are connected by no objective, rational principles, but in their combination simply follow the workings of the imagination and obey its mechanical laws.

And the same is true to an even greater degree of our religious ideas. . . . Man did not begin as a philosopher and it is a delusive and vain hope that he will ever end as a philosopher. He is not subject to the domination of an abstract reason, but to the power of appetites and passions. And appetites and passions are not only the source of the first religious ideas and dogmas; they are still the root of all religion.

Religious conceptions are not shaped and fostered by thinking and by the moral will. It is the emotions of hope and fear which have led men to adopt beliefs and which support their continuance in faith. Here we have the real foundation of religion. Religion is rooted neither in logical nor in ethical grounds; it merely has an anthropological cause. It arises from the fear of supernatural powers and from man's desire to propitiate these powers and subject them to his will. . . . Superstition and fear of demons are the real roots of our conception of God. . . .

Such is the "natural history of religion," as Hume portrays it; he believes he has overthrown natural religion once and for all and shown that it is nothing but a philosophical dream. . . .

3. M. Spinka[1] studies Kant's doctrine of God. He rejected the three traditional arguments for the existence of God and for them substituted

---

[1] Matthew Spinka: cf. ch. x, 3, n. 1.   This excerpt is from *op. cit.*, pp. 113–127.

"moral" arguments. Moral consciousness must postulate the existence of God as the guarantor of the ultimate fulfillment of happiness and of the eternal life in which the tragic shortcomings of our earthly existence shall be made good.

Immanuel Kant. The greatest revolution that occurred in philosophical thinking after the debacle of empiricism caused by Hume was the work of Immanuel Kant.[2] . . . Kant became an adherent of the rationalistic school of Wolff, that Philistine philosopher of barren Reason. It was under such circumstances that Kant developed a strong distaste for, or rather aversion from, all emotional and mystical elements of pietism which prevented him ever after from comprehending their proper place in religion. . . . His own religious views, further affected by Rousseau, developed in the direction of moralism, the sense of the ethical foundations of human life conceived in terms of imperative duty, of reverence for "the starry heavens above and the moral law within."

In his philosophical thought Kant matured slowly. He began as . . . a Wolffian; but soon added to rationalism adherence to the tenets of Lockean empiricism, which, however, he knew mainly through David Hume. It was Hume, Kant confessed, who was instrumental in "waking him from his dogmatic slumbers." But Rousseau exercised even greater influence upon his thinking.[3] . . . Rousseau's notion of conscience as opposed to all external authority of the current *mores* became basic for Kant in the form of the "categorical imperative." Kant also credited Rousseau with teaching him "the gospel of man," understanding man as an essentially moral being, ethically autonomous and therefore free. Man was thus part of the noumenal realm, and as such was a being of infinite worth. . . .

Confronted with the debacle of Lockean empiricism as presented in the skepticism of Hume, Kant set himself the task of reconstruction. Without surrendering the basic principles of empiricism, he thought he saw an escape from the *faux pas* that had led to the Humean debacle. At first he hoped to put the whole matter right in one volume. But as he worked away at the critical problem, the subject matter differentiated itself into three *Critiques* and later into his *Religion within the Limits of Reason Alone*. It took him the greater part of his remaining life to accomplish the task he had blithely thought of completing in a relatively short time.

The *Critiques* form a unity, dealing

[2] Immanuel Kant was born in 1724 and died in 1804. As a *Privatdozent* at the University of Königsberg his central courses were on logic, metaphysics and ethics but he also lectured on physical geography, anthropology, mathematics, physics and mechanics. His *Religion within the Limits of Reason Alone* (1793) was the only book that brought him into conflict with the civil authorities. He was working away at a complete restatement of his philosophy, in view of recent developments made by Fichte and the young idealistic movement, when death interrupted his labors in 1804.

[3] Cf. Ernst Cassirer, *Rousseau, Kant, Goethe* (Princeton: Princeton University Press, 1945).

with a single theme; as such they must be considered together. The questions he sought to answer have to do, first of all, with the limits of scientific — what he calls pure —knowledge; since this is derived from experience plus reason and understanding, it is necessarily limited to the empirical or what he calls the phenomenal realm. This is the burden of his *Critique of Pure Reason,* on which he worked for eleven years and which was at last published in 1781. But since noumenal reality, being immaterial, is not capable of being subjected to empirical inquiry, a different method of treatment is required: it is the practical reason, or morality, which yields answers to the metaphysical problems. This is then the theme of the *Critique of Practical Reason* published in 1788. And finally his attempt to deal with esthetics and religion (as distinct from morality) is the subject not only of his *Critique of Judgment* but also of his *Religion Within the Limits of Reason Alone.* . . .

Since our knowledge is wholly of the phenomenal world and never can reach the noumenal reality, it can deal only with the sensory data and "cannot prove anything regarding man's immortality, transcendental freedom, an intelligible world, or an unconditioned Being. . . . Speculative reason can never afford us knowledge of the nature of ultimate reality; but for identical reasons materialism, too, can never prove its case."[4]

Accordingly, Kant proceeds to at-tack and reject the three traditional arguments (long held to be proofs) for the existence of God, since they rest upon the objective, i.e., phenomenal grounds. "I have therefore found it necessary to deny knowledge, in order to make room for faith," he writes in the Preface to the second edition of his *Critique of Pure Reason.*

The ontological arguments of Anselm which he knew only in the Cartesian version, he declares to be fallacious as resting on "a confusion between the logical necessity of thought and the ontological necessity of existence."[5] The cosmological argument of Thomas Aquinas — that is, the argument from various contingencies of particular things depending for their existence upon a self-existent Being — is inapplicable, because the category of causality belongs only to the phenomenal world, not to God, who is of the noumenal realm. The teleological argument is dealt with in the *Critique of Judgment.* . . . Nature exhibits, Kant writes, countless examples of purposiveness. . . . And yet . . . "That crude matter should have originally formed itself according to mechanical laws, that life should have sprung from the nature of what is lifeless, that matter should have been able to dispose itself into the form of a self-maintaining purposiveness — this . . . (is) contrary to reason." "Absolutely no human reason . . . can hope to understand the production of even a blade of grass by mere mechanical causes."[6] How then shall the teleological argu-

---

[4] Theodore M. Greene, tr., *Kant's Religion within the Limits of Reason Alone* (La Salle, Ill.: The Open Court Publishing Company, 1934). Introduction, p. xli.

[5] *Ibid.,* xlii, n. 1.
[6] *Kant's Critique of Judgment,* J. H. Bernard, tr. (London: Macmillan and Co., Ltd., 1914), p. 326.

ment be regarded? Kant, rejecting both the mechanical and Spinozan hypotheses, inclines to accept the theistic explanation as the most satisfactory, not as knowledge, however, but as faith. Nevertheless, he declares that theism is "certainly superior to all other grounds of explanation."[7]

To sum up: neither scientific knowledge nor speculative reason is able to prove the existence of God, for God is not part of the objective world with which our cognitive apparatus deals. This is not to say that God cannot be apprehended by man at all; only that he cannot be known by human mind. For Christian theology this is nothing new. The anonymous, fourteenth-century, English mystic who wrote *The Cloud of Unknowing* expressed it by saying, "By love He can be gotten and holden; by thought, never". . . . And Kant points out that were it otherwise, it would be detrimental to religion: "Once prove God's existence out of the mouth of non-moral nature and you have a non-moral God of no use to the religious consciousness. . . . . It is all to the good that man is forced to depend upon moral proofs of God's existence and nature for an adequate theology and a sound basis for religious faith."[8]

Such a new, and in his judgment sound, basis for the existence of God and the moral realm Kant provides in his *Critique of Practical Reason,*[9] which establishes not only the existence of the noumenal realm, but also asserts the method of our attaining it.

[7] *Ibid.,* p. 305.
[8] *Religion within the Limits of Reason Alone,* p. li.
[9] 1788.

This then places Kant, along with Plato, among the few outstanding philosophical dualists. In the opinion of Nicolas Berdyaev, these dualist philosophers were the greatest minds of the entire history of Western thought, for they distinguished by a philosophical method the two kinds of reality — material and metaphysical. To be sure, Kant's successors (just as Plato's), quietly subverted the master's dualism into monism. Nevertheless, it is Kant's glory that he provided on philosophical grounds the proof of the metaphysical (or as he called it, the noumenal) reality, even though from the point of view of Christian faith it is not adequate; nevertheless, it makes the adequate statement possible. . . .

In developing the implications of the categorical imperative, Kant holds it as axiomatic that the moral obligation necessarily implies moral freedom, without which it would be a mere mockery. If we felt compelled to live virtuously without being able to do so, it would imply a radical evil in the moral universe. . . . In the phenomenal realm we are subject to physical necessity that we loosely term natural laws; in the noumenal realm we are morally free.

Yet virtue is not *wholly* its own reward, but is a condition of happiness. For, if virtue deserves to be crowned with happiness, it is a matter of common and fairly frequent observation that a life of virtue is not always so rewarded. Is, then, moral law a mockery, an illusion, a sorry jest of some cosmic demiurge? Never! In order to remove the intolerable doubt as to the integrity of the moral law, moral consciousness must postulate the existence of God as the guarantor of the ultimate and inevitable fulfillment of happiness, and of the eternal life in which the tragic shortcomings of our earthly existence shall be made good. These "moral" arguments for the existence of God and for immortality are Kant's substitutes for the ontological and cosmological "proofs" he had rejected.

The argument suffers from the fatal weakness that it is a deduction from the premise of the sense of moral law, rather than a self-sufficient fact. Anyone who does not acknowledge the premise, or does not make the deduction from it that Kant made, need not acknowledge the existence of God and immortality. Furthermore, if one acts solely from a sense of duty, then it must be without regard to whether happiness or unhappiness results. And if happiness is necessarily presupposed either in this life or the next, then the sense of duty is no longer the *sole* motive. On the other hand, if virtue need not necessarily result in happiness, neither God nor immortality is essential to the scheme. Nevertheless, for himself, Kant did make the deduction. . . .

In conclusion, then, what is Kant's contribution to religious thought, in general, and Christian apprehension of it, in particular? First of all, as Berdyaev has recognized, Kant established on empirical grounds, without recourse to religious presuppositions, the existence of two kinds of reality — phenomenal and noumenal. It was the latter that provided the ground for a spiritual interpretation of the cosmos

congenial to the religious view of life. To be sure, Kant's successors immediately proceeded to convert his dualism into monism — either of the idealistic or the materialist kind. But Kant's own conclusion, that scientific (pure) reason cannot perceive true reality (*ding an sich*), but possesses knowledge only of the phenomenal world, is a solid achievement, although some scientists and most nonscientists still look upon scientific knowledge as the only "objective" kind there is. Nevertheless, since God is Spirit, and therefore not an object perceivable by sense-perception, He cannot be "known" scientifically. Kant thus repudiates the Thomistic assumption that knowledge of God's existence is inferential from sense-perception (*per ea quae facta sunt*). He grounds such inference upon the moral sense of mankind, although in his last unfinished work he comes close to holding that man may know God intuitively. Nevertheless, his lifelong mistrust of mysticism and "enthusiasm" have kept him from acknowledging rightly this approach to the question which would have resulted in some form of existentialism. Accordingly, his critical reconstruction has led him to regard religion as morality, and his essential Pelagianism ("I ought, therefore I can") has caused him to assume that all men are potentially capable of realizing, as a duty dictated by rational morality, the Sermon on the Mount. And although he occasionally has conceded the need of "supernatural" aid in the process of transforming the evil nature of man into one animated by altruistic motives, he has remained a stranger to the insights of Paul and Augustine in regard to the antinomy of law and grace. His influence on theological thinking of his and subsequent periods has been profound, but has been fraught with a preponderance of philosophical over purely theological concepts. . . . Kant has rendered religion a most valuable service.

4. C. Welch[1] studies the trinitarian doctrine of Schleiermacher and Hegel. Schleiermacher is convinced that the doctrine of Trinity in itself is an unnecessary and unwarranted addition to the faith. Hegel's doctrine of the Trinity is a philosophical truth, resting entirely on general philosophical premises, and it does not correspond essentially to the Christian doctrine of the Trinity.

Schleiermacher. The two factors which in early nineteenth-century theology were most directly responsible for subsequent questioning of the importance and validity of the doctrine of the Trinity were the development and growing acceptance of the methods of biblical criticism and the writings of Friedrich Schleiermacher.[2] Historical analysis of the Bible did not originate in the nineteenth century, but the period with which we are concerned marked the transfer of theological leadership to the German universities, and in this freer atmosphere the method of "objective" historical research was widely accepted for the first time.

This fact is of vital importance for nineteenth-century theology. It was the successful application of literary criticism to the gospel texts, more than the attacks of the rationalists or even the works of Schleiermacher, which breached the walls of the traditional concepts of revelation. It was the abandonment of the literal and final authority of the Scriptures which made plausible the effort of the Hegelian theologians to establish doctrine on another basis, which opened the door to the liberal picture of Jesus of the Ritschlians and the *religion geschichtliche Schule*, and which is at the root of contemporary concern with the nature of revelation. Conversely, the popularity of the new methods of Schleiermacher and the Hegelians made the "higher criticism" appear less offensive by minimizing its effect on the essentials of the faith.

The first major blow to the doctrine of the Trinity was the elimination of the Fourth Gospel as a primitive his-

---

[1] Claude Welch began this work as a dissertation presented for the degree of Doctor of Philosophy in Yale University in 1950. The work was thoroughly rewritten and recast and was published as *The Trinity In Contemporary Theology* (London: SCM Press, Ltd., 1953). This excerpt is from pp. 3–13 of that book.

[2] Friedrich Schleiermacher (1768–1834) is regarded as the father of modern liberal theology. Among his many works are *On Religion: Speeches addressed to its Cultured Despisers, Soliloquies, The Christian Faith.* Of *The Christian Faith* Hugh Ross Mackintosh has said that "Next to the *Institutes* of Calvin, it is the most influential dogmatic work to which evangelical Protestantism can point" (*Types of Modern Theology*, N. Y.: Charles Scribner's Sons, 1937), p. 60. The controversy about his "pantheism" still rages.

torical source. Johann G. Herder had seen as early as 1796 that the Gospel of John cannot be reconciled as an historical source with the synoptics, and that it was, at least partly, a theological work. But not until Strauss was the question decided and the true character of the Gospel widely recognized.[3] In every case of comparison of the synoptics with John, Straus's decisions were unfavorable to the latter, and through F. C. Baur's work, the general position of the historical superiority of the synoptics was firmly established. The inevitable effect of this upon the doctrine of the Trinity is readily apparent, for John's Gospel had been from the beginning the happy-hunting ground for those who sought trinitarian proof-texts. When doubt was cast upon the authenticity of Jesus' utterances concerning himself in the Fourth Gospel, serious question was raised about a fundamental root of the doctrine of the Trinity. . . .

Friedrich Schleiermacher's attitude toward the doctrine of the Trinity is suggested by his relegation of the dogma to an appendix at the conclusion of *The Christian Faith*. There are at least two considerations involved in this classification. The traditional scheme of dogmatics (e.g., Calvin, Thomas Aquinas) treated of the Trinity in conjunction with the general discussion of the being and attributes of God. This is quite improper, thinks Schleiermacher, for the doctrine cannot be intelligibly viewed until after account has been taken of Jesus Christ and the Holy Spirit. But this fact

alone would not justify reducing the dogma to an appendix. The controlling motive in Schleiermacher's judgment of the Trinity is his conviction that the doctrine in itself is an unnecessary and unwarranted addition to the faith. It means well, one might say, but is misleading and over-reaches the mark.

There is a genuinely essential element expressed in the dogma, viz., "The doctrine of the union of the Divine essence with human nature, both in the personality of Christ and in the common Spirit of the Church,"[4] for the idea of redemption in Christ and of the Church as the bearer of redemption requires such a union. That it was truly the divine essence which was so united is the element that the doctrine was established to defend.

But the ecclesiastical dogma, which alone justifies the use of the term Trinity, goes far beyond this, tracing the union with Christ and the union with the Church back to eternal distinctions, in God, posited independently of such unions. It is not, therefore, *"an immediate utterance concerning the Christian self-consciousness but only a combination of several such utterances."*[5] Since Christian theology consists in the explication of the contents of the Christian self-consciousness, the doctrine of the Trinity can be assigned no important place. Schleiermacher is willing to go all the way here, asserting that even if the fully developed doctrine arose definitely out of the teachings of Jesus and the apostles, it would still not

---

[3] D. F. Strauss, *Leben Jesu* (1835).

[4] *The Christian Faith*, no. 170, 1.
[5] *Ibid.*

properly be a doctrine of faith. We should have to accept it on the basis of the testimonies about "supersensible fact," but our fellowship with God would be *no different* from what it would be without such knowledge. The essentials of the Christian faith are thus altogether independent of this doctrine.

We may identify several facets of Schleiermacher's thought which lie behind his insistence that the doctrine of eternal distinctions in the divine nature can neither be read off directly from the contents of Christian self-consciousness nor be shown to be in essential relation thereto. One is the pervasive subjectivism which haunts his theological method. . . . Referring to the doctrine of the Trinity, he writes. . . . "We have only to do with the God-consciousness given in our self-consciousness along with our consciousness of the world; hence we have no formula for the being of God in himself as distinct from the being of God in the world."[6] . . . Schleiermacher clearly approaches the doctrine of God with a priori limitation of the knowledge which man may have of God in himself — a limitation derived in part from Kant and in part from a pietistic conception of theological method.

Closely related to this is another reason for Schleiermacher's refusal to admit that the phenomena of Christian experience imply significant distinctions in God: he does not see any real distinction between the presence of God in Christ and God in the Church. For him, there is no differ-ence which is significant for the nature of God, between the *forms* of union. The presence of God in Christ, i.e., his God-consciousness, is not essentially different from the presence of God in the Christian. . . . Any attempt to draw distinctions would inevitably lead to anthropomorphism.[7]

This suggests the hidden domination of Schleiermacher's thought by rationalist principles. He eschews speculation, but God is always for him the absolute unity. "God is the unconditioned and the absolutely simple."[8] In him there can be no distinctions or difference. . . . If from the standpoint of the feeling of dependence all ideas of divine attributes represent nothing objective in the self-identical Original Being, and, on the other side, God as the causal nexus of nature is absolutely simple being, what place can there be for the doctrine of the Trinity?

In *The Christian Faith* Schleiermacher says little about the *content* of trinitarian doctrine. Commenting briefly on some of the difficulties in the traditional view, he concludes that it is untenable but declares himself favorably disposed toward the "Sabellian" interpretation of the doctrine.[9] . . .

---

[6] *Ibid.*, no. 172, 1.

[7] *Ibid.*

[8] *Ibid.*, no. 96. See also nos. 56; 167.

[9] See "Ueber den Gegensatz zwischen der Sabellianischen und der Athanasianischen Vorstellung von der Trinität," *Sämmtliche Werke*, 1:2, 485–574. This essay was translated, with extensive notes, by Moses Stuart, under the title "On the Discrepancy between the Sabellian and Athanasian Method of Representing the Doctrine of the Trinity," *The Biblical Repository and Quarterly Observer*, VI, 19 (July, 1835), Andover, 1–116.

But Schleiermacher's most important influence came from his estimate of the role and importance of the doctrine of the Trinity. . . . In response to the attacks of rationalism upon Christianity, Schleiermacher forced consideration as to whether religion was not *sui generis*. He insisted on the distinctive nature of Christianity as an historical positive religion, hence free from subjection to philosophy and speculative reason. He abandoned the method of deducing doctrine from propositions of scripture or reason and sought to establish theology as a strictly empirical discipline.

Thus Schleiermacher opened a method of approach to Christianity which did not presuppose the concept of an infallible revelation in scripture. And in so doing, he did not see how the new method left any place for the doctrine of the Trinity. Succeeding theologians, who accepted in principle the abandonment of the old concept of revelation and the revision of methodology, tended also to accept Schleiermacher's judgment that upon such a basis it was impossible to defend the notion of Trinity in any sense which justified the use of the term. . . .

In sum, then Schleiermacher's reduction of the Trinity to a doctrine of the second rank was especially important because it was so closely associated with certain far-reaching (and fundamentally valid) *formal* revisions of theological method: the abandonment of piecemeal deduction from verbally inspired Scripture, and the organization of doctrine about a single principle — Jesus Christ. His attitude toward the Trinity was not . . . determined by these principles, but by other and extraneous considerations. Yet for a long time, those who accepted the principle of his methodological approach (especially Ritschl and Liberalism generally) accepted also Schleiermacher's dicta about the Trinity.

Hegel. The philosophy of Georg Wilhelm Friedrich Hegel[10] offered an attractive possibility for surmounting some of the problems raised by the older rationalists, by Schleiermacher and by the biblical critics. Their combined result with respect of the doctrine of the Trinity had been to deprive that doctrine of its traditional historical basis. Hegel's program seemed to provide a means for preserving many of the basic concepts of the Trinity and of the Incarnation. If the metaphysical aspects of theology could not be supported according to the principles of Schleier-

---

[10] Georg Wilhelm Friedrich Hegel was born in 1770 and died in 1831. His theological manuscripts of the period 1793–1801 were published in 1907, under the title: *Hegel's Early Theological Writings.* They included: a *Life of Jesus* (1795), in which Jesus was portrayed as a preacher of Kantian morality; *The Positivity of the Christian Religion,* in which Hegel's Greek ideal of a "folkreligion" and Kant's moral doctrine were blended together and contrasted favorably with Christianity; *The Spirit of Christianity and Its Fate* (1800). His *Phenomenology of Spirit* (1807) described the voyage of discovery by which the cultured mind is brought finally to the standpoint of the absolute spirit. In the *Encyclopaedia of the Philosophical Sciences* (1817), he provided a conspectus of his entire system, in its three main divisions: logic, philosophy of nature, and philosophy of spirit. This note is based on J. Collins: *A History of Modern European Philosophy,* Bruce, 1954, p. 600 f.

macher, they became central in Hegel's interpretation of religion.

The doctrinal formulations of theology are, for Hegel, symbolic and pictorial representations of the highest truths. Philosophy enables faith to understand itself for the first time. This does not mean that the religious symbols are untrue; on the contrary, Hegel asserts, "In faith, the true content is certainly already found."[11] . . . Philosophy, therefore, does not actually set itself above the truth of religion. . . . The trinitarian symbols of religion are far more truthful than the categories of the "understanding," which by virtue of their terms of externality fail to comprehend the true nature of God. The Christian doctrine of the Trinity expresses the true thought that God is not the abstract unity, the barren identity without difference conceived by rationalism or by Judaism, but a richer concrete entity composed of inner movement and process.[12]

The doctrine of the Trinity is the ultimate truth; the proof of this is the whole of philosophy, which shows the essential nature of every definite conception or notion. But it must always be understood that the categories of theology are only pictorial. The relation of Father, Son, and Spirit is "a childish natural form"; Spirit does not, of course, actually enter into such a relation. The content of faith is true, but the form of faith is inferior to the form of thought. Philosophy does set itself above the *form* of faith. In this assertion we

see the other, and perhaps the fundamental, side of Hegel's attitude toward religion . . . "thought is the absolute judge before which the content must verify and attest its claims."[13] Religion gets its ultimate justification, not from itself, but from philosophy. Philosophy is the final court of appeal. Faith and doctrine are strictly subject to its jurisdiction. . . .

The clear implication of this relation between philosophy and theology is that Hegel's doctrine of the Trinity is a philosophical truth, resting entirely on general philosophical premises. The truth of that doctrine can be established and elaborated in complete independence of religion. Indeed, it can be understood and *known* to be true *only* by the speculative reason through the analysis of the nature of logic and concrete actuality. "God" means Absolute Spirit, which posits itself in three forms, according to Hegel. Spirit is the eternal process of self-differentiation and resumption, of "diremption" and reconciliation. God is the activity of pure thought, and knowledge implies the existence of an object or Other. But God has not gone outside himself in being in the other; what is distinguished is identical with that from which it is distinguished — this is the form of love, such that the identity is posited or brought forward into actuality.

These three moments in the life of Spirit are what is figuratively represented by the religious terms Father, Son, and Holy Spirit. They suggest the inner movement or dialectic of Absolute Spirit, by which process

[11] *Lectures on the Philosophy of Religion*, III, 148.

[12] Cf. *ibid.*, I, 19 ff.; III, 12 ff.

[13] *Ibid.*, III, 148.

Spirit determines itself, and the Universal as totality is Spirit.

The question may be raised whether this conception of the nature of Absolute Spirit corresponds essentially to the doctrine of the Trinity. This question must be answered in the negative. Hegel undoubtedly felt that his teaching secured the essential Christian truth the more firmly. Certainly the distinctions which he sees in God are immanent in his Being and some of Hegel's terminology is reminiscent of the traditional *psychological* analogy[14] and of classical discussions of the generation of the Son and the unity of Father and Son in the Spirit. But at least two crucial differences must be noted.

First, Hegel apparently means to equate the second person of his trinity with finite existence. The Son is identified with the force of particularization, and the kingdom of the Son, the Otherness or other-Being, is physical nature and finite Spirit.[15] . . . A more orthodox interpretation might be drawn from some portions of Hegel's argument,[16] and Hegel is notoriously open to diverse interpretations, but the prevailing immanentism and monism of his thought suggests that for him the generation

of the Son and the "creation" of the world are not essentially distinct. The processes of nature and history are at least "organic to the dialectical process in which the Divine self-consciousness is itself constituted and eternally realized."[17]

Second, the conception of an "economic" Trinity — i.e., the Trinity of operation, or the divine threefoldness as it relates to the work of God in history — has been abandoned or altered beyond recognition. The divine *oikonomia* for Hegel has relation not to the revelation and redemption in Christ and the inspiration of the Holy Spirit, but only the general world-historical process. . . . Hegel does attach considerable significance to the rise of the idea at the time of Christ, who perceived the unity of God and man. . . . But he also asserts categorically that "it is in the first instances a matter of no importance whence that doctrine (of the Trinity) may have come: the only question is, whether it be essentially, inherently true."[18] Since all history is the basis of the God-man of the divine self-manifestation, no single point in it can be final and the connection with Jesus is little . . . more than accidental.

Hegel believed sincerely that the religious doctrine of the Trinity . . . was at least analogous to the doctrine now established by philosophy.

---

[14] That is, the interpretation of the Trinity by analogy from a threefoldness of finite personality. This was first given elaborate expression by St. Augustine in books IX–XV of *De trinitate,* in terms of memory, understanding, and will.

[15] *Ibid.,* III, 2; and part C., no. II: Creation.

[16] Cf. his discussion of God in his Eternal Idea in-and-for self (*Phil. of Rel.,* II, 7 ff.).

---

[17] C. W. Lowry, art. "Trinity" in *Encyclopedia of Religion,* Vergillus Ferm, ed. (1945), 795.

[18] *Phil. of Rel.,* I, 39. Cf. III, 29 ff.

(5) J. Collins[1] studies Nietzsche's rejection of God and of absolute truth. Nietzsche admitted he was an atheist and by instinct, and like Comte he based his whole philosophy upon the instinctive rejection of the reality of God. He repudiated the idea of God as being antivital and inimical to human culture. Zarathustra's message of the "death of God" meant the desuetude of all practical belief in the idea of God.

Nietzsche. Nietzsche[2] liked Schopenhauer's[3] frank denial of God and his systematic effort to construct an antitheistic world view. Schopenhauer's honesty contrasted favorably with the hypocrisy of those who paid lip service to God but were practical atheists in their daily lives. As for himself, Nietzsche admitted that he was an *atheist,* as a matter of course and by instinct. He identified the instinct in question as the feeling of hubris or rebellious pride, which over-

[1] James Collins is Associate Professor of Philosophy at Saint Louis University. He is the author of *A History of Modern European Philosophy, The Existentialists,* and other works. This selection is taken from his book, *A History of Modern European Philosophy* (Milwaukee: The Bruce Publishing Co., 1954), pp. 784–790, 795, 798–799.

[2] Friedrich Wilhelm Nietzsche (1844–1900) taught at Basel for ten years, until ill-health forced him to resign. There followed a steady stream of literary production, increasing loneliness and alienation from old friends, and finally madness. His main doctrines on the will to power, the superman, the aristocratic moral idea, and the eternal recurrence of the same situation, were given expression in *Thus Spoke Zarathustra* (1883–1885). *The Anti-Christ* and his autobiography, *Ecce Homo,* reflected his distorted conviction of having a mission against Christianity.

[3] Arthur Schopenhauer was born in 1788 in Danzig. In 1819 there appeared his philosophical masterpiece, *The World as Will and Presentation.* The crux of his philosophy is the transition from appearances to the thing-in-itself, together with the identification with cosmic will, so as to lead to an irrationalistic, voluntaristic and

came him whenever he was told that one must accept God and must not call his existence into question.[4] Nietzsche understood this necessity of acknowledging God's existence, to mean a call to blind, conventional submission, rather than a recognition of the cogent, speculative evidence of his existence and the consequent moral obligation upon one's freedom. Hence his reaction took the form of steeling his mind against any objective consideration of the evidence for God's existence. . . . Like Comte, Nietzsche based his whole philosophy upon this instinctive rejection of the reality of God.

Despite the fact that his atheism is emotionally underived from anything prior to this instinctive closing of his mind, it is derived philosophically from a definite metaphysical premise. . . . Nietzsche proposed to substitute sovereign becoming for Hegel's sovereign reason. . . . He converted the description of the world as the region of constant becoming into a demonstration that this world is self-sufficient and in no need of causal explanation. . . . Hence Nietzsche did not examine the causal proof of God's existence, and find it wanting. Instead he absolutized the process of becoming itself, and then concluded pessimistic metaphysics.

[4] *The Genealogy of Morals,* III, 9 (Samuel translation, in *Philosophy,* 115–116).

that philosophy need not seek beyond it for a transcendent principle. Becoming is there for Hegel and the evolutionists, but Nietzsche added that it is sovereignly and sufficiently there, so that causal analyses are superfluous. . . . If our experience bears no implications beyond the sphere of becoming, then philosophy does not deal with God but only with the idea of God. Hence Nietzsche consistently reduces the theological problem to a psychological one. He deems it a sufficient analysis, when he offers an explanation of how belief in the idea of God arose, what this idea signifies, and what the consequences are of a denial of theistic belief.

This psychologizing of the problem of God is in the tradition of Voltaire, Hume, and Feuerbach, although for Nietzsche it is an unavoidable metaphysical consequence of so defining the real that a transcendent, immutable God could not figure as a real principle in any inquiry. Nietzsche pictures the idea of God as arising, sometimes from the fear of ancestors, and sometimes as a compensation for the miserable conditions of earthly life. In the latter instance, men project their desires for perfection into another region, attribute total power over the conditions of existence to a transcendent entity, and end by fearing the very product of their imagination. Believers fail to reflect upon the contradiction of supposing that God is omnipotent and benevolent toward men, and nevertheless that he allows men to live in suffering and ignorance of the truth. By setting up a contrast between the here and the hereafter,

the idea of God drains human energies away from earthly tasks. "The concept 'God' was invented as the counterconcept to life, all bound together in one horrible unit."[5] Hence Nietzsche repudiates the idea of God as being antivital and inimical to human culture. *UNRELATED.*

He extends this bitter line of attack to include the notion of absolute truth. The veneration paid by both philosophers and scientists to disinterested, objective truth, is the final place of refuge for theism. Nietzsche usually links together "Platonic metaphysics," the Christian notion of God, and the ideal of absolute truth, as containing variations on a common theme. They agree in sponsoring belief in a "beyond," a "really real" world which stands in noticeable contrast with the here-and-now "apparent" world, emptying the latter of all significance and value for men. . . .

In this polemic, Nietzsche made a remarkable anticipation of the views of John Dewey and other American naturalists who also charged that the idea of God and an absolute truth

[5] *Ecce Homo* (Philosophy, 143–144). A systematic analysis of Nietzsche's arguments against God is made by H. Pfeil, "Nietzsche's Gründe gegen Gott," *Philosophisches Jahrbuch*, LIII (1940), 45–61, 198–209. Pfeil regards Nietzsche's biologicopostulatory atheism as the methodological counterpart of Kant's ethicopostulatory theism. Nietzsche offers three sorts of arguments: historical (belief in God has a nonrational, affective origin), metaphysical (the world is a self-sufficient whole of becoming), and dysteleological (the world is full of evil, suffering, and antipurposive factors). These objections rest upon the postulated description of the world as a plenum of becoming, animated only by the will-to-power and the values it creates.

are hostile to culture and mark a failure of nerve. There is no denying that the idea of God does serve some people as an anodyne and excuse for escaping from their social responsibilities. . . . But Nietzsche passed from what occurs by way of corruption, in some cases, to the unqualified verdict that belief in God and an absolute measure of truth must always and necessarily lead to these consequences. . . .

Belief in a transcendent, perfect God is incompatible with Nietzsche's own metaphysics, but the issue is whether this metaphysics is the sole basis for appreciating temporal and finite values. The Nietzschean and Christian views of the cosmos are countervaluations: they are not related as a prizing and a despising of the world. Their conflict is over whether or not the components of our experience are creatures, bearing witness to their creator, not about whether or not there is any significance and value in the world of becoming.

Nietzsche personifies his antitheistic standpoint in the character of *Zarathustra*, whose message is *the death of God*. Zarathustra comes down from his mountain retreat, to share the fruits of his meditations with the sons of men. In dithyramic periods, he preaches thus: "I conjure you, my brethren, *remain true to the earth*, and believe not those who speak unto you of superearthly hopes. Poisoners are they, whether they know it or not. . . . Once blasphemy against God was the greatest blasphemy; but God died, and therewith also those blasphemers. To blaspheme the earth is

now the *dreadfulest* sin, and to rate the heart of the unknowable higher than the meaning of the earth."[6] By "the death of God" is meant the desuetude of all practical belief in the idea of God. Nietzsche points to the discrepancy between profession of such belief and the actual interests of European men of our age. Their real gods are power politics, riches, sensual pleasure, and war. But his message is not that they should foreswear these false idols, and return to the worship of the true God. To have urged that, he would have had to abandon his own definition of the idea of God, in favor of the reality of God himself. But within the Nietzschean perspective, there is only the idea of God — and it is irretrievably dead, once men cease to give it credence, in their own hearts.

The real significance of loss of faith in God is *cultural nihilism* and the *downfall of all values*. Nietzsche's aim is not to deplore this predicament but to intensify it, to the point where his own Promethean solution will alone seem viable to bold spirits. The "death of God" is only conceivable on condition that all values, including the highest, are creations of man. Man is confronted with no objective norms of belief and conduct. . . . The cosmos as such is a chaos of becoming, but man can will to make it intelligible, to construct concepts, and thus to endow experience with meaning and value. Human history made a fatal mistake, when it erected the

[6] *Thus Spake Zarathustra*, Prologue, 3 (*Philosophy*, 28). Hegel had also spoken about "the death of God," in terms of the negative moment in his dialectic.

idea of God into the supreme value. In modern times, there has been a secret recession from this idea, but, as yet, no open repudiation. Zarathustra bids men turn away openly from belief in a transcendent God, and forge for themselves a completely immanent, voluntaristic system of values and goals.

Nietzsche's conception of an atheistic world of human values is best understood as an experiment of thought and imagination, carried on within the framework of Kantian and Schopenhaurian epistemology. Let us suppose, he asks us in effect, that there is no noumenal source — neither Kant's thing-in-itself nor Schopenhauer's cosmic will — for the matter of sensation. Then the latter may be regarded as a true sampling of the original flux of the cosmos. Since it is a chaotic and completely unorganized becoming, it does not contain any permanent, essential structures. The latter must be provided by the decision and project of the human subject (to use language that also fits Jean-Paul Sartre's atheistic humanism). Hence all meanings are purely human in provenance, immanent in content, and evolutionary in tendency.

The incompatibility which Nietzsche sees between a world of becoming and a permanent, essential principle of intelligibility in finite things is inevitable, only on condition that the fact of becoming be interpreted in this modified Kantian way, as the flow of the matter of sensation, cut off from any intelligible foundation. Similarly, there is an essential antagonism between belief in God and

respect for the finite world, only when the latter is construed as a field of appearances, composed solely of the surging cosmic matter of sensation and the formal structures provided by human decision. By postulatory definition, such a matter-form composition would bear no reference beyond itself. Nietzsche would require us to be loyal, not toward the earthly situation of common human experience, but toward the experimental construct which would result, if "appearances" alone were real, and were constituted entirely by the human resolution to tame the flux of sensations and inject meaning therein.

This hypothesis does mark the death of the idea of God, if by that phrase is meant the final despair of nineteenth-century philosophy over fitting the living God into the Kantian machinery of the matter of sensation, the forms of human subjectivity, and the intelligible ideals. . . .

Although he paid his respects to Jesus as a human person, Nietzsche made passionate denunciations of Paul and Christianity. He linked Judaism and Christianity together, as the main forces which achieved "the slave revolt in morals." By vindicating the moral value of sympathy, self-denial and altruism, Judaeo-Christianity spread the standards of slave morality to all classes of society. It undermined the eugenic soundness of the race, by lending moral and religious sanction to the care of the sick, the weak and the poor. This ascetic ideal despises all earthly and human values. Christian faith is "a continuous suicide of reason." . . . . It is little wonder that, holding this distorted conception of the Christian faith and its consequences for the self, Nietzsche should feel revolted at it. . . .

The Nietzschean treatment of the Christian influence upon morality is equally one-sided and arbitrary. Present-day Christianity is presented as though it contained no internal powers of reform and regeneration. . . . In dealing with what he regards as the primitive message of Christian faith, he relies mainly upon Pascal, Schopenhauer, Wagner, and Dostoevski for his conception. They provide him with an abstraction, called "*the* Christian ascetic ideal," which he never compares with the integral Christian teaching. . . . Nietzsche accords himself the right to sublimate and transfigure pain and bodily urges, whereas the Christian concern with the same problem is presented as a suppression and defaming of the body. Nietzschean man recognizes the positive value of overcoming and disciplining oneself, whereas Christian man is never permitted to have the same insight.

6. C. Bonifazi[1] studies Kierkegaard's view of God in comparison with Nietzsche's. Both deny the validity of any objective proofs for the reality of God; the former because proofs are harmful to true faith, the latter because "God is dead." Both criticize the popular concept of God as love. But Kierkegaard upholds the orthodox belief in the Trinity, and at heart of his faith stands the Paradox of the Incarnation.

In the objective thought of the Hegelian the individual had been lost to view; mankind was left with an objective world process to be contemplated disinterestedly. . . . Kierkegaard[2] affirms that to objectivize our own existence is impossible; it is only by virtue of our own existence that the one other existence which matters, that of the incarnate God-Man can be realized. "The exister who chooses the objective way to God enters upon the approximative reflection which aims at bringing God to evidence, an aim which will not be attained in all eternity, because God is subject, and therefore exists only for subjectivity in inwardness."[3] Only through an act of faith arising out of the intensity of a man's existence, can the paradox presented by Christianity

[1] Conrad Bonifazi made a comparison of Kierkegaard and Nietzsche and presented it as a thesis to the University of Bristol. As far as the end of Chapter 9 it was approved by the University for the award of the degree of Master of Arts. It was published as a book, with the title *Christendom Attacked — A comparison of Kierkegaard and Nietzsche* (London: Rockliff, 1953). This excerpt is from that book, pp. 26–27, 31–32, 57–58, 73–74, 76–82, 84–85, 172–173.

[2] Søren Aabye Kierkegaard was born in 1813 in Copenhagen and died in 1855. He was one of the great pioneer thinkers of recent times and has had an immense influence on both Catholics and Protestants. Among his works may be singled out *Either/Or, Two Edifying Discourses, Fear and Trembling, Training in Christianity, In Vino Veritas, Dread, Christian Discourses, Attack on Christendom, Philosophical Fragments, Judge for Yourselves, Works of Love.*

[3] *Concluding Unscientific Postscript*, p. 193 f.

be understood. Religious faith is not continuous with rational belief. It cannot be reached by any approximations of proof or probability, only by a "leap." "Faith," asserts Kierkegaard in the *Fragments* "is not a cognition but an act of freedom, an expression of the will." . . . The more proof one can produce for the object of faith, the less room there is for faith, which is gradually exchanged for knowledge. . . .

The majesty of God demands implicit obedience, and the theme of *Training in Christianity* is the *imitatio Christi*, wherein Kierkegaard insists that Christ can be imitated only in his lowliness and suffering and death.[4] . . . Against this conception of Christianity as a life of suffering, of acknowledged helplessness before God, and of utter dependence upon divine grace, a Christianity whose demands were absolute and unconditioned, Kierkegaard beheld a religion that was an easy-going compromise with the world, whose adherents sought advancement and personal well-being despite the sacrifice of Christ which stood at the source of their supposed inspiration. . . .

"The greatest Protestant Christian of the nineteenth century!"[5] exclaims H. A. Reinhold of Kierkegaard; and Theodor Haecker, the Roman Catholic scholar, in *Kierkegaard the Cripple* admits Kierkegaard to be one of the greatest Christians but casts a slur upon him because "he lived in heresy." . . .

Kierkegaard contended for no sec-

[4] *Journals*, 1336.
[5] *The Commonweal*, Vol. XXXV, p. 608.

tarian interest; his chief desire was to see resuscitated the Christianity of the New Testament. Nietzsche's attack had no sectarian basis; but understood the power of the Protestant Reformation in terms of a renewal of Christianity when it might have decayed. They look to the Reformation as carried through by Luther: as far as Kierkegaard's works are concerned, Calvin might not have existed; Nietzsche alludes to him on four occasions.[6] Catholics and Protestants have taken them both to heart. M. Chaning-Pearce says that, in his theology, Kierkegaard "has supplied the fuel for the most advanced thought in both Catholic and Protestant camps, for both Thomists and Barthians."[7] . . .

There is a sense in which every man must know God; a man could not deny God, states Dr. Emil Brunner, "had he not an original knowledge of him."[8] Man's godlessness is a witness to God.[9] Atheism itself is a kind of theology, and contains much that is important for a right understanding of religion. . . . Kierkegaard and Nietzsche attack the concept of God; their reasons for criticism differ, but the force behind their challenge springs directly from a common concern for men. Kierkegaard attacks the error of worshiping a mere concept of God instead of God himself, for

[6] R. Guppy, *Index to Nietzsche's Works*, p. 35.
[7] *The Terrible Crystal*, p. 20.
[8] *Revelation and Reason*, p. 56.
[9] Cf. E. Lampert, *The Apocalypse of History*, p. 65; "The dignity of man spells a two-fold capacity for revolt and humility in the face of God: defiance and self-abandonment in love are the indelible signs of his true God-given manhood."

to mistake a concept for a person not only permits intellectual assent to masquerade as living faith, but also produces hollow men. Nietzsche challenges the concept of God by asserting that it has no foundation in reality and is, therefore, hostile to life.

Kierkegaard's viewpoint is unfolded in passionate antithesis to Romantic Idealism; Nietzsche's gospel is no less a reaction to Hegelian Rationalism. Their work is a cross-roads of vital problems rather than a logical and progressive exposition. With glowing personal passion they vindicate the irrational and the immediate as existence, life and personality, against reason, which in its claim to universal validity, absorbs and annuls what is singular in each individual. . . .

God is beyond rational comprehension. Kierkegaard affirms that between God and man there is an "infinite qualitative difference," and although in Jesus Christ the God-Man we have a revelation of Eternal Truth in time, the unity of God and an individual man, the revelation is an absolute paradox which neither thought nor reason can grasp. . . . Familiarity with God is to be deplored. "It is impudence to wish to fraternise with God" (Kierkegaard).

There can be no "proofs" of the existence of God. Truth no longer remains truth when the veil has been withdrawn from it. Kierkegaard maintains that if God exists, it is impossible to prove it logically, because we must have some fixed point from which to begin. From the mere thought of God we can arrive only at his conceptual existence, never at his actual existence. But we would never begin to prove God's existence unless we were already convinced that he existed.[10] . . .

Though there can be no proofs of God's existence, this is not, in Kierkegaard's case, to deny the objectivity of God in himself, but the final truth of God is revealed only to the man who believes. "When an existing individual has not got faith, God is not, neither does God exist although understood from an eternal point of view God is eternally."[11] . . .

If reason is insufficient to prove the existence of God, neither is he demonstrable from nature. Certainly nature is God's handiwork, according to Kierkegaard, but only the work is immediately present, not God. "In his omnipotence he created this visible world — and made himself invisible."[12] . . . With all his deep feeling for nature, Kierkegaard recognizes in creation a mighty power, but does not prove from it the existence of a "humanitarian" God. . . . Both Kierkegaard and Nietzsche turn to history, but do not find that it holds proof

---

[10] Students of the history of philosophy have often confessed to the feeling that the massive and often passionate assurance of God's reality which has been professed by a majority of its leading figures did not really rest upon the arguments which they so painstaking contrived for the establishment of His existence, these arguments being rather in the nature of afterthoughts, subsequent to their belief in Him rather than the cause of it, and therefore in the language of the new psychology, not so much reasons as rationalisations. . . ." John Baillie, *Our Knowledge of God*, pp. 132–133.

[11] *Journals*, 605.

[12] For *Self-Examination and Judge for Yourselves*, 230.

of the existence of God. "In relation to the absolute there is only one tense: the present" (Kierkegaard).

Both Kierkegaard and Nietzsche, therefore, deny the validity of any objective proofs for the reality of God: the former because proofs are harmful to true faith, the latter because, briefly, "God is dead." From the speculative standpoint both demand a leap of faith: Kierkegaard's affirmation and Nietzsche's denial of God become dogmatic assertions; they dogmatize, respectively, as to the existence and nonexistence of God.

Hegel had emphasized an immanental conception of God who stood in closest relationship with man and the world. The divine was immanent within the human, and, despite the acknowledged imperfections of man, the human was capable of entering into communion with the Absolute Spirit of the Universe.

Kierkegaard protested that "man is not to be merged into God by way of a sort of pantheistic disappearance, or by the obliteration of all his individual traits in the divine ocean";[13] he resisted the illusion of pantheism with the concept of the individual who chooses himself as a creature in relation to the infinite and personal absolute, God. Man's union with God proceeds through personality, through a heightened awareness of self. . . .

Kierkegaard upholds the orthodox belief in the Trinity, Father, God-Man, and Holy Spirit, but his treatment of this belief is decidedly practical rather than metaphysical. God

is "certainly personal"[14] and the individual stands before God in complete dependence and the closest relationship. "From a Christian point of view, the whole of learned theology is really a corollary, and is declined like *mensa*."[15] . . .

Kierkegaard joins Nietzsche in criticism of the popular concept of God as love: God is a name for "everything men and women think of when they hear the word 'love' (Nietzsche); "the bourgeois' love of God begins when vegetable life is most active, when the hands are comfortably folded on the stomach, and the head sinks back into the cushions of the chair, while the eyes, drunk with sleep, gaze heavily for a moment towards the ceiling" (Kierkegaard). . . .

At the heart of Kierkegaard's faith stands the paradox of the Incarnation; in "complete unrecognisableness" God reveals himself to men. . . . Kierkegaard describes how God is apprehended. Without purity no man can see God, and no man takes notice of God without becoming a sinner.[16] The first step is that a man should fear God: "in order really to love God it is necessary to have feared God."[17] Eternal Truth has been presented to men in the absolute paradox of the God-Man, and the uncertainty of God thus created should arouse infinite interestedness in the individual since his eternal blessedness is bound up with it. He is thus driven to relate himself not just in thought, but in his inner existence to the object of

---

[13] *Journals,* 220, and cf. *The Point of View,* 137.

[14] *Journals,* 1388.
[15] *Ibid.,* 1375.
[16] *Stages on Life's Way,* 461 (note).
[17] *Journals,* 150.

his concern. The eternal truth of God thus becomes a matter of subjective relationship, and no longer one of objective understanding. . . .

What is Kierkegaard's significance in this context? One of the most impressive aspects of the present comparison has been Kierkegaard's anticipation of Nietzsche's offensive, and the forging of weapons suitable for counter-offensive measures. This was possible because the spiritual climate to which Nietzsche gave definition was that in which already Kierkegaard had done battle.

He had waged his warfare in defense of the supernatural against the natural, the transcendence of God against the immanence of the rational philosophers, the personal God as opposed to pantheism; he had stressed the uniqueness of the God-Man, the reality of sin and salvation, Divine Love as against human love, and the holiness of God as against the sentimentality of the "beautiful soul." . . . With all his capacity he had striven to uphold the category of the Individual against the beginnings of a socialism without God. Through the haze of a volatilized Christianity he struggled to press men back upon the fundamentals of their faith; he aimed at bringing the Church to take account once more of the heart of that revelation which the fourth-and-fifth century Church Fathers had suffered to express in Christological and Trinitarian terms, and to confront men with the truth which Protestant reformers had agonized to say, that all men from the highest saintliness to abysmal wickedness live by the mercy and grace of God whom we encounter on his own terms, where and when he deigns to reveal himself.

As regards weapons: taking his stand upon the ground of orthodoxy, Kierkegaard defied attack upon the Gospel made by an outraged moral sense with his presentation of the God-Man as absolute paradox; that scepticism which assailed Christianity in the absence of rational proof for doctrinal assertions, he disarmed totally by pretense of rational agreement which, suddenly unmasked, was seen to be nothing other than faith's discontent with unintelligibility. Accepting the forces which militate against Christianity, Kierkegaard transmuted them into powers which heighten the passion of Christian faith.

Whereas the pertinence of Kierkegaard's work for this age may well lie in his analysis of despair, his emphasis upon the category of the Individual is apposite to the needs of contemporary Christianity, for with this category not only did he defend the human person against the ravages of a socialism without God, but also brought into focus the constituent cell of the Body of Christ — the Single One!

XII

GOD IN CONTEMPORARY PROTESTANT THEOLOGY

1. K. Barth[1] studies the knowability of God, and maintains that only by the grace and mercy of God effectual in his self-revelation is God knowable to us. Hence he flatly contradicts the doctrine of the natural knowability of God set forth in Vatican I. He rejects its natural theology because it is a construct which obviously derives from an attempt to unite Yahweh with Baal, the triune God of holy Scripture with the concept of being of Aristotelian and Stoic philosophy.

The Knowability of God. . . . "God is knowable" means: "God can be known" — he can be known of and by himself. In his essence, as it is turned to us in his activity, he is so constituted that he can be known

---

[1] Karl Barth was born in Basle, Switzerland, May 10, 1886. He became professor of theology successively at the Universities of Göttingen, Münster, Bonn, and finally of Basle. His best known works are *Der Römerbrief* and *Die kirchliche Dogmatik*. The exhaustive list of his writings until the end of 1955 was composed by Charlotte von Kirschbau, *Antwort, Festschrift, Karl Barth* (Zollikon-Zürich, 1956), pp. 945–960. This excerpt is from his *Church Dogmatics*, Vol. II, 1, *The Doctrine of God* (Edinburgh: T. & T. Clark, 1957), pp. 65, 69, 75–84.

by us. . . . But now we cannot be too definite when we go on to say that we are thinking of the grace of God when we say that God is knowable. . . . For it is by the grace of God and only by the grace of God that it comes about that God is knowable to us. . . .

We possess no analogy on the basis of which the nature and being of God as the Lord can be accessible to us. . . . Moreover, we have no analogy on the basis of which the nature and being of God as Creator can be accessible to us. . . . Moreover, we have no analogy on the basis of which the nature and being of God as the Reconciler can be accessible to us. . . . And finally we have no analogy on the basis of which the nature and being of God as the Redeemer can be accessible to us. . . .

In this discussion, the opponent whom we have not so far named is the doctrine of the knowability of God which has found its classical and sharpest expression in the basic theology of the Roman Catholic Church. Our identification of the truth by which the truth is revealed to us with the good-pleasure of God is in flat contradiction to what is said in the *Constitutio dogmatica de fide catholica* of the Vatican Council, *cap.* 2 *De revelatione: Eadem sancta mater Ecclesia tenet et docet, Deum, rerum omnium principium et finem, naturali humanae rationis lumine e rebus*

creatis certo cognosci posse. And we have done what is condemned in a canon of the same Council[3]: *Si quis dixerit, Deum unum et verum, creatorem et Dominum nostrum, per ea quae facta sunt, naturali rationis humanae lumine certo cognosci non posse, anthema sit.* In contrast to this doctrine, we have affirmed that God can be known only through God, namely in the event of the divine encroachment of his self-revelation. There can be no question of any other *posse*, i.e., a *posse* which is not included in and with this divine encroachment. Let us now try to clarify in which sense and on what grounds we oppose this doctrine.

What we have said is that the accessibility of the nature and being of God as Lord, Creator, Reconciler, and Redeemer is not constituted by any analogy which we contribute but only by God himself. Now when we compare this with what the *Vaticanum* says, the first thing to strike us is that right from the very outset in our outline of the problem of the knowability of God we have been dealing quite unequivocally with the Christian concept of God. Right from the very outset we have been speaking of the one, triune and true God in his work and action as they are knowable in his revelation. Of this God and of his truth we have said that he is knowable only by the truth, i.e., only by his own grace and mercy.

---

[2] April 24, 1870, Denz. No. 1785:3004: The same holy Mother Church holds and teaches that God, the origin and end of all things, can be known with certainty by the natural light of human reason from the things he created.

[3] *De rev.* I, Denz. No. 1806:3026: If anyone says that the one and true God, our creator and lord, cannot be known with certainty by the natural light of human reason through the things that have been made: let him be anathema.

Now the *Vaticanum* does not wish to speak about another God, or about only a part of this one God. But its procedure in the noetic question is different from that in the ontological. To that extent it certainly intends to make a provisional division or partition in regard to the knowability of God, and this will inevitably lead to a partitioning of the one God as well. For it cannot be overlooked or denied that in the second passage to which we referred, although God is once called *Dominus noster,* everywhere else and decisively he is no more or not yet more than *rerum omnium principium et finis,* or *creator.* And in regard to this one side of God a knowability of God is affirmed other than that which is grounded in the revelation of God. The primary reference of our contradiction is to this partition. Of course, we too understand by "God" *principium et finis omnium rerum* and also *creator.* But God is not only this. He is also God the Reconciler and Redeemer. We have taken the unity of God seriously, not only in theory but in practice. We have answered the question of the knowability of God in the light of his unity, and for that very reason we have had to answer it in the way we have. Every single thing that we have said has been conditioned by this total view. . . .

Therefore, whatever may be the content of his answer, we have to put to our Roman Catholic opponent the following question: In defining what we have to understand by "God" in this question of his knowability, how can we possibly take any other

view? How can we carry through the division — even if it is only meant to be provisional — which enables us in the first instance to investigate the knowability of God the Creator in *abstracto*? Are we really speaking of the one true God if even provisionally we think of only one side of God — in this instance of God the Lord and Creator? Are we really speaking of the real Lord and Creator? . . . On what ground do we think we can speak about his knowability in this abstraction, in the light of only one side of God?

The Word of God testified in holy Scripture gives us no reason to think this, unless it is heard and read very differently from how it is meant to be heard and read. . . . It speaks of God the Reconciler and Redeemer no less than of God the Lord and Creator. . . . How can that partition of God be effected from the Scriptures?

If, according to Roman Catholic doctrine, it has to take place, will it not be on some other ground than that of Scripture and therefore of the Word of God? Is not the *Deus Dominus et creator* of this doctrine the construct of human thinking — a thinking which in the last resort is not bound by the basis and essence of the Church, by Jesus Christ, by the prophets and apostles, but which relies upon itself? And although the knowability of this construct can rightly be affirmed without revelation, do we not have to ask what authority we have from the basis and essence of the Church to call it "God"? Obviously, in the doctrine of the Roman Catholic Church this partition is already presupposed when the doctrine is put. . . . It is definitely not summoned and authorised to make this partition by God's revelation. . . . But if Jesus Christ as attested by the prophets and apostles is the basis and essence of the Church, then this different sort of knowing is alien to Christian doctrine and it is impossible for the Church to make the partition. . . .

If we again except the formula *Dominum nostrum*, there is not a single word in the *Vaticanum* to suggest that the God referred to is engaged in a work and activity with man, which is for man a matter of life and death, of blessedness and damnation, nay more, which is for God a matter of his honor and therefore of the miracle of his love, and from which we cannot abstract for a single moment when it is a matter of the relationship of God and man and in particular of the knowability of God. Apparently Roman Catholic doctrine can and must make this abstraction. It does, of course, know about this work and activity, and the necessity and reality of the divine action. But it is able to postpone its treatment of it, deferring it for later consideration. . . . It first establishes the fact of the existence of God, i.e., of the beginning and end of all things, God the Creator. In the light of this affirmation it then decides that God is knowable — knowable even without his revelation. . . .

But then the following questions arise: How is it that the formula *Dominus noster* was not taken seriously in the *Vaticanum?* How is it that Roman Catholic theology does not seriously and unambiguously investigate the being of the God who acts among us and toward us as his one true being, besides which there is no other? How is it that it abstracts from the fact that he is this God, i.e., the God who does these things, the God who condemns to death and leads from death to life, that God who loves us in incomprehensible mercy? Can we set all this aside in order first to consider the being of this God in itself and as such? . . . Can we compare with that being, and therefore set against it, the certainly very modest part of all other being, and therefore our own part in being in particular? Can we say, therefore, that they belong together, that they are on the same plane? Only if we accept this can theology take its stand on the ground where the God who is to be known and the man who knows can be considered and compared and, therefore, apprehended together, prior to and quite irrespective of any particular act of God to restore this fellowship. Only if we accept this, can the analogy of being be identified with the knowability of God apart from his revelation.

But how can we accept this? By the mere fact that we are in being, how can we possibly stand on the same plane as God in his being? . . . How can this being, which is the origin and boundary for all being, have only a part as we do in some being in general? How can this being, therefore, come to stand on the same plane as our own being? . . . And where then is the comparability between his Creator-being and our creature-being, between his holy being and our sinful being, between his eternal being and our temporal being? Where then is the analogy on the basis of which the knowledge of God is possible to us? If there is a real analogy between God and man — an analogy which is a true analogy of being on both sides, an analogy in and with which the knowledge of God will in fact be given — what other analogy can it be than the analogy of being which is posited and created by the work and action of God himself, the analogy which has its actuality from . . . God alone, and therefore in . . . faith alone? . . .

The intolerable and unpardonable thing in Roman Catholic theology is that the question is put in this way, there is this splitting up of the concept of God, and hand in hand with it the abstraction from the real work and activity of God in favor of a general being of God which he has in common with us and all being. To put the question in this way is to commit a twofold act of violence which means the introduction of a foreign god into the sphere of the Church. The fact that knowability is ascribed to this god, apart from his revelation, is in no way surprising. In itself it is even quite proper. This god really is knowable *naturali humanae rationis lumine e rebus creatis* apart from God, i.e., apart from God's special help. But to affirm that the true, whole God, active and effective, the Head and Shepherd of the Church, can be knowable in this way is only possible if he has already been identified with that false god. What thanks do we owe to that god for the benefit and the grace and mercy of his revelation? . . . And the really wicked and damnable thing in the Roman Catholic doctrine is that it equates the Lord of the Church with that idol and says of him therefore the very thing that would naturally be said of it. This is the decisive difference between them and us. . . .

Our primary contradiction is not of the "natural theology" of the *Vaticanum* as such. This is only a self-evident consequence of our initial contradiction of its concept of God. We reject this because it is a construct which obviously derives from an attempt to unite Yahweh with Baal, the triune God of holy Scripture with the concept of being of Aristotelian and Stoic philosophy. The assertion that reason can know God from created things applies to the second and heathenish component of this concept of God, so that when we view the construct on this side we do not recognize God in it at all, nor can we accept it as a Christian concept of God. . . .

2. E. Brunner[1] studies the problem of a *"theologia naturalis."* Both biblical evidence and the Christian Idea of the Creator force us to admit the reality of a revelation in Creation. But between the revelation in Creation and the natural man there stands the fact of sin. Hence, there is no valid natural theology.

---

[1] Cf. Ch. IX, 4, n. 1. This excerpt is from *op. cit.*, pp. 132–136, 149–150.

The "Natural" Knowledge of God.
In recent times, and rightly, the question whether — from the standpoint of the Christian faith — God can be known outside the historical revelation, is to be answered in the affirmative, or in the negative, is now regarded as a fundamental problem and, like few other problems of this kind, has led to varied and passionate controversies. . . . Since I myself, by the use of a misleading idea, am bound to admit that I have caused some of the chief misunderstanding, I feel obliged to make yet another attempt to clear up the difficulty.

First of all, we must make a clear distinction between two questions which, unfortunately, are continually being confused with one another; the question of the revelation in Creation, and the question of man's natural knowledge of God. While one side was mainly anxious to deny the validity of a *"theologia naturalis,"* the other side was chiefly concerned to affirm the reality of the revelation in Creation. Now some theologians believed (mistakenly) that their denial of a *"theologia naturalis"* obliged them also to deny the reality of the revelation in Creation; this was due to their mistaken idea that the acknowledgment of a revelation in Creation must necessarily lead to the recognition of a *"theologia naturalis."* I myself, however, helped to foster this mistaken equation of the revelation in Creation with Natural Theology (which I contested from the very outset), to this extent, that in the first edition of *Natur und Gnade* I described the Christian doctrine of the revelation in

Creation by the misleading expression of a "Christian *theologia naturalis."* On the other side, however, it is evident that the correction of this unfortunate phrase, to which I drew special attention in the second edition of this brochure, has not been noticed.

The affirmation of a revelation in Creation has, in itself, nothing whatever to do with a belief in Natural Theology. A theology which intends to remain true to the biblical witness to revelation should never have denied the reality of revelation in Creation. All efforts to contest the biblical evidence for such a revelation must lead to an arbitrary exegesis, and to forced interpretations of the text of the Bible.

But even apart from explicit Biblical evidence, the Christian Idea of the Creator should itself force us to admit the reality of a revelation in Creation; for what sort of Creator would not imprint the mark of his Spirit upon his creation?

The question whether the "natural man," that is, the man who has not yet been affected by the historical revelation, is in a position to perceive this divine revelation in Creation as such, in accordance with its nature and its meaning, is a quite different question. This question, therefore, has not been answered when we have answered the former question in the affirmative, because between the revelation in Creation and the natural man there stands the fact of Sin. . . . Sin not only perverts the will, it also "obscures" the power of perceiving truth where the knowledge of God is concerned. So where a man supports the view of the reality of a *"theologia naturalis"* in the sense of correct, valid knowledge, he is actually denying the reality of sin, or at least its effect in the sphere of man's knowledge of God. Thus, on the one hand, the reality of the revelation in Creation is to be admitted, but, on the other hand, the possibility of a correct and valid natural knowledge of God is to be contested.

Now, however, the problem is complicated by the fact that when we have said that we must question the possibility of a valid knowledge of God (to the natural man), we have not said all there is to say. There is, it is true, no valid "natural theology" but there is a Natural Theology which, in fact, exists. The place to discuss this, however, is not in connection with the doctrine of God, for here it has no theological validity, but in connection with the doctrine of man; for "natural theology" is an anthropological fact, which no one can deny. Human beings, even those who know nothing of the historical revelation, are such that they cannot help forming an idea of God and making pictures of God in their minds. The history of the religions of mankind provides incontrovertible evidence of this fact. The formation of theological ideas is an empirical fact of the reality of sinful humanity. This fact cannot be denied; all that we can contest is how it should be interpreted. . . .

The chief passage in the Bible which deals with this question — Romans 1:19 ff — gives the interpretation which alone can stand the test of theological examination. The fact that sinful human beings cannot help having thoughts about God is due to the revelation in Creation. The other fact, that human beings are not able rightly to understand the nature and meaning of this revelation in Creation is due to the fact that their vision has been distorted by sin. . . .

The apostle cannot be interested in the theoretical question: how are we to explain the *"theologia naturalis"* of the pagan sinful man or woman; but the question which interests him is this: How should we address the man to whom the message of Jesus Christ is to be proclaimed? This question he answers thus: Sinful man is responsible for his sin, because in the revelation in Creation the possibility is given him of knowing God. He is responsible for his idolatry: he is *anapologetos,* "without excuse." Thus, according to the biblical teaching, the doctrine of general revelation becomes actual in anthropology. Human responsibility is based upon the general revelation. . . .

It is very cheering to note that Karl Barth, in his exposition of the narrative of the Creation in Genesis 1:26 ff. has come to the same conclusion. The fact that man has been created in the Image of God (taught in this passage) means responsible existence, the "Thou"-relation with the Creator, which is the basis of the "Thou"-relation with one's fellow man; and *this* fact: namely, that we have been created in the Image of God, cannot be lost.[2]

The Fall does not mean that man ceases to be responsible, but that he ceases to understand his responsibility

---

[2] *Kirchl. Dogma.,* III, I, p. 224.

aright, and to live according to his responsibility. . . . The idolatrous images of man — whether they be the massive structures of wood or brass, or the idolatrous abstractions of speculative theology — accuse man, because to him has been given another possibility of the knowledge of God. It is sin which makes idols out of the revelation in Creation.

This biblical view of the natural man, and of his *"theologia naturalis,"* can, and must, be examined in the light of historic facts. What is the result of this examination?

The history of religions shows that mankind cannot help producing religious ideas, and carrying on religious activities. It also shows the confusion caused by sin. The multiplicity of religious ideas of God, and of the "gods" is so vast, and so contradictory, that it is impossible to gather it all up in one positive conception, as the result of research; to reach such a result by a process of elimination is not the task of religion itself but of philosophy. Whither it leads will be shown directly.

Within this welter of religious conceptions of God it is impossible to discover one common denominator. The "higher religions" are contrasted with the primitive religions, and the contradictions are too great to be overcome. There is no common element which could do justice at the same time to the polytheistic personalism of the one, and the monistic impersonalism of the other.[3]

From the beginning of Greek philosophy men have continually tried to reach a clear and certain knowledge of God, not along the path of religion, but by the way of philosophy, by speculative thought, and thus to overcome the irrationalism of the purely religious formation of ideas. These philosophical doctrines of God now confront one another in irreconcilable opposition. Above all, none of them can possibly be combined with the Christian Idea of God. The relation of the "God" of Plato or of Aristotle with the God of the Biblical revelation is that of the Either-Or. The same may be said of every other idea of God which has been attained purely by philosophical speculation. The reason for this [is that] . . . the God of thought *must* differ from the God of revelation. The God who is "conceived" by thought is not the one who discloses himself; from this point of view he is an intellectual idol.[4] . . .

Proofs for the Existence of God. In the chapter *"de existentia Dei"* usually the various proofs for the existence of God are formulated. This proceeding is based upon the strange idea that the existence of God must first of all be established before we can speak of his nature as manifested in his revelation. This enigma is solved as soon as we become aware that such thinkers are not dealing so much with the question of the nature of God on the basis of his revelation, as upon the basis of metaphysical speculative ideas. The doctrine of the "metaphysical" Being of God . . . is not only by its content, but also by the methods of its metaphysics, not

[3] Cf. my *Religionsphilosophie protestantischer Theologie*, pp. 51 ff., and *Offenbarung und Vernunft*, pp. 215 ff.

[4] Cf. *Offenbarung und Vernunft*, pp. 43 ff., and ch. 20–23.

theology. If one has departed so far from the proper path of theology, from the exclusive orientation towards revelation, then the presupposition of the proofs for the existence of God, in order to make his existence seem more solid, is not such a great aberration, after all.

Actually, however, behind both these points there lies the same misunderstanding. The existence of God, of which faith speaks, proves itself only as completely sufficient where the nature of God is manifested: in revelation. In apologetics, indeed, relations may be established between the revealed faith, and rational metaphysics, with its proofs for the existence of God; but within Christian doctrine itself there is no place for them.

The God in whom we believe cannot be "proved," and the God who can be proved is not the God of faith. We do not want, first of all, to be convinced of the existence of God by proofs, and after that to believe in the God of revelation. The existence of God becomes certain to us in and with the revelation in which he manifests himself to us as the living Lord, and proves himself to us.

Whatever value the "proofs" may have, they are of no concern for faith. Faith does not want to hear about them. The God who is "proved" by human reason is not the God who reveals himself to man as his Lord.

But even the distinction between "metaphysical" and "ethical" statements about God arises from the same misunderstanding. If we have to do with the God of revelation, who is the Lord, the sovereign "I" — where is the possibility of making a distinction between the "metaphysical" and the "ethical"? Is the Sovereign Being of God "metaphysical," or is it "ethical"? This distinction is only possible where one starts from a neutral — actually from a metaphysical, speculative — concept of being, but not where — from the very outset — one has to do with the revelation of the Lord. The Being of God as Lord, if we must use this somewhat dubious distinction at all, is both metaphysical and ethical. Metaphysically speaking, it is the ONE WHO IS who alone gives existence to all other forms of being. Ethically speaking, it is the will of the Lord from which every kind of ethos is derived.

3. G. Weigel, S.J.[1] studies the theological significance of Paul Tillich. He finds him an original theologian who has produced a remarkable synthesis of Protestant thought and doctrine from the days of the reformers to our own time. For him, God is ontologically the ground of being, phenomenologically the object of man's ultimate concern. But

---

[1] Gustave Weigel, S.J. (1906–1964), was an eminent Catholic theologian, who was Professor of Dogmatic Theology at the Catholic University of Chile, 1937–1948, and Professor of Ecclesiology at Woodstock College, 1948–1964. He was a peritus at Vatican II. He was the author of numerous articles and of *Faith and Understanding in America; The Modern God; Churches in North America; Catholic Theology in Dialogue.* This excerpt is from his article, "The Theological Significance of Paul Tillich," in *Gregorianum*, Vol. 37 (Rome: Pontificia Universita Gregoriana, 1956), pp. 35–47.

is God personal in this theology? God is suprapersonal. Is this the God of theism? This is the God above and beyond theism.

The Theological Significance of Paul Tillich.[2] It can be maintained without rashness that he is the most impressive figure in today's Protestant theology. . . . Wherein lies the importance of Tillich? In the fact that he has made an all-embracing system of Protestant thought and doctrine. . . . He is really bringing together all the elements of Protestant thinking from the days of the reformers to our own time. What is more, this synthesis takes into consideration the Catholic elements which are latent in Protestant belief, though often unrecognized. A unified rational synthesis of the diverse and seemingly contradictory stands and tenets of the Reform tradition in its life of four centuries is a major event. Has anyone ever attempted it before? . . .

---

[2] Paul Tillich was born in Germany in 1886. He taught at Berlin, Marburg, Dresden, Frankfurt, and for more than twenty years at Union Theological Seminary in New York. In 1954 he accepted a call to Harvard University as a University Professor. From Harvard he went to Chicago University. He died in 1965. His publications are voluminous. A catalogue of his works up to 1952 can be found in C. W. Kegley & R. W. Bretall's *The Theology of Paul Tillich*, pp. 353–362. Among his works are *The Protestant Era; The Courage To Be; The Shaking of the Foundations; Love, Power and Justice; The New Being; Dynamics of Faith.* For American Catholic critiques of Tillich cf. G. Weigel, S.J., *Contemporaneous Protestantism and Paul Tillich: Theol. Studies* XI (1950), 177–202; Id., *Recent Protestant Theology: ibid.,* XIV (1953), 573–585; G. Tavard, A.A., *The Unconditional Concern. The Theology of Paul Tillich: Thought,* XXVIII (1953), 234–246.

Second, Tillich has achieved his system in the only way it could be realized. He takes an ontological approach to his task. . . . This is undoubtedly a new note in recent Protestant theology. Tillich's ontology is neither Platonic nor Scholastic; it is existentialist, but it is a formal ontology and it is chosen deliberately and consciously.

Third, Tillich is original. He is indebted to many theologians: Kähler, Barth, Niebuhr, and others. However, he is not the follower of any one man. He embraces positions which are typical of other theologians but his stand is bigger and frequently not to the taste of the theologians whose thought he has absorbed. . . . The thing that must be stressed is his positive doctrine that theology is the rational effort to unite humanly and organically the data of revelation. . . .

Revelation for Tillich is God's self-manifestation to man. This manifestation is through existentialist encounter and it is immediate. God is presented to us under two aspects. First of all, God ontologically is the ground of being, the *prius* of all thought and reality, the unconditioned "no-thing" to which all things must be referred. Concerning this God we can think and express ourselves only symbolically, for human conceptions are utterly inept to deal with this primal matrix of reality. Concepts can and must be used by the theologian, but they must be used in a "method of correlation." This method demands that the doctrine cohere with the data of the history of revelation, be consistent logically with all the rest of theology, be relevant definitely to all man's concerns as these derive from his total and actual experience.

Second, on the phenomenological side, God is the object of man's ultimate concern — not really the object but rather the first subject. What concerns man ultimately, that is divine and that is the exclusive phenomenological norm for theology. Where reality is considered in obedience to concerns less than ultimate, we have no theology and whatever is said in terms of ultimate human concern is *eo ipso* theology. (It is not necessarily good theology, but it belongs to the theological plane of human thought.)

There is a negative consequence of this positive, ultimate theological principle. In line with Barth's thinking but not identical with it, natural theology for Tillich is an unhappy delusion; for it is a complex of fallacious reasonings. The attempt to prove the "existence" of God or the immortality of the soul involves a logical impossibility. . . .

On last analysis, God is reached existentially, aconceptually and immediately by man. But that is hardly the full statement of the matter. Man is a creature of history and community, so that God's self-revelation is made socially and in history through progressive stages. The fuller revelation of God demands a *kairos,* an apt historical moment, in which the reality of God is experienced in a peculiar way. Consequently, Tillich does not refer immediately to man's personal and individual experience of God for his theological construction. Individual experience is only a sharing in the continuous solidarity of the corporate human achievement of God. Individual experience is a carrier of total human experience and so individual experience is a medium but not the source for theological investigation. The specific content of historically progressive revelation, carried by experiencing persons, is given to us in three ways: first, in the Scriptures; second, in the continuous life of the Church; third, in the cultural postulates of communities. These are the three sources from which the theologian derives the data relevant to what concerns man ultimately.

Is God personal in this theology? Tillich considers the question to be a pseudo-question. God is suprapersonal. He cannot be called properly either personal or impersonal. Such categories are finite and natural and therefore useless in a discussion of the reality of God, though symbolically the divinity should be described as personal; for only such description makes God significant for man's ultimate concern. However, such a description is only a pointer to the numinous, not a statement about his inner reality.

Is God triune? He is if we mean that the human preoccupations with power, justice, and love have their ultimate answer in the one ground of being. However, the Trinity is not a metaphysical statement concerning God but only a phenomenological statement about man in terms of his ultimate concern which drives him to meet his last ground in mortal and sinful anxiety.

This encounter is epistemologically a peculiar thing, though historically quite common. It is not natural in the sense that it conforms to the structure of judgment whereby we luminously synthesize the events which make up the finite order. Nor is it an elevation of man into the order of divine reality. This latter notion, absolutely basic in the Catholic notion of the supernatural, is rejected by Tillich as blasphemous and absurd unless taken symbolically. Man reaches God because man is hounded by anxiety.

This anguish has three drives: death, which must overcome life inevitably; guilt, which witnesses man's estrangement from the being he would be; skepticism, which hopelessly seeks for an ultimate truth whereby his existence can become meaningful. When fear of death, guilt, and skepticism attack man in their most formidable and final strength, man sees that it *is he* who fears, so that extreme fear itself affirms existence and, therefore, meaning and justification. In the ground of being there is power, meaning, justice, and love. This is the self-revelation of being-itself, which is another Tillichian word for God. The phenomenal subject who is a finite, guilt-ridden man is thus shown to be rooted in an ontological subject greater than he. Man's being (which really means his existence) is a participation of an existence inconceivably transcending the phenomenally subject. The recognition of this truth is not essential knowledge, i.e., through conceptual categories. . . .

The ultimate subject, the ground of existence, is not contemplated; it is only existentially apperceived as illuminating the being of man. This experience is totally grasping but not a bizarre transport.

Is this the God of theism? No, this is the God above and beyond theism. The God of theism can and should be doubted, and in that doubt through existential reflection, the God beyond theism reveals himself.

Is not this solipsistic subjectivism? No, for the existentialist reflection can only be produced by a *kairos,* an historical moment which by its structure is social and in history and society spontaneously induces the reflection. True, nature alone can lead man to revelation, but it is a man conditioned by culture. The more usual ways toward revelation involve more than a consideration of nature. Some men come to it by moral endeavor which, because of the human situation, is never truly successful but only ambiguous. Some men meet revelation in social history either by immediate contact with a man who has achieved revelation or by the recorded witness to revelation which is the Bible. The majority find it in the life of the Church which is a concrete community under the impact of the Bible message.

Here we have the newer Protestant conception of the Bible. Its propositions are not the revelation, which is carried only by experience, original or dependent. In the Scriptures witness is given to the original experience, which as a stimulus excites a similar experience in others who thus depend on the revelation of others. Hence, the Scriptures are pointers whereby the reader can be led to the encounter with the self-revealing God. The Bible considered as a collection of propositions can be called revelation only in an improper sense; for revelation is always an existential experience. . . .

All that we have stated so far belongs to the propaedeutic of theology. It does not offer us a doctrine, but only the loci and rules for the formulation of doctrine. The data of doctrine Tillich derives according to the principles already cited. The teaching of the Scriptures in so far as it has impact on the continuous life of the Church, made manifest in the perennial vital tradition, is datum. Consequently, Tillich sincerely and enthusiastically holds the Apostles' and Nicene creeds. He believes in God the Father, Creator of Heaven and Earth. He believes in Jesus Christ as the only Son of God. He believes in the Holy Ghost as proceeding from the Father and the Son. He believes in the holy Catholic Church. He even has no difficulty in believing in the assumption of the Virgin Mary. However, here is the rub. He believes that these are symbolic statements. Literally understood, they are for Tillich nonsense or blasphemy.

It is this capacity for affirmation and negation which makes Tillich simultaneously fascinating and frightening. Everything is affirmed and yet everything is denied. This fact does not escape Professor Tillich, and he considers it the proper use of the theory of analogy, which is the only way in which we can speak of the divine, the exclusive object-subject of theology. Analogy affirms and denies, and only in and through analogy can we speak seriously and significantly of God. . . .

What is the essence of Christianity, which from what has been said must not be identified adequately either with Catholicism or Protestantism? It is New Being. This term is the pure essence of Tillich's theology. For a Catholic reader the term can be puzzling. It inescapably brings up the doctrine of Paul from which the term is borrowed, and it also suggests Thomistic ontology. Of course, Tillich wishes the term to be both Pauline and ontological, but the ontology is not Thomistic. It is existentialist. There is no pretense of giving us a system of categories, abstract and strictly rational. Existentialist ontology is vibrant, living, and immediately relevant to the anguish of existence. To be means to exist; to exist means to live; to live means to feel the drives, pushes, and pulls which define the human situation.

This is why Tillich's ontology sounds so familiar and yet so strange to Catholic theologians. Their ontology is calmer and less involved with the emotions and feelings of the harassed mortal who thinks. This is why the Tillichian doctrine of analogy is like and unlike that of Thomas. Tillich from the existentialist point of view reduces Thomistic analogy to the only value it can have in an existentialist scheme. It is the device of symbolic expression where the proposition has no rational content.

It is yet significant; for it acts as a pointer to the ultimate existent which is grasped in existentialist awareness that prescinds from the limitations implied in all category systems. . . .

Where does Jesus Christ fit into this scheme? He is the definite answer to the divine-human question. This must be understood correctly. The man Jesus of Nazareth is not the answer. He was a man like all others, with their defects, virtues, shortcomings, and aspirations. To declare him to be God is blasphemy and idolatry. However, with him and in him came the revelation of God rendered definitively luminous in the minds of Christ's disciples who saw in the man Jesus, Jesus as the Christ. It is Jesus as the Christ who definitively reveals God to the world. It is Jesus as the Christ who saves men by showing them man's true response to God. In Jesus as the Christ man rises to the God-dimension of reality, and is thus a New Being. . . .

Because Jesus as the Christ accepted life even when it upset all his own desires and schemes, he rose above the threatening anxieties of human existence. He died indeed, but his existence was in God, and in consequence, he rose from the dead; and all who join themselves to him in his faith, who trust in God when trust itself seems meaningless, become one with him in New Being. This being transcends the finitude of the human situation, ever exposed to inevitable death, loveless loneliness, and meaningless search. . . .

What is Christian life? It is New Being. This means that man, hemmed in by the absolute meaninglessness of existence as seen in its phenomenological dimension, threatened by inevitable non-being because of death, solitary in his estrangement from all things by his individuality, accepts in love and trust the unseen meaning, the abiding existence and the love, which lie at the heart of existence beyond its phenomenological dimension. This is the eschatological aspect of Christianity. This is salvation, produced by faith (i.e., trust) alone. The Christian dogmas of heaven, hell, final resurrection, are not statements concerning physical situations. They are eschatological pointers to New Being. . . . Eschatology is the consideration of man beyond history, not the promise of a new history. . . .

Neeless to say, few if any Protestants will accept completely the Tillich synthesis, but he has shown what Protestantism through evolution now is.

4. J. Macquarrie[1] studies Bultmann's existential approach to God's mighty acts, incarnation, atonement, resurrection. Bultmann sees three elements in the New Testament account of these acts, the mythical, the objec-

[1] John Macquarrie of the University of Glasgow recently published a book on Bultmann, *The Scope of Demythologizing: Bultmann and his Critics* (Harper & Brothers, 1961). This excerpt is from a prior work of his, *An Existentialist Theology, A Comparison of Heidegger and Bultmann* (London: SCM Press Ltd., 1955), pp. 164–182, 189–192.

tive-historical, and the existential-historical. Though he excessively devaluates the second element, he does not entirely eliminate it. But the primacy belongs to the third element, for it makes these acts significant for my existence today.

While Bultmann[2] does not explicitly mention Heidegger's philosophy of history, it is not difficult to show that some such understanding of history underlies his interpretation of New Testament theology. And indeed that is to be expected in the existential approach to theology, in which the theologian goes to the pages of the New Testament, including its historical passages, with the question of human existence in mind. In the first of his two essays on demythologizing, Bultmann describes the world which we meet in the writings of the New Testament.[3] It is essentially the world of Babylonian cosmology — the flat earth surmounted by the inverted bowl of the firmament, and sandwiched between heaven above and the underworld below. Strange invisible powers are at work both in human affairs and natural events, angels from above and demons from below. Miraculous and occult happenings are attributed to their agency — yes, and everyday happenings too. . . .

Bultmann says that the world-view of the New Testament is mythical. No doubt it is, but it would be misleading not to realize that the modern world-view has its myths as well, and

may be perfectly unintelligible to men who live two thousand years after our time. A strang object in the sky is not interpreted now as a sign from the gods, but as a flying saucer. Whether more or less mythical than the world-view of modern men, the world of the New Testament is not our world but a museum of antiquities.

But, of course, it does not therefore follow that the New Testament has nothing to say that is significant today. . . . The story of the ascension, for instance, as narrated in St. Luke's Gospel and the Acts of the Apostles, implies the New Testament world-picture. . . . The problem of demythologizing might be expressed as the problem of disentangling the primary historical from the secondary historical in the New Testament. The primary historical consists of possibilities of existence which are repeatable, present to me today as they were present to others in the past. The central theme of the New Testament is such a possibility — the possibility of forgiveness and the new life which God offers to men in Christ. It is that in the New Testament history which is significant for the existence of modern man, that is to say, a present possibility of decision for him. What Bultmann is striving to do is to spotlight this essential primary historical in the New Testament, to separate it from the now meaningless

[2] Rudolf Bultmann was born in Germany in 1884. He is an outstanding contemporary existentialist theologian. Among his many works are *Theology of the New Testament; Essays: Philosophical and Theological; Jesus and the Word; Jesus Christ and Mythology.*

[3] *Kerygma und Mythos*, I, Hamburg, 1951, pp. 15–16.

secondary historical and so make it a real possibility of decision for man today. And if that be so, his work is not destructive of the historical element in the New Testament, but the reverse. . . .

The Mythical and the Historical. God has acted in a decisive and unique manner in Jesus Christ. That is the foundation of the Christian religion, and because of that it stands on a different level from all human philosophies, actual or possible. But how are the mighty acts to be understood theologically? Bultmann's interpretation seems to depend on the possibility of distinguishing three elements in the New Testament account of these acts of God.

First, there is the mythical element. . . . The mythical is defined by Bultmann as a way of thinking in which the other-worldly and divine are represented as this-worldly and human.[4] . . . He goes on . . . to speak of the flat earth under the vault of the firmament — in other words, the Babylonian cosmology. But this is not myth within the sense of his own formal definition. It is primitive science or primitive world-view, not a description of the divine in terms of this world, but a description of this world itself as these early thinkers imagined it to be.

Having regard for this confusion in Bultmann's usage, we shall have to look for the meaning which he attaches to the term myth not only in his formal definitions but also in the broad way in which he speaks of the mythical. . . . We take it to

[4] *Ibid.,* I, p. 15.

include: (a) what might be called myth proper, the representation of the divine and other-worldly in human and this-worldly terms; (b) everything in the New Testament which implies those first-century concepts which now belong to a world that is no longer, and are not acceptable or intelligible to the modern mind. . . .

A difficulty immediately arises, for who is going to say just what is and what is not acceptable and intelligible to the modern mind? On some matters there might be fairly general agreement. The story of the ascension . . . is literally intelligible only if we accept the Babylonian cosmology, and since we live in the post-Copernican era, it is literally unintelligible to us — though, of course, that is not to deny that it may be intelligible in some other way. There are other matters on which there would be very little agreement. Consider, for instance, the miracles of Jesus. Bultmann apparently rejects them as not acceptable to the modern mind. But that is to ignore the fact that in this scientific age thousands go to Lourdes every year, and that in Protestant Churches also there is a very real interest in what is called spiritual healing. There seems to be nothing unacceptable about it to many modern minds. . . .

The truth is that at this point we perceive in Bultmann's thought not the influence of existentialism but the hang-over of a somewhat old-fashioned liberal modernism. He is still obsessed with the pseudo-scientific view of a closed universe that was popular half a century ago, and anything which does not fit into that tacitly assumed world-picture is, in his view, not acceptable to the modern mind and assigned to the realm of myth. Let us frankly acknowledge that there is myth in the New Testament, in both senses of the term which we described, but Bultmann himself is perhaps too ready to assign to the mythical element in the New Testament narrative events which may really belong to the second element to which we now turn.

This second element we shall call the objective-historical (*Historisch*). The narrative element in the New Testament, as Bultmann acknowledges,[5] is entirely different from the mystical narratives of Greek or Helleistic deities, since it centers in a definite historic person, Jesus of Nazareth. The mighty acts may, therefore, be studied as objective happenings by the scientific historian, as indeed the Apostles' Creed implies when it states that our Lord "suffered under Pontius Pilate." The event is given a definite place in world history.

Among the mighty acts, the cross is the one which can most readily be understood as an objective-historical event. That Jesus aroused opposition by his teaching, that he was betrayed, arrested, tried, and put to death — there is nothing mythical about that, considered as a fact and apart from interpretations of it. It is perfectly intelligible and acceptable as it stands, whether one's world-view is that of the first or the twentieth or any other century. But is theology particularly interested in the objective-historical?

. . . It is precisely in their character as saving events that theology is interested. . . . It is not the objective-historical element in the mighty acts that is of primary importance for theology.

This primacy belongs to the third element, which we shall call the existential-historical (*geschichtlich*). By this we mean that element in them which makes them significant for my existence, that is to say, which sets before me a present possibility. . . . Insofar as the cross and resurrection are saving events and proclaimed as such, they are not past occurrences of world history but open to man as present possibilities — namely, of forgiveness and a new life. They are thus understood as existential-historical happenings. . . .

But does the primacy of the existential-historical for theology mean that we can do without the objective-historical and the mythical altogether? In the New Testament the three elements are all interwoven. Can theology either dispense with any one of them or isolate any one of them?

We begin with the mythical element. . . . While Bultmann also counts much of the record as mythical, he does not deny that it has value, and his aim is to restate its content in a form free from mythical expressions, if that is possible. . . . The myth is therefore to be translated into a statement which concerns my existence. And further, Bultmann thinks that the New Testament itself leads the way in demythologizing, in that it sometimes expresses the significance of the myth for human existence in a form which does not appear to be mythical. . . .

But what about myths of the other type, in which the divine is represented as this-worldly? Can this other type . . . be eliminated?

Bultmann himself seems to concede that we can speak of God's actions only in mythical terms.[6] . . . We can only speak of him by analogy or symbolically in categories drawn from *Vorhandenheit* (objects in nature) or *Existens* (man himself), as when we say that he is the First Cause or that he is our Father in heaven. But already in the use of such symbols we are into the realm of the mythical. . . . It is impossible to get away from such metaphors, as long as we seek to speak directly of God and his acts. Human thinking is such that here myth and symbol are inevitable[7] . . .

Bultmann believes — as every Christian theologian must — that God has acted in Jesus Christ. . . . Yet the presupposition itself can only be expressed in mythical form — as that Jesus Christ is the Son of God, or that God has sent him. We can, never, therefore, eliminate the mythical, and indeed we reach the conclusion that all existential exposition of the Christian faith rests upon an assumption which is only capable of mythical or symbolic expression. . . .

[6] *Ibid.*, I, p. 40.
[7] Even to make such a simple statement of the Christian message as that "God sent his Son" involves (*a*) a symbol drawn from *Vorhandenheit*, the idea of sending or transferring from one place to another; and (*b*) a symbol drawn from *Existenz*, the idea of sonship, a relationship between two human beings.

We turn next to the objective-historical. Can it be eliminated? . . . Bultmann frankly acknowledges that the existential-historical significance of the cross has its origin in the objective-historical event of the crucifixion of Jesus.[8] But he makes it clear that he attaches little importance to the objective-historical happening as such. . . . To preach the cross as saving event is to propagate an illusion unless the origin of that saving event was an actual happening — namely, God's once-for-all act at Calvary. Bultmann, I believe, recognizes this, but tends to obscure it by excessively subordinating the objective-historical to the existential-historical.[9]

[8] *Kerygma und Mythos*, I, p. 43.
[9] The discussion here may seem to require further clarification. We are trying to contrast two possible positions. The first is that of the man who begins from his experience of a saving event as present in the hearing and receiving of the Word in the act of faith, and who infers from that an origin for that event in objective world-history. But he may not be particularly interested to know the precise "how" of that objective event though he believes "that" it took place, for, as Tillich says, "propositions about a past revelation give theoretical information; they have no revelatory power." (*Systematic Theology*, I, p. 141). The second position is that of the man who begins with the assertion that an objective event once occurred, and bases his faith — or his theology — on that. The latter seems to be dependent on the results of historical research in a way in which the former is not, yet the former has not abandoned the objective-historical altogether because, as Bultmann says, Christianity differs from Greek myths in having its origin in an objective event of world-history. But here the guarantee of the once-for-all event in world history is provided by the reality of the present saving event, which posits the once-for-all event as its origin. Both faith and theology are thus liberated from dependence on historical research.

The argument here links up with and reinforces an earlier criticism of Bultmann.[10] It was said that he stripped our Lord of the numinous character which the records assign to him, and represented him as little more than a teacher of practical philosophy, and we contended that this picture of the historic Jesus is inadequate. . . . The existential-historical (the Jesus of faith) presupposes an objective-historical origin (the Jesus of history). . . . That does argue that there must be a greater degree of continuity between the Jesus of history and the Jesus of faith than Bultmann seems willing to allow.[11] . . .

Bultmann . . . appears unable to believe that we can attach any objective-historical meaning to the birth and resurrection stories of the New Testament. Yet since he certainly does attach existential-historical significance to these stories, he must find some objective-historical event as their origin . . . We have on several occasions protested against Bultmann's excessive devaluation of the objective-historical origins of Christian faith. . . . He does not, however, eliminate this element. . . . His aim is not to destroy the historical foundation of our religion, but to exhibit it in its cosmic dimensions as authentic repeatable possibility, significant for the existence of men today. In his own words, it is the case "of a historical Person and his Destiny being raised to eschatological Rank."[12]

5. J. A. T. Robinson[1] wonders whether the traditional language of a God that came in from outside is relevant, if Christianity is to be meaningful to men of today. He asks: Must Christianity be "supranaturalist"? "mythological"? "religious"? He believes we should break with traditional thinking and move to a position "beyond naturalism and supranaturalism" in our thinking about God and Christ.

Up There or Out There? The Bible speaks of a God "up there." No doubt its picture of a three-decker universe, of "the heaven above, the earth be-

[10] Did Jesus have no consciousness of being the Messiah? Was there no reflection of such a consciousness in his teaching? . . . These questions are surely not unimportant, but Bultmann does not seem to take them very seriously. They are somewhat dogmatically brushed aside, and it is asserted that Jesus had no consciousness of being the Messiah . . . His negative attitude to these questions compared with his preoccupation with the existentialist elements in the teaching of Jesus suggests that Bultmann may be unconsciously biased in his presentation because of the influence of existentialism in his thought.

[11] It appears to me that as soon as the historian admits the objective-historical real-ity of the figure of Jesus, he must also admit that he was a big enough figure to found the Christian religion — or to put the same thing in another way, he must recognize an objective historical which can support the weight of the existential-historical.

[12] *Theologie des Neuen Testaments*, I, 1948, p. 301.

[1] John A. T. Robinson, Bishop of Woolwich (1919–   ) is the author of *Liturgy Coming to Life* and *On Being the Church in the World*. This excerpt is from the book that has stirred up immense discussion most everywhere, *Honest to God* (Philadelphia: The Westminster Press, 1963), pp. 24, 29–37, 64–70.

neath and the waters under the earth" was once taken quite literally. . . . Even such an educated man of the world as Luke can express the conviction of Christ's ascension . . . in the crudest terms of being "lifted up" into heaven, there to sit down at the right hand of the Most High[2]. . . . Moreover, it is the most mature theologians of the New Testament, John and the later Paul, who write most uninhibitedly of this "going up" and "coming down."[3]

For the New Testament writers the idea of a God "up there" created no embarrassment — because it had not yet become a difficulty. For us too it creates little embarrassment — because, for the most part, it has ceased to be a difficulty. . . . *For in place of a God who is literally or physically "up there" we have accepted, as part of our mental furniture, a God who is spiritually or metaphysically "out there"* . . . The coming of the space-age has destroyed this crude projection of God — and for that we should be grateful. For if God is "beyond," he is not *literally* beyond anything.

But the idea of a God spiritually or metaphysically "out there" dies very much harder. . . . Every one of us lives with some mental picture of a God "out there," a God who "exists" above and beyond the world he made a God "to" whom we pray and to whom we "go" when we die. . . . This picture of a God "out there" coming to earth like some visitor from outer space underlies every popular presentation of the Christian drama of salvation. . . .

The abandonment of a "God out there" represents a much more radical break than the transition to this concept from that of a God "up there." For this earlier transposition was largely . . . a change in spatial metaphor, important as this undoubtedly was in liberating Christianity from a flat-earth cosmology. But to be asked to give up any idea of a Being "out there" at all will appear to be an outright denial of God. . . .

But suppose such a super-Being "out there" is really only a sophisticated version of the Old Man in the sky?. . . . Suppose the atheists are right . . .? Suppose that all such atheism does is to destroy an idol, and that we can and must go on without a God "out there" at all? Have we seriously faced the possibility that to abandon such an idol may in the future be the only way of making Christianity meaningful . . .? Perhaps after all the Freudians are right, that such a God — the God of traditional popular theology — *is* a projection. . . .

Some Christian Questioners. . . . I know that as a bishop I could happily get on with most of my work without ever being forced to discuss such questions. . . . But they were questions that had long been dogging me. . . . Let me instance three pieces of writing, all brief, which contain ideas that immediately found lodgement when I first read them and which have since proved seminal not only for me but for many of this generation.

The first of these in date for me (though not in composition) was a sermon by Paul Tillich, which appeared in his collection *The Shaking*

[2] Acts 1:9–11.
[3] Jn 3:13; 6:61 f.; Eph 4:9 f.

of the Foundation.[4] It was called "The Depth of Existence" and it opened my eyes to the transformation that seemed to come over so much of the traditional religious symbolism when it was transposed from the heights to the depths. God, Tillich was saying, is not a projection "out there," an Other beyond the skies, of whose existence we have to convince ourselves, but the Ground of our very being.[5] I remember at the time how these words lit up for me. . . . They seemed to speak of God with a new and indestructible relevance and made the traditional language of a God that came in from outside both remote and artificial.

Next, I must register the impact of the now famous passages about "Christianity Without Religion" in Dietrich Bonhoeffer's *Letters and Papers from Prison.*[6] . . . Bonhoeffer was saying . . . suppose men come to feel that they can get along perfectly well without "religion," without any desire for personal salvation, without any sense of sin, without any need of "that hypothesis"? Is Christianity to be confined to those who still have this sense of insufficiency, this "God-shaped blank," or who can be induced to have it? Bonhoeffer's answer was to say that God is deliberately calling us in this twentieth century to a form of Christianity that does not depend on the premise of religion, just as Paul was calling men in the first century to a form of Christianity that did not depend on the premise of circumcision. . . .

Then, third, there was an essay which created an almost immediate explosion when it appeared in 1941, though I did not read it in detail till it was translated into English in 1953. This was the manifesto by Rudolf Bultmann entitled, "New Testament and Mythology."[7]

Once more Bultmann seemed to be putting a finger on something very near the quick of the gospel message. For when he spoke of the "mythological" element in the New Testament he was really referring to all the language which seeks to characterize the gospel history as *more* than bare history like any other history. . . . And his contention was that this whole element is unintelligible jargon to the modern man. In order to express the "trans-historical" character of the historical event of Jesus of Nazareth, the New Testament writers used the "mythological" language of pre-existence, incarnation, ascent and descent, miraculous intervention, cosmic catastrophe, and so on, which, according to Bultmann, make sense only on a now completely antiquated world-view. . . . The relevance of Bultmann's analysis and of his program of "de-mythologizing" to the whole question of God "out there" from which we started is obvious enough. If he is right, the entire conception of a supernatural order which invades and "perforates"[8] this one must be abandoned.

---

[4] Published in England in 1949 and now available in a Pelican edition (1962).

[5] *Op. cit.*, pp. 63 ff. (Pelican edition).

[6] Ed. E. Bethge (1953; 2nd ed. — to which all references are made — 1956). The American edition is entitled *Prisoner for God.*

[7] *Kerygma and Myth* (ed. H. W. Bartsch), Vol. i, pp. 1–44.

[8] The phrase as used by Bultmann in a subsequent and more popular presentation of his thesis, *Jesus Christ and Mythology* (1960), p. 15.

But if so, what do we mean by God, by revelation, and what becomes of Christianity?

Must Christianity be "Supranaturalist?" Traditional Christian theology has been based upon the proofs for the existence of God. . . . We must start the other way round. God is, by definition, ultimate reality. And one cannot argue whether ultimate reality *exists.* . . . Thus the fundamental theological question consists not in establishing the "existence" of God as a separate entity but in pressing through in ultimate concern to what Tillich calls "the ground of our being." The traditional formulation of Christianity, he says, has been in terms of what he calls "supranaturalism." . . . God is posited as "the highest Being" — out there, above and beyond this world, existing in his own right alongside and over against creation.[9] . . .

This way of thinking . . . *is* criticized by those who reject this supranaturalist position as a rejection of Christianity. . . . Professor Julian Huxley expressly contrasts "dualistic supranaturalism" with "unitary naturalism."[10] The existence of God as a separate entity can, he says, be dismissed as superfluous; for the world may be explained just as adequately without positing such a Being. . . . Any notion that God really exists "out there" must be dismissed: "gods are peripheral phenomena produced by evolution."[11] . . . True religion . . . consists in harmonizing oneself with the evolutionary process as it develops

ever higher forms of self-consciousness.

"Naturalism" as a philosophy of life is clearly and consciously an attack on Christianity. . . . The real question is how far Christianity is identical with, or ultimately committed to, this "supranaturalist" way of thinking.

Must Christianity be "Mythological"? . . . The center of today's debate is concerned with . . . how far Christianity is committed to a mythological, or supranaturalist, picture of the universe at all. Is it necessary for the biblical faith to be expressed in terms of this world-view . . .? Bultmann . . . answers boldly, "There is nothing specifically Christian in the mythical view of the world as such. It is simply the cosmology of a pre-scientific age"[12] The New Testament . . . language is not, properly speaking, describing a supernatural transaction of any kind but is an attempt to express the real depth, dimension, and significance of the *historical* event of Jesus Christ. . . . The transcendental significance of the historical event is "objectivized" as a supranatural transaction. . . .

Must Christianity be "Religious?" What does Bonhoeffer mean by this startling paradox of a non-religious understanding of God?[13] . . . Bonhoeffer speaks of the God of "religion"

---

[9] *The Courage to Be* (1952), p. 175.
[10] *The Observer,* Sunday, July 17, 1960, p. 17.
[11] *Ibid.*

[12] *Kerygma and Myth,* Vol. i, p. 3.
[13] I have made no attempt to give a balanced picture of Bonhoeffer's theology as a whole, which cannot be done by concentrating, as I have been compelled to do, on this final flowering. See J. D. Godsey, *The Theology of Dietrich Bonhoeffer* (1960); E. Bethge, "The Challenge of Dietrich Bonhoeffer's Life and Theology," *Chicago Theological Seminary Register,* Vol. li (Feb. 1961), pp. 1–38 (for the best brief introduction); *The Place of Bonhoeffer* (ed. Martin E. Marty, 1963).

as a *deus ex machina*. He must be "there" to provide the answers and explanations beyond the point at which our understanding or our capacities fail. But such a God is being pushed further and further back as the tide of secular studies advances. In science, in politics, in ethics the need is no longer felt for such a stop-gap or long-stop; he is not required in order to guarantee anything, to solve anything, or in any way to come to the rescue.

. . . *The Man for Others. Christmas and Truth* . . . Traditional Christology has worked with a frankly supranaturalist scheme. . . . Still the traditional supranaturalistic way of describing the Incarnation almost inevitably suggests that Jesus was really God almighty walking about on earth, dressed up as a man. Jesus was not a man born and bred — He was God for a limited period taking part in a charade. He looked like a man, he talked like a man, he felt like a man, but underneath he was God dressed up — like Father Christmas. However guardedly it may be stated, the traditional view leaves the impression that God took a space trip and arrived on this planet in the form of a man. Jesus was not really one of us; but through the miracle of the Virgin Birth he contrived to be born so as to appear one of us. Really he came from outside. . . .

But suppose the whole notion of "a God" who "visits" the earth in the person of "his Son" is as mythical as the prince in the fairy story? Suppose there is no realm "out there" from which the "Man from heaven" arrives? Suppose the Christmas myth (the invasion of "this side" by "the other side") — as opposed to the Christmas history (the birth of the man Jesus of Nazareth) — has to go? Are we prepared for that? Or are we to cling here to this last vestige of the mythological or metaphysical world-view as the only garb in which to clothe story with power to touch the imagination? Cannot perhaps the supranaturalist scheme survive at least as part of the "magic" of Christmas?

Yes, indeed, it can survive — as myth. . . . As Christmas becomes a pretty story, naturalism — the attempt to explain Christ, like everything else, on humanistic presuppositions — is left in possession of the field as the only alternative with any claim to the allegiance of intelligent man. . . . To do it justice, let us then take the naturalistic interpretation of Christ at its highest and most positive. This has even been ready to use the epithet "divine" of Jesus — in the sense that he was the most Godlike man that ever lived. . . . According to this view, the divine is simply the human raised to the power of "x". . . . Yet . . . modern humanistic naturalism has found less and less need to speak of Jesus as in any sense "divine." The belief that we are at this point and in this person in touch with *God* has increasingly been left to the religious minority that can still accept the old mythology . . . as true.

6. **E. L. Mascall**[1] studies the secularized theology of Bishop Robinson, Dr. Van Buren, Dr. Harvey Cox and others. He concludes that they seriously misjudge the nature of the present situation, offer totally inadequate remedies for its ills and almost completely ignore the resources that are waiting to be explored in the classical Christian tradition.

Reflections on the "Honest To God" Debate. The debate which thrust itself into the arena of general public interest with the appearance of the Bishop of Woolwich's famous little paperback *Honest to God* is, I believe, in essence simply a manifestation in the contemporary setting of scientific technology and industrialist democracy, of an activity in which the Church has been continually engaged, with varying success, throughout her history. . . .

Christians, of all people, ought not to be afraid to face facts. And the basic fact is that the "Secular City" is here. Dr. Harvey Cox's remarkable book with that title, in spite of a great deal that seems to me to be unsatisfactory in both its evaluations and its policy-program, gives a most striking picture of the way in which, under a vast variety of different forms, the same basic fact of secularization governs the life of all our modern urban technopolitan cultures. Father Karl Rahner[2] and Father Charles Davis[3]

have eloquently insisted that . . . the acceptance of this situation as God's will for the contemporary Church is a must that should be undertaken, not grudgingly or regretfully, but joyfully and constructively. . . .

The secularization of modern society thus makes the Church's evangelistic task very different from what it has been in the past and it makes it in many ways much more difficult. The difference can be seen when we reflect on the fact that, in the early Church, the chief error that had to be combated, and the chief sin into which unstable Christians were likely to lapse, was idolatry. Men would worship anything that was going. . . . Today the difficulty is in getting them to understand that there is anything to worship at all. . . . Today it is the people, as much as the philosopher, that considers all religions equally false. . . .

It is against this background that we must try to assess the movement typified in various ways by the Bishop of Woolwich in *Honest to God,* by Dr. Paul van Buren in *The Secular Meaning of the Gospel,* and, less wholeheartedly, by Dr. Harvey Cox in *The Secular City.* . . .

The Bishop and Dr. van Buren differ in many ways from each other, but they share the conviction that it is hopeless to try to persuade twentieth-century men and women to

[1] Eric Lionel Mascall is an Oxford University Lecturer in the Philosophy of Religion and a Priest of the Oratory of the Good Shepherd. Among his works are *He Who Is; Existence and Analogy;* and *Christ, The Christian And The Church.* This excerpt is from *Thought,* the Fordham University Quarterly (New York: Fordham University Press, 1966), pp. 181–197.

[2] *Mission and Grace,* I, pp. 3 ff.

[3] In his F. D. Maurice Lectures of 1966 at King's College, London, shortly to be published.

accept the Christian religion in anything like its traditional form. They appear to differ on the question whether some new, secularized type of Christian apologetic is desirable or feasible. The Bishop clearly thinks it is and tries to construct it; Dr. van Buren, however, explicitly says he is concerned not with modern man who is outside the Church but with modern man who is inside the Church, more or less, and is wondering what he is doing there.[4] They are, however, both agreed that the secularist outlook of modern man — the outlook that is concerned simply with the world that our senses disclose to us in the brief span of time that stretches for each of us from the womb to the death bed — is correct or at any rate inevitable.

Neither of them thinks of questioning whether the outlook of modern man is false or inadequate; each of them, though in different ways (and the Bishop less consistently than Dr. van Buren), offers a reinterpretation of Christianity in secularist terms which it is hoped that modern man, outside or inside the Church, will find it easy to accept. Dr. van Buren, who appears to have been captivated by the philosophy of linguistic empiricism just at the time when philosophers are beginning to lose faith in it,[5] shows remarkable skill in producing ingenious, if not always convincing, formulas which are alleged to be logically, though secularistically, equivalent to the sentences of the Bible and classical theology, though one is left wondering what he would make of such a state-

ment as that of Paul that "if in this life alone we have hope of Christ we are of all men most miserable."[6]

What chiefly stands out from this policy of "reductionism," as it has been called, is the extreme anxiety of the writers to hold on to the traditional formulas of Christianity (or at any rate to some of them), even when it has been decided that the traditional interpretation of them is no longer acceptable. . . . The classical Christian formulas were intended to have factual content; to describe the substitution of a nonfactual content as "interpretation" seems to be a sheer misuse of words. . . . This whole question has been very well dealt with in Dr. Hugo Meynell's book, *Sense, Nonsense and Christianity*.

With the desire of the secularizers of Christianity to address modern man, whether inside or outside the Church, in a way that he will find intelligible and relevant it is impossible not to sympathize if one is a Christian at all, but there is something remarkably naïve about the way in which they set themselves to the task. It is taken by them as axiomatic that the outlook of secularized man is to be accepted without question, and that if the Christian faith is to survive at all it must somehow or other be forced into line with it; it seems never to occur to them to ask whether the outlook of secularized man may need to be radically transformed if it is to become compatible with the Christian religion. . . .

In such a situation as this it is a perfect godsend to the secularizers to

---

[4] *The Secular Meaning of the Gospel.*
[5] Cf. the symposium *Clarity Is Not Enough*, edited by Dr. H. D. Lewis.

[6] 1 Cor 15:19.

find ready to hand a radically unintellectual version of Christianity in the writings of Dr. Rudolf Bultmann. Three main elements can be distinquished in Bultmann's theology and they are all equally welcome to the secularizers. There is first an almost complete skepticism about the historicity of the gospel narratives, resulting in the conclusion that all we can really know about Jesus is that he existed and was crucified; the alleged ground for this is the application of the method of Form-Criticism to New Testament study. Then there is an obstinate disbelief in the supernatural, whether in the life of Jesus or anywhere else; this is vaguely supposed to be somehow connected with the development of modern science. Third, there is a deep-seated prejudice against any emphasis being laid on the use of the intellect in religion; this leads to the introduction of the existentialist philosophy of Heidegger as the only respectable matrix for Christian theology. It is indeed only the introduction of this third element that salvages anything of Christianity from the ravages of the first two. When traditional belief has collapsed in sin and shame under the twin onslaught of form-criticism and science, a Second Adam comes to the fight and to the rescue in the shape of existentialism, with the comforting news that Christianity does not consist in believing anything; all we have to do is make existential decisions in response to the preaching of the *kerygma*, and questions of truth and falsehood simply do not arise. It is perhaps interesting to note that, for Dr. van

Buren, the philosophical Second Adam comes not in the shape of existentialism but in the more Anglo-Saxon guise of linguistic analysis, but the result is much the same. However incompatible the two may be as philosophical doctrines, they have in common the blessed characteristic of having no place for theological assertions. For existentialism theological assertions are irrelevant, for linguistic analysis they are meaningless; by both they are rejected, and that is what really matters.

Which of the three Bultmannian elements is taken by a secularizer as primary will no doubt depend on his background and interests. . . Most theologians, however, outside the Roman Communion have been formed chiefly by biblical study and it will therefore be well to pay a little attention to the biblical aspect. And here it needs to be said quite plainly that the skeptical conclusions of the more extreme formcritical scholars have been given much more weight than they deserve.[7] . . . I am not, however, a New Testament scholar and it was easy to write off my arguments as those of an unqualified amateur. I have, therefore, been interested and encouraged to find my main theme argued, quite independently and with a great wealth of illustration from biblical material by two scholars whose competence in the New Testament field is unquestioned. These are the two professional brothers, R. P. D. and Anthony Hanson,

[7] For an up-to-date and balanced assessment of the new movements in biblical study I would heartily recommend *Apologetics and the Biblical Christ* by Fr. Avery Dulles, S.J.

who contributed the central essays to the symposium *Vindications,* edited by the latter. One of the most illuminating passages is that in which Dr. R. P. D. Hanson . . . convicted the extreme form critics of "a scepticism about historical evidence which is not apparently shared by contemporary students of ancient history" . . . "But," he continues, "strongest of all the motives for historical scepticism in the minds of New Testament scholars has been the Lutheran distrust of the search for an objective basis for faith. It should be remembered that the vast majority of early form-critics were Lutherans, and the majority of leading form-critics still are Lutherans."[8]

It is painful to have to make such a point as this in these ecumenical days, but it is nevertheless necessary. The tendency to treat religion as simply a matter of man's inner consciousness and of his personal confrontation by God is deeply rooted in many types of Protestantism. . . . It is significant that Mr. David E. Jenkins in his brilliant little book *Guide to the Debate about God* has seen the chief source of modern secularized Christianity to be the writings of Schleiermacher. . . .

There are many halfway houses on the road to a completely secularized Christianity, and one of these is provided by the Bishop of Woolwich's mysterious formula that, while we must not talk about "a personal God" we must say that God (whom the Bishop defines as "ultimate reality") is personal. Some words of Dr. A. M. Farrer's seem to me to be very

illuminating here. "It is a popular attitude nowadays (he writes) even with professed believers to wallow in theological indecision and in particular to refuse to affirm anything about the personal nature of God. But if belief does not assert that everywhere and in all things we meet a sovereign, holy, and blessed will, then what in the world does it assert? If we don't mean this, let us confess ourselves atheists and stop confusing the public mind."[9] . . .

It is indeed true that the immediate concern of every individual man must be with the decisions that he has to make and the attitude that he is going to adopt. But . . . it is not sufficient for him to secularize his theology; it is also essential that he shall have a theology of the secular, that is to say that he must have a reasoned and coherent view, based upon the Christian revelation, of the world as a whole and of its origin, its resources, and its destiny.

He must, therefore, not deny the concept of the supernatural and devise a purely natural version of Christianity to take its place; there is laid upon him the far more arduous task of working out in the conditions of his own time and place the appropriate relation between the two orders. He is called, not to naturalize the supernatural but to supernaturalize the natural. . . .

The intentions of the Christian secularizers are no doubt excellent, but, objectively considered, their program verges, as I see it, closely upon apostasy. And for all their attacks

---

[8] *Op. cit.,* pp. 63–65.

[9] *A Science of God?,* pp. 92–93.

upon ecclesiasticism, institutionalism, clericalism, and the like, it amounts to a desperate attempt at survival at any price. . . .

But is there, we may inquire in conclusion, any prophet of our time who can point a way out from this absorption of the supernatural into the secular, this substitution of man for God as the primary object of religion. . . ? If there is, I would suggest that his name is Pierre Teilhard de Chardin. . . . He appears to have been more successful than any other thinker of our time in combining, perfectly naturally and without any intellectual strain, the insights of traditional Christianity and of modern physical and biological science. . . .

I wish, therefore, in conclusion to make it quite plain what my quarrel with them is. I believe that they seriously misjudge the nature of the present situation, that they offer totally inadequate remedies for its ills and that they almost completely ignore the resources that are waiting to be explored in the classical Christian tradition. In support of this judgment I may perhaps be permitted to refer to [my] book.[10] . . . The secularizers have . . . had something of a *succés de scandale,* but there are already indicators, of which the writings of Mr. David Jenkins and the two Professors Hanson are examples, that the tide is beginning to turn.

In a work which the Bishop of Woolwich has described as "the most significant constructive contribution yet made by a British writer to a theology of the secular" . . . the author writes: "The background for my image of modern man is the Germany of the pre-war years, and that of the Third Reich and the brutality and terror of the Nazi regime."[11] As it is now more than twenty years since the downfall of the Nazi regimes . . . there would seem to be a good deal of point in Mr. Alasdair MacIntyre's contention that to rely upon writers such as Bonhoeffer for guidance today is really to flee from reality. "Bonhoeffer's Christianity (wrote MacIntyre) is, then, intelligibile only in one sort of context. Outside that context it lacks precisely any specific differentia from the way of life of sensitive generous liberals. It does not issue in atheism as the conclusion of an argument (as Bultmann's theology does), and it does not present atheism in theological language (as Tillich's theology does), but it fails in the task for which it was designed and in our sort of society it becomes a form of practical atheism, for it clothes ordinary liberal forms of life with the romantic unreality of a catacombic vocabulary.[12] MacIntyre may perhaps be drawing from the writings of Bultmann and Tillich implications that they themselves would not accept, but I think he is fundamentally correct in his suggestion that the secularizers are nothing like as contemporary in their outlook as they imagine. Such a verdict might not cause very much distress to a traditionalist, but to a modern secularizer it is a sentence of death.

---

[10] *The Secularization of Christianity* (New York: Holt, Rinehart and Winston, 1966).

[11] R. Gregor Smith, *Secular Christianity,* p. 15.

[12] *The Honest to God Debate,* p. 222.

7. **T. J. J. Altizer**[1] **sketches a radical Christian's view of the death of God. To confess the death of God is to speak of an actual and real event that has actually happened both in a cosmic and in a historical sense. The radical Christian proclaims that God has actually died in Christ to his transcendent epiphany. Faith can name this movement as the metamorphosis of God into Satan, as God empties himself of his original power and glory.**

The Death of God. What can it mean to speak of the death of God? . . . First, we must recognize that the proclamation of the death of God is a Christian confession of faith. For to know that God is dead is to know the God who died in Jesus Christ, the God who passed through what Blake symbolically named as "Self-Annihilation" or Hegel dialectically conceived as the negation of negation. Only the Christian can truly speak of the death of God, because the Christian alone knows the God who negates himself in his own revelatory and redemptive acts. Just as a purely religious apprehension of deity must know a God who is transcendent and beyond, so likewise a purely rational and non-dialectical conception of deity must know a God who is impassive and unmoving, or self-enclosed in his own Being. Neither the religious believer nor the non-dialectical thinker can grasp the God

[1] Thomas J. J. Altizer is a native of Cambridge, Mass, and an Episcopalian layman. He received the degree of A.B., A.M., and Ph.D. at the University of Chicago, and since 1961 has been Associate Professor of Bible and Religion at Emory University, Atlanta, Georgia. Among his works are *Mircea Eliade and the Dialectic of the Sacred* and *Oriental Mysticism and Biblical Eschatology.* This excerpt is from his book, *The Gospel of Christian Atheism* (Philadelphia: The Westminster Press, 1966), pp. 102–120.

whose actuality and movement derives from his own acts of self-negation. Thus it is only the radical, or the profane, or the nonreligious Christian who knows that God has ceased to be the active and real in his pre-incarnate or primordial reality. . . .

To confess the death of God is to speak of an actual and real event, not perhaps an event occurring in a single moment of time or history, but notwithstanding this reservation an event that has actually happened in both a cosmic and a historical sense. There should be no confusion deriving from the mistaken assumption that such a confession refers to an eclipse of God or a withdrawal of God from either history or the creation. Rather, an authentic language speaking about the death of God must inevitably be speaking about the death of God himself. The radical Christian proclaims that God has actually died in Christ, that this death is both a historical and a cosmic event, and, as such, it is a final and irrevocable event, which cannot be reversed by a subsequent religious or cosmic movement. True, a religious reversal of the death of God has indeed occurred in history, is present in the religious expressions of Christianity, and is now receding into the mist of an archaic, if not soon to be forgotten, past. But such a religious reversal cannot annul the event of the death of God; it cannot recover the living God of the old convenant, nor can it reverse or bring to an end the progressive descent of Spirit into flesh. . . .

Once again we must attempt to draw a distinction between the original or primal death of God in Christ and the actualization or historical realization of his death throughout the whole gamut of human experience. Remembering the radical Christian affirmation that God has fully and totally become incarnate in Christ, we must note that neither the Incarnation nor the Crucifixion can here be understood as isolated and once-and-for-all events; rather, they must be conceived as primary expressions of a forward-moving and eschatological process of redemption, a process embodying a progressive movement of Spirit into flesh. At no point in this process does the incarnate Word or Spirit assume a final and definitive form, just as God himself can never be wholly or simply identified with any given revelatory event or epiphany, if only because the divine process undergoes a continual metamorphosis, ever moving more deeply and more fully toward an eschatological consummation. . . .

Let us openly confess that there is no possibility of our returning to a primitive Christian faith, and that the Christ who can become contemporary to us is neither the original historical Jesus nor the Lord of the Church's earliest proclamation. Given our historical situation in the twilight of Christendom, we have long since died to the possibility of a classical or orthodox Christian belief, and must look upon both the New Testament and early Christianity as exotic and alien forms of religion. . . .

Already we have seen that the modern radical Christian has evolved an apocalyptic and dialectical mode of vision or understanding revolving about an apprehension of the death of God in Christ, and it is just this self-negation or self-annihilation of primordial reality of God which actualizes the metamorphosis of an all-embracing Totality. . . . The radical progressive metamorphosis of Spirit Christian envisions a gradual and into flesh, a divine process continually negating or annihilating itself, as it ever moves forward to an eschatological goal. . . .

If we conceive of the Word or Spirit as moving more and more fully into the body of the profane in response to the self-negation of God in Christ, then we can understand how the Christian God gradually becomes more alien and beyond, receding into a lifeless and oppressive form, until it finally appears as an empty and vacuous nothingness. . . . Let the contemporary Christian rejoice that Christianity has evolved the most alien, the most distant, and the most oppressive deity in history: It is precisely the self-alienation of God from his original redemptive form that has liberated humanity from the transcendent realm, and made possible the total descent of the Word into the fullness of human experience. The God who died in Christ is the God who thereby gradually ceases to be present in a living form, emptying himself of his original life and power, and thereafter receding into an alien and lifeless nothingness. . . .

Once the Christian has been liberated from all attachment to a celestial and transcendent Lord, and has died in Christ to the primordial reality of God, then he can say triumphantly: God is dead! . . . True, every man today who is open to experience knows that God is absent, but only the Christian knows that God is dead, that the death of God is a final and irrevocable event, and that God's death has actualized in our history a new and liberated humanity. . . . The Christian can live and speak by pronouncing the word of God's death, by joyously announcing the "good news" of the death of God, and by greeting the naked reality of our experience as the triumphant realization of the self-negation of God. . . .

Atonement. When the Incarnation and the Crucifixion are understood as dual expressions of a common process, a kenotic or negative process whereby God negates his primordial and transcendent epiphany thereby undergoing a metamorphosis into a new and immanent form, then the incarnate manifestation of Word or Spirit can also be understood as an eschatological consummation of the self-negation of God, extension of the atoning process of the self-annihilation of God throughout the totality of experience. . . .

Already we have seen that faith can name this movement as the metamorphosis of God into Satan, as God empties himself of his original power and glory and progressively becomes

manifest as an alien but oppressive nothingness. We must understand this whole movement as an atoning process, a forward-moving process wherein a vacuous and nameless power of evil becomes increasingly manifest as the dead body of God or Satan. . . .

Yes, God dies in the Crucifixion: therein he fulfills the movement of the Incarnation by totally emptying himself of his primordial sacrality. . . . The Crucifixion is an act of atonement, an act reversing the primordial sacrality of God. . . . Only with the extension of this reversal into every alien sphere will the actualization of the atonement be consummated. . . . Satan must undergo a final metamorphosis into an eschatological epiphany of Christ. . . .

So long as Christianity knows the Crucifixion as a vicarious sacrifice for a totally guilty humanity, as the innocent sacrifice of the eternal Son of God to a just but merciful Father, it can never celebrate the definitive victory of the Crucifixion; for such a redeemed humanity remains in bondage to the transcendent Judge, and must continue to be submissive to his distant and alien authority, ever pleading for mercy when it falls away from his absolute command. . . . Not until the Christian recognizes the Crucifixion as enacting and embodying the self-negation of the sovereign and transcendent Creator can he celebrate an atonement which is the source of the abolition of all confinement and repression. . . .

The radical Christian repudiates the Christian dogma of the resurrection of Christ and his ascension into a celestial and transcendent realm because radical faith revolves about a participation in the Christ who is fully and totally present to us. Speaking in the traditional symbolic language of Christianity, we could say that radical faith transposes the traditional vision of the resurrection into a contemporary vision of the descent into Hell: the crucified Christ does not ascend to a heavenly realm but rather descends ever more fully into darkness and flesh. By this means we can see that the continuing descent of the Word into flesh clearly parallels the historical actualization of the death of God and God's final appearance in our history in a totally alien and lifeless form. . . .

XIII

GOD IN CONTEMPORARY CATHOLIC THEOLOGY

1. J. J. Smith[1] compares Brunner's doctrine concerning the original revelation in creation with Catholic theology on that point. He finds such a close agreement between the two views that it is very difficult for Brunner to maintain a mediating position between Barth and Catholic theology.

Primal Revelation and the Natural Knowledge of God. Protestant and Catholic theologians today are seek-

[1] Joseph J. Smith, S.J., of Loyola House of Studies, Ateneo de Manila, is the author of the article, "Primal Revelation And The Natural Knowledge of God: Brunner and Catholic Theology," which appeared in *Theological Studies,* Vol. 27, September, 1966 (Woodstock, Md.: Theological Studies, Inc.). This excerpt is from that article, pp. 339–357.

ing a more thorough knowledge of each other's thought in an effort to work together toward a more adequate understanding of the revelation given in Christ. At the same time they seek to delimit more clearly the areas of disagreement that separate them. One of these areas is the doctrine concerning the primal revelation and the natural knowledge of God. In this area the Catholic theologian finds a special interest in the position represented by Emil Brunner of Zurich; for Brunner over a period of years has consistently defended a mediate position between that of the earlier Karl Barth and Catholic theology. Moreover, the Catholic theologian can learn much from a study of a position which is at the same time so near and yet so far from his own.

Emil Brunner's doctrine concerning the original revelation in creation has been formulated and polished in controversy with Karl Barth that received its impetus in 1934 from Brunner's *Natur und Gnade* and Barth's response: *Nein! Antwort am Emil Brunner.* In 1937, at the conclusion of *Der Mensch im Widerspruch,* Brunner felt that "the opposition between Barth and me consists mainly in two points: that I, in opposition to Barth, but in harmony with the Scriptures and the Reformers, maintain that God even now is manifest in His creation, and secondly, that I do not view the human existence of man as a bagatelle, but as theologically relevant fact, which can only be understood from the idea of the image of God."[2] . . . Brunner specifies that this primal revelation is still present to us in two forms: in man created according to God's image, and in the created world as the manifestation of the divine power and wisdom. This article will limit itself to a discussion of the second form of the primal revelation.[3]

Created World as Manifestation of God's Power and Wisdom. The whole Christian tradition is unanimous in recognizing a revelation of God in the created world. The Church Fathers, the Scholastics, and the Reformers all insist on this point, because Scripture teaches it beyond the shadow of a doubt.[4] . . . Apart from the Old Testament, he believes that the clear testimony of Paul in his letter to the Romans[5] should be sufficient to convince any Christian. . . . Brunner is aware that creatures veil God as much as, or more than, they reveal him. But the infinite qualitative difference between Creator and creature, the vast chasm that separates them, is no reason for denying what Paul affirms, "that precisely the divinity of God, his invisible nature, his superiority over the world manifests itself in the works of creation.[6] . . . Creation bears the imprint of its Creator because of his creative will and his creative act."[7]

For this reason, Brunner can see no cause for mistrusting or denying the doctrine of the analogy of being. He finds that it has been the commonly held doctrine of the Church from the beginning, and that it expresses nothing else than the fact that it has pleased God to create the world in such a way that it reflects

---

[2] *Der Mensch im Widerspruch* (Zurich, 1937), p. 541.

[3] It is to be noted that in the course of time it has been Barth who has modified his position. In 1950, in Vol. 3, Part 3, of the *Dogmatik, he is willing to admit a* manifestation of God in creation which only the believer can perceive, whose eyes have been opened by the revelation in Christ. Cf. *Dogmatik* 3/3, 58–59; H. Bouillard, *Karl Barth* 3 (Paris, 1957), 131–132.

[4] *Offenbarung und Vernunft,* p. 60.

[5] 1:19 ff.

[6] Cf. *Der Mittler* (Tübingen, 1927), p. 13; *Offenbarung und Vernunft,* p. 64.

[7] *Offenbarung und Vernunft,* p. 68.

"His eternal power and divinity." But, Brunner adds, this does not mean that man actually sees God in creation as he really is. It does mean that creation is an objective vehicle or means for the revelation of God, whether man recognize it as such or not.[8]

But if men do not perceive the objective revelation of God in creation, it is not because they do not possess the subjective capacity to do so. . . . For this purpose God has given him an intellect. Through this special possession of man, the objective "revelation of creation" becomes "general revelation"; for the objective means of revelation and the subjective capacity of knowing are ordered to one another.[9]

And yet . . . man does not truly know God from creation. Brunner insists that man possesses no true natural knowledge of God, that there is no "natural theology." "Rather, man's sin consists precisely in this, that he suppresses the knowledge of God that arises in him through God's revelation, so that the revelation that God has given for a knowledge of himself becomes for man the origin of his idolatry."[10] . . .

There can be no doubt that Paul's affirmations imply that without the revelation in Christ it is extremely difficult or morally impossible for sinful man to arrive at a true knowledge of God from the sole revelation in creation. For this reason, the First Vatican Council affirmed that it is due to the revelation in Christ that the divine realities which are not in themselves inaccessible to human reason can be known by all "without difficulty, with firm certitude, and without mixture of error."[11] . . .

Therefore, in affirming the radical possibility of a correct natural knowledge of God, the Catholic theologian does not "deny by that very fact the reality of sin, or at least its effects in the sphere of our knowledge," as Brunner believes.[12] But . . . he is not necessarily affirming that this possibility was ever activated in history independently of grace.

What he is affirming is that . . . the possibility of the natural knowledge of God is the transcendental condition of the knowledge of faith. "The knowledge of faith demands and implies, as its transcendental condition, a natural knowledge of God, a knowledge proper to man, which most often remains implicit, but is susceptible of rational explicitation."[13] . . .

Thus, the possibility of a knowledge of God in faith demands and implies a double condition: (1) the revelation and grace of Jesus Christ, and (2) the natural ability of the human reason to know God. The first conditions faith as an event; the second is the transcendental condition of faith as *meaning*, and as meaning *for us*.[14] This possibility of a natural knowledge of God constitutes the subjective foundation of the Christian faith as the transcendental condition of the knowledge of faith. . . . It is the in-

---

[8] *Ibid.*, pp. 68–69.
[9] *Ibid.*, p. 69.
[10] *Ibid.*, p. 66.

[11] Denzinger-Schönmetzer, *Enchiridion symbolorum* (32nd ed.; Freiburg, 1963), no. 3005.
[12] *Dogmatik*, 1, 138.
[13] Bouillard, *Karl Barth*, 3, p. 138.
[14] *Ibid.*, p. 103.

ternal condition by means of which man can discern the God of the Bible from idols and acknowledge him without making him an idol.[15] . . .

This does not mean that in the process by which man comes to believe in the Christian faith a natural knowledge of God must chronologically precede the knowledge of faith. In this respect, Brunner's critique of certain Catholic theologians . . . is completely justified.[16] But it means that at least the knowledge of faith implies and contains the rational element of the natural knowledge of God. Naturally, this latter need not be explicitated; it is not required that we possess a reflex consciousness of it; nor is it necessary for it to have been systematized in the form of organized, rational knowledge.[17] But it is essential that this original, implicit seizure of God by the intellect be present and that its explicitation be possible. Otherwise "we would possess no basis for judging the validity of the recognition of a divine revelation in history; nothing would authorize us to affirm that the God of the Bible is our God."[18] . . .

What enables Brunner to give an apparent reasonableness to his insistence on the absolute impossibility for man to acquire a true and valid natural knowledge of God is his excessively exigent definition of "true and valid" knowledge of God. For Brunner, a true knowledge of God must be a knowledge of God as the living, per-

sonal, holy, and merciful Lord and Father precisely as manifested in the Christian revelation. Furthermore, it must be a knowledge which is the abolition of sin.[19] But this is to demand not merely a true knowledge, but a more perfect and complete knowledge. There is here an apparent identification of incomplete knowledge and untrue knowledge. Naturally, there is a vast difference between the knowledge of God resulting from faith in Jesus Christ, and the knowledge of God that can be attained from the primal revelation in and through the created world. The latter tells man nothing of the interior or the triune God, of his definitive attitude toward sinful man, of his redeeming love and mercy. . . . Reason alone cannot establish a friendship between God and man; nor does its light involve vital communion.[20] And yet, though the knowledge of God possible from creation will always remain inadequate (as, however, is all our knowledge of God), it is nevertheless correct, valid, and true. . . .

Brunner appears to take it for granted that any natural knowledge of God from reason proceeds from man's initiative alone, whereas in fact man is always merely the one who reacts to the manifestation of himself initiated by God in creation. For this reason, natural knowledge of God need not be regarded as an autonomous attempt by man's reason to construct for itself and by itself a knowledge of God. . . . It can be the recog-

[15] *Ibid.*, p. 112.

[16] *Natur und Gnade*, p. 33.

[17] L. Malavez, "Le croyant et le philosophe," *Nouvelle revue Théologique*, 82 (1960), 911–912.

[18] Bouillard, *Karl Barth*, 3, 102.

[19] *Natur und Gnade*, p. 19.

[20] M. Corvez, "Foi en Dieu et connaissance naturelle de l'existence de Dieu," *Lumiére et vie*, 14 (1954), p. 20.

nition of the personal God who makes signs to me through his creation.[21] The knowledge that results from the encounter with such a sign is not an abstraction, but the concrete apprehension of God; at least it can be. . . .

Brunner's insight remains true: "The true God can only be known in his descent to us."[22] But this descent occurred, not merely in the revelation in Christ, but in the revelation in creation as well. And, as Brunner also teaches, this revelation is not merely a thing of the past, but is continually present to every man. . . .

Therefore, the final word must be: "Idea of the Good, the First Mover, the Necessary Being, One Superior to being, Universal Principle, Deity without form or name — God of the Patriarchs, God of Moses and Isaiah, Sovereign Master, Awe-inspiring Judge, King of History, Father of Jesus . . . from the one to the other there extends an abyss; and yet it is, or at least it can be, the same God."[23]

In this "at least it can be" lies the difference between Brunner and the Catholic theologian. The latter insists on this "at least, it can be," because the negation of the possibility for the human reason in reaction to the revelation in creation to arrive at a true and valid natural knowledge of God, logically leads to a skepticism in the

domain of religion. If human reason cannot naturally know God without revelation in Christ, how can it know God even with the revelation in Christ? . . .

Actually, it is very difficult for Brunner to maintain a mediating position between Barth and Catholic theology. Once he has admitted an objective revelation in creation to which corresponds in man a subjective capacity to know it, and once he adds to this that despite sin man actually knows enough about God to make his idolatry inexcusable, i.e., to make him responsible, it would seem that he has already admitted with Paul the possibility and the actuality of a natural knowledge of God. When he denies that this is a true and valid knowledge of God, the reader can only ask: How can a knowledge which makes man inexcusable not be a true and valid knowledge? Perhaps it is not an adequate knowledge of God's Name, for it is true that this is only given in the historical revelation in Jesus Christ. Certainly, it is not a saving knowledge which removes sin and brings communion with God, for that too can only be given, after man's fall, by the revelation in Jesus Christ. But if the knowledge makes man inexcusable for his sin, it must be true.

2. G. Moran[1] is concerned with the problem of relating revelation to the unevangelized. He thinks that in the ordinary actions of the unevan-

21 De Lubac, Sur les chemins de Dieu, p. 109; cf. H. D. Robert, "Connaissance et inconnaissance de Dieu, au plan de la raison," in L'Existence de Dieu, pp. 349 ff.
22 Offenbarung und Vernunft, p. 315.
23 De Lubac, op. cit., p. 137.

1 Gabriel Moran, F.S.C., is professor of Philosophy and Theology at De La Salle College, Washington, D. C. This excerpt is from his book, Theology of Revelation (New York: Herder and Herder, 1966), pp. 162–175.

gelized and in their social and religious structures God's grace is at work and his revelation in Christ is experienced albeit implicitly. God lives among his people in the intimacy of a person-to-person relation that penetrates to the heart of man.

Revelation to All the Earth. . . . In the first place, we have discovered in modern times that the unevangelized of the Christian era are not the exception but the majority of mankind. Catholic theology has not advanced a great deal on this point since Thomas proposed for his "man in the woods" that "God would either reveal to him through internal inspiration what had to be believed, or would send some preacher of the faith to him."[2] But as Victor White has remarked, "we know of many millions more men in different sorts of woods than St. Thomas ever imagined."[3] Second, if the case of the unevangelized is not the exception to which God supplies an *ad hoc* solution, it may throw light upon the Christian life as well. "If a man is saved in ignorance of the Christian message, then what happens in his heart must be essentially identical with the justification of the Christian. Any other position, it seems to me, would be heretical. Even the man who is saved apart from the Christian message is justified by faith and baptism."[4]

The supposition of a "primitive revelation" in the naïve form in which it was put forth in an earlier century is hardly credible today.[5] Catholic theology, however, continues to insist that man achieves salvation only in the assent to God supernaturally revealed. The reduction of the number of supernatural truths that would be of minimum necessity for salvation does not come to grips with the real problem which is how a supernatural revelation plays any part at all in the "good pagan's" life. The doctrine of "baptism of desire" as the means to salvation is a statement of the question rather than the answer.

If we were to accept only what the earlier treatises have said on revelation, there would seem little possibility of relating revelation to the unevangelized except by positing a special divine intervention to supply it. On the other hand, the more extensive development of a theology of revelation that we have seen in contemporary Catholic writings has within itself the principles of a solution to this question. This answer is a highly significant one not only in speculative theories on God's salvific will, but also in the immediate practical problems of missionary work and catechetical procedure.

We may take note first of all that Catholic belief predicates a "natural

[2] *De Ver.*, XIV, 11, ad 1.

[3] Victor White, "St. Thomas's Conception of Revelation," in *Dominican Studies*, I (January, 1948), p. 32.

[4] Gregory Baum, " 'Honest to God' and Traditional Theology," in *Ecumenist*, II (May, 1964), p. 67.

[5] See Wilhelm Schmidt, *Primitive Revelation* (St. Louis: B. Herder, 1939), pp. 1–41; Karl Rahner, *Offenbarung und Überlieferung* (Freiburg: Herder, 1965), p. 17; Charles Davis, *Theology for Today* (New York: Sheed and Ward, 1962), p. 117.

revelation of God" in the universe, that is, the possibility of knowing God by the light of reason.[6] . . . The problem of the unevangelized, however, is not resolved by this so-called natural or general revelation of God. The teaching of the Church is that salvation comes through Christ, that is, through a sharing in the revelation that takes place in the consciousness of the risen Lord and is mediated to the world through Church and gospel. This is the heart of the question which needs further examination.

According to Catholic belief, God has established for man an end that gives absolute completion to his nature. . . . If the natural and supernatural are not simply juxtaposed externally, man's nature cannot remain unaffected by the fact that he is living in a supernatural order and that God wills no other end for him than a share in the life of the Trinity.[7] The call of God has been realized in the incarnation such that the attainment of the end is not just a possibility but has actually been accomplished, even though the individual must ratify this by his free decision. In Christ's life and more definitively in his death-resurrection, all of humanity has been assumed into a new relation with God.

The experience which man now has of his own person is not the

same as it would have been in a state of pure nature. Long before the fact of a supernatural order is brought before him as objective knowledge, he has already taken up a position with reference to it because it is a "given" of his concrete, personal structure. There is a remarkable passage in Thomas in which he says that, at the age of reason, "the first thing that occurs to a man to think about, then, is to deliberate about himself. And if he then direct himself to the due end, he will, by means of grace, receive the remission of original sin; whereas if he does not then direct himself to the due end, as far as he is capable of discretion at that particular age, he will sin mortally, through not doing that which is in his power to do."[8] Whatever precisions we would make on this "age of reason," there is a way indicated here which has reference to all people including the unevangelized. Thomas is suggesting that every person is faced with the Christian mystery of revelation in terms which are connatural to him prior to any scriptural or doctrinal instruction.[9]

Man does not stand neutral before God; he must take a position for or against his end which is in fact supernatural. The unevangelized man who seeks God, who holds himself open to the possible revelation of God, who ratifies the entelechy of his concrete existence by moral decisions, has already experienced God's revelation and has already accepted God's grace. The

---

[6] See Denz.-Schön., no. 3004.
[7] See Louis Malavez, "La gratuité du surnaturel," in *Nouvelle revue théologique*, LXXXV (1953), pp. 561–586; Karl Rahner, "Concerning the Relationship between Nature and Grace," *Theological Investigations*, Vol. I, pp. 297–317; J. P. Kenny, "Reflections on Human Nature and the Supernatural," in *Theological Studies*, XIV (March, 1953), pp. 280–287.

[8] *S.T.*, Ia–IIae, q. 89, a. 6, c.
[9] See Avery Dulles, S.J., "The Theology of Revelation," *Theological Studies*, XXV (March, 1964), p. 52.

"signs of revelation" for such a man are the conditions of his own moral life: his weaknesses, his struggling, his ideals which in fact go beyond the purely human. He meets God at those hard edges of experience which can never be transmuted into an extension of himself.

In the context of a supernaturally oriented existence, the most ordinary actions of man's life bear a dimension which is more than natural. Above all, however, in the profound human experiences of trust and love, fidelity and courage, suffering and death, there emerges a relation to an absolute ideal beyond the human even though the individual's expression of it may be badly distorted or poorly articulated.[10] Here God's grace is at work and here God's revelation in Christ is experienced, albeit implicitly. What must not be forgotten by the Christian, therefore, is that those who have never heard of an historical revelation may achieve a more genuine repentance, humility, and sanctity than those who have. The Christian has no reason for pride; he has been chosen not on the basis of merit, but in order to serve as God's witness in bringing to explicit consciousness what has already been accomplished

or is being accomplished by God's grace.

This experience of God's revelation which occurs in man's decision regarding his own person is never an isolated act. . . . There is a constant interchange between men that modern civilization has increased in astounding proportions. . . . The whole social structure becomes the medium of communication between men and a dominant influence in the life of the individual. . . . The anonymous order of the non-personal structure ceases to be morally neutral or of negligible concern.[11] God has redeemed man in his entirety, in the sociability of his nature, and in the "worldliness" of his concerns. By taking hold of man, the Spirit necessarily took hold of man's world.[12] There is a difference, of course, in the degree or kind of revelation that can be mediated by various objects and events in the universe, but the central and indispensable element in every revelatory situation is man, the recipient to whom God addresses himself. . . .

If the social structure in general is capable of entering into the revelatory experience of men, then evidently the religion which men profess can also embody elements of an objectified revelation. . . . Intermingled with the ignorance and failure of human frailty are supernatural moments of grace embedded in the religious structures. . . . Religions undoubtedly vary greatly in their capability of bringing about a genuine relation to God, but

---

[10] See Karl Rahner, "Christianity and Non-Christian Religions," in *The Church. Readings in Theology*, compiled at the Canisianum (New York: P. J. Kenedy and Sons, 1963), pp. 131–132; Urs von Balthasar, *Word and Redemption*, p. 43: "Everything in the created order, with the exception of sin, is enabled through Christ, to be an expression of God, most of all what we would think to be most remote from him: the cross, opprobrium, anguish, death."

[11] See Remy C. Kwant, *Encounter* (Pittsburgh: Duquesne University, 1960), p. 72.

[12] Rom 8:19–23.

precisely which elements are authentic and which are corruptive is not always easy to determine.

What does need unequivocal affirmation is that non-Christian religious experience can bear within itself a genuine though obscured supernatural revelation; that non-Christians are saved not simply in spite of their religion, but by means of their religion insofar as it is a preparatory stage for a definitive revelation; that other great world religions must be part of God's salvific activity and are therefore to be respected and preserved until a better revelation can emerge from these peoples' lives before God.[13]

The foregoing thesis has nothing to do with a bland universalism or religious indifferentism. The Church and every Christian is called as missionary and servant to a world which longs to hear (even though implicitly) the word of the gospel. To this non-Christian world the Church speaks the words which Paul once spoke in Athens: "What you already worship in ignorance, that I am now telling you of."[14] . . . A man cannot form someone else into a Christian, but he can expose the other to the light which can help him to reflect upon the grace-filled depths of his own existence and that of his brothers. . . . With all men and with all religions the Church today must enter into dialogue.[15]

God's revelation does not stand outside man as an object to be known by a special inner light. . . . It is only as a consequence of God's indwelling (which is not to be confused with being located in a container) that there arises an inner light of faith and an outer mediating object. . . .

The study of God's "indwelling," therefore, is not one peripheral question in theology, but the center of theology, the rediscovery of what the Bible and the great theologians have said of the relation of God and man. God lives among his people in the intimacy of a person-to-person relation, in the exchange of knowledge through gestures of love that penetrates to the heart of man.

3. L. Dewart[1] studies the problem of the integration of Christian theistic belief with the everyday experience of contemporary man. He suggests that this integration requires not merely the *demythologization of Scripture* but the more comprehensive *dehellenization of dogma*, and specifically that of the Christian doctrine of God.

[13] See *Constitution on the Church*, ch. II, Art. 16; see also S. T. Balasuriya, "Toward a Wider Ecumenism," in *Ecumenist*, III (January, 1965), p. 24: "We may and must say that the people who are born into the religious and social environment of these religions receive through them a message of hope and life. God who has taken hold of the people in Christ may lead them in this way to actualize the kingdom in their heart, at least to some extent."
[14] Acts 17:23.
[15] See *Declaration on the Relation of the Church to Non-Christian Religions*, Art. 2.
[1] Leslie Dewart of St. Michael's College in the University of Toronto, is the author of *Christianity and Revolution, The Lesson of Cuba*. This excerpt is from his book, *The Future of Belief* (New York: Herder and Herder, 1966), pp. 7–23, 28–29, 37–50, 130–148.

Christian Theism and Contemporary Experience.[2] This book [*The Future of Belief*] attempts to sketch an approach to what may be among the most fundamental theoretical problems which challenge Christianity (and specifically the Catholic Church, with which I shall be predominantly concerned here) in the present age, namely, the problem of integrating Christian theistic belief with the everyday experience of contemporary man. . . .

In brief, the problem is, at its most basic level, whether one can, while complying with the demand that human personality, character, and experience be inwardly integrated, at one and the same time profess the Christian religion *and* perceive human nature and everyday reality as contemporary man typically does. In his assumption that this is a contradiction in terms, Sigmund Freud spoke for modern man. . . .

The trouble with religious theism is that, having once . . . served man as a means of coping with utterly real perplexities, it has perpetuated itself beyond his needs. With increased self-consciousness and increased mastery of the world . . . man can devise more adequate means than religion to grapple with the same problems. . . . But, continues Freud, it can be hoped — in fact, it can be foreseen — that human progress will eventually assert itself. The only future that can be reasonably forecast for the illusions of belief is that the heightening of hu-man consciousness will in due time dispel it. . . .

It is not my intention here to enter into polemics. On the contrary I intend to show that Freud's observations are largely correct. . . . No less unexceptionable a Catholic thinker than Jacques Maritain has, though hardly in so many words, admitted that the Christian morality of beatitude . . . can take the illusionary form described by Freud.[3] . . .

This book advances, first, the suggestion that the integration of Christian belief and contemporary experience must logically begin . . . from — the integration of the *concept* of God with contemporary experience. . . . Tillich's contribution to the cause of bringing the Christian faith to its proper level of contemporary self-awareness cannot be belittled. . . . However, it appears that Tillich did not reach the root of the problem of experience and faith, and that in this precise, if limited sense, his theology is insufficiently radical. . . .

Hence, this book advances, second, the suggestion that the integration of Christian belief and contemporary experience, especially in what concerns the concept of God, could not be successfully attempted by a Christian theology which, however radical and novel in every other respect, assumed any fundamental principle or essential part of that very mode of philosophical enquiry (and particularly the classical epistemologies and metaphysics) on which was erected the concept of God which can no longer be in-

[2] See Chapter XII for Protestant views on this matter, especially the essays by Robinson, Mascall, Altizer. (Editor's note.)

[3] See *Moral Philosophy* (London, 1964), p. 79.

tegrated with contemporary experience. . . . For if the project of integrating faith and contemporary experience is going to be ultimately successful, it must be sufficiently radical. To be sufficiently radical, it must get to the root concept of God. And to be sufficiently radical respecting the conceptualization of God, it must radically depart from the philosophic world-viewing which has given the traditional Christian faith in God a cultural form which no longer serves well that Christian faith.

In one respect, therefore, the thought of Dietrich Bonhoeffer should be considered . . . an improvement over Tillich's basic doctrine. For Bonhoeffer recognized clearly two things: (a) that if, rejecting fideism as well as the dichotomization of faith and experience, we project the integration of Christian faith and contemporary experience, then contemporary experience must be accepted *as given* and *as an integral whole*,[4] and (b) that, therefore, no part of the Christian faith, not even the concept of God, should escape re-examination and re-conceptualization at the most fundamental level.[5] . . .

In the light, thus, of this analysis of some of the difficulties of both

the typically Protestant and the typically Catholic approaches to the problem, this book advances, finally, the suggestion that the basic methodological concept which Christian philosophy might use in order to integrate Christian theism and contemporary experience must be sufficiently comprehensive to deal, beyond the strictly scriptural aspect of the problem, with its dogmatic and historical dimensions.

More concretely, it will be suggested that the integration of theism with today's everyday experience requires not merely the *demythologization of Scripture* but the more comprehensive *dehellenization of dogma,* and specifically that of the Christian doctrine of God. . . . Dehellenization may well be described, without a negative reference to the past, as the conscious historical self-fashioning of the cultural form which Christianity requires *now* for the sake of its *future.* In other words, dehellenization means, in positive terms, the conscious creation of the future of belief. . . .

The Abnormal Underdevelopment of Christian Theism. . . . The Christian religious experience must always take a given cultural form, without which there can be no religious experience at all. Therefore, like every other religious faith, the Christian belief in God is relative to some given *concept* of God: God cannot be believed in unless he be somehow conceived. . . . Consequently, the development of the concept of God is crucially important in the development of Christian dogma. Underdevelopment or inadequate development of theism is the principal form of the unwarranted and

---

[4] This is surely the important principle behind Bonhoeffer's idea of "Christianity without religion."

[5] This is surely the truth that has been inflated by rhetoric in certain circles of the post-Bonhoeffer movement — though a truth which its critics have not always fully recognized. Herbert McCabe's assessment of recent theological debates in this vein introduced much good sense into the discussion, as did Justus George Lawler's "Theology and the uses of history," *Continuum,* IV, 1 (Spring, 1966), 92–101.

inexpedient inadequacy of the Christian faith. . . .

It is possible to allude briefly to what was possibly the single most important factor tending to arrest the development of dogma in general and that of the concept of God very particularly. I refer again to the conclusion of historical research that the catholicization of Christianity from Paul to Augustine necessarily meant the adoption of a hellenistic cultural form. . . . [But] to say that the hellenic form of Christianity is inadequate to the present moment is not in the least to say that it was inadequate in the first four centuries of Christianity. . . .

It must be also understood that if it is much more difficult to dehellenize Christianity than it was to hellenize it, the reason has much less to do with the will and the initiative of Christians than with an intrinsic characteristic of the hellenic form: hellenization naturally and logically tended to lend Christianity the conviction that it should not develop further or transcend its hellenic form. For hellenization introduced into Christianity the ideals of immutability, stability and impassibility as perfections that all Christians and Christianity as a whole should strive for, since these were the typical and central perfections of God himself.[6] . . .

---

[6] And yet stability was by no means the most powerful idea within the culture of Greece herself. Possibly the concept of *ananke*, natural necessity (especially in its mythological form, *moira*, fate) filled that role. But in Greek *speculation* immutability and self-identity were the central properties of divine being. Therefore, they became central to hellenized Christianity, because the idea of God was central to Christianity in the first place.

The development of dogma stimulated and made possible by the hellenization of Christianity meant, from another viewpoint, its petrification. For example, the swifter the Christian faith developed toward the formulations of the Trinity and the Incarnation — the heart of the Christian doctrine of God — reached at Nicea, Constantinople, and Chalcedon, the firmer its self-implication in a partly conscious, partly unconscious, commitment to a supposedly final conceptualization of its belief in the Christian God and in the person of Jesus, its founder and Christ. The briefest examination of the matter should suggest how this occurred.

The Underdevelopment of the Dogmas of the Trinity and the Incarnation.

Now, the word used by the author of the prologue to the Fourth Gospel to designate the Word which — proceeding from God yet not being other than God himself — must be said to *be* God, was *logos*. . . . As adopted by Christian theology, and in the first place by the Fourth Gospel, *logos* . . . signified the consubstantiality of the *Incarnate* Word and God, for "the Word was made flesh." And *logos* signified this not by reason of its gnoseological, but of its metaphysical connotations. In short, if the God of Christian belief was the self-communicating God who revealed himself to man not only by sending messages, but also by being present to us in all things at all times, and ultimately most fully and completely by coming to us, . . . then the Christian God who revealed himself to us in the person of

Jesus was in reality that which in hellenic usage was already — indeed, had traditionally been — called the *logos*. The philosophers had never realized it, but "the logos was God." . . .

The theism of the New Testament goes so far beyond the Old Testament monotheism which it so perfectly assumes, that its ultimate basis must actually be considered not as the *unicity* of God (monotheism) but the *self-communicating procession of God* ("trinitarianism"). . . . As Karl Rahner has put it (using the orthodox distinctions which emerged in order to conceptualize the foregoing): the New Testament doctrine of the Trinity "begins with the three Persons (three Persons, who are of a single divine nature) or better, with the Father, who is the source from which the Son, and through the Son the Spirit, proceed, so that the unity and integrity of the divine nature is conceptually a *consequence* of the fact that the Father communicates his whole nature."[7]

The concepts provided by the hellenic culture, especially that of the *logos* and those which led to distinction between *person* and *nature*, served admirably well to bring into full consciousness and to formulate the foregoing Christian faith in the Christian God. We have not to date managed to do *better*. On the other hand, this does not mean that the formulation of the doctrine in the hellenic terms of *word*, *nature*, and *person* has not had serious disadvantages, even from early times, and increasingly so in more recent ages. We have *not managed* to do

---

[7] *Theological Investigations*, I, p. 146.

better. It is because we have not done better since the fifth century that the future development of the doctrine of the Trinity must *begin* with Nicea and Constantinople as from a point of departure. . . . The doctrine of the Trinity, the absolutely basic doctrine of the Christian faith, has through underdevelopment become inadequate to the point that it must be seriously suspected of causing some scandal — not simply that of incredibility but that of irrelevance and senselessness.

The contemporary inadequacy of conceptualizing the second person as the *Word,* for instance, should be fairly clear from what has been said above. There is nothing in our contemporary experience corresponding to the *logos* of the Greeks that could be fittingly or intelligibly called *Word*. To say that at the beginning of time the *Word* already was, and that the *Word* was God, should be most significant and important to someone who first assumes that there *is* a Word. To someone who does not perceive the world by means of such a concept these propositions cannot reveal very much about God. . . .

In any event, it is not simply a question of the concepts used to think of the various "persons" of the Trinity. There are more basic inadequacies concerning the concept of the Trinity as a whole. I will mention here only two ways in which conceptualizing the God of Christian belief in the hellenic form of trinitarianism has been disadvantageous. . . .

The first made its appearance long ago. It consisted in that the formulation of the doctrine in the opposed concepts of nature and person — God is three consubstantial persons — automatically lent itself to understanding the Trinity as a sort of property of the divine nature: the position of the tract on the Trinity in St. Thomas's *Summa Theologiae* is symptomatic of this tendency.[8] In time, the Trinity became the doctrine of "one God in three persons." Thereafter the Christian concept of God no longer "begins with the three Persons." . . . The concept of a "trinitarian" God personally involved in human events out of the abundance of his reality was bound to become gradually subordinated to that of a monotheistic Supreme Being eternally contemplating himself in heaven while keeping a tight rein on his refractory, restless subjects here below. Trinitarianism was effectively weakened into a modified monotheism.

The other disadvantage of the conceptualization of the Trinity in hellenic forms has not taken effect until more recently. . . . As long as cultural contact was maintained (as it was during the middle ages) with the hellenism in which *natura, substantia,* and *persona* were realities of common experience, the weakening of trinitarianism did not have noticeably ill effects. But in recent times the same condition has no longer obtained.

Person has long ceased to mean *prosopon* or *persona,* and *personality* cannot today remotely convey the idea of a *mode of subsistence.* . . . To him who is formed by the twentieth century, *person* means . . . a center of consciousness and, therefore, a center of *exercised* existence, life, presence, freedom and reality. . . . A person, thus, cannot be a termination of nature. On the contrary, nature is a termination of personality — and a person, moreover, terminates itself and makes its nature in and through existing.[9]

The Christian believer of today, therefore, can repeat faithfully the formula: one God in three persons. But, (except as noted), in his actual and effective religious life he cannot very well avoid the thought that . . . three persons must be three beings, even if they all share one and the same substance and nature. . . . In a word, we suffer from *cryptotritheism.*[10] . . .

The term *Trinity* now . . . tends to obscure the fundamental Christian idea that God *does* manifest himself and that he does so precisely as Trinity . . . and that the different persons *are* different modes (albeit not successive ones) of his self-communication.

4. L. Dupré[1] asks how Christianity must develop so as not to betray its original message. He agrees with Leslie Dewart that the old theory of

<hr>

[8] "That which belongs to the unity of the divine essence having been considered, it remains to treat of . . . the Trinity," *S.T.,* I, 27, *prooemium.*

[9] Gabriel Marcel, *Being and Having* (New York, 1965), pp. 154–174.

[10] Karl Rahner and Herbert Vorgrimler, *Theological Dictionary* (New York, 1965), p. 472.

[1] Louis Dupré, Professor of Philosophy at Georgetown University, is the author of *Contraception and Catholics.* This excerpt

development — as mere explicitation of what is implicit — is inadequate. But he questions the sufficiency of Dewart's own solution and especially of his view that religious truth is a conceptualization of experience. He thinks religious symbols must be retained, insofar as they are part of the revelation, but that new religious symbols must be created in order to retain or restore the meaning of the old ones.

The God of History. Christians claim that theirs is an historical religion, distinguished from the non-historical, cyclic world view of the Greeks by the definitive, irreversible meaning of temporal events. Yet, no sooner is someone willing to believe this and to consider Christianity as historically determined and historically developing, than believers lose faith in their own assumption that God *can* speak an historical language. Their perplexity in the face of present-day reinterpretations of scriptural texts and ecclesiastical documents shows that they had never accepted evolution and relativity as essential characteristics of the historical, but had simply redefined history so as to fit a purely static concept of religion.

Now, it must be admitted in all fairness to the perplexed believer that religion is much more than an historical process: it is above all a dialogue with the transcendent, initiated by a revelation from a *trans-historical* divine sphere. Still in the Judaeo-Christian tradition this revelation itself occurs as an historical event. God reveals himself through the history of a particular people and, within this history, in a definitive way through the acts

and words of one man. Insofar as the revelation takes on an historical character, it must be received into that dynamic process through which man constantly creates and recreates his values. . . .

If the divine message is to make sense at all it cannot be a meteoric block "hurled at the world," but it must be actively received within a particular universe of discourse that will restrict it by its own limitations. There is no such thing as a purely passive reception of truth. Man alone can make truth, even though he must be divinely inspired to make *revealed* truth. But if this is the case, it follows that the *expression* of a revealed truth depends largely on the capacity of the receiving subject and this capacity is always to some extent culturally circumscribed.

Can there be a definitive expression of God's revelation, a final truth about what he has communicated to us? If *definitive* and *final* are understood in the sense of a total adequacy between the expression and the expressed, no single historical expression can ever exhaust God's revelation. Not even divine authority precludes concrete statements concerning man and his values from being subject to further evolution, for man himself continues to develop. On the other hand, the revelation (and the authentic tra-

is from his article, "The God of History," in *Commonweal*, Vol. 85, No. 18, February 10, 1967 (New York: Commonweal Publishing Co.), pp. 516–522.

dition) must be expressed adequately enough to remain authoritative for later generations.

This conclusion applies even to the words of Christ. As a man Christ could not but think and speak *within* the framework of a particular time and culture. . . . If Christ preserved the specific character of human nature, as the Council of Chalcedon clearly states,[2] then I do not see how the notion of an omniscient Christ unbound by any cultural limitation can escape contradiction. I also wonder what then the Gospel of Luke means when it states: "As Jesus grew up, he advanced in wisdom."[3]

Man's relation to God can be expressed only within a particular language, that is, an interpreted set of symbols. This holds true even if the Man who expresses this relation is also God. . . . Through the Incarnation God is able to speak to man from person to person, but the language is human and bears the mark of a particular person who lived in a particular culture. . . . Christ is absolutely authoritative in *what* he expressed and in that it was *He,* the God-man, who expressed it. But his particular way of expressing it is, as all expression, co-determined by individual and cultural characteristics.

The Historicity of the Gospel. The same is even more true of the reports of Jesus' words and deeds in the Gospels. . . . Whether all the details are historical or not . . . is irrelevant. . . . The authority of the Gospels is not based on historical or theological qual-

ities but on the faith of those who read it as an authentic expression of God's revelation in Christ. . . .

Each dogma shows the mark of the cultural conditions in which it was formulated. Often no correct interpretation of an authoritative document can be given without a good deal of information on the historical — and very contingent! — circumstances in which it was issued. . . .

The words of Christ and the basic directions of his Church guide man authoritatively in his relations with God. . . . But the symbols in which this view or, in phenomenological terms, this *intentionality* is expressed are, as all human symbols, determined by a cultural tradition. This is not to say that they are false or even inadequate. If a revelation is to take place at all, the symbols in which it is expressed must have at least that minimum adequacy which enables them to transmit the message effectively to later generations. But beyond that, every generation has the task of capturing the message of the revelation anew.

The difficulty, however, is to distinguish intentionality from expression. . . . It is . . . insufficient to assume that the intentionality of revelation and of authentic magisterium is divinely determined whereas the expression is not. . . . In giving expression to God's revelation man is as creative as he is in building the world. . . . Inspiration does not eliminate the creativity (good or bad) of a literary work; it merely guarantees that this work is an authoritative expression of an original religious impulse.

---

[2] Denz.-Schön., no. 148:301.
[3] Lk 2:52.

But this intimate mingling of divine inspiration and human creativity makes the question all the more urgent: How must Christianity develop so as not to betray its original message? How can we separate the relative from the absolute? The old theories claim that development consists merely in making explicit what is implicit and that nothing basically new is ever introduced.

In his remarkable study *The Future of Belief,* Leslie Dewart convincingly shows how inadequate this explanation is. Yet, I am not sure that his own solution, interesting as it is, is altogether sufficient. . . . To say that "Christianity was a *mission,* not a *message,*" as Dewart does,[4] is not entirely correct. Christianity may not have a doctrine (that is, a systematic body of knowledge), but it definitely has a message. Scripture is not merely "the report of an event that happens"; it also provides the authoritative interpretation of that event. . . . The relatively small consideration which Dewart gives to the problem of scriptural and traditional authority may be due to the fact that, for him, religious truth (like any other truth) is defined as the conceptualization of *experience.* But is it sufficient to say that "Christian belief is a religious experience?"[5] To the believer faith is always considerably more than a religious *experience.* An objective experience is experience *only to the extent that it grasps its object,* whereas the object of the religious act remains mostly transcendent to the experience. This

is the very reason why the religious message has to be *revealed.* It is also the reason why the original expression of the message must be more than the "conceptualization of an experience." The symbolization of Christianity and its evolution cannot be determined by the experience alone because it expresses more than a mere experience. . . .

As all other symbols, the religious symbol conveys an immediate, intrinsic meaning, for example, that God is Father, Son, and Holy Spirit but, unlike other symbols, it attempts to attain through this obvious meaning a content that cannot be directly expressed. The religious experience, therefore, lives in a constant tension with its forms of expression. . . . This basic ambiguity is what makes religious language so unscientific even when it attempts to be scientific. But it also enables religious symbols to develop organically and to renew themselves from within, while scientific symbols can only be discarded as soon as there is a basic shift in signification. . . .

The concept of *trans-substantiation,* originally intended to explain Christ's presence in the Eucharist by means of Scholastic terminology, acquired throughout centuries of Christian tradition a religious meaning which still speaks even to those who long ago stopped thinking in terms of substance and accident.

I, therefore, think that it would be wrong (granted that it would be possible within the tradition) to abandon a notion that has become a religious symbol more than a scientific concept.

---

[4] P. 8.
[5] P. 113.

Its religious transformation leaves the term so scientifically vague that theologians have sufficient freedom of interpretation, whereas a new definition would simply be another attempt to fix a datum of revelation in precise philosophical terms.

Because of the flexible nature of religious symbols, evolution *can* take place without any abandonment of traditional symbolism. Insofar as the symbols are part of the revelation, they *must* be retained if contact with the original message is to be preserved. However, the traditional character of revealed religion by no means implies that no new symbols ought to be created. Since the *experience* of the transcendent is always expressed in terms of the *self* and the *universe* that is being transcended, modern man's entirely different outlook on both compels him to look for new religious symbols in order to retain or restore the meaning of the old ones. But the creation of religious symbols is ultimately the task of the religious man himself and of the religious community. The reason why the writings of Teilhard de Chardin have proven so fertile in new religious language is that they express above all a religious experience. . . .

Is it possible to go even further, beyond, tradition, and to envision the possibility of new *beginnings*? If the last words of revelation were written in the first century or shortly thereafter, then only development of the tradition is possible. But are we willing to accept the conclusion that even for those who will live one million years from now, no new revelation will have occurred? Christians know that even now God's Spirit is actively present in the Church, urging its members to explore new horizons. But his light has traditionally been understood to illuminate only a message delivered in times past. . . . Could epiphanies only occur in the past, and has God really spoken his final word in this world? Could there ever be a new Pentecost?

5. K. Rahner[1] ponders the unchangeable God and his becoming. The Unchangeable can be changeable *in another*. The Absolute, while retaining the perfect freedom of his infinite non-relativity, has the possibility to become the other, the finite. The primordial phenomenon in our faith is the self-divestment, the becoming, the kenosis, the genesis of God himself who can become by positing the other that he himself becomes, though he, the origin of all, does not become.

God *became* man. . . . But can God become something? This question has always been answered in the affirmative by pantheism and all the other world views that consider God an essential part of history. But at this point the Christian and the theistic philosopher find themselves in a more difficult position. They profess God as the

---

[1] See ch. II, A, 1, n. 1. This excerpt is from his book, *Spiritual Exercises* (New York: Herder and Herder, 1965), pp. 104–113.

"unchangeable one" who just is, the "pure act" who, in the absolute security of his infinite reality, possesses from eternity to eternity the fullness of his own being, without having to become and without having to seek anything else. . . .

Still, it remains true: "And the Word became flesh". . . . It would be very difficult to deny that traditional scholastic philosophy and theology get very obscure when it comes to this point. They explain that the change and becoming take place only in the creature that is assumed, not in the Word who assumes. Thus, everything is supposed to be crystal clear: Without any change in himself, the Word assumes a created reality that does change even while it is being assumed. And so all change and history and suffering still remain on this side of the absolute abyss that separates the unchanging necessary from the changing, conditioned world.

But it still remains true that the Word *became* flesh, that the history of the development of this human reality was His own history, and that our time became the time of the Eternal, and our death became the death of God who does not die. . . . This question is one of realizing how the statement about the unchangeableness of God can be reconciled with the fact that what took place on this earth in the development and history of Jesus is the history of the Word of God himself, and is *his* own *becoming*.

If we take a good look at this fact of the Incarnation, then we simply must say: God can become something; the Unchangeable can be changeable

in another. With this statement, we come to an ontological principle that a purely rational ontology perhaps could never discover as one of its basic starting points or fundamental principles. What this really means is that the Absolute, while retaining the perfect freeom of his infinite non-relativity, has the possibility to become the other, the finite. God has the possibility in the very act of divesting himself, giving himself away, of positing the other as his own reality.

The primordial phenomenon that we should begin with here is not the concept of an assumption that simply presupposes what is to be received and then atttributes it to the assumer; for in such a situation it is never really assumed, since it is rejected by God's unchangeability (which is conceived undialectically and as completely isolated for itself alone) and can never affect him in his unchangeability. But the primordial phenomenon that we find in our faith is rather the self-divestment, the becoming, the kenosis, the genesis of God himself who can become by positing the other that he himself becomes, though he, the origin of all, does not become. Because he pours himself out and at the same time remains infinite fullness (since he is love, that is, the will to fill that which is empty, and since he has the means to fill with), the other comes into being as his own reality. He constitutes that which is different from himself because he retains it as his own; or, put the other way around, because he truly desires to have the other as his own, he constitutes it in its own true reality.

God himself goes out of himself as the fullness that gives itself away. Because he can do this, because his ability to become in an historical way is his basic and primordial possibility, for this reason he is defined in holy Scripture as love — a love whose lavish freedom is simply indefinable. And therefore, his power to create — the ability to produce the other out of nothing without losing anything of himself, is only a derivative, limited, and secondary possibility that is founded on this primordial possibility, even though the former could be actualized without the latter. Therefore, the possibility of being assumed by God, of being the material for God's own history, resides in the very essence of the creature. God always projects the creature by means of his creative power as the grammar of a possible self-expression. Perhaps this could be a starting point for reaching an understanding of the fact that only the Word of God became man and only he could become man.

The immanent self-expression of God in its external fullness is the condition of his external self-expression, and the latter is only a condition of the former. Even though the positing of creatures is the work of the Godhead without distinction of Persons, still the possibility of creation has its ontological basis in the fact that God, who has no beginning, expresses himself in himself and for himself, and thus posits the original, divine difference in God himself. And when this God expresses himself outside of himself, then this expression is the expression of this immanent Word; it is not just any word that could be attributed to one of the other Persons. Only from this standpoint can we better understand what it means to say: The Word of God "becomes" man. Certainly, there are men who are not the Word of God. Certainly, men could exist even if the Word had not become man, just as the less can always exist without the greater, even though the less is based on the possibility of the greater and not vice versa.

If the Word becomes man, then his humanity is not something pregiven; it is something that becomes and originates in essence and existence, if the Word divests himself and to the extent that he does so. This man, precisely as man, is the self-divestment of God, because God externalizes himself when he divests himself; he manifests himself as love when he hides the majesty of his love and reveals himself as an ordinary man. Otherwise, his humanity would merely be a garment, a masquerade, a sign that indicates the existence of something, but does not really reveal anything about the one who is there. . . . And the fact that he states as his own reality just what we are opens up our essence and our history to the freedom of God. It says what we are: the sentence in which God could expose himself and express himself into the emptiness that necessarily surrounds him. For he is love, and therefore he is necessarily the wonderful possibility of the free gift of self.

At this point, penetrating man to his most profound and obscure mystery, we could define him as that which proceeds from the freedom of

God when God's self-expression, his Word, is spoken with love out into the emptiness of Godless nothingness. Someone has termed the Logos the abbreviated Word of God. The abbreviation, the cipher of God, is man, that is, the Son of Man — and in the final analysis, men exist only because there was supposed to be a Son of Man. Actually, we could say that when God desires to be non-God, then man begins to be — that and nothing else! This, of course, does not mean that man is reduced to the level of the vulgar and the common; it really means that he is brought back to the mystery that always remains incomprehensible. Such a mystery is man.

Now, if God himself is man and remains man for all eternity, then theology may not make light of man. For if it did, it would be making light of God who remains the impenetrable mystery. For all eternity, man is the expressed mystery of God — thus participating in the mystery of his supporting ground. Hence, man must always be accepted in love as an inexhaustible mystery. . . . It is only in this obscurity — of God — that we can grasp that this finite man is the finiteness of the infinite Word of God himself.

Christology is the end and the beginning of anthropology, and this anthropolgy in its most basic form, that is, Christology, is theology for all eternity. This is the theology that God himself proclaims when he speaks his Word as our flesh into the emptiness of Godlessness and sin. This is the theology that we ourselves then pursue in faith, provided that we do not think we can find God by simply ignoring the man Christ. . . .

Because the Word creates in his Incarnation in the very act of assuming and dispossessing himself, the axiom for every relationship between God and creatures is operative here in a radical and unique way. This axiom is: Nearness to God and distance from him, the subordination and the independence of the creature, are not opposed to one another, but increase together. Therefore, Christ is more of a man than anyone else, and his humanity is the most independent, the most free, not in spite of the fact that it is assumed, but because it is assumed and posited in being as the self-expression of God. . . .

Man is a mystery. No! He is *the* mystery. He is this not only because he is needy openness toward the mystery of the incomprehensible fullness of God, but because God spoke this mystery as his own reality. . . . Thus, the Incarnation of God is the absolute mystery and also the most obvious mystery. . . . If the desire for the nearness of God . . . sees how this nearness manifested itself . . . in the flesh and in the hovels of the earth, then only in Jesus of Nazareth . . . can one find the courage to bend one's knee and tearfully pray: And the Word became flesh and pitched his tent among us.

6. C. Mooney[1] studies Teilhard's view of "creative union," Christogenesis, Pleromization. The theory of "creative union" attempts to explain the three mysteries of creation, Incarnation, and redemption in terms of a single evolutionary movement toward the final Plenitude of Christ. At the Parousia Christ will bring Christogenesis to an end and unite all of mankind in the fullness of his Body-Person.

Christogenesis.[2] Teilhard's[3] analysis of the Church as a phylum of love is what is primarily responsible for his speaking of the evolutionary process as Christogenesis. From this point of view too, the mystery of God's continuous creation is intimately linked with Christ's work of redemption and is not simply the unfolding of a pre-existent

[1] Christopher F. Mooney, S.J., is professor of theology at Fordham University, New York City. His research on Teilhard de Chardin was begun during his doctoral studies in Paris, at the Institute Catholique. He has contributed numerous articles to religious publications. This excerpt is from his book, *Teilhard De Chardin And The Mystery of Christ* (New York: Harper & Row, Publishers, 1965), pp. 168–181.

[2] Teilhard insists that the evolutionary process must be described as "a Christogenesis in which the Upward and the Forward become reconciled." Since Christ is Prime Mover of evolution, "he *ipso facto* acquires and develops in the fullest sense a real omnipresence of transformation. Under his influence and attraction, every energy, every event of our lives is suranimated. In the last analysis cosmogenesis, discovered along its principal axis to be biogenesis and then noogenesis, culminates in Christogenesis, the object of every Christian veneration." See *Reflexions sur l'ultrahumain*, 1951, Oeuvres, vii, 22; *Le Christique*, 1955, 8.

[3] Pierre Teilhard de Chardin, S.J. (1881–1955) was a scientist of high distinction, with a special interest in the problems of evolution. He spent most of his life abroad in scientific research. Among his many works we may mention *The Phenomenon of Man; The Divine Milieu; Hymn of the Universe; L'Apparition de l'Homme; La Place de l'homme dans l'univers; Le Vision du passé.*

plan. The outcome is indeed to be the the Plenitude of Christ, but this Plenitude is conditioned by the extent to which men freely choose to be transfigured by Christian charity and thereby participate in God's creative power. For Teilhard such participation is the necessary but insufficient condition for the coming of the Parousia, and the world will end only when men have, through charity, freely pushed the movement of radial energy to its point of planetary maturation.

It is important to underline this first outlook of Teilhard because it differs considerably from the second point of view we are now about to consider. The object of Teilhard's analysis from his second vantage point is not Christian action in the world, but the eternal creative action of God; not the Church's task in the evolutionary process, but God's design from all eternity, to direct this process towards the Parousia.

Christogenesis is to be seen now not in so far as it is an accomplishment of man's freedom, but in so far as it is a work of divine omnipotence and love, and the key concept of "organic phylum" is to be replaced by that of "Pleromization." It is characteristic of the ordinary economy of Christian life," wrote Teilhard in 1940, "that certain elements of revelation which have long lain dormant should suddenly receive a powerful development according to the needs and demands of a new age. It seems to me that in our time this is the role reserved to the great concept of the Christian Pleroma, which is such an integral part of dogma, . . . the mysterious synthesis of the created and the Uncreated — the complete fulfillment (at once qualitative and quantitative) of the universe in God."[4] The slow maturation of the universe into this "mysterious synthesis" at the Parousia he calls "Pleromization," and its analysis constitutes the final phase of his effort to rethink the mystery of Christ in terms of genése.

For purposes of clarity we may divide his treatment into two main parts. There is first a metaphysical theory which Teilhard calls "creative union," the starting point of which is a strong affirmation of Christ's election at the beginning of time to be Head of all creation. The theory itself then attempts to explain the three mysteries of creation, Incarnation and redemption in terms of a single evolutionary movement toward the final Plenitude of Christ. The second part of Teilhard's approach to Pleromization is a tentative speculation concerning the planetary maturation of mankind. In his system this will take place at the moment of the Parousia, for it is then that Christ will bring Christogenesis to an end and unite all of mankind in the fullness of his Body-Person. We shall now examine in greater detail these two parts of his analysis.

[4] La parole attendue, 1940, in Cahiers, iv, 26.

The starting point of Teilhard's theory of "creative union" is the data of revelation concerning Christ's relationship to the whole of creation from the very beginning of time. Here Teilhard puts special emphasis on Colossians 1:15–17. Early essays are filled with allusions to these verses as well as to Ephesians 2:19 and I Corinthians 8:6. . . . "The prodigious extent of time before the first Christmas was not void of him but penetrated throughout by his powerful influence." . . . . "(God) willed his Christ, and in order to have his Christ he had to create a world of the spirit, men in particular, in which Christ would germinate; and to have man, he had to launch the enormous movement of o r g a n i c life . . . and for the latter to spring up the whole tumult of the cosmos was necessary" . . . "Everything takes place as if God were ontologically engaged (in the cosmos) even before his Incarnation."[5]

This insistence of Teilhard upon Christ's role in creation calls attention to an aspect of Paul's thought which . . . is receiving considerable attention today.[6] Paul seems clearly to affirm a

[5] La Vie cosmique, 1916, in Ecrits du temps de la guerre, 1916–1919 (Paris, Grasset, 1965), 48; Science et Christ, 1921, Oeuvres, ix, 60; Mon Universe, 89, 108; Contingence de l'univers et gout humain de survivre, 1953, 4; Teilhard also speaks of Christ as "Alpha and Omega" in Note sur le Christ universel, 1920, Oeuvres, ix, 30.

[6] See Benoit, Corps, Tete. . . , 31–40; Dupont, Gnosis, 453–576; V. Warnach, O.S.B., "Kirche und Kosmos," in Enkainia, ed. Hilarius Emonds, O.S.B. (Düsseldorf, 1962); Andre Feuillet, "L'Eglise plerome du Christ d'apres Eph!" — Nouvelle Revue Theologique, lxxviii (1956), 446–472, 596–610; Joseph Huby, S.J., Les Epitres de la capitivité (Paris, 1935), p. 40; J. B. Lightfoot, St. Paul's Epistles to the Colossians,

pre-existence for Christ, and apparently it is always the concrete, historical God-Man of whom he is thinking, never the Word independent of his humanity. How this is to be explained theologically is a question for which there is as yet no satisfactory answer. Teilhard's own theory is that "every cosmic particle, even the tinest electron, is rigorously co-extensive with the totality of space and time" . . . . But "in the case of Christ, this co-extension of co-existence has become a co-extension of domination," and the reason Christ's Body has such a privileged position in the universe is to be traced to "the transforming effect of the Resurrection."[7]

This relationship of Christ to the whole of creation provides the key to an understanding of Teilhard's theory of "creative union." To treat this theory as a purely rational analysis, as some have done,[8] is to distort it completely and to create theological difficulties which do not in fact exist. "The philosophy of creative union . . . is nothing but the development . . . of what the Church teaches us concerning the growth of Christ." It is the philosophy of the universe conceived in the function of our knowledge of the Mystical Body. This "philosophical extension of faith in the Incarnation," as Teilhard also

and to Philemon (London, 1904). Exegetes have noted that whenever Paul speaks of the pre-existence of Christ, as in Colossians, he is always thinking of the concrete, historical God-Man and never of the Word independent of his humanity. Cf. for example, Joseph Bonsirven, S.J., _Theology of the New Testament_ (Westminster, 1963, p. 232): "St. Paul knows nothing of this Word existing in the bosom of the Trinity; when he envisages a pre-existence, he is always speaking of Jesus Christ, who was consequently mediator of creation, for example, even before his appearance on earth." See also B. Brinkmann, "Die kosmische Stellung des Gottmenschen in Paulinischer Sicht," _Wissenschaft und Weisheit_, xiii (1950), pp. 6–33, especially 8–9; F. X. Durrwell, C.SS.R., "Le Christ, premier et dernier," _Bible et Vie Chrétienne_, ix (1963), 16–28, especially 22–25; A. Grillmeier, S.J., "Zum Christusbild der Heutigen Katholischen Theologie," in _Fragen der Theologie Heute_, ed. J. Feiner, J. Trütsch, F. Böckle (Einsiedeln, 1957), 269–270; Emile Mersch, _The Theology of the Mystical Body_ (St. Louis, 1952), 135–141. The unity of creation and salvation has also been shown to be a major theme of the Old Testament. See Lucien Legrand, "La Création, triumphe cosmique de Yahve," _Nouvelle Revue Theologique_, lxxxiii (1961), 449–470.

[7] *_Comment je vois_, 1948, 4, n. 4, 35. Hans Küng has attempted an explanation of Christ's pre-existence by making use of Cullmann's study of the New Testament mode of conceiving time and eternity. See _Rechtfertigung_, 277–295 (Eng. trans., 285–301), and Cullmann's _Christus und die Zeit_, 52–59 (Eng. trans., 61–68). In the _Summa Theologica_ (III, q. 24, a. 1–4) St. Thomas relates Christ to the totality of time and space by reason of his eternal predestination. And Karl Rahner has recently observed that, on the scale of an evolution which should continue millions of years, the Incarnation actually took place at the beginning of true human history, that is to say, when man had just commenced taking charge of the world in which he found himself in order to shape his own destiny. See "Die Christologie innerhalb einer evolutiven Weltanschauung," _Schriften zur Theologie_, Vol. v (Einsiedeln, 1962), 218.

[8] Claude Tresmontant so treats and so distorts the theory of creative union in his _Introduction_ . . . , 112–115 (Eng. trans., 89–93). See also his "Le Pére Teilhard de Chardin et la théologie, _Lettre_, i (1962), 11–38. Teilhard's references to the Pleroma are not, as Tresmontant says, forced into his theory, but constitute its starting point.

calls it,[9] is therefore meant to deal with God's continuous act of creation not only on the level of reason but also on that of revelation. . . . "The world is still being created and it is Christ who brings himself to completion in it. . . . "From top to bottom things find in Christ their sole principle of stability: *In eo omnia constant.*" The world is "above all a work of creation continued in Christ."[10]

Hence, were it not for the data of revelation regarding Christ's presence at the beginning of time and the existence of his Pleroma at the end of time, Teilhard would never have conceived his philosophy of creative union. . . . Although creative union may be placed *logically* prior to Teilhard's theology insofar as it is a metaphysical theory, it is in fact an integral part of his overall theological effort to clarify the concept of Christogenesis.[11]

Teilhard begins his exposition by defining being in terms of a movement indissolubly associated with it, that of union. Thus, in its active sense, being would mean "to unite oneself or to unite others," while in its passive sense it would mean "to be united or unified by another." Teilhard adds immediately that "others" in the active formula applies even to God, but only in regard to "Pleromization," not in regard to "Trinitization."[12]

He then distinguishes four successive "moments" in his metaphysics of union. The first moment is a recognition of a divine and self-sufficient First Cause, that is to say, an acceptance of the philosophic option of a persona Omega . . . The second moment, "in conformity with 'revealed' data," is a recognition that the existence of this Center, "who is both beginning and end," consists in the act of opposing and uniting himself triunely to himself. However, it is in the third and fourth moments that Teilhard begins to explain how, in and through the Pleroma of Christ, God can be said to "complete" himself in the action of creation. Here is the complete text: "By the very fact that he unifies himself interiorly, the First Being *ipso facto* causes another type of opposition to arise, not within himself but at his antipodes (and here we have our third moment). At the pole of being there is self-subsistent Unity, and all around at the periphery, as a necessary consequence, there is multiplicity: *pure* multiplicity, be it understood, a 'creatable void' which

---

[9] Mon univers, 82. The first text is from *L'Union creatrice,* 1917, in Ecrits du temps de la guerre, 196. When Teilhard says (in MU, 72) that his theory is simply the result of his reflection upon the relationship between matter and spirit, what he omits to tell the reader is that he is thinking here as a Christian and is therefore making use of two sources of knowledge.

[10] *La Vie cosmique,* 1916, in ET, 49; *L'Union creatrice,* 1917, in ET, 196; *La Lutte contre la multitude,* 1917, in ET, 128; *Pantheisme et Christianisme,* 1923, 11; *Essai d'integration de l'homme dans l'univers,* 1930, 4th lecture, 13.

[11] Creative union may also be situated within the more limited context of Teilhard's approach to the mystery of evil, and this is the approach of George Crespy (*Pensée théologique. . . ,* 113–122). Teilhard does this himself occasionally, although in this context the theory loses some of its force as a clarification of Christogenesis.

[12] *Comment je vois,* 1948, 17 and note 26. In the same note Teilhard puts his two formulas "more clearly" in Latin: *plus esse — plus plura unire* and *plus esse — a plus a pluribus uniri.*

is simply nothing — yet which, because of its passive potency for arrangement (i.e., for union), constitutes a possibility, an appeal for being. Now everything takes place as if God had not been able to resist this appeal, for at such depths our intelligence can no longer distinguish at all between supreme necessity and supreme freedom (except by recognizing the presence of the Free in the infallible sign of an accompanying love)."[13]

In classical philosophy or theology, creation or participation (which constitutes our fourth moment) always tends to be presented as an almost arbitrary gesture on the part of the First Cause, executed by a causality analagous to "efficient" and according to a mechanism that is completely indeterminate: truly an "act of God" in the pejorative sense. In a metaphysics of union, on the contrary — although the self-sufficiency and self-determination of the Absolute Being remain inviolate . . . — in such a metaphysics, I say, the creative act takes on a very well defined significance and structure. (It is now seen to be) "Pleromization" (as Paul might have said), that is to say, the giving of reality to participated being through arrangement and totalization. Pleromization is thus the fruit of God's reflection, not upon himself but outside himself; it appears somehow as a sort of replica or symmetry of Trinitization. Somehow its actuation fills a void and it

finds its place in the scheme of things. At the same time we can give it expression by using the very terms which served us to define being. To create means to unite.[14] . . .

In regard to the relationship of God to the material world, Teilhard begins by saying that creation is a reflection, an image of the life of the Blessed Trinity. This is what imposes upon it that metaphysical structure by which it must necessarily move from multiplicity to unity, and more precisely toward an ultimate unity with God. This is the sense of Teilhard's statement in 1942 that "evolution is not 'creative' . . . but is the expression of creation in space and time."[15] Thus far there is no difficulty for traditional Christian teaching; Thomas made practically the same statements, although obviously not in Teilhard's evolutionary framework.[16] . . .

However, the assertion that the world's movement toward unity "completes" God in some way is unusual

[13] The words in brackets were added by Teilhard as a footnote to the word "freedom." The French *multiple* in this and the following texts is translated either as "multiplicity" or as "many," depending on the context.

[14] *Ibid.*, pp. 18–19.

[15] *La Place de l'homme dans l'univers*, 1942, *Oeuvres*, iii, 323–324. The allusion is to the "creative evolution" of Henri Bergson, with whom Teilhard differed greatly, as we have seen in ch. 2, note 49. . . . In regard to the Person of Christ the difference is radical: Teilhard always speaks of Christ as an object of faith; Bergson always as an object of philosophy. See Henri Gouhier, *Bergson et le Christ des Evangiles* (Paris, 1961), 98–99, 164, 191.

[16] *Summa Theologica*, I, q. 45, a. 6 deals with the interior life of the Trinity as motive and image of creation, while a. 7 deals with the reflection of the Trinity in every creature; q. 93, a. 1 and 2 deal with man as God's image. I–II, q. 1, a. 7 and 8 deal with the necessary movement of all things created toward their own highest unity, which means union with God who is One in an absolute sense; see also q. 2, a. 8.

and needs to be clarified. Again it must be kept in mind that Teilhard is referring always to the building up of the Body of Christ in the present supernatural order. . . . From these texts[17] it is clear that what Teilhard is doing is nothing more nor less than simply asserting in an evolutionary context the paradox which is already contained in Paul: the Pleroma of Christ cannot constitute an intrinsic completion of God himself, but it will nonetheless in some real sense be a real completion. But why go to such lengths to insist on the second half of the paradox? The answer is that Teilhard wants to do away once and for all with the idea that God's continuous act of creation is one of *absolute* gratuity. It is important to note here the operative word. For Teilhard has no intention whatsoever of denying the sovereign freedom of God the Creator. What he means is that, from all eternity, creation in God's mind is creation in Christ, and that consequently it cannot be considered an "arbitrary act." . . .

What Teilhard is denying, therefore, is not the abstract idea of God's freedom in creation, but the concrete idea that he is personally independent of this present world whose destiny from all eternity was to be created in Christ. Nor does he wish by this to compromise in any way the added gratuity of the present supernatural order. . . . Up to a certain point there is no God (i.e., considered in his Pleroma) without creative union, no

creation without (God's) incarnate immersion into it, no Incarnation without redemptive compensation. In a metaphysics of union the three fundamental "mysteries" of Christianity are seen to be but three aspects of a single mystery of mysteries, that of Pleromization, or the reduction of multiplicity to unity.[18]

Note here that the emphasis here is upon the unity of these three mysteries in the divine plan for the human race. What is being questioned is not their gratuity but their separability in the present supernatural order. "Creation, Incarnation, redemption each mark a higher degree in the gratuity of the divine operation, but are they not also three acts which are indissolubly united in the appearance of participated being?" In this sense the ultimate mystery of God's dealings with man is to be found "not precisely in the mechanism of creation or of the Incarnation or redemption, but in 'Pleromization,' by which I mean the mysterious relationship of 'repletion' (if not completion) which links the First Being with participated being."[19] We have

---

[17] MU, pp. 73–74; MD (*Le Milieu divin*), p. 149; *La Route de l'Ouest*, 1932, 20.

[18] *Comment je vois*, 1948, 20–21. An almost identical statement appears in *Christianisme et evolution*, 1945, 7–8, although here Teilhard states explicitly what we have added in brackets: "Without creation something is strictly lacking to God considered in his Plenitude, i.e., in his act of union, not in his being."

[19] *L'Ame du monde*, 1981, in ET, 231; *Reflexions sur le peche originel*, 1947, 7. See also *Quelques vues générales sur l'essence du Christianisme*, 1939, 1–2; *Du cosmos a la cosmogenes*, 1951; *Oeuvres*, vii, 272. In this sense the mystery of original sin would also be inseparable from this "mystery of mysteries," since the first sin of man exists from eternity in God's

therefore "one single process, which is Christogenesis, considered either in its moving principle (creation), or in its unifying mechanism (Incarnation), or in its uplifting struggle (redemption)."[20]

"Creative union," "Pleromization," "Christogenesis," are therefore synonymous terms to describe the exercise of Christ's power as organic Center of the Universe, a continuous influence which is both creative, unitive, and redemptive, and which culminates in his plenitude at the Parousia. "Be-cause all the lines of the world converge and knit themselves together in him, it is he who physically and literally gives his own stability to the whole structure of matter and spirit. It is consequently in him as 'Head of creation' that the fundamental cosmic process of cephalization, in its universal extent and supernatural depth, and yet in harmony with all the past, culminates and draws to its close."[21] . . . "The total Christ can be consummated only at the end of the world's evolution."[22]

7. P. De Letter[1] sees in God's self-gift the key concept in the supernatural and Christian economy. He sketches three modern ways of conceiving and expressing the self-gift of God to the creature. De la Taille's builds on the analogy drawn from the composition of finite being, while Lonergan's is based on the analogy drawn from our natural knowledge of God. Rahner's rests on the analogy drawn from what revelation teaches us about the procession of the Word, and in a way it synthesizes the other two explanations.

Contemporary theology is fairly well agreed that the key concept in the supernatural and Christian economy is that of God's self-gift to men, particularly in the three cardinal mysteries of that economy: the Incarnation of God's Son, the life of grace, and the vision of God. . . . To explain or express the nature of the divine self-gift, one current of theological thought follows up Father M. de la Taille's concept of the supernatural

---

[20] *Introduction á la vie chrétienne*, 1944, 3. This perspective of Teilhard explains for the most part expressions such as the following: ". . . the work of man's salvation in which creation consists." (*ibid.*, 9); "By the Incarnation, which has saved mankind . . ." (*La Vie cosmique*, 1916, in ET, 49); "Like creation, of which it is the visible surface, the Incarnation is coextensive with the duration of the world." (MU, 92) . . .

foreknowledge of the Incarnation and redemption. This is not, however, the way Teilhard wishes to universalize original sin; for him it is not moral evil at all, as we have seen in chapter four, but the physical imperfection of the cosmos at the moment of creation.

[21] *Super-humanite, super-Christ, super-charite*, 1943, Oeuvres, ix, 211.
[22] *Le Christique*, 1955, 7; *Comment je crois*, 1934, 24. A third form of the same affirmation appears in *Introduction á la vie chrétienne*, 1944, 3.
[1] P. De Letter, S.J., professor of theology at St. Mary's College, Kurseong, India, has published a good deal on matters theological and spiritual. This excerpt is from his article, "The Theology of God's Self-Gift" in *Theological Studies*, Vol. 24, (Woodstock, Md.: Theological Studies, Inc., 1963), pp. 402–422.

proposed in 1928,[2] and looks to an analogy drawn from the composition of finite being, the analogy of act and potency, form (or quasi form) and matter (quasi matter). These basic concepts, it is believed, offer an apt expression of the mystery of God's self-communication to men.[3]

This approach has been challenged of late by Father B. Lonergan in two of his manuals, on Christ and on the Trinity.[4] He refuses the analogy drawn from created things and their composition (essence and *esse*, matter and form) as unsuited for the purpose, and looks instead for an analogy in what we naturally know of God in whom being and knowledge and willing are one. His basic idea is that, in the case of the Incarnation, the divine infinite *esse* of the Son is the reason and intrinsic constitutive cause of the hypostatic union, on which, however, there follows of necessity a secondary *esse*, a substantial act, by way of *terminus* (terminating result). So, too, in the divine mission of the Holy Spirit or the divine indwelling through grace, his relation of origin constitutes his mission with, as a nec-

essary condition, the *terminus ad extra*. In a word, instead of speaking of (uncreated) Act and (created) actuation or of divine quasi form and created foundation of the union, Father Lonergan speaks of the (uncreated) intrinsic constitutive cause of the divine self-gift and the (created) terminating result. . . .

We propose here to compare and contrast briefly the two approaches . . . to see where the two conceptions agree and where they differ. . . . A recent study of Father Karl Rahner on the theology of the Incarnation may serve as a further illustration.

Analogy from Finite Being. In the mind of Father de la Taille,[5] the composition in the finite being of act and potency opens a way for conceiving and expressing the self-gift of God to the creature. Every creature and particularly the rational creature, is in obediential potency to its Creator. The pure and uncreated Act, God, because pure and unmixed with any potency, can communicate himself as Act or perfection to the obediential potency of the rational creature, not as the form of the creature (this would suppose imperfection in God) but as its Act . . . and even then not as "received" or limited by the creature's limited capacity, but as actuating (without informing) by a created or limited communication of himself. A created actuation which is the reality in the creature of the self-communication of the Act (not a link standing between the two) is received in the obediential potency of the creature,

[2] M. de la Taille, S.J., "Actuation crée par Acte incrée," *Recherches de science religieuse* 18 (1928), 253–268; English by C. Vollert, S.J., *The Hypostatic Union and Created Actuation by Uncreated Act* (West Baden, 1952), pp. 29–41 (referred to as *Hypostatic Union*).
[3] Cf. our article "Created Actuation by the Uncreated Act: Difficulties and Answers," *Theological Studies,* 18 (1957), 60–92.
[4] B. Lonergan, S.J., *De constitutione Christi ontologica et psychologica* (Rome, 1965), esp. pp. 63–82; *Divinarum personarum conceptio analogica* (Rome, 1957), esp. pp. 206–215. We refer to these two works as CC and DP.
[5] We may abstain here from detailed references to de la Taille and in general refer to *art. cit.* above.

and thus the creature is really trans-formed or perfected by and united with the uncreated Act.

This concept of the divine self-communication, Father de la Taille held, applies to the three key mys-teries of our faith . . . the Incarnation . . . the vision . . . the life of grace. The analogy, therefore, of composi-tion of act and potency, in the mind of Father de la Taille, illustrates the union of the uncreated Act with the creature. God as infinite Act com-municates himself to the obediential potency of the creature, and the re-sult is . . . that the uncreated Act unites himself to the creature immedi-ately so as to perfect or divinize it. *Analogy from Natural Knowledge of God: Hypostatic Union.* Father Lonergan considers the above analogy insufficient for a proper expression of God's self-gift.[6] It is from what we know about God by our natural reason that we must start — an approach which apparently is the exact opposite of the former. We briefly sum up

6 We do not attempt here to summarize the twenty-seven points of Fr. Lonergan's deduction from "the principle of the com-position of the composite" (CC, pp. 77–82). For our purpose it should suffice to state, as accurately and clearly as possible, first the starting point of his reasoning, and then the three main points of his system (indicated by him): the constitutive cause of the (hypostatic) union, the created term *ad extra,* and the relation between the two . . . This should suffice for the com-parison and contrast with the corresponding three points in de la Taille's concept: the uncreated Act (communicating Himself); the created actuation, or created grace of union or created sanctifying grace; and the relation between the two, the latter being both the ultimate disposition for and the result of the former (cf. *Hypostatic Union,* p.37).

what he says in order to "explain" the mystery of the Incarnation.[7] . . .

Because in God to know and to will and to be what is necessary, and to know and to will and to be what is contingent mean one act of know-ing and willing and being and not two, it is by one and the same act of being that the Word is both God and man (God of necessity, man con-tingently), and that one act is the in-trinsic and constitutive cause of the hypostatic union of the two natures in one person. In terms of divine self-gift we may translate: it is by becoming man contingently in virtue of the same act of divine *esse* by which he is God, or by taking unto himself the humanity so that it exists by his own divine act of existence, that the Word gives himself to the human nature. . . . Therefore, the infinite *esse* of the Son is the intrinsic constitutive cause of the hypostatic union.

But besides the intrinsic cause of the union, there must also be a created term. . . . This term must be the real foundation of the real union of the humanity with the Word, a substantial and supernatural act of existence, created, of course, and distinct from the uncreated *esse* of the Word, and corresponding to the obediential po-tency which is the very essence of the human nature. And this sub-stantial act of existing is received in the human nature so as to exclude from that nature its own connatural *esse.*[8] . . . In his conclusion Father Lonergan says that this extrinsic term

7 CC, pp. 69–82.
8 CC, pp. 73–76.

does not differ from the secondary non-accidental *esse* which Thomas allows in the *Quaestio disputata de unione Verbi incarnati*.[9] (If so, then apparently neither does it differ from what Father de la Taille called the "created actuation": a secondary *esse* not as act but as actuation.)[10]

Within this very large margin of agreement there are also differences, resulting mainly, it would seem, from a basic difference in approach. Perhaps we might characterize this difference by the terms "static" and "dynamic." Father de la Taille studies the supernatural reality of the divine self-gift in the first place *in facto esse*, as it exists statically. Father Lonergan studies it as it is *in fieri* or dynamically, for he considers in the first place the divine missions, thus naturally placing the emphasis on the divine Gift and inclining to reduce the role of the created gifts.[11] . . .

Father de la Taille expresses this communication of the divine existence to the humanity by the term actuation, or communication of the Act: the Act communicates or gives himself to the humanity or assumes the humanity into his own *esse*. Father Lonergan refused the idea of actuation of the finite by the Infinite. This actuation, he says, would mean that "in the Word incarnate . . . God through the divine *esse* is infinite in act, and through his human nature he must be something finite and potential."[12] . . . When Father Lonergan says that "by the divine *esse* of the Word . . . one and the same person is God of necessity and becomes man contingently,"[13] does he not say in other words that this divine *esse* unites unto itself the humanity, i.e., the uncreated Act communicates himself to the humanity? And if this way of understanding Father Lonergan is not mistaken, then both the expression of the mystery of the hypostatic union in terms of Act and actuation, and the expression in terms of the Word being by the same act or *esse* God of necessity and man contingently, would seem to be admissible. Then we should say that on this point also the difference is more verbal than real. . . .

Analogy from the Revelation of the Word. To the above theologies of God's self-gift, one resting on the analogy drawn from the composition of finite being, the other on the analogy drawn from our natural knowledge of God, we may add . . . Father Karl Rahner's view. This in a way synthesizes the two previous explanations. Perhaps we may characterize it by saying that it rests on the analogy drawn from what revelation teaches us about the procession of the Word within the Trinity.[14] . . .

---

[9] *CC*, p. 82.

[10] *Hypostatic Union*, p. 40.

[11] One might well ask whether Fr. Lonergan would not lessen this emphasis were he to write a theology of grace or of the vision that is, of the creature in grace or in the vision.

[12] *CC*, p. 64: ". . . in Verbo incarnato . . . et per esse divinum Deus infinitus est actu, et per essentiam humanam aliquid finitum in potentia sit necesse est. . . ."

[13] *CC*, p. 70.

[14] We suggest this phrase, which is not in Rahner, to keep in line with the two previous theologies of the divine self-gift, as named by Fr. Lonergan, *CC*, pp. 63, 69.

Quasi-formal Causality. As far back as 1939, Father Rahner proposed a way of conceiving the scholastic idea of uncreated grace drawn from the concept of quasi-formal causality. . . . Nor has he changed his mind on this point. In 1960 he writes: In glory and therefore also in grace, there is, besides the divine efficient causality which produces the created gifts, a quasi-formal self-communication of God to men. Thus, uncreated grace is not just a consequence of created grace, it is the central gift in the life of grace.[15]

Self-Gift and Incarnation of the Word. Father Rahner notes that in pre-Augustinian tradition it was taken for granted that only the Word, and not another divine Person, "could" become man and begin a human history."[16] . . . The Incarnation means that God while being changeless becomes changeable; that he empties himself (kenosis) to become another (genesis); that he strips himself to give himself. . . . Creation is nothing else than the constitution of the context needed for the self-expression of God, and the creature is of necessity an obediential potency open to this divine self-gift.[17] . . .

This theology of the divine self-gift, whose dogmatic and theological foundations would require fuller development,[18] is a third approach to the mystery of the supernatural; in its own way it synthesizes the first two. It includes the approach from the analogy of the finite being's composition of act and potency: the divine self-gift is the Act or quasi-form of the spiritual creature or man, whose very essence it is to be an obediential potency to the divine. It includes likewise the approach from the analogy of our natural knowledge of God: God's Son becomes man by the very act of *esse* by which He is God. . . . Father Rahner's analogy from the procession of the Word, who is the Father's self-expression within the Trinity, involves the idea that the self-gift of God in the Incarnation of the Word, or his self-expression ad extra, is constituted by his self-expression *ad intra* (the generation of the Word) extended freely and contingently to the humanity of Christ and, through Christ, in an accidental way to all his members.[19]

---

[15] Cf. "Natur und Gnade," *Schriften* 4 (Einsiedeln, 1960), 209–236 (reprinted from *Theologie heute* 2 (Munich, 1960), esp. p. 220. The role of the divine *esse*, which is very nearly the same as that indicated by Fr. Lonergan, will appear in what follows below on the Incarnation of the Word.

[16] *Schriften*, 4, 138 f.

[17] Cf. *Schriften*, 4, 142. Rahner's idea is clear and suggestive: man as man (or as a spiritual being) is of necessity a *potentia obedientialis* for the reception of the Infinite,

and so also, or even in the first place, for the hypostatic union.

[18] The point to be made in greater detail is that the supernatural order is of necessity, i.e., connaturally or from the nature of things as far as we can conceive these supernatural realities, an incarnational order: no supernatural order without the Incarnation (of the Son).

[19] Thus Fr. Rahner's conception incorporates the whole positive part of Fr. Lonergan's theology of the divine missions, without setting aside the analogy from act and potency.

8. G. Salet[1] presents the Trinity as a mystery of love. Following the great medieval theologians he finds in genuine love not a demonstration but a way of picturing the Blessed Trinity for ourselves. The mystery of the Blessed Trinity is precisely this, that it is the complete realization of perfect love.

The Trinity: Mystery of Love. There is only one God. There are three divine Persons in God, truly distinct from each other, the Father, the Son, and the Holy Spirit. They are united by relations of origin: the Father begets the Son, the Holy Spirit proceeds from the Father and the Son. Each of these Persons is truly God. All of them and each of them possesses one and the same divinity. This is the dogma of the Blessed Trinity which every Christian must believe. . . .

God is Love. Scripture gives us another definition of God: "God is Love." And this is, without a doubt, the most profound and most inspiring definition of all for us. Augustine said: "You wish to think of God. Why do you allow your thoughts to wander here and there? God is not at all what you imagine, not at all what you think you understand. Do you wish to have some foretaste of what he is? God is Love." . . . "The great Johannine phrase is truly the most profound that man can utter and the only one, in the last resort, that is worth clinging to: God is Love."

Following the great theologians of

[1] Gaston Salet, S.J. is the author of *The Wonders of our Faith* and editor and translator of *La Trinite, Richard of St. Victor.* This excerpt is from his article, "The Trinity: Mystery of Love" in *The Idea of Catholicism,* ed. by W. J. Burghardt, S.J., and W. F. Lynch, S.J. (Meridian Books, Inc., 1960), pp. 133–138.

the Middle Ages, then, we can examine genuine love to find in it, not a demonstration, but a way of picturing the Blessed Trinity for ourselves. We can discover in this divine Trinity the perfect realization of the dream which is pursued by every heart which loves, as well as the living model which every true love should imitate.

What is perfect love? It is a complete mutual giving. This supposes, at one and the same time, the presence of distinct persons and the absence among them of all selfishness: "To be aware of another in one's self and one's self in the other, to be united and joined together yet still distinct, to have all in common yet merging nothing." Love is union but not absorption. To give oneself totally, it is necessary to be and to remain completely oneself; to give oneself totally, it is necessary to keep nothing back for oneself.

Love is a "we." It demands, then, the "I" and the "thou." It also demands the suppression of the "mine" and "thine," those chilling words, Augustine would call them.

This is the ideal that orientates, sometimes completely unconsciously, sincere love in all its manifestations. It does not demand two beings who remain juxtaposed, nor two beings merged into one, but two beings who are distinct and conscious of their distinction in order to be united to each other in their very act of giving.

For human love, however, this ideal is only an inaccessible limit. We are always shut up within ourselves by a selfishness which is never completely destroyed. We are always hemmed in by the very circumstances of our nature, which makes us individuals incapable of communicating all that we are, and who remain completely unintelligible to one another. . . .

Perfect Love in the Trinity. Distinction, but not remoteness; union, but without confusion; "I" and "thou," but without "mine" and "thine" — what is idle fancy on the human level is a reality in God. The miracle of the Blessed Trinity is precisely this, that it is the complete realization of this perfect love.

The dogma tells us: only one God, only one nature, three Persons.

Here, then, are three Persons who really exist, who are distinct from each other in an irreducible fashion, and not by a mere metaphor or a way of looking at or imagining the mystery. Truly the Father is not the Son, the Son is not the Father, the Holy Spirit is neither the Father nor the Son. In other words, there are three "I's" set, as it were, opposite one another.

But these are not selfish egoisms that confront one another, nor juxtaposed beings that are mutually exclusive, but bountiful beings who are constantly giving themselves.

They possess the same divine nature, that infinite richness which can communicate itself entirely, since it is infinitely spiritual, and which forbids any idea of division and sharing, of joint ownership and participation, because it is infinitely simple. That divine nature cannot be possessed except in exactly the same way and integrally by each of the persons and by the three persons at the same time.

Accordingly, we ought not to speak of harmony, but rather of subsistent communion. For each of the divine persons possesses this richness only in an unselfish way, only in order to love the others in a total giving of himself. For example the Father, in his entirety, is paternity, and is not paternity completely turned toward the Son? Thus each Person exists only in his relation to the others. It is in existing for the others that each one is in himself. Since he does not seek his own reality in himself, it is in the others that he finds himself. Each of the persons is not a selfish withdrawal into himself, but a complete pouring out of himself toward the others.

This plurality of persons loving each other, however, does not result in a plurality of gods. If God is subsistent Love, how could he help but be infinite unity? All love is unifying; it brings about "unanimity" among the most dissimilar things. What should we say then of infinite Love? Is it not unity itself?

Divine Love and Our Love. . . . Our essential attitude, the great obligation which sums up all of Christianity, is love. Since the Blessed Trinity is divine Love itself, the dogma of the Trinity is the revelation of this Love; it is, as it were, the central message of the Trinity. "How can I recommend love to you in a more urgent way than by calling God Love?" asks a Father of the Church.

The love of the divine persons for each other is poured out toward us. They have given us themselves, their very beings, no more, no less than that. "God so loved the world that he gave to it his only-begotten Son."[2] When the Father gave us his Son, who is his own Image, he gave us himself. And the Son, who has brought us to an understanding of the love of the Father by sacrificing himself even unto death, sends us his own Spirit, this Holy Spirit, who is the Spirit of the Father and of the

2 Jn 3:16.

Son, who is their Love and who is called by his own proper name, the Gift.

In the face of this love of the divine persons, how can we fail to understand that our service of God, our religion, does not consist in the love of slaves, in services and rents paid to the last penny, in rituals and empty forms, but that it is, above all and essentially, a personal love? Nothing can interest God more than this human person made in his own image, nothing can influence him more than this heart which he has created. "Are you looking for something to give to God"? asks St. Augustine. "Give him yourself."

INDEX

Abercrombie, N., Molina's doctrine of divine concurrence, knowledge, and predestination, 242 ff

Abelard, apologist for Christianity, 165; and Bernard of Clairvaux, 163; condemnation of, 163; inspiration, 164; rationalism, 163 f; Roscellin, 162 f; Trinitarian dogma, 165 ff; and William of Champeaux, 162

Abraham, and God, 2; history, 29 f; polytheistic ancestors, 3

Act, actuation, 354; quasi-form of man, 355

Actuation, of finite by infinite, 354

Age of Reason, 246 ff

Agape, meaning of, 66

Ahern, B. M., Gospel and Exodus typology, 29 ff;

Alexandria, Council of, 362, 99

Allah, bodily qualities, 149 f; human arts, 148; Paradise, 148

Altizer, T. J. J., atonement, 322 f; death of God, 320 ff

Analogy, from finite being, and De la Taille, 352 f; natural knowledge and Lonergan, 353 f; revelation of word, for Rahner, 354 f; in Tillich, 364; of Trinity, in St. Augustine, 117 f

Analogy of being, and Barth, 293 ff; and Brunner, 325; meaning, 325

Analysis, linguistic, and theological assertions, 317

Anselm, St. dialectician, 157; ontological argument, 159 f; as a theologian, 157

Apologists, distinctions within the deity, 91; eternal generation of Son, 91; *Logos* idea, 90; personality of Word, 92; subordination, 91; and the Trinity, 92

Apostasy, and secularizers, 318

Appropriations, in St. Augustine, 115

Aquinas, St. Thomas, analogy, 176; and Aristotle, 175; divine processions, relations, persons, 189 f; Christian philosophy, 175; existential interpretation of Exodus, 179 ff; five ways of establishing God's existence, 182 ff; *Haec sublimis veritas,* 180 ff; Maimonides, 175; man at the age of reason, 330; "man in the woods," 329; nature and attributes of God, 183 ff; Plato, 175; synthesis of Aristotle and Catholic thought, 178; theologian, 177 f; theology of the peaceful, 179

Arguments for the existence of God, 193 and Kant, 274 f

Arians, 99

Arianism, 96 f; and Nicaea, 97 f

Arius, 96; question of, 104 ff

Athanasius, St. rule of faith, 107

Atheism, and Bultmann, 319; of Nietzsche, 283 ff; and Tillich, 319; as theology, 288

Atonement, for Altizer, 322 f

Augustine, St., and creation, 124 ff; and distinction of divine persons, 115; divine appropriations, 115; and divine operation *ad extra,* 124; and divine processions, 116 f; and evolution, 125 ff; and God's existence and nature, 119 f; mutual divine relations, 115; nature before persons, 122 f; and predestination, 238 f; predestination and damnation, 127 ff; psychological theory of processions, 124; and separation of grace from Christ, 238; and "*Sola gratia,*" 238; and the Trinity, 121 ff; and trinitarian analogies, 117 f; trinitarian starting point, 114; trinitarianism, 114 ff; and unity of divine nature, 115

Bañez, and divine premotion, 248 f; on God's plan and causality, 246 ff; and Molina's doctrine, 247 ff; and predestination, 247 ff; and universal salvific will, 248

Baptism, of desire, 329; formula of, in Matthew, 35; of Jesus, and three divine persons, 37 f

Barrett, C. K., on Father, Son, and Spirit in John, 84 ff; on the Spirit in the Synoptics, 45 ff

Barth, K., and analogy, 293 ff; and the knowability of God, 292 ff; and Vatican I, 293 ff; and Vatican I's natural theology, 296; revelation in creation, 298

Becoming, for Nietzsche and Hegel, 283 f

Bernard, St., "the last of the Fathers," 170; as theologian and mystic, 170 ff

Biel, G. and his doctrine of predestination and justification, 206 ff; as nominalist theologian, 207 f; and Scotus' supralapsarianism, 212

Biffi, G., and the three divine Persons in New Testament, 34 ff

Body of Christ, 350; and Kierkegaard, 291

Boehner, P., on God in William of Ockham, 201 ff

Bonhoeffer, D., his Christianity, 319

Bonifazi, C., on Kierkegaard's view of God, 287 ff